International Studies in Law and Literature

VOLUME 2

The titles published in this series are listed at *brill.com/isll*

Law, Literature, and History

A Fateful Rendezvous with the Shoah

By

Richard H. Weisberg

BRILL | NIJHOFF

LEIDEN | BOSTON

The Library of Congress Cataloging-in-Publication Data is available online at https://catalog.loc.gov

Typeface for the Latin, Greek, and Cyrillic scripts: "Brill". See and download: brill.com/brill-typeface.

ISSN 2773-191X
ISBN 978-90-04-52516-0 (hardback)
ISBN 978-90-04-52517-7 (e-book)
DOI 10.1163/9789004525177

This book is printed on acid-free paper and produced in a sustainable manner.

For Cheryl

Contents

Preface: Sources and Methods

I begin with the question asked by one of my guides along the path to understanding this difficult subject: "Who am I to say so?" James Carroll, whose *Constantine's Sword*[1] lies side by side on my desk with several other masterpieces of religious frankness, wondered aloud about his own "credentials" in challenging from the inside the behavior of his beloved Catholic Church. His entire book, and perhaps especially its first half-dozen chapters, adopt a highly personal auto-biographical tone that I will endeavor to replicate at the beginning of my own work. Carroll, deeply upset by the construction of a Carmelite crucifix at Auschwitz in the mid-1980's, thought first about how his traditionally Catholic upbringing left him ignorant and unprepared to think about Jewish people in an informed way:

> As is obvious by now, I had been raised with an anachronistic idea of Judaism: the Scribes and Pharisees, worship at the Temple, the stereotype of the vengeful Old Testament God. Catholics like me knew nothing of the living tradition of Jewish thought and observance, ignorance that reflected the Christian assertion that after Jesus, Israel had been superseded by the "new Israel," the Church.
>
> SWORD, 47

Then, still in autobiographical mode, Carroll identifies a single moment that provoked his inquiry, here occasioned by the sight of a *crucifix at Auschwitz*:

> The small crosses were taken away by Polish officials, but the large cross remains at Auschwitz to this day. What does the cross of Jesus Christ mean at such a place? What does it mean to Jews? What does it mean to Christians? Or to Polish Catholics? Or to those for whom religious symbols are empty? What does the cross there signal about our understanding of the past? And what of the future? If Auschwitz has become a sacred center of Jewish identity, what does the cross there imply about the relations between Judaism and Christianity? These questions were on my mind one November morning as I stood alone before that cross .... I could imagine the eyes of a Jewish protester as he detected in prayers offered before the cross at Auschwitz echoes of the old refrain "Jews out!" – only now it was Jewish anguish that was expected to yield before Christian

---

1 *Constantine's Sword, The Church And The Jews* (Boston: Houghton Mifflin, 2002).

> hope? If Auschwitz must stand for Jews as the abyss in which meaning itself died, what happens when Auschwitz becomes the sanctuary of someone else's recovered piety?...Perhaps the voice a troubled Christian most needs to hear is that of the Jew who says the Holocaust must be made to teach nothing. SWORD, 5–6
>
> But that the Holocaust requires us, personally as well as institutionally, to understand how such events were prepared for by other events is an absolute moral legacy. The question posed itself not to me but to history: How did the cross of Jesus Christ become the cross at Auschwitz?
>
> JAMES CARROLL, *Constantine's Sword*, p. 54

Carroll's entire book suggests that, at least for him, the Holocaust is a source of teaching. And my work, in his footsteps, furthers that teaching. My "crucifix-at-Auschwitz" moment came, less shockingly for me perhaps than for Carroll, when I blanched each time I read the over-used adjective "Judeo-Christian." For others, too, the hyphenated adjective smarts. As Arthur Cohen put it some years ago:

> How can it be that Christianity, regarding itself the successor and completion of Judaism, should have elected to take into itself the body and substance of that Jewish teaching which it believed to be defective, which it regarded itself as having in measure rejected ... How can it be that Judaism, the precedent in principle and progenitor in history of Christianity, should have remained not only independent of but unassimilated by the doctrinal vision and historical pressure of Christianity? ... Where Jews and Christians divide, irreparably, is that for Jews the Messiah is yet to come and for Christians he has already come. That is irreparable.[2]

With each successive repetition of "Judeo-Christian," unable to shake off my increasing crucifix-at-Auschwitz-type revulsion, I realized the necessity for this book-length refutation of that seductive but oxymoronic phrase. I also sensed that my intensive practice of the field of "Law and Literature" replicated in a different set of disciplines James Carroll's integration of his own practice in the priesthood. As this book pervasively integrates "Law and Literature" scholarship into discussions of the Holocaust, so I will rely on such pioneering

2 See Arthur A. Cohen, *post*, Introduction, n. 14; see also https://www.commentary.org/articles/arthur-cohen/the-myth-of-the-judeo-christian-tradition/.

scholars as Frank Kermode,[3] on the under-appreciated prophetic Protestant scholar Franklin Littell,[4] on Bart D. Ehrman,[5] on the irrepressible Shakespearian Harold Bloom (whom I met in his apartment in Greenwich Village late in his life and who encouraged me, in signing the book I think he will someday be best known for, to proceed with this book project),[6] and on David I. Kertzer.[7] Each in his way has argued that the progression in early Christian thought from a total rejection of the older religion to a felt need to retain it and to map the "Old Testament" onto the New wreaked havoc with theology, history, and common sense. This retention of the "Old" while proclaiming something "New" was hardly necessary given the vast divide between the new faith system and so much of what came to be (often virulently) detested in the "Old." Once the decision was made to link them, though, a grammatical way of accommodating the strategy came to be embodied by the adjective *"Judeo-Christian." This must be reformed.*

But the progenitor of us all in taking the axe to the hyphen in "Judeo-Christian" is Friedrich Nietzsche, the brilliantly straightforward German Lutheran who wrote a century before the Holocaust of Jewish-Christian differences, always favoring the People of the Book to Protestant and Catholic authorities and contemporaries. Warped into being an anti-Semite by distorted readers of his magnificently philosemitic aphorisms, Nietzsche sharply distinguished between the heroic Old Testament, which he adored, and the "New," which lacked everything vital (including the truth!) that was to be found in the Jewish Bible. He prophesied a catastrophe for Europe, calling out in many works the duplicity and the *ressentiment* of early Christian story-tellers and exegetes, especially in *The Genealogy Of Morals*, *Dawn Of Day*, and *Beyond Good and Evil*.[8] This philologist, philosopher, and aphorist was sickened by the deliberate and (in his view) absurd misreadings of the Jewish sacred texts to fit the program of Christianity at its origins and as it progressed into full power over

3 Kermode, *Pieces Of My Mind: Essays And Criticism*, 1958–2002 (N.Y.: Farrar, Straus & Giroux, 2003). For more on Kermode, see here Chapter Two (A).

4 *The Crucifixion Of The Jews: The Failure Of Christians To Understand The Jewish Experience* (N.Y.: Harper & Row, 2001). See especially Chapter Two (B).

5 *Misquoting Jesus: The Story Behind Who Changed The Bible And Why* (N.Y.: Harper Collins, 2005).

6 *Jesus And Yahweh* (London: Penguin, 2005).

7 *The Popes Against The Jews: The Vatican's Role In The Rise Of Modern Anti-Semitism* (N.Y.: Knopf, 2001).

8 *The Genealogy Of Morals*, Trans. Francis Golffing (N.Y.: Doubleday, 1956). *Beyond Good And Evil*, Trans. Marianne Cowan (Chicago: Regnery, 1966). *Dawn Of Day*. See in the same exact vein, Harold Bloom, *Jesus And Yahweh*, *op. cit.*, Preface, n. 6.

the continent of Europe and its minions. The spread of Christianity, for thinkers like Nietzsche, was predicated in large part on a *textual lie*:

> However much the Jewish scholars protested, everywhere in the Old Testament there were supposed to be references to Christ and only to Christ and particularly his cross. Wherever any piece of wood, a switch, a ladder, a twig, a tree, a willow, or a staff is mentioned, this was supposed to indicate a prophecy of the wood of the cross; even the erection of the one-horned beast and the brazen serpent, even Moses spreading his arms in prayer, even the stick on which the Passover lamb was roasted – all are allusions to the cross and as it were preludes to it! *Has anyone who asserted this ever believed it?* But they were conducting a war and paid more heed to their opponents than to the need to stay honest.
>
> NIETZSCHE, *The Dawn of Day*, aphorism 84, emphasis added

The select few who write about this set of hermeneutic distortions may seem (as we shall see Harold Bloom pointing out in *Jesus And Yahweh*) to be fighting a losing battle. Has not Christianity won the day, parrying every such attack, and matching interpretive victories with martial conquests, all in support of what Bloom calls the "resentful child" of the "vast and magnificent Tanakh"[9]? One of those stratagems, indeed, is the very phrase "Judeo-Christian," which hides millennia of cruelties inflicted by the latter, quite selectively and as a specific object of resentful malice, upon the former, who generally wish only to be left alone with their own traditions as they understand them – not as imposed by degrading interpretations. I join to Bloom's strangely overlooked efforts here some exemplary literary works that inform my approach to the historical and political issues in this book.

Far from a passive observer of the courtroom and its often legal-religious dimension, I am also an occasional litigator, and I have participated actively in several US federal cases on behalf of Holocaust survivors or their heirs against various European institutions for genocidal wartime misconduct. These experiences have brought me together with people on all sides; one of the most successful cases, involving stolen Jewish bank accounts during the dark French period known as "Vichy,"[10] set in motion a still ongoing

9 Bloom, *Jesus And Yahweh*, *op. cit.*, Preface, n. 6, p. 33, using the Hebrew short-form "Tanakh," for the entirety of the Jewish Bible.

10 Bodner vs Banque Paribas, EDNY (2000), per Judge Sterling Johnson. This decision in favor of Holocaust victims led to settlements by 26 banks who had ripped them off under color of Vichy law.

restitution mechanism[11] in which to the present day I have been privileged to play a central role.[12] (The latest meetings in Paris were in June 2024.) With the cooperation of the French and American governments, and many individual actors of good will, the French agency known as CIVS[13] has restituted hundreds of millions of Euros to victims of the wartime Vichy regime's antisemitic laws. Relatedly, through a program I innovated at the Benjamin N. Cardozo Law School in New York,[14] I teach and write about the striving for a rule of law that might answer people's hopes for "Never again!" after they learned of the horrors of the Holocaust.

I have also helped bring performance and drama to Law and Literature by staging scenes from such works as *The Merchant of Venice* and then leading a debate among lawyers, judges, and story-tellers about the legal approach of Venice to the beleaguered Jew who tries to enforce his contractual rights against the Merchant, Antonio.[15] The many "moot courts" based on stories such as Melville's *Billy Budd* have also brought to a wider audience the dilemmas that Christian law *creates*, paradoxically perhaps, as it steps forth self-importantly to *resolve* conflicts within a fictional setting.

Just as the intensely personal approach of James Carroll identified as the generative moment for his shock at seeing a crucifix at Auschwitz, so everything in my life as scholar and secular Jew has led me to shock and distress at the use of the adjective "Judeo-Christian." I have been privileged to lead a full postwar life in the academies, the courthouses, and the administrative agencies in the United States and abroad. Non-traditional in my practice of Jewish rituals, I have had the immeasurable good fortune throughout my life to study Jewish sacred texts with Orthodox rabbis and scholars. One of these, Rabbi Simon Langer, prepared me for my Bar Mitzvah in New York some years after he had prepared the grandson of Alfred Dreyfus in Marseille just after Hitler had occupied Paris. In 2008, I met Charles Dreyfus, and the coincidence emerged of our two secular lives so affected by the same Orthodox influence. Thanks to Rabbi Langer and other teachers – including my beloved

11 On "The Washington Accords of January, 2001," which resolved the victims' case against Banks during Vichy, see Eizenstat, *Imperfect Justice: Looted Assets, Slave Labor, And The Unfinished Business Of World War II* (N.Y.: Perseus Books, 2003), pp. 336–7.

12 https://www.civs.gouv.fr/images/pdf/Programme20ans.pdf Remarks of Prof. Richard Weisberg, 11/19/2019. For my work beginning in 1995 as a litigator and then progressing to a quasi-diplomatic role, the French government awarded me the Legion d'Honneur in 2008.

13 Commission pour l'Indemnification des Victimes de la Shoah.

14 Cardozo Law Institute in Holocaust and Human Rights (C.L.I.H.H.R.), founded 2003.

15 *New Yorker*, "The Talk of the Town," Dec. 22 and 29, 2008.

older brother of blessed memory, Rabbi David B. Weisberg – I am reasonably conversant with the Biblical texts in their original Hebrew. I have written about the "Old" and "New" testaments in three prior books and in many articles.[16] My most recent book, *In Praise Of Intransigence*,[17] set me to thinking out loud about the ways religious upbringing affects otherwise secular lives. I argued there, and have developed my argument in view of the many responses to the book, that there is a fundamental difference between Christian and Jewish ways of seeing the world, that this difference comes to the surface cyclically, as it did during the Holocaust, and that, finally, it constitutes so fundamental a divide as to be unbridgeable. All of my professional work sustains me in that very non-ecumenical claim, which I hope to prove in the pages that follow.

Still, answers to the "Who am I to say so?" (again, James Carroll) question lie more in experience than in disciplined training. I ask the reader's indulgence as I intersperse into what follows more than one glimpse at what has shaped me individually. For, as the theologian Donald Dietrich has said in commenting on Carroll's idiosyncratic approach: "Carroll's historical analysis can be characterized as very personal, since his own life has become the lens through which he 'reads' the facts. But such an approach is not bad .... Carroll has concluded that the Catholic Church itself has used an ahistorical theology to function in a world of contingent events and so has frequently hurt people. A personalized approach to history may help provide the remedy to some of the evils that have been perpetrated."[18]

The cruelties imposed on Jews through the thousands of years since Saint Paul and others "proved" that Jewish sacred texts somehow predicted and justified the new faith's belief-system and values have often been announced by some of the wisest and most daring of Christian "insiders."

Some born to the Christian faith have gone further even than James Carroll in their critique of the vast religion. Some have proclaimed the death itself of Christianity. When Friedrich Nietzsche, the son of a Lutheran minister, proclaimed the death of God, he had in mind a *specifically Christian trinity* and all it had wrought in Europe over an agonizing 1900 year span. My thoughts here develop theirs into a post-Holocaust Jewish perspective, that of a "Law and Literature" scholar and activist whose own claims to "the truth" derive from his work in the fields of this amazing inter-discipline as it inter-relates, fatefully, with history.[19]

---

16 Vichy, *op. cit.*, Introduction, n. 16. *Failure Of The Word, op. cit.*, Introduction, n. 4.

17 *In Praise Of Intransigence: The Perils Of Flexibility* (N.Y.: O.U.P., 2014).

18 "Antisemitism and the Institutional Catholic Church," *Holocaust And Genocide Studies* (publication of U.S. Holocaust Memorial Museum), v 16:3, pp. 415–26.

19 See text at note 1 to this book's Introduction.

Acknowledgements

This book could not have been dreamt of without the support of dozens of people. The love of my wife, Cheryl, my sons, Dan, Benno, and Sam, and grandchildren Owen, Wes, Henry, Jacob, Rose and Joey, sustained me and brought me to what you now see before your eyes as my readers.

The ideas forming the backbone of this text sprung from the minds of my real and figurative teachers. I was privileged to absorb, at once or gradually, *unmediated* lessons from such great teachers as Yves Bonnefoy, Robert Cover, J.V. Cunningham, George Gibian, Ruth Bader Ginsberg, Isabel Gordon, Geoffrey H. Hartman, Wolfgang Holdheim, Rabbi Simon Langer, Alan Levitan, Franklin Littell, Benno Schmidt Jr., and Telford Taylor. While not formally categorized as my teachers, many friends and colleagues added to my learning and assisted me through the twists and turns of such a project. All credit goes to them, and all mistakes should be blamed on me. These allies include Marguerite Allen, Eric Freedman, Jeanne Gaakeer, Peter Goodrich, Dominique Gros, Haider Ala Hamoudi, Arthur Jacobson, Sanford Levinson, Clayton Koelb, Michael Pantazakos, Anton Schuetz, Karen-Margrethe Simonsen, Ditlev Tamm, Robin West, George Williams, and the late Christian Biet, Rabbi David B. Weisberg, and William Witteveen.

The move from inspiration and writing to this book's production and launch involved notable contributors without whom there would be nothing but a manuscript gathering dust in my study alcove. Over a two-year period, the University of Pittsburgh's Pitt Law Administrative Services (PLAS) worked in tandem with me to produce clean copies of draft after draft of the book. Special mention goes to Karen Knochel and LuAnn Driscoll.

I am indebted in multiple ways to my editor, María José Falcón y Tella. Her willingness to read the manuscript in various iterations and to burn the midnight oil fashioning it into final form is deeply appreciated. Others who read the manuscript *in medias res* and commented on it generously include Vivian Curran, Elaine Scarry and Jonathan Weisberg. Irreplaceable support also came my way from Sara Braun, Richard Danzig, Claire Estryn-Freedman, Arnie and Jo Sohinki, Bea Timmer, and Rachel Weisberg.

I greatly enjoy the act of writing, as well as the primary and secondary research that often informs it. But without all these dear "influencers," most or all of the "*tam*" (Yiddish for "zestful flavor") would have been sadly lacking. So thanks again to all those who edified this endeavor.

Introduction

Grasping my methods and interests in this book *avant la lettre*, Prof. Christine Krueger presciently linked *to history* "Law and Literature" scholarship at its highest level of generality:[1]

> "*Lest Law and Literature Forget: Richard H. Weisberg and History.*" Putting his project of law and literature into a historical context, Weisberg asserts, "The events of [the 20th] century have more than fulfilled the prophetic signs emerging from Melville, Dostoesvky, and Kafka – that the West was ready for a cataclysm, and that the innocent of the world would suffer horribly during the death throes of the dominant culture" ... This is one form of historicist thinking – looking at literature of the past for explanations of the present and ethical principles for law's future. "Our goal, so far unreached," Weisberg concludes, "is justice.'" Weisberg represents a major line of thought about history in the field of law and literature.[2]

Prof. Krueger, writing in one of four encyclopedic compendia of "Law and Literature" studies published just during the past half-dozen years,[3] has correctly identified not only a method but also an *aim* of my work. The content of the present book-length exploration falls completely within the usual dimensions of a "Law and Literature" study, with history as its focal point and a more just exercise of what Law and Literature has called the "narrative disciplines"[4] as its goal. Primer – what exactly *is* "'Law and Literature' and History"?

The modern iteration of "Law and Literature" began in the United States in the 1970's and 1980's and then spread productively to the UK and the continent of Europe as well as to China, South America, the Antipodes, and elsewhere. It is truly a worldwide, inter-disciplinary venture, involving scholars and

---

1 See, e.g., Christine L. Krueger, "Law and Literature and History," in Kieran Dolin, ed., *Law and Literature* (N.Y.: Cambridge U. Press, 2018), pp. 64–66 and *passim.*

2 *Id.*, p. 65.

3 These are: Anker and Meyler, eds., *New Directions in Law and Literature* (N.Y.: Oxford U. Press, 2017); Kieran Dolin, ed., *Law and Literature, op. cit.*, Introduction, n. 1; Goodrich, Gandorfer, and Gebruers, eds., *Research Handbook on Law and Literature* (U.K.: Elgar, 2022); Olson, *From Law and Literature to Legality and Affect* (U.K.: Oxford U. Press, 2022).

4 See Richard Weisberg, *Poethics: And Other Strategies of Law and Literature* (N.Y.: Columbia U. Press, 1992), ch. 1 and *passim.* See also Weisberg, *The Failure of The Word* (New Haven: Yale U. Press, 1984).

 | DOI:10.1163/9789004525177_002

performers in Literature and theater as well as law professors and legal activists arguing in court. The history behind the "movement," as it is often called, highlighted at its origins an increasing postwar sensitivity to the Holocaust, born of a laudable and hard-won influx of information about what happened during World War II, country by country, from Great Britain [!] in the West[5] to the killing fields of central and eastern Europe.

A gradually workable factual record of these enormities revealed how, within our own lifetimes, Europe's Christians actively participated in what became known as "genocide."[6] Jew-hatred replaced "Judeo-Christian" as an accurate hyphenated phrase. Those of us in the Law and Literature "movement" who were most sensitive to our place in postwar history became the reporters, the theoreticians, the activists, and the scholars working within the subject matter of this enterprise.

Central to the methods of this book – (and to Law and Literature scholarship as a whole) is the linkage of two usually unassociated disciplines, law and literature, which the field has united through their reliance on words, and on the structures of language to convey an entire perspective that organizes previously chaotic realities into a coherent narrative form.[7] Practitioners of "Law and Literature" are interested in how the edicts of authority and the words of story-tellers recount and convey the reality around them. Exclusively grounded in *verbal* expression, both law and literature stand united in their influence upon the way people generally think, speak, interpret texts, and understand the issues of the day and how to respond to them.

The field can be sourced to figures like Cicero,[8] who unified both fields into his own person, but this book follows comprehensively Robert Cover's argument that the Jewish sacred texts also unify these only seemingly separate disciplines into what he calls "Nomos and Narrative."[9] Its 20th century iteration has been variously sourced to my PMLA essay co-authored with Jean-Pierre Barricelli as the field re-commenced, an essay which gave full honors to John

5 See further, Chapter Nine, which treats an epistolary novel set on the occupied British Channel Islands, whose local British officials helped identify Jews, some of whom were eventually deported to Nazi camps in the East, all with the help of British bureaucratic and legal reasoning, from 1940–45.

6 See, e.g., Douglas Irvin-Erickson, *Rafael Lemkin and the Concept of Genocide* (Philadelphia: U. of Pennsylvania Press, 2017).

7 See *Poethics, op. cit.*, Introduction, n. 4, and selections from all the recent works cited at Introduction, n. 3.

8 The great Roman orator and lawyer lived from 106–43 B.C.E.

9 "Nomos and Narrative," in Minow, Ryan, and Sarat, eds., *Narrative, Violence, and The Law: The Essays of Robert Cover* (Ann Arbor: U. of Michigan Press, 1995).

Wigmore and of course Benjamin N. Cardozo.[10] Typical of the very thoughtful more recent accounts of the field is Julie Stone Peters' well received essay in the PMLA,[11] and Brook Thomas's excellent description in the Anker and Meyler volume.[12] Thomas, a distinguished writer in this field from the literature side of the inter-discipline, notes the sustaining of the emerging field through its turn to history:

> In 1982, Richard Weisberg and comparative literature professor Jean-Pierre Barricelli produced "Literature and the Law" for an MLA volume on *Interrelations of Literature*. About this time, others tried to move beyond formalism in literary study by turning to history. Engagement with legal history was one way to provide a new sense of literature's relation to culture in general. A groundbreaking work was Robert A. Ferguson's *Law and Letters in American Culture* (1984), which restored to our attention a "now-forgotten configuration of law and letters that dominated American literary aspirations from the Revolution until the fourth decade of the nineteenth century." The mid-1980s saw a flurry of activity .... With professional journals and professional organizations, a law and literature movement was well underway....[13]

This book argues that an ultimate contribution of the field of "Law and Literature" to intellectual history inevitably involves the most fraught questions of *religious identity*. I establish in these pages, employing interdisciplinary strategies, that because of early and consistent Christian manipulation of Jewish sacred texts, the new religion supposedly based on the older one developed into Judaism's direst enemy. The myths of "supersessionism," Talmudic "literalism," and the Jew as a "materialist" who worships a legalistically cruel Jewish God have persisted and have inflicted on the Jewish people across the centuries not

10 Barricelli and Weisberg, "Law and Literature," in Barricelli and Gibaldi, eds., *The Interrelations of Literature* (PMLA, 1982), p. 150. Also often cited are two earlier 20th century American sources for the "modern" renaissance of the inter-discipline: John Wigmore, "A List of 100 Legal Novels," *Illinois Law Review* (1908 at 574 and 1922 at 26) and Benjamin N. Cardozo, "Law and Literature," in Margaret E. Hall, ed., *Selected Writings* (Matthew Bender, 1975), p. 339. Many commentators date the modern iteration of the field to the publication of J.B. White, *The Legal Imagination* (Boston: Little Brown, 1973), a text that continues to inspire.

11 See the PMLA exchanges among Peters, Peter Brooks and myself, vol. 120, 442–53; 1645–6 (2005) and vol. 121, 546–9 (2006).

12 *Op. cit.*, Introduction, n. 3.

13 Brook Thomas, "Minding Previous Steps Taken," in: Elizabeth S. Anker and Bernadette Meyler, eds., *op. cit.*, Introduction, n. 3, pp. 36–38.

only hermeneutic but also *actual physical* cruelty. Jews, through a mendacious set of interpretive distortions, came to be seen by generations of European Christians as greedy, non-spiritual, earth-bound, and stiff-necked. They were also, according to a close reading of many Gospel passages, "Christ-killers." All the richness and the beauty of Jewish traditions and practices were reduced – where anything even modestly positive was asserted – to a single contribution: "the Law," Law not as the ennobling and cherished backbone of an ethical people but instead Law as merely hairsplitting and vengeful, ripe to be replaced by some spiritually "elevated" quality of Christian "love."

The modern inter-discipline of "Law and Literature" – or so I further argue in these pages – uniquely brings to light the necessity of removing forever the false association of the two religious traditions freakishly embodied in the hyphenated adjective "Judeo-Christian," which deliberately sweeps under the rug of history the calumnies wrought by hypocritical protestations of Christian "love" or "mercy" never intended to include non-converting Jews. The mythical linkage through that single hyphen of two vastly opposed belief systems has been noted by other writers.[14] Very recently, Prof. Magda Teter contributes much to debunk the easy-going bonding implied falsely in the hyphenated adjective. But in the absence of any profound use or even brief mention of *stories* to enrich her analysis, her approach cannot, in my view, encompass such a subject in its tragic fullness.[15]

"Law and Literature" methods permit me here to make this assertion in perhaps its most cogent form. Just as my work of history, *Vichy Law and the Holocaust in France*,[16] began with Albert Camus and one of France's other

---

14 See, e.g. Arthur A. Cohen, *The Myth of the Judeo-Christian Tradition and Other Dissenting Essays* (N.Y.: Schocken, 1971). In the same vein, see James Loeffler, "The Problem with the 'Judeo-Christian Tradition,'" *Atlantic*, 8/1/2020. See Jacob Neusner, *Jews and Christians; The Myth of A Common Tradition* (Valley Forge: Hymns, 1991). See also Rochelle L. Millen, *Reviewing Nietzsche, God, and The Jews* (1994): "I find the term Judeo-Christianity problematic; it tends to emphasize continuity in the Christian theological sense; a meaning even Nietzsche with his notion of 'slave morality,' I believe would have decried," in Modern Judaism, vol. 17 (1997), p. 97. From the antipodes, also quite recently, see https://www.abc.net.au/religion/is-there-really-a-judeo-christian-tradition/10810554

15 Magda Teter, *Christian Supremacy: Reckoning with The Roots of Antisemitism and Racism* (N.J.: Princeton U.P., 2023). See also Timothy P. Jackson, *Mordechai Would Not Bow Down: Antisemitism, The Holocaust, and Christian Supersessionism* (N.Y.: Oxford U. Press, 2021), who dedicates his excellent book to Harold Bloom and to the eleven murder victims at the Tree of Life Synagogue in Pittsburgh.

16 U.K. and N.Y. (Gordon & Breach and the N.Y.U. Press), 1996. The archival genesis of this book is recounted briefly in a number of reviews, including Richard Bernstein's excellent

great people of letters during the 20th century, Leon Blum, and just as it progressed to analyze as *texts* various authoritative statements that contradicted each other and lied about Jews but that found their way into French lawbooks and theological discourse during Vichy, so throughout this book stories about history illuminate the words of the Holocaust's sustaining religious and legal leaders.

In addition to accounts like Brook Thomas'[17] in anthologies about the field generally, this book – *of course!* – analyzes *individual stories*. For the first time – in extended form, I treat Camus' *The Plague*, Daniel Silva's *The Confessor*, Mary Ann Shaffer and Annie Barrows' *The Guernsey Literary and Potato Peel Society*, Bernhard Schlink's *The Reader*, Bernard Malamud's *The Fixer*, Jonathan Littell's *The Kindly Ones*, and Rolf Hochhuth's *The Deputy*. Some other stories I have treated frequently need refreshing here in view of disputes about my approach to them raised recently: *The Merchant of Venice, The Fall* (these latter two worthy again here of quantities of ink), *Billy Budd Sailor, The Tin Drum*. To this group of plays and prose stories I add a discussion of the Shakespeare sonnet that most dizzyingly captures themes of law and religion from elsewhere in his work, Sonnet 134.

I also take note of scholarship about works I do not have space to treat myself in depth but that reflect the approach of my book as a whole, in some cases replicating almost precisely my methodology of recognizing how central to developing understandings of key stories is a post-Holocaust set of revelations about the catastrophe in World War II Europe. For example, Richard Ashby in 2021 reports on sea changes relative to *King Lear*[18] criticism in the '60's and '70's that responded to newfound knowledge about Christian cruelty (institutional and otherwise) towards Jews during the War: His account of a major shift away from some redemptive, Christian assessments of *Lear* makes

---

essay in the *New York Times*, "Giving Collaboration a Bad Name," https://www.nytimes.com/1997/03/26/books/giving-collaboration-a-bad-name.html

17 *Op. cit.*, Introduction, n. 13. The pioneering work applying imaginative fiction to the Holocaust is Lawrence Langer, *The Holocaust and the Literary Imagination* (New Haven: Yale U. P., 1975). Langer's book, like this one, treats various novelists (but none discussed here) who attempt to grapple with the Holocaust. I hope my book will sit side by side with Langer's on the shelves of those who wish to think about the contribution uniquely made by imaginative fiction to the understanding of seismic events. See also Arthur A. Cohen, "An Esthetic Atrocity", review of Langer in the *NYTimes*, 1/18/76.

18 I do treat *Lear* briefly in Part Two of the book.

claims about a canonical work that readers of this book will come to recognize often about virtually every work treated here.[19]

On this informed, post-Holocaust reading of a canonical work, the ending of the play "*shatters, more violently than any earlier apostasy may have done, the very foundations of Christian faith itself.*"[20] As perspicuous in 2024 as it was in the 1960's and '70's, this key conclusion about *Lear*, to which I return in Part Two on Shakespeare, extends to many stories found in the rest of this book.

Of primary importance to my readers here is an inquiry into the gradual development within Christianity towards a largely figurative and allegorical misapprehension of what they came to call the "Old Testament," an interpretive process that began with the Gospel writers themselves and then extended across the centuries to Saint Augustine and beyond. The literal meanings of the Jewish Bible were abandoned if they did not serve the purposes of Christian "spiritualism" and the announcement of Jesus-as-Messiah. As is obvious in a commonsensical way, the meanings so adduced defy rational understanding. Further, as we shall see in Part One, the new religion displayed, fatefully, a deep distrust of *law itself.*

All of the stories treated here have to do in one way or another with the consequences of creating a system of law when law itself as an institution and an ideal has been programmatically cheapened, undermined, and debased. The result in almost every story is a cruelty unimaginable to those like the Jews who were accused of being narrowly legalistic and vengeful. Innocents suffer, and in this way all the stories, too (whenever written), relate centrally to the Holocaust, either explicitly after World War II or as a prophetic foreboding of disaster that precede the event. All serve to support the main argument I make here, which is that Europe's Christian institutions and deliberately mendacious manner of interpreting texts (and reality itself) led directly to the catastrophe across Hitler's Europe. In some cases, I rehearse and answer responses to my own analyses of canonical works in "Law and

19 Ashby, *King Lear After Auschwitz* (Edinburgh: Edinburgh U. Press, 2021). "Over the 1940s and 1950s, *King Lear* was typically read 'positively' as a story of Christian redemption, even being conscripted as a bulwark of traditional social and moral values in the face of a catastrophic modernity, represented most disturbingly by the camp system and Auschwitz. But in the 1960s, the play began to be read 'negatively', as violating the type of schematic Christian worldview that would finally see Lear redeemed through his sufferings. .... *It was only in the 1960s and the 1970s that the full scale of the atrocities committed during the Second World War began to be more widely known.* The Adolf Eichmann trial in 1961, famously covered by Hannah Arendt in *Eichmann in Jerusalem*, and the Frankfurt Auschwitz trials of 1963–5 increased public awareness about the unparalleled suffering and degradation of the Nazi camps. The scale of destruction unleashed in the Holocaust [yields] the prognostication ... of Edgar in *King Lear*: and worse may be yet."

20 Richard Ashby, *id.*, emphasis added.

Literature" such as *The Merchant of Venice* and *The Fall* [*La Chute*], building on earlier arguments and bringing to the reader's attention lucid and accessible interventions about them by others since the last time I wrote in a monograph about these classics. Such exchanges also involve in somewhat shorter form chapters on Grass' *The Tin Drum* [*Blechtrommel*], Bernhard Schlink's *The Reader* [*Der Vorleser*], Jonathan Littell's *The Kindly Ones*, Camus' *The Plague* [*La Peste*]. In the process – and only somewhat in a lighter vein – this book also familiarizes its readers with the *popular culture* subset of "Law and Literature,"[21] through three small masterpieces in the genre that represent Catholic anguish and Anglican cruelty during the War: *The Confessor* by Daniel Silva, *The Deputy* by Rolf Hochhuth, and *The Guernsey Literary and Potato Peel Pie Society*, an epistolary novel that introduces us to the still largely untold tale of antisemitism and genocide in the *British Channel Islands* from 1940–45. In some ways the most representative piece of fiction I treat here, *The Confessor*, creates a new Pope (Paul VII), who shakes up the Vatican by moving to open the secretive wartime archives on the behavior of Pius XII (a theme also treated in the blockbuster play from the mid-1960's, Rolf Hochhuth's *The Deputy*). "Paul VII" intends to address the Jews who remain in Rome in their Great Synagogue for the purpose of confessing the Church's sins and asking retribution for its "sow[ing] the seeds of the poisonous vine known as antisemitism and provid[ing] the water and nourishment those seeds needed to take root and thrive in Europe."

From the stage, to the modern novel, to the domain of popular culture, stories guide us into understandings unavailable elsewhere of weighty matters that no reflective person can ignore or deflect. When epochs end, we should deploy all available stocks of understanding. The portentous questions, where have we been and where are we headed, defy "specialized" resolution. Stories have been overlooked in mainstream public discourse for much too long, the bastion of a small cadre of literary analysts. I belong to that cadre. As such, I have fought for the maintenance of stories even as many literature professors have turned from them to what they call "theory." We will see that no theoretical breakthrough of these several "post-modernist" decades has even vaguely approached the dynamic understanding brought to human behavior by the great stories situated in the "canon," nor has managed even to fathom the

21 See for example a widely read piece of scholarship incorporating popular culture methods, Michael Asimow and Richard Weisberg, "When the Lawyer Knows the Client is Guilty: Client Confessions in Legal Ethics, Popular Culture and Literature," *Southern California Interdisciplinary Law Journal*, vol. 18 (2009), pp. 229–58. The link is: gould.usc.edu/why/students/orgs/ilj/assets/docs/18-2%20Asimow.pdf. On the law in film more generally, see, e.g., *Symposium; In Flagrante Depicto; Films on Trial*, Peter Goodrich, Ed., Cardozo Law Review, vol. 31 (2010).

cataclysmic change that is in the air, nor has effectively challenged the mainstream values already deeply undermined by the stories we are now going to re-read together. Without stories such as these, we simply would not have the wherewithal spiritually to work with what our logical and historical sides see to be true. I am content the appeal to stories will be vindicated and – if you do not always agree with my readings – you will at least be intrigued by the medium of imaginative fiction.

So, in all their fullness and world-wide dynamism, both components of what has been called the "Law and Literature Enterprise" (sometimes dichotomized with perhaps too great simplicity, as the Law-as-Literature and the Law-in-Literature[22]) have permitted me to think and write about both interpretive theory and the history of hermeneutic distortion. In many of the standard stories treated by Law and Literature scholars across many decades, the legal complexities of the work rise eventually to the level of religious struggle and even theology. There is no better methodology for facing up to this book's fateful material than "Law and Literature."

Unfortunately, as I finish these pages in the Summer of 2024, the rise of "Christian nationalists" in the U.S. necessitates mention here, as the unedifying newest purveyors of an ancient prejudice chant "Jews will not replace us,"[23] a mantra whose only virtue is in proving that "Judeo-Christian" is a false flag. The Charlottesville mob evokes – along with a cadre of covert as well as overt political figures and advisors who use Christianity to get votes for their favored candidate – the millennia-long lies directed against the "People of the Book," who just want to be left alone. I do include, of necessity here, some paragraphs on how false political claims during the Trump period mimic, probably intentionally, the tactics of the first Christian storytellers.[24] A fuller account of "white nationalism" and its obvious sources in New Testament and Christian writings must await another day, another book.

---

22 See, e.g., my non-relative Robert Weisberg, "The Law-Literature Enterprise," *Yale Journal on Law and Humanities*, v. 1:1 (1979).

23 See, e.g., Adam Gabbatt, "Jews Will Not Replace Us,", *The Guardian*, 8/16//17. Finally, see – from the antipodes in 2019 on this issue, Philip C. Almond: abc.net.au/religion/is-there-really-a-judeo-christian-tradition/10810554.

24 Here one must keep a close eye on Trump's enduring signals-caller, Steven Bannon, a devout Roman Catholic who is covertly guiding his man towards a still-possible overturning of democracy in 2024. For a good history of "White Christian nationalism," defined as "the original form of identity politics that validates only one identity, the white Christian nationalist, as the true inheritor of the white 'Founders' nation," see Joe Winikka-Lydon, E. Hodges, and R.G. Cravens, "Old Bigotries Melded with New Conspiracies Burgeon White Christian Nationalism," in *Southern Poverty Law Center*, "The Year in Extremism, 2022," p. 38.

PART 1

Christianity and Auschwitz: The Decline of a Faith

CHAPTER 1

"God is Today in eclipse in Christendom"; or "A Boat About to Sink"

A Christendom's Failure to Grapple with the Holocaust's Religious Implications: Sharp Declines in Christian Adherents

Country by country, Western Europe and the United States have been experiencing sharp diminutions in Catholic and Protestant adherents, as the following quotes snapshot. Of course, reasons for this are over-determined and may include other (although related) factors besides younger peoples' growing understanding of Christianity's central place in the Holocaust. But the thesis of this book indicates that Holocaustic understandings from west to east (including Great Britain!, where informed adherents to the Anglican Church may have been sobered to learn – as we shall here – of the treatment of Jews in the British Channel Islands from 1940–45) trickle down to individuals, particularly since there has been a continuation of practices that helped bring on Hitler's genocide.

> The revision of a contentious Good Friday prayer approved this week by Pope Benedict XVI could set back Catholic-Jewish relations, Conservative Judaism's international assembly of rabbis says in a resolution to be voted on next week. The prayer calls for God to enlighten the hearts of Jews "so that they may acknowledge Jesus Christ, the savior of all men."
>
> NEELAQ BANERJEE in *The New York Times*, February 9, 2008

> As Spaniards Lose Their Religion, Church Leaders Struggle to Hold On
>
> SAMUEL LOEWENBERG in *The New York Times*, June 26, 2005

> The Roman Catholic Church in Britain is facing its greatest threat since the Reformation, according to research. Over three decades, Mass attendance has slumped by 40 per cent, baptisms by 50 per cent, Catholic marriages by 60 per cent and confirmations by 60 per cent.
>
> RUTH GLEDHILL in *"WorldWide Religious News"* 2006

> Americans Are Losing Their Religious Faith … They are drifting away from churches, they are praying less and they are less likely to say religion

 | DOI:10.1163/9789004525177_003

is very important to their lives .... Most of the research is on Christians because they account for roughly 90% of believers in the United States. ... This "dechurching," as they call it, is apparent in most denominations, reducing the numbers of Presbyterians and Episcopalians and also of evangelicals like southern Baptists.

NICHOLAS KRISTOF in *The New York Times* August 24, 2023

In five decades, the number of people with no religion in Britain has grown from just 3 per cent of the population to nearly half, according to a new survey. Among adults aged under 25, nearly two-thirds define themselves as "nones," or people with no religious affiliation.

RUTH GLEDHILL in *"Christian Today,"* October 17, 2014

Western Europe, where Protestant Christianity originated and Catholicism has been based for most of its history, has become one of the world's most secular regions. Although the vast majority of adults say they were baptized, today many do not describe themselves as Christians. Some say they gradually drifted away from religion, stopped believing in religious teachings, or were alienated by scandals or church positions on social issues.

Pew Research Center survey of religious beliefs and practices in Western Europe, May 29, 2018

Europe's march towards a post-Christian society has been starkly illustrated by research showing a majority of young people in a dozen countries do not follow a religion. In the UK, only 7% of young adults identify as Anglican, fewer than the 10% who categorize themselves as Catholic. The figures are published in a report, Europe's Young Adults and Religion, by Stephen Bullivant, a professor of theology and the sociology of religion at Saint Mary's University in London. Religion was "moribund," he said. "With some notable exceptions, young adults increasingly are not identifying with or practicing religion." The trajectory was likely to become more marked. "Christianity as a default, as a norm, is gone, and probably gone for good – or at least for the next 100 years," Bullivant said.

HARRIET SHERWOOD, *The Guardian*, March 20, 2018

Lord, your Church often seems like a boat about to sink, a boat taking in water on every side.

BENEDICT XVI (CARDINAL RATZINGER), *The Atlantic*, January–February 2006, p. 83

> That God is today in eclipse in Christendom, the sensitive perceive…
>
> FRANKLIN LITTELL, *The Crucifixion of the Jews* 1975

> I'm not sure Christianity will survive.
>
> LITTELL, *"Holocaust's Legacy: A Struggle for Faith," N.Y. Post*, March 26, 1975

> Years after his death [in 2007], Abbé Pierce [a celebrated symbol of Catholic charity] is facing a sudden profusion of sexual harassment and assault accusations – a stunning fall from grace that has…unsettled a country that once hailed him as a symbol of virtue. 'The image of purity that he had is crumbling.'
>
> *The New York Times*, September 19, 2024

B Closing the French and Vatican Archives, Avoiding the Truth

There is an intimate relationship between the theology of Christianity, which includes its distortions of the Jewish sacred texts as well as the deeply implicit antisemitism of its own Gospels, and how truth is generally attained or deliberately hidden. As we have just seen, emerging generations are gradually losing faith in the various Christian religions. I argue that an increasing awareness of atrocities against Jews on the continent of Europe considerably influenced this falling off in belief and practice, and that many Europeans got tired of mainstream Christianity's many falsehoods. Meanwhile, specialists like myself had to grapple with overt mendacity.

Examples of deliberate falsification of Catholicism's contributions to the slaughter of the six million include the bizarre sealing of *archival* sources relating specifically to World War II. Beginning in the early 1980s, I personally encountered the complete shutdown of the French National Archives for the Twentieth Century for the period 1940–44. Only towards the end of the 1980s, as I shall report in this book's section on Albert Camus and Vichy history, were these archives partly opened; with some very good luck in gaming the bureaucratic obstacles, I entered the dusty files that had not been touched since the end of the War. Why this selective refusal, in the birthplace of Rene Descartes and of the European Enlightenment, to let people find a pathway to the plain truth? I wondered then, and continue to ask this question of my readers: what deep-rooted, anti-rational drive fenced off the truth and furthered falsehood? What millennia-long traditions of hermeneutic distortion and textual mis-readings found expression in these archival closings? Were the self-protecting secular acts of the French government aberrational, or were they reflections of non-secular strategies that had dominated the continent for almost 2000 years? Where does religious mendacity bleed into archival secrecy?

The struggle to enter into the archives of the Roman Catholic Church displays even more poignantly the barriers created by thousands of years of lies. What did the Popes and their gate-keepers fear? Information that might prove that Pius XII was a very poor candidate for sainthood? Worse, that the Vatican allowed Jews to perish and also benfited financially from the genocide at its doorstep? That the Church, beginning when everyone knew the Nazi cause was lost, began creating for potential war criminals a perverse lifeline to South America? Why did it take until mid-2020 for a trickle of Vatican wartime documents to see the light of day?[1] Did the Vatican, like the postwar France of DeGaulle and Giscard d'Estaing, have reason to fear the truth?

In precise opposition to the authoritative walling off of crucial documents stands the agonizingly slow revelation of the truth by some of those who liberated the camps and their associated documentarians, by courageous film-makers, writers, and eventually historians of the central reality of wartime Europe. The genocidal realities emanating from World War II Europe – that grand old Europe of Goethe and Beethoven, of Montaigne and Hugo, of Cervantes and Lope de Vega, the continent of elegant aristocrats, Cartesian rationalism, and polite speech – emerged only when General Eisenhower joined the troops liberating the concentration camps and (to his great credit) insisted that people see what he had seen there.

In various iterations and through repeated screenings, something gradually took hold in the spirits of postwar Europeans. Way beyond our specialized class of researchers, ordinary people had reason to question the status quo they had long accepted. World War II – infinitely more than the conflict of '14-'18 that temporarily produced a "lost generation" – broke the back of ancient European traditions that had gotten away with preaching "love" and "mercy" for far too long.

Watching films of a soldier in a handsome uniform, brought up in the churches of Christian countries like Germany, deliberately shooting a bullet into the brain of a small child who then falls into a pit splattered by the grey matter of dozens of other victims, growing numbers of Europeans came to doubt the *veracity* of mainstream Christianity's claim to "love your neighbor [including your enemy] as yourself."

1 David Kertzer, "What the Vatican's Secret Archives are About to Reveal," *Atlantic*, 3/2/2020.

This change in the *inner certainties* of western men and women dwarfed the far more obvious and seemingly positive advances in their material lives. The way I am writing this book in 2024, for example, benefits from improvements of information gathering and even word processing that were barely imaginable to my grandparents during their lifetimes; but what makes a human being tick responds to the universal inner clockwork of the heart and the spirit.

Displayed during the 1946 war-crime trials at Nuremberg, the film clips taken upon the liberation of Auschwitz-Birkenau guaranteed that every sentient human being in Europe and the Americas would *know* what western culture had wrought.[2] More recently film makers have brought this reality to countless millions in movie theaters, on platforms, and on television.[3] Excellent story-tellers such as Rolf Hochhuth and Daniel Silva[4] speculated brilliantly about what went through the mind of Pope Pius XII as he personally observed from his balcony the round-ups of Rome's Jews and failed to protest or even speak publicly about them. Guenther Grass' trilogy, and especially the unmatchable chapter in *Blechtrommel* [*"The Tin Drum"*] called "Faith, Hope, and Love," stand as perhaps the best representation we have (through fiction) of the falsities of Christian piety and their link to the gas chambers.[5]

What would we do without stories? – a rhetorical question invoked in these pages – is especially perspicuous when we find that story-tellers (including film-makers and novelists like Camus) were the first to reveal the deliberate obfuscation of the Holocaust's *actual factual record*. The archives were closed by authoritative fiat, but the truth was finding its way to people's spirits.

C I Become a Player: the Unique Truth Value of "Law and Literature"

On the graduate school faculty in French and Comparative Literature from 1970–75 at the University of Chicago,[6] I taught Camus' 1956 story *La Chute* [*"The Fall"*] to students preparing for their PhD. With hitherto no particular

---

2 "'We will show you their own films': Film at the Nuremburg Trials" (Historical film footage), *U.S. Holocaust Memorial Museum* (encyclopedia.ushmm.org).

3 Alain Resnais, *Nuit Et Brouillard* ("Night and Fog"), 1956. Marcel Ophuls, *The Sorrow and The Pity*, 1969. David Elstein, *The World at War* (BBC series narrated by Lawrence Olivier), 1973. Arnold Schwartzman, *Genocide*, 1981. Claude Lanzmann, *Shoah*, 1985. James Moll, *The Last Days*, 1998. Ken Burns, Lynn Novick, Sarah Botstein, *The U.S. and The Holocaust* (PBS documentary series), 2022.

4 See Chapter Seven.

5 See Chapter Ten.

6 Ph.D, 1970, Comparative Literature, Cornell U.

personal or professional ties to the European Holocaust, I saw that the story, essentially a Rousseau-like confession but narrated by the lawyer, Jean-Baptiste Clamence, spoke directly to the indifference of France's Catholic population to the death of at least 80,000 Jews under color of Vichy law from 1940–44.

"Some of my best friends are French" – but what compelled me to take on the subject of Vichy wrongdoing was precisely their unwillingness to discuss this aspect of *The Fall* and of Vichy with me. All other subjects were always on the table, but the wrongdoing of their parents (not them personally!), coupled with the Gaullist myths of French heroism, and the archival closings, removed Vichy from the conversational map.

Not having lost any of my own extended family to the Holocaust, I became a player for three reasons: First, this "the fork sticks in the air" syndrome, the absolute refusal during meals with French friends to engage them in the topic of Vichy and indeed the shocked discontinuation of the very act of eating at its mere mention; second, Albert Camus, my literary "influencer," whose works I was teaching to graduate students; and third, French lawbooks that, unique among those in Europe, simply kept publishing during the years 1940–44, unchanged from prior and subsequent years except for the addition of a bizarre new substantive legal topic: "juifs."[7]

My curiosity, born of an upbringing in New York City and its best public schools (including the Bronx High School of Science) and of conversations around my parents' dinner table, provoked me to open the door to truth about the country whose language and culture I had savored since my mother sent me to a private French tutor in second grade. Eventually, and by then armed with a law degree,[8] I began an odyssey through French archives previously closed to all other researchers that helped me to complete a book on Vichy wrongdoing[9] and to become a player (to the present moment of authoring this text) in the restitution to Jews who were ripped off under color of Vichy law, losing in many cases not only their lives but also large chunks of their material wealth, including paintings, bank accounts, businesses, precious personal and family objects, stamp collections, first edition books, sewing machines, farm property – you name it. My work indicated that, with the exception of about 5% of the people who were *actually* in the Resistance,[10] France as a whole

7 See, e.g., *Journal Officiel* and *Gazette Du Palais* for each wartime year. Other countries in Hitler's Europe discontinued such publications, but not France. It was legal business as usual during Vichy and from Paris to the provinces that business grew considerably because so much new litigation and client contact had to do with "Jews".

8 J.D., Columbia, 1974.

9 *Op. cit.*, Introduction, n. 16.

10 Henri Rousseau, *The Vichy Syndrome* (Cambridge: Harvard U. Press, 1994).

and on its own participated in the pillage. The Catholic religious upbringing, discourse, and practice of 90% of the French assisted them not only to fail to resist the Nazis but to take on as a fully Franco-French phenomenon the genocide on French soil.[11]

D Europe's "Totentanz"

In Europe, the seat of the Holocaust, mainstream religion has been performing a kind of *Totentanz* – or dance of death – "avoiding the central reality"[12] of its sure eventual demise. The religion itself in almost all of its varieties is based on severe interpretive distortions of Jewish sacred texts. No wonder that the Holocaust has inspired a diminution in the ranks of the believers! But even among the increasing cadres of lapsed Christians, the lay religion of American-inspired markets and materialism conspired in a different way to forestall recognition that incurably awful things had happened during the 20th century, and that only those who faced the sickness and changed were going to get better. Not surprisingly, then, thinkers on the "left," who believed neither in God nor the market, tended to be the skeptics, while more centrist secular Europeans leaned towards American-style entrepreneurialism as their new faith. In Germany for example, there has been a vibrant impulse towards the best hopes of a continuing enlightened world. Unable to sustain many of their cultural traditions because Nuremberg, American postwar occupation, a divided country, and their own honest acceptance of guilt denied them that luxury, Germany has forthrightly become a European leader in the always difficult task of admitting to shameful conduct. Among countries who have tried to restitute Jewish families for genocidal losses, Germany by 2023 is by far the leader, monetarily and in terms of memory.[13] Full honor and credit, yes, but even there – among nominal Lutherans as well as Catholics – slippage into antisemitism and historical negationism[14] hint at a failure fully to expunge the disease that brought Hitler to power and left him there for 12 full years!

---

11 See Chapter Six on Camus for far greater detail regarding the French archival and historical and literary record during and after the Vichy years.

12 Weisberg, "Avoiding Central Realities," *Human Rights Quarterly*, vol. 5 (1983).

13 See, e.g., "Survivors of Holocaust to Receive $1.2 billion in German Reparations," *Nytimes*, 9/16/22, p. A7. This was of course hardly the first payment made by postwar Germany to the victims. See generally Stuart Eizenstat, *Imperfect Justice, op. cit.*, Preface, n. 11.

14 Germany, like France, has seen a recent renewal in far-right antisemitic language and deeds.

But in France, the *Totentanz* has been far less constrained in its negationist moves than has been true in postwar Germany. France hid its active participation in the Holocaust, where Germany could not; so there were many more features of the death-dance that could be displayed without fear of world-wide condemnation.

A provocative new dance craze appropriate to mention here is deconstuctionist theory, whose major proponents were my own teachers at Cornell and Zurich (Paul de Man and Geoffrey Hartman), a complex dance that attracted American graduate students such as myself and others who then spread the craze to their own students. Eventually – end even before what came to be known as the "DeMan Scandal"[15] – I was writing about ways in which deconstructionism in most of its iterations was part of the larger Totentanz,[16] and missed the mark in its own right, paradoxically joining with long-standing Catholic interpretive traditions that deliberately aim to alter reality, traditions that still affect France and other major countries in the western world. Frank Kermode, shared this perspective, and at one point wrote with sarcastic elegance about Derrida's mis-readings of Nietzsche:[17]

> Derrida more than once recalls Nietzsche's "active forgetfulness," which is said to protect us from history, so enabling us to act and "to make room for a new thing." The question may be whether the philosophy of Derrida should not, like the philosophy to which he argues that literary criticism is historically enslaved, become part of that history which we should "actively forget," in order not to lose that present which, as Nietzsche says, cannot be had without forgetfulness. There is then a kind of knowledge, doubtless mendacious but humanly useful, which is only to be had by forgetting.

Nietzsche counsels forgetfulness not to make way for the new but instead to rid the self of ressentiment when it is too obsessed with a perceived insult or an object of envy and rancor. As Kermode sardonically observes, it was to make way for the "new" – whether it be the "New Testament" or the "new" theoretical dance – that always drove Derridean reading strategies.

15 Several years after his death, the esteemed deconstructionist was discovered to have written antisemitic articles early in the occupation of Belgium.

16 Weisberg, "DeMan Missing Nietzsche: 'Hinzugedichtet' Revisited," in Koelb, ed., *Nietzsche as Postmodernist* (1990).

17 Kermode, *Pieces of My Mind, op. cit.*, Preface, n. 3, p. 317.

Americans uninterested in French theory (i.e. the vast majority of people outside Literature departments) ended the 20th century having already produced histories and successful lawsuits directly relevant to an understanding of the Holocaust, perhaps particularly as the genocide had developed in Vichy France itself.[18] While the faddish French theory swept American campuses, inevitably implicating in diametrically opposed wartime-related ways the leaders of the Yale U-based deconstructionist movement[19] a contrary, *fact-based imperative* among North American scholars and lawyers brought about the impetus for finding what the French archives actually at long last revealed to be fact and not "theory."[20] Undaunted by any sense of guilt or remorse for their parents' generation, a shame that as I have experienced personally kept normally gregarious French friends from wanting to utter a word about Vichy, American scholars and lawyers forged ahead and opened doors to the truth. No wonder that this created resentment in French and other Europeans, at the time quite happy to see the subject obscured, occulted, omitted, or even obliterated.

18 See, e.g., the seminal work of the Columbia historian Robert Paxton on Vichy; see also Marrus (a Canadian scholar) and Paxton, *Vichy France and The Jews* (Cambridge: Harvard U. Press, 1981); Weisberg, *Vichy Law and The Holocaust in France*, *op. cit.*, Introduction, n. 16. The latter – the current writer – went on to litigate a half dozen cases in U.S. federal courts on behalf of Holocaust survivors or their heirs.

19 Paul de Man was posthumously shamed for antisemitic wartime articles he had written as a young man in a Brussels newspaper; and Geoffrey Hartman was a direct victim of the Holocaust, having escaped death as a German Jew only by being included in the "Kindertransport" from Berlin to London in 1939. Neither DeMan nor Hartman wrote about the Holocaust directly, DeMan for obvious reasons of obfuscation of this past and Hartman delaying this until his magisterial work, *The Longest Shadow* (Bloomington: Indiana U. Press, 1995), where he cites my work as part of in an extended discussion of Vichy, *id.*, ch. 5. He and I had become close friends and discussed issues central to this book many times over 30 years, including especially as partners at a residence at the Rockefeller Foundation villa in Bellagio, Italy, in 1996.

20 The phenomenon of European closed archives is treated frequently in these pages, *e.g.*, as part of the discussion of Silva's novel, *The Confessor*, in Chapter Seven and the Channel Islands wrongdoing, revealed by the French archives, in Chapter Nine. See also Section B of this Chapter.

CHAPTER 2

The Jewish Bible Put Through the Wringer

A Frank Kermode's Account

Contemporaneously with North American scholarship and litigation relating to the European Holocaust, other prominent English-language writers within the field of literary criticism also contributed centrally to a grasp on Jewish-Christian conflicts. Although he probably did not know of the wrong-doing wrought against Jews in his nation's Channel Islands, Sir Frank Kermode felt it vital to his enterprise in 2003 to say the following about the long, tortured skein of Christianity's violence to Jewish sacred texts:

> When whole systems of belief are involved, as in the case of the Bible they always are, the difficulties [of discerning meaning] are multiplied. Christianity decided … [to] keep the Jewish Bible, and thenceforth the question of the nature of its relevance to a non-Jewish religion became a permanent problem, with much bearing on the matter of plain sense. If the Law was abrogated, the relevance of the Old Testament lay primarily in its pre-figurative relation to the New; it became, more or less, a repository of types, but it contained other elements not easily given up – moral instruction and a history of God's providence and promises. And from quite early times there was some resistance to the copious allegorizing of the Alexandrian tradition, some respect for the *sensus historicus*. The school of Antioch limited allegorical interpretations to the sort of things licensed by Paul, for example in his reading of the story of the sons of Sarah and Hagar. Theodore of Mopsuestia sought to understand the Old Testament historically …
>
> … [D]espite the success of allegory, the importance of the literal sense was habitually affirmed, most influentially by Augustine, a contemporary of Theodore …. Augustine was an historian and as an exegete he held that an understanding of historical reality must be the foundation of any attempt to provide spiritual interpretation. [*B*]*ut he also ruled that no interpretation should transgress against "charity": any literal-historical sense that was inconsistent with virtuous conduct and the true faith should be treated figuratively* … [A]s J.S. Preuss describes it: the plain sense of some of the Old Testament is edifying in itself, but the remainder has value only because it means something other than

 | DOI:10.1163/9789004525177_004

> it seems to be saying; the literal, grammatical, and historical senses include what should not be figuratively interpreted and also what must be so interpreted. *But that which is edifying is so only because it already conforms with the New Testament, and the unedifying has to be made edifying by figurative meanings in New Testament terms. Thus the extended context determines the plain sense, which, in the case of the Old Testament, resides effectively in the text of the New. There was a Jewish or carnal sense ...; but the true sense was Christian and spiritual, and that sense could be represented as the plain sense. The figurative becomes the literal.*
>
> KERMODE, 236–7, emphasis added

There is much to unpack in this phenomenally rich passage. A starting point is its last two sentences describing the interposition of pejorative Christian imagery upon almost all of the "Old Testament." Reminding his readers that the early Christian authorities decided that their new religion would retain what was "Old" – they did not have to do this, after all! – Kermode understands that eventually the "superseded" religion of Judaism had to be described as "carnal," as "literal" in a material way that provokes the more "spiritual" successor religion to reduce the older compendium of sacred texts to a commonsensical reading *only* when that vibrant, living, heroic, and ethical history does not "contradict" the "Christian and spiritual" approach to theological meaning.

For the Jews, on the other hand, there need not be such an absolute distinction between law and spirit, body and soul, literal textual meaning and imaginative interpretations. Saint Augustine set up some of these seeming "oppositions" at around the time Constantine was establishing for Europe the previously beleaguered Christian faith. Kermode wants us to see that the system of "allegory" – the reading into the Jewish texts of non-literal understandings defying any common sensical hermeneutics – prevailed over the "literal" in almost any passage from the Jewish Bible that conveyed the history of a people and that in the process offended if allowed to keep its literal meaning the claims of the new religion.

For Kermode, it was Saint Augustine who might have privileged the "literal" – i.e. the "truth" – in these passages but then made the key move of excluding from an ordinary understanding passages that could be read to offend against "charity," "virtuous conduct and the true faith." As I shall explore much more fully in my next sections, the "carnal" included the law – which was rejected in its so-called literalism – and the rest of Jewish history was falsified by being incorporated into the figurative or the allegorical.

The fantastical result called out and brought down by Nietzsche more than a century before Kermode, distorted Moses' staff to be a precursor of the Cross, Jesus to be present with Abraham, the prophet Isaiah (Kermode's example in the quoted passage) to be announcing Christ-as-Messiah, and the sacred 10 commandments to be worthy of reduction to two only. All of the magnificence of the Jewish sacred texts, by this process, is stripped bare, denigrated, and falsified.

Most significantly for European history, the law becomes not a firm structure of human conduct to be tempered always by the Jewish God's mercy and by narrative understandings of legal meanings,[1] but instead a fabricated beast of duplicity – an instrument of the ever-resisting Jew, the carnal, the Pharisaic, the stiff-necked adherent of a system that by the Augustinian declension no longer deserved close attention but instead justified finding "spiritually" adduced meanings to suit the "true faith."

Christians throughout the millennia, whether meaning good or ill to the Jewish adherents in their midst, were trained from childhood on to see the "Old Testament" as part of their religious heritage but only insofar as it could be authoritatively interpreted to fit the new religion's claims, especially but not only the purely supposed announcement in the Older text of Jesus-as-Messiah.

Put slightly differently, as I have in some earlier writings, Christian exegetes had to adopt a *more flexible* approach to the interpretation of sacred texts. When Saints Paul, John and the other Jews who at the beginning knew and/or loved Jesus took a look at their own sacred texts, which in many cases had existed for eight centuries or more while Jesus walked the earth, they faced a dilemma of meaning. Not much of the Jewish Bible pointed to their man as the Messiah. In fact, then and now, when Jews speak of the Messiah, they more have in mind an epoch than an individual. Maybe it was just what I am calling here religious intransigence, but if you were an ordinary Jew at the time of Jesus, and if you had not personally been down your own Damascus road, you just didn't think in Messianic terms. The dots in your holy texts did not connect at this great teacher's feet. So, as I have discussed, the saints had to wreak some havoc with the traditional textual understandings they had learned as kids.

Here is where flexibility entered the religious game big time. The Gospel writers had to employ a maximum of interpretive flexibility to bring unexpected meaning to sacred texts. With Saint John, they opened a second battle-front. They made the undermining of traditional Jewish interpretive practice just as

1 Cover, "Nomos and Narrative," *op. cit.*, Introduction, n. 9.

vital to the new religion as was the claim that the old texts somehow predicted Jesus-as-Messiah in his specificity.

Everything changed when Constantine institutionalized the new religion and brought victory on both fronts.[2] Billions of people would think of Jesus as their personal savior. This is a happy development, or might have been if it had remained on that level of revelation. Saving the Hebrew texts, as Geoffrey Hartman has ironically put it,[3] Paul brought them to the countless uncircumcised who may have otherwise remained pagans. Individual lives have been enriched; culture has magnificently reflected the exaltation – although also of course, the extreme taste for suffering – of the new faith. If they could have left others alone, Christians might have become a light to the nations. Remember, though, that a religion *cannot not* be intransigent at its core, and one of the core tenets of Christianity is that the "good news" must be brought to heathen and Jew, Asian or African, whatever the cost.

But something else proved even more costly for western culture than the proselytizing of the unwilling. Saint John's second front, the one that ensconced textual flexibility (some might call it sloppiness) as an interpretive principle, left some very important values in shambles. Stability in the interpretation of important texts, Saint John's stories teach, is a bad thing. What began as a logically necessitated strategy of textual deconstruction during the first century extended forth until the Protestant Reformation, setting in place the very idea of distortion as a reading strategy.

For a while now, I have been writing and lecturing about this "flexible hermeneutic," as I call it.[4] I have made the claim, and I have elaborated on it in these pages, that, paradoxically, Roman Catholicism is nowhere more intransigent than in its insistence on *flexibility* in reading the law, in reading ethics, in acting within the political realities of the given age.[5] The Church's behavior during the Holocaust is the best example we have of this ill-advised flexibility. The higher instincts of many in Rome yielded, flexibly, to the perceived needs of the moment. Just as the earliest Christian writers sacrificed textual plausibility to the sea change they were seeking, reality at first was deliberately undermined by post-Holocaust national leaders. But soon, the film clips of Nazi soldiers in handsome uniforms destroying lives of Jewish men, women,

---

2 *Constantine's Sword, op. cit.*, Preface, n. 1.

3 See Geoffrey Hartman, *Saving the Text* (Baltimore: Hopkins, 1982).

4 See, e.g., *Intransigence: Or the Perils of Flexibility, op. cit.*, n. 41. See also in the context of discussion of Bernard Malamud's *The Fixer*, chapter Eight.

5 See chapter six.

and children in central and eastern Europe, and of the gas chambers in Poland brought a common-sense downturn in the postwar practice of Christianity in Great Britain and on the continent. Did the attentive viewer put two and two together? Didn't he or she learn in Church that the Jews and their traditions, where they were not utilized to announce Jesus-as-Messiah, were unworthy of full status in a "spiritualized" Christian world that failed to stop in its tracks such inconceivable atrocities?

B The Pauline Paradox: Resisting Jesus' "Reverence for the Law" While Preserving all the Older Legal Texts

Common to an otherwise highly variegated set of early Christian writers is a deep skepticism about *the law*. To the extent these writers perceived "legalism" in the Jewish traditions and also in the practices of some Jews who lived at the same time as Jesus, they often associated the law with an allegiance to a kind of *material literalism* dictating a believer's every move in life. They wanted to replace this with their spiritual message, emphasizing "love" over strict commandments and – in the argument of this book (following others like Harold Bloom) – also creating an interpretive strategy that avoided "legalism" by permissively engaging in non-literal and often nonsensical readings of texts. So even while asserting the "Old" predicted the New, they rejected a fundamental component of the entire Jewish Bible, which is a reverence for God's law.

Although I am hardly the one and this is not the place to resolve Paul's conflicting statements about law one way or the other, what does seem fair to say, on the current state of the scholarship central to my enterprise in this chapter, is that Paul and Jesus may have disagreed sharply about how to *value* the law. For one thing, as Bart Ehrman observes:

> Some Christians went so far as to insist that Judaism, the old religion of the Jews, had been completely circumvented by the appearance of Christ [supersessionism]… For some scribes of this persuasion, the parable that Jesus tells of new wine in old wineskins may have seemed problematic: *"No one places new wine in old wineskins …. But new wine must be placed in new wineskins. And no one who drinks the old wine wishes for the new, for they say, 'The old is better'."* (*Luke*, 5:38–39) How could Jesus indicate that the old is better than the new? Isn't the salvation he brings superior to anything Judaism (or any other religion) had to offer? Scribes who found

> the saying puzzling simply eliminated the last sentence, so that now Jesus says nothing about the old being better than the new.[6]

But even when fiddling with texts, which I am arguing throughout Part One (here with the help of Ehrman and Bloom) became fully justified as a central methodology of Christian hermeneutics early and throughout the centuries, the Christians were faced with too much of their own evidence tending to show that Jesus – unlike Paul – *revered the Law*. Jesus may have wanted the "new wine" he introduced, in other words, to be encased, indeed, by the "old wineskin" of the Jewish sacred texts he honored.

Harold Bloom brings out best among recent scholars, this dichotomy between Jesus and his brilliant chief propagandist, Paul:

> Though individualistic to a degree where he refigured the messianic vision, Jesus outdoes the Pharisees (his closest rivals) in honoring the Law. His genius fused love for his father, Yahweh as *abba*, with love for the Law, oral and written, and love for his people.
>
> BLOOM, *Jesus and Yahweh*, p. 13

This "reverence for the Law," a phrase I used somewhat controversially to describe my own belief system as it informed my thesis in *The Failure of the Word* on that book's 20th anniversary,[7] was not shared by Paul even if he was not fully antinomian:

> Paul turned to the Gentiles. Jesus, as even the Synoptic Gospels make clear, did not ... Though my [Bloom's] personal distaste for Paul and the violently anti-Jewish Gospel of John, is considerable, I will brood on their Jesuses ... The first observation that I am moved to make is that all of the New Testament is obsessed with its anxious relationship to the Law and the Prophets ....
>
> BLOOM, *Jesus and Yahweh*, 13;36

6 Ehrman, *Misquoting Jesus*, *op. cit.*, Preface, n. 5, p. 96. See also Jeremy Waldron, "'Dead to the Law,' – Paul's Antinomianism", *Cardozo Law Review*, v. 28 (2006).

7 See "Symposium issue on the 20th anniversary of *The Failure of the Word*," in *Cardozo Law Review, vol.* 26 (2005), *e.g.*, at pp. 2247 and 2267. *Failure* was published by Yale University Press in 1984 and reviewed in this prophetic sense by, *inter alia*, A.W.B. Simpson, in TLS, 3/29/84, p. 342.

On this reading, Paul's skepticism about the Jewish law and of its textual base carried with it a decision, as we have seen Kermode describe it,[8] to retain Hebrew ideas and even the full material text (sometimes grossly distorted for their purposes) of the Jewish Bible. For, although the "New Testament" narratives beginning with Paul underwent – according to Ehrman's study – "thousands" of changes, at the time of Jesus himself "Judaism was unique in that it stressed its ancestral traditions, customs, and laws, and maintained that these had been recorded in sacred books [that included most importantly] the laws that God gave Moses indicating how his people were to worship him and behave toward one another in community together. These were sacred laws, to be learned, discussed, and followed – and they were written in a set of books."

Saint Paul, a brilliant tactician as well as writer, became the primary alleged source of this transformation of a great written tradition – along with what was then as much as eight centuries of commentary, written and oral – into a highly dubious emerging religion that might have done as well without the "Old" but had good reasons to maintain it once it figured out how to distort the Jews' moral and historical language.

My Protestant teacher Franklin Littell, at whose feet I sat in his "Christian responsibility for the Holocaust" yearly seminars in Philadelphia, observes that Paul needed to use "considerable skill" in order "to graft believing gentiles into an essentially Jewish history of salvation."[9] Harold Bloom, channeling Nietzsche explicitly, is far less gentle:

> Of course, Nietzsche is extreme. But can he be refuted? Paul is so careless, hasty, and inattentive as a reader of the Hebrew Bible that he very rarely gets any text right; and in so gifted a person this kind of weak misunderstanding can only come from the dialectic of the power drive, of the will to power over a text, even when the text is as formidable as the Torah. There is little agonistic cunning in Paul's misreadings of the Torah; *many indeed are plain howlers*.[10]

How could anyone get things so badly wrong? Can we excuse Paul because he thought the end of days was at hand? Does an emergency excuse falsehood? Unlike many of the other foundational writers, the Saul who became Paul believed that Jesus would herald the end of days, the time when men beat their swords into plowshares, study war no more, etc. Can we condone Paul, when

---

8 Kermode, *op. cit.*, Preface, n. 3.

9 Littell, *op. cit.*, Preface, n. 4, p. 29.

10 Bloom, *op. cit.*, Preface, n. 6, p. 80, emphasis added.

he saw with his own eyes that the world was not ending, yet he continued to lie about Jewish sacred texts? Even after the crucifixion, in identifying potential Christian communities in Europe, Paul continues to work with the old, sacred texts to make them fit, somehow, the known reality of Jesus' presence on earth. His eschatology having been disproved, we might say, his hermeneutics had to prevail; or, in plainer terms, when the world neither ended nor changed as the old texts said it would upon the coming of the true Messiah, those texts had to be manipulated through a new and radical method of reading them. The beleaguered and impassioned first Christians, as recognized by the Christian prophet Nietzsche to have distorted out of a sense of emergency such sacred Jewish texts as the Pentateuch, book of Isaiah, and the Psalms, wound up instantiating interpretive distortion.

Perhaps even more tragically, respect – or as I call it *reverence* – for Law diminished. Later Christian iterations of "Law" – as this book shall trace them perhaps especially through *The Merchant of Venice* in Part Two – bore little resemblance to the rich textured Jewish traditions Paul extinguished. Despite Christian falsehoods about Jewish legalistic harshness, laws promulgated and applied under nominally Christian regimes turned out to be far more cruel.[11] You cannot "do" law without a respect for it! So it is not by chance that Carroll, thinking at the end of his journey about the cross at Auschwitz, associates it with Pius XII's antinomianism, the Pontiff's formal reiteration that the Jews and their Law were superannuated:

> I began this book at the mercy of an instinctive wish that the cross at Auschwitz could be made simply to disappear ... My wish is different now, the product not of instinct but of this history. The cross at Auschwitz, transcending whatever benign intention attaches to it, embodies supersessionalism, medieval absolutism, the cult of martyrdom, the violence

11 The classic *accurate* understanding of the *merciful* application of what Christians wrongly posit as some cruelly legalistic, "eye-for-an-eye" Judaic approach to punishment is the "bloody Sanhedrin" story: "The word Sanhedrin may trigger negative associations for those brought up to recall the legislative body that handed over Jesus to his Roman executioners. Yet in Jewish tradition the Sanhedrin was one of the triumphs of ancient Judaism. The legal processes it dealt with became the foundation stone of Jewish jurisprudence. Its reputation for delving into the most complex issues, in order to find for an accused person, was legendary. *The Talmud says that a Sanhedrin that sentenced someone to death once in 70 years was considered a bloody Sanhedrin.* Mordechai Beck, "Face to Faith," *The Guardian*, opinions, 6/9/07. The Christians perversely undermine this beautiful tradition, turning light into the darkness of their own practices. Law without a reverence for law is the law we see throughout this book, infinitely cruel.

of God, the ancient hatred of Jews, and the Christian betrayal of Jesus Christ. This is the cross that was stolen by the emperor Constantine, perverted by the crusaders, and blasphemed by the editors of *La Croix* [a viciously antisemitic religious paper who falsely accused Dreyfus and provoked decades of Jew hatred see Pierre Sorlin, *La Croix Et Les Juifs*, Paris, Grasset, 1967]. Pius XII, in the encyclical *Mystici Corporis Christi*, issued in June 1943 at the roundup of Jews was peaking, declared "... but on the gibbet of his death Jesus made void the Law with its decrees, [and] fastened the handwriting of the Old Testament to the Cross, establishing the New Testament in His blood .... On the Cross, then, the Old Law died, soon to be buried and to be a bearer of death." In the name of the cross, even in 1943, Jews were implicitly being accused of causing death, and not just Jesus'. And in recent years, by self-proclaimed Christian friends of Jews, the cross has been imposed on them, whether they wanted it or not ... The cross has thus been twisted into an apologetic tool and a source of slander. It has consistently been made to serve the purpose of power. Auschwitz is the final disclosure of this truth.

[602–3] CARROLL

CHAPTER 3

Jews are Not for Jesus; Jesus is Not for Jews

A "We Christians Need Jewry First"

Why, once again, in the Charlottesville's mob, do Christians seem to define themselves not through any positive features of their own belief system but in opposition to a negative image of Jews? – "Jews will not replace us!"[1] Franklin Littell, a Protestant revolutionary thinker among my influencers, puts it this way in a statement that holds at least some glimmer of hope for better respect among Christians for the Jews:

> The relationship of Christendom to the Jewish people has been so wretched for so long that a number of outspoken Jewish leaders say frankly that they expect nothing and desire nothing from the Christians except that they keep their distance. We need each other to be sure, but we Christians need Jewry first. The Jewish people can define itself in history without Christianity: Christians cannot establish a self-identity except in relationship to the Jewish people – past and present, and whenever the Christians have attempted to do so, they have fallen into grievous heresy and sin.
>
> FRANKLIN LITTELL, *The Crucifixion of The Jews*, p. 66

On a similar note, the Unitarian minister R. Travers Herford says:[2]

> Whatever part Christianity was intended to play in the providential design for mankind, that part could only be played if there were present also, and at every stage, a living Judaism. Christian efforts to convert the Jews or to destroy Judaism were in reality attempts at suicide .... The Church has always regarded a living Judaism as a continual danger. But a dead Judaism would have been to her a fatal disaster.

1 See *op. cit.*, Introduction, n. 23.
2 Herford, *The Truth about the Pharisees* (N.Y.: Menorah Assoc., 1925), p. 43.

 | DOI:10.1163/9789004525177_005

1 *An Honest View of Inalterable Difference*

I hope by this book to expunge forever the hyphen that has falsely linked irreconcilable religions through the bogus adjective "Judeo-Christian." I lack faith – almost literally – in a phrase that tries by its very punctuation to link belief systems irredeemably opposed one to the other and understood as different by both parties to the presumed linkage.

Except for my "Law and Literature" methodology, I am not unique, certainly not at this mid-2024 date, in scrutinizing Christianity's long relationship to Judaism and in distrusting protestations of mutuality between the religions. Harold Bloom's greatest book, *Jesus and Yahweh*,[3] everywhere argues that the differences are immense, that – here channeling Jaroslav Pelikan and Wayne Meeks[4] – they commence with awful Christian misreadings of Jewish sacred texts, that the Jews' own readings are far sounder and deserve enduring respect, and that Christian interpretive exaggeration is both esthetically displeasing and ultimately quite costly for Jews throughout history.[5]

From the other side of the divide, Friedrich Nietzsche largely concurred. This son of a Lutheran minister, whose "life affirming ideals" began with his early reading list of "the first book of Moses, … Cicero, [and] the *Iliad* –," wrote with characteristic bluntness:

> In the Jewish "Old Testament," the book of divine justice, there are people and things and speeches in such a grand style that Greek and Indic literature have nothing to equal them. One stands in awe and reverence before these enormous remains of what man once had been, and one has sad thoughts about ancient Asia and its tiny promontory Europe which insists on distinguishing itself by way of "human progress" from Asia. On the other hand, whoever is only a scrawny, tame domestic animal with the needs of a domestic animal (like our "cultured" men of today, including the Christians of cultured Christendom), has nothing to surprise nor distress him when he views these ruins. One's taste for the Old Testament is a touchstone as to "great" and "small." Perhaps the cultured man of today will find the New Testament, the book of grace, much more in accordance with his heart. (It has much of the regular, tender-hearted, stuffy odor of the devotee and the small soul.) *To have pasted this New*

3 Bloom, *Jesus and Yahweh*, *op. cit.*, Preface, n. 6.
4 Bloom, *id.*, pp. 72–74.
5 Bloom, *id.*, describing how and why the brilliant early Christians distorted the Jewish texts, commandeered and "enslaved" them, to use his terminology.

> *Testament (a rococo taste in every sense) together into one book with the Old Testament, and to call this the "Bible," "the Book," is possibly the greatest recklessness and "sin against the Holy Ghost" that literary Europe has on its conscience.*
>
> NIETZSCHE, *Beyond Good and Evil, Aphorism* 52, emphasis added

From Nietzsche's iconoclastic soul a truth emerged, perhaps for the first time in such a direct way among Christian thinkers: it is a sin to place together in the same grammatical or bibliographical place two traditions so diametrically opposed in their styles, their heroes, their values and – perhaps especially – their opposed embracing, versus deliberate falsification, of textual truths.

And as to their very theologies? Trude Weiss Rosmarin put it this way in her 1943 book, *Judaism and Christianity: The Differences*:[6]

> The chief and fundamental difference between Judaism and Christianity is that the former is committed to pure and uncompromising monotheism and the latter subscribes to the belief in the Trinitarian nature of the Divine Being. Trinitarianism, that is to say, the Belief in and worship of "God, the Son, and the Holy Spirit," are as basic and important to all types and denominations of Christianity, as they are contrary to all and everything Judaism holds sacred. To the unconditional monotheism of Judaism the doctrine of the Trinity is profoundly objectionable, because it is a concession to polytheism or, at any rate, an adulteration of the idea of the One, Unique, Indefinable, and *Indivisible* God .... Judaism has always fought, and with all the weapons at its disposal, against the Christian idea of incarnation, that is to say, of God's coming into human life. The thought that "God was made man" is shocking beyond words to the Jew who believes that God is One and Unique, and that this Uniqueness consists also in His utter difference from anything and everything in existence and anything and everything man can possibly fashion in his mind and label "God." How, then, can the Jewish and Christian ideas of God be reconciled, or how can it be said that the "two religions are truly, basically one?"

To the Jewish mind – scholarly, sectarian, or secular – Weiss-Rosmarin's formulation is as true as 2 + 2 = 4. Only such ingrained cliches as the adjective

6 Middle Village, N.Y.: Jonathan David Publishers (1972).

"Judeo-Christian" divert attention from what amounts to an unavoidable clash of theologies. And sincere Christian theologians have been no less forthright:

> These two religious systems have confronted each other for nineteen centuries, have influenced each other profoundly, both internally and externally, and still exist side by side, offering rival divine revelations and *apparently no nearer to a reconciliation than they were at the beginning* .... Judaism and Christianity can never blend without the surrender by the one or the other of its fundamental principles.
>
> PROF. R. TRAVERS HERFORD, 1925[7]

2 *The Metaphor of "Oil and Water" in its Most Relevant Historical Context*

Ironically, in the midst of his country's most antisemitic and cruel period, Vichy's foremost government lawyer put the "oil and water" image to the service of justifying the persecution, arrest, and eventual deportation of Jews under color of vicious French laws not – as history has by now made inarguably clear[8] – required by any German "Diktat." A chief architect of those laws, the second Justice Minister and pre-War liberal Joseph Barthelemy, evokes and exemplifies my major themes here:

> We must speak seriously, serenely, amicably, fraternally, but also frankly and courageously about the Jewish problem. Most of us have had Jews among our friends. I have had friends of that race and I hope to keep them. It's a fact nonetheless that for centuries they have refused to meld into the French community. "Put a glass of oil into a tub [barrique] of water, a chief rabbi used to say to me proudly, the oil will remain separate. Double the quantity of water, triple it, increase it a hundred fold, the glass of oil will never mix itself into the vile liquid. So it is with our race." This is the fact that the French government had to face .... I am obsessed in writing these things by the specter of great Jews who are my colleagues, partners, or friends, like the great Bergson, that undeniable glory of French philosophy and literature, and I add, one who thinks French [*pensant francais*]. The Marshal [Petain] foresaw [and he helped implement, Barthelemy is saying] ostracizing measures [*des mesures d'exception*] ... I also have a heavy heart when I think of the tragedy of so many individual

7 *Op. cit.*, ch. 3, n 2, pp. 34–5.

8 Marrus and Paxton, *op. cit.*, ch. 1, n. 18; Weisberg, *Vichy Law, op. cit.*, Introduction, n. 16.

> situations. I need all my reason to think that it was really necessary to take such measures, even against one's will, to heal surgically this suffering French soul of the sickness that has taken us where we are. The law is cruel. Those who bear responsibility for the destiny of the country have judged it necessary.[9]

Aside from my focus here on the dichotomy of "oil and water" – which is elaborated apropos of *The Merchant of Venice* in Part Two of the book – Vichy Justice Minister Barthelemy's pronouncement is typical in two other, far less accurate, respects. His assertion that "the law is cruel" could only have been made by a non-Jew, and Barthelemy was a practicing Catholic. Jews do *not* think that the law is inevitably cruel. On the contrary, it is to be *revered* as a pathway to justice. Also, Vichy's guardian of that law as Justice Minister bemoans (falsely) the necessity of sacrificing Jews, although otherwise completely innocent beyond their legalized status as outsiders, to that cruelty.

Both these corollaries indeed exemplify Barthelemy's primary image of "oil and water." The metaphor of inevitable difference pervades both Jewish and non-Jewish strands of thinking through the ages. It is a difficult metaphor, but truth about fraught issues is often tough to absorb. It is far more honest than the palliative adjective "Judeo-Christian," which attempts to cover over reality by mendaciously building a bridge constructed by hypocritical and fragile materials. Jews will do much better, I argue, when Christians accept forthrightly the differences instead of hiding the grotesque results of their claim that the older religion somehow is part of the new set of beliefs, interpretive principles, and stories that Christianity from its origins falsely associated with Jewish sacred texts and practices.

3 *Jewish Indifference to the "New Testament"*

I think many if not most Christians lack an understanding of the way a preponderance of Jews (and perhaps other non-Christians and non-believers) feel about the New Testament. Apart from the very occasional Jewish scholar who has chosen to specialize in the New Testament (and recognizing that Muslims may well look more closely at the teachings of Jesus, whom they honor as a prophet), Jews display less variation in feeling than one might expect. The best word for it is *indifference*. Not hatred, not fear, not even really curiosity. Most Jews never crack the spine of any edition of the Christian Bible,[10] no matter

9 *Vichy Law, op. cit.*, Introduction, n. 17, pp. 142–3, italics added. See Berard letter.

10 For non-specialist Jewish scholars whose very efforts offset my generalization here, I recommend the late Robert Burt, *In The Whirlwind* (Cambridge: Harvard U. Press, 2012),

how frequently in history one has been forced on them or – more benignly – one is offered to them, say at motels or by curbstone proselytizers. Sure, there may be a glance at certain sections (if required) in a Great Literature course. Non-Christian music-lovers might know every lyric of "Amazing Grace" or Handel's "Messiah." Paintings evoke magnificently certain key symbols, such as the Annunication, the Pieta, the Crucifixion, or events such as the Clearing of the Temple, the Last Supper, or the Resurrection. Secular Jews such as myself tend to understand, in broad strokes, that the early Christian writers sought love in the world and that they had a spiritually elevated leader who had actually walked the earth and whom they considered to be the son of God. There is not much else, not much about what probably counts most to Christians: the "second coming," the usurpation of the Jewish Bible, the Apocalypse, eschatology, nothing at all except perhaps Dante's fantastical map of the afterlife, or the account of Purgatory by the ghost of King Hamlet.

Jewish indifference to the texts that have so influenced billions is a small miracle that even today challenges rational explanation. In many earlier European generations, Jews were forced by the Roman Catholic Church to listen to sermons directly attacking their own beliefs while furthering the perspective of the New Testament. Well into the 19th century, as Kertzer reports, "Any Jew who failed to attend on the day assigned him or her was to be assessed a heavy fine, with a third of the fine going to the 'secret informer' who reported the delinquent to the authorities." [*The Popes against The Jews*, 84–5]

Many of the "forced sermons" took the Jews' own weekly readings of their Bible and slanted the texts towards a Christological interpretation. The strategy, which my book scrutinizes in a variety of historical situations, at least seems to pay the Jews the "compliment" of taking their own sacred texts to heart. The New Testament relies heavily on the Jewish Bible. Why the absence of reciprocal interest, even (or especially) when the newer stories have been forced on the keepers of the older texts?

The vast majority of Jews thus "exposed" to the Christian message exited unmoved. And the fortunate many who were not forced into such repulsive situations simply did not read the otherwise influential "new" version of the Bible. Harold Bloom, in what for me is his greatest contribution (late in his life) to understanding texts, echoes this Jewish combination of indifference except when forced to confront the "new" faith and deep concern about how Christianity has deformed the magnificent texts of the Jewish sacred Bible.[11]

---

especially chapters 9 through 11. And Harold Bloom's *Jesus and Yahweh* plays a major role here, *op. cit.*, Preface, n. 6.

11 *Jesus and Yahweh*, *op. cit.*, Preface, n. 6.

Another answer, I think, has to do with a sense, informed more by long tradition than by entry into the texts themselves, that the Christian use of Jewish sacred texts is distasteful and implausible. Secular Jews who rarely pick up their own Bible still have an innate sense of how to read their own stories. Christian readings of the "Old Testament" – at least in the schematic way Jews tend to understand them – make no sense. The Messiah exists, for example, as a common icon. But Jews know deep down and in a way that just will not be altered that the Messiah makes the world better. If one comes along – and there have been many claimants through the years – he or she or it had better make sure the lion lies down with the lamb and swords are beaten into plowshares. There's no second chance in the Jewish texts, not for Moses (who breaks the tables of the Law and thus for all his goodness, modesty, and leadership is not permitted to enter the Holy Land) and surely not for some putative Messiah who fails to do the job the first time around.

Sustaining all forms of Christian belief is a set of Jewish textual predicates so divorced from their origins as to leave the proponents of the "older" Bible (standing on its own!) amazed into indifference. Christianity's ascension to majority status, which began 325 years or so after Jesus during the reign of Constantine, still had to be undergirded by an insistent evangelicism based on an astounding reversal of the Jewish Bible's meanings. Instead of quiet contentment borne of their personal revelation and salvation, most Christian sects still insist on converting the heathens. A religion that simultaneously usurps and coerces another cannot endure forever.

Esthetics/Taste. Nietzsche put his finger on yet another reason many if not most Jews do not read the New Testament: *esthetics*. We have only so much time, and after all there is so much we want to read. You may adore Thackery while for me it is Trollope. Maybe a line or two of this or that text shows us enough to lead us elsewhere. Our life as readers involves us in choices based on taste: Nietzsche nailed the esthetic distaste of the Jew brought up on the magnificence of the Torah to the somewhat strange stories in the New Testament;

> The Old Testament is another story. I have the highest respect for that book. I find in it great men, a heroic landscape amid one of the rarest things on earth, the naivete of a strong heart. What is more, I find a *people*. In the New Testament, on the other hand, I find nothing but petty sectarianism, a Rococo of the spirit, abounding in curious scrollwork and intricate geometries and breathing the air of the conventicle; to say nothing of that occasional whiff of bucolic mawkishness of the epoch (and the locale) and which is not so much Jewish as Hellenistic. Here humility and braggadocio [*Wichtigtuerei*] are bedfellows; here we find

> stupendous volubility of feeling: the trappings of passion without real passion; an embarrassing amount of gesturing; obviously there is a lack of good breeding all the way through.
>
> NIETZSCHE, *On the Genealogy of Morals*, 3:22

Nietzsche located the esthetic problem in the New Testament. Harold Bloom later adds that such secular American writers as William Faulkner had the same comparative problem; Bloom:

> The New Testament is a remarkable (though uneven) literary achievement, but no secular reader (who knows how to read) could judge it to be of the aesthetic eminence of almost all of the Hebrew Bible .... William Faulkner expressed a persuasive preference for the immensely varied stories of the Hebrew Bible as compared with *the* Greek New Testament, which strives to tell one story and one story only ... [As to] the virulent intensities of John, [he merely fulfilled] the incessant misreadings of the Jewish Bible [inaugurated by Paul].[12]

Its stories often have a certain strange beauty – they can also be quite ugly, as we shall see. But the beauty is born of individual revelation and thus hard to translate to the non-initiated. For the Jewish Bible's histories and laws we find the unsatisfying replacements of localized events reported so variously in the sacred texts of Christianity that the historical features are implicitly denigrated.

B The Example of John

In *In Praise of Intransigence*,[13] I cite numerous passages from the Gospel According to Saint John that throw stones at the Jews in his midst, sometimes exhibiting an almost gratuitous resentment, as the writer "angrily'[14] (Harold Bloom) exposes what seem like hypocritical patterns in "Pharisaic" practice, patterns however that make for a "false" report rather than one imbued with verisimilitude.[15]

In John 7, to take but one of many examples, Jews respond to the idea that Jesus might be the Messiah with some exceptionally well-reasoned, textualist

12 *Jesus and Yahweh, id.*, 30, pp. 36–42.
13 *Op. cit.*, Preface, n. 17.
14 Bloom, *Jesus and Yahweh, op. cit.*, Preface, n. 6, p. 5.
15 Bloom quoting Ralph Meeks, *id.*

skepticism. The conditions under which Jews had already for eight centuries built up their hopes and their prophetic construct of the Messiah were simply not met by Jesus Christ, no matter how great a teacher and Rabbi he was. There were many false messiahs roaming the region (this has hardly stopped well into the 21st century C.E.!). Maybe, in telling the story of one you may have thought was the Messiah, at least some tolerance could be vouchsafed the Jews who just were not convinced. The opposite is the reaction, however. Not disappointment but outright *ressentiment*; not some concession to the long traditions and expectations of Judaism but instead rage.

This is not pretty! In John's account, Jews are at best nitpickers. In verses 40–44, for example, they Pharisaically (according to John, inaugurating this calumny against Jewish modes of reading) split hairs about whether the Messiah was supposed to descend from David and come from Bethlehem. Opposition to Jesus is both derived from the Jewish prophetic tradition and linked to the interpretive strategy of sticking to the text. Christian commentators label this a quibble: "there is a division among the people over superficial matters," says one. But for the Jewish reader ensconced in long traditions of textual understanding, it is no mere "quibble" to try to restore interpretive integrity to their own Bible.

I proceeded in *Intransigence* to credit the local Jews' so-called stubborn opposition to the Jesus-as-Messiah claim. The distorted interpretation of parts of *Isaiah* (chs. 52 and 53) and *The Psalms* (e.g., 69:8,9), does not get the job done in the face of legitimate insistence upon adhering to these sacred texts' otherwise ensconced meanings that have nothing whatsoever to do with Jesus! As Bloom puts it:

> The first observation that I am moved to make is that all of the New Testament is obsessed with its anxious relationship to the Law and the Prophets, and seeks to resolve a complex anguish resulting from that overwhelming influence.
>
> *Jesus And Yahweh*

Isaiah does not pronounce the coming of Jesus. Instead, as Franklin Littell asserts, its "suffering servant," its "despised" subject is the Jewish people in exile:

> Is [not] the Jewish people, after all and in spite of two millennia of Christian calumny, the true Suffering Servant promised in Isaiah?[16]

16 Littell, *op. cit.*, pp. 16–17.

As I argued in *Intransigence*:

> Saint John could not of course foresee that his own frustrated response to Jewish non-acceptance might someday help bring about the genocide of his own people. But he was obviously very annoyed that most Jews just could not even contemplate such distortions as his own of their own sacred texts. The Jewish refusal over the next nineteen centuries of Christian mis-readings only fueled what had by then become majoritarian resentment. But to take these lines with John's understanding required more *textual flexibility* than the minority's experts (or, I imagine, most reading communities dealing with familiar and precious stories) were willing to show. These were, after all, sacred texts received not without creative variation but nonetheless within *certain hermeneutic bounds* that were being stretched to fantastical limits by the intervening and – so the Christians hoped – "superseding" interpretation.[17]

My argument further characterized John as conducting a two-front war, in which the destruction of the Jewish interpretive tradition is equally as important as – indeed intertwined with! – the claims for the divinity of Jesus. Strangely, it was just as important to do away with hermeneutic accuracy as it was to proclaim the coming of the Messiah (which was a contradiction, to the Jewish mind, of how and when such an event would occur according to their own texts!).[18]

The strategy of elevating "spirit" above "letter" assisted Christians across the millennia to distort sacred Jewish understandings of the texts that – strangely and unnecessarily – Christians nonetheless chose to incorporate into their "Bible":

> Opposed to the "Letter," on this view, was the "Spirit." The elaborate system of laws established in the older "Testament" could be denigrated, and it was "replaced" or at least "fulfilled" by the commandment to "Love thy neighbor," a value that of course the ancient text repetitively revered on its own. Yet the beautiful-sounding new spirit, deliberately uncoupled from the old system of well-understood ethics and law, could not really work on earth. Justice, for example, needed as the centuries developed,

17 *Intransigence, op. cit.*, ch. 1, n. 2.
18 *Id.*

to be on its guard against the "Spirit," because Christian versions of the spirit usually signalled bad news to all earthly outsiders.[19]

The Jews, who to their immense hermeneutic credit are slow to change – if it ain't broken, don't fix it! – have tended to couch grotesque "advances" in interpretive understandings of their own sacred texts somewhat in the manner of the following words of a respected thinker on the Talmud:

> A viable system of law must not sacrifice either its spirit or its letter. Hasty compromises, unfounded alterations, and whimsical abandonment of legal traditions lead only to chaos. In order for a legal system to endure and flourish, it is necessary for the law to be flexible, elastic, and fluid, as well as definitive, clear, and steadfast.[20]

No one has cast better than Harold Bloom (that latter day prophet!) the dichotomy between John's implausible reading strategies and those of the calmly resisting Jewish peoples:

> As John's Jesus graciously is about to tell them, the Jews' father is the devil. They scarcely can be blamed for answering "Abraham is our father." … Jesus responds by calling them liars, again surely rather gratuitously, and then by ensnaring them in John's subtlest entrapment:
>
> Your father Abraham rejoiced that he was to see my day; he saw it and he was glad." The Jews then said to him "You are not yet 50 years old, and have you seen Abraham?" Jesus said to them, "Truly, truly, I say to you, before Abraham was, I am.[21]

The response to *Jesus and Yahweh* has been relatively muted. But Bloom anticipated this: his argument posits a seemingly thorough victory of Christian hermeneutics, despite all the flaws he notes, many of which have been picked up in very recent books[22] and in my own work, notably the one you are reading; but in an O.Henry switch, he predicts that Yahweh will again move to restore His people's sound traditions.[23]

19 *Id.*
20 Samuel N. Hoenig, *The Essence of Talmudic Law and Thought* (N.Y.: Jason Aronson, 1993).
21 *Jesus and Yahweh*, *op. cit.*, Preface, n. 6, pp. 84–5, citing John, 8:56–58.
22 See sources *op. cit.*, Introduction, n. 15.
23 See text at Preface, n. 10.

Yahweh may not yet have spoken his final word upon this matter.

The project of re-opening and exposing to the light of common sense the millennia-long Christian attack on hermeneutic soundness may seem Quixotic, although the presence in this book of so many earlier distinguished Quixotes is encouraging. (I stand in, too, for those who tilted at this windmill in relative anonymity.) Our collective endeavors implicate the individual belief systems of too many Christians, including some who otherwise would be most attracted to the light behind the newly re-opened door. On the other hand, should we ignore the fact that Jews living and dead have also had to suffer the slings and arrows of Christianity's attacks on their most precious beliefs and practices?

During the Holocaust, the Jews may have hit rock bottom (please excuse the metaphor, entirely and tragically apt considering the killing fields of Belarus in 1941 and 1942, when Jewish men, women, children, and babies fell to the stony and cold earth with Christian bullets in their skulls!), but I think that, as a Shakespearian, Harold Bloom is saying their Yahweh may arise again and that, in the words of Edgar in *King Lear*, a true suffering servant who reminds some 21st century viewers of those pathetic innocents whose bodies were sent to the unyielding pit of death on the killing fields of eastern Europe:

> The lamentable change is from the best,/The worst returns to laughter.
>
> *King Lear*, IV, I, 5–6

May this chapter, and perhaps this book, be a small contribution to the return to the hermeneutic wars of Yahweh and his mercy-laden justice!

PART 2

The Two Sides of the Judeo-Christian: the Judaic and the Christian through the Lens of Shakespeare

Introduction to Part II

The book's focus from here to the end is on individual stories, the basic stuff of the "Law *in* Literature." History continues to be linked intimately to each such story, and the aim of my analysis continues to be *how* these stories mean,[1] how through the effect of their language and form they manage themes that would otherwise be almost impossible to convey. I begin by treating at considerable length a text debated almost as widely as the Scriptures, Shakespeare's complex comedy, *The Merchant of Venice*. I take my reader on the magical mystery tour that is this problematic play. The trip is worth the time and the imaginative input I hope it will inspire in each reader. Every major theme of this book is covered in the discussion of *Merchant* over two long chapters, not only allusively but in depth. At far less length but still sufficiently for my task, I treat also one phenomenal, law – infused sonnet (#134) and several other plays, *Measure For Measure*, *King Lear*, *Hamlet,* and *The Tempest.*

As we go through *Merchant,* we will find the literal embodiment (on the stage) of the oil-and-water opposition I have referenced earlier. No text so challenges readers regarding claims such as those embodied in that dichotomy than does *Merchant,* and it deserves the ink I drop into the uneasy mixture. No matter how familiar with it my readers are, or if they need a good refresher, the two Chapters of Part Two will go through the whole play again, vitally connecting it with this book's earlier pages.

---

1 John Ciardi and Miller Williams, *How Does a Poem Mean?* (N.Y.: Riverside Press, 1959).

CHAPTER 4

"Oil vs Water" in *The Merchant of Venice*

A Why Every Great Actor Wants to Play Shylock

Accused of being "antisemitic" – in my view with terrible inaccuracy albeit by writers I deeply admire and have had the pleasure of meeting (Harold Bloom, Anthony Julius[1]), the play in less simplistic terms should be thought of not only as representing the inalterable difference between Christian and Jew but of being *pro-Jewish*. I have written extensively on the play and benefitted from responses to my claims[2] . This chapter, and in different terms the next chapter, help me to further these dialogues.

Merchant fascinated King James – he of the "authoritative" version of the Bible – to the extent that, alone among Shakespeare's plays, he insisted on seeing it twice.[3] It has provoked audiences ever since, and its meanings still puzzle us while its comic plot somehow manages to delight us at the same time. Its "villain," Shylock compels our often admiring scrutiny, even though we know we are supposed to hate him. He has the best lines, and every great actor

1 Julius, *Trials of The Diaspora; History of Antisemitism in England* (London: O.U.P., 2010), pp. 178ff.; Bloom, *Shakespeare, The Invention of The Human* (N.Y.: Riverhead, 1999).

2 See perhaps most prominently my "Then You Shall be His Surety: Oaths and Mediating Breaches in *The Merchant of Venice*," in *Poethics and Other Strategies of Law and Literature, op. cit.*, Introduction, n. 4; "Antonio's Legalistic Cruelty: Interdisciplinarity and *The Merchant of Venice*," in *College Literature*, vol. 25 (1998), p. 12, repr. in Myrsiades, ed., *Undisciplining Literature* (N.Y.: Peter Lang, 1998), p. 180; and "The Concept and Performance of the Code in *The Merchant of Venice*," in Watt and Raffield, eds., *Shakespeare and The Law* (U.K.: Hart Publishing, 2007), p. 289. All have been widely discussed. See, e.g., Geoffrey Hartman, "The Tricksy Word: Richard Weisberg on *The Merchant of Venice*," *Law and Literature*, vol. 23 (2011), p. 71; Cormack, Nussbaum, and Strier, eds., Shakespeare and The Law (Chicago: U. of Chicago Press, 2012), at p. 5 and p. 199, where Richard Strier argues against my "Legalistic Cruelty" that "the exact financial terms of Shylock's punishment are quite unclear." I disagree, despite Strier's pronouncement, and maintain on these pages that Antonio in assessing these penalties knows exactly what he is doing and that the result for Shylock as a matter of property law is disastrously clear. Paula Bolduc, "The Cruelty of Mercy: Oxymoronic Paradoxes," https://digitalcommons.salve.edu (2008); Nicoleta Cinpoes, "Defrauding Daughters Turning Deviant Wives?: Reading Female Agency in *The Merchant of Venice*," SEDERI, 21 (2011), p. 133.

3 Alscher and Weisberg, "Why King James Insisted, as with No Other Skakespearian Play on Seeing '*The Merchant of Venice*' Twice," in Carpi, ed., *Property Law in Renaissance Literature* (2005).

 | DOI:10.1163/9789004525177_006

in every generation covets the role. F. Murray Abraham, for example, "always knew he wanted to play Shylock … [As the actor, who took the role whenever offered it, to brilliant reviews, says:] 'Some people are so angry about this play that they say it shouldn't be presented … But that's close to book-burning, as far as I'm concerned. This was one of the first plays that presented a Jew as a normal person. Until then, Jews had been portrayed as something less than human. [*Merchant*] was revolutionary.'"[4]

Merchant, although generically a comedy, implicates entire institutions, including law, religion, and even comic theater itself. On a basic plot level, it begins when a Venetian Jewish money lender, Shylock, agrees if the wealthy merchant Antonio will guarantee the deal, to tender a loan of 3000 ducats to a young fortune-hunter named Bassanio. The latter wishes to court the beautiful heiress Portia, whose estate near Venice, on the island of Belmont, now accepts suitors to her hand in marriage. Short on ready cash and shorter still on credit-worthiness, Bassanio has to entreat a loan from his older friend Antonio, the Merchant of Venice himself. Antonio induces "the Jew" (as he is often called by the Venetian Christians) to lend the younger man the money by inserting his own credit and the pledge of a pound of his flesh into the bargain. Bassanio, flush with the needed ducats, adorns himself and his group of cronies, hires a gondola or two, and heads out to woo Portia. His behavior in general, as Frank Kermode puts it,[5] "shows us why the Christians in this play are, on the whole, such an unlikeable lot."

In the "casket sub-plot," Bassanio manages to choose correctly from among three treasure chests, which Portia has laid out in front of all of her suitors because her father's Will requires this little game before she can get married. To her great delight, Portia observes men she dislikes wrongly choose the gold or the silver casket. She tarries a bit with Bassanio, whom she clearly loves – perhaps hinting broadly that the lead casket is the one to choose. Bassanio, not exactly brilliant but good-looking and also quick to take help of any kind, verbal or monetary, picks the lead casket and gets to marry Portia and glom on to her fortune in the process.

These are happy times, as befits a comedy. There are also other romantic couplings, beautiful language, clowns, music, a mardi gras, and a casual sense of a loose mainstream morality – the Venetian Christians are nothing if not flexible. Standing apart from this comic mix, Shylock, – who does not lack

4 Alexander Stevens, "F. Murray Abraham Brings Shylock to Boston," *The Patriot Ledger*, 3/31/11.

5 Kermode, *op. cit.*, Preface, n. 3.

humor – is a fairly stubborn, and even "intransigent"[6] money lender on the still-famous Venetian bridge, the Rialto. A proud Jew in an alien environment, his family and his religion sustain him against the slights of the Christian establishment, which range from personal insult to group hatred to sloppy dealings in general, at least as Shylock sees things; as it has often been played often on the stage, *Merchant* could easily be made into Shylock's tragedy,[7] so powerful and so wronged is his character.

Yet, this play must be understood for what it is: a *comedy* in which, like the world itself over the past centuries, the ethical, the faithful, and the law-abiding are *necessarily* cast away to make life simpler and wealthier for the Christian majority.[8] In my reading, Shakespeare understands that it is the Christian world's inevitable *choice* to turn a figure like Shylock into a villain, because its own morality – like that of an evening of comedy – can find no room for such steadfast seriousness.

Comedies need problems, and indeed the play spirals downhill soon after Bassanio chooses the correct casket and wins the hand (and the purse) of the woman whose golden locks he has greedily compared to Jason's fleece. The couple have not even consummated their marriage – although Portia has given her new husband a ring which he is never to part with– when they receive terrifying news. Antonio's credit for Shylock's loan, in the form of five ships at sea (which in all probability have been launched to plunder colonial wealth abroad),[9] all founder. The Jew demands his pound of flesh. of no small concern to Shylock or to the audience – although Portia herself knows none of this "back-story" – the Jew's vengeful wrath is based on Antonio's admitted habit of spitting on him in the marketplace and his own daughter's running off (along with a big chunk of his portable wealth) with a young Christian charmer, Lorenzo. Shylock feels an anguish that Shakespeare's audience is also meant to feel. So things are looking very bad for Antonio.

Portia hears of this dilemma and sets her extraordinarily supple mind to a solution that will liberate her new husband's spirits so they can make ready for the honeymoon bed, unencumbered by woeful thoughts of Antonio's fate. Although such bliss proves to be an elusive goal, the witty new bride does find

---

6 *Intransigence, op. cit.*, Preface, n. 17.

7 See, e.g., Jaya Ghosh, "*The Merchant of Venice* Strikes the Right Tone as a Tragedy," *The Rogers Review* (3/29/22).

8 See my discussion in *Poethics, op. cit.*, Introduction, ch. 10, n. 4. See also the following two endnotes.

9 Judith Koffler, "Terror and Mutilation in the Golden Age," *Human Rights Quarterly*, vol. 5:2 (1983), at p. 127.

a way to defeat the seemingly blood-thirsty Shylock. Disguised as a kind of "guest-judge" or "*amicus curiae*," she tricks the Jew in open court into demanding "the law," then seems to support him on behalf of the court, and then (somewhat fantastically) declares the law to be against him. He can have his pound of flesh, the "lawyer" informs the Jewish plaintiff, but only if he measures it exactly and also draws no blood. As almost all prominent legal scholars have said of this ploy for well over a century, it simply does not stand as a plausible interpretation of the bond.[10] Were Portia's reading of the contract to hold, no piece of real estate, for example, could ever be transferred without describing every single tree, wall, fixture, nail, and appliance on it in detail. The fictional Prof. Kinsgfield of "The Paper Chase," and every one of my contract-law colleagues, would be appalled.

We must remember, though, that we are analyzing a *comedy*.[11] And Portia's ploy seems at first (until we remember how unjustly Shylock has been treated by Venice and by Antonio) to be at least poetically "just." So he is defeated on the contractual quibble, a bit of nitpicking far exceeding anything a Pharisee, as I signaled in Part One, could ever have imagined. Shylock then learns from the "judge" that, under the terms of a disgraceful Venetian law Portia has in her side pocket, the Alien Statute – a text cited in full later that is an antisemitic element throughout this analysis – strips the Jew of all his wealth, half going to the Merchant, half to the state. And, on a whim of Antonio's to which we shall return, Shylock must also convert to Christianity.

Shylock retains a modicum of his dignity throughout the ordeal. No ordinary comic villain, he continues to have the best lines, even during the trial that is his undoing. Noting how Antonio and Bassanio sentimentally out-do each other in exaggerated expressions of mutual love that include the new husband's open wish to sacrifice his wife, if she were there, to save his friend's life, Shylock takes the time to say:

---

10 The tradition of pro-Shylock legal interpreters of the comedy is led by the famous 19th century jurist Rudolf von Ihering, whose spirited defense of the Jew over several editions of his most prominent book is reported in greater detail in these pages under the heading "The German Tradition", below. See von Ihering, "Der Kampf uns Recht." See also my "Lawyers and Judges Address Shylock's Case," in Nahshon and Shapiro, eds., *Wrestling with Shylock; Jewish Responses to "The Merchant of Venice"* (U.K.: Cambridge U. Press, 2017).

11 On the Donatan tradition of comedy's avoidance of death, see J.V. Cunningham's brilliant *Woe or Wonder* (Denver: Swallow, 1951), pp. 36–70; and see Stephen Greenblatt's superb complementary discussion of *Merchant* in *Will in The World* (N.Y.: Norten, 2016), pp. 34 and 279–287.

> These be the Christian husbands. I have a daughter –
> Would that any of the stock of Barrabas
> Had been her husband rather than a Christian!

Shylock cares about family, marriage vows, and loyalty, and he does so up to and throughout this trial scene, in which supposedly he is hell-bent to take his pound of flesh. These are among his major "sins," from a Christian point of view. Recognizing how opposed the two linked religions are, Shylock wishes his daughter on any kind of husband except these mainstream loose speakers and flexible oath-breakers. Meanwhile, the audience may still have ringing in its ears during the trial Shylock's best known speech about the dignity and fellow-feeling of all of God's creatures, his plea for the common dignity of humanity, "Hath not a Jew eyes?" [III, I, 54] But the Christians, nominal believers in what this speech conveys, disdain extending to any non-converted Jew this prayer for kindness and human equality.

All these lines and all these ways of tying them together lie right there in the text of the play. So even though the "villain" is tricked and brought down, the complexities of his value system remain as a challenge to the less than sterling opposed combination of Christian values. As we shall see, Portia in the final Act certainly seems to have been impressed by the man her wit alone manages to defeat at trial. She will insist (against the odds) that her new husband opt for loyalty and direct commitment as Shylock has throughout the life she now knows much more about than she did before meeting the Jew. It is a "comedy" yes – but one even Shakespeare's immediate audience (including King James) might have had to see twice to understand.

B Is this Play "antisemitic"? Anti-Christian?

1 *"Hath Not a Jew Eyes?"*

Scholars if challenged to opine have generally been willing to call the play antisemitic. They are wrong. But even those otherwise sensitive interpreters like Harold Bloom and Anthony Julius who have called the play "antisemitic" can't stop themselves from writing reams about Shylock.[12] I have entered the fray and my earlier efforts have been answered by many others.[13] Shylock, again,

12 Bloom, *op. cit.*, n. 1.

13 Hartman, "The Tricksy Word," *op. cit.*, ch. 4, n. 2. See also François Ost on *Merchant*, and indeed on Law and Literature more generally: see, e.g., "*Le Marchand de Venise:* Le Pari et La Dette, Le Jeu et La Loi," *Mcgill Law Journal*, vol. 62 (2017), p. 1103.

is the centerpiece of our attention not only for himself but because one's assessment of the Jew naturally flows from and inevitably affects our judgment of the Christian characters. Harold Bloom has quite amazingly said this of the play:

> One would have to be blind, deaf, and dumb not to recognize that Shakespeare's grand, equivocal comedy *The Merchant of Venice* is nevertheless a profoundly antisemitic work. Yet every time I have taught the play, many of my most sensitive and intelligent students become very unhappy when I begin with that observation ....[14]

The syntax and ordering of these two sentences tell us how hard it is for even a professed and proud Jew to declare that Christianity is different from Judaism, and that a text demarcating these differences does not automatically turn out to be anti-Jewish!. For in no other story, besides the Gospels themselves, has the opposition between two belief systems been made clearer. And the result, in Bloom's own word – backed by the reaction of his best students – is "equivocal"! Still, the eminent Shakespearian tells us this magnificent rendering of the old story of the Jewish money-lender is patently antisemitic. Nonsense!

For too long, Jews have been ashamed to state some obvious truths; yet Shakespeare, does so. Shylock's excessive wrath against Antonio is a grave fault. Consider the "equivocal" sources of that wrath, however. Before a religious man such as Shylock would even dream of being physically violent in any way, he had to be pushed beyond human tolerance by the majoritarian Christians who rule everything in his life besides his deeply ethical sense of Jewish values. All this is in the play itself! In Act I, scene iii, where the bond is sealed among Antonio, Bassanio, and Shylock, the latter offers his *friendship* to the Christians, after a lifetime of bearing their insults. Antonio brutally rejects this Jewish offer to love one's enemy, although it lies at the supposed core of Christian values:

> Shylock: Fair sir, you spet on me on Wednesday last
> You spurn'd me such a day, another time
> You call'd me dog; and for these courtesies
> I'll lend you thus much monies?
> Antonio: I am as like to call thee so again,
> To spet on thee again, to spurn thee too.
> If thou wilt lend this money, lend it not
> As to thy friends, for when did friendship take

14 Bloom, *op. cit.*, ch. 4, n. 1, p. 171.

A breed for barren metal of his friend?
But lend it rather to thine enemy,
Who if he break, thou mays't with better face
Exact the penalty.

Shylock: Why, look you how you storm!
I would be friends with you, and have your love,
Forget the shames that you have stain'd me with.
Supply your present wants, and take no doit
Of usance for my moneys, and you'll not hear me.

2 *Shakespeare Knew no Jews*

We do not know if (and if so how) Shakespeare could have learned so well the back-story of Jewish persecution in places like Venice, but there is more than enough of the "equivocal" in this exchange to make Bloom the "blind, deaf, and dumb" one. There were very few Jews in Renaissance England, because they had been given the boot two centuries earlier. Bloom points out that one of the only Jews left around, Dr. Lopez, was drawn and quartered when his influence upon Queen Elizabeth as court physician threatened far more powerful interests. Shakespeare probably knew of this court scandal, which evokes in its way the reward Jews ultimately received for trying to do good works in a Christian world.

Instead, the Jew was forced into the profession of money-lending, having few other options. Christians on the continent periodically forced them into ghettoes and – as we have seen – compelled them to listen to the New Testament sermons that tried to contradict their own Sabbath interpretations of the Jewish Bible. Shylock is complex enough a character to make us imagine, admittedly in a thought experiment, that his creator had read some contemporaneous record akin to the following brief historical description of "usury" from Kertzer's *The Popes against the Jews*:

> The old aristocratic elites in Europe had long looked disdainfully on finance and banking. Indeed, in a number of lands they had for centuries turned to Jews – dubbed "court Jews" for their service to the rulers – to perform these functions. Among the Jews' other advantages was that they were not hampered by the Christian religious prohibition on lending money at interest, a major stumbling block to the development of international commerce. Prohibited by law from owning land and kept out of the trades controlled by guilds, the Jews found in finance and money-lending the only economic path to prosperity open to them. [79]

Shylock's trade was "friendly" to Christians like Antonio in at least two ways: it facilitated the merchants' own businesses and it made the Christians feel better about their lofty morality. The dirty work explicitly accomplished by Jews, Christians like Antonio were liberated to amass such "nicer" millions by looting native populations abroad, exactly what Antonio's colonializing ships were trying to do until they foundered.[15]

What makes Shakespeare especially cogent about the themes of this book, however, is not so much his feel for Jewish-Christian economic relations. It is instead what we would expect from a playwright: his sensitivity to the differences *in speech* between the Christian and Jewish characters. Shylock speaks directly, using earthy images if he uses images at all; during the trial, for just an example, he speaks as follows while the Christians mask the casual violation of marriage vows in the ethereal language of generosity to friends:

> You have among you many a purchased slave
> Which like your asses, and your dogs and mules
> You use in abject and in slavish parts, because you bought them
> ... The pound of flesh which I demand of him
> Is dearly bought, 'tis mine, and I will have it.
>
> IV, I, 90

This is a rhetoric of direct criticism of his Christian interlocutors, who demand of Shlyock some explanation for his pursuing the trial to its gruesome penalty stage. The "antirrhetic form" characterizes his speech. It is not without ethical force, but it contradicts to its very syntax the elevated discourse of every Christian character in the play with but one exception – the yappishly antisemitic Gratiano, whom Shylock pithily dismisses during the trial as follows:

> Til thou canst rail the seal from off my bond
> Thou but offend'st thy lungs to speak so loud
> Repair thy wit, good youth, or it will fall
> To cureless ruin. I stand here for law.
>
> IV, I, 139

His words are acute, but he does not realize that his own, infinitely better schooled "wit" will – if it is not cured – bring *him* to ruin. The Christians do not want wit from a Jew. Christians have too much to hide to hear their own faults, or anything else, described by a Jew. Sixteen centuries after Saint John falsified the Jewish Biblical tradition in defense of Jesus, polite and convenient lies had

15 Koffler, *op. cit.*, ch. 4, n. 9.

become traditional in Catholic circles such as the comedy's world of Venetian law and commerce.

The linguistic differences between Shylock and the Venetian male protagonists crystallize the larger dilemma of how they see and read the law. The directness, the earthiness, the "thereness" of Shylock's speech reflects an ethics of material commitment to the meaning of words and especially of legally sanctioned words. Oaths and promises, bonds and rings, the performatives and the symbols of promises to others – these virtues only begin to look like their opposite in a topsy-turvy environment privileging casual breaches and textual distortion.

C Shylock Has No Rights the Court in Venice is Bound to Respect

1 *Legal Analysts of the Play Have Bestowed These Rights on Him, However*

The trial scene has to some extent divided lawyers from other analysts. In general, distinguished readers trained in the law have been supporters of Shylock. From the 19th century's Rudolf von Ihering to our own generation's Daniel Kornstein,[16] they tend to take his side, despite the pound of flesh, either because they feel that on the terms of the play itself Shylock has a justifiable claim or *because the Jew never intends to cut Antonio*.[17] Either way, these readers agree that Shylock instead wants to teach everybody a lesson about the way mainstream Christians use words to falsify and divert from what is real. Shylock's "back story" about being repeatedly mistreated on the Rialto, which is fully recounted early in the play, as well as his edginess when "the Christians are in the streets," and above all what he has learned of Christian behavior from Lorenzo's theft of his daughter and his ducats (violating two or more of the Jewish God's commandments without blinking an eye!) – all of this perfidy stands revealed in the developing comedy. Lawyers look to a full factual record. It is there.

Almost all legally trained commentators across national traditions agree, at a minimum that Portia's argument about the meaning of the contract amounts to sophistry or even cruelty. Alfred Polgar, a Jewish Viennese essayist writing in

---

16 Kornstein, *Kill all the Lawyers?: Shakespeare's Legal Appeal* (N.J.: Princeton U. Press, 1994).

17 See discussion at the end of this sub-section of Prof. Anton Schuetz' view that *Shylock never intended to cut. and that to think he would is itself antisemitic.* See "Structural Terror," in Goodrich, Barshack, and Schuetz, eds., *Law, Text, Terror* (U.K.: Routledge, 2006), pp. 84f.

the 1920s, sums up the already prevailing view by labeling Portia's contractual argument "rabulistisch" – petty hairsplitting, demagogically vile.[18] Similarly Kornstein, a contemporary American lawyer and critic, articulates a view common to 21st century legal commentators:

1. Liberty of contract is of bedrock importance to Shylock ... [whose] legal stance is far from the harsh caricature often portrayed. Any outsider to a commercial community like Venice (or China today, for example) must be able to rely on the freedom of contract, and especially on impartial judicial treatment even on behalf of the outsider, where merited on the terms of the deal.
2. Throughout the *Merchant*'s trial scene, everybody in the court, from the Duke on down, recognizes that any display of favoritism during this dispute will bring untold hardship to the commerce that is Venice's mainstay.
3. But Portia then points out that the contract says a pound of flesh but nowhere mentions blood. Therefore, she rules, Shylock must cut precisely one pound of flesh – no more, no less – and without shedding any of Antonio's blood, an obvious impossibility ... [This] is transparently absurd ... like granting an easement on land without the right to leave footprints.

Von Ihering, the distinguished German professor of legal philosophy who surely gained no new fans in the late 19th century by taking Shylock's side – but he gained dozens of acolytes in the 20th and 21st century legal communities – articulates this overview of Portia's contractual quibble and brings it down to the level of two key points. First, no character in the Venetian courtroom (Act IV) argues that the pound of flesh provision is unenforceable. (Both continental and English law had in fact periodically countenanced such provisions.) So however legitimate the revulsion against the taking of flesh, Von Ihering, and others, do not emphasize this as a reason to negate the contract. (And neither do the Duke or Portia!)[19]

Next, Professor Von Ihering himself a Jew – inherited from the poet Heine a keen sense of Shylock's power as the character in the play who stands for ethical and legal rightness. The analytical precision as well as the passion of his pro-Shylock position are palpable in Von Ihering's central idea, that Shylock's "is the language which an injured sense of right always speaks in all times and places; the force, not to be shaken, of the conviction that the law must forever

18 Polgar, "Der Kaufmann von Venedig," in *Weltbuehne*, 20:2, 1924, p. 150.

19 Could it be that no character at the court, except for the hysterically antisemitic Gratiano, actually believes that an observant Jew will take a fellow human being's flesh?

remain the law; the lofty strain and pathos of a man, conscious that he pleads not merely for his own person, but for the enacted law." Von Ihering's consistent vision of justice held that the outsider can rely on nothing but the law. To see in Shylock's insistence on his day in court the excessive tribal narrowness posited by many critics is, for von Ihering, a complete misreading of Shakespeare's meaning. Those with power can bend and break the law, using their flexible interpretive skills to sustain their positions; but those already situated at the periphery of society must seek to enforce the law to the letter when they have it on their side, which occurs infrequently enough. Flexible distortion of law will always work against society's outsider, who legitimately fights it with every ounce of strength available. And private law, for example liberty of contract, often affords the outsider a forum to assert rights that would be otherwise lacking.

But to calm her new husband down, Portia uses all of her considerable intelligence and skill to spare the life of a man she already has ample reason to dislike. She has been observing the unseemly closeness of the two men, and Antonio's call on Bassanio's affections even as against Portia's. (Worse will occur out of her eyesight as the trial scene ends). And at least the audience to a comedy, which in traditional terms dating to the Romans,[20] should not have its enjoyment marred by seeing bloodshed on stage, has been saved the experience of potentially watching the Merchant lose a pound of flesh. But another character, the Jew, is destroyed spiritually and materially by Portia's efforts.

Anton Schuetz, a late 20th and early 21st century legal thinker who teaches in London at Birkbeck, goes even further in Shylock's defense than have his legally-trained predecessors. Schuetz argues, and I believe with perfect logic, that Shylock if given the chance would never have cut into Antonio. He just wants his day in court, his only chance to gain the respectful attention of those who hate him for his religion and ethnicity.

2 *Anton Schuetz and the Alien Statute Elaborated: Shylock Would Not Have Cut!*

Shylock in his typically direct and honest way, immediately calls his effort to substantiate his rights a "losing suit against [Antonio]." But he demands pursuing it to teach the Christians that there is rightness to a perspective they have deliberately and brutally quashed, which is that of von Ihering's righteous outsider demanding the Law. (IV, I, 60) Nothing stops him, if he is so hell-bent on self-destruction, to kill Antonio in open court apart from any legal process!

---

20 See J.V. Cunningham, *Woe or Wonder*, *op. cit.*, ch. 4, n. 11.

He has pointed out long before, at the very genesis of the contract in Act One, that there is no commercial value to such a pound of flesh and that therefore the penalty provision that is negotiated in that scene, is nothing more than a "merry bond" and that by not charging interest he is actually extending his friendship to a Christian, who he assumes will not refuse his enemy's offer of love:

> O father Abram, what these Christians are,
> Whose own hard dealings teaches them to suspect
> The thoughts of others! Pray you tell me this:
> If he should break his day, what should I gain
> By the exaction of the forfeiture?
> A pound of man's flesh taken from a man
> Is not so estimable, profitable neither,
> As flesh of muttons, beefs, or goats. I say
> To buy his favor I extend this friendship.
> If he will take it, so; if not, adieu.
> And for my love, I pray you wrong me not.
>
> I, III, 168

Shylock knows, even before the Christians led in court by Portia lay it on thick, that the offer of thrice the bond by the still profligate Bassanio – using his new wife's money – pragmatically makes more sense than the pursuit through to a verdict of his civil remedies. He is not as greedy for material benefit, however, than his stereotype as a Jew pronounces. He wants his rights. He wants a verdict from the Venetian court. Will they be afforded? Is there such a thing as Christian law, even-handedly distributed to all who seek commerce with Venetians?

Portia's dubious interpretive dealings in distorting the contract not only eliminate any risk to Antonio's life but also forestall our knowing whether Shylock would ever have done a violent deed so opposed to his own religious scruples, and most notably to the Sixth Commandment.

Less well known perhaps than any other legal commentator mentioned so far in this chapter, Prof. Anton Schuetz builds brilliantly upon the Germanic tradition of Heine, of Polgar, and especially of von Ihering, in an essay on the play originally published in 2006.[21] Schuetz understands that Shylock is seeking the court's attention and respect, and raises the question whether he truly

---

21 Schuetz in Goodrich, ed., *op. cit.*, ch. 4, n. 17. For Heine, see further at ch. 5, n. 1.

intended to cut Antonio's flesh: But Schuetz pre-empts the question by laying a predicate for it that assumes in the very asking of it an antisemitic bias:

> The problematic question which comes up, reads: what is really the difference between believing that the Jew Shylock, if he were not stopped, would have killed Antonio, and believing, as did entire urban populations in the earlier Middle Ages, in the narratives – infamous and transparently pogrom-motivating – of Christian babies being the victims of Jewish ritual slaughter?[22] ... What, then, would Shylock have done if he had been allowed to wield his knife? Shakespeare leaves us at a complete loss on this point. Even so, the contention that Shakespeare himself believed Shylock to be a potential killer, is a non-sequitur and an arbitrary reply to an improper question.

We don't know and on this view perhaps should not even be asking whether Shylock would have cut. The important element we do know is "the statutory predicament of being a Jew in Venice." Shylock's only chance of gaining respect in Venice – after all he has tried earlier to gain Antonio's friendship and been grotesquely rebuked by that "virtuous, generous Christian" – seems to have been to obtain the court's acknowledgment of his contractual rights. With such a judgment in hand, he would have desisted from an act in violation of his ethical condition as a Jew. And that positive ethic is everywhere available to the average audience member!

We must never forget Prof. Schuetz' dreadful predicate for the formulation of the "Would Shylock Have Cut" question. She who asks it is revealing thereby her antisemitic inclinations. But we never get to an actual dramatically rendered answer.

Poor Shylock, who perilously acts as his own lawyer during the trial, and in the process naively takes the bait of Portia's disguised offers to him to see her as a friend, as a "Daniel," is unaware that his overt position as an outsider has been inscribed in a Venetian statute! When Portia, having anyway already resolved the problem through her "wretched quibble" pulls the Alien Statute out of the hat, he learns to his amazement that he has no rights that Venice needs to recognize. And this sets up Portia's test of Antonio: whether the Christian merchant can in fact do "mercy" – a test which, as we shall see in the next section, Antonio miserably fails.

---

22 See Chapter Eight below, on Bernard Malamud's *The Fixer*.

For Schuetz, the trial scene is about the progressively dwindling chances of an outsider, perhaps particularly a Jew in a universe hermeneutically controlled by Christian readers, to gain full dignity and perhaps even a measure of legal equal protection of the law. Until a complete change takes place, Shakespeare shows us, Christian majorities will not accept Jewish interpretations, however plausible they may be.

D Religion Trumps Law in *The Merchant of Venice*

1 *Shylock Craves the Law but Receives Christian "Mercy"*

"Let me see if your courts will follow the law," Shylock repetitiously intones during the trial. When Portia's exaggerated reading of the contract wins the day, Shylock the Jew can only ask, incredulously, "Is that the law?"[23] As a Jew he naively expected better of Christian institutions and the way they implement their laws.

The Venetian court and its main players have something else entirely in mind than the law. The theological turn of which I spoke throughout Part I now finds apparent expression in a secular court of law. Portia begins to turn the tables on law in her poetically lovely but factually irrelevant answer to Shylock's question about what compulsion should drive him to show mercy?. In the play's most famous speech, Portia draws on both Biblical "testaments," but the thrust of her language finds a "fulfillment' of law through more "spiritual" if less identifiable virtues like love and mercy:

> The quality of mercy is not strained,
> It droppeth as the gentle rain from heaven,
> Upon the place beneath ....
>
> IV, I, 182–5

The disguised Portia's words are of an immense beauty, but how can someone as used to Christian hypocrisy as Shylock give them any weight at all, particularly in the setting of a contract dispute against a man like Antonio! Shylock's rejoinder to Portia is perspicuous, matching except for the smaller number of

---

23 A structurally almost identical moment occurs, as we shall see, in Malamud's *The Fixer*, when the Jewish protagonist, Yakov Bok, is forced by a prosecutor to hear a priest's absurd misreadings of Jewish texts and asks with similar wonderment how anyone could believe such nonsense. See Chapter Eight.

words used her own eloquence: "My deeds upon my head! I crave the law,/ The penalty and forfeit of my bond." Shylock will face his Maker in due course. When that day comes, he will want the mercy Portia now insists he show to Antonio, a man in whom Shylock can see no merit. Even if there were something in the Merchant for the Jew to admire, Shylock is neither a monarch nor a Deity, so why "must" he show mercy at all? This is a civil lawsuit, not a morality play! So at this precise moment, Shylock says, the issue of his own human frailties is not before the court.

Shylock has every reason to believe the "law" is on his side, whatever his ultimate fate may be before a Divine judge. His own Deity is one of equal justice and mercy, so what Portia preaches he already understands. She does not know, or chooses to ignore, the numberless, lovely textual evocations of the Jewish Bible in favor of mercy. She preaches to the choir, but her sermon is irrelevant to the legal issues now before the court.

Shylock, who has no lawyer – they only appear centuries later in his defense[24] – will have to learn the hard way, and in open court, exactly how Christian "mercy" plays itself out. Portia's hair-splitting, nonsensical treatment of the bond having rendered it unenforceable on its terms (no drop of blood, not an ounce more or less than a fair pound of flesh), she imposes on the "alien" Shylock a special statute against any non-Christian Venetian who threatens an "insider's" life. The state and Antonio are thus permitted to dispose of the Jew's entire fate; Shylock becomes a criminal defendant, through the bizarre workings of Christian law, and this at the climax of a trial in which he began as a civil plaintiff. The Christian gentleman Antonio, having narrowly escaped what he, perhaps wrongly pre-judging his adversary, sees as a seemingly certain death, quickly takes the offensive, in every sense of that word. The "alien statute" gives the Christian insider the right to take half the alien's wealth, but he does not have to do this at all. In fact, the Duke, speaking for Venice under the statute, not only immediately pardons Shylock's life but also reduces to a mere fine the half of the Jew's wealth that the statute assigned to the state. Will this true lenity influence the Christian Merchant to do the same? Portia wants to find out – in fact, her repulsion about her husband's courtroom behavior with Antonio provokes her curiosity generally about this wealthy old Christian. (There is no other salient reason for her to have extended Shylock's suffering, once the contractual quibble prevailed and she has won the day, into the realm of this bizarre and prejudiced statute.) She wants to test Antonio as

---

24 See Weisberg, "Lawyers and Judges Address Shylock's Case," in Nahshon and Shapiro, *Wrestling with Shylock*, *op. cit.*, ch. 4, n. 10, p. 105.

a Christian. So after Venice quickly reduces Shylock's exposure for its own half to "a fine" and also forgives him his life, the following line occurs:

> Portia: *What mercy can you render him, Antonio.*
> IV, I, 376, emphasis added

Portia's use of the word "mercy" puts Antonio – and I would think audiences from 1600 to the present – on notice that a "Christian moment" is underway. To test a Jew, the play seems to say, put him in a situation in which the law seems to control his finer instincts as a human being. Reciprocally, however, to test a Christian you must mention a word like "mercy" and see what he does with it. We will return at the appropriate moment to the textual and "spiritual" substance of Antonio's response, noting for now only that, as most viewers recall, the Merchant forces Shylock to convert to Christianity, But we await the right juncture in the next chapter to see, not only for this play but for Shakespeare's vision throughout his works, the full import of Antonio's cruel legality. Suffice to say it is hardly merciful.[25] And Shakespeare, brilliantly noting the sharp divergences between Jewish oil and Christian water, as we shall see, comes out in favor of the Jew's value system.

2 *Two Grim Conversions: from Mercy to Cruelty and from Judaism to Christianity*

Antonio's cruel display of what Portia was asking him for – "mercy" – involves on the comic stage an iteration of one of Christian Europe's worst iniquities against Jews, the forced conversion. The best you can say for this remarkable and unexpected maneuver is to surmise that many in Shakespeare's audience would have seen forced conversion as beneficial for a Jew. The worst you can say is that it is a nauseating stretch of Antonio's newly empowered imagination to use even a harsh law like the Alien Statute in this shocking way. The statute only gives him dominion over Shylock's wealth, as we shall review thoroughly in the next chapter. Small surprise that Shylock by the end of the scene is "not well." Portia, by now recognizing *Antonio* as a threat to herself and her marriage, may have started to feel queasy as well. She never had anything particular against the Jew – to the contrary as we shall see when we get to Act V. Yet it was her contractual quibble and her use of the Alien Statute that gave such a man as Antonio so much power over the Jew. Then, after asking for a show of Christian "mercy," she hears instead a series of cruel resolutions harsher

25 "Antonio's Legalistic Cruelty," *op. cit.*, ch. 4, n. 2.

in their way than anything an unprovoked Jewish "legalism" could have conjured. If Shylock, she may be thinking, has been excessive in his insistence on the pound of flesh, this Christian merchant also fails in the primal duty of his Christian creed: kindness even to enemies.

3 *Forced Conversions, Historically*

Portia and Shylock, if they were real people instead of characters, would have also been aware that in this very city-state of Venice as well as elsewhere in Italy at the time, forced conversions often took the form described extensively in Kertzer's *The Popes against the Jews*,[26] which devotes an entire chapter to the practice as it actually existed into modern times:

> Rome's House of the Cathechumens was founded by Pope Paul III in 1543, and kept under close papal control .... Throughout the seventeenth and eighteenth centuries, Rome's House of the Catechumens baptized about ten or a dozen Jews per year, many from Rome but others from lands far and near .... Conversion offered the poor Jew an escape from the poverty of the ghetto, and the chance to enjoy the freedoms that came with being a Christian ... [Over the centuries, women and children increasingly became subject to forced baptism.] The feeling of dread that hung over the ghetto ... produced by the frequent nocturnal visits of the police and the seizure of women and children, continued for as long as did the Papal States. [42–3;59] ....

E Conclusion: In Merchant's Comic Medium, and Only There, Christianity Must Prevail over Judaism

I have been arguing that *The Merchant of Venice* offers "comedically" the emergence and victory of Christian over Jewish values. No surprise so far. This in itself does not make the play antisemitic. I have emphasized that the genre of comedy best supports, indeed it mandates, this victory. In the context of a comedy, which requires frothiness, hypocrisy, looseness, flexibility, and of

---

26 Kertzer, *op. cit.*, Preface, n. 3. James Shapiro's authoritative *Shakespeare in a Divided America* engages this key moment in the trial scene by suggesting that Shylock "has agreed to convert," but the Jew's consent arises from extreme legalistic coercion. (N.Y.: Penguin, 2021), p. 125. John Gross' excellent *Shylock* is equivocal on audiences' responses through the years to Shylock's "enforced baptism," but he is quite wrong about historical Christianity's "reluctant toleration" of Jews, a strange formulation indeed (N.Y.: Simon and Schuster, 1992), ch. 7.

course marriages, mainstream characters live in deeply flawed ways that have the veneer of politeness and even beauty. Who would want anything else as a theater-goer: "tragedy tomorrow, comedy tonight!," we have demanded. But far more provocatively, who would want anything else for society as a whole? Who would have wanted Shylock's sobriety, righteousness, and lawfulness, to have won the day and dictated the everyday lives of Europeans?

An articulate, smart, ethical character created by someone who probably had never met a Jew in his life, Shylock carries his virtues to an extreme forced upon him by the represented and the real world of Catholic Venice. He has to be "defeated," but the real question of the play remaining ahead of us is whose set of underlying values gets redeemed as we look more closely at Antonio's "resolution" – beyond even the forced conversion of Shylock, and beyond that to the often overlooked final moments of Act IV and then the Belmont-centered final Act of the comedy. It is to those scenes that we return, but to get there meaningfully they must first be nested in the "oil and water" substances in conflict throughout this entire book.

Most of the play, as I shall emphasize next, brilliantly identifies the stark differences between Christian and Jew. But the comedy ends with Portia increasingly attuned to the value system of the Jew she has helped defeat. The ending of the play provides a bonding between the Jew Shylock and, surprisingly, the heiress-disguised-as-lawyer who helped defeat him, the gent(i)le Portia.

CHAPTER 5

The Risks of Mediation, Triangulation, Abdication and Indirection in Shakespeare's Plays and Sonnets

A After Their "Oil vs. Water" Start, How Portia Bonds with Shylock, or the Comedy's Remarkable Grasp on Religious Difference

1 *A Commanding Jewish Presence on Stage*

Jews had been banned from England in the late 13th Century. Recall that there was one famous – or infamous – Jew at Elizabeth's court, Dr. Lopez, whom *Merchant* alludes to derogatorily during the famous trial scene in Act IV, when the hysterical anti-Semite Gratiano calls Shylock's soul "wolfish," perhaps an allusion to the Latin lupus and hence to Lopez. Others, hiding their true beliefs, may have prayed together as Jews in some inaccessible places. There is no evidence that Shakespeare, himself, knew any Jews.

This makes all the more remarkable the complex portrait we have just rehearsed of the Jew Shylock. Although on stage only sporadically, the character compels the audience's full attention. Shylock the Jew mandates a deep respect despite the apparent wish to take human flesh, a highly unlikely and completely self-destructive act (as opposed to a contractual provision) he would likely not have seen to its violent end had he been given the chance.

This intense focus on a character who could easily be simplified into pure maliciousness derives from the Bard's remarkable grasp on how a Jew does business, prays, and acts in situations fraught with personal, legal and eventually religious consequences. How does the Jew behave in positions forced upon him by the mainstream Christian community? How does he earn a living? How does he bring up his children? Who are his fellow congregants and how do these members of his "tribe" enforce his own values? What are the everyday conflicts he endures. And of special interest for a playwright depicting him, *how does he speak?*

There were Jews, of course, in the Venice of the play's settings. They were allowed to be money-lenders, but little else was left open to them professionally. Their syntax and argumentative style, like Shylock's, reflected a material and sometimes literalistic cast of thought. They did not in general have occasion to elevate their discourse to the sometimes metaphoric levels of the

 | DOI:10.1163/9789004525177_007

Christian gentlemen around them. Their speech patterns, at least in public, mirrored the stereotypical vision of Jews: non-spiritual, legalistic, bound more to the earth than to the heavens, etc.

Shylock does not let on to those he calls "Christian intercessors" (III, III, 12) the spiritual reality of his actual existence as a Jew, but the play in its fullness lets its audience know how he really feels. He will not be told of mercy (III, III, 1), and we now know why, having traversed the Christian characters' dubious invocation of that lovely concept during the trial scene. Occasional play-goers through the years seize this inner Jew feelingly, as was reported by Heinrich Heine of a woman in a luxury box in London who, as the trial scene ends, rose tearfully from her seat to cry out for Shylock: "Oh the poor man"[1]! But in general, he stands before us, unaccommodated and unaccommodating, uncompromising with Christian merchants and their friends, unyielding and uninfluenced in the way he speaks to them by turns of speech that might more gain him their respect or even – if he wishes it – their love.

As we have seen, the mainstream approach to the comedy, although challenged by myself and many others, opts for a perception of Jewish and Christian difference that values positively – as the play may not – the side of the majority religion. And this brings us back to "oil and water"[2] and to the ineluctable divide that does, indeed, exist, between Christian and Jew and that makes the hyphenated adjective "Judeo-Christian" such a farce. But the question on the table right now is, which set of opposed values does the play really support?

2 *"Oil and Water" Schematized*

Integrating what we have now said about MERCHANT into the discussion, let us now be specific about the sharp dichotomies between the Judaic and the Christian perspective implicit in the image of oil and water. Let's call the Jewish set of values, schematized in *Merchant*, "Oil," and the Christian opposites "Water." Here is a chart that flows, so to speak, from this dichotomy. It is proposed as reflecting Shylock vs the Christians in Merchant but also, on the themes of the rest of this book, too, a wider history of enmity caused by these differences.

Although some of the traits may have been imposed as a kind of caricature by one religious group on the other, I am listing the opposed points to say that both *Merchant* and history generally support these dichotomies;

1 Heine, *Shakespeare's Maidens and Women* (1838).

2 See my introduction of this dichotomy, via Vichy Justice Minister Joseph Barthelemy, in Chapter Three.

OIL – THE JEWS	WATER – THE CHRISTIANS
Justice-seeking	Love
Talmudic, Law-based	Spiritual, Seeking mercy (equity)
Bound up with History[3]	Escaping earthly history through faith
Repair the world (Tikun Olam)	Overcome the world in favor or the next world[4]
Slow to Change[5]	Ahistorical, rapid changes
Unity of Body and Soul	Docetism:[6] the split of body and soul
Clever/smart as positive traits	Skepticism towards intellectuals
Tribalism	Universalism
When life is good, that's good	It's bad to be too well off; better to suffer
Materialistic	Skeptical, theoretically, about earthly things
Literal	Allegorical when necessary, to avoid obvious textual meanings
Uncompromising	Inclined to allow negotiation, even of first principles

3 Franklin Littell on Protestant faddishness and neglect of history: Having destroyed history by neglect of memorization and recollection, having weakened even serious study by neglect of the biblical languages, having allowed spiritual and moral tone deafness to grow like cancer, we fancy ourselves as "Enlightened" men and women. We are in fact simply impoverished and rootless, "like a wave of the sea driven with the wind and tossed" (James 1:6). Every fad that comes along in the currents of the general society is seized upon, for a short session stressed as proof of the church's "relevance," and then quickly dropped as a more brightly flashing lure enters the stream of consciousness, *Crucifixion*, p. 21.

Littell's predecessor in outspoken-ness from within, Friedrich Nietzsche, diagnosed a Christian "disease of the eye" – a trained dissociation from the real world. The thinkers both suggest that the combination of Protestant attraction to whatever comes along and Catholic privileging of the next world over present reality have diminished European and American Christian practice.

4 Remember, this is possibly over-stated here, particularly as to many activist Protestants [Jimmy Carter].

5 Nietzsche; And the Jews are beyond any doubt the strongest, toughest and purest race now living in Europe; they know how to assert themselves in the midst of the worst possible conditions (better, in fact, than in more favorable ones). That they can do this is due to certain virtues of theirs, virtues which others would like to label as vices nowadays. Above all, due to their resolute faith, which need not be ashamed before "modern ideas"; they change, when they change . . . according to the principle *"As slowly as possible". Aphorism 251, Beyond Good And Evil*, italics added. Franklin Littell sees the "oil and water" component of this trait through the eyes of a Protestant clergyman: "In stubborn fashion, and in spite of flirtations with assimilation at different seasons and in different places, the Jews have clung to history, earthiness, concrete events. And Israel, which came into being as part of a specific series of historical events, cannot properly be judged by persons whose dominant thought patterns are ruled by a flight from history." The Crucifixion of The Jews (95–6).

6 Although heretical, this first millennium Gnosticism symbolizes here a more generalized split in Christianity.

Although not a theologically endorsed chart, these oppositions reflect some obvious features in *Merchant*: Shylock during the trial seeks "the law," "justice," the literal text of the contract, and (apparently) the material fruit of the penalty clause – Antonio's flesh – and he is accused by the Christians in the courtroom of lacking any "mercy," any willingness to compromise, any interest in avoiding the letter of his contract's language.

Four related but distinct features of oil and water conflicts have been left to the end of this provisional list, because I think they deserve individual elaboration in the rest of this Chapter. These are as much so or more a part of Merchant as the earlier components of the dichotomy:

Oil: Direct Speech	Water: "Elevated" Rhetoric
Oil: Allegiance to CODES	Water: These Can be Violated at will
Oil: DIRECT TALK WITH GOD, unmediated	Water: Needing Christ, the Saints, etc.
Oil: Distrusting all secular "Middlemen"	Water: Preferring Mediation, Triangulation

The Bard may not have known any Jews, but he knew the differences – unbridgeable – between them and Christians. Section B traces, in terms of the play, Shakespeare's special competence in locating the "Direct speech" vs "Elevated rhetoric" dichotomy. The remaining sub-sections treat the unalterable differences – always as presented by Shakespeare – connected to *codes*, a *direct* relationship with God, and secular differences about what I call "*triangulation.*"

These four principal "oil vs water" divergences lead us back to the end of the comedy and to Portia's overcoming them through a strongly implicit bonding with Shylock.

B Direct Speech: Shylock's Strength and Weakness vs the Christians' Elegant if Falsifying Words

The lovely but falsifying ("water") approach to the use of words is exemplified very early in *Merchant* when the youthful rogue and bankrupt Bassanio approaches his rich older friend Antonio, hoping that despite many prior financial catastrophes the Merchant will once again agree to lend him money. Bassanio needs the cash – 3000 ducats – to perfect a scheme of courting and winning the beautiful Portia whose marital choice is dictated from the grave by her father's Will. The winning suitor needs to present himself at her palatial island estate, Belmont.

Well, you cannot appear in Belmont in rags. And you need a troupe of fellow-travellers and a ride out to the island. All of this takes cash, or at least a whole boatload of credit cards. Everyone knows Bassanio's dismal credit history, including Antonio, but if the young adventurer finds the right words, maybe the Merchant will help him out.

What are those "right words"? Certainly, among Christian gentlemen, they are NOT the fairly direct paraphrasing, honestly, of Bassanio's needs. Even Bassanio, who is not the brightest bulb in the Venetian firmament, has learned this as he has come to maturity amidst Christians. A more "elevated" form of discourse is required. Meanwhile, the audience to a comedy – you and I – is dreamily ready for poetic speech, anyway. The Christian characters provide it. Two birds with one stone:

> Bassanio: In my schooldays, when I had lost one shaft
> I shot the fellow of the selfsame flight
> The selfsame way, with more advised watch
> To find the other forth; and by adventuring both
> I oft found both. I urge this childhood proof
> Because what follows is pure innocence.
> I owe you much, and like a willful youth
> That which I owe is lost; but if you please
> To shoot another arrow that selfsame way
> Which you did shoot the first, I do not doubt,
> As I will watch the aim, or to find both
> Or bring your latter hazard back again
> And thankfully rest debtor for the first.
> …
> In Belmont is a lady richly left;
> And she is fair, and fairer than that word,
> Of wondrous virtues. Sometimes from her eyes
> I did receive fair speechless messages.
> Her name is Portia, nothing undervalued
> To Cato's daughter, Brutus' Portia;
> Nor is the wide world ignorant of her worth,
> For the four winds blow in from every coast
> Renowned suitors, and her sunny locks
> Hang on her temples like a golden fleece,
> Which makes her seat of Belmont Colchos' strand,
> And many Jasons come in quest of her.
> O my Antonio, had I but the means

To hold a rival place with one of them
I have a mind presages me such thrift
That I should questionless be fortunate!

Bassanio's speech signals to the audience not only that they appropriately will be hearing beautiful words throughout the play but that they must be on guard to detect the real strategies behind such recitations. The bankrupt roue Bassanio knows how to press the buttons of his much older mentor and frequent creditor. You don't say straight out, "I need your cash or credit to make whole my earlier debts to you, which I can do by courting a rich girl, winning her, and gaining all her money." This is not the approach of Christian speakers throughout the play. Only Shylock, the Jew, speaks directly and honestly.

Poetry comes from Christian mouths. Bassanio's beautiful figure of the arrow shot into the air towards a lost arrow so that in finding the second both can be redeemed hides his greed but affects the audiences – Antonio, as well as us in the theater – with its beauty. It sets our thoughts into the ether, the heavens, the romantic azure.

Shylock understands these Christian figures of speech, detests them, will not use them even when his self-interest might favor them, and chooses as soon as we meet him (Act I, scene III) and until the very end of the trial scene Act IV, scene I) to abjure "elevated" rhetoric. But in a Christian world, hiding realities through words, or the way we interpret words, is a truer coin of the realm than Shylock's ducats, honestly won.

Antonio yields to his young friend's plea. But Antonio himself never lets on the true nature of his own commerce. We picture his ships bobbing along on the high seas – again appealing images of the waves. Where do his ships go? What do they bring back, and who supplies the luxury needs of Venice and Venice's commercial partners when Antonio's ships come back laden with wealth?

We have to pierce the lovely veil of Christian language to seize the truth of Christian dealings in the world. Even Shylock's sometimes brutal criticisms of "Christian intercessors" underplay the justified dread any Jew would feel when surrounded by such lies. These lies can quickly balloon into physical cruelty and even annihilation. (Almost every postwar story treated in this book reiterates this lesson. Shylock narrowly avoids physical death when the Duke spares him his life, although he is destroyed as he says himself by the rest of what Antonio does to him at the end of the trial scene; the 20th century taught story-tellers that elevated language or the rationalization by lawyers of Nazism's brutal language results in the deaths of millions.) Shylock's verbal and interpretive honesty brings him defeat, degradation, disgrace, disempowerment and the destruction of his essence as a Jew.

C In *Merchant*, Oil Sticks to Codes; Water Runs off Them

1 *External, Written Codes*

Various codes, formal and informal, influence characters' decisions on how to behave publicly or privately throughout the play. Whether driven by strong internally generated commitments or by codified contractual or statutory law, characters think of codes as a kind of "marching order" dictating correct conduct. As soon as a code appears, implicitly or explicitly, the audience is on notice as to appraising the soundness of the character's choices. Already seen this way, we perceive more than a legal dimension to this – how a character responds to an internally felt or externally imposed code is often an earmark to that character's *religious* belief system.

In terms now familiar to my readers here, the distortions imposed by "flexibly" interpreting a contract or a code can derive, methodologically, from a divide between Jewish allegiance to Law and Christian scepticism about it. As in many other plays from all epochs, codes demand of often reluctant protagonists a kind of loyalty to a previously created (by the individual herself) or stipulated by, say, a legal or religious document that inscribes more formally a set of norms.

Explicit legal codes in *Merchant* include the "Alien Statute" that Portia cites further to disgrace the already successfully defeated Shylock during the trial scene. A non-statutory code, of course, is the contract between Shylock and Antonio, created between private, competent adults to guide their behavior. Famously (or infamously) the bond sworn to by Antonio in Act 1 commands him, if he fails to pay 3000 ducats to Shylock within three months, to forfeit a pound of his flesh to the Jew. A third externally imposed code is Portia's father's Last Will and Testament, which she accepts although it dictates from the grave her choice of a husband.

2 *Strange Bedfellows in the Service of a Private, Internal Marriage Code*

I have already explored all three of the *externally* imposed codes (Alien Statute, contract, Will) in the play. But here I want to explore the *internally* generated "marriage code," a way of acting that is dictated by the private value system of two marriage partners. Although they may be bound by their vows, these are integrated or negotiated as further understandings carry them through the years. Portia and Bassanio are just starting out in life, but they have one private sign and symbol already of their code, and that is the ring that Portia gives her successful suitor just before they hear of the impending catastrophe in Venice. (III, II, 171)

Shockingly, the identification of the *ring* as guidepost to a code of marital values leads to the *bonding* of two seemingly opposed major characters, Portia and Shylock! Only the symbolic foregrounding of various characters' "rings" produces an alliance (pun intended!) between Portia and the Jew. Oil and water finally merge as substances in this one breath-taking way.

Antonio's role in coercing Bassanio to give away his wedding ring just after the trial scene ends reveals how different Portia is from the Merchant, whom she only has supported because of his so-far incompletely explored close friendship with her new husband. Even prior to the explicit linkage to Shylock embodied in *his* wedding ring, she feels the nausea not only of her own hermeneutic excesses in construing the contract[7] but also of Bassanio's overt willingness to sacrifice her – he of course does not know that his wife is there at all, since she is in disguise – to save his friend from the Jew's knife:

> Bassanio: Antonio, I am married to a wife/Which is as dear to me as life itself,/But life itself, my wife, and all the world/Are not with me esteemed above thy life./I would lose all, nay sacrifice them all/Here to this devil, to deliver you.
>
> IV, I, 288–93

The beginning (but hardly the end!) of an understanding of Portia's emerging knowledge *of Shylock's similar feelings about marriage,* starts with her aside to Bassanio's outrageous speech:

> Portia: Your wife would give you little thanks for that/If she were by to hear you make the offer ….
>
> *Shylock's Aside Concurs with Portia's:*
>
> Shylock: These be the Christian husbands!/ I have a daughter – /Would any of the stock of Barrabas /Had been her husband rather than a Christian!
>
> IV, I, 288–97

7 Portia has come to court in disguise to take on the male world and save her husband's friend. But by the end of the trial, her own excesses and the corruption of that friend, have become patently obvious to her,. Contrary-wise, the Jew she has defeated has exhibited before her observant eyes the very values of oath-keeping and marriage loyalty she hoped for—prior to learning of Antonio's example—from Bassanio. She is too self-critical and simply too smart to rest easy with her own interpretation in open court.

Shylock's sarcasm about Bassanio (and the violently antisemitic Gratiano, who also freely and figuratively sends his new wife to heaven to save his old friend) reflects what the viewer already knows from Act III : Shylock defines his inner code through a commitment to his wife signified by their exchange of rings:

> Tubal ... There came divers of Antonio's creditors in my company to Venice that swear he cannot choose but break ... One of them showed me a ring that he had of your daughter for a monkey.
>
> Shylock. Out upon her! Thou torturest me, Tubal. It was my turkis [turquoise], I had it of Leah when I was a bachelor. I would not have given it for a wilderness of monkeys.
>
> III, I, 113–123

Portia's amazement that a gentleman of Venice can deal so casually with her new husband's promise relating to *her* wedding ring is exacerbated into her heart-break when she finds out, after the trial ends, that Antonio has manipulated his young friend to give that ring away to the lawyer (Portia in disguise) whose flexible construction of various external codes (including the contract) has just saved his life in open court.

Bassanio offers the "judge" a gift, anything (s)he might ask for having saved his dear friend's life in court. Portia tests her new husband, who so far has been bartering her and her ducats away for Antonio, by demanding his new wedding ring. Maybe Jessica sold her dad's ring for a monkey, but the audience has the right to hope against hope that Bassanio will decline to part with that by-now highly meaningful symbol of conjugal devotion. He does resist, at first.

Then – predictably – the porte-parole for Christian "mercy" and generosity, Antonio, once again intervenes. He has trouble keeping out of the young man's affairs, as we know. (Another intercession lies just ahead in Act V!) He successfully coerces the new husband to give the "judge" his new ring. Portia just afterwards receives the ring with enormous sadness.

In Act V, on Belmont itself, Shylock is gone but not forgotten. Portia spends most of the final scene teaching Bassanio about the value of wedding rings, a lesson already learned in the Jewish household eventually fully destroyed by a continuum of Christian acts. At Antonio's urging after the happy resolution of his own fate, Bassanio had gifted his new wedding ring to the "judge" who won the day for the Christians. Now the youthful adventurer must pay the piper, for Portia, having been disguised as that judge, now possesses that ring. She ruefully and skeptically seeks assurances of Bassanio's improvement. Not alone among the remaining characters and with a full heart, Portia points to the older values she has seen embodied in her adversary at the trial, a man whom she almost reluctantly had to defeat. Ethics, loyalty, direct obligation, a devotion to performatives and symbols like wedding vows and the ring itself, these things matter to Portia. Bassanio must promise her never again to betray her by breach, symbolically or otherwise, of their vows. Will Bassanio and Bassanio alone agree to ratchet up his ethics? Or will he let the chance slip through his embarrassingly un-ringed fingers?

Not to worry, Bassanio. Antonio will again step forward and pledge himself for you. He almost died for your sins, after all! Now he can display the (Christian) *chutzpah* to get between a man and his wife! In as amazing a set of lines as this amazing play produces, he *intervenes* – remember, reader, this is bad, not good! – as follows:

> I once did lend my body for his wealth
> Which but for him that had your husband's ring
> Had quite miscarried. I dare be bound again,
> My soul upon the forfeit, that your lord
> Will never break faith advisedly.
>
> V, I, 249

As one who has had the privilege of staging parts of this play on several occasions, I have suggested to the actress playing Portia that there must be at least 15 seconds of complete, uncomedic silence as she tries to absorb these words. She must look Antonio up and down several times during this rare pause in the verbal action, as one might look directly in the eyes of someone who has just uttered the most patent falsehood. She hopes, perhaps, for self-awareness, from even someone as impervious as the Merchant has been to the real effect of his various pledges. How can she manage to reform her husband with a guy like this standing next to him all the time, easing the pain of full commitment and personal integrity that she wants from Bassanio, syphoning it off – first legally, now metaphysically? But Antonio is too steeped in the values of mediated code-breaking to "get it." So Portia comes back with the most ironic line of the play:

> Then you shall be his *surety*.
>
> italics added

In a work replete with legalistic references, that final word (used by her earlier in the play[8] – she knows the full significance of this legalism) explicitly evokes a lawful relationship of creditor to both a primary debtor and one who

8 I, II, 77.

"guarantees" the loan for the latter. It is defined, both in Shakespeare's time and today, as follows:

> Surety: A person who binds himself for the payment of a sum of money, or the performance of something else, for another who is already bound for the same.
>
> *The Law in Shakespeare*, ed. CUSHMAN DAVIS, 1883

Exactly, of course, what Antonio "did" for Bassanio when the young man's credit-rating otherwise would have hopelessly flunked the Shylock-test. Portia, as we recall, has just had to expend considerable energy to save Antonio and her husband from the rotten fruits of that earlier surety-ship. Antonio might have learned the lesson of direct obligation and helped her to teach it to the young adventurer. Instead, she finds the unrepentant intervenor once again placing himself between Bassanio and the person to whom he owes a direct obligation. And now that obligation is marital love, not merely a commercial debt.

Portia's patience for this man who obviously has so infected her husband's moral system, has run dry. She will have none of it. It is time for Bassanio to stand for himself; it is time for the couple, unhindered by third-person intervention, to consummate their marriage and to proceed to a conjugal life in this way similar to Shylock's with Leah. "Mediation," a term used mostly in a positive sense, cannot really help two directly obligated individuals to keep their faith one to another.

Portia gapes as she gazes incredulously at this last gasp of control attempted by Antonio over her husband, with whom she insists on direct obligation. She will have to get rid of Antonio to stand any chance that Bassanio will adapt to her value system. The Merchant has grotesquely exacerbated his earlier offer to stand as Bassanio's commercial surety. He will not learn the lesson of how negative the consequences were of that triangulated agreement. Now he is back, "politely" promising to stand in for her husband on the level of love and personal commitment! This will not stand. He has to be thrust off her island of Belmont.

Is the comedy in its last stages suggesting that "mediated religion" also must be questioned? I think so. Shylock, the marginalized Jew, believes in the direct responsibility of each individual to keep his vows, both to others and to God. He had to be defeated, on the terms of the comedy and perhaps of the world more broadly, because the marginalized and victimized expression of his ethics can lead to excess and inappropriateness. Suppose, on the other hand, his ethics were mainstream? Portia tries this thought experiment on her own island, apart from the male Venetian enclave she has seen in all its corruption. Speaking finally "in her own voice" – undisguised, unmediated by her father's Will or the masculine conventions of Venetian courtrooms – she opts for unmediated devotion to individual responsibility.

It is no wonder that she does not greet with explicit warmth to her island her husband's friend, whose life she has just saved. Yet many mainstream critics find a way to support or at least include Antonio at the comedy's end. Alone among title characters of Shakespeare's comedies he stands without a spouse, but maybe he can be edged back into Portia's good graces? This is a tough critical task.

Nonetheless an excellent representative writer back in the day, Lawrence Danson, tries it out.[9] Danson finds no reason to dislike Antonio and wants him, literally, to stick around as the three actually wedded couples appear to head off to bed (perhaps – they don't seem so eager to do so, strangely), presumably without the cloying presence of the Merchant. Danson is representative of most critics (maybe not so many stage directors) in concluding that Antonio surely has his flaws, but his "risk-taking" on behalf of his young friend and protégé Bassanio signifies the values of Christian love and generosity, against which he is faced by a "stony villain" who stands for something else. At the end of the play, all the major characters (except Shylock, who has been defeated and does not appear throughout Act V) share a Belmont version of the kumbaya moment as the curtain falls.

From the perspective of all other Shakespearian comedic title characters, though, Antonio uniquely remains unmarried as the play ends. It is unclear to directors what to do with this "hanger on" and literal "fifth wheel" to the married couples around him. As one who had a hand in a mini-production of the play,[10] I advised exiling him to the side of the stage; but who am I to say so?: mainstream Shakespearians, such as Danson, have the Merchant involved in a figurative "dance" with the three married couples. But wouldn't Portia – by any measure of her legitimate Shylock-like demand for honesty and loyalty on the part of her new husband – insist on ejecting the Merchant from Belmont?

Shylock is gone but not forgotten. The legalistic language he tried to bring to Venice has strongly and strangely influenced the Christian characters' words as the play ends. Portia follows her use of the term "surety" with a suggestion that the group of married couples answer "inter'gatories" about the trial; Gratiano in fact provides a "first inter'gatory" to his new wife, Nerissa: will she come to

9 Danson, *The Harmonies of "The Merchant of Venice"* (New Haven: Yale U.P., 1978). See also cites from Stephen Greenblatt, ch. 4, n. 11; John Gross, ch. 4, n. 26; and James Shapiro, ch. 4, n. 26.

10 See coverage of this in *The New Yorker, op. cit.*, Preface, n. 15.

bed with him right away or, given the imminence of dawn, should they wait 'til tomorrow? "These be the Christian husbands," among whom even the brashest and most antisemitic start to mimic Shylock's speech habits.[11]

D The Jew's Direct Relationship with God

1 *Shylock's Belief System Is Direct and Will Not Tolerate "Christian Intercessors"*

Shylock complains, in his typically memorable and vivid honesty, about "Christian intercessors." [III, III, 15] He is deeply distrustful, particularly in matters religious,[12] of some third party influence over the Jew's direct relationship with his God. Urged by Portia to let go and find an easy way out, he sticks to his oath and his bond: "Cursed be my tribe if I forgive him!" (I, III, 47)

No wonder Portia's insistence that he show "mercy" is rebuffed. A Christian telling him, a devout Jew, about mercy? His sacred texts, and his Deity, embody mercy. And he has pledged to do Antonio in, although it is quite unclear he would ever take this – against his own belief system – to its cutting edge climax in open court. "My deeds upon my head! I crave the law ..." he quite logically if unhelpfully for his case declares after Portia's highly elevated but hypocritical speech insists on his compromising his claim against one who has humiliated him on the Rialto just because he is a Jew; Shylock believes in God and is directly responsible to that omniscient Being. The relationship is one-to-one, always and forever. Shakespeare has wondrously perceived and brilliantly represented the difference between Jew and Christian in this respect. This is why Shylock makes clear to Antonio and Bassanio, early on, that although he may deal with them in their commercial affairs, he will not "eat with you, drink with you, nor *pray with you*." [I, III, 34]

The Jew's direct relationship with his God is basic. Prayer involves conversation with or supplication of that One, indivisible, omnipotent, and omnipresent Being. There are no graven images to pray to, there are no saints, there is nothing to help the individual Jew except his reverence for and deeply personal commitment to that Being. You don't triangulate this God, you don't

---

11 The very end of the play is replete with legalistic language all tending to delay the two new couples' repairing to bed actually to consummate their marriage. Shylock's way of speaking, but not his approach to conjugal love, has influenced the ordinary talk of the Christians, who now use words like "inter'gatory," and phrases like "and charge us there upon inter'gatories," [V, I, 295–end] as though they were their native argot instead of a legacy from the Jew. The effect of all the legalisms is to ward off going to bed with one another.

12 See the following sub-section for how this plays out in secular practices.

place entities supernatural or otherwise between yourself and your God. All of this is *Judaism 101*, as we shall see immediately.

2 *Job, in Agony, Errs Grievously by Seeking a Mediator Between Himself and His God*

Where characters in the Jewish Bible *do* begin to flirt with "intercessors," they go horribly wrong. The most poignant and fully understandable attempt brings us to the awesome (in the older sense of *furchtbar*) case of Job. ....

In the ninth chapter of the Biblical book of Job, verse 33, the title hero yearns for a "mokhiach," an intercessor, to stand between him and God. Job's struggle has only produced more suffering. God may hear his pleas, but at this nadir of spiritual strength he wants *someone else* to vouch for him. He needs something more than run-of-the-mill aid and comfort. He needs a full-fledged mokhiach – [King James: daysman; New Revised Standard: umpire; Septuagint: "Would that he our mediator were present, and a reprover, and one who should hear the cause between both."] Stretched thin, Job in his limitless suffering wants help. He yearns to deflect his pain onto a mediator; he craves relief from the unavailing direct relationship to God, and he wishes to triangulate, to take the pressure off, to lay it all on someone else. Job's moment of weakness reveals a human need: when everything seems lost, and when the arbiter of your fate seems most judgmental of you, or when you no longer have the will or the means or the strength to proceed on your own in the relationship, a third force would be most welcome. The problem doesn't change, but the responsibility for its resolution is *outsourced*.

Christians triangulate every day when they are in need.

But the Jewish scholars were not kind to Job (as a character) in his moment of extreme weakness; "Dust should be put in the mouth of Job," Rav opined,[13] "because he makes himself the colleague of Heaven [by praying, against all tradition] 'Would there were a mocheach, a triangulator, between us, that he might lay his hand upon us both.'" Job's need to triangulate his relationship to God of course has always commanded the favorable attention of the Christian commentators, who after all saw just this kind of mediation/triangulation/intervention/ outsourcing as central to their faith. They *love Job at that precise moment*, finding in their all-too-typical way that his suffering and call out for a mediator[14] between himself and God somehow prefigured their deepest

---

13 See https://www.sefaria.org/Bava_Batra.15b.15?lang=bi [The William Davidson Talmud].

14 See for example a recent comment on these verses in Job at https://www.placefortruth.org. The 2017 commentator notes several ways in which Job can be used to preach about Jesus and that primary among these is Job's "longing for a mediator."

messianic claims for Jesus, somehow transmogrified into one of their infinite discoveries of Jesus-within-the-Hebrew-Bible (which is its own form of hermeneutic mediation/ "outsourcing" on a grand scale); they saw triangulation as central to their faith. Paul – to Timothy – put it this way: "For there is one God, and one mediator between God and men, the man Jesus Christ."[15]

E The Bard's Consistent Skepticism about Triangulation of any Kind

We have just seen that the Christian interpreters (or at least many of them) turned Job's brief flirtation with a mediator to triangulate his relationship with God into a "teachable moment" for the whole idea of Jesus Christ as the being to whom all Christians delegate or triangulate a superannuated direct relationship to God. In our metaphorical terms. Shakespeare, seen as a unified voice across all the works, abhors triangulation and expresses how disastrous it always is in theological, legal, and even or especially romantic situations.

In this sense, the Bard, like many of the writers I treat throughout this book, prefers "Oil" (Judaism) to "Water" (Christianity). Oil sees the urge to an intercessor between God and Jew as at best humanly understandable during moments, like Job's, of extreme personal distress, but nonetheless a no-no; water spills the episode from Job over onto a basic tenet of the new faith. What I am demonstrating, in thinking about 9:33 of Job, for example, is that the Bard might have been perfectly at one with Talmudic sages such as Rav, whom we just saw, in the Babylonian Talmud, criticizing Job for seeking a mediator.

1 *Shylock Would Not Take Job as a Role Model*

In *Merchant*, the figure who most likely would have found Job going astray from the perspective of his own traditions is Shylock. Shylock can moan about his fate, and he can wonder why God has put him where he is. But he is his own man. Like Job, he reaches a spiritual nadir: in the first scene of Act III when Tubal gives a discouraging report, and just prior to letting the worst out – Jessica's sale of Leah's turquoise for a monkey – we hear Shylock say, "The curse never fell upon our Nation till now, I never felt it till now … no satisfaction, no revenge, nor no ill luck stirring but what lights on my shoulders, no sighs but of my breathing, no tears but of my shedding." But unlike Job, he bears responsibility directly, unmediated by intercessors, whose influence he explicitly shuts out, using that word – intercessors – dismissively. "My deeds upon

15 Paul and book of *1 Timothy* 2:5–6.

my head. I stand for law", he will soon say at a crucial moment (IV, I, 205), consistent with his whole unmediated character. His sole interlocutor is God, "unmix'd," to recall now Shakespeare's words from an analogous context, "with baser matter." (*Hamlet*, I, V) Shylock eschews third-person intervention and insists on "owning" his relationship to God and to others. This cannot be said of the Venetian male characters with whom he is forced to deal, and since they call the shots he is brought down, though Portia in Belmont has something to say about this, and especially about that meta-triangulator Antonio, whom she will sarcastically call Bassanio's "surety" – third-person guarantor – as the comedy ends. Evaluating as she now can the Merchant and the always bartering Christian husbands, she is coming into spiritual harmony with the man her fate required her to bring down to defeat.

Portia wants direct obligation, symbolized by the ring, a symbolism present since Shylock first mentioned Leah's turquoise. He reiterates in open court his allegiance to marriage vows and hatred of the "Christian husbands" who so easily traduce them. Shylock keeps his oaths; Portia wants this but does not find it. Her husband and his best protector, Antonio, consistently distort, denature, delegate and devalue their oaths and commitments; she becomes acutely aware of this in open court when her Bassanio more or less writes her off to save Antonio and then gives away her ring at the Merchant's intervening insistence. Act V displays her wish to avoid further triangulated trouble in her life. To this extent anyway, though it may be too late to help him, Portia bonds with Shylock the Jew.

2 *Secular Relations Must Never be "Triangulated"*

To grasp the astounding turn taken in Shakespeare towards Jewish "oil" and away from Christian "water," I first return to the moment at the end of Act IV, when Antonio is asked by Portia to do "mercy" towards Shylock. As we saw in the prior chapter, Antonio fails every test and also refuses to follow the actual mercy bestowed by Venice itself upon the Jew. He forces conversion on the Jew, a miserable sight even for many in the original Christian audiences, though some supercessionists among them might have thought it was a great idea. But now we must turn to the "triangulated" and "mediated" two remaining features of Antonio's non-merciful resolution.

Given power over Shylock by the Alien Statute, will Antonio use it brutally, or will the title character show Christian mercy? Portia goes on to see Antonio fail the test imposed on all Christians. As we have foregrounded in the prior chapter, Antonio fails to run with her hint to him to show Shylock mercy.

Portia. What mercy can you render him Antonio?
Antonio. So please the Duke and all the court
To quit the fine for one-half of his goods
I am content;[16] so he will let me have
The other half in use, to render it
Upon his death unto the gentleman
That lately stole his daughter.
Two things provided more: that for this favor
He presently become a Christian;
The other, that he do record a gift
Here in the court of all he dies possessed
Unto his son Lorenzo and his daughter.
IV, I, 378–88

Read these lines again. How, you may then ask yourself, can a man just saved by a legalistic trick from the jaws of death, how can such a man come up with such a scheme! Consider the three-part resolution Antonio contrives. He sets himself up as trustee for half of Shylock's wealth, settling the principal on Shylock's death and all that the Jewish money-lender may have earned after the trial upon "the gentleman [!]/That lately stole his daughter." "These be the Christian trustees!," Shylock is probably thinking at this point, bound in their "equitable" task to contravene every wish of the person providing the wealth. Even more likely, Portia herself – who by now may know the "back-story" of Lorenzo's theft of both Shylock's daughter and part of his treasure, including Leah's ring – must be wondering how "mercy" is to be found anywhere in such a scheme.

As I have analyzed in detail elsewhere,[17] Antonio perversely seizes on the institution of the *trust*, which as its name implies then and now permits a third person to administer a certain fund for the *well-being* of another. Similar to his interventions throughout the play on behalf of others (usually Bassanio), Antonio's mediating acts tend to create conflict, not resolution. Astoundingly, he will sin again in exactly this way during the play's final scene.

16 These lines are lovely but they are not to the point, even remotely. Antonio merely reiterates what the Duke has just done! But what will *he* do?

17 See generally Weisberg, "The Dangers of Mediation and Triangulation in Shakespeare," in *European Judaism: A Journal for the New Europe*, vol. 51, No. 2, Autumn 2018, pp. 59–66 (Publ. by Berghahn Books).

To fathom the relevance of this non-merciful moment not only for the play but way beyond – to Shakespeare in all of his works – I employ a term for the resolution of a deeply human but flawed package of needs: "triangulation," which is defined here as the deflection onto a third force of a direct obligation previously binding two as yet unmediated parties (call them "A" and "B"). To exemplify, the two parties can be the worshiper and his God, the debtor and his creditor, the lover and his beloved, the governor and those he governs. The deflection onto a third force or person can occur because of the triangulating desires[18] of "A" or "B" or even of both of the formerly unmediated pair, or by virtue of an outside intervention, as when a court requires a third person to take on duties over which two previously responsible parties apparently no longer have competence, for example a guardian ad litem to protect the interests of the children of divorcing parents, or as when the law imposes such classic interventions as a trustee to manage the affairs of a bankrupt corporation or of a viable person who needs managing.

Often this definition works for synonyms of triangulation such as mediation, delegation, arbitration and outsourcing, but for a book section on Shakespeare, the geometric image of the triangle fits best, because it intentionally evokes the ultimate form of spiritual outsourcing (to Jesus and various saints) that Jews like Shylock have resisted for two millennia. Visualize the original direct obligation (e.g. the reciprocal stance of Job and God, or more generally "parties A and B") as a straight line at the base of what is then made into a triangle by some individual or social force; the third party ("C," for example Christ?) is conjured sometime after the original binary relationship has been forged.

3 *Extending the Scope of the Bard's Distaste for Triangulation*

Throughout Shakespeare's works, we are shown the risks of diluting direct obligation by calling in a third party to overtake the relationship's previously defined binary. Both in the public and the private realms, characters or poetic voices wreak havoc when they choose to abdicate, triangulate or otherwise voluntarily yield duty, love or sovereignty to third persons. The *paradigm involves a perfectly adequate party deciding – not always for any clear reason – to outsource personal or legal power to a third person chosen (again) for reasons that leave ambiguous the desirability of the decision.* The result, throughout Shakespeare, is *always* disastrous, as triangulation destroys both the integrity of the anterior direct obligation and any remnant of sound behavior in the bargain.

18 Rene Girard wrote influentially of "triangulated desire" in an entirely relevant way. See *Mensonge Romantique Et Verite Romanesque*, translated as *Deceit, Desire, And The Novel* (Baltimore: Johns Hopkins Press, 1976).

The role of "surety," the most important example in *Merchant*, is so vital to Shakespeare as to be mentioned twice by Portia. (Soon we turn to its use in romantic experience through Sonnet 134, which builds on Portia's flabbergasted aversion to Antonio's reinventing himself as a surety for Bassanio, this time in Act V as a guarantor of the young man's responsibility to Portia, if this were even possible.)

As the following dramatic instances of triangulated sovereign power – perhaps especially in the problem comedy *Measure for Measure* – reveal, subjective judgment overtakes the rule of law, predictability diminishes, and outsiders who had counted on the direct authority of a ruler see themselves hopelessly ejected from any scheme of rational treatment or just interpretation of texts. This association of interpretive falsehood with political corruptness carries with it religious overtones when, for example in *Merchant*, Christian distortions of the law win the day over Jewish pleas for just recognition of the law. Indeed, within Shakespeare's work, the distorting *hermeneutic* methods of the third party, again call him, her, or it: Job's "mokhiah," Shylock's "intercessor," the "trustee," the "surety," etc, are indistinguishable from the unsound exercise of their unnaturally acquired power.

When King Lear gratuitously abdicates his throne, at the outset of the tragedy, in favor of two of his three daughters, disaster quickly descends on the Kingdom. Abdication of responsibility and of power by a reasonably still-sound ruler is *never* a beneficial development in Shakespeare. Maybe the outcome might have been less fraught had Lear's third daughter not intuited that what her father was doing was wrong and had instead played along. Or perhaps Cordelia does not even understand her father's voluntary surrender of power? Like all of us, Lear may be "crawl[ing] toward death," (1.i.35) but he is still competent, crafty, and prideful. (In the many stage productions I have been fortunate to attend, octogenarian stars such as Christopher Plummer easily lift from the stage the dead Cordelia, and this having just gone through four acts that would tax the strength of a far younger actor! Lear is by any standard as competent as the actors who so superbly play him.) There is no good reason for the transfer of sovereignty. *Lear innovates a baleful pattern within government of elevating his own comforts while simultaneously leaving his duties to others.* Comfort as a motive behind the disruption of a prior direct line between ruler and people will not do, then or now, as – in the realms of social science – Leslie Green in the UK and Paul Verkuil in the US have recently shown about twentieth – and twenty-first-century governmental outsourcing.[19]

19 Leslie Green, *The Germ of Justice* (N.Y.: O.U.P., 2023).

To quote Green: "Absenteeism in legislatures is routine, and those who cannot go AWOL eagerly subcontract their work to private entities, from 'outsourcing' policy development to publicity firms and think tanks, to contracting for enforcement with private prisons and armies. The idea that our political leaders actually have a fundamental duty to govern and to bear the responsibilities of doing so seems quaint." Shakespeare prefigures the identification of serious difficulty in the theological and political realms (and Sonnet 134 shows us also in the realm of romantic love, once triangulated) when power is abdicated and yielded to a party hitherto uninvolved in a relationship of duty and responsibility. For Shakespeare, political entities disintegrate when adequate leaders delegate, abandon or (as in *Hamlet*) fail to pursue legitimate power. When Claudius "popped in between th'election" (V, I) and Hamlet's hopes, he apparently had been able to work his wretched will even upon Denmark's elders, who skipped over Prince Hamlet and chose the dead King's brother as the new monarch. Obviously, this has plagued Hamlet ever since, although he first mentions it only at this very late moment in the play.

As soon as the election triangulated (in our terms) the normal line of succession, the Prince needed to move quickly, but he was too distraught by his mother's overhasty marriage to Claudius to do anything except futilely ponder suicide – "O that this too, too solid flesh would melt, thaw, and resolve itself into a dew" (I,ii,129) Hamlet's responsibilities upon the death of his father were directly to his people, yet his uncle as interloper and disrupter of this direct line of obligation successfully triangulated the power of the unmediated expectation. Instead of the direct, unmediated ("oil") line between Hamlet and the Danish subjects, the triangle ("water") has flowed to the wretch and the usurper.

A way of understanding Hamlet's delay, as many including myself have written, is that he becomes distracted and fascinated by triangulated power.[20] His unresolved fatal flaw causes untold agony, and at least a handful of relatively innocent deaths, and more than this disrupts the order of the state by leaving Denmark in the murderous hands of corruption, greed, and ignobility.

In the problematic "comedy," *Measure for Measure*, there is a plot-generating moment structurally similar to that which begins *Lear*: the Duke of Vienna decides to delegate power to his deputy, Angelo. The Duke's stated reason might be a bit more understandable than Lear's: he describes himself as having become a lax ruler in that certain laws are still on the books but have remained

20 Weisberg, "Hamlet and Ressentiment," *American Imago*, v. 29 (1972), p. 318. This analysis approximates but is quite distinct from Ernest Jones' Freudian approach in *Hamlet And Oedipus* (N.Y.: Doubleday, 1954).

unenforced. Rather than reforming either these often superannuated laws or this weakness in his own (otherwise) perfectly adequate exercise of power, the Duke delegates it to one who quickly proves disastrous. In *Measure for Measure*, the worlds of theology, politics and love are subjected to the whims of the Duke's strange mediating choice, Angelo. As with Lear, though, the ostensibly self-ejecting ruler does not disappear. There is true triangulation in this sense, too, as elsewhere, the phenomenon is to be observed in Shakespeare: the original mutually obligated pair – the Duke and his people – is overtaken by a shakier less well-defined figure of authority, one of Job's desired middlemen. The residents of Vienna, like Lear's former subjects, do not quite know where their fealty lies. (Even where, as in *The Tempest*, the leader does not abdicate or formally delegate power but merely disappears to pursue his books, Prospero as much as causes the corruption that follows his abandonment of Milan. Yet another Antonio intermeddles, and the result, again would be poor were the audience to *The Tempest* more actively reminded of what its magical hero left behind for the Milanese to sort out.) In a triangulated world, real or theological, judgment is warped, replaced by all kinds of merely subjective speculations. Who is in charge? Is there a law? To what or to whom do I turn?

These risks, all of which have been updated into twentieth – and twenty-first-century contexts of privatized government,[21] include:

1. the increasingly subjective nature of authority;
2. the privatization of public decision-making;
3. the randomness and diminishing predictability of legal edicts;
4. the suffering of those outside the power structure.

The Duke's governance in *Measure for Measure* has been flawed, but at least it is transparent: people directly ruled by him have learned what to expect. Ironically, only when he triangulates authority to Angelo do long-forgotten laws become enforceable, and even these on the mere whim of his delegate. Escalus, a fair judge in the old system who was passed over despite the Duke's praising him, confesses he has no idea how the new system will affect his authority. Triangulation produces chaos. The rules of the game are no longer publicly conveyed, and the subjectivity of the triangulated structure emerges confusingly. Who is to be protected? Who is to be punished? Is there only a private basis for authority, or does law continue to provide an ethical and transparent vehicle for resolving problems?

21 See Paul Verkuil, *Outsourcing Sovereignty* (N.Y.: CUP, 2007), *passim*.

F Fulfilling *Merchant* through Act V and Sonnet 134

1 *"The Middleman of Venice": the Final Act of Merchant Recapitulated*

As we have seen, there are strong links between two problem comedies, *Measure and Merchant*, in both of which triangulation plays a nefarious role. So in Act IV of *Merchant*, full interpretive power over the bond openly agreed to by Antonio and Shylock is first bestowed on an interloper to the court, Portia, who compounds her astounding reading of the contract by further delegating to Antonio the interpretation of the Alien Statute. Vienna's inexplicable confidence in Angelo is hence replicated by Portia's *outsourcing* to Antonio ultimate power over Shylock's fate, undoubtedly hoping (like the Duke of Vienna regarding Angelo, or really against all hope) that the revivified Merchant will actually do some good in the Christian spirit of things. What occurs, as in Vienna, is the exact opposite of the triangulator's expectations. We have instead seen Antonio, the supposed Christian gentleman, destroy Shylock's personhood.

Portia, who stood amazed – as was Shylock – by the give-and-take in open court between the man she thought was hers and his puppeteer, the Merchant, is as disappointed in Antonio's "mercy" as the Duke of Vienna was in Angelo's cruel and hypocritical edicts.

Antonio compounds one mediating deed with others, all in the service of controlling Bassanio. Why does the middleman do this? Why does he even decide to show up on Belmont in Act V? Why does he not leave the newly married couple alone and console himself as trustee of Shylock's wealth by remaining in Venice and making the Jew's life even more of a living hell? We do not know precisely, beyond recalling that Antonio always wants to be the bosom companion of Bassanio, but we do know how he behaves on Belmont.

Rather than smooth out the ambiguities and ironies of what Harold Bloom grudgingly calls this "equivocal" comedy, the "fifth act," as encumbered by the "fifth wheel" Antonio, only deepens them. Portia first has explained to the always eager Lorenzo and Jessica that the Jew's wealth has been triangulated away to them, via Antonio's intermeddling at the end of the trial. When Portia tells Lorenzo of his windfall from Shylock, Jessica's husband calls the gifts to him "manna in the way/Of starved people." It is hard to laugh off the Biblical allusion here, which makes the material wealth of the Jew Shylock into food for the thieving couple. As it has been since Paul, Jewish legal and Biblical texts furnish forth Christian rhetoric. And as things developed over the centuries, so too here: Jewish substance feeds Christian hungers.[22]

---

22 See further, *op. cit.*, text at Preface, note 14 and see below, sub-section (3) on actual theft by Christians in Vichy during the Holocaust.

Portia's behavior amidst this less-than-fully happy set of endings guides us towards Shylock, however, and away from the earlier comic values of mediation, ethical flabbiness, and a lack of direct responsibility or real sympathy. Her ironic gibe at Antonio's intermeddling, her ban on oath-breaking, these will be Belmont's ratification of the worldview of the just-defeated Jew. In her domain, Shylock's ethics, without his understandable excesses, will prevail.

Portia may have needed to defeat Shylock, but everything from then on until the end of the play – including this crucial final scene on Belmont – proves her implicit admiration for the Jew whose devotion to marriage and wedding rings replicates her own! She needs to teach her new husband (if at all possible, given Antonio's baleful presence and continuing intermeddling) that some codes cannot be flexibly re-invented, distorted, betrayed through tricks of thought or action. The marriage code, symbolized by the ring,[23] is (as it was for the old Jew, Shylock) one of her "non-negotiable," "zero-tolerance" code principles. If given half a chance and if she ejects Antonio, her husband will learn that only direct commitment counts, that there are no romantic "sureties" allowed, and that a more "Jewish" approach to marriage is mandated.

2 *Sonnet 134 and the Cruelty of Triangulated Romance, or "Surety" Strikes Again*

Act V's use of "surety" in *Merchant* is elaborated in a superb sonnet, which calls forth the word "surety" once again to provoke and fascinate us just as it did when Portia uttered it twice in *Merchant*. Attend to the disastrous unfolding of events in Sonnet 134, a legalistic poem – remember that is a good thing! – where the Shakespearean voice regrets the whole idea of triangulation as it relates to love. The poem gives the word "surety" pride of place and seems to suggest that although it is possible to love under the influence of a mediator, triangulated love is suspect, whether human or divine.

> Sonnet 134. So now I have confessed that he is thine,
> And I myself am mortgaged to thy will,
> Myself I'll forfeit, so that other mine
> Thou wilt restore to be my comfort still;
> But thou wilt not, nor he will not be free,
> For thou art covetous, and he is kind;
> He learned but surety-like to write for me,

23 Gary Watt has argued that the ring in this context meant more to Shakespeare's audiences "as a well-known method of transferring title to freehold land," but allows that it also would have been seen as a "betrothal ring," hence identical to what Shylock received of Leah. See Raffield and Watt, *Shakespeare and The Law* (London: Hart Publishing, 2008).

Under that bond that him as fast doth bind.
The statute of thy beauty thou wilt take,
Thou usurer, that put'st forth all to use,
And sue a friend came debtor for my sake
So him I lose through my unkind abuse.
Him have I lost; thou hast both him and me:
He pays the whole, and yet am I not free.

You may need one trained in law to get through this, but it is a thing of beauty to all readers. The terms employed by me already throughout these chapters on Shakespeare, and the vision I have suggested about direct vs indirect (oil vs water) responsibility, may prove helpful in grasping the desperate plea of the poem's speaker to save his friend from the grasp of his beloved.

My reading of the poem can be summarized as follows, using familiar terminology for the three players within the poem:[24] The voice of the sonnet (the "poet") finds himself in a double-bind. The object of his love (the "Dark Lady") has ensnared a dear friend of his (the "friend"), and now both are trapped by the lover's beauty and her greed. The friend entered the triangle when the poet asked him for an endorsement. The friend "learned but surety-like to write for me" [line 7]. Even here early on, it is worth pausing to equate this situation to the one we saw several times in *Merchant* from start to finish, when Antonio stands up for his protégé ("writes for" him– literally – when he swears to the bond that puts his life at risk to procure Bassanio's loan of 3000 ducats). I always picture the Bard at work simultaneously on the sonnet and the comedy, and there are scholarly sources who agree with me.[25] The sonnet dovetails with the Act V intercession of Antonio between Bassanio and Portia, who

24 See, e.g., description of these and other "Dark Lady" sonnets in Evans, ed., *The Riverside Shakespeare* (Boston: Houghton Mifflin, 1974), p. 1746.

25 Dating the writing of the sonnets is a risky business, but there are sufficient sources putting its composition at roughly the same period as that of *Merchant*. A scholar and TV producer, Dr. Steve Sohmer says, "So much of the drama of *Merchant* is pre-figured in the language of this poem [#134] that it seems to demand a connection between this Dark Lady and … the loansharking world of the play Shakespeare wrote in 1596, perhaps within months of writing Sonnet 134," *Reading Shakespeare's Mind* (U.K.: Manchester U. Press, 2018). Others concur with a date sometime in the decade of the 1590's: "The sonnets printed last in the 1609 collection (from ##127–154) were the earliest composed," according to an Auckland scholar, Macdonald Jackson. See Paul Edmondson and Stanley Wells, eds., *All The Sonnets of Shakespeare* (U.K.: Cambridge U. Press, 2020), which seems to hypothesize for the grouping of these Dark Lady sonnets their authorship between 1590 and 1595. Comparing sonnets such as # 134 to plays using similar "key words and phrases," in my view, makes 1596–8 almost a sure bet as to the sonnet's period of authorship.

simply wants a direct vow of loyalty from her new husband. Antonio stands, again "surety-like" for the irresponsible youth. The structural similarities, as we will shortly see, do not end there, but the sonnet's triangulation also thus involves a "surety" – the friend – who becomes ensnared by the Dark Lady, and this tweaking of the structure could not possibly have happened in *Merchant* because Antonio's interest lies exclusively with Bassanio, and even if he loved Portia, her repugnance for him makes any triangulation of this sort dramatically and comedically impossible.

When, however, the friend writes words of praise to the Dark Lady about the poet, she brings the hapless friend, too, "Under that bond that him as fast doth bind" [line 8]. They are both entrapped. So, now playing themselves out poetically, we find all the dangers so far rehearsed by me whenever triangulation – or mediation, or abdication, or outsourcing – replaces the connection between two parties who previously were directly connected. The poet sings mournfully of his ill-fated decision to make his friend his "surety" with the Dark Lady.

Line two, "And I myself am mortgaged to thy will," describes through a familiar figure the anterior unmediated position one might expect in a romantic relationship, or, in our terms here, the binary baseline before it has become a triangle. The poet is hopelessly in love, and the line's legalism ("mortgaged to thy will") evokes his continuing "indebtedness" to the Dark Lady. Many of my readers – like those of Shakespeare in his day[26] – will recognize this commercial metaphor. You are buying a house and you need to find a mortgage to help you close the deal. The bank, usually, is the place your needs begin and end. You become the bank's debtor and the security for the repayment of your loan is your newly acquired property. Early in the poem, the only wrinkle or foreboding about this direct obligation of one lover to another is that a third person is immediately introduced (in line one). It would be as though the mortgage I get from the bank, say, requires me to deal with another party in order to make my payments.

The "he is thine" dictates our understanding of "mortgaged to thy will." The choice made by the desired object of the poet's love will dictate whether the direct earlier relationship between them continues or is disrupted by the Dark Lady's turning to the other, the friend who threatens the earlier direct love relationship. The poet must take responsibility for the whole mess, because it was his delegation to that friend to find good things to tell the Dark Lady about

26 O. Hood Philips, *Shakespeare and the Lawyers* (London: Methuen, 1972), *e.g.*, chs. 8 and 9 on terms like "mortgage" and others in this chapter as employed by Shakespeare. For "surety," see the still totally accurate definition found in *The Law in Shakespeare*, p. 95 and text around ch. 5, n. 15.

the poet that has led to disaster. Now, much too late, he realizes in the terms of the sonnet, that the mission he set for his friend was "my unkind abuse" [line 12]. (Bassanio oh so briefly tries to dissuade Antonio from standing in for him when Shylock offers the loan – I,iii,155 – but the self-serving young man goes ahead with the "unkind abuse" of Antonio.)

The first two lines, which thus portend a traditional triangulated love affair, immediately yield to line three, which surrenders the poet's well-being to that of his friend. The poet stands ready, in legal terms, to "forfeit" his lover's mortgage and let his rival take it over. Without any choice as between them by the Dark Lady, in other words, the poet wants to surrender to his "other mine" all the romantic gifts he had once enjoyed, if that will at least result in the friend's finding peace. The poet is equally committed to the other as he is to the Dark Lady, or at least equates the two in the expression "that other mine." And that "other," as we learned in line one, has also been ensnared – to his peril – by the one both of them now desire.

So the poem is about another kind of legal relationship, not that of creditor/lender but instead the triangulated entanglement of a third person, the "he" of line one ("So now I have confessed that he is thine"). As we have seen this legal structure work among Antonio, Bassanio and Shylock in Act I of *Merchant*, the binary debtor-creditor or mortgagor-mortgagee explodes outward to the "surety-like" triangulation made explicit in line seven of the poem ("He learn'd but surety-like to write for me"). A surety, both as Portia uses the word ironically in the final act of *Merchant*, [V, I, 254] or as it is used in the sonnet, has no place in what should be the unmediated love of two romantic partners. Nothing in Shakespeare – whether in the public world of power or the private world of love – *nothing* works well when triangulation occurs.[27]

There will be no happy ending as we move towards this sonnet's final couplet. The triangulated chaos for which the poet is responsible will surely not be cleaned up by the Dark Lady: "For thou are covetous, and he is kind" [line 6]. Continuing into another area of law, the poet describes the Dark Lady as one who promiscuously lends her favors to men like the poet and (now) his friend. "The statute of thy beauty thou wilt take,/ Thou usurer, that put'st forth all to use" [lines 9–10] She, on this figure, not so much gives the gift of her beauty to many as she (like Antonio over Shylock's wealth at the end of the trial scene) creates a "use" – a trust – that brings her usurious wealth while totally destroying those whom she controls. The friend now also appears as her debtor, one

27 As to the novel, Rene Girard is not to the contrary in his *Mensonge Romantique Et Vérité Romanesque*, *op. cit.*, ch. 5, n. 18.

whom she is figuratively suing [line 11] for the "use" of her beauty, however briefly.[28]

Arriving now at the closing couplet: it is a remarkable summary of the sad situation reached by parties originally bound to each other directly who decide – one, or both – to triangulate their love. Poet has lost his friend; the Dark Lady possesses both; the friend especially is at risk for the moment (line 11), but the poet is still paying his share of the interest for the loan of her beauty that started the whole business. A happier ending was not in the cards, given the cruel source of the poet's feelings; but he at least could have left his friend out of it.

And maybe this is the ultimate lesson for Christian "intercessors," like the young evangelical who casually stopped me on the street today to get me to bring Jesus into my life: just leave me alone! I can be your friend, but not if you insist on bringing me in to your own private affairs, your own belief systems, your own commercial dealings, your own affairs! Maybe Shakespeare is suggesting in all the works treated in Part Two, that, at least when left alone, the Jews – the oil that will never blend with the Christians' water – have done well, perhaps including even the example of Job at his nadir, to stand through the centuries for directness – hermeneutically, theologically, personally, and ethically.

3 *Legalized Triangulation During the Holocaust: the Example of the "Aryan Trustee" Over Stolen Jewish Wealth*

As is pervasively argued in this book, great stories change the meaning and value-orientation of our understandings. That is why we read! So, words like "mediator" as well as others that sound good to us are put in play and astound us into revaluations. In *Merchant*, laudatory nouns such as "mercy" and "equity" and "surety" and "trust" are dramatically deconstructed, and their questionable effect on the interactions of people identified and contrasted with institutions like law, which may be flawed but which aspire to regulate people's behavior not through the subjective whims of majority spoke-persons but rather justly and directly through codes and customs and commentaries that enrich through their interweaving of stories and norms the lives of generations.

What our close look at the law in *Merchant* has revealed so far: the Alien Statute as implemented non-mercifully by the newly liberated Antonio, has led not only to Shylock's forced conversion but also to the naming of Antonio as trustee over Shylock's wealth. The Jew, whose portable property already has

28 Recall Antonio's dictating a "use" of Shylock's present and future-earned wealth, through the trust he is creating over Shylock as the trial scene cruelly ends. [IV, I, 385].

gone missing into the hands of the Christian husband of his daughter now is forced to give the couple almost everything else he owns and indeed will own at his death. The triangulated relationship created by every trust is downgraded here into a manipulative and deliberately cruel control over Shylock, the source of all the wealth.

Our last sub-section here crosses the t and dots the i of "triangulation" and even specifically of the institution of the trust by moving forward into history and perceiving how prescient Shakespeare was in flagging the use of Jewish wealth in *Merchant* to feed Christian needs and in (more generally) conveying in poetry and the plays a sense of doom every time direct obligations are triangulated.

In *Merchant*, a lifetime of Shylock's hard-earned material wealth is transmuted, through the actions of Antonio, into "manna, in the way of starved people," as Lorenzo wolfishly[29] but poetically puts it. (V, I, 295). Just as the comedy is ending, Jessica's husband finds out that the Jew, by operation of Venice's court, somehow has made the couple the beneficiary of a trust administered by Antonio but for their eventual benefit. His reaction perfectly replicates the historical celebrations at many a Christian household during World War II when Jewish property fell into their hands, also by operation of what passed for "law" in each country of Hitler's Europe.

Raul Hilberg, the great historian of the Holocaust in Europe, reminded us that extermination, the last phase of any genocide, is *always* accompanied by the theft of the property of the victimized group.[30] Untold billions of dollars in Jewish wealth were "aryanized" in various countries, including, as we shall see in this book, Great Britain itself (the Channel Islands), Vichy France, the low countries (alluded to in Camus' *The Fall*), the Reich, just about everywhere in Christian Europe, including "neutral" Switzerland. I have played a small role in restoring to Jewish victims or their heirs a part of the Vichy banks' windfall.[31] And I still meet with French officials in Paris every year to pursue that work.

To my literary imagination, tracking the process of all this "legalized" wartime theft almost immediately reminded me of Shylock's fate under the Alien Statute – as cruelly implemented by Antonio – during the trial scene of *The Merchant of Venice*. Eerily similar to Antonio's use of the "trust" to control Shylock was the French mechanism of the "aryan trustee," who took over specific

29 The word "wolfish" was associated earlier in the play with Shylock (Dr. Lopez 's name sounds like "lupus" and the rabid anti-Semite Gratiano uses the term to describe Shylock, which does not disturb the Jew one wit. [IV, I, 130–45 a)]

30 Raul Hilberg, *The Destruction of The European Jews* (Chicago: Quadrangle Books, 1961).

31 See text at Preface, n. 12.

Jewish properties and totally controlled their administration. The legalized take-over involved a deformed and denatured version of the trust by which, under color of a cruel set of laws, a third-person who was an "aryan" took control of the wealth of someone whom those same laws had identified as being Jewish.[32]

When I started my research, inspired by Camus, into Vichy legal wrongdoing, I had no access to the Vichy-era section of the Twentieth Century French archives – no one did in the early 1980's – but I gained the precious assistance of the Centre de Documentation Juive contemporaine ("CDJC"), a terrific source of knowledge that still exists and has been expanded into a Holocaust Museum just off the Seine on the Right Bank. The CDJC files included hundreds of index cards from the wartime years that memorialized the transfer of wealth from the Jew and his or her business or possession to the aryan trustee, known as the "administrateur provisoir" or "A.P." The A.P.'s name and address, as well as those of the Jew and the business, were inscribed on each card. Thousands of ordinary French citizens, counting only Paris and the close-in suburbs and towns, signed on to twist their Jewish neighbors' property into "manna" that fed their greed.

Why would they do this? Surely, it was not to take on a responsible position in hopes that eventually the property would be returned to the Jewish owner; in fact, we know that this almost never happened. At the time of the liberation, many properties had been fraudulently used up by the trustee himself or herself, transferred to others for ridiculously low prices, or, in the case of portable property – here tracking Shylock's experience with the Christian couple Jessica and Lorenzo – "disappeared" altogether.

Although the mid-1941 statute putting this scheme in place and signed by the pre-War liberal second justice minister, Joseph Barthelemy,[33] contained in a minor provision potential penalties for abuse of the A.P. function, this was rarely triggered, as would be understandable given the position penniless Jews found themselves in who might indeed have wanted (like Shylock?) to test the procedural fairness of clearly biased courts.

Feeding on Jewish wealth in Vichy France took many, often less codified forms – the casual stripping by a concierge of precious personal objects like candlesticks and silverware and ceremonial gold cups as soon as a Jewish family was arrested and presumed never to be returning, to their apartment,[34] the

32 See *Vichy Law, op. cit.*, Introduction, ch. 7, n. 17.

33 See my *Vichy Law, op. cit.*, ch. 1, n. 7, chs. 4 and 7.

34 Maurice Rajsfus, *Jeudi Noir* (Paris: Harmattan, 1988) recounts just this experience, a rapidly ripped off apartment discovered when – unexpectedly – he and his older sister were

theft by a rival small-business owner of such objects as sewing machines, dental equipment, automobiles – but the A.P. case in point is a matter of historical record. And those records have greatly assisted in postwar judicial activity hoping to return some of the wealth to its rightful owners. All of this could not have been better predicted than by Shakespeare four centuries earlier down to the last legalistic detail of a depraved version of the "trust" to mediate, triangulate, divert Jewish property. But, again, why did so many Europeans behave this way?

A simple fact has been insufficiently acknowledged: the root cause for the tragedy lies in the basic attitude honest Christians take toward Jews, then and now. People grow up with New Testament stories that depict Jews as hateful, guilty, and blind. They are hair-splitters, Talmudic, legalistic, and, worst of all, Christ killers. It is hard to move beyond the incredible force of these stories. Their mythic appeal colors the emerging adult's optic. In pre-War Europe, even the most "enlightened" countries and traditions stood ready for the eternal recurrence of Jew-hatred. Tolerance, epitomized in the Enlightenment ideal of the autonomous and equal individual, collapsed in the Europe of the 1920s and 1930s. In fact, the Enlightenment ideal ironically led to extreme bitterness when it turned out that the liberated Jew could outdo the entrenched Christian once he or she was permitted to act as an equal. The "emergencies" of the between-the-wars period contributed the spark that ignited the already explosive mix.

Distrust always exists when Christian thinks about Jew. Equally as troubling but unequally produced, the Jew also distrusts the Christian. "I hate him for that he is a Christian," we have seen Shylock say in and of the *Merchant of Venice*. But Shylock's antipathy is grounded in his own direct experience of Christian persecution, while the Christian's arises from an early educational mix of myth and religion. To distrust a Christian, if you have had the luck of avoiding personal tragedy, you need only access historical data; but as a Christian – even among the millions we have shown have abandoned an active allegiance to their faith – you have been hard-wired from infancy to distrust a Jew. These are stories you pick up on your mother's knee. If you have a problem with envy, you do not even *need* a successful Jew to trigger spiteful thoughts, and in fact you do not even need a *living* Jew at all! (Antisemitism in contemporary Poland

---

allowed as children under the age of 16 and born in France to return home after 10 tortuous and terrifying hours with their just arrested parents, and thereby to avoid the fate of their parents and 11,000 other Jews during the "big round-up" of July 1942 in Paris. The apartment was there, but not the precious family mementos, the valuable remnants of a happier time.

and Hungary is on the rise, even though Hitler and the Poles and Hungarians made sure there would be no or few Jews left after the Holocaust.) It is a short step to cyclical violence when economic deprivation upgrades resentment and envy into hatred.

The Jew as scapegoat in Europe. What else is new? Yet we have not come to understand it much, and we certainly have tried politely to avoid the frank explanation I give throughout this book: Jew and Christian are inalterably different. I hope I have shown that Shakespeare endorses this viewpoint, which would only be disheartening if its result were any worse than the false flag of "Judeo-Christian" solidarity. The solution to the scapegoating problem, therefore, lies not in the "dialogue" or temporary sense of optimism we see in some places today.[35]

Christian scapegoating of the Jew comes with the territory of being Christian. It is cyclical. It overwhelmed even the highly cultured and technologically sophisticated European of the '30's and '40's. Law and Literature, in perhaps its most salient historical mode, has identified the best wisdom about this problem. It lies in Shakespeare, it relates to the terrible effects of rejecting not only Jews but also their values of direct communication, direct prayer, and ethical existence through a sound Law that brings one closer to God.

35 Back in 2008, to take but one example, thoughtful writers like Tony Judt were still opining – in the *Ny Review of Books* ("The 'Problem' of Evil in Postwar Europe," Feb. 14, 2008) – that all is again well in Europe for Jews. He was wrong then and might not repeat his mistake were he alive and writing today. And at roughly the same time, Pope Benedict XVI was cutting back on the Church's brief flirtation under John XXIII with real Christian love for the Jewish people. The German Pope wanted Jewish souls to soften. He wanted the re-installation of the old Good Friday prayer so that all Catholics again understand and vouch for the idea that Jews need to be fundamentally changed. There is in this something distasteful at best; a man brought up in the shadow of Hitler could not fathom that the Third Reich's negation of the Jew drew on just such traditional Catholic attitudes. The Jew is other, the Jew is lesser, the Jew's status is itself beneath that of others.

PART 3

Nine Stories Pitted against the Very Grammar of Judeo-Christian as Adjective

Introduction to Part III

Part III's first set of discussions, which deal with the two postwar novels of Albert Camus that most clearly bear on Vichy France's misbehavior from 1940–45, reports in some detail findings connected to my work on the European Holocaust, and particularly the ways in which Catholic France (with some wonderful individual exceptions) managed to accommodate the beast within. I have learned by getting into archives no one had seen since the War that the words Catholics used, both at the pulpit and among the rank-and-file, helped even basically decent people to stand by as their own gendarmes arrested Jews right in front of their faces. Christian mercy gave way rapidly to a discourse of accommodation to the Hitlerian genocide. I am going to analyze that discourse and to figure out how Paul's commandment to "love thy neighbor" often turned into its opposite. The key catastrophe for the Jewish people of the 20th century may, as we try to come to understand it better, mark the gradual end of the era of the great Christian faiths that grew from Judaism supposedly to spread love among all peoples.

CHAPTER 6

Camus as Primary Direct Source Regarding France During the Holocaust

A Stories Crack the Code of Silence on Fraught Issues

Picture a long conversation over lunch with one of your best and most loquacious French friends. You have talked about everything through the years, from the political to the personal. Suddenly, your friend turns mum. You have noticed this before, but it occurs only when you bring up a specific subject. Although you can't understand the silence in the face of the subject, you keep trying and failing. This is what I have labelled in these pages the surprising "fork stuck in the air syndrome" that occurred during restaurant conversations with my close French friends in the 1970's just at the mere mention of "Vichy." People otherwise willing to discuss anything at all with me declined even to open their mouths to finish a bite of food. The mere mention of France's dark and shameful period closed their mouths. Not much was available to meet my curiosity then, except the wartime-related works of Albert Camus. I began, just as I was cracking the archival codes and gaining entrance where none before had dared (or had the good luck!) to go,[1] I wrote about Camus's masterful 1954 novel, *La Chute*.[2] While others of his generation, and the younger folks, too, remained silent, Camus spoke up. In a key section of *The Fall*, the narrator – who happens quite significantly to be a lawyer – confesses that during France's attack on the Jews under its jurisdiction in World War II, he flirted with resisting the Nazis but talked himself out of it. I stressed his lawyer-like ability to rationalize even the most transparently evil of decisions; part of his professional training allowed him to avoid going "underground" almost as a matter of rhetorical antipathy to anything but the heights, as he liked to call the rest of his life. Camus chose a lawyer-as-protagonist and narrator because, I argued, he was pinpointing as a reason for the "Fall" of his country French wartime legal reasoning (a kind of "dessicated Cartesianism," said the *NYTimes* book reviewer for my later book on Vichy[3]); I wanted to find out a lot more

1 See *op. cit.*, ch. 1, n. 4 and ch. 4, n. 6.

2 *The Failure of the Word, op. cit.*, Introduction, ch. 7, n. 4.

3 NYT book review by Richard Bernstein of *Vichy Law and The Holocaust in France, op. cit.*, Introduction, n. 17.

 | DOI:10.1163/9789004525177_008

about actual legal reasoning during the Vichy period. The archives[4] beckoned me, thanks to Camus.

Camus in *The Fall* gives his lawyer-protagonist-narrator the name "Jean Baptiste Clamence." Not much interpretive creativity is thus required to associate law with religion, and to see that Camus intertwines the two in the culpable sphere of Dantesque sin and punishment. When, provoked by Camus to try to enter the closed off Vichy-era files in the 20th Century French archives and then to write about Vichy from 1982-1984, I already thus had come to suspect that *French law and religious authority might well prove to be at the heart of France's fall from grace.*

Camus' 1956 story opened my eyes to the inter-relation of law, literature, history and religion in Vichy France. When only a handful of others deemed it wise even to *broach* the subject, he made it an explicit part of what I still believe is his greatest novel.[5]

1 *A French Lawyer, Channeling Jean-Baptiste Clamence, Conveys a Twisted Picture of Catholic Morality*

Upon entering the hitherto closed off space of the 20th Century French archives, I learned that Camus had been correct on both fronts in launching a subject through his fiction that almost all others preferred to avoid. I learned that not only law but also religion was culpable in the destruction of at least 80,000 Jews under color of Vichy law from 1940–44.

A real-life lawyer, which did not shock me given Camus' brilliant choice of lawyer-narrator in *The Fall*, led the way here, too. Leon Berard, Vichy's emissary to the Vatican, answered an inquiry from Vichy's leader Marshal Petain about the Vatican's possibly objecting on moral grounds to Vichy's laws against the Jews.[6] Never a devout Catholic, the ancient "hero of Verdun" who had "given to France the gift of my person" in mid-1940 as all was crumbling around the shamefully defeated nation, still seems to have left the door of decency opened just a hair. As the Marshal's own laws, camps, and expropriations were in full genocidal sway, what small inner voice in mid-1941 led him to assign this lawyer such a fraught task?

Would the Vatican at its highest levels endorse his laws, which had already stripped Jews throughout the country of property, career, and liberty itself?

4 See discussion on archives in Chapter One (B).

5 For more on his earlier story, *La Peste* (*The Plague*), see the next sub-section.

6 On Vichy's promulgation – with no German pressure on them at all – of almost 200 laws against the Jews, laws that went beyond the German precedents, see my *Vichy Law and The Holocaust in France, op. cit.*, Introduction, n. 16.

Petain takes the unusual step of asking his emissary to Rome about the Vatican's perspective on Vichy French racial legislation.[7]

Leon Berard spends the summer of 1941 (as Jews throughout Europe – including in Rome – began their worst few years in recorded history) at the Vatican researching the question. At the helm was Pius XII, whom several story-tellers covered in this book have focused on.[8] Berard's thorough-going research broached a topic that, except in this unique circumstance, was being utterly covered over by that Pontiff. Berard, a talented lawyer and diplomat, weeds out a truthful answer when all around him might have been flummoxed by the Vatican's secrecy, falsehood, and collaboration. Berard hears that racism itself is unacceptable to the Church. And that all those who had come to Christ, from whatever former level of sub-standardness, were equal in the eyes of the Faith. Given these absolute tenets of Catholicism, maybe the Church will advise Marshal Petain that his laws are wrong in its eyes? The door is open for a response consistent both with morality and the Church's own doctrine!

By September, 1941, Berard has completed his survey of Church officials. In a letter I found only in the French archives, he writes to Petain. The missive is of sufficient importance to our study to cite at some length. Consider the old French leader pondering the news from Rome. Without any Nazi intervention, his government in Vichy had already promulgated some 50 laws against the Jews. 150 more were to see the light of day, right up to Allied bombing on Vichy courthouses in 1944![9] But so far, no deportation trains had rolled eastward from French soil. There was time for a turnaround in French law that would protect the Jews. There was time to correct and even eliminate the fully functioning French judicial and administrative system to which the Germans had been only too happy to delegate most of the antisemitic work – including in the zone of France they fully occupied. Imagine this: what if the highest levels in Rome privately would tell him that his policies violated Catholic doctrine and placed his immortal soul at risk!

Berard's conclusion was as follows

> As an authorized person at the Vatican told me, they mean no quarrel with the Jewish laws.
>
> *Vichy's Emissary to the Vatican to Vichy's Leader*, Summer 1941

7 There is a strikingly similar moment in Daniel Silva's *The Confessor*, pp. 291–3.

8 See Chapter Seven, through the works of Rolf Hochhuth and Daniel Silva.

9 *Vichy Law and the Holocaust in France*, *op. cit.*, Introduction, n. 16.

Law, the Church, and the Jews come together in the figure of Berard, and in the message he gives Petain. Camus in *The Fall* had been on to something about his countrymen. Way ahead of time, he introduced through his protagonist, Jean-Baptiste Clamence this same dreadful combination of lawyer-like rationalization, verbally manipulative skills, and an effortless ability to do harm against the most innocent groups in his midst.

I have studied Berard's lengthy letter to his leader. But each time I re-read it, I stand amazed. Go ahead, he concludes: Go ahead and isolate your Jews. Deprive them of their careers and their possessions. Put them in hideous prison camps within your country, knowing that many will die there. Accommodate even a worse fate for these people by identifying who should be "sent to the East." It's OK. On the pathway to the ultimate victimization of the Jews, the Church at its highest levels gives you not only the green light but also the comfort of its theological rest-stops along the way. The Vatican has taken a close look, and its clinical perspective lights your way towards genocide. Your soul, and that of our country's Catholic majority, have nothing to fear.

Indeed, the summer of 1941 gave the Catholic Church sufficient time to rationalize for Berard such a reversal of common morality and its own apparent doctrine. Here are relevant passages from Berard's letter to Petain:

> 2 September 1941. M. le Maréchal: By your letter of 7 August 1941, you honored me by requesting information touching questions and problems that might be raised, from the Roman Catholic perspective, by the measures your government has taken regarding the Jews. I have had the honor of sending you a preliminary response where I observed that nothing has ever been said to me at the Vatican that would imply, on the part of the Holy See, a critique or disapproval of those legislative and regulatory acts. *Now I can affirm that at no time has the pontifical authority been either concerned or preoccupied with that part of French policies, and that no complaint or request coming to it from France has so far given it such an opportunity ....*
>
> A. The Church and Racism. There is a fundamental and basic opposition between Church doctrine and "racist" theories. The Church, by universal definition, professes the unity of all human beings. The same Redeemer died for all men; the Gospel is announced to "every creature" .... All these precepts are incompatible with a concept that could derive from the conformity of the skull and the nature of the blood and the aptitudes and the vocation of peoples, their religion itself, to establish finally a hierarchy of the races, at the top of which is found a pure and royal race called "Aryan." [There are then quotations to this effect

taken from the words of Pius XI in *Mit brennender Sorge* in 1937, as well as from other authoritative declarations.] The Church thus has condemned racism as it has condemned communism.

From its teachings about racist ideas one should be far from deducing, however, that it necessarily condemns any specific measure taken by any particular state against what it calls the Jewish race. Its thinking on this involves distinctions and nuances that must now be noted. The subject must be treated clearly [sic?].

B. The Church, the Jewish Problem, and Antisemitism.

It would be vain to extract from Canon Law, theology, pontifical acts, a group of precepts that resembles legislation on Judaism or the Judaic religion. It would even be difficult to find easily, regarding this subject, a clearly marked doctrinal body.

The first principle that appears, and the surest, is that in the eyes of the Church, a Jew who has been authentically baptized ceases to be a Jew and becomes part of "Christ's flock." But one should not conclude from this that the Church regards religion alone as the thing marking Israel off in the midst of the nations. It does not believe that Jews constitute simply a "spiritual family," as do in our case, for example, Catholics and "reformed" Christians. It recognizes that among the distinctive traits of the Jewish community there appear not so much *racial* as *ethnic* particularities. It discerned this long ago and has always taken this into account. [Bérard then recounts various periods in which such measures as the *numerus clausus* or special signs on apparel were adopted by Catholic authorities such as, respectively, Saint Thomas of Aquinas and the Lateran Council.] ....

D. What Disjunctions Can One Find Between Catholic Doctrine and the French Law of 2 June 1941 on the Jews?

[Bérard reviews the law's exclusionary sections.] In principle, there is nothing in these measures that the Holy See would criticize. It believes that in promulgating such measures a State uses its legitimate power and that a spiritual force should not interfere with the internal politics of States. And, then too, the Church has never professed that the same rights must be given to or recognized in all citizens. It has never ceased teaching dignity and respect for the individual. But it surely does not understand matters in the fashion, strictly speaking, of the spiritual followers of Rousseau and Condorcet .... Yet the law of 2 June 1941 begins with the legislator's giving a juridical definition of the Jew as expressly linked to the notion of "race." Still, if we compare the law of 2 June with that of 3 October [1940] (which it replaced), we see that the new text has

> reduced the reliance on "race." If a Jew proves that he belonged, prior to 25 June 1940, to the Catholic faith, or to the Calvinist or Lutheran faiths, he is no longer "considered as a Jew," as long as he does not have more than two grandparents of the Jewish race. In this case, the law attached legal significance to "conversion." *It remains the case that a Jew, if duly converted and baptized, will still be considered a Jew, if he is the issue of at least three grandparents of the Jewish race, that is having belonged to the Judaic religion.*
>
> *There, one must admit, is a contradiction between French law and Church doctrine.*
>
> E. Practical Result of This Contradiction. Conclusion. I just pointed out the sole point at which the law of 2 June 1941 contradicts a principle held by the Roman Church. But it does not follow from this doctrinal divergence that the French state is threatened with ... even a censure or disapproval that the Holy See might express in one form or another about the Jewish laws .... *As an authorized person at the Vatican told me, they mean no quarrel with the Jewish laws.*

Berard ascertained that the Vatican *found a way to rationalize through interpretive methods the Church's awareness that Petain's laws were immoral,* to find a way to let them prevail nonetheless. Although Vatican thinking claimed to deplore "racism," there was a way out. The slippery hermeneutics this book has located in so much of Catholic reasoning about the Jews, and in Christian distortions of Jewish sacred texts more generally, is encapsulated in the "thesis/hypothesis" principle adduced by Berard from Vatican sources. *Tens of thousands of Jews in Vichy France alone would be sacrificed to this principle!:*

2 *For the Catholic Church, Realpolitik Trumps Morality*

Although a lawyer and not a theologian, Berard is a quick study as a summer researcher in 1941 Vatican City. He has been taught how opposites can simultaneously exist in Church doctrine. It is a twofold lesson: Jews can exist as long as they become Christians; and moral principles can exist as long as *Realpolitik* does not trump them. He has been told, during that Summer of 1941 when so much hinged on the teaching and when there was still time to reverse the awful flow of events, of the Church's distinction between "thesis" and "hypothesis." In the harrowing space provided by this theological distinction, the Church's alleged rejection of all racism can be adjusted to accept any given state's actual, racist legal practice. If events on the ground require the moral rule to be bent and perhaps broken, so be it. There is another interpretive rule that transmutes religious virtue into the base metal of *Realpolitik*. As Guenther Grass surmised, and as I write about later in these pages,[10] Christian love turned effortlessly into Christian hate at the exact moment that the alchemist, Adolf Hitler, most counted on the transformation.

The *hermeneutic* of easy manipulation is ingrained in both entities: Church and State, each preserving its historical functions, can reach a détente through the meta-interpretive distinction between "thesis" and "hypothesis." Once again, the early Christian flexibility in understanding texts, morality, and ethics has reared its head.

B Camus Equates Vichy's Legal Speech with the Vatican's Thinking

We have seen, and Camus displays novelistically that law, too, responded on the ground to high theory among Vatican church officials! What was meaningful for Vichy legal actors was the Catholic method of reading texts itself. For this method helps explain the hermeneutics of Vichy lawyers (who, after all, were predominantly Catholic and in some notable cases, devoutly so) both as to their capacity to read texts a certain way and as to their quick acceptance of a particular kind of religious victim.

Something far more native to their education and training would have to appeal to them to make the system as pervasively anti-Jewish as it eventually became. Change of this magnitude would occur by appealing to a two-pronged French disposition to read texts a certain way.

Catholic reading strategies assisted Vichy, then, not only morally and pragmatically in affirming its program but even more integrally in providing a way to effectuate the program on every level of legalistic practice. How perfect, too, in isolating the Jew as *Talmudic* other! For the main component of this strange figure's durability was precisely the Jew's ability – at least over the long haul – to interpret the text as the barometer of a legislated and ethical daily routine, the Text as it was originally written and not as it had been "accommodated" into the New Policy.

1 The Plague (*1947*) *Precedes* The Fall (*1956*)

The Failure of the Word, and its analysis of two Camus stories (*The Stranger and the Fall*) has recently been translated into French.[11] It had been earlier

10 See Chapter Ten.

11 *La Parole Defaillante*, transl. Françoise Michaut (Toulouse: Editions L'Epitoge, 2019).

translated into German[12] and much earlier than that into Italian.[13] (A translation into Chinese is pending as this book's publication date approaches.) Its focus through the medium of stories on law, legal distortion, ressentiment, and the victimization of Jews during the Holocaust has been much discussed by reviewers both in the U.S. and in the countries where the book has been translated.[14]

One response to my analysis of *The Fall*, though, coming from north of the border, has provoked me into remedial action in the pages of this book. About 20 years ago, a Canadian critic, Dwight Newman,[15] criticized me for the focus on *La Chute* (and even of *L'Étranger*) when he believed *La Peste – The Plague* – should have had pride of place in *The Failure of the Word*, since it is at least as germane to the Vichy period as the other two novels. I cite him at length because his critique has the merit of being correct – although as we shall see for the wrong reasons – because I am now about to atone for that earlier omission, and because his assessment of legal themes in *The Plague* will help my readers to recall and enter into a Camus novel that is often thought of as an allegory of the Vichy period and its infliction upon Jews of the epidemic of legalized racism.[16]

> Weisberg chooses to study *The Outsider* [Canadian translation of *L'etranger*] … [but] entirely neglects another work by Camus that has a profound legal content but simply does not have a legal protagonist …. *The Plague* on its face is a story more medical than legal, for its plot, as the title suggests, revolves around a tale of a town called Oran that is struck by the plague. However, when we are prepared to look past skin depth, we find a work with a deep-seated legal content and much to say about matters related to the law. The work's law related content … can be divided into seven important aspects. First, the text does have a surface legal content after all, one which is based on the town's measures to

12 *Rechtsgeschichten*, transl. Walter Popp (Berlin: Suhrkamp, 2013).

13 *Il Fallimento De La Parola*, transl. Andrea Fabbri (Bologna: il Mulino, 1990).

14 Reviews of all translations include some substantial review essays, such as Michael Stolleis' of *Rechtsgeschichten* in the *Frankfurter Allgemeiner Zeitung*.

15 "Existentialism and Law – Toward a Reinvigorated Law and Literature Analysis," *Saskatchewan Law Review*, v. 63 (2000), p. 87.

16 See the very recent volume, *Critical Insights: The Plague*, ed. Robert C. Evans (Grey House Publishing, 2023), *passim*. For Camus' own allusion to "fascism and the collapse of western values," see *id.* at 212, "Language and the Duty of Memory," by Peter Dunwoodie.

> control the plague, and in this the text lays bare the flexibilities[17] of the law in dealing with crises. Second, the text also illustrates the nature of legal discourse as highly abstracted from the realities with which it deals. Third, in a theme particularly apt to Law and Literature consideration, the text reveals some of the power of language and, it follows, of the language of the law. Fourth, further from the surface and at a more metaphorical level, the text deals with using, and actually itself uses, language to witness to injustices. Fifth, in an ironic twist on this, the text exposes but does not deal with certain other injustices – in particular certain issues of race, class, and gender. Sixth, building on all of the preceding at a more philosophical level, the text develops the dilemmas resulting from the interaction between the existentialist hero and legal (and other) institutions. Seventh, the text implicitly holds out possibilities of a positive social vision in legal reform.

Newman is correct that this still quite incredible 1947 story anticipates much about law that ripens into the far more palpably "law-related" 1956 tale, *The Fall* and at the same time builds on much to be found in the 1942 Vichy-era novel, *The Stranger*. But as to the law-related components of *The Plague*, the most important, perhaps, is the figure of an "examining magistrate," or "juge d'instruction." M. Othon, who plays a key role not only in implementing edicts about the plague and seeking out those who may have violated them but also in his own right as a family man whose tragic loss to the plague of his young son constitutes one of the most poignant and detailed descriptions in the story.

M. Othon provides, for a change, a palpably human variation on one of Camus' favorite figures from *The Stranger*,[18] the examining magistrate who seals Meursault's fate though a series of deliberate and heartless distortions of the defendant, culminating in the fatal verdict on Meursault: he is "M. l'antichrist." In the earlier work, as I fully analyzed in *Failure*[19] Camus' judge-figure incorporates negatively a combination of religious hypocrisy (the crucifix) and creative but unfortunate legalistic distortion. (And as I also explore in this book, other 20th century novelists – such as the American, Bernard Malamud – were drawn to the European examining magistrate.[20]) But *The Plague*

17 For the dangers of flexibility and the occasional strengths of its opposite, see my *Intransigence, op. cit.*, ch. 1, n. 2, and various sections of the present volume.

18 *Failure, op. cit.*, Introduction, n. 4.

19 *Id.*

20 *The Fixer*, see chapter 8. Malamud may have been influenced by Camus in *The Plague* (not of course *The Stranger*!) in rendering a fully sympathetic version of this key legal official, whom novelists usually love to pillory as narrative falsifiers. See also Balzac, Kafka.

gives the judge a heart and even a soul. Although portrayed early in the novel as a pedantic follower of rules – even at his dinner table, the examining magistrate tends to correct the manners of his children in a kind of legalistic manner (*The Plague*, p. 28), Othon grows and is humanized by the extended and painful period of his son's submission to the Plague.[21]

2 *Father Paneloux, a Conflicted Priest in the Face of an Epidemic*

Besides the legal elements helpfully brought to my attention by the Canadian Dwight Newman, there is much more in *The Plague* that commends our attention, given the present book's focus on religion during and preceding the Holocaust in Europe. Camus' 1947 book was published very soon after the catastrophe when little was known about French contributions to Jewish deaths, and those who knew about it were keeping it quiet. The strong allegorical element in the story caught the attention of reviewers[22] as well as eventual critics. But what were the invasion of the rats and the subsequent Oran epidemic allegorizing? It could be anything, because as Camus reminds us at the beginning of the story, quoting Daniel Defoe about the shattering strengths of fiction generally to help us understand reality:

> It is as reasonable to represent one kind of imprisonment by another, as it is to represent anything that really exists by that which exists not.
>
> ROBINSON CRUSOE

Even on a superficial level, it is not hard to associate Oran's fate with that of victims of any country invaded by Hitler (if the rats signify the Nazis).[23] But even this is too vague and even unlikely for a writer like Camus, who was primarily if not exclusively interested – as we see in *The Fall* – in the comportment of his *countrymen* during the War.

To judge this self-critical component of any ultimate allegorical meaning, we need not await *The Fall's* condemnation of the law. The most important character in *The Plague* is not any lawyer or judge but instead the *priest*, Paneloux. If we are to carry the allegorical level of the story just a bit, it is Paneloux's two

---

21 See, e.g., Gene Fendt, "The Women in *The Plague*," in Robert C. Evans, *Critical Insights, The Plague* (MA: Salem Press, 2023). Fendt provides an excellent description of how Othon softens, after the strict period in which he expects his wife to be "married to the law, towards a series of personal decision observed by Dr. Rieux, that totally change him. *Id.*, at 147.

22 See, e.g., a review by Charles A. Brady, writing in a NY publication, reported in Evans, ed., *op. cit.*, ch. 5, n. 16, at p. 22.

23 Rebecca Totaro, "Camus and Plague Literature," in Evans, ed., *op. cit.*, ch. 6, n. 16, p. XIX.

sermons to the entrapped townspeople of Oran that lead to a direct comparison to the *priesthood during Vichy*, which is a central focus of this book, first on the highest levels of the Church we have just described but now on the local level: what did priests say to their congregants about their responsibilities to each other and to people directly threatened by "plagues" – natural or humanly inflicted?

Paneloux is a Jesuit priest with many followers in plague-struck Oran. He is described as a "local celebrity" (p. 78). In the course of the story, Father Paneloux gives two sermons, described in detail, as he tries to find a Christian set of lessons for Oran's people during the epidemic. We will track the priest's progression from a fiery prophetic orator of old to a much more consoling and flexible preacher once the Plague has progressed. Then we will see this progression to reflect the actual discourse of French parish priests during the Vichy years.

As described by critic Mark Orme:[24]

> In Paneloux' first sermon ... the disease is interpreted by the priest as divine retribution. "Calamity has come on you, my brethren, and my brethren, you deserved it." In this first sermon, the plague is deemed "the flail of God" and a punishment for the criminal indifference of the townspeople, with the heavy downpour rattling against the Cathedral windows reminiscent of Old Testament Flood imagery. ... Striking a condemnatory tone, the priest plays on the fears of his parishioners to rationalize, through divine association the arrival of plague. Yet the effect of this first sermon on the local community is a moot point. While the magistrate Othon deems it to have been "absolutely irrefutable,[25] others merely took from the occasion "the fact that they had been sentenced, for an unknown crime, to an indeterminate period of punishment."

I believe that Camus' allegory was in part asking the fateful question (three years after France had been liberated and revelations of tens of thousands of Jewish victims of the Vichy regime were beginning to leak out) of whether the disproportionately dominant religion throughout France had sufficiently challenged its followers to accept some moral responsibility, to internalize it, and to do something about it. Paneloux' first sermon, a kind of old-fashioned (almost Jewish?) prophetic berating of his parishioners, challenged them to

24 Orme, in Evans, ed., *id.*, p. 124.
25 See my analysis of the stricter examining magistrate, Othon, in the previous sub-section.

atone for Divine retribution by acting in the world to improve the plague-torn city of Oran.

However, Paneloux' first sermon probably turned his parishioners off, and by the time of his second sermon, his tone had softened considerably. The much gentler approach of the palliative second sermon, we now know, is far more representative of local parish discourse during the Plague of Vichy than was his first fire and brimstone sermon. Facing a flock that had been reduced by 25% from the earlier attendance, Paneloux now seeks not a Judaic reaction of personal responsibility from his parishioners but rather a quiescent, more Christian, sense of resignation. As Orme surmises about this change:

> ... [T]he moral certainly on which Paneloux' first sermon is predicated is replaced with a far more morally ambivalent mentality following the death of Judge Othan's son, Jacques, an event which shakes Paneloux' retributive mentality to its very foundations ... Interestingly, while listening to Paneloux' second sermon, Rieux [the narrator] considers that the priest was "dallying with heresy" in the way that he attempts to correct the earlier absolutist interpretation of the plague as divine retribution.[26]

Although I doubt the correctness of Orme's interpretation of the priest's change – it is more the result of his realizing that he is losing his audience in pursuing a righteous tone – this quibble is far less important to me here than in noting that the conciliatory tone of the second sermon accurately reflects local Catholic discourse as Vichy progressed. Any Catholic impetus to challenge the faithful to accept responsibility for the epidemic of hatred sweeping France (and there are almost no examples of this) gave way rapidly to a discourse of Christian self-forgiveness and passivity. Camus was on to something, both in his representation of the judge, Othon, and of the priest Paneloux. The empirical findings that I describe now will help us both to clarify the allegorical intent of the story-teller in *The Plague* and to see, historically, what parishioners heard in churches every Sunday.

26 *Op. cit.*, ch. 6, n. 24, pp. 124–5.

C Religious Conditions on the Ground: What the Parish Priests Said to the Faithful during the "Plague" of Vichy France

Vesna Drapac[27] is the historian who most contributes empirically to a knowledge of the actual weekly experience at the local level of Catholic parishioners during Vichy. Crucially for our thesis here. Drapac has no particular problem with characterizing the French Catholic church as "compliant, accommodating and opportunistic in the face of the Vichy regime and German occupation. What the church's 'politics of presence' really meant during the Occupation was that members of the hierarchy and, alongside them, key Catholic notables, were drawn to the reactionary rhetoric of Vichy which openly courted Catholics." (389)

Drapac's singular contribution is to situate the discourse of Catholic prelates during Vichy on the most local level, and she does this in two senses, first what highly placed officials such as cardinals said directly to parish congregations (as opposed to what they said to either the Pope or to Vichy government officials) – which we have exemplified elsewhere in this chapter – and second what *parish priests* themselves preached to their flock as the war progressed:

> The people, gathered in their spiritual home in their *quartiers*, were united. That unity did not signify uniformity of religious motivation, much less political homogeneity. Nor could it have. Rather, it signified a general attachment to a discernible (and familiar) national religious tradition which defined Catholics and which was under threat, [Note here the similarity to Oran's Catholics in church in Camus' novel.] Their collective identity was expressed on occasions of communal worship and this could not be lost on observers or participants. *On such occasions their responsibilities were outlined.*
>
> p. 391, emphasis added

The scholarly task of Drapac, in studying Catholic sermons on the most local level during Vichy, is precisely to identify what *were* "their responsibilities." What would the parishioner take with him or her from a Sunday in church during Vichy? Camus, in the realm of the novel (which Drapac's methodology

27 See, e.g., Vesna Drapac, "Religion in a Dechristianized World: French Catholic Responses to War and Occupation," *Journal of European Studies*, vol. XXVI (1996), pp. 389–416. My response to Drapac's French-language findings is in Roth and Maxwell, eds., *Remebering for the Future* (U.K.: and N.Y.: Palgrave, 2002), vol. Two, p. 509.

does not include), imagines through the two sermons given by Paneloux a very similar inquiry: what do the Catholics of Oran learn from their local priest about proper comportment during the plague? In both cases, the real and the imagined, parishioners were advised to behave like Christians. But what did this actually mean in the substantive context of emergency and disaster? Drapac continues:

> People were expected to remain active, doing what it was in their power to do to alleviate the suffering of neighbors and compatriots further afield. They had choices and if they chose to do wrong they would be judged accordingly. Finally, we have the link between patriotic and religious duties which could prove a potent combination in an occupied city where the enemy seemed all powerful. (391–2)

Drapac concedes that no parish church was in any way "a direct target of the Germans and collaborators in the first instance." She does not concede the conclusion, however, that the impetus in these unthreatened venues was to produce merely "pieux paroissiens du Marechal [the Marshal's pious little parishioners]." (392) Drapac endeavors to challenge some basic assumptions consistent with the relative passivity and acceptance of the average Catholic to the enormities of Vichy and Nazi persecution. However, her assessment of the influence a Sunday in church – what people heard from their local priests, what they discussed together going and coming, how they assimilated the religious experience into the rest of their activities – does not differ much from Camus' suggestion in *The Plague* that Paneloux may have scored some points in his two sermons but not enough to inspire on a religious plane some active Christian response to the suffering of others. Rather, her conclusions, based on her commendable study of local church rhetoric, are either vague or completely consistent with a merely "spiritual resistance" (394) or with the stereotypical little parishioner of the Marshal.[28] Drapac continues:

> Catholics, along with their compatriots, were shocked and humiliated by the defeat. [Then came] Petainism, and the associated sense of relief was widespread. But the Vichy regime did have something special to offer Catholics and appealed to them in its propaganda .... There was not jubilation at the fall of the republic. At [sic] parochial level talk was of the

28 See my commentary on Drapac, in "Differing Ways of Reading, Differing Views of the Law: The Catholic Church and its Treatment of the Jewish Question During Vichy," *op. cit.*, n. 27.

> great sadnesses, the great suffering, the dislocation, the disarray and the turmoil. (396)

Drapac hardly seems to be describing an environment in which the average parishioner was being asked to go beyond vague, highly self-protective responses that eventually in her own words gave way to "'an understandable sense of relief mixed with shame, pain and anger ... All hope was now lost and a great silence took hold. It was the silence of those who no longer expect anything and whose misfortune is complete.' [citing *La Semaine religieuse de Paris*, 4 April 1942, 215]." (403) Her findings point to what even the early postwar Camus of *The Plague* posited as a paradox: greater attention by the not-yet-infected Oranians to themselves as somehow on a par with the sufferings of the actual victims of the epidemic.

The postwar vision of Camus, if nothing else, casts into question the bland, tepid, and self-congratulatory nature of Drapac's conclusions. In the first sermon delivered by Paneloux in *The Plague*, Camus' parish priest was looking for quite a bit more from his parishioners. He challenged them, almost as might Isaiah himself, to take direct responsibility and act to improve the situation in Oran. But in the second sermon, he speaks much more as one of Drapac's actual parish priests during Vichy. "We must accept that bad things happen," he tells his flock. No more retribution; they need not look to themselves. (Thought experiment here: what if Catholic parishioners had been challenged, as did the early Father Paneloux, to take personal responsibility for the disaster and the cruelty of Vichy?) The best we can do is pray for the victims of the plague and await better times.

Dr. Rieux, reporting on Paneloux' second sermon in *The Plague*:

> All trials, however cruel, worked together for good to the Christian. And, indeed, what a Christian should always seek in this hour of trial, was to discern that good .... The sufferings of children were our bread of affliction, but without this bread our souls would die of spiritual hunger."... Paneloux, directly from the second sermon: "We must aspire beyond ourselves towards that high and fearful vision. And on that lofty plain, all will fall into place, all discords will be resolved, and truth flash forth from the dark clouds of seeming injustice.
>
> *The Plague*, 200–06

The Christian can always make do in the face of the suffering of others, in part by somehow making *himself* the victim! This is water versus oil, again. "Seeming" injustice can be tolerated as the believer finds redeemed in it her most basic faith. Many years after *The Plague*, in *The Fall*, Camus' Jean-Baptiste Clamence comes to realize that a merely "spiritual resistance" – Paneloux' combined message to his flock – unmoved to actions in the world utterly failed to assist those suffering from the particular plague of Vichy genocidal antisemitism. What are we to make, then, of Drapac's parish priest during Vichy?

Drapac concludes:

> While it was recognized that the beauty of services and offices might enable some Catholics momentarily to transcend the daily drudgery of life during the ordeal, there was always the expectation that the spiritual lessons would remain with those who had been present and then filter out into the wider community. What was significant was the very public affirmation of absolute moral and religious values in the presence of an enemy whose ideology enshrined their opposites. (404)

Children's suffering is God's will, but let's always affirm absolutely that such suffering is wrong. If brought on by a plague – or by the Nazis (again, how about by Vichy?) – we must whisper in church and to our neighbors that this is wrong. But the "thesis" of absolute evil is always softened by the "hypothesis" of needing to survive in the world.[29] Imagine more than an "affirmation" but instead a call to action. What if a small trickle of France's Catholics, who comprised 90% of the population, had been inspired by some parish priest's direct words of revulsion in the face of Nazi Germany and Vichy France. This is Camus' powerful thought experiment in his postwar stories that implicate the dark Vichy years. But Drapac dilutes the issue and becomes strangely unhistorical when she points almost exclusively, as in the next cited paragraph, to *German* wrongdoing. Somewhat along the lines of Daniel Silva's story, treated in the next chapter about Vatican myopia in the face of genocide,[30] Drapac's local Catholic parishioners do not appear to have learned in church that the "enemy whose ideology enshrined their opposites" was *France itself*: Paris gendarmes arresting Jews in the streets and in their apartments, French prison camps where 3000 Jews were dying, French railroad trains that were taking beleaguered Jews to "the East." Instead, at best in descriptions such as the following, a still diluted vision of German evil, and only *German* evil, seemed to trickle down to some local Catholics:

---

29 See (A)(1) of this chapter for an elaboration during Vichy of this Roman Catholic palliative interpretive principle.

30 Pius XII may be paying a price for his wartime indifference and inaction: no sainthood.

> Girls in Catholic youth works … observed the feast of the Assumption in 1943, described as the "fourth year of sadness"… and at Christmas their thoughts turned to those "behind barbed wire or at the machines [in Germany]." They prayed that God "would look compassionately on his children who were dying in inhuman battles." They thought about the "immense prison camps in Germany" of the "long-suffering and their continuous privations." … There could not be one single legitimate Catholic response (active resistance) to the crisis … By its nature the Church embraced diversity and could not call upon Catholics to act as one. As there was not one path towards sanctity, it followed that there were many models for exemplary behavior in times of hardship [religious historical models follow]… When it was evident that the enemy would be driven out, there was unambivalent joy. Church bells rang … and God and his mother were thanked for sparing Paris from the worst (though people still prayed for peace). (410)

Guenther Grass and Albert Camus would not have been amazed by such a set of observations. Grass satirizes this Catholic perspective in his brilliant chapter "Faith, Hope, and Love," which is treated soon in Chapter 10. And Camus would not allow that Paris, or France generally – anymore than his Oran during the Plague – had been spared the worst. For Camus, inconsolably, what had taken place was the Fall of *France*. For the parishioners listening to Paneloux's two sermons in Oran, some measure of Catholic spirituality may have led them to conclude that the Plague could have been far worse. But this is precisely what Camus' stories challenge. For those real victims of Vichy France and fictional victims of Oran's Plague, things could not have been any worse. But we are asked to imagine *how they should have been better.*

This is a key assertion of Law and Literature on its date with history. I do not ever assume that I would have been one of the heroes. But I have learned from writing about Vichy history, and from reading Camus that everyone could have resisted actively, that most failed miserably, and that a merely spiritual resistance (if that oxymoron makes any sense at all), coupled with a deliberate avoidance of central realities, collaborated in the disaster.

In this, from its highest levels to its weekly parish sermons, French Catholicism failed during the War to inspire the vast numbers of the faithful towards active rather than banal spiritual resistance. In *The Fall*, Jean-Baptiste Clamence, Camus' ultimate signpost to legal and religious shame during Vichy, conveys through his confession the specificity of these combined failures: In reading the following passage, consider whether the brilliant lawyer-protagonist's behavior – or that of other more devotional Catholic lawyers who went on to do Vichy's dirty work – might have been different if the atmosphere in Catholic discourse during Vichy reflected more Paneloux' first sermon than his second:

> *Clamence's* confession: I was tempted by the Resistance .... I arrived in the unoccupied zone with the intention of finding out about the Resistance. [Note, this is Clamence's high-point, his "thesis," his inflexible resolve!] But once I did that, I hesitated. [Oh-oh! Flexibility creeps in; here comes his "anti-thesis"] The idea began to seem a little crazy and, to be frank, romantic. I think, above all, that underground action simply went poorly with my personality .... I admired those who gave themselves over to this heroism of the depths. [A purely rhetorical construct, typical of Vichy's lawyers and prelates!] But I could not imitate them.

I am not surprised that, as to Vichy's fall and with it that of France, its dominant religion, and its eloquent wrongdoers, Camus says it all.

CHAPTER 7

Two Works of Popular Culture Probe Realities of Holocaust Era Coverups: *The Confessor* and *The Deputy*

A Popular Culture Has Its Place in "Law and Literature"

Many of my readers will know that the modern Law and Literature movement has always welcomed the study of more "popular" story-telling genres, such as film, TV shows, Netflix and streaming platforms, detective fiction, experimental theater, and prose works that occupy a kind of highly respectable boundary between "serious" (or even "great") Literature and the wider public's yearning for entertainment about important topics. The representation of lawyers in fiction – one of the foundational merits of the Law *in* Literature,[1] for example – includes canonical Great books treated in these pages, but also somewhat lighter or one might say "secondary school level" classics such as a work like *To Kill a Mockingbird*,[2] which presents Atticus Finch, the most familiar name among fictional U.S. lawyers, whose strengths and weaknesses still capture the popular imagination well beyond the classroom. Popular culture venues include, of course, film and play versions of *Mockingbird* as well as three dozen films about law and lawyers in the U.S. and abroad, including superb works like *The Verdict*, *Absence of Malice*,[3] *Anatomy of a Murder*, *Erin Brokovich*, *Mr. Klein*, and many others.

One of the most frequently cited of my own articles in the field falls into this "popular culture" mode. I examined, with Michael Asimow, the pressing subject of what to do, professionally, "When the Lawyer Knows the Client is Guilty?[4] Our sources ranged from movies like *Michael Clayton* and *The Devil's Advocate* to "Serious Lit" via Susan Glaspell's *A Jury of Her Peers* and Dostoevski's most complex and fascinating defense attorney Fetyukovich in *The Brothers Karamazov*. The synergy of pop culture and Serious Lit worked well, and we still have many "hits" for that article.

---

1 John Wigmore, "A List of 100 Legal Novels," *Illinois Law Review*, vol. 2 (1908), p. 574.

2 Harper Lee, To *Kill a Mockingbird.*

3 See my 2000 article "The 'Verdict' is an: Civic Implications of Civil Trials," https://via.library.depaul.edu/cgi/viewcontent.cgi?article=1593&context=law-review.

4 Asimow and Weisberg, *op. cit.*, Introduction, n. 21.

 | DOI:10.1163/9789004525177_009

I thus give pride of place here to two fine writers of popular fiction, Daniel Silva and Rolf Hochhuth. And then, in Chapter Nine, I track an epistolary novel about a literary reading group in occupied Great Britain – yes; you read that right! – via Mary Ann Shaffer and Annie Barrows' *The Guernsey Literary and Potato Peel Pie Society*, another work of popular fiction bearing strongly on the themes of this book. More than 60 years ago, Hochhuth produced a blockbuster play about the wartime Pope, Pius XII called *The Deputy*.[5] Several decades later, Silva in *The Confessor*[6] writes about a fictional Pope, "Paul VII," whose initiative in reaching out to apologize to Rome's Jews for his predecessor Pius XII's silence and inaction dovetailed with Silva's protagonist's tracking down and resolving an awful secret connected to active Catholic wrongdoing in producing the Wartime genocide.[7] Both works are exceptionally well researched, and although their authors would be the last to suggest that they count as real histories, they do not stray too far from as much historical knowledge as was available to them when they wrote these works.

Silva's stories often deal with the interplay of Vatican politics, access to archives about Pope Pius XII, the history of European art, the State of Israel,[8] and the Catholic religion's relationship to the truth and to the Jews. Obviously,

---

5 N.Y: Grove Press (in translation), 1964.

6 N.Y.: Putnam, 2003.

7 Silva, chapter 6.

8 Beyond this mention relating to *The Confessor*, and the text of this footnote, I do not treat the State of Israel in these pages, except here to remind my readers that both liberal Protestantism and the Catholic Church have had a fraught relationship with "the very idea" of such a separate Jewish entity since virtually the beginning of the Zionist movement. Franklin Littell says this of the Quakers, as a salient example:

"The Quakers are noted for – among other things – ethical sensitivity, for courage to confront unjust rulers, and for producing fruits of Christian service far beyond the natural energy of their small numbers. Yet [the initial, 1970 edition of their *Search for Peace in the Middle East*] was faulted, and justly, by both Christians and Jews for being blind to basic facts about the Middle East problem. Most significant, the report ignored the fact that the Middle East conflict had produced Jewish refugees as well as Arab refugees. From all the evidence, the Quaker working party simply forgot the hundreds of thousands of Jewish refugees as they built up a case harshly critical of Israel in the name of Arab refugees. And the meaning of the fact that almost all Israelis [were then] refugees or the descendants of refugees from Christendom and Islam escaped them entirely although the central argument of the report was humanitarian. How could this happen? It happened, and happens regularly among well-meaning liberal churchmen, because Christians are sub-consciously accustomed to accept as normal the misery of the Jews. Men of the Free churches, like men of the legally established churches, are riddled with anti-Jewish prejudices which they have not even acknowledged – let alone repented of." [88] And, as to the Catholic Church, Kertzer reports:

Kertzer, *The Popes against the Jews:*

I am a fan. With the publication a score of years ago of *The Confessor*,[9] I found a pop culture book that was delving into all the issues I cared about and (eventually 20 years later) would write about in these pages. The work is so impregnated with lawyers, legal reasoning, and the usual stuff of Law and Literature that I reviewed it (favorably) for the leading daily serving practitioners in New York.[10]

B Silva's Tale of "Pope Paul VII"

The Confessor tells the story of a hypothetical Pope, Paul VII, who is committed to a public recognition of the Vatican's sins towards the Jews historically and especially during World War II. As "Paul VII's" decision to address on these

"And then there is the audience that the Pope [Pius X] had with Theodore Herzl [the leader of the Zionist movement] on January 26, 1904. We won't be able to stop the Jews from going to Jerusalem [said the Pope], but we could never favor it... The Jews have not recognized our Lord, and so we cannot recognize the Jewish people. The Pope continued: The Jewish faith was the foundation of our own, but it has been superseded by the teachings of Christ, and we cannot admit that it still enjoys any validity. Herzl asked the Pope if he knew anything about the Jews' current situation. Yes, replied Pius X... Indeed we also pray for them, that their spirit see the light. This very day the Church is celebrating the feast of an unbeliever who became converted in a miraculous manner – on the road to Damascus. And so, if you come to Palestine and settle your people there, we will be ready with churches and priests to baptize all of you." (p. 225)

Prior to the massacre of Oct. 7, 2023 of over 1,300 Israelis, and the western world's grotesque turn against Israel beginning that very evening!, I would not have programmatically affixed the label "antisemitic" to most criticism of Israeli policies and actions; as I have said, I share strong misgivings especially about Israeli treatment of the Palestinians, and I have done a small measure of work (including face-to-face discussions with Palestinian academics in the West Bank) to try to bring together two peoples whose affinities far outweigh their differences. But I have reluctantly come over to the view held by some Jews and Christians since 1948 – and then particularly after Oct. 7, 2023: something sickeningly deep must be there in Christians who earmark Israel for special obloquy. Political analysis and even harshly critical attacks are one thing; irrationality in the scapegoating of a country that stands alone in sharing the democratic values of many stone-throwers is quite another. Sensitive Protestants such as Franklin Littell, have emphasized the special place for the State of Israel he finds to be at risk: *The restitution of Israel is the event which challenges Christians to take events, history, and the world seriously again. The sterility of a "spirituality" in which nothing important happens between the Ascension and the Second Coming has been exposed to sight. ... No one can be an enemy of Zionism and be a friend of the Jewish people today.* (Littell, *The Crucifixion of the Jews* [96–7]

I have started a separate book on the connection of antisemitism to anti-Zionism.

9 N.Y.: Putnam, 2003.

10 N.Y.L.J., June 6, 2003, p. 3.

subjects a shabbat service at Rome's Synagogue gains currency, all the reactionary forces of the Church secretly convene to prevent what they see as a catastrophic reversal in Church policy towards both the Jews and the Holocaust. A real life recent Pope, John Paul II, had expressed similar impulses, but then became associated with the cross at Auschwitz that so infuriated James Carroll, the "Christianizing of the Shoah," and the traditional Church's attempt to take over Judaism as "the New Israel."[11]

Knowing of the very real risks of a premature death-in-office, Silva's "Paul VII" was nonetheless already heading on a given shabbat to preach to the remnants of Rome's Jews. He was going to offer to them and their Chief Rabbi an explicit Papal atonement for Pius XII and the wartime Church's behavior. The event, mortally opposed and feared by many of Silva's high-level Cardinals and Vatican officials such as archivists who had kept the Vatican data on Pius XII closed off, now seemed almost inevitable.

The protagonist of *The Confessor*, Gabriel, who appears in many of Silva's stories, is an Israeli counter-terrorism double agent who works in Europe under the cover of his expertise as an art restorer. Gabriel has taken part in some of the most significant episodes in Israeli spy-agency history, including the capture of Adolf Eichmann in South America (p. 227), and the killing of villains akin to Osama ben Laden (p. 24) in their evil actions and intent. His quiet work restoring a Bellini in Venice, literally and figuratively "shrouds" his violent life in the protection of the Jewish state he serves. Gradually, Gabriel becomes heavily involved in the network of cardinals, Vatican security officials, and hard-right spies and killers who, he figures out, are all conspiring to keep secrets about the War from the public, and especially to keep "Paul VII" from his rendezvous at the synagogue, perhaps going so far as to assassinate him.

Ever at the beck and call of the secret services of the State of Israel he so reveres, Gabriel is drawn from his Venetian Bellini project into the mystery of a death in Berlin of a professor who is writing a book about the behavior of a specific monastery that hosted an infamous wartime gathering whose agenda was the extermination of Europe's Jews. His inquiry into the professor's murder leads him to these same suspicious, hard-right Vatican cardinals and their violent aides. Gabriel hears of course of "Paul VII's" initiative and wanders over to the Ghetto in Rome to pray at the sparsely-attended Great Synagogue and to discuss history, theology, and current events with the Chief Rabbi.

---

11 See Prof. Sergio Itzhak Minerbi, "Pope John Paul II and the Jews: An Evaluation," in *Jewish Political Studies Review*, 18 (2006).

The rabbi took Gabriel by the elbow and together they walked slowly around the edge of the square. "The Jews of Rome were rounded up ... at five-thirty on the morning of October 16th [1943] .... [T]he terrified Jews in the back of the trucks pleaded with the Pope to save them. All evidence suggests he knew full well what was taking place in the ghetto that morning. It was, after all, under his very windows. He did not lift a finger to intervene .... Two days after the roundup, the Jews of Rome were loaded onto rail cars at the Tiburtina station for the journey east. Five days after that, one thousand and sixty souls perished in the gas chambers at Auschwitz and Birkenau".... Gabriel: "But many survived, did they not? .... Was it because of an order from the Vatican [that so many ordinary Italians helped save Jews]? ... The Rabbi: "That is what the Church wishes us to believe, but I'm afraid there is no evidence to suggest the Vatican issued instructions to Church institutions to offer shelter and comfort to Jews fleeing the roundup. In fact there *is* evidence to suggest that the Vatican issued no such order .... There are numerous examples of Jews who sought shelter in church properties and were turned away. Others were told they had to convert to Catholicism in order to stay.[12] Had the Pope issued a directive to throw open the doors to Jews, no mere nun or monk would have dared to disobey him .... Pope Pius XII never found it in his heart even to speak out against the mass murder of Europe's Jews." Gabriel: "Why not?" The Rabbi: "I'm afraid his Holiness did not much care for us. Remember, he was raised in a Catholic Church that preached antisemitism as a matter of doctrine. He equated Jews with Bolshevism and bought into all the old hatred that Jews were interested only in the material .... Why should he risk himself, and more importantly his Church, for a people he believed were guilty of history's greatest crime – the murder of God himself?" (116–8)

12 *The Confessor* takes a very skeptical look at postwar European claims that, even if the Pontiff might have been more pro-active, Catholic venues such as monasteries and convents secretly protected Jews from Hitler. In fact, one account says only 6–11% of Europe's pre-War generation of children survived, compared with 33% of adults: https://www.jewishvirtuallibrary.org/hidden-children-of-the-holocaust. As to those children who did survive, did they have to convert? When their parents or other relatives came to take them back after the War, did they meet resistance, refusal, or demands for payment? See *id.* See also the Vatican's 1946 instruction to French Catholic authorities not to hand baptized Jewish children back to their parents. Sylvia Poggioli on NPR, 1/21/05, https://www.npr.org/2005/01/21/4461958/document-renews-debate-on-vatican-role-in-wwii.

C Hochhuth's Version of Pope Pius XII

Silva's imagined conversation, as good popular culture stories (and films) very often do, dramatizes dreadful questions. How much is still unknown about the wartime Vatican and its leader? To what extent are his attitudes fairly common not only among Pontiffs but also the kind of cardinals and lesser prelates that agitate to prevent "Paul VII's" public acknowledgment of culpability?[13] These fraught matters arise in perhaps the best known literary representation of Pius XII, Rolf Hochhuth's play, *The Deputy*.[14] *The Deputy* represented on stage in the 'Sixties a Pontiff who resists all calls to speak out against the cruelties he knew about well before 1943, when Rome's Jews were rounded up right under his balcony. A character who tries to insist on such clear opposition to Jew

---

13 See, in the context of Vichy's church at the uppermost levels, a very similar conversation taken from the archives I researched: Cardinal Gerlier of Lyon was one of the first clerics to bring closer to the world of real people the *flexible* hermeneutics of the leadership. On 6 October 1941, this "brilliant lawyer" and cleric sat down and conversed with Xavier Vallat – head of Vichy's infamous anti-Jewish bureaucracy – about Marshal Petain's laws. The conversation – as narrated by Vallat, reveals both Cardinal Gerlier's Pétainist leanings and the complex flexibly adduced acceptance of religious persecution that I claim was more central to the suffering than even the positive statutes of which he spoke:

Me [Vallat:}: [The lawyer Leon Berard, Petain's Ambassador to the Vatican] relies doctrinally on Saint Thomas Aquinas for one .... *Implicitly this signifies that no provision of the French law is blameworthy to the Vatican.* Of course, the Ambassador makes clear that the desire of the Vatican is for us to apply that Law with justice and charity. His Eminence interrupts me, his face becoming less affable: There's the complex part [*le point délicat.*] No one knows better than I the enormous harm the Jews have done to France.... No one supports more zealously than I the policies of Marshal Pétain. [Gerlier then brings up the paucity of exemptions under the statute, which were designed to permit categories of worthwhile prior conduct to be exempted from the hideous treatment of Vichy's antisemitic laws.] Vallat replies, "on my honor as a Christian" that only five such cases were clearly exceptional, whereas "in none of the multitude of other cases I have seen would it have been reasonable to characterize as exceptional the services rendered by the claimant." Gerlier wants Vallat to know that he was referring to war veterans, and Vallat tells him that these are Article 3 exemptions and would he care to give Vallat specific names? Gerlier alludes to one case, and Vallat says that if the Conseil d'État and the Vichy government ministry and the Marshal confirm, the exemption will be granted....]

His Eminence: By the way, Pastor Boegner came to see me, also troubled like me, by numerous visits from poor types who see no other choice but suicide.

Me: To my knowledge, there have not yet been any suicides of Jews in the free zone, and if there were, there are certainly fewer than in Germany at the time of the new laws. And, although Your Eminence knows that I feel deference and even zeal about the advice You are giving me, I am absolutely indifferent to the opinion of Pastor Boegner, who has written to us that "all Christians, we have been spiritual Semites." His Eminence smiles.

14 *The Deputy*, translated by Richard and Clara Winston (N.Y.: Grove Press, 1964).

hatred is Count Fontana, a lawyer counseling overt Papal opposition to Hitler as follows;

> Fontana: Your Holiness, may I ask in all humility: Warn Hitler that you will *compel* five hundred million Catholics to make Christian protest if he goes on with these mass killings! Pope (senses that he must answer this seasoned adviser to the point he is embarrassed, vexed; he speaks as if he has frequently explained the matter, and nevertheless he overcomes his irritation to the point of going up to Fontana and placing a hand on his shoulder): "Fontana! An adviser of your insight! How bitter that you too misunderstand Us. Do you not see that disaster looms for Christian Europe unless God makes Us, the Holy See, the *mediator*.?[15] The hour is dark. To be sure We know they will not touch the Vatican. (Hitler has only recently renewed his guarantee.) ... Germany today *is* Hitler .... Hitler alone, dear Count, is now defending Europe .... In March [1943] We publicly declared that We have nothing, nothing at all to do with the aims of Great Britain and the United States .... We always tell the President's Envoy, Eminence [a Cardinal who takes the side of the Pope, and not Fontana]! Herr Hitler must not be disposed of unless the Reich survives his downfall as a buffer state between the East and West ..." (209)

Hochhuth is painting a Pontiff who not only fails to speak out publicly but whose words generally begin to lose all meaning in the context of a required specificity. The following stage direction points to the larger issue, embraced by writers from Shakespeare to Camus to Silva and many others, of the cheapening of language utilized by Christian "intercessors" to hide their motives and hypocrisy:

> It is inevitable that the scene suddenly takes on an unreal, in fact a phantasmagoric atmosphere. Words, words, a rhetoric totally corrupted into a classic device for sounding well and saying nothing. It is a blessing that in this scene it is technically impossible to show some of the victims in the background: families in tatters, from infants to old men – several hundreds of thousands of European families .... So it was in Europe from 1941 to 1944. (212)

---

15 See my Chapter Five section on mediation and triangulation as devices to destroy Shylock in *The Merchant of Venice*.

Why this immensely influential wartime Pontiff could not summon the will to denounce Nazism and the deportations that in effect were taking place right under his balcony in Rome – and whether much more recently these tragic omissions disqualify Pius XII from being elevated to sainthood[16] – these questions are raised by Hochhuth and Silva. They motivate "Paul VII" to seek the forgiveness of the few remaining Jews in Rome.

Both fictional works create a dialectic of inaction vs action, cynical clericalism vs heroic honesty, and, inevitably, Catholic vs Jew. They will still appeal to many readers because they present ongoing issues with real dramatic flair. They deserve their place as Law and Literature continues to confront history.

16 The move to elevate Pius XII to sainthood seems to have stalled; James Carroll points quite early to *why*, see *Constantine's Sword, op. cit.*, Preface, n. 1, p. 44.

CHAPTER 8

Malamud's *The Fixer*: the Blood Libel and Christian Flights of Fantasy

Ce que je reproche au Christianisme, c'est qu'iI est une doctrine de l'injustice." Camus, "Carnets, 1942–45

In Part One, we saw that distortions of Jewish sacred texts have harmed real – and not only fictional – persons. No recent work of fiction, however, relates this truth as imaginatively, cogently, and accurately as does Bernard Malamud's *The Fixer*, to which we now turn.

A Histories

1 *A 20th Century American Novel Censored for False and Hypocritical Reasons*

Late in his highly productive and creative life, the American novelist Bernard Malamud was censored off the library shelves of a Long Island (New York) public high school. When told they had removed his 1966 novel, *The Fixer*, Malamud thought it might have had something to do with the very occasional sharp language in the text. But, as is always the case when books are censored, burned, or removed from circulation, the censors told a lie about "why" they did it. They said the book was "antisemitic." Malamud is said to have smiled wanly at this news, quietly declaring: "If anything the book is anti-Christian." Throughout this heart-stopping tale, Malamud sustains an oil vs water[1]clash of values, and it is odd that any parents might have read it to end in antisemitism. Instead, as any fair reading of the novel sustains, the tilt is in favor of "oil" (the Jewish perspective) throughout.

1 For "oil and water," see *op. cit.* text at ch. 3, n. 8, relating to *Merchant* and first use of this phrase in Chapter Six by Vichy justice minister, Joseph Barthelemy.

 | DOI:10.1163/9789004525177_010

Litigation that went all the way to the U.S. Supreme Court restored this small masterpiece to Island Tree's high school students.[2] And to us.

The First Amendment struggle to save *The Fixer* has compelling doctrinal elements that are beyond the scope of this book. What lies squarely with my task here is to raise the question of why the American white Christian majority occasionally goes on a rampage against imaginative fiction that offends its members. A disturbingly relevant topic in 2024, we find school boards in states like Florida and Texas replicating the ignorance of past times, such as the censorship of Malamud, the erasure of Charles Darwin, the banning of curricula that include thought-provoking writers like Toni Morrison, Richard Wright, or Angela Davis.

In Malamud's case, a few parents decided to tar as "antisemitic" a story casting certain *Christian* practices into disrepute. Could it be that "Judeo-Christian" plays tricks on politically correct parents and school-boards, who would prefer not to see religious conflict represented at all in the high school curriculum because it might unsettle youthful minds from the dominant narrative of white Christian hegemony? From such a twisted perspective, *The Fixer*, like such predecessors as *The Merchant of Venice*, might better be censored than to permit critiques through fiction of Christian modes of law, speech, and interpretive cruelty. We need to be on guard against the censors, those who want to keep the truth from the eyes of children and adults alike.[3]

Fortunately, along with his better-known story (and film, *The Natural*), *The Fixer* remains on the shelves and in the bookstores and this despite censorship attempts that understood and did not appreciate Malamud's wish to axe the hyphen from the relationship between two opposing religions. He performed this wish not by negative portrayals of Jews; but instead of their perennial torturers the Christians. Law and theology nowhere better converge than in this story, except perhaps in the figure of Camus' examining magistrate in *The Stranger*, who hysterically waves a crucifix in Meursault's face!

2 *The Last Russian Czar Re-invokes the Awful European "Blood Libel": the Actual Trial of Mendel Beilis A/K/A Yakov Bok*

The hero of Malamud's narrative, the fixer Yakov Bok, stands in for the real Jew, Mendel Beilis, who in 1913 was put on trial in Kiev fighting for his life

2 *Board of Education, Island Trees Union Free School District #26 et al vs Pico*, 457 US 853 (*Scotus*, 1982).

3 A similar message will be conveyed when our next chapter briefly recounts the censorship – again in the U.S. – of the film version of Guenther Grass' *The Tin Drum*.

against the spurious charge of killing a Christian boy to extract blood for Jewish ritual purposes, Beilis was one of thousands across the history of Christian Europe to face such charges, and he may have been one of the last to do so. (There was a subsequent notorious blood libel in the American state of Georgia just before World War II!)[4] In the early 20th century, Czar Nicholas II – an ignorant and antisemitic man – fought a doomed rear-guard effort to preserve his realm from revolutionary socialist forces. Collaterally, the struggle helped him to keep alive one of Christian Europe's most vicious iniquities, the spreading of a specific lie about Jews. Called the "blood libel," the ancient falsehood had originated further west, in the writings of Thomas of Monmouth around 1150 in England, migrating thence to France,[5] and gradually spreading like a Camus-ian plague eastward eventually to attack Russia's Jews, As the fable went, Jews needed to kill Christian children particularly around Passover/Easter time to provide blood for the Passover matzoh.

Absurd on its face, the blood libel never quite lost steam, and this novel helps show which forces kept it alive for so long. In fact, the czarist state leveled this ritual murder charge against Mendel Beilis, "an ordinary man working in a brick factory in Kiev, Russia, who was suddenly thrust into the international spotlight."[6] Like the fictional Bok, Beilis was a hard working factory supervisor when, in early spring 1911, he heard about the discovery in a nearby cave of the body of a boy named Andrusha (Andre) Yushchinsky. Like Bok, Beilis was hiding his Jewish identity (of which he was otherwise proud) because Jews were outlawed from living and working in the Kiev district of his employment; he had no other infractions on his record when he was arrested in July, 1911 for the ritual murder of the boy.

There were by then other, more viable suspects, including members of the boy's own family and its shady close acquaintances. But in the months between the discovery of Andrusha's body and the arrest of Beilis, traditional forces of late Czarist antisemitism had involved themselves in the investigation. The

4 See David Fraser, "The Blood Libel in North America: Jews, Law, and Citizenship in the Early 20th Century," *Law and Literature*, vol. 28 (2016), p. 33.

5 Hannah Johnson, *Blood Libel: The Ritual Murder Accusation at the Limit of Jewish History* (Ann Arbor: U. of Michigan Press, 2012). Johnson's book was part of a discussion including the Beilis family descendants as well as lawyers and historians. See "A Thousand Years of Infamy: The History of the Blood Libel, *Law and Literature*, vol. 28 (2016).

6 David Zaklikowski, "An Overview of the Notorious 1913 Ritual Murder Trial," in *Footprints: Colorful Lives, Huge Impact* (N.Y.: Hasidic Archives, 2017).

Czar became in this way a key player throughout the case; as my colleague, Vivian Curran puts it:

> At the time of the Beilis Affair, the Russian government feared the revolutionary rumblings, and Tsar Nicholas II personally was a rabid anti-Semite who equated Jews with revolutionaries, and whose aggressive hostility to Jews no doubt was responsible for pushing many of them into the camp of the revolution. [ftnt omitted] When the body of young Andre was discovered, the government decided to find a Jewish culprit for the crime. And when the Kiev police and judiciary found none, the Minister of Justice simply fired and transferred the judge or examining magistrate and police detectives. [ftnt omitted] ... So-called experts, often complete incompetents, were paid by the police to testify that Jews consumed the blood of Christian children at their religious rituals. [ftnt omitted] Nicholas II had invested 12 million rubles to disseminate antisemitic propaganda, with ritual murder figuring most predominantly in it. [ftnt omitted] ... And yet, despite all this, there remained a strange amount of judicial independence.[7]

Doing the Czar's work on the ground in Kiev were the forces of virulent antisemitism in the early 20th century, and such groups as the "Black Hundreds" and their local leader Vladimir Golubev of the "Double Headed Eagle," had influenced the investigators away from the more logical suspects.[8]

B A Pre-Trial Investigation Rendered Accurately by the Novelist

As we have seen here already via readings of Camus –- in this sense influenced by Dostoevski[9] – novelists have relished portraying the continental figure of the examining magistrate (French, juge d'instruction; Russian: sudebni sledovatel'). Think of Camus' crucifix-wielding magistrate in the interrogation of the hapless, Meursault in *The Stranger*; think of his significant examining magistrate, Othon, in *The Plague*; and, I can merely list here (in the interests of space) examining magistrates in Balzac, Kafka, Tolstoi, Hugo, and Solzhenitsyn, I add

7 Vivian Curran, "At the Crossroads of Law and Society: The Trial of Mendel Beilis," *Law and Literature*, vol. 28 (2016), p. 91.

8 Zaklikowski, *op. cit.*, p. 209.

9 *Failure of The Word, op. cit.*, Introduction, n. 4.

at length to that list in this chapter Malamud's amazing character, Malamud's Bibikov.

What so attracted European novelists about a figure native to their country's criminal procedure but unlike any similar Anglo-American figure? Malamud is the most inspired of American writers to catch the spirit of his continental forbears and to see the creative potential implicit in the narrative powers granted to the examining magistrate.[10]

The actual years-long Beilis criminal process, and the weeks-long trial culminating it, for which we have the full transcript,[11] basically track with almost perfect accuracy the real criminal procedure that focuses on the examining magistrate, and the panoply of prosecutors and defense counsel with whom he deals. Each key legal figure has his analogue in the story. Beilis may have been very unlucky in being in the wrong place at the wrong time when he was arrested, but he had some good luck in having had a decent man and good lawyer assigned to his case, the examining magistrate Vasily Feneko. Feneko's unlikely sympathy for the Jew, and his awareness of the absurdity of such charges still being levelled as the new century was starting, are accurately represented in Malamud's fictional examining magistrate, Bibikov. The voice of justice in the story, and one of its only heroes (besides Bok himself), Bibikov insists on facts and law. A man of law in the best sense, he rejects fantasms, crooked expertise, and even political pressure from the highest governmental level. In his first interview with the accused Jew, Bibikov self-identifies as an ally of the Jew:

> Nodding to the prisoner, [Bibikov] said quietly, "Whatever happens, you must have fortitude." "My God, what can happen? I'm an innocent man." Bibikov shrugged. "It's a touchy thing." "Have mercy, your honor; I've had little in my life." "Mercy is for God, I depend on the law. The law will protect you." [71]

Sounding like Shylock, but seemingly spared the latter's stigma as Jew and outsider, the examining judge represents every finer instinct of fair process through law. Mercy must be for another day, he says. I believe Malamud had in mind, when penning this dialogue, Shylock's rejoinder to Portia's elegant speech: "My deeds upon my head! I crave the law." For people in trouble, and indeed for all of us, the abstraction "mercy" and its analogue "love" cannot

10 See my elaboration in *The Failure of The Word. Id.*, Part Two.

11 An account of the actual Beilis case is found at archives.org/stream/BeilisAffair/Beilis%20Affair_djvu.txt.

effectively replace law fairly administered on earth. Mercy is too easily twisted into its opposite. We need to depend on law.

Bibikov, whose own fate in the novel provides one of 20th century American fiction's most scintillating moments, uses his considerable power as examining magistrate to come to the aid of Yakov Bok. Recognizing that Bok (like Beilis) broke the law only in living in a part of Kiev where Jews were excluded, the examining magistrate tries to limit the force of the powerful libel absurdly directed at yet another victim of Europe's infamous treatment of the Jewish people. However, most of the rest of the Czarist prosecution team lined up against Bok, and Beilis, including the lead prosecutor, Chaplinksky (Grubeshov in the novel). Taking their marching orders from Nicholas II, such prosecutors gave the defendant little real hope of acquittal. During the pre-trial investigation, they summoned witnesses who furthered the bizarre story of the blood libel.

C Christian Superstition, and Manipulation of Jewish Texts, Redux

Perhaps the most important of the prosecution witnesses was Father Anastasy, Malamud's fictional embodiment of Christian superstition and a so-called czarist "expert" on Jewish religious matters; Father Anastasy was at least in part based on Justin Pranaitis, a Catholic priest whose "expertise" dotted Beilis' real trial and whose ignorance of Jewish traditions was only matched by his superstitious account of their trumped-up iniquities:

> Father Anastasy: "If the bowels of the earth were to open to reveal the population of human dead since the beginning of the world, you would be astonished to see how many innocent Christian children among them have been tortured to death by Christ-hating Jews.
>
> The ritual murder is meant to re-enact the crucifixion of our dear Lord ... It is said that the murder of the gentile – any gentile – hastens the coming of their long-awaited Messiah, Elijah, for whom they eternally leave the door open but who has never, during all the ages since his first coming, bothered to accept the invitation to enter and sit in the empty chair. Since the destruction of their Temple in Jerusalem by the legions of Titus there has been no sacrificial altar for animals in their synagogues, and it has come about, therefore, that the killing of gentiles, in particular innocent children, is accepted as a fitting substitute." [130]

We have here, from the pen of an American novelist, a Slavic twist on the now-familiar lies about Jewish texts and traditions. Nested in the middle of the preliminary legal investigation into the alleged guilt of Yakov Bok, the priest's peroration – at the invitation of the antisemitic prosecutor Grubeshov – also fits perfectly into the pages of this book.

Law and religion merge throughout the novel. The "expert" completely distorts the Jewish Bible, but this fabrication merely replicates the earliest Christian manipulations of Jewish sacred texts, which I have exemplified and emphasized earlier in these pages. Such fabrications gained life through the centuries, and real Jews were punished because of them.

As in the actual trial, so in the novel, Bok-Beilis is given a chance to respond to the "expert," whose ignorance and grotesque fabrications about the Jewish need for Christian blood highlight the prosecution's case. Bok responds with a *Shylock-like veracity* in front of a similar Jew-hating audience:

> It's all a fairy tale, every bit of it. Who could ever believe such a thing? Not me." His voice quavered and his face was bloodless .... "It's all right to theorize with a fact or two but I don't recognize the truth in what's been said. If you please, your reverence, everybody knows the Bible forbids us to eat blood. That's all over the book, in the laws and everything. I've forgotten most of what I knew about the sacred books, but I've lived among the people and know their customs. Many an egg my own wife would throw out to the goat if it had the smallest spot of blood on it .... [119–20]

Bok's amazement that such superstition might be an actual part of the case against him mirrors Shylock's incredulous "Is that the law?" when Portia pulls various unlikely rabbits out of her hat to defeat him in *The Merchant of Venice*.[12] Thanks to the presence of sympathetic lawyers like Bibikov – Shylock had no lawyer, of course – his rejoinder forces even more absurd words from the priestly "expert":

> Father Anastasy: There are those among us, my children, who will argue that these are superstitious tales of a past age, yet the truth of what I have revealed to you – I do not say it is all true – must be inferred from the very frequency of the accusations against the Jews. [118]

Stories, again, get the job done. Malamud nails a perverse component of Christian reasoning through the centuries: Challenged as to the actual veracity of the blood libel, Father Anastasy argues that if a lie hangs on long enough and gets repeated, well there must be something to it, right? How often have

12 See Chapter Five on Shylock's relatively simple use of language compared to the often flowery but clearly wrong or at best irrelevant speech of the Christians.

totalitarian governments in the 20th and 21st centuries successfully invoked, to Christian audiences, this spurious reasoning?

Facts have lost their value over time. Superstitions, distortions, repetitions of lies: these become the stuff of public speech, including in secular courts of law during the Christian era.

D Malamud's Bigger Picture: Christian Legality Divorced from Law

Something good dropped out of the calculus when law itself was denigrated formally by writers like Saint Paul.[13] He feared the end-of-days yet kept many antinomian words in his writings that have influenced generations. Once the world decided to keep spinning and Jesus Christ did not bring about the messianic age as the Jewish texts prophesied, people still needed a legal system of one kind or another. What happened in Christian Europe bore no resemblance to the elegant and even merciful adumbration of Law by the Hebrews over the centuries,[14] which Christians had been taught to reject, using disgracefully false language such as hairsplitting, Pharisaic, materialistic, and eventually the ultimate insult "Talmudic."[15] Stories strip bare what happens when law is interpreted by those who, as a matter of belief and principle, deny law's preciousness and sanctity. Among the cruelties of European law from west to east over the millennia – and putting to one side such punishments as drawing and quartering, flaying, and the rack – Malamud's novel locates the following:

1. *Interpretive flexibility* has struck again. A trait that seems quite positive at first, "flexibility" underlies the critique of Christianity so far presented here. By flexibility, I mean – as in the ordinary usage of the word – an ability to go with the flow, to adapt to new circumstances, to assimilate data in such a way that it can be used helpfully in developing situations. It is a quality many westerners tend to admire. It is part of our enlightenment approach, valued in most secular pursuits as well as in many 20th century philosophical movements, such as pragmatism.[16] To say that a western religion is "flexible," therefore, is quite possibly to be complimenting it. Why do I consider such a good thing to be so bad? The interpretive

13 Part One.

14 See *op. cit.*, ch. 2, n. 11.

15 In Vichy justifications of the antisemitic laws that led to around 80,000 Jewish deaths, the charge of "Talmudic" was leveled against Jewish systems of law in order to justify special laws against them. See my *Vichy Law*, *op. cit.*, n. 16, chs. 2 and 10. Geoffrey Hartman called these verbal absurdities "writing desk murders". *Op. cit.*, ch. 2, n. 3, p. 75.

16 Morris Dickstein, *The Revival of Pragmatism: New Essays on Social Thought, Law, and Culture* (Durham: Duke U. Press, 1998).

distortions provided by such Christian "experts" as Father Anastasy on Jewish texts as the fictional priest in *The Fixer* – who was based on a real witness at Beilis' trial – require an infinite flexibility in twisting one meaning into a fantastical shape unimagined by the original author or tradition. As I showed throughout Part I, flexibility is a Christian reading strategy adopted 2000 years ago for the finding in Jewish sacred texts of Christian doctrinal meanings.[17] Flexibility also characterized the jurisprudential approach of Hitler's favorite lawyer, Carl Schmitt.[18]

2. Jewish texts are distorted and an entire ethical tradition turned on its head. Because of this ability, born of the Gospels themselves, a lie could endure that Jews kill Christian children and use their blood in rituals.
3. Absurd Logic. The very durability of the libel, to the Christian mind, proved its claim, as though they had invented the Big Lie long before Hitler. Malamud strikes a chord by having the religious "expert" close his peroration by saying that even though some of what he said about Jews using blood in their mazzah might actually be false, that doesn't matter

---

17 In thinking about the risks of flexibility, I ask my readers, preliminarily and briefly, to consider a still – current issue: the treatment of prisoners at Guantanamo and other venues of the war on terror. I have written about the "torture debate," as it has been called, and my specific complaint has been that the modification of America's long-standing avoidance of torture has occurred because Bush administration lawyers such as John Yoo were too "flexible" in their treatment of long-standing policies forbidding the practice. I saw this ability to work creatively but unethically on issues that have long been settled in a positive way – eg America does not do torture – as a function of a risk run by lawyers (as well as certain religious traditions such as the ones discussed in this chapter): the risk of submerging all first principles into any felt current need. In this case, the need to gather information overwhelmed the legal rules, so those rules were discarded through broad interpretive gestures. (The NY Times in early August 2006, opined in a main editorial called "Listening to the Lawyers" that the Bush administration's legal interpretations of already existing codes and treaties permitted a definition of "the difference between coercion and torture [that] is way too flexible." See Weisberg, "Loose Professionalism," in Levinson, ed., *Torture A Collection* (N.Y.: OUP, 2004), p. 299.

18 But then Hitler and others in Hitler's Europe showed the deep structure of things. You could *never* be an insider, whatever you did, if you were born into "Talmudism". If you believed in law and in some allegiance to sound ways of interpreting it, you were always already an outsider. Hitler detested lawyers in general; but he had his own, a certain Carl Schmitt. And that brilliant master of jurisprudence reiterated Catholic flexibility – fulfilled it, to use Paul's word about Jesus' completing the law somehow – by reducing everything legal in Nazi Germany (and there was plenty that looked like law there and in Vichy France and elsewhere in Hitler's Europe) to the "Fuhrerprinzip," to the judge's highly personal sense of how Hitler would have wanted the case to come out. Flexibility had reached its pinnacle. Hitler's legal system was no aberration. It was the fulfillment of Christian Europe's programmatic replacement of the subjective, redeemed individual for the texts and the constraints of the law! See, on Schmitt's influence upon Hitler, Ingo Mueller, *Hitler's Justice* (trans., Cambridge, Harvard U. Press, 1991).

because the assertion has been made so often it might as well be thought of as true anyway.

4. Grotesque mis-statements that turn reality completely on its head. Yakov Bok reminds the investigators that not only do Jews not use blood, they ritualistically avoid it. His former wife, he explains simply and directly, would throw out an egg that even had the tiniest fleck of blood in it.
5. Permeability to outside influences of prejudice that go beyond the legal procedure itself.

E Beilis / Bok is Acquitted

Sometimes reality shines through and justice is done even in the topsy-turvy world of Christian law. On October 28, 1913, a Russian jury took about 75 minutes to acquit Mendel Beilis on all charges. (Interestingly, *The Fixer* ends before Bok's long-desired trial begins, and the reader of the novel does not know of this actual acquittal.) Most of the credit for the historical happy ending goes to Beilis who endured – as does Bok in the remarkable representation of his pre-trial misery provided in *The Fixer* – years of isolation, solitary confinement, religious prejudice, scant or disgusting food, and especially not knowing if he would ever be formally indicted and thus be given his own lawyer. Eventually, Otto Gruzenberg led a team of excellent defense counsel, all appearing pro bono.

There were other heroes, too. Examining magistrates who fought off their superiors to pierce the veil of superstition and lies and re-direct focus on the victim's sleazy family; the press, which both in foreign newspapers and in Russia kept featuring both the pre-trial investigation and the trial; some co-religionists of Beilis, who managed to get through the system of guards and of solitary confinement to lend him support and solace and especially news of the outside world that helped the defendant in his single-minded task of never confessing and of getting his formal indictment, his defense counsel, and his trial.

Yakov Bok, falsely accused, endures years of imprisonment, humiliation, and what we today would call cruel, inhuman, and degrading treatment. Today, too, we are familiar with stories of indefinite incarceration and techniques of interrogation seemingly at the margins of anything resembling "law." Stories such as these have a universal quality because they deal with more even than the struggle between Christian and Jew at very sad moments in history. They signify that – at the very heart of that struggle – there is a larger core of opposition: law versus something not really law; law versus a bogus substitute (mercy) or versus an "ultra-legal" harshness more terrible than anything the Mosaic God could have produced.

CHAPTER 9

The Guernsey Literary and Potato Peel Pie Society Introduces Its Readers to the Antisemitic Use of British Law and Tradition

A "Great Griefs Lie Silent"

The Commandant of Guernsey had ordered all Jews to report to the Grange Lodge Hotel[1] and register. According to the Commandant, our ID cards would merely be marked 'Juden' and then we were free to go home. Elizabeth knew my mother was Jewish …

Islander John Booker to the protagonist Juliet Ashton, pp. 90–91 …

> As Seneca says, 'Light griefs are loquacious, but the great are dumb.'
>
> Id., p. 150

I follow the methodology of this book as a whole in introducing, through fiction, the history of the British Channel Islands during World War II. To that end, I also replicate my embrace of popular culture by adding to Silva and Hochhuth a work that perhaps does not attain their level of craft but that has caught the imagination of a public that had no clue otherwise about its specific geographical locale as connected to World War II. The work was never completed by its original author, which does make some of it seem a bit haphazard, but it is still a very good story, and I want to show my readers precisely why that is so for my purposes here.

The epistolary novel by Mary Ann Shaffer and Annie Barrows, *The Guernsey Literary and Potato Peel Pie Society* (made into a film in 2018[2]), follows an exchange of letters that includes various residents of the occupied British Channel Island of Guernsey during World War II. The complicated title refers to an incident early in the book, when a few of the characters run into a German patrol. Past curfew, they need to think on their feet and come up with an excuse. Whereas in fact they had been clandestinely celebrating and eating

1 The authors of the novel should be congratulated. This "fictional fact" comports with the actual history of the Island as to its Jewish or suspected Jewish population. See further in this chapter.

2 N.Y.: Random House, 2008.

 | DOI:10.1163/9789004525177_011

a pig, they tell the authorities, whose Lugers are drawn, that their breaking of curfew was for a meeting of a literary society, and that they had lost track of time. The soldiers buy the story. But to give themselves future cover, they decide to create a kind of book club, which lends the novel its title.

The main characters in *Potato* are Elizabeth McKenna, who cooks up the story of the then non-existent book club, and Juliet Ashton, an emerging London-based popular story-teller in her early thirties who had no relationship whatsoever with the Islands until made aware of them as a possible topic for her postwar new book. Eventually, the Guernsey occupation story emerges through a series of letters to Juliet written by each member of the book club.

The Channel Islands, which also include Jersey, Alvernay, and Sark, lie not too much to the north and west of the French coastline. French influence, as we shall see soon relative to the wartime antisemitic laws that in part were imported from Vichy to the Islands, emerges in the Guernsey newspapers we now have accessed more than in the Islanders' diet, which is British to the core. There are two bright line differences between the Occupied Guernsey of the novel and any earlier Islander epoch: German guns are situated against the English Channel, and Jews are being persecuted by statutes written and published widely in English and administered and condoned by long-standing British councils on the Island, which employ British bureaucratic and legal reasoning.[3]

Mention of Jews in the novel is sparse, but local colo(u)r is plentiful.[4] We can recognize pleasurably, even if like most of us we have never been there, the gorgeous green plushness associated with such an Island, the pubs, the gossip, the cows, and of course the potatoes. The grim reality behind this quaintness is more than hinted at, as the Londoner Juliet comes to recognize. Under the Nazi jackboot, new and grim elements are added: difficulties of the curfew, the rationing of everything from gasoline to eggs, and the bizarre German instructions occasionally juxtaposed with the familiar English signs and signals.

Eventually, even the small vessels traditionally found in the port were to transport a few unfortunates, identified under Island law as "Jews," to some destination to the east (via France). A handful of Islanders were deported, and these tragic victims died in the camps. The epistolary exchanges – with one notable exception! – ignore this grim antisemitic background. But history

3 For the best history of this situation, see David Fraser, *The Jews of The Channel Islands and The Rule of Law*, 1940–45 (U.K.: Sussex, 2000).

4 The historically accurate Guernsey genocide has been recreated for 21st century audiences in many venues. An exercise puts U.S. students and lawyers to the test. See next note. See Brooks, Weisberg, Princeton event; and Freedman and Weisberg, N.Y.C. Bar event.

shows that the relegation to a mere detail of the plight of the Islands' Jews provides a realistic snapshot of most of the Islanders, including their governing bodies and officials, despite the historical likelihood that they read in their newspapers of special laws directed against the Jews in their midst[5] and saw with their own eyes that Jews had been set apart, that their businesses had been taken from them and "aryanized," and that some of these Jews "went missing." There was no reason not to know what was happening. But for most, like the letter-writers in the novel (except for the half-Jewish character, John Booker), Jews were a mere detail.[6]

B Actual *British* Bureaucratic Wrongdoing on Guernsey

1 *The Archives, again, to the Rescue*

My own research in the French 20th Century National Archives and at Yad Vashem in Israel uncovered a surprise: a small file in English that pinpointed the dilemma of Guernsey's Jews or of those suspected of being Jewish from 1940–45, and what penalties awaited them. Part of that file are newspaper articles focusing on laws and orders, all of which were freely available to Guernsey's residents and would quite definitely have been read by all or at least most of the letter writers to Juliet. Typical is the "Third Order" of April 26, 1941, which defines a Jew according to the individual's grand-parental heritage, an imported technical feature that came from neighboring Vichy.[7] Several of these definitions were published alongside headlines like "Rationing of Cigarettes, Cigars, Cigarillos, and Tobacco," and other relatively trivial features of law on the Islands.

The laws that sent Jews to the camps, and that, *not* trivially, terrorized "suspected Jews" whose mixed grandparental heritage placed them at risk of deportation or of seeing their businesses curtailed and their wealth expropriated,[8] were in part borrowed from Vichy definitions of "Jew" but were

---

5 See Weisberg, "The Hermeneutic of Acceptance and the Discourse of the Grotesque, with a Classroom Exercise on Guernsey," *Cardozo Law Review*, vol. 17 (1996), p. 1875.

6 In fact in the novel, much more narrative space than to the Jews is given to the horrible fate of Russian and Polish prisoners of war on *Sark*. (pp. 53; 106; 215)

7 See Chapter Six, on *The Plague* and *The Fall*.

8 See Weisberg, *op. cit.*, on Guernsey, ch. 9, n. 5. See also generally, Fraser, *op. cit.*, ch. 9, n. 3. A case I have written about is that of Mrs. Violet Woolnaugh, whom the archives identified as an Anglican but who, because of her having a Jewish mother, was investigated by Guernsey's *British* authorities as being a suspected Jew who was at risk, thereby, of losing her Inn. Weisberg, *op. cit.*, ch. 9, n. 5.

published on these Islands in English. Various orders specifically relating to Jews on Guernsey were published in the *Guernsey Evening Press*.[9] The laws were administered on the Islands by *British* councils that were fully recognizable to – and elected by – the local population, following the governing structure on the Islands for many prior centuries.

We know now, indeed, that the laws against the Jews could not have been written or applied without the "rubber stamping" of the Bailiffs of Guernsey (Victor Carey) and the larger island of Jersey (Alexander Coutanche) and their respective attorneys general, sheriffs, and governing councils. They were complicit as co-decision makers. On Guernsey, Carey and his attorney general Ambrose Sherwill, along with a few private lawyers who profited from these laws, followed – or traduced – their finest traditions into the unfortunate corners of antisemitic persecution.[10] According to the authoritative voice on the betrayal of British legal traditions in wartime Guernsey, David Fraser:[11]

> Local lawyers and legal officials in the Channel Islands, loyal to the British monarch, played a key and seemingly unquestioning role in implementing Nazi antisemitism .... Identifying Jews and Jewish businesses became part of daily routine for Island lawyers .... [T]he Bailiff or Attorney-General passes on lists of Jews and Jewish property to the Germans.

2 *Protest to the Occupiers was Possible without Substantial Risk*

Islander officials and councils had the ability to protest against these laws, as indeed happened about other issues such as rationing. At Grange Lodge on Guernsey, which is mentioned by the half-Jew John in the epistolary novel, p. 90–91, protests on rationing of food brought about considerable alteration in the Occupiers' behavior.[12]

From the first time the Guernsey council met to discuss the ever-growing number of decrees about the Jews on the Islands, a vote was taken whether to approve or disapprove these laws. One of nine members protested repetitiously against these decrees that were (in Fraser's book's sub-title) "*quite contrary to the principles of British justice*."[13] His name was Sir Abraham Laine (a non-Jew)

---

9 Fraser, *id.*, p. 47.
10 *Id.*, at chapters 2–8.
11 *Id.*, p. 7.
12 See Hazel R. Knowles Smith, *The Changing Face of the Channel Islands Occupation* (N.Y.: Palgrave, 2007), p. 66.
13 Fraser, *op. cit.*, ch. 9, n. 3.

a respected elderly member of the council. Of his intransigent[14] insistence on keeping up the Island's great traditions of fairness, due process, and stiff upper lip, Guernsey's Attorney General (who folded his tents during the War, and far worse!) said this afterwards:

> ... If I had [objected to the antisemitic laws] presumably the Germans would have threatened the ... [council] by marching in soldiers. [query, sic?] Nevertheless, I still felt ashamed that I had not done something by way of protests. [But] Sir Abraham Laine ... openly and categorically refused his assent and stated his grave objections to such a measure .... As I sat listening to him, I realized how right he was.[15]

The epistolary novel's London-based protagonist Juliet might well have fashioned her entire prospective new novel on Laine, if she had researched a bit further: But Laine was so beyond her range of interest, because the Jews were also not particularly on her radar screen, that he (or a fictional counterpart to Laine) merited no mention.

3 *The Novel's Brief Recognition of the Islanders' Responsibility for Jewish Lives*

Greatly to the credit of the epistolary novel's co-authors, nonetheless, there is at least some recognition of the collaboration of British authority figures on the Islands with the Vichy-Nazi laws that terrorized local Jews. But like an embarrassing detail cast aside that deserves mention only to provide thoroughness to a narrative that then escapes its shame altogether, the letters move on too quickly to other subjects. And although some of them go on to recount major characters' wartime imprisonment at Belsen and Ravensbruck, their experiences at these death camps, although horrible, do not feature any emphasis on Jews as the primary victims of British (in this case) or Europe-an-wide antisemitism. John Booker, the character whose mother is Jewish and who therefore would, if not forewarned by Elizabeth, have had his identity card stamped "Juden" by British authorities (the only mention of these laws in the novel – (p.90–2) – is sent to Ravensbruck not because he is possibly a Jew but for other reasons disconnected to race or religion (p. 148).

Juliet is drawn to her topic and begins to research the history and government of these British territories. All of this work, and probably any eventual

---

14 I mention him with great respect among my list of wartime intransigent keepers of their countries' great-re-War traditions. Weisberg, *Intransigence*, *op. cit.*, ch. 1, n. 2, pp. 87, 103.

15 Knowles Smith, *op. cit.*, ch. 9, n. 12, p. 144.

book this main character might write, have nothing to do with the "detail" (or as I call it in my headnote to this Chapter through Seneca, the "great grief") that is British officially legalized antisemitism during WWII.

What Juliet uncovers are the following, largely accurate administrative data:

> Guernsey's ruling body, such as it is, is named the States of Deliberation but called the States for short. The real head of everything is the President of the States, who is elected by the STATES and called the Bailiff. In fact, everyone is elected, not appointed by the King. (p. 112)

Like so many people in so many countries in Hitler's Europe, there were on Guernsey local figures of authority who had the agency – the ability to choose to avoid wrong-doing and stick to their best traditions. The epistolary novel may not ultimately point that way as clearly as other stories treated here, but it does not totally avoid the "detail" that speaks volumes. And it leads today's readers to the discovery that British territories, and British officials and lawyers, are part of Christian Europe's wartime shame.

CHAPTER 10

Two German Novelists Represent World War II History

A Nietzsche Anticipates Their Themes

Appropriately, we enter the Third Reich itself through the portal of three German writers, one of whom has already been central to this book and the others of whom must be read by everyone interested in my subject.

The iconoclastic 19th century philosopher, Nietzsche, has been my lifelong mentor. I have written about him throughout my own career and have received plaudits as well as complaints for my readings of his stunningly prescient aphorisms. His transcendent prose has graced this work already, although the very verb "graced" would have bothered no one more than Nietzsche himself, that brick-thrower at everything Christian. Lately, the post-moderns have co-opted him, trying to find deconstructionist tendencies in a man who was trained in philology and believed in the meaning of words and the value of their author's intention when we try to understand them. Nietzsche, to the postmodern mind, attacked everything; in fact, he was selective. We have seen already his great love for the Jewish texts and the Jewish people – only after his death would the Nazis and his own warped sister's changes in his work dare to make him, falsely, into an anti-Semite.

Like the Jews he so admired, Nietzsche believed in law. He is the great instigator and supporter of codes of justice. Not every code wins his affection, nor should all laws blindly be accepted by us. But he gives us, as few thinkers about law ever have, a way of *assessing* the codes we are presented with, of *evaluating* them and making our own decisions about what constitutes good rather than bad laws. We have seen him praising the Jewish Bible precisely as the locus of "divine justice" and the Jewish people for their ability "to change, *when* they change ... according to the principle 'As slowly as possible.'" What he was looking for in a code to follow should appeal to us today: a code free of rancor and reactive hatreds (this is why he hated the nascent antisemitism already appearing during his lifetime in German political circles), one that brings a bounded liberty to the individual:

> Historically speaking, all law ... is a battle waged against the reactive emotions by active people who have employed part of their strength to curb

 | DOI:10.1163/9789004525177_012

> the excesses of reactive pathos and bring about a compromise. Wherever justice is practiced and maintained, we see a stronger power intent on finding means to regulate the senseless raging of rancor [*ressentiment*] among its weaker subordinates ... by the establishment of a code of laws which the superior power imposes upon the forces of hostility and resentment whenever it is strong enough to do so; by a categorical declaration of what it considers to be legitimate and right, or else forbidden and wrong. Once such a body of law has been established, all\acts of high-handedness on the part of individuals or groups are seen as infractions of the law, as rebellion against the supreme power. Thus the rulers deflect the attention of their subjects from the particular injury and, in the long run, achieve the opposite end from that sought by vengeance, which tries to make the viewpoint of the injured person prevail. Henceforth the eye is trained to view the deed ever more impersonally [unpersoenlicher].... It follows that only after a corpus of laws has been established can there be any talk of "right" and "wrong."
>
> *Genealogy of Morals*, 2.11:207

Nietzsche on justice is Nietzsche at his most Judeo-classical – a hyphenated phrase he might have welcomed in lieu of "Judeo-Christian." Justice does exist on earth, not after we die. But it requires the establishment of a good code of laws, judged as such because it evokes what is positive in people and because it totally lacks rancor, bitterness, and reactive venom. Any code, such as that of the Third Reich, lashing out vindictively at certain minorities, is a code to be rejected. The American constitution at its origins, or the Napoleonic codes of Nietzsche's continent, Europe, had much to commend them but also, in their deprivations of racial and gender minorities, much that needed change.

What of the "Old" compared to the "New" testaments, those "codes" that far exceed in their influence even constitutions and statutes? As we elaborated earlier in detail, Nietzsche is absolutely clear. The first – warts, human weaknesses, and all – is worth living by. Changes needed over time? Of course. But in the main a positive code steeped in ethical understandings and encouraging the best in people, including the necessity of prophetic and even heroic actions to change what is corrupt in those ruling over the code and the people. Meanwhile, as for the "newer" code, for Nietzsche, it disqualified itself in its reactive venom against the older code and the people trying to maintain its strictures. The *ressentiment* against the law-keepers is palpable, as we have seen in Saint John's gratuitous slurs against the very people whose holy book he purported to need in order to "prove" the claims he was making about the divinity of Jesus.

None of this is simple, but all of it informs our understanding of Nazi Germany, as rendered by Grass and Schlink. It takes a lifetime of choice and of thoughtfulness to develop within us the capacity to make moral and interpretive judgments. For example, why is the prophetic tradition of Judaism more positive than the actions of Gospel writers much later who in their way also tried to speak what they saw as truth to power? Could it be the demonizing of a group of Jews just because they insisted on keeping the Law? Or so many gratuitous broadsides at the Jews generally? Why the need for so much hatred as part of a religion overtly preaching love as a commandment more powerful than all of the older ones? What counts is thoughtfulness about these matters – *rumination* as Nietzsche once called the process. This "*Wiederkauen*" – this chewing over – helps us make choices and also helps us to stick with them rather than be pulled here and there by whatever new thing shows up on our doorstep.

B From Different Generations, Two German Voices

I now examine the novels of exemplary German writers who deal, explicitly, with one aspect or another of the Holocaust. Of such authors, especially, it might be asked whether there is some special responsibility to cabin the creative urge, to restrict as he might not in dealing with an ordinary subject, the imagination and its potential distortions and exaggerations These two writers, I believe, recognized that obligation but nonetheless endowed their works with the only pathway to their readers that privileged fiction above other genres such as history or documentary films. In Grass' use of religion at the end of a key chapter of *The Tin Drum*, and Schlink's use of law and legalistic passivity towards the end of *The Reader*, we find avenues of understanding that lead in their unique ways to the questions I am asking in the present book.

1 *Guenter Grass and* The Tin Drum*: "Faith, Hope, and Love"* are *the Gasman*

In a recent dissertation, David Lloyd Barry argues that Grass' staggeringly comprehensive novel *Blechtrommel* is a "narrative of memory" that has primary value in inspiring further understandings of the Holocaust.[1] In *Gunther Grass and His Critics*,[2] Siegfried Mews compendiously recounts critical approaches

1 Barry, "Unencumbered by History: Identity, Modernity, and the Holocaust in Guenther Grass' Die Blechtrommel…." UCLA, Germanic Languages, 2015, a Ph. D. dissertation.

2 Siegfried Mews, *Guenther Grass and His Critics* (N.Y.: Camden House, 2008).

to this masterpiece. We are indebted to Dr. Barry's generalization about memory and to Dr. Mews' impressive annotated bibliographies. All assessments of *The Tin Drum*, including theirs, pass through the stunning chapter "Faith, Hope, and Love." There is no sharper, more bitter sally at Roman Catholicism than is to be found in that chapter to which we shall shortly return.

Conversely, news of Guenter Grass' wartime secrets have now reached all who might be interested.[3] The great scribe of German guilt never hid his own service in the Hitler Youth or the Wehrmacht. Like Cardinal Ratzinger's though, his wartime story tended to be relatively benign. Benedict XVI had no choice, we are told, but to serve in the Hitler Youth. Who is to throw stones at ordinary young people trying to survive in the horrifying and choice-reducing world of Nazi Europe? "Few see taint in Service by Pope in Hitler Youth" read a headline in the April 21, 2005 *New York Times*.[4]

Many hid their tracks. Two of my own teachers in the field of Comparative Literature in the 1960's – not exactly as fraught an enterprise, you might think, as novel writing or the Papacy – wound up eventually being uncovered as, respectively, antisemitic wartime writer in Belgium and youthful member of the SS.[5] Grass himself revealed, probably *a contre coeur*, his service in the Waffen SS. One member of the Hitler Youth grew up to be a Pope. The young SS-man became the conscience of his country, particularly through the incredible prose in his wartime-era novels, the *Danzig Trilogy*.

There were some who have tried to explain, rationalize, or at least "contextualize" Paul de Man's youthful antisemitic scribblings, although the articles by the later deconstructionist critic offer a glimmer of his mature brilliance while they go about suggesting that European art would probably be better off if the Jews just went away. As a former student of de Man, I still revere his memory as a generous teacher and careful advisor to me.[6] I was as

3 See Alan Riding, "Guenther Grass Under Siege After Revealing SS Past," *NY Times*, 8/17/2016. "In novels, plays, essays and newspapers interviews, Guenther Grass has often told Germans what they did not want to hear ... For many on the left, since the 1960's, he has come to represent the conscience of a country with much to lament.... But now at 78 Mr. Grass has stunned Germany by confessing ... that in the final months of World War II, when he was 17, he was drafted by the Waffen SS, the military branch of the notorious Nazi corps that played an important role in the Holocaust ... Mr. Grass is hardly the first former SS soldier to have covered his tracks ..."

4 P. A 12.

5 Paul de Man and Hans Robert Jauss; for the latter, see "Tout Comprendre, c'est Tout Pardonner," Brill.com (2017), *Philological Encounters*, pp. 388–402.

6 In Ithaca and Zuerich on the Cornell Ph.D. program.

disheartened with news of Grass and the SS as I was when the de Man "scandal" broke about four decades ago.

Still, Grass' treatment of the themes of this book stands as among the high-points of all of postwar literature. I believe that without his intimate knowledge of what overwhelmed the German people in the Hitler-time, he would not have been able to see feelingly the juxtaposition of Christian faith with the genocide of Jews.

It has been comforting to distance Hitler's killers from the very idea of Christianity because other explanations sit easier and give us comfort. Yet "Hitler's Willing Executioners" as Daniel Judah Goldhagen, aptly called them[7] while paying close attention to the Christian component of their willingness, were brought up in Christian households. Nazi iconography, their displays, their ceremonies, their rhetoric – all cleverly drew on the single most important part of the Volk's childhood mythic upbringing: the people's Christian faith. Each conquered country tapped into this common understanding. Each responded with greater or lesser efficiency but with roughly equal acceptance to the essential component of the myth: the Jew as other, the Jew as Christ-killer, the Jew as successful interloper, the Jew as ripe for periodic and bloody vengeance.

The following passage from *The Tin Drum* deserves memorization and reflection:

> *Faith, Hope, Love* or Santa Claus is the Gasman
>
> [The setting is the morning after Kristallnacht, the infamous smashing of Jewish synagogues and Jewish heads by Nazi thugs, so it is late in 1938…] Outside, it was a November morning. Beside the Stadt-Theatre, near the street-car stop, some pious ladies and strikingly ugly young girls were handing out religious tracts, collecting money in collection boxes, and holding up between two poles a banner with an inscription quoted from the thirteenth chapter of the First Epistle to the Corinthians, "Faith … hope … love." Oskar read and played with the three words as a juggler plays with bottles: faith healer, Old Faithful, faithless hope, hope chest, Cape of Good Hope, hopeless love, Love's Labors Lost, six love. An entire credulous nation believed, there's faith for you, in Santa Claus. But Santa Claus was really the gasman. I believe – such is my faith – that it smells of walnuts and almonds. But it smelled of gas.

7 Goldhagen, *Hitler's Willing Executioners: Ordinary Germans and The Holocaust* (N.Y.: Knopf, 1996).

The full chapter, the full novel, and ultimately the trilogy as a whole should be read to feel the intensity of this connection between religion and the ultimate evil of the Holocaust, a connection I take to be Grass' highest artistic achievement. The words that helped Europeans to support the beast in their midst were primarily religious. The abstractions Christians had been taught were lovely, but in the event they failed to signify. It is interesting that the churches, because too many Christians were victimized, did manage to put a halt to Hitler's euthanasia program.[8] But there is too much against the Jews in the Gospels and too little, too absurd, too vague, or too trivial a redemptive element in words like faith, hope, love.

As my method throughout this book of "Law and Literature" and History has revealed, forces came together during the Holocaust that began throughout the Reich that November night and morning, forces that seem almost pre-destined to have emerged. Maybe we need to look back with a measure of forgetfulness merely to go on. But writers like Grass, situated in the belly of the beast, insist on irking the "Ninevites," and we are in his debt despite (or because) of his own participation in the horrors.

Historians and theologians join story-tellers in grappling with these events. They are still a minority in their various crafts. Most want to move ahead, to put aside the seemingly unexplainable and to focus on other things. Some, like Prof. Robert Wistrich of the Hebrew University in Jerusalem, who goes even beyond James Carroll by suggesting that better choices throughout history would not have forestalled Christian behavior towards Jews because the enmity was always already ingrained, are willing to ask the ultimate questions, as I believe Grass and all the other writers I have treated also try to do:

> There is [among some ecumenical theologians and historians] a categorical repudiation of the portrayal of Judaism as Christianity's negative other. At times I have to wonder whether the wish is more powerful here than the reality. One must ask whether that history which is recounted … of Judaism as the quintessential negative other of Christianity really was avoidable. [James Carroll, in *Constantine's Sword*, for example,] argues the case for an alternative history, for places where opportunities were not taken, choices were not made, and he gives some examples. But I, perhaps like many professional historians, remain skeptical about those alternatives, even while accepting that there is indeed choice in history. This particular history of Christianity's perception of

8 On this, see, e.g., *Ingo Mueller, Hitler's Justice*, pp. 126–28.

> Judaism is one where the dominant weight of the tradition, certainly until fairly recently, was so overwhelming that one has to wonder whether these alternative options were really as possible as he makes them appear.[9]

2 *Bernhard Schlink's* The Reader

Bernhard Schlink is my age. Born as World War II was ending, we have similar perspectives on many issues and have collaborated on a variety of projects. He often teaches and lectures where I do in New York City and in Pittsburgh, and I have lectured at his Law School in Berlin. And if 1944 was your birth-year, you share a sensitivity to the horrifying film clips – perhaps photographed on the day of your birth! – that we now have of other less fortunate children being crammed into Hungarian cattle cars on their way to certain death at Auschwitz. "Born in 1944" provides a link[10] that has not been severed even by such major biographical differences as Bernhard's unexpected recent success as novelist or the differing postwar memories that have formed our childhoods.

Where Guenther Grass responds to the Nazi period as one who was old enough to serve in Hitler's armed forces, Schlink writes about it as the child of those who experienced the Third Reich. His masterpiece, *The Reader*, sets in opposition an adolescent protagonist and at least two formative adults who lived through Hitler's horrors. Michael's love affair with a much older woman eventually leads to a series of confrontations with his own father. Michael learns of his lover's past as a concentration camp guard, and he then begins to scrutinize the ways of thinking that permitted even a decent man like his father to abide the Nazi beast. Like Grass' brilliant descriptions of everyday Germans during the War, Schlink's narrative gets to the source of genocide, to the atmosphere that caught up so many otherwise ordinary people.

Novelists want the truth to get out. Michael's story throws light on dark places untouched even by such controversial histories as Goldhagen's *Hitler's Willing Executioners*.[11] Where Goldhagen extended genocidal guilt to the ordinary German, Schlink's character takes it upon himself, upon his own generation of Germans, although Michael and his peers never held a gun to the head of a Jewish baby or dropped zyklon B into a room packed with completely innocent fellow human beings.

---

9 Robert Wistrich, *Antisemitism: The Longest Hatred* (N.Y.: Schocken, 1994).

10 He was instrumental in spearheading, and wrote a Preface for, the German translation of my *The Failure of the Word* [*Rechtsgeschichten* (Berlin: Suhrkamp, 2017)].

11 *Op. cit.*, ch. 10, n. 7.

My appreciation of *The Reader* has marked a C-Span forum[12] and various less publicized symposia in which I have played a role. I have situated the novel's strengths within the field of "Law and Literature," and I believe it still deserves a place there today. Schlink's antihero, Michael, belongs in the ranks of those I had called "the lawyer-as-protagonist,"[13] a peculiar breed of leading men (few if any such female protagonists) whose legalistic proclivities provoke them to favor complexity over simple human interactions. (Here in Part Three, other such texts are analyzed, especially Melville's *Billy Budd, Sailor* and Albert Camus' *The Fall.*) The result for the other characters such "lawyer-figures" encounter is usually disastrous.

"He goes to law school!," I said of Michael.[14] In my reading, this decision by the youthful protagonist explains a great deal about the Holocaust-related action (or inaction!) by Schlink's protagonist. After that decision, the plot produces the usual inverse proportion in such figures of intellectual growth to natural empathy. Michael's marriage ends. He can make no affirmative choices at Hanna's trial. He feels numb when visiting the death camp near Strasbourg. All that is left inside him is shame, his own and that of the country he lives in and of that country's mother tongue, whose degradation under Hitler still survives although 6,000,000 do not, in part because of what Guenther Grass identifies as the obscenities promulgated in Sutterlin Script.[15]

Comparisons have been in order of Michael to Hamlet, Captain Vere, Mr. Jaggers, and (from pages of this book), Jean-Baptiste Clamence, protagonists who are either formally trained in law or – like the Danish Prince and the British ship captain – so trained to think like a lawyer that they might just as well be posthumously awarded their law degrees. Hamlet's quick wit and verbal subtleties, like those similar traits in Vere, turn him not only from the crying needs of the less complex people around him – Ophelia being the most poignant victim of his "quillities and quiddities."[16] Vere's destruction of the non-verbal but magnificent foretopman Billy Budd is now a matter of "Law and Literature" record, and it will be reiterated in our final chapter.

Michael becomes cold even as he becomes legalistic. Like these other characters, he lures people into a sense of dependency on his superior intellectual

12 My readers can still access this 1998 event, "The Next Generation", on https://www.c-span.org/video/?99309-1/holocaust-germany-generation.

13 Failure, *op. cit.*, Introduction, n. 4, redux.

14 *Op. cit.*, ch. 10, n. 12, and attached link.

15 This Part, Subsection (B)(1). Grass was for obvious reasons fascinated and (like Schlink) bothered by using the same German script utilized obscenely by the Nazis.

16 Act v, scene I at Ophelia's gravesite, imaginatively but futilely identifying "the skull of a lawyer!".

abilities, but he turns away from them at their keenest moments of need. Michael at Hanna's trial pre-figures Michael's meeting Hanna the day before she is due to leave prison – he is there but not there. He is doubly absent for Hanna. Her suicide, like Ophelia's, bears the mark of the lawyer.

I have elaborated on this idea in a written symposium on *The Reader* in the journal *Law and Literature*,[17] in which I addressed the matter of "Forgiveness and Memory" in Schlink's novel. Does it "intend" to render complex (like Michael) what seems most clear: the inexcusable culpability of Hanna's war crime? Although the focus of the inquiry seemed to shift from Michael to his paramour and former camp guard, what counts even more is Michael's absence for Hanna, his failure to tell the judge that Hanna is illiterate and hence could not have organized in writing the camp guards' collective iniquity. as the prosecution contended.

Crucially, Michael seeks out his father's advice on whether he should intervene at the trial to exonerate Hanna or at least to reduce her penalty. Somewhat in a Kafka-esque play on father-son relations,[18] Schlink locates the father as yet another figure – a philosopher in the older man's case – of enormous intellectual capacity but little in the way of affect. He seems to want Michael to let Hanna's trial develop without his son's *deus ex machina*, doubtlessly symbolizing a generation of "bystanders" to such enormities as Hanna's. He, tragically channeling the indifference of so many "good Germans" to the fate of the Jews, prefers to stand aside and let things develop as they will, even where an obvious moral wrong demands correction. The father does not believe in intervention. Michael does not intervene. By passing down his "bystander" status, Michael's father sins again.

Like the good philosopher he is, Michael's father has evidently built this holding back into a veritable ethos. He has not been much of a father to Michael, making the boy line up for an appointment with him as though he were just another student waiting to see the great man. He does not want Michael to be much of a *mensch*, either. Michael's failure to speak up when he goes to see Hanna's judge assures her sentence, which is in this way not real but only symbolic justice.

Now the generation of the Hitler-time is directly implicated in the plot of Schlink's story. The episode has little to do with whether the reader is supposed to forgive Hanna, the subject of ongoing debate foregrounded by such

17 Vol. 16 (2004).
18 Kafka, "The Judgment," in *Collected Stories*.

writers as Cybnthia Ozick.[19] Rather, and in my view far more importantly, we must ask whether forgiveness is due the "bystanders" to the genocide, who include Michael's father. Should they be exonerated because they were not perpetrators?

Earlier in this book, of course, I had to grapple with the bizarre assertion made implicitly or expressly by Catholic religious leaders – some of them "bystanders" or worse like Pius XII – that even *perpetrators* deserve forgiveness. Schlink, like myself in the camp who roundly say "No!" to such an obscenity – presents, therefore, the subtler question. Michael's father – whose Wartime record seems unblemished by any "active" wrong-doing, displays the fatal inability to act that characterized so many Europeans from 1933–45.

Schlink does not directly touch on that generation's religious upbringing and indeed does not further explore why they failed to react beyond what I am emphasizing here, the disease of intellectual over-thought characteristic of Michael as a lawyer and of his father as a philosopher. But one of my teachers, throughout this book, Franklin Littell, speaks in another context of the Lutheran/Protestant transgressions in Nazi Germany. Speaking after the War, in the mid-'Seventies, about what he saw as virtually a complete absence of recognition by Protestants of the War's lessons, he writes:

> This is precisely the problem in the ecumenical councils today: the lessons of the Holocaust ... have not been mastered in most churches; the terrible guilt of Christendom and its centuries of false teachings about the Jews has only been admitted by those who learn of Nazi ideology and practice at first hand .... In America, where the delusions of 19th century culture-religion are still regnant, only the impact of the preliminary stage of a new church struggle has served to move some churchmen to reflection and reappraisal ....
>
> But the crucial long-range question is how the Christians are to re-establish their credibility vis-à-vis humanity, signalized in the concrete historical situation by the way they re-work their relationship to the Jewish people. *The Holocaust was the consummation of centuries of false teaching and practice.*
>
> LITTELL, p. 64–65, emphasis added[20]

19 *Law and Literature, op. cit.*, ch. 5, n. 8, prominently the excellent writer Daniel Stern "Some Notes Toward a Response to *The Reader*," *id.*, pp. 203–5.

20 In the "Law and Literature" setting of Schlink's story, perhaps in particular, I must emphasize the resistance of wartime German Judge Kreyssig, who from the bench itself and as late as 1942, resisted Hitler's euthanasia program and also took steps publicly to oppose

Franklin Littell would not want us to forget the courage of Protestant towns like Le Chambon-sur-Lignon, either; nor does this book scant the immeasurable courage shown almost uniquely by one or two Protestants in Germany (Lothar Kreyssig) or the Channel Islands (Sir Abraham Laine), and in fairness one amazing Catholic protester in Vichy, my hero Prof. Jacques Maury.[21] However, as to such precious acts of defiance, Philip Hallie has reminded us that they are, fundamentally, *simple* and not so hard as one might otherwise imagine:

> If we would understand the goodness that happened in Le Chambon, we must see how easy it was for them to refuse to give up their consciences, to refuse to participate in hatred, betrayal, and murder, and to help the desperate adults and children who knocked on their doors in Le Chambon .... Goodness is the simplest thing in the world, and the most complex, like opening a door.[22]

Novelists want the truth to emerge. Even though not polemicists, their medium is the most accurate reflection of the age. When they are good story tellers, like Schlink, their aim is flawless. The significance of his work involves not so much flagrant wrong-doers such as Hanna – though the novel does not forgive her[23] – but instead an entire generation – like the one of Schlink's parents – who saw, knew better, equivocated through linguistic contortions worthy of Michael's father (and of Jean-Baptiste Clamence in *The Fall*), felt insufficiently towards the Jews specifically, and did nothing.

I am not saying that Schlink provides the stunning imagination of a Guenther Grass to his country's harrowing recent past. But his novel, with a boost from Hollywood, remains worthy into this century of re-reading and reflection.

---

the direction Nazis were taking to subvert law and destroy Jews. Kreyssig, perhaps not uncoincidentally, was a Lutheran. For the full story see my in *Praise of Intransigence, op. cit.*, ch. 1, n. 2, pp. 105–7, and see Ingo Mueller, *op. cit.*, ch. 10, n. 8. Elsewhere in Hitler's Europe, Protestants were more likely than the Catholic majority to *stick to* the core value of their religion and come to the rescue of beleaguered Jews. The story of Le Chambon-sur-Lignon has rightly been told often in film and in books. See, e.g., Caroline Moorehead, *Village of Secrets: Defying The Nazis in Vichy France* (N.Y.: Harper Collins, 2014). The film rendition of this story is *Weapons of The Spirit*, directed by Pierre Sauvage in 1987.

21 See Vichy Law, *op. cit.*, Introduction, ch. 2, n. 17. I was privileged five years ago to give a major welcoming address at Maury's home law school in Toulouse.

22 Philip Hallie, *Lest Innocent Blood Be Shed* (N.Y.: Harper and Row, 1979), p. 284.

23 Towards Hanna, Schlink's is a "sympathy that does not condone". *Law and Literature, op. cit.*, ch. 5, n. 8, pp. 229–35.

CHAPTER 11

The Kindly Ones: a Christian Lawyer Shoots the Heads off Babies on the Eastern Front

> [A Ukrainian POW in 1942 in conversation with the lawyer-protagonist Aue, an SD member on the eastern front:] "What difference, at bottom, is there, between National Socialism and socialism in a single country?" "In that case, why are we locked together in such a death struggle?" "You're the ones who wanted it, not us. We were ready to make compromises. But it's as once before, with the *Christians and the Jews; instead of joining forces with the People of God with whom they had everything in common, to form a united front against the pagans, the Christians preferred, no doubt out of jealousy, to let themselves be paganized and to turn against the witnesses of truth, to their own misfortune. That was a huge waste.*" "I'm guessing [responds Aue] that in your comparison, the Jews are you?" "Of course. After all, you took everything from us, even if only to caricature it ...."
>
> [p. 393] emphasis added[1]

∵

Jonathan Littell's blockbuster 2009, novel *The Kindly Ones* tracks over almost 1000 pages the wartime progression into total evil of a man who had been trained as a lawyer. This conceit opens up all of the themes of this book: how verbally gifted but perversely complex actors brought about – far more than single madmen shrieking patent lies and yet immediately captivating sophisticated Christian Europeans – the horrors of World War II. Littell, as the headnote to this chapter shows, also does not hide from connecting the dots to Christian hatred of Jews. Verbal acuity, and a lawyer-like ability to see all sides of an issue tend throughout world literature to exacerbate rather than to resolve potential violence. We must seek, as Littell does throughout a novel

1 By Jonathan Littell, Translated by Charlotte Mandell (N.Y.: McClelland & Stewart, 2009).

 | DOI:10.1163/9789004525177_013

that spans the continent (with many very accurate scenes set in Vichy, French being a native language for the novelist here), to understand why narrative gifts have loaned themselves so easily to horrid causes instead of to the pursuit of the good. Religion *always* is a factor in explaining this conundrum. As the Ukrainian prisoner of war surmises in the paragraph above, Christians blundered at their origins by wasting an opportunity to join with the Jews – "the witnesses of truth" – and instead viciously turned on the People of the Book and hence on Law, interpretive soundness, and justice itself. Using the dominant metaphor here, oil was isolated and made hideous, while water predominated and was made "kindly." The "kindliness" of the emerging Christian religion also involved a component of genocide I noted earlier in this book: the paganistic theft of Jewish property in the process of exterminating the owner. Greatly to this novel's credit, Jonathan Littell includes in its pages the intermixing of murder with expropriation:

> Of course there were some genuine anti-Semites in the Kommando: Luebbe, for example, another Untersturmfuehrer, seized the slightest occasion to rant against the Hebrews with extreme virulence, as if the whole of world Judaism were nothing but a vast conspiracy aimed at him, Luebbe ... And then there were some who stole from the Jews, kept gold watches, rings, money, even though everything was supposed to be turned in to the Kommandostab to be sent to Germany. ... But officers too kept things.
>
> *Kindly Ones*, 88–9

Why is Aue, the awful protagonist, presented as a lawyer? There is some of Michael's coldness, as we see him emerge from law school in Bernhard Schlink's *The Reader*. Perhaps a more fitting precursor of Aue, particularly given Littell's fascination with Vichy, is Camus' Jean-Baptiste Clamence in *The Fall*. And the consanguinity of Aue and Clamence extends explicitly to their perversion of the very notion of law. Together with many others trained in law, including historical figures like Werner Best, Aue winds up participating in genocide, explicitly the brutal murder of Jews in Ukraine, a connection to current events in 2024 that will interest many contemporary readers. Additionally, Aue – although hardly a devout Christian – joins predecessors like Clamence in having been brought up as a Catholic; his father was a Protestant, however, so neither religion emerges unscathed. Mainstream Christianity, and mainstream legal thinking and speaking, share a guilty place in the murder of millions.

Law – except of course for canon law, which falls outside the purview of my book – was "replaced" in Catholicism, but by what, exactly? This book has noted, and I believe Jonathan Littell's novel suggests this, that law without any foundation in history and tradition, law as practiced by those who have been taught to detest law, turns into cruelty and sometimes extreme genocidal cruelty. How would the continent of Europe, deliberately shorn of roots in Judaism that could have been utilized for the common good (see the headnote for this chapter) inculcate any idea of the underpinnings of legal justice? This did not happen, and two millennia of "kindly" Christian law present us with the opposite of the professed yet inchoate "mercy" that supposedly characterized Christianity. This is what *The Kindly Ones* tells us and the reason for its protagonist being a lawyer run amok in a lawless, genocidal culture. All we have left are such elevated abstractions as "mercy," or "equity," or "love," and we can add here in the spirit of Guenter Grass "faith" and "hope" as well – beautiful ideals masking an intensely subjective view of things all too often abused by the powerful. Law at its best constrains power and protects the outsider. The "new" Testament did away with those constraints. Your only chance was to join with the insiders, and sometimes they forced you to do it at risk of your and your family's lives.

It has been comforting to distance Hitler's killers from the very idea of Christianity because other explanations sit easier and do not disturb our *sang froid*. As we have seen, however, the effect of superb stories is to jar us out of our smugness and to pay attention to troubling truths unavailable to us through any other medium. "Hitler's willing executioners[2]," as the historian Goldhagen aptly called them, were brought up in Christian households. Hitler cleverly drew on the single most important part of their childhood mythic upbringing, their faith. Not only in the Reich but also in Italy and France, leaders adapted public display strategies that deliberately flattered the Catholic majorities and Protestants majorities;[3] each conquered country utilized this common strategy. Marshal Philippe Petain, the octogenarian "savior" of France after its disgraceful defeat, used the ancient religious imagery of the nation's deep pre-Revolutionary past to shore up "hope" among his overwhelmingly Catholic people. Saint Joan, Saint Louis, and other icons chosen precisely for their appeal as martyrs or absolute Catholic rulers,[4] presented on stamps, in speeches, in artwork and artisanal creations the not so covert message that France under the Marshal's leadership would be brought into the "new Europe" only by rejecting its Republican past and reverting to its Catholic traditions.

---

2 Goldhagen, *op. cit.*, ch. 10, n. 7.

3 See, e.g., Mueller, *op. cit.*, ch. 10, n. 8; Michael Stolleis, *The Law under the Swastika* (Chicago: U. of Chicago Press, 1992) at *e.g.*, pp. 7, 66.

4 See, e.g., my *Vichy Law, op. cit.*, Introduction, n. 17, pp. 20–22; 140–42.

Puppet leaders or awful collaborators at the street level in central and eastern Europe – the venue for much of Jonathan Littell's novel – needed less subtlety to employ Christian iconography against native Jewish populations. Each of Europe's peoples responded with greater or lesser enthusiasm but with roughly equal acceptance to the essential component of the genocidal belief system: the Jew as other, the Jew as Christ-killer, the Jew as successful interloper, the Jew as ripe for periodic and bloody vengeance.

But was this not the work of anti-Christian demons who added to Pogrom-like murder the cool technologized methods of the mid 20th century? Easier to ponder a continent gone temporarily out of its senses than one that was responding precisely *within* the confines of its traditions! For if the European "final solution" were the result of a continent gone temporarily mad within a new context of technological advances that for the first time permitted widespread dissemination of horrible political talk and also precise planning for the murder of all of the continent's Jews, we would have little to learn from the event. It would be like the act of a normal person who had gone temporarily insane. But if these developments merely appropriated an already situated set of Christian tropes and beliefs, we would expect decades of examination (such as are now occurring not only in this book but in the many cited in these pages), perhaps resulting in a gradual admission that there is a chronic sickness here needing radical cure. So if Christian-Jewish otherness is emphasized as the primary reason for Auschwitz, all our postwar assumptions about ecumenicism, dialogue, acceptance of the other in his or her particularism – all these good things crumble when we look too closely at the facts, and we are left with a world of Christian-Jewish relations that is bound to further destructiveness unless we honestly confront the problem.

Most postwar approaches to the Holocaust, once the subject was removed from the lists of taboos or cover-ups, emphasized other explanations. The deconstructionists, as I mentioned, began by avoiding the Holocaust in their mainstream writings, except for the later Geoffrey Hartman in his magnificent *The Longest Shadow*,[5] and then adapted their indirect discourse to the avoidance of the main issues. As Christine Krueger correctly described my "rebuttal of post-modernist anti-foundationalism,"[6] I identified a fallacy in post-modernist ways of thinking and writing that erroneously blamed the Holocaust on a Hitlerian "declarative, absolute" rhetoric that therefore needed forever to be avoided at all ethical costs. Instead of speaking clearly as Hitler did, we all needed to complicate our discourse. But the evidence showed

5 See Hartman, *op. cit.*, ch 1, n. 19.

6 Christine Krueger, *op. cit.*, Introduction, n. 1, p. 65.

that the Holocaust "emerged at least as much from complex, creative, and even deconstructive strategies of oppressive speech."[7] On this view what was needed was, precisely, a clear and direct declaration about the causes of the disaster, which were religious in nature. Contraindicated was the complex, often unscannable, diction of deconstructionism.

Earlier in postwar intellectual analysis, Hannah Arendt had emphasized the banality of bureaucratized evil. For Raul Hilberg, still a seminal historian and theoretician of genocides and particularly World War II Europe's version of them,[8] Hitler's brutal success arose more from economic than from cultural or religious factors.

The range of stories discussed in this book prevents deflection of the root causes onto less controversial explanations that do not go to the heart of many people's faith and belief systems. When Jonathan Littell creates as genocidal protagonist a lawyer and Christian intellectual named Aue, and when that "hero" goes on to discharge bullets into Jewish bodies and brains, we can no longer rest easy with explanations that miss the central point, the central cause, the *ne plus ultra*. It is because story tellers reveal such truths that their work deserves recognition. When it comes to Hitler's genocide, they have tended to see things more like Daniel Goldhagen than like Arendt or Hilberg, as excellent as these non-fiction writers are. Narrative media, such as stories, convey best the linguistic and theological roots of the European genocide. Thus these stories often transmit their "fictional truths" to us by promoting to the very center stage of evil an articulate, wordy, Christian lawyer or lawyer figure. Jonathan Littell joins with Camus, Schlink, Silva, Hochhuth, Malamud, and others in associating mainstream religious traditions with perversions of law and legal reasoning, drawn with specificity to implicate the murder of innocents.

Thus it is not hard, after we have travelled together so far and so long through the pages of this book, to situate Jonathan Littell's massive novel within a literary tradition. It is one that is precious to my project: it links law and history with storytelling, and it endeavors to bring meaning, where none of those three narrative disciplines on its own could do so, to the awfulness of the European Holocaust. There are overtures, too, to a variety of classical comparisons: Europe as a dysfunctional, continent-wide House of Atreus? The legalistic Christian protagonist, Dr. Maximilien Aue, as Camus' genocidal lawyer, Clamence, or Shakespeare's homicidal Macbeth or a sinister combination of the Bard's Richard II and Richard III? Or making the grotesque a joke, as

7 Weisberg, "Literature's 20 Year Crossing into the Domain of Law," in Freeman and Lewis, eds., *Current Legal Issues; Literature and Law* (U.K.: Oxford U. Press, 199), vol. 2, pp. 55–56.

8 Hilberg, *op. cit.*, ch. 5, n. 33.

Littell situates Gogol's crazy humor somehow within nightmare worlds even the Russian could not have experienced or predicted?

Each example brings us closer to the mark, a precedent fully evoked in this story otherwise so full of literary references but slow in naming its horrific primary source. Gogol gets us almost there, and it is not for nothing that, among Aue's randomly violent final acts, he bites the Fuehrer's "bulbous nose" during a freakish scene in the bunker as the Nazi world sinks into oblivion. Thoughts of Gogol's masterfully bizarre story "The Nose," with its disembodied title hero, attack our imaginations – we are getting closer!

By this time, we have traversed, with increasing willingness and fascination, more than 900 pages of murderous madness. We have been the constant companions of a totally repulsive narrator whose calm personality and legal education somehow have provoked rather than prevented his genocidal mania. We have walked with him through the killing fields of western Russia where his ascension to rank and power in Hitler's Sicherheitsdienst (SD) begins with his coup de grace to thousands of Jewish victims wiped out as were over a million other babies, children, women, and men forced first to dig their own graves and those of their families, and this long before Zyklon-B or Auschwitz were even gleams in Heydrich's or Eichmann's or Himmler's eyes. We have learned of Aue's private as well as his public perversions, and we stroll with him through his family house in the south of France where he strangles his own mother, having already murdered her despised second husband.

A law student become murderer who somehow merits our benumbed but all-encompassing attention as though the pages of a long novel are reflecting endless moments in one of our worst nightmares? A double homicide projected into the vicious mass murders in Byelorussia and then in Sobibor? The logic of the law adumbrated into impersonal slaughter?

Yes, dear reader: We have rejoined and updated Dostoevsky, whose feverish law student, Raskolonikov, slaughters not only the old pawnbroker but also her totally innocent half-sister early in the pages of *Crime and Punishment*. Dostoevsky accustomed us to homicidally violent lawyers who snuff the life from innocents, and Jonathan Littell, with the Holocaust freshly in the history books and very much on his mind, takes the next steps, influenced well by the imaginations of other postwar purveyors of legalistic violence covered in this book: Camus, Grass, Malamud, and Schlink. Repelled, we still want to know more and more about their violence because it reflects the intellectualized viciousness of our species at its worst. *The Kindly Ones* maps the tradition from the Greeks to the late 19th century novel, and then beyond onto the geography of Hitler's genocidal Europe. Our mesmerized eyes, which had followed Raskolnikov from the double murder onward to his punishment in Siberia, now find an Endloesung, a final solution to our own exploration of the darkest rather than the most sublime extremes within us.

So, when Aue brings a copy of Flaubert's *A Sentimental Education* with him through his personal "end-game," a crazed and murderous march from his sister's country house to Berlin as the victorious Russians close in on that seat of Hitler's 1,000-year Reich, Littell has chosen another law-school protagonist as distraction. Flaubert's Frederic Moreau again replicates both Aue's place as distorted "Bildungsroman hero" and Littell's quest to build a recognizable literary form around an ungraspable historical enormity. Littell's legalistic anti-hero finds comfort in Flaubert's realism, for what Aue has seen and done would have boggled the brain of Moreau, whose immersion in the chaotic Paris of 1848 seems like a cakewalk compared to Aue's violent wanderings through Hitler's Europe. Thus do literary and actual history conjoin: In the space of less than a century, Europe's revolutionary ideals have turned to ash.

Littell has done his factual homework. As an historian of wartime France myself, I vouch for the accuracy of almost every Vichy-related figure evoked – from Celine to Maurras to Sartre to Petain to Brasillach and then to the real life lawyers who complement Aue, such as Werner Best (chief of the Paris occupation until he moved on to Denmark), who raise Littell's narrative question, "What man of sane mind could ever have imagined that they'd pick jurists to assassinate people without a trial?"

Littell's lawyers and judges dominate his story, permitting him to show that the space between reason and madness is paper-thin. The writer has mastered the intricacies of Nazi "law" and included every jurist of note, from Hitler's legal philosopher, Carl Schmitt, to the ranting People's Court judge, Roland Freisler. His pages accurately adumbrate the debate between those who "just followed the law" – however immoral – and those many other judges who anticipated what the Fuhrer would have wanted in any given case and thereby inflicted even greater terror on defendants precisely because they did not even need a written law to go by. Aue's over-the-top self-indulgence is thus constantly balanced by his perfectly rational and fully historicized legalistic perspective. This period cannot be portrayed accurately without both of these elements, and in my view Aue's wildness and his logic are necessarily and proportionately combined.

Imaginatively recreating from a firm factual base, the writer accurately represents Aue's personal relationships with men like Eichmann, Rudolph Hoess – the commandant of Auschwitz – Himmler, Speer and others high and low on the Nazi flow-chart of civilian death productivity. Furthermore, every bridge, every town, every dialect destroyed by the Final Solution has been meticulously recovered. There will be quibbles, but this is not a work of law or history, and a wrong detail or two does not detract from this record. Much more significant might be our response to the larger issues that no sentient reader can ignore, despite horrors not even evoked here that make for occasionally difficult reading.

Each reader will have strong responses to the representation of this fraught historical period. But when I found myself shaking my head "No," it was just as I shook my head "No" to the double-murder Dostoevsky's protagonist thrusts on us in the early pages of *Crime and Punishment*. I wanted nonetheless to go on, deeper and deeper, because truth was emerging. This truth is anticipated in Dostoevsky's Ivan, the intellectual Karamazov brother who tortures his gentle sibling Alyosha by recounting tales of men who grab babies from their mother's bosoms and throw them onto pitchforks and into fires. Littell's unfortunate task, brilliantly rendered, was to bring us in nauseating detail the embodiment of Ivan's nightmares – not a crazy man but a "hero of his time." Littell's murderous lawyer stands as a precursor – fifteen years after the book appeared – to clever lawyers endeavoring to support Donald Trump's efforts to bring down the Republic; much more to the point, strategists then and now embolden murderers of Jews in the name of protecting Christianity. "Jews will not replace us!," they shouted at Charlottesville. Jews can be murdered at will even in their places of worship, as though there were no disconnect between the Ukrainian venue of death and destruction and the seemingly calmer environment in Pittsburgh Pennsylvania, where I am writing these words during Rosh Hashanah, 5785. *The Kindly Ones* identified, as is true of all the stories I have treated here, an enduring illness.

CHAPTER 12

Melville's Mediterranean News Revisited

A 40 Years of Back and Forth on *Billy Budd, Sailor*

Since the appearance four decades ago of *The Failure of the Word*,[1] there have been several mini-generations of commentary on my approach to Melville's earthshaking story, *Billy Budd, Sailor*.[2] Some of these responses, in my opinion, will not stand the test of time as serious readings of the story or of my own analysis. Richard Posner, although a long-time friend and colleague, goes down as one of those whose readings – both of my arguments and, far more grievously, of the stories themselves – are almost always tone deaf.[3] Others, like the various responses of Robin West, are brilliant and beautiful in their own right.[4]

Easily the best researched and possibly also the most significant of very recent responses is that of Richard McAdams and Jacob Corre.[5] These co-authors, whose work on the tale proceeds apace, bring new light to bear on the law as referenced and applied in the story. They mention my "novel interpretation of the general background of the story and Vere's actions" and accurately rehearse the debates regarding those factors, remaining agnostic on them but advancing many of the technical and historical findings in my book that touch on the British Naval Law Melville references compendiously during the trial scene (chapter 21 of the story).[6] McAdams and Corre are on track significantly to increase our archival knowledge of the law Melville utilizes so knowledgeably and explicitly within the story.

B Why the Tale is Vital to this Book's Endeavor

Jonathan Littell's *The Kindly Ones*, which we have just discussed, proves if it were necessary to do so, that *Billy Budd, Sailor* retains vital life 135 years

1 *Op. cit.*, ch. 3, n. 3.

2 My favorite remains, because you "never forget your first" perhaps, AWB Simpson's in *TLS* right after the book's publication in 1984; see "The Darker Side of Western Law," *op. cit.*, ch. 2, n. 2.

3 Posner, *Law and Literature: A Misunderstood Relation* (Cambridge: Harvard U. Press, 1990).

4 Robin West, *Caring for Justice* (N.Y.: N.Y.U.P., 1997).

5 "New Light on the Trial of Billy Budd," in LaCroix, Masur, Nussbaum, and Weinrib, eds., *Canons and Codes* (N.Y.: Oxford, 2021), ch. 3.

6 *Id.*, p. 53.

 DOI:10.1163/9789004525177_014

after its completion. Littell's articulate lawyer twists reality, in part influenced by his religion, and participates in the slaughter of innocents. The setting is historically real. So, in the Melville tale, a verbally manipulative ship's captain – whose talents are so like those of a lawyer that observers quoted in the story say his pedantry would have been better served in a land-based career like law – [63 in the authoritative edition of Hayford and Sealts][7] runs roughshod over fairness and justice to maintain absolute control over his ship, the *Bellipotent*. Eventually, a false report of the proceedings becomes "gospel" through the workings of a deceitful official naval journal.

By returning to where it all began, then, I wish here to bring a fitting coda to my linkage throughout this book of law, literature, history, and the problems posed by 2000 years of Christian interpretive practice. *Billy Budd*, for all the intrigue that leads to Billy's unjust conviction and hanging after a masterfully hypocritical trial led by the articulate Captain Vere, speaks better even than those stories treated so far to the bedrock distortions not only of authoritative interpreters generally but of Christian interpreters specifically. Linked strongly as well to *The Merchant of Venice*, the story elaborates in its self-proclaimed "considerate"[8] way how Christians in power bring bizarre interpretations of law to bear against relatively powerless "outsiders." *Budd* and *Merchant*, both of course written long before the Holocaust in Europe, exemplify the forebodings in our mainstream stories about the destruction of innocents deliberately wrought by those who have the power to distort texts and who have been traditionally taught to manipulate them against their plausible meanings and towards self-serving subjective ends, whether legal, religious, or political.

7 All references within the chapter are to the definitive Hayford and Sealts, eds., *Billy Budd, Sailor* (Chicago: U. of Chicago Press, 1962).

8 The story is perfectly self-conscious about its own narrative method: "truth uncompromisingly told" can only be conveyed indirectly; the more fraught the dramatic moment the more it becomes necessary to flatter the needs of the reader who might otherwise shudder to think about the story's controversial meanings. Digressions prevail over more linear plot lines and the narrative voice must convey or feign ignorance just when the reader might crave omniscience. The "considerate" narrator permits the reader to escape the story's truths but also uniquely offers the scrupulous reader a universe of insights that are troubling and otherwise not widely available. I have no doubt, and have argued so consistently, that the tale associates Christian modes of thinking, speaking and interpreting with this need to be "considerate," to deflect direct truths rather than pronouncing them forthrightly. See *The Failure of the Word, op. cit.*, ch. 3, n. 3, ch. 8.

C The Story's Deceptively Simple "Plot-Line"

Set on a British man-of-war at the end of the 18th century, the tale fascinates as a sea story, a battle of opposing types, a legal drama, and – most controversially – an account of powerful men reading and mis-reading texts to impose their will on others who dare to resist.

Written from around 1885 until Melville's death in 1891, and published posthumously in 1924, the tale pits the villainous shipboard master-at-arms, John Claggart against the physically and morally attractive titular foretopman. The former's irrational rancor eventually leads to a false accusation that Billy is a mutineer, the most terrible charge possible in the British Navy, especially then, as mutineers influenced by French Revolutionary ideas threatened the stability of the Empire. The ship's *seemingly* well-balanced Captain disbelieves Claggart and summons Billy to defend himself. But the lad, organically perfect except for his stutter, cannot speak up; instead he strikes and kills the master-at-arms, a capital crime. Vere convenes a drumhead court and insists to his carefully chosen jury that they convict and execute Billy. Vere speaks as elegantly as any novelistic lawyer – or as any Venetian Christian character for that matter – and his superior rank and superficially convincing arguments steamroll the highly reluctant jurors to do what their conscience abhors. Everyone loves Billy, whom Vere is the first to label "an angel of God," a force of moral good on the ship compared to Claggart's covert evil.

Like Portia's strategy to bring down Shylock at trial, Vere's argument bifurcates. He first concludes that the law of the case – the Articles of War – can only be interpreted to require Billy's conviction and hanging. But his hand-picked and highly subservient jury shows skepticism. So he shifts to a pragmatic appeal to their self-interest: if Billy is not hanged, he claims, the crew may join other mutinous sailors and seek an advantage over an apparently weak captain. This argument, like so many other false flags presented by self-interested, verbally gifted characters, manages to win the day. Billy is convicted, despite the strong misgivings of the subservient jury.

D The Narrator Makes Things Complicated

On one level, the tale is about the sacrifices required when crises call exceptional states of "law and order." Or at least that is Vere's argument, and it succeeds. Billy is hanged at dawn, his ever-loyal acts completed with the dying words, "God bless Captain Vere!" The sailors, usually a quiet lot, are moved by the sight (ironically) to as near a mutinous mood as they had ever experienced.

Vere musters them back to work. Eventually, wounded in battle, he dies with the words "Billy Budd, Billy Budd" on his lips.

As with *Merchant*, so here, law or the appearance of law plays a central role. How are the texts of the law to be read? Both masterpieces link religion explicitly to the dilemma. Is Vere forced to execute Billy, or – like the Venetian court – does he twist the law, using Law's noble name to bring about an injustice? If, as the narrative suggests, there is more egotism than law to his method, what does that say about the morality of mainstream decision-makers?

Obviously, we once again have a story that far exceeds even its scintillating basic plot line. Melville's narrator delights in "digressions," in a host of sidebars, detours, and secondary characters that eventually help us to answer the main questions about law and religion. Quickly, for example, the three principal characters are joined by the dazzling presence of Admiral Sir Horatio Nelson, whose legendary ability to quiet mutinous tendencies just by showing up on troubled ships seems to be set in direct opposition to Vere's need, later on, to destroy Billy on a vessel where no one seems set on mutiny at all. Nelson is there as a "foil" to Vere, an indication that there are ways to lead people through the most dire circumstances without sacrificing what is best within and among them.

My work on the story emphasized Nelson immediately, noting that he is a major character, of course taken from history, whom the narrator chooses to discuss early at great length before Captain Vere or Claggart have even been introduced! (In a relatively rare misunderstanding of my analysis, McAdams and Corre underestimate the importance I give to history and figures like Nelson.) He stands, like the three historical heroes I have honored in this book: imbedded, easy to miss despite their obvious centrality, hiding in plain sight as examples of how heroism and sound thinking shine through even in the worst of times. These are Sir Abraham Laine from the Island of Guernsey, Prof. Jacques Maury from Vichy France, and Judge Lothar Kreyssig from the belly of the beast itself, Nazi Germany.[9] All used their skills and whatever power they had to avoid killing innocents. Admiral Nelson accomplished this just by showing up on troubled vessels and without requiring Vere's impulse to destroy life in the process. Vere uses "law" to kill.

The text is hardly "just" a sea story, hardly "just" a superb representation of the space between positive and natural law; instead it deconstructs two millennia of writing and interpretation and sets modern (and post-modern) hermeneutics apart from earlier, sounder interpretive modes such as the *classical*.

---

9 See text on all three including Maury, at *op. cit.*, ch. 12, n. 2.

Admiral Nelson must be taken from the margins of the text and placed at its center, a figure who proves that distortion, dissimulation and public relations are not the sole ways of accomplishing things in this world. And that is not the only work the careful reader is "considerately" required to do.

Nelson would never have hanged Billy. Vere feels constrained to do so. One is heroic and sincere; the other, "bookish" (in the narrator's view), "pedantic" (in the eyes of other sailors), and "unhinged" (according to the ship's surgeon on hearing his captain's insistence on a drumhead court martial).[10] The doctor's assessment situates Vere as one of literature's many rational-seeming authority-figures who may be hiding something:

> As to the drumhead court, it struck the surgeon as impolitic, if nothing more. The thing to do, he thought, was to place Billy Budd in confinement, and in a way dictated by usage, and postpone further action in so extraordinary a case to such time as they should rejoin the squadron, and then refer it to the admiral. He recalled the unwonted agitation of Captain Vere and his excited exclamations ["Struck dead by an angel of God! Yet the angel must hang!], so at variance with his normal manner. Was he unhinged?

Vere's generally cool demeanor, however, disguises from everyone else his burning animus in this case, and the surgeon cannot summon the courage – as do certain deck officers in Herman Wouk's popularly known story, "The Caine Mutiny" – to challenge the captain's bizarre distortion of law and custom. Billy's crime, as the Articles of War dictated, required in a non-mutiny capital case that the matter be handled by the port admirals, not the ship's own captain and his hand-picked court. Melville knew the statute from personal experience and the surgeon speaks for him in this passage.

So the proceedings (like those of the only occasionally rational recent Supreme Court, which not coincidentally include three Catholic Trump appointees) have only the *veneer* of law about them. Yet Vere claims to be "fulfilling" the law, to use Pauline terms, in insisting on the death of the good Billy and the wonderful values the foretopman embodies. Vere hides his fear of the men on his ship and his resentment of his rival Nelson under the mask of

---

10 See the short but crucial chapter 20, inserted just before his own death into the story by a Melville who wished explicitly to raise the question of Vere's sanity or insanity in pursuing such a bizarre proceeding against Billy. The most articulate and rational-seeming individual, who feels himself under extreme stress, can act in the most irrational way. If he has authority, innocents will suffer.

the law. At first he sounds like Shylock, insisting on the letter of the naval statute; but eventually he looks more like the Venetian Christian readers of legal texts: one whose religiously based distrust of the law produces weird readings of it when self-interested ends are at stake.

E Religion and the Law: Melville's Stunning Naval Journal Takes us to the Gospels

Such covert overturnings of the law emerge from religious sources, Melville tells us in a compelling chapter set after Billy's trial and execution. Provocatively entitled, "The News from the Mediterranean," the text reveals an alternative reading of the events on Vere's ship. *Everything gets reversed.* In this authoritative naval account, Billy becomes the villain of the piece and Claggart an upstanding hero. A superb example of "considerate communication," the Naval Journal makes its readers feel better about the "necessity" of Billy's execution. It is as though Vere himself scripted this distorted "testament" as a justification for his moral and legal weakness. But we, having just completed the narrator's account, know that Billy was questionably tried, was a moral innocent, and was sacrificed for the good of fearful officers wishing to maintain their authority in times of crisis.

"The News from the Mediterranean," as I argued almost 40 years ago in *The Failure of the Word*,[11] is nothing else than Melville's version of the Gospels, those value-altering stories of the "news" emerging from the middle east and then Mediterranean Europe at the time of Saint Paul. In the Gospels and related writings, considerateness to the reader's sensitivities overwhelms truth. And a man with the initials "J.C" – the villainous John Claggart of Melville's version – has been authoritatively transformed by the Mediterranean News into a hero.

We know that Melville had a lifelong struggle with Christianity. He sought alternative modes of living, especially at sea and on remote islands where he found a freedom missing from the constrained Protestantism of his upbringing. From the islanders of his stories "Omoo" and "Typee" to Queequeg in *Moby Dick* to the sailors in this tale, the writer had set in opposition the unrepressed non-Christian life to the overly complicated resentments of "citified man," epitomized by those who use the law to regulate and tyrannize others. His own father-in-law, a distinguished Massachusetts high court chief judge – Lemuel Shaw – had described to Melville his dilemma in being "forced" from the beach

11 *Op. cit.*, Preface, n. 6.

to return fugitive slaves to their putative masters before the Civil War. But did not Judge Shaw, like Captain Vere, in fact have choices? What makes law misfire is the grotesque manipulation of it by resentful authorities who manage to produce outcomes far harsher than emerged from the older, pre-Christian precedents. Those older traditions, too had to be quashed.

When Melville tells us that "Truth is forced to fly like a scared white doe in the woodlands; and only by cunning glimpses will she reveal herself as in Shakespeare and other masters of the great Art of telling the truth – even though it be covertly and by snatches [Moby Dick, Hayford and Parker, p. 542]," he admits the extreme difficulty of telling his readers directly what is most in his heart. So his uneasiness with the Christan religion finds expression only subtly throughout *Billy Budd*. The story's theme of "considerate communication" holds that audiences cannot be hit over the head with unpleasant truths. So the entire narrative only "covertly and by snatches" has anticipated the Claggart-Christ connection that is palpable once the master-at-arms becomes the hero of the "News from the Mediterranean."

The symbol of repressed violence on board Vere's ship, John Claggart bears the initials of the hero of the Gospels. And there is more to the identity of Claggart and Christ than this, enough to establish Melville's "covert sally" through the story's considerate overturning of the Christian table of values. The narrator refers to Claggart as "a certain X," a code letter for Christ since the time of Constantine. Claggart is called "the man of sorrows," supposedly a pre-figuring from the book of Isaiah of Christ, as we saw in Chapter Two. The master-at-arms is around 34 at death, like Jesus, and much of his early life and conditions of birth are shrouded in mystery. But how can a clear villain be a Christ figure?

Before adumbrating for my readers these other "considerate" links between the story's villain and the great founder of a religion, I want even those who may never pick up the story to realize that such a claim is, for professional literary folks, as significant and unsettling as if one were to tell a Christian that – well, exactly what I am saying throughout this book! A long tradition of associating Billy – not Claggart – with Christ was being undone here, as well as a suggestion that Melville's complex and ironic writing probably hints at a much more radical overturning of values than we would get if the story were merely a war story or an *explicit* attack on its readers' religious beliefs. Furthermore, I emphasize Melville's attempt to associate Christian methods of interpretation with harsh, strange and somehow non-Jewish yet legalistic readings – akin to Portia's of the contract – that the law itself does not require or even permit if it were treated soundly. (It was this latter suggestion that bothered Judge Posner, who disliked contemplating an attack on authoritative readers of the law such as Captain Vere!)

I could only get a fair reading (much less a publication) of my association of Claggart with Christ by first nesting it within the theory of "considerate communication." As a 27-year-old assistant professor of Comparative Literature at the University of Chicago, I submitted to several learned journals a manuscript called "Melville's Subtle Heresy: John Claggart as Jesus Christ." Summoning the narrative evidence of Claggart's initials, his age at death, the uncertainty of his origins, his earning the epithets "a certain X" and the "man of sorrows" [Isaiah, 53:3, "a phrase commonly applied to Christ, as in Moby Dick, ch. 96, H & S, p. 171], and his heroic place in the gospel-like "News from the Mediterranean," I offered a radical reading of the story not different from that published years later in my book from Yale, *The Failure of the Word*. For those very early attempts, I received from the learned journals what seemed like instant rejections, supported by something like the following reader's report: "Prof. Weisberg scores a few points but he lost me altogether when he argued that Claggart was the hero of the story." Of course, I had nowhere promoted Claggart from the complex *villainy* accorded him in the story. But I realized that it was impossible to *communicate directly* a meaning so disheartening to the story's professional (and its other) readers. As Mel Gibson proved a while ago, a version of religious history that preserves the integrity of Jesus while spewing hate at others still makes for good box office. So traditionalists thought it better to think of Billy himself as the Christ-figure. My reading inadvertently produced a false syllogism in the professional reader's brain: "Weisberg says Claggart is Christ; Christ is a hero; Weisberg says Claggart is a hero." The burden was on me to argue better that Melville, with his lifelong dissatisfaction with Christianity and attraction to classical and pagan lives, might have at one and the same time produced a villain who was ALSO a *figura christi*. The narrative method of considerate communication bettered the chances that such a radical claim might, if not credited, at least be heard on its own terms. So it is with much modern and postmodern communication: Melville saw that the tougher the message conveyed the less it would be heard if conveyed directly. Again, though, this is not to be taken as the inevitable burden of human communication or interpretation. There have been better and more direct periods for writing and understanding, and they will return. This promise in effect is made by Harold Bloom in *Jesus And Yahweh*, when he assures us that the Jewish Deity and a sounder system of interpreting sacred texts will again have their day:

> Historically, both the New Testament and the Qur'an have pragmatically eclipsed the Hebrew Bible, but these successes are neither aesthetic nor necessarily spiritual, and Yahweh may not yet have spoken his final word upon this matter. We all know that history rides with the big battalions

> and, for a time, favors those who win the big wars, but history is an ironist almost of Jesus' genius, and the signs of an apocalyptic war between Christendom (to call it that) and Islam are now omnipresent.
>
> BLOOM, p. 37

Melville, like Shakespeare, is a pre-Holocaust writer who, in predicting calamity for the innocents of this world, undermined Christian values. He shows that the Gospels themselves made a hero ("J.C.") of one who upset hitherto positive values by destroying their embodiment. J.C. contrives to end the world as it had existed. That world, like Billy himself, had many strengths as well as some imperfections, but the cure for the latter proved worse than the disease. Vere could have saved the day by keeping Billy and what he stood for alive. Like Constantine, however, he made a choice for the "new." The process he began successfully inculcated Claggart-Christ's values, in the same way Constantine's fourth century decision to make Europe Christian ended the era of Judaeo-classical values and brought on centuries of repression, suppression, distortion, and hypocrisy. The official text, the "Mediterranean News," stood as the record of this transformation until the *Billy Budd* narrator's version in this tale restored the true picture, if we will only be willing to see it.

Melville adopts the Christian perspective only to undermine it. He must do this covertly. Christian modes of communication do not allow direct statements of unpopular belief. Claggart is the "X," the "man of sorrows," the hero of the Gospels. But he, unlike Nelson and unlike Billy, is not a force for good on the ship. His values prevail, but they do not work for the general betterment. Authorities adopt what he stands for: "law and order," sharp repression of instincts, violent suppression of the charismatic, the natural, the intrinsically human. Law can be manipulated because law no longer really counts where everything depends on the interpretive power of the man (or woman) in charge. Billy is defeated, much as Shylock was, and his memory endures despite authoritative accounts that exult in his destruction.

CONCLUSION

On Reverence for Law

Even some of my most loyal followers have wondered about my frequent use of the phrase "reverence for Law."[1] How could I maintain such a posture having in so many of my interpretations criticized the legal protagonist and the legal material within so many mainstream stories? I need to reemphasize, as these pages conclude, my belief that the Jewish allegiance to Law is the single marker of ethical soundness on earth compared to chaos, distortion, trickery, narrative violence, and the death of innocents. Even Jonathan Littell's awful lawyer, Aue, realizes this about the sacred People he willfully destroys:

> When the Jew submitted to the Law, he felt that this Law lived in him, and the more terrible, hard, demanding it was, the more he loved it.
>
> *Kindly Ones*, p. 102

What goes terribly wrong in these stories is not the "Law" identified within them but the authoritative perversions of those who control the Law and bring it to heel in the service of their own frequently unstated subjective impulses. My theory throughout this book is that two millennia of interpretive distortion facilitate and eventually excuse these interpretive wrongdoers. Even when Jewish institutions and some Israeli governments betray their own finest traditions, tens of thousands of righteous Jews take to the streets to correct the unacceptable deviation from the norm of reverence for Law. But in the Christian west, there is no reverence for Law. Subjective distortions of sacred texts, foul misinterpretations of human beings brought under the Christian "law's" harsh control, authoritative flights of fancy – these are taken in from the cradle through the stories Christians learn that justify ignoring the Law in favor of legalizing banditry.

The storytellers I have treated here reinstate a reverence for Law by representing the religious and legalistic conditions that bring on its destruction. As Melville in particular suggested, there have been better times for Law and for narrative honesty than we are living through today. But if the Holocaust compels in thoughtful people some kind of explanation, this book may add a small measure of understanding and a call to action in the direction of the Law.

I do firmly believe such a time is now upon us.

---

1 See, e.g., Robin West, "In Praise of Richard Weisberg's Intransigence," *Law and Literature*, vol. 29 (2017), p. 21. See also West's masterpiece, *Caring for Justice*, *op. cit.*, ch. 12, n. 4.

 | DOI:10.1163/9789004525177_015

Bibliography

Almond, Philip C., "Is There Really Such a Thing as a 'Judeo-Christian Tradition'?," Australian Broadcasting Corporation (February, 2019) https://www.abc.net.au/religion/is-there-really-a-judeo-christian-tradition/10810554

Alscher, Peter and Weisberg, Richard, "Why King James Insisted, as With no Other Shakespearean Play, on Seeing '*The Merchant of Venice*' Twice," in Daniela Carpi, ed., *Property Law in Renaissance Literature* (Lausanne: Peter Lang, 2005).

Anker and Meyler, eds., *New Directions in Law and Literature* (New York: Oxford University Press, 2017).

Arendt, Hannah, *Eichmann in Jerusalem: a Report on the Banality of Evil* (N.Y.: The Viking Press, 1963).

Ashby, Richard, *King Lear After Auschwitz* (Edinburgh: Edinburgh University Press, 2021).

Asimow, Michael and Weisberg, Richard, "When the Lawyer Knows the Client is Guilty: Client Confessions in Legal Ethics, Popular Culture and Literature," *Southern California Interdisciplinary Law Journal*, v. 18 (2009).

Barricelli, Jean-Pierre and Weisberg, Richard, "Law and Literature," in *Interrelations of Literature* (N.Y.: PMLA, 1982).

Beck, Mordechai, "Face to Faith," *The Guardian* (June 9, 2007).

Bernstein, Richard, "Giving Collaboration a Bad Name," Review of Richard Weisberg, *Vichy Law and the Holocaust in France, Ny Times*, March 26, 1997.

Bloom, Harold, *Jesus and Yahweh* (London: Penguin, 2005).

Bloom, Harold, *Shakespeare: The Invention of the Human* (N.Y.: Riverhead, 1999).

Bolduc, Paula, "The Cruelty of Mercy: Oxymoronic Paradoxes," *Texas Law Review* (2008).

Brooks, Peter, "Law and Literature in Dialogue," PMLA, vol. 120 (2005), p. 1645.

Burt, Robert, *In the Whirlwind* (Cambridge: Harvard University Press, 2012).

Camus, Albert, *The Fall* [1956] (transl., Justin O'Brien; N.Y.: Vintage Books, 1956).

Camus, Albert, *The Plague* [1947] (transl., Stuart Gilbert; N.Y.: Alfred A. Knopf, Inc., 1991).

Camus, Albert, *The Stranger* [1942] (transl., Matthew Ward; N.Y.: Vintage Books, 1988).

Cardozo, Benjamin, "Law and Literature," in Margaret E. Hall, ed., *Selected Writings* (New York: Matthew Bender, 1975).

Carroll, James, *Constantine'S Sword, The Church and The Jews* (Boston: Houghton Mifflin, 2002).

Ciardi, John and Williams, Miller, *How Does A Poem Mean?* (New York: Riverside Press, 1959).

Cinpoes, Nicoleta, "Defrauding Daughters Turning Deviant Wives?: Reading Female Agency in *The Merchant of Venice*," Sederi, v. 21 (2011).

Cohen, Arthur A., *The Myth of the Judeo Christian Tradition, and Other Dissenting Essays* (New York: Shocken, 1971).

Cohen, Arthur A., "The Myth of the Judeo-Christian Tradition," *Commentary* (1969).

Cormack, Nussbaum and Strier, Richard, eds., Shakespeare and The Law (Chicago: University of Chicago Press, 2012).

Cormack, Nussbaum and Strier, Richard, eds., Review essay, *The Holocaust and The Literary Imagination*, Lawrence L. Langer, *The New York Times Book Review* (1/18/1976), p. 19.

Cover, Robert, "Nomos and Narrative," in Minow, Ryan and Sarat, eds., *Narrative, Violence, and The Law: Essays of Robert Cover* (Ann Arbor: University of Michigan Press, 1995).

Cunningham, J.V., *Woe or Wonder: The Emotional Effect of Shakespearian Tragedy* (Denver: Swallow Paper Book, 1964, originally published in 1951), pp. 36–70.

Curran, Vivian, "At the Crossroads of Law and Society: The Trial of Mendel Beilis," *Law and Literature*, v. 28 (2016).

Danson, Lawrence, *The Harmonies of "The Merchant of Venice"* (New Haven: Yale University Press, 1978).

Dickstein, Morris, ed., *The Revival of Pragmatism: New Essays on Social Thought, Law, and Culture* (Durham: Duke University Press, 1998).

Dolin, Kieran, ed., *Law and Literature* (U.K.: Cambridge University Press, 2018).

Dolin, Kieran, ed., *A Critical Introduction to Law and Literature* (id., 2012).

Drapac, Vesna, "Religion in a Dechristianized World: French Catholic Responses to War and Occupation," *Journal of European Studies*, vol. xxvi (1996).

Dunwoodie, Peter, "Language and the Duty of Memory," in Robert C. Evans, *Critical Insights, The Plague*, p. 212.

Edmondson, Paul and Wells, Stanley, *All the Sonnets of Shakespeare* (U.K.: Cambridge University Press, 2018).

Ehrman, Bart D., *Misquoting Jesus: The Story Behind Who Changed The Bible and Why* (New York: Harper Collins, 2005).

Eizenstat, Stuart E., *Imperfect Justice: Looted Assets, Slave Labor and the Unfinished Business of World War II* (New York: Perseus Books, 2003).

Ette, Ottmar, "'Tout Comprendre, C'est Tout Pardonner':The Case of Jauss," (*Brill, Philological Encounters*, 2017).

Evans, G. Blakemore, ed., *The Riverside Shakespeare* (Boston: Houghton Mifflin, 1974).

Evans, Robert C., ed., *Critical Insights: "The Plague"* (Mass.: Salem Press, 2023).

Fendt, Gene, "The Women in *The Plague*," in Robert C. Evans, id. *Critical Insights*.

Ferguson, Robert, *Law and Letters in American Culture* (Cambridge: Harvard University Press, 1984).
Fraser, David, *The Jews of the Channel Islands and The Rule of Law*, 1940–45 (UK: Sussex, 2000).
Fraser, David, "The Blood Libel in North America: Jews, Law and Citizenship in the Early 20th Century," *Law and Literature*, vol. 28 (2016).
Freeman, Michael and Andrew Lewis, eds., *Law and Literature, Current Legal Issues, Volume 2* (U.K.: Oxford University Press, 1999).
Gabbatt, Adam, "'Jews Will Not Replace Us': Vice Film Lays Bare Horror of Neo-Nazis in America," *The Guardian* (August 16, 2017).
Ghosh, Jaya, "*The Merchant of Venice* Strikes the Right Tone as a Tragedy," *The Rogers Review* (March, 2022).
Girard, Rene, *Deceit, Desire and The Novel* (transl. from *Mensonge Romantique Et Verite Romanesque*; Baltimore: Johns Hopkins Press, 1976).
Goldhagen, Daniel, *Hitler's Willing Executioners: Ordinary Germans and The Holocaust* (New York: Knopf, 1996).
Goodrich, Barshack, and Schuetz, eds., *Law, Text, Terror* (U.K.: Routledge, 2006).
Goodrich, Peter, ed., "Symposium: *In Flagrante Depicto*, Films on Trial," *Cardozo Law Review*, vol. 31 (2010).
Goodrich, Peter, Gandorfer and Gebreuers, eds., *Research Handbook on Law and Literature* (U.K.: Elgar, 2022).
Grass, Gunther, *The Tin Drum* [1959] (trans. Ralph Manheim, London: Secker and Warburg, 1961).
Green, Leslie, *The Germ of Justice* (N.Y.: O.U.P., 2023).
Greenblatt, Stephen, *Will in The World* (N.Y.: Norton, 2004).
Gross, John, *Shylock* (N.Y.: Simon & Schuster, 1992).
Hallie, Philip, *Lest Innocent Blood Be Shed* (New York: Harper & Row, 1979).
Hartman, Geoffrey, *The Longest Shadow* (Bloomington: Indiana University Press, 1995).
Hartman, Geoffrey, "The Tricksy Word: Richard Weisberg on *The Merchant of Venice*," *Law and Literature*, v. 23 (2011).
Hayford & Sealts, eds., *Billy Budd, Sailor* (Chicago: University of Chicago Press, 1960).
Heine, Heinrich, *Shakespeare'S Maidens and Women* (*transl. in the Works of Heinrich Heine*, Leland, ed.; London: William Heinemann, 1906, pp. 377–400; originally published in 1838).
Herford, Travers, *The Truth About the Pharisees* (N.Y.: Intercollegiate Menorah Association, 1925).
Hilberg, Raul, *The Destruction of the European Jews* (Chicago: Quadrangle Books, 1961).
Hochhuth, Rolf, *The Deputy*, (transl., Richard and Clara Winston; New York: Grove Press, 1964).

Hoenig, Samuel N., *The Essence of Talmudic Law and Thought* (New York: Jason Aronson, Inc., 1993).
Ihering, Rudolf von, *Der Kampf Uns Recht* [1872] (transl. as "The Struggle for Law," in Shakespeare, *The Merchant of Venice*, Furness, ed.; New Variorum, N.Y.: Dover, 1964), p. 409.
Irvin-Erickson, Douglas, *Rafael Lemkin and The Concept of Genocide* (Philadelphia: University of Pennsylvania Press, 2017).
Isaiah, Book of, (Soncino, I.W. Slotki, transl. and ed.), original Hebrew; U.K.: Chesham Press, 1961).
Jackson, Timothy P., *Mordechai Would Not Bow Down: Antisemitism, The Holocaust, and Christian Supersessionism* (New York: OUP, 2021).
Johnson, Hannah, *Blood Libel: The Ritual Murder Accusation at the Limit of Jewish History* (Ann Arbor: University of Michigan Press, 2012).
Jones, Ernest, *Hamlet and Oedipus* (New York: W.W. Norton, 1976).
Judt, Tony, "The 'Problem' of Evil in Postwar Europe," *New York Review of Books* (2/14/08).
Julius, Anthony, *Trials of the Diaspora: A History of Antisemitism in England* (U.K.: Oxford University Press, 2010).
Kermode, Frank, *Pieces of My Mind: Essays and Criticism, 1958–2002* (New York: Farrar, Strauss & Giroux, 2003).
Kertzer, David I., *The Popes against The Jews: The Vatican'S Role in the Rise of Modern Antisemitism* (New York: Knopf, 2001).
Kertzer, David I., "What the Vatican's Secret Archives are About to Reveal," *The Atlantic* (March 2, 2020).
Knowles Smith, Hazel, *The Changing Face of the Channel Island Occupation* (New York: Palgrave, 2007).
Koffler, Judith, "Terror and Mutilation in the Golden Age," *Human Rights Quarterly*, v. 5 (1983), p. 27.
Kornstein, Daniel, *Kill all the Lawyers?: Shakespeare's Legal Appeal* (Princeton: Princeton University Press, 1994).
Krueger, Christine, "Law and Literature and History," Dolin, ed., *A Critical Introduction To Law and Literature* (U.K.: Cambridge University Press, 2011).
Lacroix, Masur, Nussbaum, and Weinrib, eds., *Cannons and Codes* (N.Y.: OUP, 2021).
Langer, Lawrence L., *The Holocaust and the Literary Imagination* (New Haven: Yale University Press, 1975).
Levine, Amy-Jill and Brettler, Marc Zvi, *The Jewish Annotated New Testament* (N.Y.: Oxford University Press, 2011).
Levinson, Sanford, *Torture, A Collection* (N.Y.: OUP, 2004).
Littell, Franklin, *The Crucifixion of The Jews: the Failure of Christians to Understand the Jewish Experience* (New York: Harper & Row, 2001).

Littell, Jonathan, *The Kindly Ones*, (trans., Charlotte Mandell; New York: McClelland & Stewart, 2009).

Loeffler, James, "The Problem with the 'Judeo-Christian Tradition'", *The Atlantic*, 2020.

Malamud, Bernard, *The Fixer* (N.Y.: Farrar, Straus, 1976).

Marrus, Michael and Paxton, Robert, *Vichy France and The Jews* (Cambridge: Harvard University Press, 1981).

McAdams and Corre, "New Light on the Trial of Billy Budd," in LaCroix *et al.*, eds., *Canons and Codes*, ch. 3.

Melville, Herman, *Billy Budd, Sailor*, first published in 1924; *see* Hayford, Harrison and Merton Sealts, Jr., eds, (Chicago: University of Chicago Press, 1960).

Mews, Siegfried, ed., *Guenther Grass and His Critics* (Rochester: Camden House, 2008) .

Millen, Rochelle J., Review essay of Santaniello, *Nietzsche, God, and The Jews: His Critique of Judeo-Christianity in Relation to The Nazi Myth, Modern Judaism*, v. 17, n. 1 (1997), pp. 97–104.

Minerbi, Sergio Itzhak, "Pope John Paul II and the Jews: An Evaluation", *Jewish Political Studies Review*, vol. 18 (2006).

Minow, Ryan, and Sarat, eds., *Narrative, Violence, and The Law: the Essays of Robert Cover* (Ann Arbor: University of Michigan Press, 1995).

Moorehead, Caroline, *Village of Secrets: Defying The Nazis in Vichy France* (N.Y.: Harper Collins, 2014).

Mueller, Ingo, *Hitler'S Justice* (Cambridge: Harvard University Press, 1991).

Myrsiades, Kostas and Linda, eds., *Un-Disciplining Literature: Literature, Law and Culture* (New York: Peter Lang, 1998).

Nahshon and Shapiro, eds., *Wrestling with Shylock: Jewish Responses to "The Merchant of Venice"* (UK: Cambridge University Press, 2017).

Neusner, Jacob, *Jews and Christians: The Myth of a Common Tradition* (Valley Forge: Hymns, 1991).

Newman, Dwight, "Existentialism and Law – Toward a Reinvigorated Law and Literature Analysis," *Saskatchewan Law Review*, vol. 63 (2000), p. 87.

Nietzsche, Friedrich, *Werke* (Berlin: DeGruyter, 1968).

Nietzsche, Friedrich, *Beyond Good and Evil* (trans., Marianne Cowan; Chicago: Regnery, 1966).

Nietzsche, Friedrich, *On the Geneaology of Morals* (trans., Francis Golffing; New York: Doubleday, 1956).

Norris, Christopher, *Paul De Man* (N.Y.: Routledge, 1988).

Olson, Greta, *From Law and Literature to Legality and Affect* (U.K.: Oxford University Press, 2022).

Orme, Mark, "Is a Priest Justified in Consulting a Doctor?: Reflections on the Case of Paneloux and Rieux in The Plague," in Evans, ed., *Critical Insights in The Plague* (Ipswich: Salem Press, 2023).

Ost, François, "*Le Marchand de Venise*: Le Pari et la Dette, Le Jeu et la Loi," *Mcgill Law Journal*, vol. 62 (2017), p. 1103.

Peters, Julie Stone, "Law, Literature, and the Vanishing Real," PMLA, vol. 120 (March, 2005), pp. 442–53.

Philips, O. Hood, *Shakespeare and The Lawyers* (London: Methuen, 1972).

Polgar, Alfred, "Der Kaufmann von Venedig," *Die Weltbuehne*, 20:2 (1924).

Posner, Richard, *Law and Literature, A Misunderstood Relation* (Cambridge: Harvard University Press, 1990).

Raffield, Paul and Watt, Gary, eds., *Shakespeare and The Law* (U.K.: Hart Publishing, 2008).

Rajsfus, Maurice, *Jeudi Noir* (Paris: Harmattan, 1988).

Riding, Alan, "Guenther Grass under Siege After Revealing SS Past," *Ny Times* (August 16, 2016).

Roth and Maxwell, eds., *Remembering for the Future, The Holocaust in an Age of Genocide* (London: Palgrave Macmillan, 2001).

Rousseau, Henri, *The Vichy Syndrome* (Cambridge: Harvard University Press, 1994).

Schlink, Bernhard, *The Reader* (trans., Carol Brown Janeway; N.Y.: Vintage, 1997).

Schmitt, Carl, *The Concept of the Political* (transl., Schwab; Chicago: University of Chicago Press, 2007).

Schuetz, Anton, "Structural Terror," in Goodrich, Barshack, and Schutz, eds., *Law, Text, Terror*, p. 71.

Shaffer, Mary Ann and Barrows, Annie, *The Guernsey Literary and Potato Peel Pie Society: A Novel* (N.Y.: Dial Press Random House, 2008).

Shakespeare, William, *The Complete Works of William Shakespeare* (U.K.: Abbey Library, 1964).

Shakespeare, William, *The Tragedies of Shakespeare*, Vol. Two (N.Y.: Random House, 1944).

Shakespeare, William, *Hamlet* [1604] (Folger Updated Edition, Mowat and Werstine, eds.; N.Y.: Simon & Schuster, 2012).

Shakespeare, William, *The Merchant of Venice* [1600] (Marcus, ed.; N.Y.: Norton Critical Edition, 2006).

Shapiro, James, *Shakespeare in a Divided America: What His Plays Tell Us About Our Past and Future* (N.Y.: Penguin Books, 2021).

Silva, Daniel, *The Confessor* (N.Y.: Putnam, 2003).

Simpson, A.W.B., "The Darker Side of Law," Review essay of Weisberg, *The Failure of the Word*, *TLS*, No. 4278 (3/29/1985), p. 342.

Sohmer, Steve, *Reading Shakespeare'S Mind* (U.K.: Manchester University Press, 2018)

Stern, Daniel, "Some Notes Toward a Response to *The Reader*," *Law and Literature*, v. 16: 2 (2004).

Stevens, Alexander, "F. Murray Abraham Brings Shylock to Boston," *The Patriot Ledger* (2011).

Stolleis, Michael, *The Law under the Swastika* (transl., Chicago: University of Chicago Press, 1998).

Tamm, Ditlev and Simonsen, Karen-Margrethe, *Law and Literature: Interdisciplinary Methods of Reading* (Copenhagen: DJOF, 2010).

Teter, Magda, *Christian Supremacy: Reckoning with the Roots of Antisemitism and Racism* (Princeton: Princeton University Press, 2023).

Thomas, Brook, *Cross Examinations of Law and Literature: Cooper, Hawthorne, Stowe, and Melville* (N.Y.: Cambridge University Press, 1987).

Thomas, Brook, "Minding Previous Steps Taken," in Elizabeth Anker and Bernadette Myler, eds., *New Directions in Law and Literature* (New York: Oxford University Press, 2017), p. 36.

Totaro, Rebecca, "Camus and Plague Literature," in Evans, *Critical Insights*, p. XIX.

Verkuil, Paul, *Outsourcing Sovereignty: Why Privatization of Government Functions Threatens Democracy and What We Can Do About It* (N.Y.: Cambridge University Press, 2007).

Waldron, Jeremy, "'Dead to the Law'—Paul's Antinomianism," *Cardozo Law Review*, v. 28:1 (2006).

Weisberg, Richard, *In Praise of Intransigence: The Perils of Flexibility* (New York: Oxford University Press, 2014).

Weisberg, Richard, *Vichy Law and the Holocaust in France* (N.Y.: N.Y. University Press, 1996).

Weisberg, Richard, *Poethics: And Other Strategies of Law and Literature* (N.Y.: Columbia University Press, 1992).

Weisberg, Richard, *The Failure of the Word: The Protagonist as Lawyer in Modern Fiction* (New Haven: Yale University Press, 1984).

Weisberg, Richard, "Triangulation as a Problem in Shakespeare's Plays and Sonnets," *European Judaism*, v. 51:2 (2018).

Weisberg, Richard, "Shylock's Jewish Lawyers: How Jewish Scholars, Judges, and Litigators have Written About and Performed *The Merchant of Venice*," in Nahshon and Schapiro, *Wrestling with Shylock* (U.K.: Cambridge University Press, 2017).

Weisberg, Richard, "A Response to Peters and Brooks," PMLA, vol. 121 (2006), p. 546.

Weisberg, Richard, "Literature's 20 Year Crossing into the Domain of Law," in Freeman and Lewis, eds., *Current Legal Issues: Literature and Law* (U.K.: Oxford University Press, 1999).

Weisberg, Richard, "Antonio's Legalistic Cruelty: Interdisciplinarity and *The Merchant of Venice*," Myrsidades, ed., *Undiscipling Literature* (N.Y.: Peter Lang, 1999), p. 180, reprinted from *College Literature*, v. 25 (1998), pp. 12–20.

Weisberg, Richard, "The Hermeneutic of Acceptance and the Discourse of the Grotesque, with a Classroom Exercise on Guernsey," *Cardozo Law Review*, vol. 17 (1996), p. 1875.

Weisberg, Richard, "Avoiding Central Realities," *Human Rights Quarterly*, v. 5 (1983).

Weisberg, Richard, "Loose Professionalism, or Why Lawyers Take the Lead on Torture," in Levinson, *Torture, A Collection*, p. 299.

Weisberg, Robert, "The Law-Literature Enterprise," *Yale Journal on Law and Humanities*, v. 1:1 (1979).

West, Robin, "In Praise of Richard Weisberg's Intransigence," *Law and Literature*, vol. 29 (2017).

West, Robin, *Caring for Justice* (N.Y.: New York University Press, 1997).

White, James Boyd, *The Legal Imagination* (Boston: Little Brown, 1973).

Widdicombe, Lizzie, "Retrial," The New Yorker – Talk of the Town (December, 2008), pp. 44–45.

Wigmore, John, "A List of 100 Legal Novels," *Illinois Law Review*, vol. 2 (1908), p. 574; repr. and revised: Weisberg and Ktretschman, "Wigmore's 'Legal Novels' Expanded: A Collaborative Effort," *University of Maryland Law Forum*, vol. 7 (1977), p. 94.

Winikka-Lydon, Hodges, and R.G. Cravens, "Old Bigotries Melded with New Conspiracies Burgeon White Christian Nationalism," *Southern Poverty Law Center: the Year in Hate and Extremism* (2022).

Wistrich, Robert S., *Antisemitism: The Longest Hatred* (N.Y.: Schocken, 1994).

Zaklikowski, David, "An Overview of the Notorious 1913 Ritual Murder Trial," *Footprints: Colorful Lives, Huge Impact* (New York: Hasidic Archives, 2017).

Index

www.ingramcontent.com/pod-product-compliance
Lightning Source LLC
Chambersburg PA
CBHW071247230926
51849CB00001B/251
9789004525160

Freedom and Security

The CSCE and the End of the Cold War (1986–1989)

Edited by

Nina Hechenblaikner
Andrea Brait

Assisted by

Julia Nora Müller

BRILL

LEIDEN | BOSTON

FWF Austrian Science Fund

Research results from: Austrian Science Fund (FWF): 10.55776/I4139.
Published with the support of the Austrian Science Fund (FWF): 10.55776/PUB1144.

Cover illustration: The Austria Center Vienna from south-southwest on August 22, 2014. Photograph taken by Robert F. Tobler. Available on Wikimedia Commons (https://commons.wikimedia.org/wiki/File:Austria_Center_Vienna_from_SSW_on_2014-08-22.png) and licensed under the Creative Commons Attribution-Share Alike 4.0 International (CC BY-SA 4.0) license (https://creativecommons.org/licenses/by-sa/4.0/deed.en).

Partially translated by Joe Paul Kroll

The Library of Congress Cataloging-in-Publication Data is available online at https://catalog.loc.gov
LC record available at https://lccn.loc.gov/2025022867

Typeface for the Latin, Greek, and Cyrillic scripts: "Brill". See and download: brill.com/brill-typeface.

ISSN 2452-2260
ISBN 978-90-04-73696-2 (hardback)
ISBN 978-90-04-73697-9 (e-book)
DOI 10.1163/9789004736979

Contents

Tables and Figures

Tables

Figures

Notes on Contributors

Andrea Brait
is head of studies at the Center for Cultures and Technologies of Collecting at the University for Continuing Education Krems. Her research focuses on historical learning, especially in museums, as well as diplomatic history with a focus on Austria's foreign cultural policy. Among other works, together with Michael Gehler, she co-edited the book *Umbruch- und Wendejahre. Österreichs Bundesländer und ihre Nachbarn 1989/91*, Wien-Köln-Weimar 2025.

Michael Gehler
is a professor of contemporary history at the Institute of History at the University of Hildesheim. His research focuses on European integration history, German and Austrian contemporary history, and international relations in the 20th century. Among other works, together with Andrea Brait, he co-edited the book *Von den Umbrüchen in Mittel- und Osteuropa bis zum Zerfall der Sowjetunion 1985–1991*, Hildesheim 2023.

Maximilian Graf
is a historian at the Austrian State Archives. His research focuses on contemporary European history, Cold War studies, international relations in the 20th century and political transitions in Central and Eastern Europe. Among other works, he published *Österreich und die DDR 1949–1990. Politik und Wirtschaft im Schatten der deutschen Teilung*, Wien 2016. For his research, he has received several awards, including the Vogelsang-Staatspreis für Geschichte der Gesellschaftswissenschaften.

Anna Graf-Steiner
is a research associate at the Ludwig Boltzmann Institut für Kriegsfolgenforschung. Among her research interests are diplomatic history, neutrality and Soviet-Austrian relations. Her publication *Brückenbauer im Kalten Krieg. Österreich und der lange Weg zur KSZE-Schlussakte*, Graz-Wien-Raabs 2024 was awarded the Award of Excellence – Staatspreis für die beste Dissertation.

Simon Graham
is a Sessional Academic at The University of Sydney. His research examines the extent to which the Stasi influenced the international order through espionage against key international organizations during the Cold War. He published the

article 'Internationalising the intelligence history of the Prague Spring', *Cold War History* 20 (2019), issue 3, p. 1–18.

Kai Habel
was a research assistant at the Graduate Institute of International and Development Studies in Geneva. His fields of research include the history of the Cold War, Neutrality and Nationalism, but also Japanese history. Among others, his research is focused on the Neutral and Non-aligned Countries at the Vienna Follow-up meeting. He is co-editor of the interview volume *Diplomatie am Ende des Kalten Krieges. Erinnerungen an die dritte KSZE-Folgekonferenz in Wien 1986–1989, Baden-Baden 2025.*

Jussi M. Hanhimäki
is a historian who teaches as a professor at the Graduate Institute of International and Development Studies in Geneva. His research focuses on the history of the Cold War, U.S. foreign policy, and transatlantic relations. Among other works he co-edited the book *Neutrality and Neutralism in the Global Cold War: Between or within the blocs?*, London 2015. For his research, he has received several awards, including the Bernath-Preis der Gesellschaft für Geschichte der amerikanischen Außenbeziehungen.

Nina Hechenblaikner
was a research associate and is a PhD-candidate at the University of Innsbruck. Her research interests include diplomatic history, the Cold War and human rights. In her most recent publication 'Diplomatie und ihre Einflüsse. Prägende Akteursgruppen *für die* Verhandlungen zur humanitären Dimension beim dritten KSZE-Folgetreffen in Wien (1986–1989)', *Zeitschrift* für *Geschichtswissenschaften* 35 (2024), p. 154–173 she shows how approaches of New Diplomatic History can be applied to the Vienna CSCE Follow-up Meeting.

Wanda Jarząbek
is a professor at the Institute of Political Studies of the Polish Academy of Sciences. Her research focusses on 1989 and its effects, Central Europe on transition, politics of memory, WW II as an object of politics of memory in different countries and the Cold War. Among other works she co-edited the book *Kommunismus und Europa: Europapolitik und vorstellungen europäischer kommunistischer Parteien im Kalten Krieg*, Paderborn 2016. In 2019, she was awarded the Ritterkreuz des Ehrenzeichens für Wissenschaft und Kunst by the Federal President of Austria.

Jonas Kaiser
was a research assistant and is a PhD-candidate at the University of Hildesheim. His research interests include the history of security and diplomacy as well as the Cold War. In his dissertation, he deals with the development of European security policy between the CDE in Stockholm and the signing of the Treaty of Conventional Armed Forces in Europe. Insights into this can be read in his most recent publication 'Von Stockholm *über* Wien nach Paris. Vertrauens- und Sicherheitsbildende Maßnahmen und das KSE-Mandat im Rahmen des KSZE-Prozesses 1984–1990', in: Fieseler/Nagornaia (eds.), *Der Zerfall der Sowjetunion und das Ende der DDR als historische Zäsuren*, Wiesbaden 2024, p- 1–13.

Miroslav Kunštát
is a historian at the Department of German and Austrian Studies at Charles University in Prague. His research focuses on Czech-German and Czech-Austrian relations after 1945, the history of churches and religion in the 20th century, as well as current political and social issues in German-speaking countries. He is the author and co-author of several publications on these topics, including *Nachbarn. Ein österreichisch-tschechisches Geschichtsbuch*, Weitra 2019.

Roland Ernst Laimer
was a student assistant at the Institute of Contemporary History at the University of Innsbruck. In his master's thesis *Die KSZE und der Umweltschutz. Korb II beim Wiener ZE-Folgetreffen (1986–1989) aus Perspektive der Ballhausplatzdiplomatie* he analyzed the negotiations on environmental protection at the third CSCE Follow-up Meeting in Vienna.

Matthias Peter
was a historian at the Institute for Contemporary History Munich-Berlin, where he contributed to numerous editions of documents on the foreign policy of the Federal Republic of Germany. Among his many publications is his published dissertation *Die Bundesrepublik im KSZE-Prozess 1975–1983. Die Umkehrung der Diplomatie*, Berlin-München 2015.

Willi Schrenk
was a research assistant at the Institute for Contemporary History Munich-Berlin. His research focuses on the history of the Cold war, German-German relation at the CSCE, and the link between the Cold War and current political events. He is co-editor of the interview volume *Diplomatie am Ende des Kalten Krieges. Erinnerungen an die dritte KSZE-Folgekonferenz in Wien 1986–1989, Baden-Baden 2025*.

Hermann Wentker
is a historian and head of the Berlin department at the Institute for Contemporary History. His research focuses on the history of international relations in the 19th century and the history of the German Democratic Republic (GDR), with a particular emphasis on church policy, foreign policy, and legal history. Together with Helmut Altrichter, he co-edited the volume *Der KSZE-Prozess. Vom Kalten Krieg zu einem neuen Europa 1975 bis 1990*, München 2011.

The CSCE Follow-up Meeting in Vienna (1986–1989)

An Introduction

Nina Hechenblaikner and Andrea Brait

1 From Helsinki to Vienna via Belgrade and Madrid[1]

The Conference on Security and Cooperation in Europe (CSCE) is regarded as one of the high points of the so-called policy of détente, the need for which had become apparent after various escalations of the Cold War in the 1950s and early 1960s. It was based on Soviet proposals for a pan-European security conference in 1954 and 1966, but the so-called West – the member states of the European Communities (EC) and NATO – responded cautiously, demanding that all relevant issues relating to human and civil rights be dealt with at the same time.[2] In 1970 the NATO Council finally agreed to a proposal made in the previous year by the Warsaw Pact to hold a conference on peacekeeping and political cooperation, on the condition that there had to be progress in the negotiations on the German question. This was achieved with the so-called Eastern Treaties of 1970, the Four-Power Agreement on the status of Berlin and the German-German Basic Treaty of 1972.[3]

After multilateral preparatory talks in Dipoli from November 1972 to June 1973, the CSCE finally began in July 1973 with a meeting of the foreign ministers of a total of 35 states (seven Warsaw Pact states, thirteen neutral or non-aligned states and the fifteen NATO states), with Canada and the USA being included at the request of the EC states. The negotiations were concluded with the signing of the Final Act on 1 August 1975 in Helsinki by the heads of state

---

1 This volume was printed, translated and copyedited with the support of the Austrian Science Fund (Fonds zur Förderung der wissenschaftlichen Forschung, FWF) (PUB 1144–P). Previously untranslated German-language sources were translated for this chapter.

2 On the prehistory of the CSCE see e.g. Peter Ruggenthaler/Anna Steiner, "Der Weg nach Helsinki. Entspannung mit Bonn als letzte Etappe auf dem Weg zur Einberufung der Konferenz über Sicherheit und Zusammenarbeit in Europa", in: Michael Borchard/Stefan Karner et al. (eds.), *Entspannung im Kalten Krieg. Der Weg zum Moskauer Vertrag und zur KSZE*, Graz-Wien 2020, p. 677–701.

3 See Thomas Fischer, "Die Sowjetunion, Österreich und die finnische KSZE-Initiative vom 5. Mai 1969", in: Wolfgang Mueller/Michael Portmann (eds.), *Osteuropa vom Weltkrieg zur Wende* (Zentraleuropa-Studien 10), Wien 2007, p. 313–339.

and government of the participating states.[4] The CSCE focussed on three relevant subject areas, which were negotiated in so-called "baskets" that also structure the final document: Basket I covered chiefly issues of security in Europe, Basket II focussed on cooperation in the fields of economy, science, technology and environment and Basket III dealt with issues of human and civil rights as well as information and cultural exchange. Finally, a Basket IV dealt with the consequences of the conference. The neutral and non-aligned states (N+N) contributed significantly to the success of the conference by tabling compromises that were acceptable to all states.[5] The Final Act was viewed favourably by both military blocs: the Warsaw Pact states saw the inviolability of their borders confirmed and the West hoped for progress with regard to the protection of human rights in the so-called Eastern bloc states. By agreeing to continue the talks, an East-West forum was established that enabled mutual influence through regular communication across the blocs, including the N+N states.[6]

The signing of the Final Act is often described as the high point of the policy of détente,[7] which was supported by the so-called Ostpolitik of the German chancellor, Willy Brandt, and the policy of so-called "active neutrality" practised by his Austrian counterpart, Bruno Kreisky, together with the Swedish prime minister, Olof Palme.[8] However, the first two Follow-up Meetings in Belgrade

---

4 Final Act of the Conference on Security and Cooperation in Europe, 1 August 1975. See e.g. Oliver Bange/Gottfried Niedhart (eds.), *Helsinki 1975 and the Transformation of Europe*, New York-Oxford 2008.

5 See e.g. Hanspeter Neuhold (ed.), *CSCE: N+N Perspectives. The Process of the Conference on Security and Cooperation in Europe from the Viewpoint of the Neutral and Non-aligned Participating States*, Wien 1987; Thomas Fischer, *Neutral Power in the CSCE. The N+N States and the Making of the Helsinki Accords 1975* (Wiener Schriften zur Internationalen Politik Vol. 12), Baden-Baden 2009.

6 Andrea Brait/Michael Gehler, "The CSCE Vienna Follow-up Meeting and Alois Mock, 1986–1989", in: Helmut Wohnout/Michael Gehler et al. (eds.), *Christian Democracy and the Fall of Communism* (Civitas. Studies in Christian Democracy 1), Leuven 2019, p. 75–92, on p. 79.

7 See e.g. Gerd Schneider/Christiane Toyka-Seid, *Entspannungspolitik*, https://www.bpb.de/kurz-knapp/lexika/das-junge-politik-lexikon/320215/entspannungspolitik/, accessed 12.11.2023.

8 See e.g. Wilfried Loth/Georges-Henri Soutou (eds.), *The Making of Détente. Eastern and Western Europe in the Cold War, 1965–75* (Cold War History Series Vol. 20), London 2008; Angela Romano, *From Détente in Europe to European Détente. How the West Shaped the Helsinki CSCE* (Euroclio Vol. 44), Bruxelles-New York 2009; Poul Villaume/Odd A. Westad (eds.), *Perforating the Iron Curtain. European Détente, Transatlantic Relations, and the Cold War, 1965–1985*, Copenhagen 2010; Steven Casey (ed.), *The Cold War. Volume IV: From Détente to the End of the Cold War* (Critical Concepts in Military, Strategic, and Security Studies), Abingdon-Oxon 2013; Stephan Kieninger, *The Diplomacy of Détente. Cooperative Security Policies from Helmut Schmidt to George Shultz* (Cold War History Series), London 2018; Maximilian Graf, "European Détente and the CSCE. Austria and the East-Central European Theatre in the 1970s and 1980s",

(1977–1978) and Madrid (1981–1983) took place under different circumstances and cannot be counted as successes.[9] Differing objectives, increasingly strident demands regarding the protection of human rights and renewed tensions in East-West relations in general – in particular the Russian intervention in Afghanistan in 1979, the NATO Double-Track Decision in 1979, the boycott of the 1980 Summer Olympics in Moscow and the imposition of martial law in Poland in 1981 – put considerable strain on the negotiations.[10] In the end, the N+N played a major role in ensuring that the CSCE process did not come to a standstill and that at least an agreement on its continuation could be reached.[11]

By the time the Vienna CSCE Follow-up Meeting (1986–1989) began, the global political environment had again changed dramatically, a process associated in particular with the reforms introduced in the Soviet Union by the new General Secretary of the Communist Party of the Soviet Union (CPSU), Mikhail

---

in: Nicolas Badalassi/Sarah B. Snyder (eds.), *The CSCE and the End of the Cold War. Diplomacy, Societies and Human Rights, 1972–1990*, New York, NY 2019, p. 249–274; Borchard/Karner et al. (eds.), *Entspannung im Kalten Krieg.*

9 See e.g. Hermann Volle/Wolfgang Wagner (eds.), *Das Belgrader KSZE-Folgetreffen. Der Fortgang des Entspannungsprozesses in Europa in Beiträgen und Dokumenten aus dem Europa-Archiv*, Bonn 1978; Jussi M. Hanhimäki, "Ironies and Turning Points. Détente in Perspective", in: Odd A. Westad (ed.), *Reviewing the Cold War. Approaches, Interpretations, Theory* (Cass Series: Cold War History 1), London ²2001, p. 326–342; Franz Ceska, "Détente und KSZE-Prozess. Österreich zwischen Helsinki (1975) und Madrid (1983)", in: Oliver Rathkolb/Otto M. Maschke et al. (eds.), *Mit anderen Augen gesehen. Internationale Perzeptionen Österreichs 1955–1990. Österreichische Nationalgeschichte nach 1945, Band 2* (Schriftenreihe des Forschungsinstitutes für politisch-historische Studien der Dr.-Wilfried-Haslauer-Bibliothek, Salzburg 6/Sonderbd. 2), Wien-Köln-Weimar 2002, p. 507–521; Wanda Jarząbek, "Lost illusions? The Polish government and human rights issues from Helsinki to Belgrade, 1975–1978", in: Vladimir Bilandžić/Dittmar Dahlmann et al. (eds.), *From Helsinki to Belgrade. The First CSCE Follow-up Meeting and the Crisis of Détente* (Internationale Beziehungen: Theorie und Geschichte Vol. 10), Göttingen-Bonn 2012, p. 305–320; Philip Rosin, "Neutralität in der Menschenrechtsfrage? Die Schweiz in Belgrad und Madrid", in: Matthias Peter/Hermann Wentker (eds.), *Die KSZE im Ost-West-Konflikt. Internationale Politik und gesellschaftliche Transformation 1975–1990* (Schriftenreihe der Vierteljahrshefte für Zeitgeschichte Sondernummer), Berlin-Boston 2013, p. 173–189; Douglas Selvage, "The Superpowers and the Conference on Security and Cooperation in Europe, 1977–1983", in: Peter/Wentker (eds.), *Die KSZE im Ost-West-Konflikt*, p. 15–58.

10 See e.g. Leopoldo Nuti (ed.), *The Crisis of Détente in Europe. From Helsinki to Gorbachev, 1975–1985* (Cold War History Series Vol. 23), London 2009; Matthias Peter, "Saving Détente. The Federal Republic of Germany and the CSCE in the 1980s", in: Nicolas Badalassi/Sarah B. Snyder (eds.), *The CSCE and the End of the Cold War. Diplomacy, Societies and Human Rights, 1972–1990*, New York, NY 2019, p. 275–304.

11 See Thomas Fischer, *Keeping the Process Alive. The N+N and the CSCE Follow-Up from Helsinki to Vienna* (1975–1986) (Zürcher Beiträge zur Sicherheitspolitik Vol. 84), Zurich 2012.

Gorbachev.[12] Expectations for the Follow-up Meeting were correspondingly high. In his opening address on 23 September 1986, the Austrian foreign minister, Peter Jankowitsch, announced that it would be "one of the largest and most significant conferences to have taken place in the Austrian capital since the Congress of Vienna of 1814/15".[13] The two major areas of negotiation at the Vienna CSCE Follow-up Meeting were undoubtedly security and humanitarian concerns. Notable successes were achieved in both: mandates were agreed for further conferences on confidence- and security-building measures (CSBMs; Stockholm II) and negotiations on conventional armed forces in Europe (CFE); in the area of humanitarian concerns, consensus was reached on human rights at the normative and operational levels, including the organisation of a series of human rights conferences.[14] The Vienna Concluding Document can be interpreted as a bridge facilitating the reorganisation of Europe after the upheavals of 1989. Although the CSCE's contribution to these developments is subject to debate,[15] the creation of a CSCE system with a human dimension and the agreement on negotiations on military confidence-building and conventional disarmament in January 1989 can be described as the beginning of the end of the East-West conflict, even if this was perceived in a completely different manner at the time than it appears with the benefit of hindsight.

---

12 See e.g. Astrid von Borcke, *Die Abrüstungsvorschläge Gorbatschows und das „neue Denken". Indizien aus der sowjetischen Innenpolitik* (Berichte des Bundesinstituts für Ostwissenschaftliche und Internationale Studien Vol. 32), Köln 1987; Vojtech Mastny, "Did Gorbachev liberate Eastern Europe?", in: Olav Njølstad (ed.), *The Last Decade of the Cold War. From Conflict Escalation to Conflict Transformation* (Cass Series: Cold War History 5), London-New York 2004, p. 402–423; Marie-Pierre Rey, "Gorbachev's New Thinking and Europe, 1985–1989", in: Frédéric Bozo/Marie-Pierre Rey et al. (eds.), *Europe and the End of the Cold War. A Reappraisal* (Cold War History Series 19), London-New York 2008, p. 23–35; Yuliya von Saal, *KSZE-Prozess und Perestroika in der Sowjetunion. Demokratisierung, Werteumbruch und Auflösung 1985–1991* (Quellen und Darstellungen zur Zeitgeschichte Vol. 100), München 2014; Andrei Grachev, "Gorbachev and the 'New Political Thinking'", in: Wolfgang Mueller/Michael Gehler et al. (eds.), *The Revolutions of 1989. A Handbook* (Internationale Geschichte/International History 2), Wien 2015, p. 33–46; Archie Brown, "Mikhail Gorbachev and the Politics of Perestroika", in: *Russian History* 49 (2022), issue 2–4, p. 123–145, doi: 10.30965/18763316-12340044.

13 Rede von Außenminister Dr. Peter Jankowitsch zur Eröffnung des KSZE-Vorbereitungstreffens im Redoutensaal, Wien, 23. September 1986, ÖStA, AdR, II-Pol 1986, GZ 803.01/51-II.7/86.

14 Das abschließende Dokument des KSZE-Folgetreffens in Wien vom 15. Januar 1989, in: *Europa-Archiv* 44 (1989), issue 5, D133-D164.

15 See e.g. Matthias Peter/Hermann Wentker, "'Helsinki-Mythos' oder 'Helsinki-Effekt'? Der KSZE-Prozess zwischen internationaler Politik und gesellschaftlicher Transformation", in: Peter/Wentker (eds.), *Die KSZE im Ost-West-Konflikt*, p. 1–14.

2 State of Research

The CSCE has long remained in the shadows of research in contemporary history. This became particularly apparent in 2009 and 2014, when numerous studies on the upheavals of 1989 were published without any significant reference to the CSCE.[16] By contrast, political science took an interest in the CSCE process at an early stage.[17] Moreover, some of the diplomats involved published their assessments and experiences.[18] There are also publications on the third CSCE Follow-up Meeting (1986–1989) in Vienna, some of which would perhaps be better categorised as sources of oral history[19] while others are works of political science.[20]

---

16 For an overview see Wolfgang Mueller, "The Revolutions of 1989: An Introduction", in: Mueller/Gehler et al. (eds.), *The Revolutions of 1989*, p. 3–30.

17 See Boris Meissner (ed.), *Oststaaten und europäische Sicherheit 1972–1975. Analysen und Dokumentation*, Köln 1977; Frenzke Dietrich/Alexander Uschakow (eds.), *Die Oststaaten, das sowjetische Bündnissystem und die KSZE vor und nach Helsinki*, Köln 1980; Jost Delbrück/Ropers Norbert et al. (eds.), *Grünbuch zu den Folgewirkungen der KSZE*, Köln 1977; Deutsche Gesellschaft für Friedens- und Konfliktforschung (ed.), *DGFK-Jahrbuch 1979/80. Zur Entspannungspolitik in Europa*, Baden-Baden 1980; Deutsche Gesellschaft für Friedens- und Konfliktforschung (ed.), *DGFK Jahrbuch 1982/83. Zur Lage Europas im globalen Spannungsfeld*, Baden-Baden 1983.

18 On this see the individual contributions in Hermann Volle/Wolfgang Wagner (eds.), *KSZE. Konferenz über Sicherheit und Zusammenarbeit in Europa in Beiträgen und Dokumenten aus dem Europa-Archiv*, Bonn 1976; Volle/Wagner, *Das Belgrader* KSZE*-Folgetreffen*; Hermann Volle/Wolfgang Wagner (eds.), *Das Madrider KSZE-Folgetreffen. Der Fortgang des KSZE-Prozesses in Europa in Beiträgen und Dokumenten aus dem Europa-Archiv*, Bonn 1984; Victor-Yves Ghebali, *La diplomatie de la Détente. La CSCE, d'Helsinki à Vienne (1973–1989)*, Brüssel 1989; Michael Zielinski, *Die neutralen und blockfreien Staaten und ihre Rolle im KSZE-Prozeß* (Nomos Universitätsschriften – Politik Vol. 13), Baden-Baden 1990; Wilfried v. Bredow, *Der KSZE-Prozess. Von der Zähmung zur Auflösung des Ost-West-Konflikts*, Darmstadt 1992; Peter Schlotter, *Die KSZE im Ost-West-Konflikt. Wirkung einer internationalen Institution* (Studien der Hessischen Stiftung Friedens- und Konfliktforschung Vol. 32), Frankfurt am Main-New York 1999.

19 For the views of an Austrian and a German diplomat involved see Stefan Lehne, *The Vienna Meeting of the Conference on Security and Cooperation in Europe, 1986–1989. A Turning Point in East-West Relations* (Austrian Institute for International Affairs Series), Boulder-San Francisco-Oxford 1991; Hans-Heinrich Wrede, *KSZE in Wien. Kursbestimmung für Europas Zukunft*, Köln 1990.

20 See e.g. Neuhold, *CSCE: N+N Perspectives*; Karl E. Birnbaum, "Die KSZE nach der Stockholmer Konferenz als Rahmen für die Zusammenarbeit zwischen Ost und West in Europa", in: *Europa-Archiv* 42 (1987), p. 171–178; Wilhelm Bruns, "Mehr Substanz in den Ost-West-Beziehungen. Zur dritten KSZE-Folgekonferenz in Wien", in: *Aus Politik und Zeitgeschichte* (1989), issue 12, p. 3–9; Michael Groth, "Fortschritte im KSZE-Prozeß. Das dritte Folgetreffen in Wien", in: *Europa-Archiv* 44 (1989), p. 95–102; Karl E. Birnbaum/Ingo Peters,

Yet for a long time, historians hardly dealt with the CSCE in any depth. In general accounts of the Cold War, it often figured as "an interlude of détente in the rivalry of the superpowers".[21] However, in order to determine more precisely the role and importance of the CSCE process in ending the East-West conflict in Europe[22] in a multifactorial context, it is necessary to analyse a wide range of sources. The project "The CSCE Process: Multilateral Conference Diplomacy and its Consequences 1975–1989/90", carried out by the Institute of Contemporary History Munich-Berlin (Institut für Zeitgeschichte, IfZ) in cooperation with the Universities of Paris IV and Erlangen-Nuremberg, has contributed significantly to advancing our knowledge. Within this framework, studies were carried out on the role of important participating states: Western and Eastern as well as neutral and non-aligned.[23] While the vast majority of previous contributions and monographs concentrated on the CSCE Conference in Helsinki from 1973 to 1975 and the Final Act of 1975,[24] with only occasional references to

"Die beiden deutschen Staaten auf dem Wiener KSZE-Folgetreffen", in: Karl E. Birnbaum/ Ingo Peters (eds.), *Zwischen Abgrenzung und Verantwortungsgemeinschaft. Zur KSZE-Politik der beiden deutschen Staaten 1984–1989*, Baden-Baden 1991, p. 71–105; Arie Bloed/ Pieter van Dijk (eds.), *The Human Dimension of the Helsinki Process. The Vienna Follow-up Meeting and its Aftermath* (International Studies in Human Rights Vol. 20), Dordrecht-Boston-Norwell 1991; Stephan Martini, *Die sicherheitspolitische Funktion der KSZE im entspannungspolitischen Konzept der Bundesrepublik Deutschland 1975–1990*, Berlin 2006.

21 Matthias Peter, *Die Bundesrepublik im KSZE-Prozess 1975–1983. Die Umkehrung der Diplomatie* (Quellen und Darstellungen zur Zeitgeschichte Vol. 105), Berlin 2015, p. 10.

22 On differing views of the CSCE see Peter/Wentker, "'Helsinki-Mythos' oder 'Helsinki-Effekt'?". See also the debates in the special issue "CSCE, the German Question, and the Warsaw Pact" of the *Journal of Cold War Studies* 18 (2016), issue 3.

23 Anja Hanisch, *Die DDR im KSZE-Prozess 1972–1985. Zwischen Ostabhängigkeit, Westabgrenzung und Ausreisebewegung* (Quellen und Darstellungen zur Zeitgeschichte Vol. 91), München 2012; Benjamin Gilde, *Österreich im KSZE-Prozess 1969–1983. Neutraler Vermittler in humanitärer Mission* (Quellen und Darstellungen zur Zeitgeschichte Vol. 98), München 2013; Philip Rosin, *Die Schweiz im KSZE-Prozess 1972–1983. Einfluss durch Neutralität* (Quellen und Darstellungen zur Zeitgeschichte Vol. 99), München 2014; von Saal, *KSZE-Prozess und Perestroika in der Sowjetunion*; Peter, *Die Bundesrepublik im KSZE-Prozess 1975–1983*; Veronika Heyde, *Frankreich im KSZE-Prozess. Diplomatie im Namen der europäischen Sicherheit* (Quellen und Darstellungen zur Zeitgeschichte Vol. 113), Berlin-Boston 2017.

24 See e.g. Jussi M. Hanhimäki, "'They can write it in Swahili'. Kissinger, the Soviets, and the Helsinki Accords, 1973–75", in: *Journal of Transatlantic Studies* 1 (2003), p. 37–58; Carla Meneguzzi Rostagni (ed.), *The Helsinki Process. A Historical Reappraisal*, Padova 2005; Bange/Niedhart, *Helsinki 1975 and the Transformation of Europe*; Andreas Wenger/Vojtech Mastny et al. (eds.), *Origins of the European Security System. The Helsinki Process Revisited, 1965–75* (CSS Studies in Security and International Relations), London-New York 2008; Nuti, *The Crisis of Détente in Europe*; Romano, *From Détente in Europe to European Détente*;

the follow-up conferences in Belgrade (1977–1979)[25] and Madrid (1980–1983),[26] the IfZ project focussed on the process character of the CSCE up to 1983, looking at both state and civil society actors. However, due to restricted archival access, the research concentrated on the years leading up to 1975 and 1983. With a few exceptions, this also applies to studies on the Warsaw Pact states.[27]

As a result, there are hardly any source-based studies on the CSCE at the end of the 1980s. This applies in particular to the third Follow-up Meeting in Vienna (1986–1989), whose significance for the end of the East-West conflict has therefore hardly been researched.[28] Research desiderata include the role of the N+N in connection with the end of the Cold War, although their

---

Villaume/Westad, *Perforating the Iron Curtain*; Petri Hakkarainen, *A State of Peace in Europe. West Germany and the CSCE, 1966–1975*, New York-Oxford 2011.

25 See Bilandžić/Dahlmann et al. (eds.), *From Helsinki to Belgrade*.

26 See Sarah B. Snyder, "The Foundation for Vienna. A Reassessment of the CSCE in the Mid-1980s", in: *Cold War History 10* (2010), issue 4, p. 493–512; Sarah B. Snyder, *Human rights activism and the end of the Cold War. A Transnational History of the Helsinki Network* (Human Rights in History), New York 2011, p. 135–157.

27 The 1980s are touched upon only in the studies by Wanda Jarząbek on Poland and Douglas Selvage and Walter Süß on the GDR: Wanda Jarząbek, "Preserving the Status Quo or Promoting Change. The Role of the CSCE in the Perception of Polish Authorities", in: Bange/Niedhart (eds.), *Helsinki 1975 and the Transformation of Europe*, p. 144–159; Jarząbek, "Lost illusions?"; Wanda Jarząbek, "Troublesome Human Rights. The Polish Strategy between the Belgrade and Madrid CSCE Follow-up Conferences", in: Peter/Wentker (eds.), *Die KSZE im Ost-West-Konflikt*, p. 121–135; Douglas Selvage/Walter Süß, *Staatssicherheit und KSZE-Prozess. MfS zwischen SED und KGB (1972–1989)* (Analysen und Dokumente Vol. 54), Göttingen 2019. On Bulgaria see Kostadin Grozev/Jordan Baev, "Bulgaria, Balkan Diplomacy and the Road to Helsinki", in: Bange/Niedhart (eds.), *Helsinki 1975 and the Transformation of Europe*, p. 160–174; Jordan Baev, "Bulgaria and the Warsaw Pact consultations on the CSCE Process. From Helsinki to Belgrade", in: Bilandžić/Dahlmann et al. (eds.), *From Helsinki to Belgrade*, p. 107–118. On Hungary and Romania see e.g. Csaba Békés, "The Warsaw Pact, the German Question and the Birth of the CSCE Process, 1961–1970", in: Bange/Niedhart (eds.), *Helsinki 1975 and the Transformation of Europe*, p. 113–128; Mihail E. Ionescu, "Romania, Ostpolitik and the CSCE 1967–1975", in: Bange/Niedhart (eds.), *Helsinki 1975 and the Transformation of Europe*, p. 129–143. On Czechoslovakia see Benjamin Müller, "Von der Konfrontation zum Dialog. Charta 77, Menschenrechte und 'Samtene Revolution' in der Tschechoslowakei 1975–1989", in: Helmut Altrichter/Hermann Wentker (eds.), *Der KSZE-Prozess. Vom Kalten Krieg zu einem neuen Europa 1975 bis 1990* (Zeitgeschichte im Gespräch 11), München 2011, p. 99–110.

28 See e.g. Altrichter/Wentker (eds.), *Der KSZE-Prozess*; Oliver Bange, "Der KSZE-Prozess und die sicherheitspolitische Dynamik des Ost-West-Konflikts 1970–1990", in: Oliver Bange/Bernd Lemke (eds.), *Wege zur Wiedervereinigung. Die beiden deutschen Staaten in ihren Bündnissen 1970 bis 1990* (Beiträge zur Militärgeschichte 75), München 2013, p. 87–104; Peter/Wentker (eds.), *Die KSZE im Ost-West-Konflikt*; von Saal, *KSZE-Prozess und Perestroika in der Sowjetunion*.

importance as mediators between the blocs has been repeatedly emphasised in the literature.[29] By the same token, there are still few findings on the attitude and influence of transnational actors such as non-governmental organisations and opposition groups in the CSCE process of the late 1980s.[30] The research situation is, of course, a result of embargoes on state documents – with the exception of those from the GDR, which is why the first research findings are already available on that country.[31] Studies on other states have therefore had to fall back on other sources.[32]

In consequence, the existing studies leave many questions unanswered. For instance, the significance of the CSCE agreements in relation to new demands for compliance with human rights and fundamental freedoms within Eastern Europe is quite controversial.[33] The role of the CSCE with regard to the

29 See Thomas Fischer, "Austria and the Helsinki Process", in: Arnold Suppan/Wolfgang Mueller (eds.), *"Peaceful Coexistence" or "Iron Curtain". Austria, Neutrality, and Eastern Europe in the Cold War and Détente, 1955–1989* (Europa Orientalis 7), Wien-Berlin-Piscataway, NJ 2009, p. 168–202; Fischer, *Neutral Power in the CSCE*; Fischer, *Keeping the Process Alive*; Gilde, *Österreich im KSZE-Prozess 1969–1983*; Jussi M. Hanhimäki, "Non-aligned to what? European neutrality and the Cold War", in: Sandra Bott/Jussi M. Hanhimäki et al. (eds.), *Neutrality and Neutralism in the Global Cold War. Between or within the blocs?* (Cold War History Series), Abingdon-Oxon-New York, NY 2016, p. 17–32.

30 Some general statements can be found in Kurt P. Tudyka, "Nichtstaatliche Organisationen und die OSZE", in: *OSZE-Jahrbuch 7* (2001), p. 503–513, on p. 503 f.; Anja Mihr, *Amnesty International in der DDR. Der Einsatz für Menschenrechte im Visier der Stasi*, Berlin 2002, p. 116 f.; Christie Miedema, *Not a Movement of Dissidents. Amnesty International Beyond the Iron Curtain* (Schriftenreihe Menschenrechte im 20. Jahrhundert Vol. 4), Göttingen 2019; Ned Richardson-Little, *The Human Rights Dictatorship. Socialism, Global Solidarity and Revolution in East Germany* (Human Rights in History), Cambridge 2020.

31 See Erhard Crome/Jochen Franzke, "Die SED-Führung und die Wiener KSZE-Konferenz 1986 bis 1989. Dokumente aus dem Parteiarchiv", in: *Deutschland Archiv 26* (1993), p. 905–914; Selvage/Süß, *Staatsicherheit und KSZE-Prozess*. See also Jens Kaiser, "Zwischen angestrebter Eigenständigkeit und traditioneller Unterordnung. Zur Ambivalenz des Verhältnisses von sowjetischer und DDR-Außenpolitik in den achtziger Jahren", in: *Deutschland Archiv 24* (1991), p. 478–495.

32 See e.g. Ralf Roloff, *Auf dem Weg zur Neuordnung Europas. Die Regierungen Kohl/Genscher und die KSZE-Politik der Bundesrepublik Deutschland von 1986 bis 1992*, Vierow 1995.

33 See Snyder, *Human Rights Activism and the End of the Cold War*; Daniel C. Thomas, *The Helsinki Effect. International Norms, Human Rights, and the Demise of Communism*, Princeton, N.J. 2001; Daniel C. Thomas, "Human Rights Ideas, the Demise of Communism and the End of the Cold War", in: *Journal of Cold War Studies* 7 (2005), issue 2, p. 110–141. On the broader topic see also e.g. Floribert Baudet, "'It was Cold War and we wanted to win'. Human Rights, 'Détente', and the CSCE", in: Andreas Wenger/Vojtech Mastny et al. (eds.), *Origins of the European Security System. The Helsinki Process Revisited, 1965–75* (CSS Studies in Security and International Relations), London-New York 2008, p. 183–198; Gregory F. Domber, "Transatlantic Relations, Human Rights, and Power Politics", in: Poul

development of the global human rights regime has not yet been substantiated with appropriate sources.[34] Similarly, the question of a new security order after the conclusion of the Stockholm Conference on Confidence- and Security-Building Measures and Disarmament in Europe (CDE)[35] and the Intermediate-Range Nuclear Forces (INF) Treaty, on which some contemporary publications exist,[36] has so far hardly been analysed with reference to the CSCE process. This volume aims to close some of these gaps, at least in part.

3 The Chapters

While this publication brings together contributions that stem directly from the research of the German-Austrian-Swiss project "The CSCE Follow-up Meeting in Vienna (1986–1989). Struggling for Human Rights and European Security at the End of the Cold War",[37] the aim was also to broaden these

Villaume/Odd A. Westad (eds.), *Perforating the Iron Curtain. European Détente, Transatlantic Relations, and the Cold War, 1965–1985*, Copenhagen 2010, p. 195–214; Christian P. Peterson, *Globalizing Human Rights. Private Citizens, the Soviet Union, and the West*, New York-London 2012; Rasmus Mariager/Karl Molin et al. (eds.), *Human Rights in Europe during the Cold War* (Cold War History Series), New York 2014. But see e.g. the assessment of Jeremi Suri, "Détente and human rights. American and West European perspectives on international change", in: *Cold War History* 8 (2008), issue 4, p. 527–545, on p. 540.

34 On the development of a human rights regime see Jan Eckel, *Die Ambivalenz des Guten. Menschenrechte in der internationalen Politik seit den 1940ern*, Göttingen 2014; Jan Eckel/Samuel Moyn (eds.), *Moral für die Welt? Menschenrechtspolitik in den 1970er Jahren*, Göttingen 2012; Peterson, *Globalizing Human Rights*; Samuel Moyn, *The Last Utopia. Human Rights in History*, Cambridge 2010; Stefan-Ludwig Hoffmann (ed.), *Moralpolitik. Geschichte der Menschenrechte im 20. Jahrhundert*, Göttingen 2010; Lynn Hunt, *Inventing Human Rights. A History*, London 2007.

35 See on the Stockholm CDE the exhaustive account by two diplomats involved, Oleg Grinevsky/Lynn M. Hansen, *Making Peace. Confidence and Security in a New Europe*, New York 2009.

36 Among contemporary studies see esp. Hans-Joachim Spanger/Vladimir Handl, *Wie weiter bei der Vertrauensbildung? Zu den Wiener VSBM-Verhandlungen und darüber hinaus* (HSFK-Report Vol. 6), Frankfurt am Main 1989; Dewitt David/Hans Rattinger (eds.), *East-West Arms Control. Challenges for the Western Alliance*, London-New York 1992; Michael R. Lucas (ed.), *The CSCE in the 1990s. Constructing European Security and Cooperation* (Demokratie, Sicherheit, Frieden Vol. 83), Baden-Baden 1993; Hans-Joachim Schmidt, "Die Anfangsphase der Wiener Verhandlungen über konventionelle Streitkräfte in Europa (VKSE)", in: Erwin Müller/Götz Neuneck (eds.), *Abrüstung und Konventionelle Stabilität in Europa* (Demokratie, Sicherheit, Frieden 63), Baden-Baden 1990, p. 11–36.

37 This was a cooperative project funded jointly by the German Research Foundation (DFG), the Austrian Science Fund (FWF) and the Swiss National Science Foundation (SNF). It consisted of the following sub-projects:

research perspectives. It was particularly important to include developments in the Warsaw Pact countries, as a sub-project of the project proposal planned for these countries was not approved by the German Research Foundation (DFG) and the project therefore had to focus much more strongly than originally planned on the NATO countries and the N+N.[38] The volume also refers to various project cooperations, including with the Ludwig Boltzmann Institute for Research on the Consequences of War (Ludwig Boltzmann Institut für Kriegsfolgenforschung).

The volume opens with two contributions which are dedicated to the CSCE process prior to the Vienna Follow-up Meeting and thus shed light on the prerequisites for the negotiations in the Austrian capital. In her chapter "Moscow and Vienna on the Road to Helsinki", Anna Graf-Steiner focuses on the importance attached to Austria by the Soviet Union in realising its idea of a European security conference in the 1960s. The analysis clearly shows, on the one hand, the persistence of Austrian diplomacy with regard to anchoring the humanitarian dimension and, on the other, the personal commitment of the Austrian chancellor, Bruno Kreisky, in the course of bilateral talks to promote the conclusion of the CSCE Final Act.

The chapter "From Helsinki to Vienna" by Herman Wentker provides an overview of developments between 1977, the start of the Follow-up Meeting in Belgrade, and 1986, the start of the Follow-up Meeting in Vienna. The focus of the analysis is on the interactions between the CSCE negotiations and the global political tensions at the time. The study shows that the agreements were by no means able to change the international order or destabilise dictatorships, but that they did form a basis for a commitment to human rights in the Warsaw Pact states, which increased the pressure on the regimes and contributed

---

Breakthrough in Human Rights? The Effects of Change in Eastern Europe on the Vienna Follow-Up Meeting (Institut für Zeitgeschichte/Universität Innsbruck, project leader: Andrea Brait, project assistant: Nina Hechenblaikner).

Cooperation and Confrontation: The Federal Republic of Germany and the German Democratic Republic at the Vienna Follow-Up Meeting (Institut für Zeitgeschichte Munich/Berlin, project leader: Hermann Wentker, project assistant: Willi Schrenk).

From Stockholm to Vienna: Confidence- and Security-Building Measures (CSBM) and CFE Mandate (Institut für Geschichte/Universität Hildesheim, project leader: Michael Gehler, project assistant: Jonas Kaiser).

The N+N: European Security and Human Rights in Vienna (Graduate Institute Geneva, project leader: Jussi Hanhimäki, project assistant: Kai Habel).

38 Since the project was based in German-speaking countries and on account of the travel restrictions in place during the Covid-19 pandemic, which covered much of the project's duration, it focuses on these countries and the relevant subjects and sources. This tendency is reflected in the present volume.

to concessions, for example at the CSCE Meeting of Experts on Human Contacts in Bern in 1986. At the same time, the study shows how stable the opposing basic positions were. With reference to the Soviet Union's abandonment of these positions even before the start of the Vienna Follow-up Meeting, the analysis provides evidence of the frequently cited "Gorbachev factor".

Maximilian Graf has chosen a biographical approach to diplomatic history for his chapter "Austria's 'Mister CSCE' Helmut Liedermann". He emphasises the influence exerted by individuals – in this case Helmut Liedermann, a senior diplomat and the long-standing head of the Austrian delegation – on the course of the CSCE process. In doing so, the analysis sheds light on Liedermann's professional career before, but especially on his involvement in the creation of, the CSCE and the subsequent process, showing how Liedermann's experiences outside the conference influenced his decisions and thus also the guidelines of the Austrian delegation. Liedermann's CSCE career was ultimately crowned by the position of executive secretary at the Vienna Follow-up Meeting. In Graf's assessment, Liedermann was one of the CSCE's creative negotiators, one who made compromises possible and always believed in the success of the process.

In his contribution "The Concluding Document of the Vienna CSCE Follow-up Meeting, 15 January 1989", Michael Gehler examines the Concluding Document's genesis from the perspective of the Austrian delegation and compares the documents of 1975, 1979, 1983, 1986 and 1989. His analysis shows that at the Vienna Follow-up Meeting, significant progress in the negotiations was made only after mid-1988, due mainly to the increasing willingness of the Soviet Union to make concessions and the pressure it exerted on those Warsaw Pact states (above all the GDR and Romania) that wanted to block them. This made it possible for the Vienna Final Document to become the most substantial of its kind besides the Helsinki Final Act, containing the most far-reaching agreements in the areas of security policy and human rights.

The next set of texts looks at individual negotiation topics, focussing on those highlighted both in contemporary discourse and in previous publications, as well as those rarely discussed in the existing scholarship on the CSCE. In her chapter "Negotiations on Cultural Cooperation at the Vienna Follow-up Meeting from the Perspective of the Austrian Foreign Ministry", Andrea Brait takes a general look at the importance of foreign cultural policy for Austria and the significance of cultural cooperation in the CSCE, focusing on the genesis of the agreements reached in this area at the Vienna Follow-up Meeting. The cultural area proves to be the one in which many forms of cross-bloc cooperation were possible and – compared to other topics – final compromises could be found early on in the negotiation process. The analysis clearly shows that not only were concrete cooperation agreements reached, but also fundamental steps taken towards the democratisation of the cultural sector.

Roland Ernst Laimer addresses a topic that has so far received little attention in research on the CSCE. His essay "The 'neglected step-child' of the Vienna CSCE Follow-up Meeting" deals with the negotiations on environmental protection and asks whether Basket II was really – as is so often claimed – of little interest to the negotiators. The focus is on the actions of the Austrian delegation. Austria, the analysis shows, was active in this area of the CSCE and made far-reaching proposals that met with fierce resistance from other participating states – an indication that Basket II was not as uncontroversial as it is often portrayed. Trade-offs between the environment and the economy often played an important role. Subsequent comparison between the proposals submitted and the Concluding Document shows which proposals could be successfully implemented.

The next two contributions address the negotiations in the areas of human rights and security, two closely linked areas that are usually at the centre of research on the CSCE. In her essay "Front Page News or Side Note?", Nina Hechenblaikner analyses the reporting of Die Presse and the Frankfurter Allgemeine Zeitung on this topic. In addition to quantitative and thematic analyses, the focus is on questions of public interest and the influence of human rights organisations. The analysis shows that both newspapers continuously reported on the Follow-up Meeting and especially the negotiations on humanitarian questions, and that various governments and delegations as well as NGOs increasingly made it their business to keep the public informed. Nevertheless, according to many participants, the conference remained a marginal foreign policy issue in terms of public perception.

In his chapter "Questions of Security", Jonas Kaiser analyses the development of the security policy dimension of the CSCE from the first proposal for such a conference in 1954 until after the Vienna Follow-up Meeting. The study emphasises that non-compliance with the provisions agreed in Helsinki led to mistrust between the participating states. The chapter also analyses how the CSCE and other security policy negotiations (such as the CDE and the CFE mandate) influenced each other. Finally, the analysis concludes that the link between security and human rights was transformed into a constructive interrelation in Vienna, contributing significantly to progress in the area of security.

The next chapters focus on the intentions and goals of individual participating states or alliances. These studies shed light on internal difficulties within the blocs and strategies for overcoming them, as well as on the interaction between the CSCE and national politics. In "Shifting Agendas?", Jussi Hanhimäki examines the role of the USA and the Soviet Union at the third CSCE

Follow-up Meeting in Vienna. The chapter analyses the foreign policy goals of the two participating states and the expectations they had of the CSCE, focussing on the topic of human rights. Special consideration is given to the influence of the reforms announced by Gorbachev, which raised high expectations among both the Western participants and the neutral states. The analysis concludes that the decisions of the Vienna Follow-up Meeting ultimately even exceeded these expectations. The United States never saw the CSCE as its main foreign policy interest but as an opportunity to exert influence on the Soviet Union. This seemed to have been achieved in Vienna.

The chapter "European Political Cooperation at the Vienna CSCE Follow-up Meeting (1986–1989)" by Matthias Peter sheds light on the efforts at coordination on the part of EC member states before and during the Vienna Follow-up Meeting. Although European Political Cooperation (EPC) was institutionally consolidated and strengthened with the Single European Act (SEA) – which came into force on 1 July 1987, at an early stage of the Vienna Follow-up Meeting – the analysis clearly shows that there were difficult coordination processes and that it was mainly in Basket II that it was possible to act as a unit with joint proposals. In other areas, national interests were decisive and therefore the states often acted independently of each other or in different. However, with the proposal that was central to the group, EPC succeeded in pushing through a mechanism for the "human dimension".

In the chapter "Divergent Neutral Strategies", Kai Habel looks at the work of the neutral and non-aligned states at the Vienna Follow-up Meeting. The study emphasises the special role of this group of states, which acted as mediators while bringing its own interests to the conference table. The analysis also shows that major divergences arose between individual states, particularly in Vienna. Using the topic of disarmament as an example, the diplomatic strategies pursued by the N+N and how they succeeded in finding and pursuing a common line are explained in more detail. The chapter also shows the challenge the N+N faced in being part of disarmament negotiations within the CSCE.

This is followed by a focus on the actions of Warsaw Pact states. In his chapter "East German Intelligence Perspectives on the CSCE Follow-up Meeting in Vienna", Simon Graham focusses on the actions of the GDR. He examines the assessments of the Main Directorate for Reconnaissance (Hauptverwaltung Aufklärung, HVA) of the GDR Ministry for State Security (MfS) against the background of the incipient changes in Eastern Europe, which were taking place against the backdrop of reforms in the Soviet Union. The analysis shows that the HVA did not pursue a clear or consistent line of argument in its internal papers: Initially, it expected that the Follow-up Meeting would not lead to any significant results; in 1988, it warned the GDR state leadership about the effects of the CSCE agreements in the area of human rights; but after its signing in 1989, the Vienna Final Document was seen as progress in terms of the further development of human rights and in terms of human contacts.

The chapter "A German-German Conflict in a Multilateral Framework" by Willi Schrenk is dedicated to the most contentious issue between the two German states at the third CSCE Follow-up Meeting. The study traces the development of the conflict, which affected all travellers to the GDR, from 1964 until after the conclusion of the Follow-up Meeting. The analysis includes both the conduct of negotiations in Vienna and external factors that ultimately led to concessions on the part of the GDR. It particularly emphasises the GDR's isolation towards the end due to its hard-line position even within its own alliance. The chapter emphasises the special nature of this area of negotiation, as bilateral conflicts were not normally negotiated within the CSCE framework.

The last two contributions are also dedicated to Warsaw Pact states. In the chapter "Human Rights, the Vienna Follow-up Meeting and Political Transformation in the Eastern Bloc", Wanda Jarząbek focuses on the negotiations on political rights and their impact on the upheavals of 1989 and the phase of political transition. It begins by analysing the human rights situation in Poland before the Vienna Follow-up Meeting before going on to look at the interactions between the negotiations in Vienna and developments in Poland. The chapter concludes that the CSCE contributed to better conditions for the political opposition. It can therefore be seen as one, but not the sole or decisive, factor contributing to political change in the Warsaw Pact states.

Mirsolav Kunštát comes to a similar conclusion in his chapter "The Vienna CSCE Follow-up Meeting and Czechoslovakia", which analyses both official state diplomacy at the Vienna Follow-up Meeting and the interactions between the events in Vienna and the actions of dissidents. The study also refers to the negotiation dynamics in Vienna, which were marked by a lack of coordination and various political tensions between individual Warsaw Pact states. Kunštát shows that until the beginning of the revolution in November 1989, critics of the regime constantly referred to the Vienna Final Document in order to highlight various humanitarian abuses and to emphasise their demands. The CSCE thus served as an important support for their arguments.

4 Conclusion

This volume is the first collection of essays to focus on the third CSCE Follow-up Meeting in Vienna. Since the expiration of the archival embargo, government files on this meeting have become accessible in many participating states, enabling research into this phase of the CSCE process. 2019 marked the beginning of the international research project The CSCE Follow-up Meeting in Vienna (1986–1989). Struggling for Human Rights and European Security at the End of the Cold War. First results have already been published[39] with more texts, which will examine different aspects of the Follow-up Meeting, in preparation.

As the contributions to this volume show, the CSCE can be studied from a wide range of perspectives and using a variety of theoretical approaches including biographical approaches, multi-archival studies and media analyses. Many of the studies collected here show a close interaction between the conference and political developments – both globally and nationally. Analyses of interests and negotiation strategies show that the participating states had different expectations of the CSCE Follow-up Meeting, which in many cases can be traced back to their assessment of the CSCE and its potential. Many contributions also point to coordination difficulties within the alliances. A thematic focus on human rights can be identified in this volume. Both country-specific and cross-bloc contributions chose this area of negotiation as their (exemplary) focus. However, the CSCE's security dimension and the interplay between these two aspects are also discussed in detail. Other contributions are devoted to topics that have so far been neglected by research. What all the chapters have in common is the realisation that far-reaching results were achieved in Vienna. This is due not least to the new dynamic between the major powers, as several contributions to this volume explain. Both the increased interest of the United States in the CSCE under President Ronald Reagan and the reforms announced by Gorbachev contributed to a change in the basic conditions for negotiations. This shows how important the views of the CSCE held by heads of government were. However, the influence of delegation members should not be underestimated either.

This insight results not only from an analysis of the documents but is also supported by diplomats who took part in the negotiations. In order to capture these voices, the project team conducted interviews with people who were involved in or associated with the third CSCE Follow-up Meeting in various

---

39 Nina Hechenblaikner, "Diplomatie und ihre Einflüsse. Prägende Akteursgruppen für die Verhandlungen zur humanitären Dimension beim KSZE-Folgetreffen in Wien (1986–1989)", in: *Österreichische Zeitschrift für Geschichtswissenschaften* 35 (2024), issue 2, p. 154–173; Nina Hechenblaikner, "Die humanitäre Dimension des KSZE-Prozesses und das Ende des Kalten Krieges", in: Beate Fieseler/Oksana Nagornaia (eds.), *Der Zerfall der Sowjetunion und das Ende der DDR als historische Zäsuren,* Wiesbaden 2024, p. 15–26; Jonas Kaiser, "Von Stockholm über Wien nach Paris. Vertrauens- und Sicherheitsbildende Maßnahmen und das KSE-Mandat im Rahmen des KSZE Prozesses 1984–1990", in: Fieseler/Nagornaia, *Der Zerfall der Sowjetunion und das Ende der DDR als historische Zäsuren*, p. 1–13.

capacities. Transcripts of these interviews approved for publication will be published in a separate volume.[40] Collecting the testimonies of different individuals should also help to capture aspects of the third CSCE Follow-up Meeting that cannot be reconstructed from files. For example, the later Austrian foreign minister Ursula Plassnik, who was involved in the Vienna Follow-up Meeting as a diplomat and drafted the opening speech for the Austrian chancellor, Franz Vranitzky, reported that she participated in the negotiations in Basket III with "great enthusiasm", as they concerned "people and their lives in this divided Europe." One of the distinguishing features of the CSCE process was that a large proportion of the provisions were (pre-)negotiated in unofficial meetings before being officially adopted in the plenary sessions. However, this approach, as well as the mood during the negotiations, can hardly be deduced from the available archive material. Plassnik, for example, remembered that even at an early stage of the Vienna negotiations she had expressed the opinion that the Berlin Wall had to disappear, even though nobody at the time could have imagined how quickly the global political situation would change.[41]

The Vienna Follow-up Meeting and its comprehensive Concluding Document can be considered the second highpoint of the CSCE process after the Helsinki Final Act. The Concluding Document exceeded the expectations of many delegations.[42] In all areas of the negotiations, provisions were agreed that potentially had far-reaching effects not only on relations between states but also on the populations of the participating states. As in the previous negotiations, the areas of human rights and security policy proved the most controversial in Vienna. They were closely interrelated, with concessions in one area often tied to concessions from the other side in the other area. However, significant further developments were also achieved in seemingly less controversial areas such as information, culture, environmental protection and the economy.

The agreements reached in Vienna included rights that seemed almost unattainable for many people in January 1989, especially in the Warsaw Pact

40 Kai Habel/Nina Hechenblaikner et al. (eds.), *Diplomatie am Ende des Kalten Krieges. Erinnerungen an die dritte KSZE-Folgekonferenz in Wien 1986–1989*, Baden-Baden 2025.

41 E-Mail from Ursula Plassnik to Nina Hechenblaikner, 2.5.2022. The editors would like to express their sincere thanks to Dr. Plassnik for giving us access to these notes.

42 Hermann Wentker, "Die KSZE als Ordnungsfaktor. Höhenflug und Bedeutungsverlust einer Idealvorstellung europäischer Politik (1989–1991)", in: Tim Geiger/Jürgen Lillteicher et al. (eds.), *Zwei plus Vier. Die internationale Gründungsgeschichte der Berliner Republik* (Schriftenreihe der Vierteljahrshefte für Zeitgeschichte 123), Berlin-Boston 2021, p. 125–141, on p. 125.

states, such as the right to freedom of movement, the free choice of residence and settlement within the borders of each state, the right to travel from one district to another and the possibility of leaving and returning to one's own country – rights that were to be curtailed only in exceptional circumstances. These measures were particularly important for family visits and reunions. In another CSCE document, the West's demand for freedom of movement was described in detail for the first time. This contributed to cross-border visitor traffic, including the possibility of reducing restrictions in a gradual process to support travellers and to facilitate personal contacts and family reunions. Three follow-up conferences on human rights were also organised: a first in Paris in 1989, a second in Copenhagen in 1990 and a third in Moscow in 1991. Although some states did not intend to implement all the provisions of the Concluding Document, key provisions soon gained practical significance. At this point, it is worth mentioning the Vienna Mechanism, which enabled the participating states to react to human rights violations between and outside CSCE events[43] and is still an important basis for the actions of its successor organisation, the Organisation for Security and Cooperation in Europe (OSCE).[44]

Not only can the Vienna Follow-up Meeting be understood as a turning point in the CSCE process,[45] it also took place at a time when the entire global political situation was in a state of flux. The CSCE follow-up process undoubtedly interacted with the reform process in the Soviet Union, initiated by the general secretary of the Communist Party of the Soviet Union, Mikhail Gorbachev, and its impact on the entire Warsaw Pact. However, this was felt in a complex form at the Vienna Follow-up Meeting: on the one hand, the Warsaw Pact adhered to the coordination mechanism tested within the framework of the CSCE and to the necessity of presenting a united front within the conference framework, while on the other hand, the Warsaw Pact states also pursued different interests in accordance with their circumstances. A development over time can be observed in this respect: while the Eastern bloc states were still quite united at the conference during the implementation phase, differences emerged in the subsequent proposal phase, intensified in the drafting phase and culminated in an open confrontation in the final phase of the Follow-up Meeting.

---

43 Rachel Brett, "The Human Dimension Mechanism of the CSCE and the CSCE Response to Minorities", in: Michael R. Lucas (ed.), *The CSCE in the 1990s. Constructing European Security and Cooperation* (Demokratie, Sicherheit, Frieden 83), Baden-Baden 1993, p. 143–160, on p. 144–145.

44 OSCE Office for Democratic Institutions and Human Rights (ODIHR), *OSCE Human Dimension Commitments*. Vol. 1, Thematic Compilation, Warsaw [4]2023.

45 Snyder, "The foundation for Vienna: A Reassessment of the CSCE in the mid-1980s", p. 493.

The question of the significance of the CSCE for the end of the Cold War has been raised many times, and the answer has usually been that it should be neither underestimated nor overestimated. No conclusive answer can be given to the question of how great the influence of the CSCE on these processes was, nor does it appear to be genuinely useful for research into the CSCE. It was one factor among many that ultimately led to the (temporary) end of the East-West confrontation.

The historical study of the CSCE is a relatively young field of research, one which offers a variety of thematic focuses and research approaches. This volume aims to help contextualise the significance of the CSCE within the web of the Cold War. It also aims to show the potential for and gaps in research on the Meeting.

Acknowledgements

The editors would like to thank everybody who contributed to the success of the conference and this volume. First, our thanks go to all the contributors, whose texts demonstrate the diversity of research into the CSCE process. That this volume could be produced is due on many levels to the FWF, which, among other things, supported the sub-project A Breakthrough in Human Rights? The Effects of Change in Eastern Europe on the Vienna Follow-Up Meeting (I 4139) as well as the printing, editing and translation of the contributions to the volume (PUB 1144–P). We would like to thank BRILL, especially Alessandra Giliberto, Petra Stiglmayer, Melissa Allieri, Peter Buschman and Wai Min Kan for their organisational help, as well as the series editors Jussi Hanhimäki and Marco Wyss, the anonymous reviewers for their constructive suggestions, and Joe Paul Kroll for proofreading and translation. We would especially like to thank Valerie Heim, Julia Nora Müller and Johanna Widmann, who supported us as student assistants throughout the editorial process.[46]

46 The authors were able to make the last additions and revisions to the content in December 2024.

Moscow and Vienna on the Road to Helsinki

Anna Graf-Steiner

When the third follow-up meeting of the Conference on Security and Cooperation in Europe (CSCE) was held in Vienna (1986–1989), it was finally Austria's turn to become the scene of a gradually dynamising CSCE process. The glasnost and perestroika policies of Mikhail S. Gorbachev, general secretary of the Communist Party of the Soviet Union (CPSU), allowed the so-called "Helsinki effect", the transformative potential of the CSCE Final Act signed in Helsinki in 1975, finally to unfold. Leonid I. Brezhnev, the Soviet leader who was the driving force behind the first CSCE Conference in Helsinki and Geneva (1973–1975), naturally had a very different idea of its value and implications when he put his signature to the document.[1] Brezhnev celebrated the signing of the Final Act as the greatest diplomatic achievement in the history of the Soviet Union, for he saw the project of a pan-European security conference as a foreign policy tool to have the European post-war borders confirmed on a multilateral level.[2] While the West considered the inclusion of the humanitarian dimension, the "Third Basket", its success, the consensus in the Kremlin was that the existence of these provisions was a matter which there was no need "to talk about in any detail at home".[3]

For Brezhnev, Moscow's road to Helsinki was a long one – and from the Soviet point of view, Austria played a decisive role in the realisation of "their" conference project.[4] Early on, the Kremlin regarded the European neutral

1 Preparatory work for this essay was conducted at the Ludwig Boltzmann Institute for Research on Consequences of War (BIK), Graz – Vienna – Raabs, in collaboration with Graz University and the City of Graz. It was supported by the FWF in the context of the project "The Role of the Neutral States in Soviet Foreign Policy Strategy, 1969–1975" ((10.55776/P31869)). This paper is based on the author's resulting publications: Anna Graf-Steiner, *Die Rolle des neutralen Österreich in der außenpolitischen Strategie der Sowjetunion, 1969–1975*. Ph.D. thesis, University of Graz, 2023, which in the same year received an "Award of Excellence – State Prize for the Best Dissertations" from the Austrian Federal Ministry of Education, Science and Research; and Anna Graf-Steiner, *Brückenbauer im Kalten Krieg. Österreich und der lange Weg zur Helsinki-Schlussakte*, Graz-Wien-Berlin 2024.

2 Michael C. Morgan, *The Final Act*, Oxford 2018, p. 74–78.

3 Anatolij F. Dobrynin, *Sugubo doveritel'no*, Moscow 2016, p. 383 (translated).

4 On Austria's role see Benjamin Gilde, *Österreich im KSZE-Prozess 1969–1983. Neutraler Vermittler in humanitärer Mission*, Munich 2013; on the Soviet view of Austria see note 1.

countries as possible advocates for a pan-European security conference.[5] This chapter will examine the question of how the Soviet Union saw the role of neutral Austria in the preparation and realisation of the (first) CSCE, what interests it had vis-à-vis the neutral actor and how successful this strategy proved.

1 European Security and the Warsaw Pact

Brezhnev became general secretary of the CPSU in October 1964 after Khrushchev was overthrown by the plenum of the CPSU Central Committee. Among other things, Khrushchev's internal opponents criticised that he had neglected European security issues in favour of the conflict with China, thereby also upsetting allies states, notably Poland and the GDR. Both had urged Moscow to take a firmer stand against NATO's plans for a multilateral nuclear force (MLF).[6] In response, the Polish government declared in February 1964 that the so-called "Rapacki plan", a plan to create a regional demilitarised zone in Central Europe first proposed by the Polish foreign minister, Adam Rapacki, at the UN General Assembly in 1957,[7] "remained fully relevant".[8] In December, Rapacki proposed to the UN General Assembly that the issue be discussed at a "conference of all European states", including the Soviet Union and the United States.[9]

---

5 On Soviet perceptions, policies and strategies toward neutral and nonaligned European countries in the Cold War see Mark Kramer/Aryo Makko/Peter Ruggenthaler (eds.), *The Soviet Union and Cold War Neutrality and Nonalignment in Europe*, Lanham-Boulder et al. 2021; on the neutrals and the CSCE see Thomas Fischer, *Neutral Power in the CSCE: The N+N States and the Making of the Helsinki Accords 1975*, Baden-Baden 2009; on Austrian neutrality see Günter Bischof/Peter Ruggenthaler, *Österreich und der Kalte Krieg*, Graz 2022; Wolfgang Mueller, *A Good Example of Peaceful Coexistence? The Soviet Union, Austria and Neutrality, 1955–1991*, Vienna 2011.

6 Douglas Selvage, *The Warsaw Pact and Nuclear Nonproliferation, 1963–1965*. (The Cold War International History Project Working Paper Series Vol. 32), Washington D.C. 2001, p. 17; Idem, "Poland and the Sino-Soviet Rift, 1963–1965", *CWIHP e-Dossier* 10, 2004, https://www.wilsoncenter.org/publication/poland-and-the-sino-soviet-rift-1963-1965, accessed 9.9.2023; Sergey Radchenko, *Two Suns in the Heavens*, Stanford 2009.

7 Michael Gehler, Neutralität und Neutralisierungspläne für Mitteleuropa?, in: Dominik Geppert/Udo Wengst (eds.), *Neutralität – Chance oder Chimäre?*, Munich 2005, p. 105–131, on p. 124; on the Polish position see Piotr Długołęcki, Diplomatic file. An Unknown Context of the Rapacki Plan, in: *The Polish Quarterly of International Affairs* 20 (2011), p. 59–71; Wanda Jarząbek, *Hope and Reality* (CWIHP Working Paper Series Vol. 56), Washington D.C. 2008.

8 Memorandum of the Polish government of 29 Feb. 1964, in: Friedrich-Karl Schramm/Wolfram-Georg Riggert/Alois Friedel (eds.), *Sicherheitskonferenz in Europa: Dokumentation 1954–1972*, Frankfurt a. M. 1972, p. 414–415 (translated).

9 Speech of the Polish FM Adam Rapacki before the General Assembly of the United Nations on 14 Dec. 1964, in: Schramm et al. (eds.), *Sicherheitskonferenz*, p. 415–416 (translated).

In early 1965 Moscow did not yet have a clear line on how to deal with the Polish proposal. Brezhnev sharply condemned the MLF at the meeting of the Political Consultative Committee (PCC) of the Warsaw Pact countries in January 1965 in Warsaw,[10] which smoothed pact relations. However, he neither mentioned a pan-European security conference nor a collective security system. The Polish initiative for a conference found its way into the final declaration of the Warsaw Pact,[11] but without defining any measures.[12]

To thwart MLF, Moscow henceforth relied on international diplomacy, including its relations with Austria. In March 1965, the Soviet ambassador to Austria, Viktor I. Avilov, suggested to the Soviet foreign ministry that Austria, as a neutral country, should be more involved in the issue of European security.[13] Avilov emphasised that the policy of neutrality pursued by Austria for the last ten years had been the main factor in the country's increased international prestige, and stressed "that the Soviet government has confidence in Austria".[14]

2 From Idea to Strategy – Brezhnev and the Pan-European Security Conference

The idea of a security conference was not announced in Moscow until the spring of 1966. Brezhnev saw the growing disagreements within NATO – France had officially announced that it wanted to leave NATO's military structures[15] – as the perfect backdrop against which to bring forward a renewed initiative. The Nordic NATO member countries in particular were under pressure

10 Brezhnev's Speech at the Meeting of the PCC of the Warsaw Pact States, 20 January 1965, Russian State Archive of Contemporary History (RGANI), F. 10, op. 3, d. 19, l. 30–47, l. 36 (translated).

11 Communiqué of the Meeting of the PCC of the Warsaw Pact States, Warsaw, 20 January 1965. Ibid., d. 18, l. 1–7, l. 5–6 (translated).

12 Andrej Zagorskij, *Chel'sinkskij Process*, Moscow 2005, p. 21.

13 Embassy of the USSR in Austria [V. I. Avilov] to the Third European Department of the Soviet Foreign Ministry, Materials for the talks of FM Gromyko with Austrian statesmen in May 1965, 31 March 1965, Archive of the Foreign Policy of the Russian Federation (AVP RF), F. 066, op. 49, p. 237, d. 7, l. 21–28, l. 22–23; see also Anna Graf-Steiner/Herbert R. Reginbogin, "Austria: The NPT, Diplomacy, and National Identity", in: Pascal Lottaz/Yoko Iwama (eds.), *Neutral Europe and the Creation of the Nonproliferation Regime 1958–1968*, London-New York 2023, p. 169–184, on p. 171.

14 Embassy of the USSR in Austria [V. I. Avilov] to the Third European Department of the Soviet Foreign Ministry, AVP RF, F. 066, op. 49, p. 237, d. 7, l. 21–28, l. 23.

15 Burkard Schmitt, *Frankreich und die Nukleardebatte der Atlantischen Allianz 1956–1966*, München 1998, p. 195.

from the Soviets.[16] So was France, as de Gaulle's conception of a new security system, if necessary without taking the United States into account, basically accommodated Soviet efforts to prevent a renewal of the NATO treaty, which would be due in 1969.[17]

At the XXIII. Party Congress of the CPSU in March/April 1966, it became the official Soviet position to seek the final confirmation of borders in the framework of a pan-European security conference. The USSR wanted to present itself as the guardian of peace and give "new dynamics" to those civil society and political forces in Western Europe critical of US hegemony.[18] Accordingly, the Warsaw Pact's PCC meeting in Bucharest in July 1966 declared a pan-European security conference a main political goal of the bloc.[19] The proposed concept included the establishment of a European security system, the withdrawal of foreign troops from Europe, the dissolution of alliances, the reduction of military forces in the FRG and the GDR, the recognition of existing borders, renunciation of violence, and an expansion of scientific-technical and cultural cooperation.[20] In the final declaration, the link between European security and the neutral states as advocates for the cause was also publicly stated for the first time.[21]

3 Multilateralisation and "the Spring of 1969"

After the Bucharest Declaration, discussions on the subject of the security conference intensified in the West. Soviet diplomacy focused primarily on France and its partial break with NATO, on the smaller NATO countries and the neutrals.[22] This marked the beginning of increasing Soviet pressure on

16 Thomas Wegener Friis, "Dänemark. NATO-Horchposten zur Ostsee", in: Stefan Karner et al. (eds.), *Prager Frühling. Das internationale Krisenjahr 1968. Band 1: Beiträge*, Köln-Weimar-Wien 2008, p. 617–631, on p. 618–619.

17 Georges-Henri Soutou, "Paris und der 'Prager Frühling'", in: Stefan Karner et al. (eds.), *Prager Frühling*, p. 355–364, on p. 356–357.

18 Brezhnev's Speech at the Plenum of the CPSU Central Committee, 12 December 1966, RGANI, F. 2, op. 3, d. 49, l. 10 (translated).

19 Csaba Békés, "The Warsaw Pact, the German Question and the CSCE Process", in: Oliver Bange/Gottfried Niedhart (eds.), *Helsinki 1975 and the Transformation of Europe*, Brooklyn 2008, p. 113–128, on p. 115; Wanda Jarząbek, "Preserving the Status Quo or Promoting Change?", in: Ibid., p. 144–159, on p. 144.

20 Morgan, *Final Act*, p. 80–81.

21 Declaration of the Warsaw Pact States in Bucharest of 6 July 1966, in: Schramm et al. (eds.), *Sicherheitskonferenz*, p. 425–435.

22 Petri Hakkarainen, *A State of Peace in Europe*, New York-Oxford 2011, p. 20; Matthias Peter, *Die Bundesrepublik im KSZE-Prozess 1975–1983*, Berlin-München-Boston 2015, p. 71–73.

Austria. Vienna showed interest in the conference project from the beginning, but repeatedly made it clear that it could not take any initiative,[23] clearly not wanting to be perceived as a mouthpiece of the Kremlin.

The suppression of the "Prague Spring" only meant a temporary suspension of détente. The Warsaw Pact sent a clear signal of relaxation to the West with the declaration of the PCC in Budapest of 17 March 1969, when the member states agreed to discuss Western disarmament plans and abandoned their demands to dissolve the military alliances and to withdraw foreign troops from Europe.[24] However, Brezhnev's actual main goals remained unchanged: the recognition of the status quo regarding the inner-German border and the Oder-Neisse line, the relinquishment of the FRG's capacity to deplay nuclear weapons and a special status for Berlin. NATO reacted cautiously positively to the conference plans and spoke out in favour of consultations on the topic at its Ministerial Council meeting in April.[25]

In parallel, efforts to win diplomatic favour resumed in the spring of 1969, especially for the small and neutral European states, with a focus on Austria and Finland.[26] On 17 April 1969, the first secretary of the Soviet embassy, Albert Dmitriev, told the Austrian ambassador in Moscow, Walter Wodak, that "the special role and function of Austria as a neutral state suggested that Austria should be proactive in the much-discussed question of convening a European security conference" – without, however, specifically stating what measures were to be taken.[27] At the same time (14–18 April 1969), the Bulgarian leader, Todor Zhivkov, visited Austria and made a similar request to Chancellor Josef Klaus, which suggests previous synchronisation with Moscow. Zhivkov,

23 Gilde, *Neutraler Vermittler;* Fischer, *Neutral Power*, p. 87–88.

24 Document No. 63: Appeal for a European Security Conference, March 17, 1969, in: Vojtech Mastny/Malcolm Byrne (eds.), *A Cardboard Castle? An Inside History of the Warsaw Pact, 1955–1991*, Budapest 2005, p. 330–331; Csaba Békés, "Der Warschauer Pakt und der KSZE-Prozess", in: Torsten Diedrich/Winfried Heinemann/Christian F. Ostermann (eds.), *Der Warschauer Pakt*, Berlin 2009, p. 225–244; Morgan, *Final Act*, p. 82–83; Thomas Fischer, "Austria and the Helsinki Process", in: Arnold Suppan/Wolfgang Mueller (eds.), *"Peaceful Coexistence" or "Iron Curtain"*, Wien 2009, p. 168–202, on p. 173; Helga Haftendorn, "The Link between CSCE and MBFR. Two sprouts from one bulb", in: Andreas Wenger/Vojtech Mastny/Christian Nuenlist (eds.), *Origins of the European Security System*, p. 237–258, on p. 240.

25 Communiqué on the North Atlantic Council ministerial meeting in Washington, Apr. 10–11, 1969, in: Schramm et al. (eds.), *Sicherheitskonferenz*, p. 70–71.

26 This refutes Thomas Fischer's thesis that Soviet interest from 1968 onwards was directed primarily at Finland: Fischer, *Neutral Power*, p. 89.

27 Talks with Soviet diplomats. Wodak to SPÖ Party Chairman Kreisky, 17 April 1969. Stiftung Bruno-Kreisky-Archiv (SBKA), VII.1 Länderbox UdSSR, Box 2, ex 1240 (translated).

however, expressed his wishes in more concrete terms: "[i]f you find, for example, that it would be appropriate to convene this conference in Austria [...] we will support you in doing so".[28] However, the chancellor apparently did not see Austria as being a position to initiate a convocation without both superpowers on board.[29]

Finland was also in the Soviet Union's sights at the same time. The Soviet ambassador in Helsinki had asked the Finnish foreign minister, Ahti Karjalainen, for Finland to "make a start" and speak out in favour of holding a pan-European security conference in the near future. Karjalainen informed the Austrian foreign ministry about this conversation via the Austrian ambassador.[30] Finland indeed made a start soon afterwards, but reinterpreted the original Soviet idea in such a way that it served Finland's interests of pursuing a policy of active neutrality more independent of Moscow.[31] On 5 May 1969, Finland approached with the European states as well as the USA and Canada, declaring itself available as a venue for a pan-European security conference. The bi- and multilateral consultation process between the Warsaw Pact, NATO countries and the neutral and non-aligned states gained momentum. Only a few days after the Finnish initiative, the first secretary of the Soviet embassy expressed his regret to Wodak that the initiator had been Finland – and not Austria.[32]

4 Austria in Moscow's Sights

Valentin M. Falin, head of the second European department of the Soviet foreign ministry, was a driving force in courting Austria. He told the Austrian

28 Minutes of conversation Josef Klaus – Todor Zhivkov, Central State Archive Sofia (CDA), F. 378b, op. 5, a.e. 386, n. d. [14.–18.4.1969], l. 20 (translated).

29 Ibid., l. 20–21.

30 Außenminister Dr. Karjalainen zur Frage der Abhaltung einer europäischen Sicherheitskonferenz, Helsinki, 21. Apr. 1969, Österreichisches Staatsarchiv (ÖStA), Archiv der Republik (AdR), BMAA, Politische Sektion, Abteilung 7 Entwicklung (II-Pol), Politische Berichte, Zl. 49-Pol/69, p. 3 (translated).

31 Kimmo Rentola, "Der Vorschlag einer europäischen Sicherheitskonferenz und die stille Krise zwischen Finnland und der Sowjetunion 1968–1971", in: Geppert/Wengst (eds.), *Chance oder Chimäre?* p. 177–202; Idem, "Finnlands Ruf nach einer Europäischen Sicherheitskonferenz im Jahr 1969", in: Michael Borchard/Stefan Karner/Hanns Jürgen Küsters et al. (eds.), *Entspannung im Kalten Krieg*, Graz-Wien 2020, p. 645–655; Thomas Fischer, "A Mustard Seed Grew Into a Bushy Tree", in: *Cold War History* 9 (2009), p. 177–201; Fischer, *Neutral Power*, p. 89–100; Morgan, *Final Act*, p. 87.

32 Amb. W. Wodak to SPÖ Chairman Bruno Kreisky, 13 May 1969, SBKA, VII.1 Länderbox UdSSR, Box 2, ex 1240.

ambassador that the "political influence of neutral states" should not be underestimated[33] and suggested to the Soviet foreign ministry in a letter dated 3 December 1969 that it should "speak out for a more active participation of Austria in the preparation of the conference".[34] Falin observed greater consultation activity on the part of the Austrian government and interpreted this as a sign that Vienna wanted to make up for its failure to take the initiative.[35] He assumed that Austria could be expected to continue its commitment to the preparation and implementation of the conference, which in turn Moscow would use for its own agenda.

Even if the Warsaw Pact officially signalled gratitude for Finland's willingness to host talks at their meeting of foreign ministers in Budapest on 21–22 June 1970, this was not a clear commitment that the preliminary talks, still less the actual conference, would take place in Helsinki.[36] Austria also openly offered itself as a possible venue – and the Kremlin was ready to make political capital out of the unresolved question, as evidenced by a Politburo decision of 17 April 1970:

> In order to influence Austria's policy and to consolidate its position of neutrality, more active use should be made of the Austrian government's interest in international negotiations, conferences, congresses being held in Vienna and in Austria's capital becoming the seat of new international organisations.[37]

The means of choice for exerting pressure on Austria was stated just as clearly: the reference to Moscow's rights under the Austrian State Treaty and Austrian neutrality.[38]

---

33 Die Sowjetunion und Österreich. Report of Austrian Ambassador to Moscow, Walter Wodak, to Foreign Ministry, Nov. 14, 1969, ÖStA, AdR, BMAA, II-Pol, Politische Berichte Moskau 1969, Zl. 46-Pol/69, p. 5 (translated).

34 Letter of V. Falin to L. F. Il'ičev, 3 December 1969, AVP RF, F. 66, op. 48, p. 103, d. 13, l. 21–24, l. 21 (translated).

35 Ibid.

36 Memorandum of the Conference of Foreign Ministers, June 21 and 22, 1970, in: Schramm et al. (eds.), *Sicherheitskonferenz*, p. 520–522, on p. 521. In this document, the participation of the USA and Canada in this conference was officially accepted by the Warsaw Pact.

37 Protocol No. 160 of the meeting of the Politburo of the CC of the CPSU, Apr. 17, 1970, RGANI, F. 3, op. 72, d. 331, l. l. 6; 39–48, l. 48 (translated).

38 Ibid., l. 45. In the same decision, the Politburo recognized that the Austrian State Treaty did not in fact provide any legal means for Moscow to prevent Austria's possible association with the European Economic Community (EEC). However, the concession remained an internal one. Towards Austria, the incompatibility between closer economic relations

A decision in favour of Vienna became unthinkable in January 1973, when Vienna had been designated as the venue for the negotiations on mutual and balanced force reductions (MBFR).[39] On 29 May 1973, it was decided that the CSCE ambassadorial negotiations would take place in Geneva.[40]

5 Kreisky as Vicarious Agent?

Aleksandr Bondarenko, head of the third European department in the Soviet foreign ministry, pleaded for more Soviet involvement in Austria in a letter to the Central Committee of the CPSU on January 3, 1973.[41] Sharply criticising chancellor Bruno Kreisky for his insistence on including the Middle East issue on the CSCE agenda, at the same time he read Kreisky's persistence as proof that the Austrian chancellor did not shy away from unpopular issues and might be won over to certain Soviet interests. Bondarenko explicitly recommended that "the interest of the Kreisky cabinet to play a more active role in European affairs" be used in conjunction with the pan-European conference.[42] As a concrete measure, he suggested a return visit by Alexei Kosygin, the chairman of the Council of Ministers, to Austria, to which he had already been invited in 1967.[43]

At the plenum in April 1973, Brezhnev took up this proposal and ordered an increase in diplomatic visits to the neutral countries to speed up the preparatory talks in Helsinki.[44] A visit by Kosygin to Austria (2–5 July 1973) was arranged at remarkably short notice, barely a month in advance.[45] The fact that it took place immediately before the end of the meeting of foreign

---

with the EEC (and the FRG) and the State Treaty's "Anschlussverbot" was to be insisted on even more strongly.

39 Haftendorn, *Two Sprouts from One Bulb*, p. 251–252; Christoph Breitenmoser, *Sicherheit für Europa*, Zürich 1996, p. 122.

40 Philipp Rosin, *Die Schweiz im KSZE-Prozeß 1972–1983. Einfluß durch Neutralität*, München 2014, p. 73–75.

41 Materials for the CC of the CPSU for Talks with Austrian Representatives. Head of the Third European Department, Aleksandr Bondarenko, to the First Deputy Head of the CC of the CPSU, Vadim Valentinovich Zagladin, Jan. 3, 1973, RGANI, F. 5, op. 66, d. 884, l. 29–35.

42 Ibid., l. 33 (translated).

43 Ibid., l. 32.

44 Brezhnev's Speech at the Plenum of the CPSU Central Committee, Apr. 26–27, 1973, RGANI, F. 2, op. 3, d. 292, l. 30–32.

45 Offizieller Besuch des Vorsitzenden des Ministerrates der UdSSR, Alexej N. Kossygin, in Österreich vom 2. bis 5. Juli 1973, June 25, 1973, SBKA, VII.1 Länderbox UdSSR, Box 2, Besuch Kossygin ex 738a 1973 Informationsmappe, Zl. 39–976-6(Pol)73.

ministers in Helsinki caused an international stir.[46] The CIA assumed an "orchestrated effort" on the part of Moscow to influence the neutrals.[47]

Washington noticed that the joint communiqué on the occasion of Kosygin's visit referred for the first time to Austria's "neutrality anchored in the constitution" and officially recognised Vienna's contacts with the European Economic Community.[48] Furthermore, in the communiqué both states declared their commitment to strengthening peace and security in Europe on the basis of the principles worked out in Helsinki. However, the only principles cited were those that happened to be Soviet priorities: the "sovereign equality" of all states, "renunciation of the use of force", "non-interference in internal affairs" and "cooperation for mutual benefit".[49] No mention was made of "human rights", "peaceful change of frontiers" or the "right of peoples to self-determination". It was precisely these principles not mentioned here that were at issue between East and West (with Austria taking the Western position) at the Helsinki meeting of foreign ministers. For the sake of "good neighbourly relations", the Vienna leadership proved quite willing (or felt compelled) to turn a blind eye when Moscow "forgot" the transformative principles.

In contrast, the Austrian CSCE delegation, led by Helmut Liedermann,[50] was particularly active in the negotiations on the Third Basket. Most of the text in the "Human Contacts" section of the Third Basket was drafted by Austrians, as was its preamble, which indeed represented"one of the finest hours of Viennese post-war diplomacy".[51] This was in contrast to the strategy of the Austrian chancellery and foreign ministry. The Austrian government did not believe that changes in the socio-political situation should be sought at the conference table, instead preferring quiet diplomacy in the humanitarian sphere.[52]

Moscow, for its part, showed surprisingly little resistance to Austrian diplomacy in this regard. Instead, the Soviet leadership focused on working towards a summit that would end the discussions and secure the status quo in Europe.

46 The CSCE Foreign Ministers' meeting in Helsinki took place from 2–7 July 1973, Chiffre der österreichischen Botschaft in Paris [Bielka] an das Außenministerium in Wien, July 4, 1973, SBKA, VII.1 Länderbox UdSSR, Box 2, Zl. 22792.

47 *Central Intelligence Bulletin* No. 0163/73, 9.7.1973, p. 2.

48 Ibid.

49 Österreichisch-sowjetisches Kommuniqué [signatories: Kosygin, Kreisky], 5 July 1973, SBKA, VII.1 Länderbox UdSSR, Box 2 (translated).

50 See the article by Maximilian Graf in this volume.

51 Günter Bischof, "Rezension zu: Benjamin Gilde, Österreich im KSZE-Prozess 1969–1983. Neutraler Vermittler in humanitärer Mission, München 2013", in: *sehepunkte* 14 (2014), issue 2, http://www.sehepunkte.de/2014/02/24330.html, accessed 9.9.2023 (translated); see also: Gilde, *Neutraler Vermittler*, p. 106.

52 Gilde, *Neutraler Vermittler*, p. 71–78.

Kreisky was seen as a suitable proxy in this effort, as he himself showed little interest in the conference proceedings in Helsinki and Geneva and in the positions of his delegation represented there. He remained disappointed that the Middle East issue was not on the agenda and from the outset would have preferred a top-level summit to "another diplomatic conference".[53] This ambiguity was closely watched by Moscow.[54]

Kreisky visited the Soviet Union from 28 May 28 to 1 June 1974. From the Soviet Union's point of view, the main result of the meeting was the public commitment of the Austrian side, namely Kreisky, to do everything possible for a speedy conclusion of the CSCE.[55] Kreisky's statement was received with horror, both in the Austrian foreign ministry and within the delegation. Not only was it contrary to the interests of the delegation, but it was feared that Moscow was trying to ensnare Kreisky for tactical reasons.[56] Soviet files show that this concern was not unfounded.

After U.S. President Nixon's stopover in Salzburg (11–12 June 1974), Kreisky personally informed Soviet chargé d'affaires V. M. Mamontov of the contents of the talks.[57] Kreisky said that he had pressed Nixon for a summit as soon as possible.[58] To Mamontov, the Austrian chancellor stated he had told Nixon and Kissinger that it was "not necessary [to] solve all the questions that are currently being discussed in Geneva", the Third Basket in particular containing "many small and simply unnecessary questions".[59] According to the U.S.

53 Ibid., p. 188 (translated).

54 See for example: Information from the Soviet Embassy in Austria, 21 February 1972, RGANI, F. 5, op. 64, d. 567, l. 28–33; Official diary of V. S. Semenov. Conversation of the Deputy Foreign Minister of the USSR [V. S. Semenov] with the Austrian Chancellor B. Kreisky, 31 January 1972, Ibid., F. 5, op. 64, d. 568, l. 8–12.

55 Political Report of the Embassy of the USSR in Austria [Mamontov], 5 July 1974, RGANI, F. 5, op. 67, d. 814, l. 162–171.

56 Gilde, *Neutraler Vermittler*, p. 188–189.

57 U.S. President Nixon visited Salzburg from 11–12 June 1974 on a stopover on his way to the Middle East. Nixon exchanged views with Kreisky on the Socialist International's recent fact-finding mission to the Middle East. The U.S. president's trip to Moscow followed from 28 June 28–1 July 1974.

58 Transcript of the conversation of the chargé d'affaires of the USSR in Austria, V. M. Mamontov, with Austrian Chancellor Kreisky, 20 June 1974, RGANI, F. 5, op. 67, d. 814, l. 136f.; see also: Memorandum of Conversation Nixon – Kreisky, June 11, 1974. Gerald R. Ford Presidential Library & Museum, NSC, Memoranda of Conversations, 1973–1977, box 4, Nixon Administration, https://www.fordlibrarymuseum.gov/library/document/0314/1552720.pdf, accessed 30.9.2023.

59 Transcript of the conversation of the chargé d'affaires of the USSR in Austria, V. M. Mamontov, with Austrian Chancellor Kreisky, June 20, 1974, RGANI, F. 5, op. 67, d. 814, l. 136f (translated).

transcript, Kreisky pleaded not to wait too long for further concessions from the East: "We can't avoid going to a conference in the long run, and if we do not do it now, we will go without any concessions."[60] In the conversation with Mamontov, Kreisky did not mention that he had cited the follow-up conferences to Nixon and Kissinger as an argument for signing the Final Act as quickly as possible. The follow-ups were needed "so the situation doesn't get frozen".[61] For Kreisky, the focus was on the CSCE process, not on the substance of the Final Act.[62]

6 Conclusion

The Final Act was eventually ready for Brezhnev, Kreisky and 33 other statesmen to sign on 1 August 1975. From the perspective of 1975, East and West could celebrate the Final Act as the crowning achievement of the policy of détente, if only because the conference ended in a spirit of general consensus.

It must have been clear to the Western actors that, in the short term, the human rights principle and the Third Basket were mere window-dressing in a deal that recognised the Soviet Union's hegemony over the states of Eastern and Central Europe. In the foreseeable future, Moscow could be expected at most to show understanding for individual "cases of hardship", but by no means to promote systemic change. That was the price one was willing to pay for détente.

Contrary to what some supporters of a "Helsinki effect" claim,[63] it was neither the Final Act nor the follow up conferences per se that thawed Europe. In retrospect, however, Austrian diplomacy in 1975 and its focus on the Third Basket proved to be far-sighted, almost prophetic. In spite of a commitment to follow-up conferences in which they might be fleshed out, the Austrian delegation did not desist from its efforts to demand substance in the humanitarian provisions of the Final Act. It seized the opportunity to enshrine these

60 Nixon – Kreisky, June 11, 1974. Gerald R. Ford Presidential Library & Museum, NSC, Memoranda of Conversations, 1973–1977, box 4, Nixon Administration.

61 Ibid.

62 On Kreisky's role, see Anna Graf-Steiner, "Kreisky, the Soviet Union, and the Helsinki Process", in: Günter Bischof/Michael Burri (eds.), *Bruno Kreisky's Foreign Policy: A Reassessment* (Austrian and Habsburg Studies Vol. 39), New York-Oxford 2025, p. 167–202.

63 Daniel C. Thomas, *The Helsinki Effect: International Norms, Human Rights, and the Demise of Communism*, New Jersey 2001; Matthias Peter/Hermann Wentker (eds.), *Die KSZE im Ost-West-Konflikt*, München 2012; Bange/Niedhardt (eds.), *Helsinki 1975*.

provisions for good, if initially only on paper. When the time was ripe for transformation and the Cold War was coming to an end, the Third Basket was able to prove its full potential. Underestimated by many – including their country's own chancellor, who would have preferred to take the negotiations into his own hands, and Brezhnev, who relied on influencing the political leadership – the Austrian delegation persevered. They laid the foundation on which the CSCE process would later emerge as a transformative force, especially during the Vienna Follow-up Meeting.

From Helsinki to Vienna

The CSCE Process in the Second Cold War

Hermann Wentker

1 Introduction

In Helsinki on 1 August 1975, 35 European and North American heads of state and government signed the Final Act of the Conference on Security and Cooperation in Europe (CSCE).[1] This marked the end of a long process of negotiation which, its prehistory since the mid-1950s notwithstanding, had been initiated by Leonid Brezhnev, general secretary of the Communist Party of the Soviet Union (CPSU) at the time. The purpose of the Final Act was to establish, even amid the conflict between East and West, a modus vivendi in Europe. At the time, both sides had secured important goals in tough negotiations. The Soviet Union and the Eastern bloc states received a guarantee of the status quo in Europe, even if they had to concede the possibility of peaceful boundary changes. Western demands, on the other hand, were met by the inclusion of human rights in the catalogue of principles (Basket I) and a commitment to improving human communication and contacts (Basket III), even if the phrasing used was far from binding. Basket II, which was of particular concern to the East, dealt above all with economic and technological exchange. Finally, Basket IV pledged the parties to periodic meetings in order to prevent the CSCE from remaining a one-off event.[2]

Since the provisions of Basket IV inaugurated a process that culminated in the 1990 Paris Charter, the CSCE was equipped with three dimensions

1 The term "Second Cold War" in the title strikes me as the most appropriate way of characterising the fundamental break with the era of détente. It began in the mid-1970s, culminated in the Soviet invasion of Afghanistan and ended with the INF Treaty in 1987. Gottfried Niedhart and Oliver Bange argue that, in view of the increased research focus on the policy of détente, the term "Cold War" should either be dispensed with completely or used only to refer to the 1950s. This, however, would not do justice to the intensity of the conflict. See Gottfried Niedhart, "Der Ost-West-Konflikt. Konfrontation im Kalten Krieg und Stufen der Deeskalation", in: *Archiv für Sozialgeschichte* 50 (2010), p. 557–594, on p. 588–594; Oliver Bange/Bernd Lemke, Einleitung, in: Idem (eds.), *Wege zur Wiedervereinigung. Die beiden deutschen Staaten in ihren Bündnissen 1970 bis 1990*, München 2013, p. 9–10, p. 13.

2 On the origins of the conference and the Final Act see most recently Michael Cotey Morgan, *The Final Act. The Helsinki Accords and the Transformation of the Cold War*, Princeton 2018.

constitutive for international relations. It fulfilled, first, a function of establishing order. The broad recognition of the political and territorial status quo in Europe meant, on the one hand, that the Western states fundamentally questioned neither the dictatorial forms of government in Eastern Europe nor the dominant role played there by the Soviet Union. On the other hand, the Soviet Union recognised the close alliance between the states of Western Europe and North America, while the neutral and non-aligned (N+N) states could feel equally secure in this status quo-oriented Europe. This entailed a shared catalogue of goals, rules of conduct and statements of intent to which all participating states pledged themselves. West Germany in particular regarded this as both an achievement and an obligation. "German security policy interests demand", stated a joint study of the ministries of defence and foreign affairs in 1976,

> that it be repeatedly made clear to the East that the treaties and agreements made – not least the Final Act of the CSCE – are the foundations of international relations, respect for which is a precondition for the functioning of cooperation between states and for safeguarding peace.[3]

In addition, there was the processual nature of the CSCE inscribed in Basket IV. By establishing a system of expert conferences and follow-up meetings, a forum was created in which East and West were committed to a perpetual dialogue which, though it might falter in times of crisis, was never wholly abandoned. Accordingly, the CSCE rules have rightly been called "a Magna Carta of East-West relations in Europe".[4]

Second, once conventional arms control had been moved to the Vienna MBFR (Mutual and Balanced Force Reductions) talks in 1973, the dimension of security policy referred only to Confidence- (later Confidence- and Security-) Building Measures, which consisted primarily of transparency through information, inspection and control of manoeuvres and troop movements. Large-scale manoeuvres were to be announced and observers exchanged,

3 Aufzeichnung der Arbeitsgruppe Auswärtiges Amt/Bundesministerium der Verteidigung, 10.2.1976, in: *Akten zur Auswärtigen Politik der Bundesrepublik Deutschland* (AAPD) *1976*, München 2007, Dok. 45, p. 196–211, on p. 207. Previously untranslated German language sources were translated by the author.

4 Peter Schlotter, "Heiße Luft oder Magna Charta? Der KSZE-Prozeß nach dem dritten Folgetreffen", in: Hanne-Margret Birckenbach/Uli Jäger/Christian Wellmann (eds.), *Jahrbuch Frieden 1990. Ereignisse, Entwicklungen, Analysen*, München 1989, p. 76.

though the Final Act's provisions to that effect were vague and its phrasing non-committal.[5]

Third, consideration of the humanitarian dimension – the commitment, that is, to improve personal contacts and communication – can be traced to a demand made by the NATO foreign ministers in November 1969 for "freer movement of people, ideas, and information" between East and West.[6] The Soviet Union felt the risks associated with such a commitment to be manageable. Andrei Gromyko, the Soviet foreign minister, saw the risk as limited because, as he reportedly said, "We are masters in our own house".[7] Thereby, and by enshrining human rights in Basket I, the CSCE opened up new possibilities for dissident groups, which could cite the Final Act in support of their protests.[8] Yet it was not only various Helsinki groups and human rights discourse in East and West that were given a boost but also movements to emigrate from Eastern bloc states, particularly the GDR.[9]

The Helsinki Final Act thus contained elements that were both stabilising and dynamic. This study deals, first, with the relation between stability and dynamics in the CSCE process between 1977 and 1986, when the international order entered a new period of turbulence known as the Second Cold War. It examines, second, to what extent rising tensions in international politics were reflected in the CSCE process. Third, it shows how, even before the Vienna Follow-up Meeting, the Soviet Union appeared ready to make far-reaching concessions, which is why this study focuses on that period's final years.

---

5 On the background see Morgan, *Final Act*, p. 95–100, 189–195.

6 Declaration of the North Atlantic Council 4./5.12.1969, https://www.nato.int/cps/en/natohq/official_texts_26760.htm, accessed 19.6.2023; cf. Matthias Peter, *Die Bundesrepublik im KSZE-Prozess. Die Umkehrung der Diplomatie* (Quellen und Darstellungen zur Zeitgeschichte Vol. 105), Berlin-München-Boston 2015, p. 82.

7 Quoted in Anatoly Dobrynin, *In Confidence. Moscow's Ambassador to America's Six Cold War Presidents*, New York 1995, p. 351.

8 Ernst Wawra, "Ein Schandfleck der westlichen Diplomatie? Der KSZE-Prozess und die Bürger- und Menschenrechtsbewegung in der Sowjetunion 1976–1982", in: Helmut Altrichter/Hermann Wentker (eds.), *Vom Kalten Krieg zu einem neuen Europa 1975 bis 1990* (Zeitgeschichte im Gespräch Vol. 11), München 2011, p. 63–73; Gunter Dehnert, "'Eine neue Beschaffenheit der Lage'. Der KSZE-Prozess und die polnische Opposition 1975–1989", in: Ibid., p. 87–98; Benjamin Müller, "Von der Konfrontation zum Dialog. Charta 77, Menschenrechte und die 'Samtene Revolution' in der Tschechoslowakei 1975–1989", in: Ibid., p. 99–110.

9 Anja Hanisch, *Die DDR im KSZE-Prozess 1972–1975. Zwischen Ostabhängigkeit, Westabgrenzung und Ausreisebewegung* (Quellen und Darstellungen zur Zeitgeschichte Vol. 91), München 2012.

2 Confrontation and Tactical Concessions: the Follow-up Meetings in Belgrade (1977–1978) and Madrid (1979–1983)

When the first Follow-up Meeting began in Belgrade on 4 October 1977, relations between East and West were already beginning to be strained by the Soviet Union's deployment of modern SS-20 ballistic missiles. Even before negotiations began, the Warsaw Pact states had agreed among themselves not to make any further concessions.[10] The US delegation, however, was emphatic in its pursuit of human rights questions, meeting with no less fervent resistance from the Soviet Union. Neither the Federal Republic with its moderate attitude nor the efforts of the N+N participants could help produce a substantial concluding document.[11] According to Per Fischer, the head of the West German delegation, there had been no real negotiations in Belgrade.[12] Although the meeting ended only with a short, vague document, the Soviet Union did not renege on the acquis de détente, for it had not left the conference and had agreed to another Follow-up Meeting.[13] Moreover, it remained committed to arms control talks with the United States, a commitment underscored by the signing of the second Strategic Arms Limitation Talks treaty (SALT II) by the two superpowers on 18 July 1979.[14]

The Second Cold War, which was triggered towards the end of 1979 by the Soviet intervention in Afghanistan and the NATO Double-Track Decision, boded ill for the CSCE process. Yet at the beginning of the Madrid Follow-up Meeting in November 1980, relations between the Western and Eastern groups of states were much less confrontative than they had been three years earlier, as the Soviet Union from the outset was seeking a mandate for a European conference on disarmament. This was motivated by a desire to burnish its image as a power for peace, which had suffered from both the intervention in Afghanistan and its own nuclear rearmament. By doing so, the Soviets hoped in turn to

10 Ibid., p. 188–191.

11 On the Belgrade Follow-up Meeting see Vladimir Bilandžić/Dittmar Dahlmann/Milan Kosanović (eds.), *From Helsinki to Belgrade. The First CSCE Follow-up Meeting and the Crisis of Détente* (Internationale Beziehungen. Theorie und Geschichte Vol. 10), Göttingen 2012.

12 Per Fischer, "Das Ergebnis von Belgrad. Das KSZE-Folgetreffen in seiner Bedeutung für den Entspannungsprozeß", in: *Europa-Archiv* 33 (1978), p. 221–230, on p. 226; Peter, *Bundesrepublik*, p. 316.

13 Ibid., p. 317.

14 Douglas Selvage, "The Superpowers and the Conference on Security and Cooperation in Europe, 1977–1983", in: Matthias Peter/Hermann Wentker (eds.), *Die KSZE im Ost-West-Konflikt. Internationale Politik und gesellschaftliche Transformation 1975–1990*, München 2012, p. 15–58, on p. 26.

strengthen their influence with the peace movement in the West and thereby to prevent Western rearmament. In order to win Western consent to such a conference, the Soviets made far-reaching concessions, particularly in Basket III, on questions of family reunification, marriage and working conditions for foreign journalists. Yet since Moscow was interested above all in securing the aforementioned conference on disarmament, these were tactical concessions that did not entail any departure from fundamental positions.[15]

Although all Warsaw Pact states followed the Soviet lead, the Soviets' concessions had taken their alliance partners by surprise and massively compromised their interests. This was particularly true of East Germany, whose leadership under Erich Honecker was well aware that the easing of restrictions on family reunifications and marriages would act as a catalyst for the country's emigration movement.[16]

Moreover, following a promising start in the summer of 1981, negotiations stalled because the United States were now demanding even more Soviet concessions but were rebuffed. The proclamation of martial law in Poland in December 1981 placed a further burden on negotiations, with Washington now eager to "punish" Moscow and to make a Concluding Document conditional on improvements in the human rights situation in the Eastern bloc. Bonn, by contrast, was loath to jeopardise the CSCE process, and the West German foreign minister, Hans-Dietrich Genscher, was able to persuade the United States not to abandon the talks.[17]

Although the delegations parted in May 1982, they agreed to resume the Meeting in November, as the Western states too were concerned not only with humanitarian improvements but also with a conference on disarmament. They were minded to implement the rearmament provisions of the NATO Double-Track Decision while signalling their continued interest in disarmament. Negotiations regained momentum in the spring of 1983. The Western states signalled increased flexibility, the Soviet Union, with its overriding interest in a disarmament conference, remained prepared to make concessions, while the N+N states offered their services as mediators in the drafting of a final document.[18] The Meeting thus ended in September 1983 not only with a substantive Concluding Document but also with a mandate for a Conference on Confidence- and Security-Building Measures and Disarmament in Europe

15 Ibid., p. 28–30.

16 Hanisch, *DDR im KSZE-Prozess*, p. 261–264, p. 273–278, p. 285–286.

17 For a West German view see Peter, *Bundesrepublik*, p. 445–491.

18 See, with a special focus on Austria, Benjamin Gilde, *Österreich im KSZE-Prozess 1969–1983. Neutraler Vermittler in humanitärer Mission*, München 2013, p. 406–430.

(CDE). Moreover, the participants in Madrid agreed to a further five smaller meetings and one regular Follow-up Meeting, to be convened in Vienna in 1986.[19] In the middle of the Second Cold War, the CSCE was thus the only East-West forum to remain from the era of détente. And once negotiations on nuclear disarmament were concluded in Geneva, the CDE became the most prominent forum in which East and West were able to discuss questions of arms control.

3 From Confrontation to Concessions: the CDE in Stockholm (1984–1986)

The CDE, which opened in Stockholm on 17 January 1984, was concerned less with disarmament than with Confidence- and Security-Building Measures (CSBMs). Whereas the provisions of the Helsinki Final Act intended to provide transparency by means of information and inspection of the other side's manoeuvres and troop movements had been framed in general terms and placed on a voluntary basis, the aim of the CDE was to specify them, make them obligatory and to "provide [them] with adequate forms of verification".[20]

For its part, the Soviet leadership sought to use the CDE as a tribunal, as Boris Ponomarev of the Central Committee (CC) of the CPSU explained to the CC secretaries of the brother parties, in which to denounce the NATO states immediately after the decision to deploy Western medium-range missiles in Western Europe and to win over the public in favour of Soviet peace propaganda.[21] As the propaganda function of the CDE was the main focus for Moscow, the Soviet foreign minister, Andrei Gromyko explicitly instructed the leader of his country's delegation, Oleg Grinevsky, at the end of 1983: "Negotiate only on the major political measures. […] Forget about any notifications and observations."[22] Furthermore, in his opening speech at the

19 These were to be expert meetings on peaceful dispute settlement in Athens, on human rights and fundamental freedoms in Ottawa, on human contacts in Bern, a seminar on security issues in the Mediterranean in Venice and a cultural forum in Budapest: Sarah Snyder, "The Foundation for Vienna: A Reassessment of the CSCE in the mid-1980s", in: *Cold War History* 10 (2010), p. 493–512, on p. 494–495.

20 Concluding Document of the Madrid meeting 1980 of representatives of the participating states of the Conference on Security and Co-operation in Europe, held on the basis of the provisions of the Final Act relating to the follow-up to the conference, 1983, https://www.osce.org/files/f/documents/9/d/40871.pdf, p. 9, accessed 23.10.2024.

21 Douglas Selvage/Walter Süß, *Staatsicherheit und KSZE-Prozess. MfS zwischen SED und KGB (1972–1989)* (Analysen und Dokumente Vol. 54), Göttingen 2019, p. 443–444.

22 Quoted in in Oleg Grinevsky/Lynn M. Hansen, *Making Peace. Confidence Building*, New York 2009, p. 121.

Stockholm Conference, Gromyko held out the prospect of further developing the "announcement of major military manoeuvres" while rejecting demands that did not serve to "consolidate trust" but were aimed only at "spying on the neighbour through a gap in the fence".[23] The background to this statement was that the Soviet Union did in fact have something to hide. As Marshal Nikolai Ogarkov explained to Grinevsky, the Soviet leadership planned to open hostilities with nuclear strikes in the event of a war with NATO.[24]

Accordingly, the Warsaw Pact states, almost all of which subordinated themselves to the Soviet leadership, countered Western proposals to increase transparency in military affairs by demanding agreements to abstain from the use of force and a ban on the first use of nuclear weapons. They had no interest in CSBMs, especially in verification measures, which might reveal details of their own military arrangements to their opponents.[25] From the outset, therefore, there was a "fundamental disagreement in the conference goals between West and East" in Stockholm,[26] with the Warsaw Pact states loath to negotiate specific CSBMs until the West had agreed to the aforementioned Soviet demands. This stance did not pay off, however, as the vast majority of the participating states were, according to Klaus Citron, the leader of the West German delegation, very keen on "reaching agreement on concrete CSBMs" while showing little interest in the Soviet proposals.[27] The Soviet Union also initially adopted an obstructive stance on procedural issues, with the result that both sides did not agreed to set up two working groups until the beginning of December 1984.[28] The fundamental confrontation between West and East had not changed in Stockholm by the end of the year, nor did Citron anticipate any major substantial progress for 1985.[29]

The replacement of Konstantin Chernenko as general secretary of the CPSU in March 1985 and of Gromyko by Edvard Shevardnadze as foreign minister in July of the same year initially had no effect on the largely stagnating talks – not

23 Rede Gromykos, 18.1.1984, in: Andrei Gromyko, *Auf dem Friedenskurs Lenins. Ausgewählte Reden und Schriften*, Berlin (Ost) 1985, p. 411.

24 See Grinevsky/Hansen, *Making Peace*, p. 118–119.

25 Horst Bacia, "Die Stockholmer Konferenz über Vertrauensbildung und Abrüstung in Europa vor der entscheidenden Phase. Eine Zwischenbilanz", in: *Europa-Archiv* 41 (1986), p. 69–78, on p. 73–75.

26 Aufzeichnung des Botschafters Ruth, 18.1.1984, in: *AAPD 1984*, Berlin-München-Boston 2015, Dok. 11, p. 51–58, on p. 55.

27 Botschafter Citron, Stockholm (KVAE-Delegation), an das Auswärtige Amt, in: Ibid., Dok. 275, p. 1264–1265.

28 Bericht Citrons vom 14.12.1984, in: Ibid., Dok. 311, note 11, p. 1445.

29 Botschafter Citron, Stockholm (KVAE-Delegation), an das Auswärtige Amt, 19.12.1984, in: Ibid., Dok. 348, p. 1597.

least because in Moscow, the military and the KGB continued to push for a tougher course in opposition to the more flexible foreign ministry.[30] Actual negotiations in Stockholm did not begin until October, and only as 1985 turned into 1986 did Moscow seem to change tack, with Gorbachev and Shevardnadze signalling to Grinevsky that they were seriously interested in reaching a settlement in Stockholm and were prepared to make concessions to do so – including in the question of verification, which had hitherto divided East and West. Yet the military leadership remained steadfast in its opposition.[31] On 15 January 1986 Gorbachev made a spectacular proposal to abolish all nuclear weapons by the year 2000, in which he also mentioned the CDE, where it was time "to take effective measures [...] to deal with unresolved issues".[32]

The diplomats at the CDE, which was to terminate in September 1986, began drafting the Concluding Document in January 1986, with the delegates of the NATO states expressing cautious optimism regarding the outcome of the Conference. Yet by March, not one substantive issue had been resolved.[33] Even at the end of May, Citron reported to Bonn that the drafting process was making no progress because the Soviet Union continued its obstruction on key points. He identified a "tentative and insecure conduct of negotiations" on the part of the East and recorded his impression "that within the Soviet delegation, the political and military sides seem not always to be in agreement".[34] This state of affairs also held true for Moscow. Although Gorbachev, addressing the Politburo on 24 April, pushed for greater flexibility in negotiations and instructed the Soviet delegation accordingly, the foreign ministry remained at odds with both the military leadership and the KGB.[35] Although the Soviet side indicated the possibility of partial concessions in Stockholm, the chief of the general staff, Sergey Akhromeyev, speaking in the Politburo on 7 August, still opposed Gorbachev's view that a limited number of inspections on Soviet territory did not pose a security risk. Ultimately, however, Akhromeyev had to give up his

30 This point is made with reference to 1984 in Selvage/Süß, *Staatssicherheit und KSZE-Prozess*, p. 447–449; for the more flexible attitude of Shevardnadze; Grinevsky/Hansen, *Making Peace*, p. 351–356.

31 Ibid, p. 393–398, p. 425–426, p. 430–450.

32 Erklärung Gorbatschows vom 15.1.1986, in: Michail Gorbatschow, *Ausgewählte Reden und Aufsätze*, Vol. 3: Oktober 1985–Juli 1986, Berlin (Ost) 1988, p. 146–159, on p. 155.

33 Botschafter Hansen, Brüssel (NATO), an das Auswärtige Amt, 24.1.1986, in: *AAPD 1986*, Berlin-Boston 2017, Dok. 21, p. 124–129, on p. 126; Botschafter Citron, Stockholm (KVAE-Delegation), an das Auswärtige Amt, 14.3.1986, in: Ibid., Dok. 71, p. 392–402, on p. 393.

34 Botschafter Citron, Stockholm (KVAE-Delegation), an das Auswärtige Amt, 23.5.1986, in: Ibid., Dok. 151, p. 778–788, the quotes p. 779, 780.

35 Grinevsky/Hansen, *Making Peace*, p. 493–499, p. 516–523.

opposition.[36] In spite of continued resistance to Western inspections on the part of the military, the CDE was able to end on 22 September 1986 with a substantial Concluding Document.[37] For the first time, the East made far-reaching concessions to the West, particularly with regard to on-site inspections.[38] As the West German foreign ministry noted, the Soviet Union had agreed to a document "that very largely reflected the Western starting position".[39]

4 Confrontation in Ottawa, Concessions in Bern

At the Meeting of Experts on Respect for Human Rights and Fundamental Freedoms in Ottawa (7 May–17 June 1985), East and West could still be found pitted against one another in the usual fashion. The Soviet delegation had been instructed to uphold the Soviet conception of human rights with particular emphasis on socio-economic human rights and to reject any criticism of Eastern bloc practices as interference with those states' internal affairs. Once more, therefore, East and West were set on a collision course in Ottawa, with a mediation proposal from the N+N states rejected by the Eastern side. No concluding document could be agreed on; the East stood isolated at the Meeting's end.[40] Remarkably, Gorbachev himself defended Soviet intransigence in Ottawa in a letter to Ronald Reagan: "However, there should be no misunderstanding concerning the fact that we do not intend and will not conduct any negotiations

36 Botschafter Citron Stockholm (KVAE-Delegation) an das Auswärtige Amt, 18.7.1986, in: *AAPD 1986*, Dok. 203, p. 1061–1070; Grinevsky/Hansen, *Making Peace*, p. 574–579.

37 Document of the Stockholm Conference on Confidence- and Security-Building Measures and Disarmament in Europe convened in accordance with the relevant provisions of the Concluding Document of the Madrid Meeting of the Conference on Security and Co-operation in Europe, 19.09.1986, https://www.osce.org/files/f/documents/5/d/41238.pdf, accessed 23.10.2024. Although the document was not signed until 22 September, it is dated 19 September 1986 because the clock was stopped during the negotiations on that day.

38 Botschafter Citron, Stockholm (KVAE-Delegation) an das Auswärtige Amt, 22.9.1986, in: *AAPD 1986*, Dok. 253, p. 1337–1343, on p. 1342.

39 Aufzeichnung des Vortragenden Legationsrats I. Klasse Hartmann, 30.9.1986, in: Ibid., Dok. 267, p. 1399–1403, on p. 1402; see also Horst Bacia, "Die Stockholmer Konferenz – Schlußverhandlungen, Ergebnis und Ausblick", in: *Europa-Archiv* 42 (1987), p. 369–378, on p. 377.

40 Yuliya von Saal, *KSZE-Prozess und Perestroika in der Sowjetunion. Demokratisierung, Werteumbruch und Auflösung 1985–1991*, München 2014, p. 61–62; Ekkehard Eickhoff, "Das KSZE-Expertentreffen über Menschenrechte in Ottawa – eine Bewertung", in: *Europa-Archiv* 40 (1985), p. 573–580, on p. 578–579.

relating to human rights in the Soviet Union."[41] Nonetheless, in consequence of the meeting, Gorbachev gave instructions to develop a distinctly Soviet conception of human rights that would allow a more forward approach.[42] Since this was not, however, made known, one West German diplomat anticipated that there would be no substantial agreement on human rights at future meetings of experts.[43] Less pessimistic was Ekkehard Eickhoff, the leader of the West German delegation, who pointed out that there had after all been a genuine if hard-fought debate on respect for human rights, as a result of which the "character of the Final Act as point of appeal for the fulfilment of human rights obligations in other CSCE states was not only left untouched but indeed strengthened".[44]

By the time of the Meeting of Experts on Human Contacts in Bern (15 April–27 May 1986), which discussed questions such as family reunifications and travel and immigration regulations, the situation had fundamentally changed. Although the Soviet delegation pursued "the buttoned-up Gromyko style" by rejecting, from the outset, Western demands for public involvement and distributing only selected speeches to the media, the "influence of the Gorbachev factor on the course of this meeting could hardly be ignored",[45] for as the Soviet ambassador, Yuri Kashlev, recalled, he had received flexible directives and hence enjoyed considerable leeway in negotiations. Although, at the beginning of the meeting, the West criticised the Eastern bloc's non-implementation of CSCE provisions, and despite East and West each finding the other side's proposals to be unacceptable, the Soviet side (unlike the GDR) indicated its willingness to make concessions. In any case, Kashlev was able to persuade the Eastern delegations to agree to a substantial Concluding Document on the basis of an N+N proposal, even if the East Germans felt that Soviet concessions went too far.[46] From the Western European (and particularly the West German) perspective, too, the Meeting concluded with a text whose provisions were more binding than those

41 Gorbachev to Reagan, n.d. [June 1985], in: *Ronald Reagan, An American Life*, New York 1990, p. 619.

42 Snyder, "Foundation", p. 499; Selvage/Süß, *Staatssicherheit und KSZE-Prozess*, p. 486.

43 Bodo Karkow in einem Runderlass vom 26.6.1985, in: *AAPD 1985*, Berlin/Boston 2016, Dok. 168, note 24, p. 884.

44 Eickhoff, *KSZE-Expertentreffen*, p. 574–575.

45 First quotation in: Andreas Doepfner, "Das KSZE-Expertentreffen über menschliche Kontakte in Bern. Einordnung, Beschreibung, Bewertung", in: *Europa-Archiv* 41 (1986), p. 515; second quotation in: von Saal, *KSZE-Prozess*, p. 63.

46 See Ibid; Selvage/Süß, *Staatssicherheit und KSZE-Prozess*, p. 503–508.

of Helsinki and Madrid had been.[47] The United States, by contrast, whose head of delegation, Michael Novak, set greater store by "practical outcomes" – i.e. the resolution of specific cases – rejected the document as containing too many loopholes.[48] This stance remained unchanged even though Novak received, immediately before the Meeting was to conclude, a list of 36 emigration applications which the Soviets had granted.[49] West German attempts to change Washington's mind were unsuccessful, again leaving the Meeting to end without a concluding document on 27 May. Yet it was no failure from the perspective of the West German government, which expected positive effects of the implementation debate and the Western proposals on the Vienna Follow-up Meeting.[50]

The Soviet leadership, which had struck observers in Bern by its willingness to make concessions, also appeared to have learnt from events. It is surely no coincidence that on 28 May 1986 Gorbachev, speaking in the foreign ministry, announced that "we are making a turnaround on human rights". He not only encouraged his audience to be less fearful in the human rights debate but also called for concrete measures to be taken with regard to family reunions as well as emigration and immigration.[51] Moreover, a department of human rights was set up as part of a restructuring of the Soviet foreign ministry in 1986, a clear indication that the Soviet Union was preparing for the Vienna Follow-up Meeting.[52]

5 Conclusion

How then to describe the balance of stability and dynamism in the CSCE process between 1975 and 1986? On the one hand, it can be seen that, far from destabilising it, the agreements signed at the CSCE and its Follow-up Conferences recognised the post-war order. Yet they did unleash social dynamics, for

47 Runderlass des Vortragenden Legationsrats I. Klasse Pleuger, 28.5.1986, in: *AAPD 1986*, Dok. 156, p. 808.

48 See Doepfner, *KSZE-Expertentreffen*, p. 517; Selvage/Süß, *Staatssicherheit und KSZE-Prozess*, p. 508.

49 Von Saal, *KSZE-Prozess*, p. 63. As one US senator observed, "This is the first time that the Soviets have resolved such cases in the context of a CSCE meeting." Quoted in: Snyder, "Foundation", p. 501.

50 Doepfner, *KSZE-Expertentreffen*, p. 520; Runderlass des Vortragenden Legationsrats I. Klasse Pleuger, 28.5.1986, in: *AAPD 1986*, Dok. 156, p. 810.

51 Grundsatzrede Gorbatschows im Außenministerium, 28.5.1986, in: Michail S. Gorbatschow, *Gipfelgespräche. Geheime Protokolle aus meiner Amtszeit*, Berlin 1993, p. 182–200, on p. 195–196.

52 Selvage/Süß, *Staatssicherheit und KSZE-Prozess*, p. 509.

instance by encouraging the formation of Helsinki groups or emigration movements. The pressure from below created by these dynamics was felt not least in the negotiations, for instance at the Bern Expert Meeting, compelling the Eastern side to make more concrete commitments on human contacts.

On the other hand, the basic positions from which East and West embarked on the Follow-up Meetings turned out to relatively stable. Neither in Belgrade nor in Madrid was the Eastern side prepared to surrender key positions. Any concessions made in Madrid were of a tactical nature, aimed at securing a propagandistically useful disarmament conference. Yet these concessions encouraged the emigration movement in East Germany, adding to that country's growing instability.

At the beginning of the CDE, which coincided with the peak of the Second Cold War, nothing had changed in the confrontation between East and West. Even Gorbachev, once he had taken office, could not simply flip the switch but had to expend considerable energy in order to overcome resistance to his policies from the military and the KGB. By accepting on-site inspections and making commitments on military transparency, Moscow could be seen to make a clear move away from its previously held basic positions – and this even before the Vienna Follow-up meeting. The background lay in the paradigm shift in Soviet policy inaugurated by Gorbachev, away from absolute security for the Soviet Union and towards a relative security that considered other states' security interests and which was to enable the government to reallocate funds from the military to the civilian sector. Against this background, the West had reason to hope that the Soviet Union and the states of the Eastern bloc would show a greater willingness to make concessions in Vienna than they had before.

Austria's "Mr. CSCE" Helmut Liedermann

A Biographical Approach to the Helsinki Process

Maximilian Graf

1 Introduction: Biographies Matter

In the beginning, the historiography of the Conference on Security and Cooperation in Europe (CSCE) was strongly shaped by the memoirs of diplomats who were part of the negotiation process. The writings of diplomats provided historians with valuable insights into the CSCE process. The most prominent examples are surely John Maresca (United States) and Jacques Andréani (France), but Michael Alexander (Great Britain), Hans-Jörg Renk (Switzerland), Berndt von Staden (Germany), Luigi Vittorio Ferraris (Italy) and Markku Reimaa (Finland) have also made notable contributions. Still, we know little about the biographical influences that made certain diplomats especially important actors of making and shaping the CSCE. Making use of multiarchival research and with more and more documents declassified, scholarship on the CSCE has grown over the past two decades and moved away from the initial focus on diplomats and their writings. Martin D. Brown and Angela Romano recently aimed to bring renewed attention to the role of diplomats, asking whether they were executors or creative dealmakers. In their pilot study on France and Great Britain, they "hypothesized that diplomats at the CSCE also served as vital communication channels, mediators and 'trouble shooters' with a shared esprit de corps that fostered relationships among the delegations of the participating states".[1]

Brown and Romano sought "to assess whether diplomats and their interactions can be counted among the factors making the CSCE 'work'". More specifically, their research agenda "scrutinizes a variety of sources to appraise the contribution made by diplomats on the ground and employs prosopographical

1 Martin D. Brown/Angela Romano, "Executors or Creative Deal-Makers? The Role of the Diplomats in the Making of the Helsinki CSCE", in: Nicolas Badalassi/Sarah B. Snyder (eds.), *The CSCE and the End of the Cold War. Diplomacy, Societies and Human Rights, 1972–1990*, New York 2019, p. 43–73, on p. 44, for full references to the publications mentioned above, see p. 62 (endnote 2).

DOI:10.1163/9789004736979_005

methods in order to relate CSCE diplomats' personal and career trajectories to their diplomatic action on site".[2] They define prosopography

> as 'the investigation of the common background characteristics of a group of actors in history by means of a collective study of their lives', and its method consists in collecting various types of information about individuals of a selected group (for example, about birth and death, social origins, education, occupations, religion, experience of office and so on), then juxtaposing and combining them in order to detect correlations with behaviours and actions of these individuals.[3]

Education, occupation, and experience of office are certainly the most relevant factors when looking at the making of Austria's "Mr. CSCE". Helmut Liedermann (1926–2019) was a distinguished diplomat whose career was intertwined with the CSCE process from the initial stages of the negotiations in Dipoli, Helsinki and Geneva to the Follow-Up Meeting in Vienna and even beyond. This chapter explores the biographical factors that made him an outstanding CSCE diplomat, revisits his key achievements in the making of the Helsinki Final Act and addresses his later role as an observer of and participant in the CSCE process until the end of the Cold War – a period during which he held posts in Belgrade, Moscow and finally Vienna, where he was tasked with preparing the third follow-up meeting.

In his groundbreaking study of Austrian CSCE policy, the German historian Benjamin Gilde has set the record straight on the importance of actors: "It was not Chancellor Kreisky who drove the country's CSCE policy and ensured its humanitarian focus, but the negotiating diplomats, first and foremost Helmut Liedermann and Franz Ceska."[4]

In contrast to many other CSCE diplomats, Liedermann did not leave his memoirs to posterity, and his factual publications on the CSCE[5] provide only

2 Ibid., p. 44.

3 Ibid.

4 Benjamin Gilde, *Österreich im KSZE-Prozess 1969–1983. Neutraler Vermittler in humanitärer Mission*, München 2013 (quotation on the back cover).

5 Helmut Liedermann, "Österreichs Rolle beim Zustandekommen der KSZE", in: Oliver Rathkolb/Otto M. Maschke/Stefan August Lütgenau (eds.), *Mit anderen Augen gesehen. Internationale Perzeptionen Österreichs 1955–1990* (Österreichische Nationalgeschichte nach 1945 Vol. 2), Wien 2002, p. 487–505; Helmut Liedermann, "Österreichs Image im ehemaligen Jugoslawien", in: Ibid. p. 523–562; Helmut Liedermann, "Von Helsinki über Belgrad nach Madrid. Die Konferenz über Sicherheit und Zusammenarbeit in Europa aus der Sicht eines österreichischen Konferenzteilnehmers", in: Peter Fischer/Heribert Köck/Alfred Verdross (eds.),

little insight into his personal actions and perceptions. Still, his remarks on the importance of personal contacts between the members of all delegations and the Austrian delegation's role as a mediator between East and West clearly support the thesis put forward by Brown and Romano. Apart from his own writings and the existing studies on Austria and the CSCE,[6] the following analysis is based on Liedermann's personal file at the Austrian foreign ministry[7] and his diplomatic reports from his various diplomatic posts from the mid-1960s until the mid-1980s. While the extensive personal file provides insights to his career and the foreign ministry's view of his role in the CSCE process, his diplomatic reports show how Liedermann perceived the situation related to Basket III in various Warsaw Pact countries before and after the Final Act. These insights enable us to understand why he became such a distinctive CSCE diplomat. With regard to the later years of the process, they also shed light on the unsatisfying implementation of the provisions of the Final Act until the Vienna Follow-Up Meeting.

2 The Making of a CSCE Diplomat

Liedermann's biography – his background and the diplomatic posts he held abroad and at home – help explain his career as a leading CSCE diplomat. The Catholic Liedermann studied law at the University of Vienna and earned his

---

Völkerrecht und Rechtsphilosophie. Internationale Festschrift für Stephan Verosta zum 70. Geburtstag, Berlin 1980, p. 427–443; Helmut Liedermann, "Some Reflections on the Humanitarian Dimension of the CSCE Process", in: Hanspeter Neuhold (ed.), *CSCE: N+N Perspectives. The Process of the Conference on Security and Co-operation in Europe from the Viewpoint of the Neutral and Non-Aligned Participating States*, Wien 1987, p. 135–143.

6 Gilde, *Österreich im KSZE-Prozess*; Anna Graf-Steiner, *Brückenbauer im Kalten Krieg. Österreich und der lange Weg zur KSZE-Schlussakte*, Graz-Wien 2023. For a broader account of the participation of the European neutrals in the Helsinki process, see Thomas Fischer, *Neutral Power in the CSCE. The N+N States and the Making of the Helsinki Accords 1975*, Baden-Baden 2009. For my assessment of Austria's CSCE policy from the making of the Final Act until the end of the Cold War, see Maximilian Graf, "European Détente and the CSCE. Austria and the East-Central European Theatre in the 1970s and 1980s", in: Nicolas Badalassi/Sarah B. Snyder (eds.), *The CSCE and the End of the Cold War. Diplomacy, Societies and Human Rights, 1972–1990*, New York 2019, p. 249–274.

7 I am grateful to the Federal Ministry for European and International Affairs for granting me access to Helmut Liedermann's personal file at the foreign ministry. Previously untranslated German language sources were translated by the author.

doctorate in 1950.[8] He remained active in this field but in the present context, it is his diplomatic career that is of particular interest.

After entering the diplomatic service in 1955, his first post abroad was in post-Stalinist Poland, where he witnessed a liberalising national communist regime under the leadership of Władysław Gomułka. In terms of international relations, Liedermann's time in Poland covered a period ranging from an early thaw to the hottest moments of the Cold War: the Berlin Crisis and the Cuban Missile Crisis. Nevertheless, Austrian-Polish relations significantly improved during those years with mutual visits by the foreign ministers. On the Polish domestic scene, the absence of collectivisation and the prominent role of the Catholic Church stood out among Eastern bloc countries. However, even in the early 1960s the first signs became visible that the Polish leadership's comparatively liberal approach was drawing to an end.[9]

In Warsaw, Liedermann served under the leading international law expert Ambassador Stephan Verosta, rising to chargé d'affaires in 1961. From this time on, reports written and signed by him personally exist. It did not escape his observation that Gomułka "has long ceased to be the hope of the Poles, as he was in 1956".[10] Not surprisingly, many of Liedermann's reports addressed the relationship between the state/party and the Church. In one of his 1961 reports on renewed and aggravating crisis between them, he concluded: It "should not be forgotten, however, that despite the existing difficulties, the situation of the Church in Poland is still a relatively good one; [...] that the Church in Poland still enjoys a far more liberal treatment than in all other Eastern bloc countries".[11] In spite of latent conflicts, he was convinced: "However, the Church will certainly not perish in Poland; on the contrary, in the long run, [...] it will ultimately only emerge stronger from this conflict."[12] During his time in Warsaw Liedermann provided the ministry "with information that went far beyond what could be expected of a young official." Furthermore, he

8 Personalakt Helmut Liedermann, Bundesministerium für europäische und internationale Angelegenheiten (BMEIA), Geschäftszahl (GZ) 171.256-7/54.

9 Maximilian Graf, "Kreisky und Polen. Schlaglichter auf einen vernachlässigten Aspekt der österreichischen 'Ostpolitik'", in: Lucile Dreidemy et al. (eds.), *Bananen, Cola, Zeitgeschichte. Oliver Rathkolb und das lange 20. Jahrhundert*, Vol. 2, Wien 2015, p. 692–706.

10 Liedermann to Bundesministerium für Auswärtige Angelegenheiten (BMAA), Warsaw, 04.05.1961, Österreichisches Staatsarchiv (ÖStA), Archiv der Republik (AdR), BMAA, Politische Sektion, Abteilung 7 Entwicklung (II-Pol), Zahl (Zl.) 27-Pol.

11 Liedermann to BMAA, Warsaw, 27.04.1961, ÖStA, AdR, BMAA, II-Pol, Politische Berichte Warschau, Zl. 24-Pol.

12 Liedermann to BMAA, Warsaw, 10.10.1961, ÖStA, AdR, BMAA, II-Pol, Politische Berichte Warschau, Zl. 36-Pol.

continuously established connections between the Vatican and the Polish Cardinal Stefan Wyszyński.[13]

Following his return from Warsaw in 1962, Liedermann became deputy head of the human resources department of the foreign ministry in Vienna. After three years at Ballhausplatz, his next posting abroad took him to the frontline city of the Cold War: Berlin. From September 1965 to March 1971, Liedermann was consul general and, as such, the Austria's leading diplomat in West Berlin. From there he was able to follow how German "Ostpolitik" was gaining momentum, forming an important part of European détente and one of the basic prerequisites for the CSCE process. His activities beyond observing political developments in Berlin were, of course, not limited to representing Austrian interests in West Berlin, but also included contacts with the GDR, which was not diplomatically recognised by Austria until late 1972.

The rigid East German regime could not be compared with the comparatively liberal Poland of the late 1950s and early 1960s. There were intractable disputes between Austria and the GDR, especially concerning the fate of some 20.000 Austrians living in the GDR, whom the regime in East Berlin regarded as East German citizens. Liedermann was tasked with all kinds of complicated and frustrating humanitarian interventions with the East German foreign office. When intervening for family visits, marriages or travel, Austria's sole leverage lay in denying East German officials their visa to Austria and thus to the West. However, this leverage became less and less effective as détente progressed and made the international recognition of the GDR only a matter of time.[14]

3 Liedermann and the Making of the Helsinki Final Act

Equipped with this experience of day-to-day Cold War diplomacy, Liedermann returned to Vienna. Following the example of other foreign ministries, a new department "to deal exclusively with the project of holding a European security conference" was set up within the ministry's political department in 1971,[15] and Liedermann was chosen to head it.[16] He held the position from 1971 to

13 Personalakt Helmut Liedermann, BMEIA, GZ 273910/22-VI.1/93.

14 Maximilian Graf, *Österreich und die DDR 1949–1990. Politik und Wirtschaft im Schatten der deutschen Teilung*, Wien 2016.

15 Personalakt Helmut Liedermann, BMEIA, GZ 57.242-1a/71.

16 Personalakt Helmut Liedermann, BMEIA, GZ 108.116-II/71.

1977, leading the Austrian CSCE delegation during the negotiations in Dipoli, Geneva and Helsinki, where he played an important role.

Liedermann's role in the multilateral preparatory talks in Dipoli and in the actual CSCE negotiations in Geneva and Helsinki has been excellently researched by Benjamin Gilde, whose analysis of Austria's CSCE politics and Liedermann's role in Dipoli can be summarised as follows: While there was great scepticism on the part of the foreign minister, Rudolf Kirchschläger, and his ministry regarding Basket III, Austrian diplomats "gradually moved from initial reticence to supporting the Western positions on Basket III and, at times, even defending them in the front line". Helmut Liedermann and his colleagues "recognized the potential of this issue and the mediation opportunities that opened up for them". Additionally, "in the interest of their own credibility and the image of their country, they felt it necessary not to lag behind the other neutrals on these issues" and gradually "they were able to occupy a special position among the neutrals in this regard and were accepted as mediators by both West and East". Despite remaining sceptical, Kirchschläger apparently relied on their assessment as well as on the political director Ludwig Steiner, "who supported the delegation from Vienna, and let them have their way". Probably Austria's greatest success during the Multilateral Preparatory Talks was the draft preamble to Basket III. According to Gilde, Dipoli "meant a great foreign policy success" for Austria, "a clear increase in international prestige and an enhanced profile as a neutral state with a special interest in humanitarian issues, which always affirmed that it had no missionary intentions". Gilde stresses:

> This result can be attributed primarily to the Austrian delegation, above all to Helmut Liedermann, who made a name for himself in CSCE circles with his knowledge of the situation and his persistence in dealing with the East, and who was also able to convince his own foreign ministry.[17]

Clearly, Liedermann's engagement was shaped by his frustrating experiences with the GDR and his recollection of how much more liberal things had been in Warsaw.

Liedermann and his delegation continued to play this role in Geneva and Helsinki. During these one and a half years, he cultivated extensive personal contacts and held numerous informal meetings with Eastern and Western participants on the premises of the Austrian delegation. The resolution of

17 Gilde, *Österreich im KSZE-Prozess 1969–1983*, p. 131–133.

the preamble crisis through the N+N "package deal"[18] was their most important mediation activity. As "Western actors in neutral clothes" within the N+N-group, Austrian diplomats contributed to making the Final Act possible. Nevertheless, Austria's mediation efforts, though considerable, should not be overestimated, since the most crucial obstacles were ultimately overcome through superpower negotiations and compromises.[19] Retrospectively, the foreign ministry highlighted especially Liedermann's role as a coordinator for the most difficult and sensitive aspects of Basket III concerning human contacts, acting by the "consensus of all delegations".[20]

4 Follow-up Meetings and the Implementation of the Final Act

Liedermann's engagement with the CSCE did not end with the signing of the Final Act in 1975. In fact, Liedermann's next posting was supposed to be The Hague, where his accreditation as ambassador had already been granted by the government of the Netherlands. However, when the Austrian ambassador to Yugoslavia caused a hunting accident in 1977, the foreign ministry dispatched Liedermann to Belgrade instead "because, as a profound expert on the CSCE complex of problems, he is ideally suited to take charge of the Belgrade Conference".[21] Additionally, the foreign ministry stressed "his previous assignments (many years in Warsaw, head of the Berlin delegation), and his excellent knowledge of the problems of East-West relations and European security".[22] Liedermann served as Austrian ambassador in Belgrade until 1981.

18 Austria had played a major role in the formulation of the preamble to Basket III in Dipoli, thereby laying the foundation for the preamble crisis. Since the text of the preamble contained virtually no restrictions, the Soviet Union demanded the inclusion of the principles of non-interference and sovereign equality. As a mediator and coordinator, the Austrian delegation, together with the other neutrals, repeatedly helped to move the negotiations forward step by step. Still, progress depended on the readiness of the Soviet Union and the United States to compromise. In the end, the Austrian delegation played a significant role in the negotiations for the joint N+N package deal, which constituted a compromise between Eastern and Western demands (acceptable for all states) but cleverly placed the respective wordings in wisely chosen sections of the preamble. The Soviet Union did not achieve the inclusion of its demands in the preamble of Basket III and the only Western concession in return was the inclusion of a reference to national laws and regulations in the Declaration of Principles of Basket I.

19 Gilde, *Österreich im KSZE-Prozess 1969–1983*, p. 159–186, p. 255–257, for the quotation see p. 439.

20 Personalakt Helmut Liedermann, BMEIA, GZ 273910/22-VI.1/93.

21 Personalakt Helmut Liedermann, BMEIA, GZ 1337.1/23-VI.1/76.

22 Personalakt Helmut Liedermann, BMEIA, GZ 1337/4-VI.1/77.

Strictly speaking, Liedermann was not part of the Austrian delegation during the Belgrade preparatory meeting, but "as the Austrian ambassador to Yugoslavia, he occasionally took part in the discussions". During the follow-up meeting (1977–1978), Liedermann again headed the Austrian delegation. In his opening statement on Basket III, he addressed questions of human contacts, information, culture and education in particular. Despite limited progress since the signing of the Final Act, he struck a hopeful note, refraining from polemics and, above all, from naming and shaming individual states.[23] During the meeting, Liedermann sketched first outlines of possible proposals for improvements in the humanitarian field. The Austrian proposals were held back for tactical reasons, to be used later as compromise papers, if necessary, once the European Community (EC) proposals became available. The EC would present maximum proposals and Austria would seek to implement them as coordinator and mediator.[24]

Austria wanted progress in Basket III, but already at the early stages of Belgrade Liedermann had learned from the East German head of delegation, Ernst Krabatsch, that the Warsaw Pact states would not agree to an emphasis on human rights. After the meeting, Liedermann warned "not to see everything 'through the lens of a rather modest conference paper'". In the end,

> [t]he most important achievement of Belgrade, [...] was the agreement on the place and time of the next follow-up meeting, which was primarily due to the Austrian delegation, which had advocated this most vehemently and had essentially already pushed it through during the preparatory meeting.[25]

The CSCE moved from Belgrade to Madrid, where the next follow-up began in late 1980. Liedermann himself moved not to Madrid but to Moscow, where he held the prestigious position of Austrian ambassador to the Soviet Union (1981–1985). In his new post, he remained one of Austria's key diplomats during the crisis of détente that overshadowed the Madrid Follow-Up Meeting (1980–1983). In an article published in 1980, Liedermann stressed that Madrid needed to revive détente and secure the progress of the CSCE process. He wanted

23 Gilde, *Österreich im KSZE-Prozess 1969–1983*, p. 332, p. 341–343.

24 Ibid., p. 352–357. On the EC and Belgrade, see Angela Romano, "The European Community and the Belgrade CSCE", in: Vladimir Bilandžić/Dittmar Dahlmann/Milan Kosanović (eds.), *From Helsinki to Belgrade. The First CSCE Follow-up Meeting and the Crisis of Détente*, Bonn 2012, p. 205–224.

25 Gilde, *Österreich im KSZE-Prozess 1969–1983*, p. 391, p. 442.

Madrid to become the new "milestone", a focus for many people's hopes and expectations.[26] However, his hope came to naught: shortly after Liedermann arrived in Moscow, the CSCE finally stalled after the imposition of martial law in Poland on 13 December 1981.[27]

Although he was no longer directly involved in the CSCE negotiations anymore, it is evident how close to his heart the CSCE still was. In a report about the end of a hunger strike by Andrey Sakharov and his wife that finally enabled the emigration permit for his daughter in law, Liedermann stated: "In the present case, foreign policy interests obviously prevailed over internal considerations." However, "Sakharov's hunger strike and its successful outcome unfortunately distort Soviet reality". Liedermann knew that applicants for family reunification often lost their jobs after submitting applications, contrary to the provisions of the CSCE. Furthermore, he stressed that the Soviet authorities – also contrary to the provisions of the Final Act – placed internal laws and regulations above the Final Act. In view of that, he recalled that the provisions of the Final Act do not allow for such a conclusion. Contrary to Soviet practice, the participating states were "required to implement the provisions of the Final Act with due regard, even if this necessitates a change in the legal situation or administrative practice of the participating states".[28]

Liedermann frequently reported about the Soviets blaming the United States for the failure quickly to achieve a final document in Madrid given Moscow's favorable view of the N+N draft.[29] Always with reference to the CSCE, Liedermann pointed to the worsening of the human rights situation, the persecution of dissidents and the breakup of Helsinki groups:

> On balance, the Soviet policy of repression against dissidents can actually be described as quite successful. The main groups have been practically crushed. Most of the known dissidents have either been arrested or gone abroad. Their successors are hardly known abroad. It now seems

26 Liedermann, "Von Helsinki über Belgrad nach Madrid", p. 443.

27 Maximilian Graf, "Österreich und die 'polnische Krise' im Kontext 1980–1983", in: Peter Ruggenthaler/Wanda Jarząbek (eds.), *Österreich – Polen. Stationen gemeinsamer Geschichte im 20. Jahrhundert*, Graz 2021, p. 201–221.

28 Liedermann to BMAA, Moscow, 15.12.1981, ÖstA, AdR, BMAA, II-Pol, Politische Berichte Moskau, Zl. 671-Res.

29 Liedermann to BMAA, Moscow, 15.03.1982, ÖstA, AdR, BMAA, II-Pol, Politische Berichte Moskau, Zl. 214-Res; Liedermann to BMAA, Moscow, 24.03.1982, ÖstA, AdR, BMAA, II-Pol, Politische Berichte Moskau, Zl. 341-Res; Liedermann to BMAA, Moscow, 15.10.1982, ÖstA, AdR, BMAA, II-Pol, Politische Berichte Moskau, Zl. 544-Res; Liedermann to BMAA, Moscow, 14.12.1982, ÖstA, AdR, BMAA, II-Pol, Politische Berichte Moskau, Zl. 660-Res.

> only logical to prevent a situation like that which arose in the 1970s, when numerous dissidents became the darlings of the Western press.[30]

Nor was progress made on humanitarian issues of bilateral concern. Hence, Liedermann asked the Austrian CSCE delegation to raise these issues in Madrid once the negotiations had resumed.[31] Soviet media constantly ignored Basket III in its coverage of the CSCE process and even the concluding document of Madrid was summarised by *Pravda* with no reference to Basket III. In consequence, Liedermann advocated using the Final Act "more than before as the basis for interventions in human rights cases and in favour of facilitating human contacts [...] Greater use of the above-mentioned document is also recommended, [...] because otherwise it may become a piece of dead paper and be forgotten."[32]

5 Executive Secretary of the Vienna Follow-up Meeting

Clearly, in Liedermann's view, the Helsinki process and especially the implementation of the Final Act had to make progress, and it seems that Mikhail Gorbachev's rise to power made him cautiously optimistic. Before the opening of the Vienna meeting, Liedermann wrote:

> Notwithstanding all shortcomings in the implementation of the Helsinki Final Act, the CSCE process has had a perceptible impact in many spheres. It is now accepted as a matter of course that the CSCE process is a thematically comprehensive forum that does not accept the East-West dichotomy as an immutable fact of life but is designed to help eliminate it.

Against the background of a newly intensified dialogue between East and West, Liedermann hoped that Vienna would contribute to fostering détente

30 Liedermann to BMAA, Moscow, 19.10.1982, ÖstA, AdR, BMAA, II-Pol, Politische Berichte Moskau, Zl. 531-Res.

31 Liedermann to BMAA, Moscow, 14.01.1983, ÖstA, AdR, BMAA, II-Pol, Politische Berichte Moskau, Zl. 17-Res; Liedermann to BMAA, Moscow, 02.02.1983, ÖstA, AdR, BMAA, II-Pol, Politische Berichte Moskau, Zl. 53-Res; Liedermann to BMAA, Moscow, 12.07.1983, ÖstA, AdR, BMAA, II-Pol, Politische Berichte Moskau, Zl. 393-Res.

32 Liedermann to BMAA, Moscow, 21.10.1983, ÖstA, AdR, BMAA, II-Pol, Politische Berichte Moskau, Zl. 482-Res.

and facilitating the implementation of the Final Act. He concluded with an appeal:

> It is in the interest of all CSCE participating States that they should succeed at the Vienna Meeting, not only in ensuring the continuity of the CSCE process, but also in moving closer and closer towards fully implementing the rules of conduct to which they committed themselves in Helsinki and Madrid, and in making substantive and successful progress along the dynamic road of the CSCE process. The idea of the CSCE process is not to replace deeds by words. It is, however, to make words credible by unreserved implementation of the commitments that have been assumed. It is only in this way that we shall be able to ensure lasting peace. And that is what the peoples of the participating States hope will be achieved by the CSCE process, as the catalyst of their expectations from a process of détente.[33]

In the run-up to the Vienna Follow-Up Meeting, "an office for the preparation of the Vienna meeting of the participating States of the CSCE, subordinate to the cabinet [i.e. the core staff] of the Federal Minister, was created" in the foreign ministry. At its head was Liedermann, who just had returned from Moscow. Next, he was appointed Executive Secretary of the CSCE Follow-Up Meeting in Vienna with the rank of "Assistant Secretary General" of the United Nations.[34] Subject to the agreement of the participating states, the Executive Secretary of CSCE meetings always was a national of the host country. He was responsible for all technical and financial matters during the meeting, which included the registration of proposals adopted and their circulation among the participants. Reservations or interpretative statements concerning given decisions had to be submitted by the participants in writing to the Executive Secretary. This made Liedermann a well-informed man and it seems that his contacts with the representatives of all participating states and the Austrian institutions involved were not limited to the coordinating and organizational tasks Liedermann had been given once all participating states had approved of his appointment.[35] His career at the CSCE was thus crowned with this "elder

---

33 Liedermann, "Some Reflections on the Humanitarian Dimension of the CSCE Process", p. 140–141, p. 143.

34 Personalakt Helmut Liedermann, BMEIA, GZ 1337/25-VI.1/85; Personalakt Helmut Liedermann, BMEIA, GZ 1337/23-VI.1/85.

35 Memo "KSZE; 3. Folgetreffen in Wien; Nominierung des Exekutivsekretärs", Vienna, 12.11.1985, ÖstA, AdR, BMAA, II-Pol, GZ 804.00/60-II.7/85; Memo "Wiener Folgetreffen,

statesman"-like diplomatic role for which he was "respected by all delegations even in difficult times".[36] Given his experience of and network within the CSCE, he was an ideal communicator during the meeting, though a full assessment of his more informal activities must remain subject to further research. Gradually Liedermann's vision for the Follow-Up and ultimately for overcoming the East-West divide in Europe materialised. In its initial stages, the debate about the implementation of humanitarian issues in Vienna did not differ much from those in Belgrade and Madrid. The West tested Gorbachev's readiness to make concessions in the humanitarian field. Against the background of accelerating reforms in Eastern Europe, expectations in the West were growing and divergences within the Socialist bloc became more and more obvious. Finally, in January 1989, all countries involved accepted a strong concluding document that once again originated from an N+N proposal.[37]

After the Vienna Follow-Up Meeting, Liedermann remained executive secretary of the negotiations on Confidence- and Security-Building Measures within the framework of the CSCE, executive secretary of the CSCE Committee for the preparation of the Paris summit in 1990, and, from mid-1991, secretary general of the Open Skies negotiations in Vienna. After successfully organising the World Conference on Human Rights held by the United Nations in Vienna 1993,[38] he retired from the diplomatic service. At the beginning of the twenty-first century, Liedermann looked back at the CSCE, recalling that

> the conference results were initially quite controversial. Some saw it as a rather worthless document that, like many others, would disappear into the archives of foreign ministries. Others feared that it would seal the division of Europe and freeze the political and territorial status quo. However, it was to turn out quite differently: not a sealing of the status quo, but the starting point for a dynamic process that led to the overcoming of the division of Europe and had unimagined repercussions inside what was then the Communist sphere. [...] The CSCE Final Act, signed at the highest political level on 1 August 1975, will not be forgotten in the assessment of the events of the twentieth century, but will be remembered as one of the most significant milestones of that period.[39]

Kandidatur Botschafter Dr. Helmut Liedermann, Zustimmung der übrigen KSZE-Teilnehmerstaaten", Vienna, 18.3.1986, ÖstA, AdR, BMAA, II-Pol, GZ 803.01/33-II.7/86.

36 Personalakt Helmut Liedermann, BMEIA, GZ 273910/22-VI.1/93.

37 Graf, "European Détente and the CSCE", p. 263–265.

38 Personalakt Helmut Liedermann, BMEIA, GZ 273910/22-VI.1/93.

39 Liedermann, "Österreichs Rolle beim Zustandekommen der KSZE", p. 492–493.

6 Conclusion

Liedermann's insider assessment of the CSCE accords with the findings of much recent scholarship on the CSCE. However, the Helsinki process was not a straight road from the making of the CSCE to the end of the Cold War. It needed diplomats capable of negotiating not only the provisions of the Final Act but also their implementation. Liedermann's experiences in Warsaw and Berlin made him an ideal CSCE diplomat regarding the challenges ahead in Basket III, to which he made significant contributions. He must be regarded as one of the creative dealmakers who made the necessary compromises possible. As a Western actor in neutral clothes, he achieved much during the negotiations. However, his experiences in Belgrade and of the Soviet Union in the 1980s also serve as a reminder of how limited progress in the humanitarian field was before the Vienna Follow-Up. Despite this, he saw the value and potential of the CSCE process and believed in its ultimate success, which he witnessed during the Vienna Follow-Up Meeting and the subsequent "peaceful revolutions" in Eastern Europe. Future comparative research on Liedermann and his fellow CSCE diplomats of both East and West will certainly enhance our knowledge about how the Final Act was made and how the struggle to implement its provisions was fought until the end of the Cold War.

The Concluding Document of the Vienna CSCE Follow-up Meeting, 15 January 1989

An Analysis of Its Drafting and an Interpretation in Comparison with Other Declarations

Michael Gehler

1 From Helsinki to Vienna, 1975–1989[1]

The Helsinki Final Act of the Conference on Security and Cooperation in Europe (CSCE) represented a political compromise between Eastern territorial and security interests and Western human rights interests. Basket I contained a catalogue of ten "principles" that were to govern relations between the participating states, including cooperation in humanitarian areas. In addition, there was a "Document on confidence-building measures and certain aspects of security and disarmament". Basket II enclosed guidelines for cooperation in the fields of economics, science, technology and the environment. Basket III included concrete facilitations for family visits and reunions and improved working conditions for journalists.[2]

This chapter answers five questions: What course did the Vienna Follow-up Meeting take? How did its Concluding Document come about? What is its structure and focus compared with other final documents (1975, 1978, 1983 and 1986)? What outcomes were achieved? These questions are answered with reference to Austrian observations and judgements.

The CSCE Follow-up Meetings in Belgrade (1977–1978)[3] and Madrid (1980–1983), which served to review and continue the policy of détente, were affected by the intensifying Cold War and failed to achieve any resounding success.[4] By the time of the Vienna Follow-up Meeting (1986–1989), Cold War

1 Previously untranslated German language sources were translated.

2 Konferenz über Sicherheit und Zusammenarbeit in Europa. Schlussakte, Helsinki 1975, https://www.osce.org/files/f/documents/6/e/39503.pdf, accessed 16.08.2023; Michael Gehler, "Meilenstein der Friedenspolitik. Vor 45 Jahren, am 1. August 1975, wurde in Helsinki die KSZE-Schlussakte unterzeichnet, ein internationaler Vertrag neuen Typs", in: *Extra. Die Wochenend-Beilage der Wiener Zeitung*, 01.08.2020, p. 33.

3 On the follow-up meeting in Belgrade, see Wilfried von Bredow, *Der KSZE-Prozeß. Von der Zähmung zur Auflösung des Ost-West-Konflikts*, Darmstadt 1992, p. 79–88.

4 Jörg Kastl, "Das KSZE-Folgetreffen von Madrid. Verlauf und Schlußdokument aus der Sicht der Bundesrepublik Deutschland", in: *Europa-Archiv* 20 (1983), p. 617–626, also published in:

DOI:10.1163/9789004736979_006

tensions were fading. It provided mandates for negotiations on conventional armed forces in Europe and confidence- and security-building measures (CSBMs), with progress made in all baskets.[5]

2 The Course of the Vienna Follow-up Meeting and the Drafting of the Concluding Document from the Austrian Perspective

Due to the negative experiences with the Madrid preparatory meeting, which had lasted nine and a half turbulent weeks, the relevant final document had defined the mandate of the Vienna preparatory meeting in "very narrow" terms, as summarised in an Austrian foreign ministry report. The agenda, task list and modalities of the Madrid meeting were to be adapted only in points "which required amendment due to the change of date and place, the drawing of lots and the mention of other meetings held in accordance with the decisions of the Madrid meeting."[6] The Vienna Follow-up Meeting was officially held from 4 November 1986 to 19 January 1989 and was organised in six sessions, with opening and closing taking place at foreign ministerial level.[7]

The Concluding Document was drafted at Ballhausplatz, the seat of the Austrian Foreign Ministry until 2005. Although the material to be discussed of the Vienna Follow-up Meeting was available in full by Easter 1987, negotiations regarding the text took a long time to begin. The conclusion of the conference had been set for 31 July 1987. However, the date passed without a single sentence of the Concluding Document having been formulated and finalised. It was not until the autumn of 1987 that the drafting work got off even to a "slow

---

Hermann Volle/Wolfgang Wagner (ed.), *Das Madrider KSZE-Folgetreffen. Der Fortgang des KSZE-Prozesses in Europa*, Bonn 1984, p. 45–54; von Bredow, *Der KSZE-Prozeß*, p. 88–96. On the end of détente and subsequently the end of the Cold War in the 1980s see John Lewis Gaddis, *Der Kalte Krieg. Eine neue Geschichte*, München 2008, p. 243–292.

5 On the CSCE Follow-up Meeting in Vienna and the new quality of the CSCE process see von Bredow, *Der KSZE-Prozeß*, p. 111–132; for a summary see Wilfried Loth, "Der KSZE-Prozess 1975–1990: eine Bilanz", in: Matthias Peter/Hermann Wentker (eds.), *Die KSZE im Ost-West-Konflikt. Internationale Politik und gesellschaftliche Transformation 1975–1990* (Schriftenreihe der Vierteljahrshefte für Zeitgeschichte Sondernummer), München 2012, p. 323–331, on p. 330–331.

6 Bericht über Verlauf und Ergebnis des Wiener KSZE-Folgetreffens, Österreichisches Staatsarchiv (ÖStA), Archiv der Republik (AdR), BMAA, politische Sektion II/Abteilung 7 Entwicklung (II-Pol.) 1989, GZ 804.00/2-II.7/89. The information can be found in BMaA-Abteilung II.7-1989, 804.00 to 804.02.02 OZ 1–120, there from photograph number (Bericht im Haus): 3222–3252 and again from (Bericht im Ausland): 3253–3362 (translated).

7 Ibid.; on Liedermann, see the article by Maximilian Graf in this volume.

start". According to Austrian diplomats, the reasons for this delay lay partly in the large number of proposals but above all in political factors.[8]

Until July 1987, the struggle of the NATO countries to reach a common position on military questions acted as a retarding force. The neutral and non-aligned (N+N) states also had difficulties in maintaining a common stance. Yugoslavia, Sweden and Finland had sought the participation of the N+N in the arms control negotiations, while Switzerland had "completely ruled out" any such participation for itself. After the NATO states, with the agreement of the Warsaw Treaty Organisation (the "Warsaw Pact"), had de facto established the concept of the twenty-three NATO states acting as autonomous negotiators within the CSCE framework, all N+N countries fell in with this solution, which Austria had favoured for some time.[9]

The Warsaw Pact states used the delay of the Western proposal on military issues to "justify slow progress" in the human rights and humanitarian fields. From the perspective of the Ballhausplatz, the considerable problems in reaching new normative agreements had "deeper-rooted reasons".[10]

The reforms initiated in the USSR by Mikhail Gorbachev, general secretary of the CPSU,[11] as well as those in the Central and Eastern European states had raised expectations in the Western camp regarding a positive conclusion to the Vienna Follow-up Meeting. On the one hand, the aim was to increase the pressure for implementation in areas where the realization of the Final Act was deficient – for instance, freedom to leave the country and freedom of religion – by means of concrete provisions, and on the other hand to set the existing "mechanism" in motion through permanent monitoring of the human rights practices of the participating states as a result of the obligation to provide information, notification procedures, and bilateral and multilateral meetings. Due to the different political developments in the socialist states of Central and Eastern Europe, however, it was uncertain whether the negotiations in Vienna would produce a reliable result. As a result of this uncertainty, the Western states adopted a wait-and-see attitude, which initially was not conducive to progress in the negotiations.[12]

The representatives of the Warsaw Pact states were on uncertain ground. The already emerging power rivalries in the Kremlin and increasing differences

8 Bericht über Verlauf und Ergebnis des Wiener KSZE-Folgetreffens (translated).
9 Ibid.
10 Ibid. (translated).
11 On the "Gorbachev Factor" see Bernd Stöver, *Der Kalte Krieg. Geschichte eines radikalen Zeitalters 1947–1991*, München 2007, p. 437–462.
12 Bericht über Verlauf und Ergebnis des Wiener KSZE-Folgetreffens.

among the Eastern delegations between "progressive", reform-oriented countries such as Hungary and Poland on the one hand and the "conservative" Warsaw Pact states such as Czechoslovakia and Romania on the other – a group that also included "with qualifications, Bulgaria and the GDR" – contributed to an atmosphere of uncertainty.[13]

It was the representatives of the neutral states with their particular commitment to the "human dimension" who enabled effective negotiations on the text to begin. On 30 July 1987, an Austro-Swiss working paper was brought to bear on Basket III, organising the now confusing negotiating material on 11 pages and suggesting possible solutions for the relevant and still unresolved issues. In autumn 1987, a series of non-papers by the head of the Austrian delegation, Rudolf Torovsky, in his capacity as coordinator, served the same purpose for controversial issues in the area of human rights such as freedom of information, freedom of expression and freedom of travel.[14]

In Basket II,[15] in which the work had been completed in Madrid after a relatively short time, negotiations in Vienna on the agreement on the drafting of the final text proved difficult. The Western camp was concerned chiefly with more openness on the part of the Central and Eastern European state systems and better conditions for economic cooperation.[16] A new focus in Basket II was environmental protection. Austria submitted five proposals regarding cross-bloc cooperation for the further development of international environmental law.[17]

A revealing interim assessment from the Austrian diplomatic perspective concluded that the course and results of the fifth session of the Vienna Follow-up Meeting from 22 January to 25 March 1988 had so far been, in Torovsky's view, "disappointing". It became clear from the individual baskets that "little concrete progress had been made in the efforts to draft a concluding document".[18]

The negotiations on military security were the most promising in terms of reaching an agreement, particularly among the states organised in blocs, which was not particularly surprising given that the discussions were primarily focussed on agreeing mandates for future substantive negotiations. According to Torovsky, an East-West climate favourable to arms control issues had a

13 Ibid. (translated).

14 Ibid.

15 See the article by Roland Laimer in this volume.

16 Ibid.

17 Ibid.

18 Zusammenfassung der Sitzungsperiode 22.1.–25.3.1988, Österreichisches Staatsarchiv (ÖStA), Archiv der Republik (AdR), BMAA, politische Sektion II/Abteilung 7 Entwicklung (II-Pol.) 1988, GZ 803.12/16-II.7/88. (translated).

positive effect in this area. In other sectors – as with Basket II, about which there had been little controversy in previous follow-up meetings – the results achieved before the end of 1987 were rounded off and consolidated with minor textual modifications, although there were some setbacks, not least the fact that the negotiations barely touched upon the proposals of the follow-up programme.[19]

Torovsky saw the CSCE and the follow-up meetings as parts of a long-term process with a "tendency towards processual development, in which phases of progress in negotiations alternate with phases of stagnation and setbacks". In his view, the negotiations in Vienna were characterised by plenary meetings and formal drafting groups, numerous informal forms of consultation, contact groups and task forces – all typical of the CSCE. Leaving aside limited problems in individual baskets, in which there was a difference between tactical reservations on the one hand and substantial political resistance on the other, Torovsky felt able to discern a possible outcome of the Vienna Follow-up Meeting in "broad outlines" as early as April 1988. The final result seemed likely to fall "somewhere between the very high expectations at the beginning of the [Vienna Meeting] and a Madrid-style outcome", but Austria's leading diplomat at the CSCE did not rule out the possibility that "hardening positions on both the Western and Eastern (or both) side(s)" might, in extreme cases, "also produce a short document with not much of a follow-up programme, as was the case in Belgrade".[20]

Against the backdrop of easing East-West relations and Gorbachev's reforms in the Soviet Union, the question was repeatedly raised why the Vienna negotiations had so far been so "tough" and why the high expectations placed in the follow-up meeting had not yet been fulfilled and "relative failure" could not be ruled out. Torovsky cited two reasons:

1. Despite improved East-West relations, especially in terms of superpower dialogue, the conflicts of interest and differences in ideology and politics remained. Relations improved primarily in the fields of arms control and the resolution of regional conflicts, while many of the CSCE's broad spectrum of issues had not yet been addressed.
2. According to Torovsky, the slowing of Gorbachev's reform efforts had brought about only "marginal improvements in relations between individuals and the state or party" by April 1988, which had "significantly reduced" the likelihood of a greater willingness on the part of the USSR and other socialist states to implement the human dimension provisions.

---

19 Ibid.

20 Ibid. (translated).

In Torovsky's view, misguided expectations regarding the positive impact of both factors and the understandable desire for a qualitative leap in the CSCE process had greatly raised the level of expectations among Western and N+N states in the initial phase of the Vienna Follow-up Meeting, just as most Central and Eastern European states also entertained heightened expectations of the Vienna Follow-up Meeting.[21]

In spite of all this, Torovsky felt entitled to hope that "more precise and clearer commitments could be agreed in each of the baskets, which should serve greatly to improve respect for the Final Act". At the beginning of April 1988, he recognised for the first time the possibility in the CSCE process of creating "a co-operative monitoring system (or at least serious moves in that direction) of compliance with the CSCE provisions on the human dimension". He also noted that "the negotiating structures in the military field which are close to being agreed upon [...] may encourage moves in the direction of conventional disarmament and a consolidation of military confidence-building".[22]

The state of repeated deadlock in the negotiations continued until the spring of 1988. A turning point was reached on 13 May, when the N+N states presented a draft Concluding Document based on the previous negotiations. The initiative led to a re-examination of the Soviet position by the representatives of the N+N and resulted in more flexible instructions, which brought new momentum to the sensitive humanitarian and human rights issues. However, the Soviet delegation had difficulties persuading its less reform-minded allies to support its new course. The greatest resistance came from the Romanian delegation, which, even a month after the presentation of the N+N document, completely rejected any relevant regulations in the area of human rights and Basket III.[23]

In the autumn months of 1988, new progress was made in the work on the Concluding Document and in the consultations on the mandate for conventional arms control negotiations, which were taking place simultaneously. The particular focus lay on fulfilling the task of holding a conference on human rights and humanitarian issues in Moscow. The proposal presented by the Soviet delegation in the opening phase of the Vienna Follow-up Meeting had initially been met with scepticism and outright rejection by the Western states, especially the United States, Great Britain and Canada. The American delegation had demanded changes to the practice of the Soviet human rights regime as a precondition for its agreement, which in practice amounted to a rejection. As a result, the Soviet delegation had pursued its suggestion with

21 Ibid.

22 Ibid. (translated).

23 Bericht über Verlauf und Ergebnis des Wiener KSZE-Folgetreffens.

reduced commitment, which might have been taken for its factual abandonment. Unexpectedly, the Soviet foreign minister, Eduard Shevardnadze, in an exchange with his partners in September 1988, insisted on holding the Moscow Conference as an integral element of concluding the Vienna Follow-up Meeting, while at the same time vigorous efforts were made to improve human rights practices, such as the release of political prisoners, the resolution of family reunification cases, the increase in the number of emigrants from the USSR and the cessation of jamming Western radio broadcasts. This change in attitude amounted to factual compliance with the American conditions and allowed the West to give its unanimous approval to the Moscow Conference. After a dispute between the French and American delegations about the relation between conventional arms control negotiations and the CSCE process, which flared up again in November 1988, the basis for the conclusion of the Vienna Follow-up Meeting was in place. In the second half of December, the N+N delegations presented a revised version of their draft, which on 15 January 1989 was adopted by all 35 participating states as the Concluding Document of the Vienna Follow-up Meeting.[24]

Although Romanian statements made it clear that the country would not implement Western aspects of the human rights agreements, and although demonstrations taking place in Czechoslovakia and the GDR were being suppressed at the same time, the adoption of the Concluding Document was welcomed as a historic event in East-West relations. This was also the general tenor of the final declarations issued by the foreign ministers of the participating states from 17 to 19 January.[25]

3 Organisation, Structure and Priorities of the Vienna Concluding Document

Including its appendices, the Vienna Concluding Document contains 81 closely-spaced pages in its German version, 41 of them form the main part. It is divided into first a section on security issues in Europe with 27 principles and their respective subsections, and second a section on CSBMs and certain aspects of security and disarmament in Europe, based on the Conference on Security and Confidence Building Measures and Disarmament in

24 Ibid., on the Vienna Concluding Document see also Michael Cotey Morgan, *The Final Act. The Helsinki Accords and the Transformation of the Cold War*, Princeton-Oxford 2018, p. 244–245.

25 Bericht über Verlauf und Ergebnis des Wiener KSZE-Folgetreffens.

Europe (CDE) held in Stockholm (1984–1986) and the assessment of the progress made, negotiations on CSBMs and on conventional forces in Europe, and meetings to exchange views and information on the progress of negotiations on conventional forces in Europe. Third, there follows a section on cooperation in the fields of the economy, science and technology, and the environment, including trade and industrial cooperation and other areas, covering 46 points. Fourth, there is a section on security and cooperation in the Mediterranean region and, fifth, one on cooperation in humanitarian and other areas, including 71 points on human contacts, information, cultural and educational cooperation and exchanges. The sixth section addresses the human dimension of the CSCE, based on the principles and provisions of the Final Act and other relevant CSCE documents, with four resolutions on developments in the human dimension, including the implementation of specific CSCE commitments and their review, as well as the functioning of the procedures described in the four resolutions (later known as the Vienna Mechanism). It also contained a commitment to discuss the information provided and to consider practical proposals for new measures aimed at improving the implementation of the commitments relating to the human dimension of the CSCE and the effectiveness of the procedures described therein. On the basis of these proposals, the Conference was to consider the adoption of new measures.[26]

A first meeting of the Conference on the Human Dimension was to take place from 30 May to 23 June 1989 in Paris, a second from 5 to 29 June 1990 in Copenhagen and a third from 10 September to 4 October 1991 in Moscow. The agenda, timetable and other organisational modalities were contained in a separate appendix (X.).[27]

A seventh section of the Concluding Document deals with the consequences. The fourth main meeting after Belgrade, Madrid and Vienna was to be held in Helsinki from 24 March 1992 to assess the functioning of the procedures set out in the four resolutions and the progress made at the meetings of the Conference on the Human Dimension of the CSCE. The stated intention was to examine ways of further strengthening and improving these procedures and to pass resolutions accordingly.[28]

26 For this and the following, see Abschließendes Dokument des Wiener Treffens 1986 der Vertreter der Teilnehmerstaaten der Konferenz über Sicherheit und Zusammenarbeit in Europa, welches auf der Grundlage der Bestimmungen der Schlussakte betreffend die Folgen der Konferenz abgehalten wurde, Wien 1989. https://www.osce.org/files/f/documents/c/a/40883.pdf, accessed 30.6.2023.

27 Ibid.

28 Ibid.

For the purpose of adapting the agenda, task list and modalities used for the Vienna Follow-up Meeting, a preparatory meeting was to be held in Helsinki from 10 March 1992. It was agreed that modifications should be made to those items requiring them due to changes in time and place, the drawing of lots and the mention of other meetings held in accordance with the decisions of the 1986 Vienna Follow-up Meeting. The duration of the preparatory meeting was not to exceed two weeks.[29]

The results were to be duly taken into account at the main meeting in Helsinki. The remainder of the Concluding Document contains eleven major appendices and two sub-appendices.[30]

4 The Final Documents Compared[31]

A comparison of the five final documents of Helsinki, Belgrade, Madrid, Stockholm and Vienna (Table 1) provides initial insights regarding the frequency of certain terms. In terms of substance, the selection can be justified as follows: These terms were to be found in most of the final documents and they

29 Ibid.

30 Ibid.

31 The analysis was based on the German versions of the documents. The overview table therefore contains both the English and German terms. Konferenz über Sicherheit und Zusammenarbeit in Europa. Schlussakte, Helsinki 1975, https://www.osce.org/files/f/documents/6/e/39503.pdf, accessed 16.08.2023; Abschließendes Dokument des Belgrader Treffens 1977 der Vertreter der Teilnehmerstaaten der Konferenz über Sicherheit und Zusammenarbeit in Europa, welches auf der Grundlage der Bestimmungen der Schlussakte betreffend die Folgen der Konferenz abgehalten wurde, Belgrad 1978, https://www.osce.org/files/f/documents/1/c/40867.pdf, accessed 30.6.2023; Abschließendes Dokument des Madrider Treffens 1980 der Vertreter der Teilnehmerstaaten der Konferenz über Sicherheit und Zusammenarbeit in Europa, welches auf der Grundlage der Bestimmungen der Schlussakte betreffend die Folgen der Konferenz abgehalten wurde, Madrid 1983, https://www.osce.org/files/f/documents/4/c/40873.pdf, accessed 30.6.2023; Dokument der Stockholmer Konferenz über Vertrauens- und Sicherheitsbildende Maßnahmen über Abrüstung in Europa, Einberufen in Übereinstimmung mit den einschlägigen Bestimmungen des abschließenden Dokuments des Madrider Treffens der Konferenz über Sicherheit und Zusammenarbeit in Europa, Stockholm 1986, https://www.osce.org/files/f/documents/4/2/41240.pdf, accessed 30.6.2023; Abschließendes Dokument des Wiener Treffens 1986 der Vertreter der Teilnehmerstaaten der Konferenz über Sicherheit und Zusammenarbeit in Europa, welches auf der Grundlage der Bestimmungen der Schlussakte betreffend die Folgen der Konferenz abgehalten wurde, Wien 1989, https://www.osce.org/files/f/documents/c/a/40883.pdf, accessed 30.6.2023

TABLE 1 Comparison of key terms in the final documents

	Helsinki 1975	Belgrade 1978	Madrid 1983	Stockholm 1986	Vienna 1989
Abrüstung (disarmament)	7	0	10	9	14
Energie (energy)	12	0	2	0	10
Entspannung (détente)	6	2	6	0	2
Fortschritt (progress)	18	0	10	2	17
Freundschaft (friendship)	10	1	5	3	5
Frieden (peace)	20	0	8	5	4
Gegenseitigkeit (reciprocity)	4	0	3	2	2
Gemeinschaft (community)	1	0	3	0	9
Gerechtigkeit (justice)	7	0	2	1	2
Gleichheit (equality)	7	0	1	2	3
Grenzen (borders)	7	0	6	6	2
Grundfreiheiten/Freiheit ([basic] liberties)	13	0	11	2	34
Integrität (integrity)	7	0	0	1	2
Klima (climate)	4	0	0	0	0
Kultur/kulturell (culture/cultural)	84	1	21	1	71
Menschenrechte (human rights)	7	0	11	1	15
Minderheiten (minorities)	8	0	1	0	8
Selbstbestimmung (self-determination)	4	0	0	0	1
Sicherheit (security)	60	11	42	31	72
Souveränität (sovereignty)	4	0	0	0	0
Stabilität (stability)	5	0	1	0	7
Umwelt (environment)	51		8	1	31
Unabhängigkeit (independence)	4	0	0	1	2
Verantwortung (responsibility)	3	0	0	0	5
Verhandlungen (negotiations)	4	0	5	1	67
Verkehr [Transit] (traffic [transit])	27	0	3	1	8
Vermittlung (mediation)	1	0	0	0	1
Verständnis/Verständigung (understanding/rapprochement)	19	0	3	1	4
Vertrauen (confidence)	19	0	18	21	24
Zusammenarbeit (cooperation)	162	11	52	8	101
Total	585	26	232	100	523

obviously represented central concerns of the participating states from both East and West as well as from the perspective of the non-aligned and neutral states. In terms of methodology, it should be borne in mind that the frequency of mentions alone does not automatically say anything about all the priorities of the participating states. In some cases, the final documents represented compromise formulas in which concessions had to be made with regard to the original objectives. Only a complete and reciprocal evaluation of all negotiation records in their various languages can provide further information on what terminology and formulations ultimately had to be softened, deleted or reinserted. A purely quantitative analysis is thus necessarily limited, especially as terms might convey qualitatively different levels of meaning across languages and have different meanings from an Eastern or Western perspective. This terminological survey therefore represents only an initial, superficial and preliminary attempt that requires further analysis and refinement. What exactly did the West, as opposed to the East, understand by "freedom" or "human rights"? This was by no means already decided and established with the Vienna Concluding Document, as its first interpretations – e.g. by the East German leadership – suggested.

These caveats in mind, what trends does this quantitative analysis suggest? "Disarmament" was prioritised in Vienna, "peace" in Helsinki – joined, in Vienna, by basic liberties, freedom, human rights, security and confidence. Based on the frequency in which these concepts were mentioned, the Helsinki Final Act and the Vienna Concluding Document can be identified as the two outstanding, most substantial, comprehensive and far-reaching documents of their kind – ground-breaking, that is, in terms of détente and security policy and decisive in terms of human rights. Vienna and Helsinki closed a circle. While Belgrade represented a clear step backwards, Madrid contributed to cohesion but did not achieve any significant progress, while the Stockholm document on "security" and "confidence" acted as an essential link and indeed a catalyst between Helsinki and Vienna.

These findings are further emphasised when all significant uses of these terms are added up: Helsinki, with 585 mentions, and Vienna, with 523 mentions, are in the lead, with Madrid and Stockholm trailing far behind with 232 and 100 mentions, respectively. The Belgrade final document appears the least substantive due to the text's very sparse content. To be fair, it must also be added that Stockholm addressed a more limited subject matter, namely "confidence building" and "disarmament". However, the importance of Vienna after Helsinki becomes abundantly clear in this type of word field analysis.

5 Outcomes

The agreement reached in Vienna went far beyond the texts negotiated in Belgrade and Madrid. It reaffirmed freedom of travel for citizens of participating states, gave them the opportunity to appeal against administrative decisions (e.g. on applications for exit visas), committed governments to tolerate Helsinki Monitoring Groups and established a procedure to monitor how well each state was implementing its CSCE commitments. The Western allies agreed to participate in conventional disarmament negotiations, a new round of talks on CSBMs and the human rights conference in Moscow. In almost all points, the agreement met the criteria of glasnost and the ideas of Gorbachev's "common European home".[32] In return, the document gave Gorbachev a new instrument to overrule his critics and justify further domestic reforms.[33]

During the 27 months of the Vienna Follow-up Meeting, relations between East and West developed with unprecedented dynamism. In complex and controversial negotiations, a Concluding Document was drawn up that translated the impetuses and impulses of previous years into provisions and regulations. This laid the foundations for further progress, particularly in terms of human rights and humanitarian issues. Agreements on human contacts, ease of travel, freedom of information and working conditions for journalists were intended to ensure greater openness between the participating states, the removal of barriers and a free flow of information between East and West. The negotiations on religious freedom, national minorities, control rights and legal remedies were starting points for the creation of pluralism and the rule of law. The newly created mechanism for the permanent monitoring of the implementation of the CSCE human rights agreements, in conjunction with an annual conference on the human dimension, was intended to strengthen the mutual responsibility of states for the fulfilment of their commitments.[34]

32 Deborah Cuccia, "The European Common House: The Soviet Prescription for Reshaping Europe", in: Michael Gehler/Wilfried Loth (eds.), *Reshaping Europe. Towards a Political, Economic and Monetary Union, 1984–1989* (Publications of the European Liaison Committee of Historians Vol. 20), Baden-Baden 2020, p. 443–459 (translated).

33 Cotey Morgan, *The Final Act*, p. 244–245; see also: Rolf Steininger, "Entspannung und Abrüstung im Kalten Krieg. Der KSZE-Prozess und seine Auswirkungen auf die innenpolitischen Situationen in Ost und West", in: Andreas H. Apelt/Robert Grünbaum/Jens Schöne (eds.), *2 x Deutschland. Innerdeutsche Beziehungen 1972–1990*, Halle 2013, p. 111–126.

34 Bericht über Verlauf und Ergebnis des Wiener KSZE-Folgetreffens; on the major breakthrough of the Vienna Follow-up Meeting 1986–1989 from the Vatican's perspective see

In military questions, the launch of negotiations by the 23 NATO states on conventional armed forces provided a new approach to a key area of European security issues. The negotiating mandate attached to the Concluding Document prepared a framework for communication that would subsequently become an important element of the arms control dialogue. The simultaneous negotiations of all CSCE states on CSBMs opened up the opportunity to follow up on the CDE and achieve further progress in the calculability and transparency of military activities and potentials. In the field of economic co-operation, regulations were drawn up for business contacts, economic information, joint ventures and compensation deals.[35]

The USSR's more conservative allies tried to prevent this move towards openness. Although most Central and Eastern European heads of state and government accepted the Intermediate-Range Nuclear Forces (INF) Treaty negotiated between Gorbachev and Reagan on 8 December 1987 (in force from 1 June 1988) and supported the Moscow Conference proposal, some Warsaw Pact states feared that Gorbachev and Shevardnadze would go too far. The East German foreign minister, Oskar Fischer, warned that the Soviets would give in to the West's "particularly extortionate" pressure on human rights, by means of which the Soviets would undermine Communist sovereignty, grant the West a "right to interfere" and a "right to complain" under the auspices of the CSCE, and ultimately help it to dismantle socialism by "infecting the socialist states with bourgeois values". The Romanian delegates, who raised similar objections, declared that they would not regard any of the agreements reached in Vienna as binding. However, given Gorbachev's determination to press ahead, opponents and sceptics had little chance of blocking the realignment of Soviet foreign policy.[36] By the time of Vienna, the so-called Eastern bloc had long ceased to exist and was visibly disintegrating, and the Vienna Follow-up Meeting itself thus contributed to the end of the Cold War.

---

also Paul Wuthe, *Für Menschenrechte und Religionsfreiheit in Europa. Die Politik des Heiligen Stuhls in der KSZE/OSZE* (Theologie und Frieden Vol. 22), Stuttgart 2002, p. 174–208; on the Concluding Document: Ibid. p. 192–194; on human rights in the CSCE process: Daniel C. Thomas, *The Helsinki effect. International Norms, Human Rights, and the Demise of Communism*, Princeton 2001; Sarah B. Snyder, "The foundation for Vienna. A reassessment of the CSCE in the mid-1980s", in: *Cold War History* 10 (2010), issue 4, p. 493–512; Andrei Zagorski, "The Human Dimension of the CSCE, 1975–1990", in: Nicolas Badalassi/ Sarah B. Snyder (eds.), *The CSCE and the End of the Cold War. Diplomacy, Societies and Human Rights, 1972–1990*, New York 2019, p. 17–42.

35 Bericht über Verlauf und Ergebnis des Wiener KSZE-Folgetreffens.

36 Cotey Morgan, *The Final Act*, p. 245.

6 Conclusion

The course of the Vienna Follow-up Meeting negotiations was essentially divided into two phases: 1987/88 and 1988/89. Initially, no decisive breakthroughs were achievable. A combination of three "positive" factors played a role in the final success from the second half of 1988 onwards. These were the resurgence of the Gorbachev effect with pressure on Eastern delegations, which led to their more or less willing concessions, the disarmament agreement between the superpowers on nuclear weapons in Europe, and the mediating influence of the neutrals in particular.

A comparison of the final documents shows that Vienna and Helsinki closed a circle in terms both of scope and of substance, while Belgrade and Madrid, in retrospect, appear as merely intermediate and transitional stages. Remarkable successes of mediation and agreement were achieved in the policy areas of "freedom" and "security", so that Vienna can be seen as the fulfilment of Helsinki, especially with a view to further negotiations on the reduction of conventional weapons systems in Europe. The Vienna Concluding Document thus also paved the way for the Conventional Armed Forces in Europe (CFE) Treaty, one of the most important international agreements in helping to end the Cold War in Europe.

Under Torovsky's leadership, the Austrian delegation was particularly committed to raising the profile of Vienna as a meeting place, presenting the outcome of the Vienna Follow-up Meeting as a success story of the Ballhausplatz for the benefit of Europe and thereby moving out of the shadow of the country's internationally largely isolated president, Kurt Waldheim.[37] However, Austrian CSCE diplomacy was not crowned by the honour of hosting the adoption of the charter declaring the end of the Cold War in Vienna. This was to take place in Paris in 1990 at the request of the French president, François Mitterrand.

---

37 Michael Gehler, "Die Affäre Waldheim. Eine Fallstudie zur Instrumentalisierung der NS-Vergangenheit zur politischen Vorteilsverschaffung 1986–1988", in: *Geschichte in Wissenschaft und Unterricht* 69 (2018), issue 1/2, p. 67–85.

Negotiations on Cultural Cooperation at the Vienna Follow-up Meeting from the Perspective of the Austrian Foreign Ministry

Andrea Brait

1 Austria's Foreign Cultural Policy[1]

Cultural diplomacy is a policy area that has received increased scholarly attention only in recent years,[2] perhaps because it is a policy area in which almost impossible to measure effects. Nevertheless, the benefits of cultural diplomacy are repeatedly asserted. Benno Signitzer, for example, emphasises that its aim is to serve general diplomatic goals.[3] Austrian activities in this policy area are also driven by the hope of positive effects in various contexts. These activities are mainly the responsibility of the Cultural Policy Section of the foreign ministry, which coined the term "foreign cultural policy", an unusual term in an international setting. From the early 1970s, under the then foreign minister, Rudolf Kirchschläger, this Auslandskulturpolitik developed into the third pillar of Austrian foreign policy alongside traditional diplomacy and trade policy.[4]

In contrast to the classic areas of tension during the Cold War, such as human rights or arms control, the cultural sector was often seen as a policy area in which borders could be overcome. The former Austrian foreign minister, Peter

1 The research for this article was conducted as part of the project "*Breakthrough in Human Rights? The CSCE Follow-up Meeting in Vienna (1986–1989)*" and was financed in whole or in part by the Austrian Science Fund (FWF) [project number: I 4139]. Previously untranslated German language sources were translated.

2 In recent years, in addition to general studies on the significance of cultural diplomacy, a number have also been published that deal with the Cold War period. Jessica C. Gienow-Hecht/Mark C. Donfried (eds.), *Searching for a Cultural Diplomacy*, New York-Oxford 2010; Simo Mikkonen/Pia Koivunen (eds.), *Beyond the Divide. Entangled Histories of Cold War Europe*, New York-Oxford 2015; Christopher Hollings, *Scientific Communication Across the Iron Curtain*, Cham 2016; Simo Mikkonen/Pekka Suutari (eds.), *Music, Art and Diplomacy. East-West Cultural Interactions and the Cold War*, London-New York 2016.

3 Benno Signitzer, "Public Relations and Public Diplomacy: Some Conceptual Explorations", in: Ansgar Zerfass/Betteke van Ruler et al. (eds.), *Public relations research. European and International Perspectives and Innovations*, Wiesbaden 2008, p. 205–218, on p. 207.

4 Andrea Brait, "'Die große Trennungslinie, die an unserer Haustür vorbeiführt, überbauen'. Zur Vermittlerfunktion der österreichischen Kulturaußenpolitik zwischen Ost und West", in: Maximilian Graf/Agnes Meisinger (eds.), *Österreich im Kalten Krieg. Neue Forschungen im internationalen Kontext* (Zeitgeschichte im Kontext Vol. 11), Göttingen 2016, p. 259–295.

Jankowitsch, is convinced that cultural exchange enabled encounters between people who would not have been able to meet by other means.[5] The Austrian foreign ministry also sees the cultural sector as an important contribution to peacekeeping. The Austrian ambassador Emil Brix, for example, emphasises that cultural diplomacy has developed from an attempt to spread a positive image of one's own country in the post-war period to the use of images and stereotypes to build trust and promote dialogue.[6] In many cases, however, it can be assumed that the importance of contacts in the cultural sphere was overemphasised, as it became clear time and again how much these contacts were burdened by conflicts in other political fields.[7] For its part, the Austrian foreign ministry was aware that the cultural sphere could not operate in an ideological or political vacuum.[8]

In contrast to the importance that the Austrian foreign ministry likes to ascribe to foreign cultural policy,[9] it has so far been the subject of little research.[10] This applies to bilateral cultural relations, on which individual studies have emerged in recent years,[11] but even more so to foreign cultural policy in the context of multilateral diplomacy. It therefore comes as no great

5 Peter Jankowitsch, "'Das Konferenzgeschehen in Wien war sehr wichtig für das, was sich dann 1989 und später abgespielt hat.'", in: Kai Habel/Nina Hechenblaikner et al. (eds.), *Diplomatie am Ende des Kalten Krieges. Erinnerungen an die dritte KSZE-Folgekonferenz in Wien 1986–1989*, Baden-Baden 2025, p. 92.

6 Emil Brix, "Austrian Cultural and Public Diplomacy After the End of the Cold War", in: Günter Bischof/Ferdinand Karlhofer (eds.), *Austria's International Position after the End of the Cold War* (Contemporary Austrian Studies Vol. 22), Innsbruck 2013, p. 95–107, on p. 105.

7 Andrea Brait, "Österreichisch-tschechische Kulturdiplomatie zwischen 1918 und 2018 aus der Perspektive des österreichischen Außenministeriums", in: *Paginae Historiae* 27 (2019), issue 2, p. 184–234.

8 Bundesministerium für Auswärtige Angelegenheiten, *Außenpolitischer Bericht 1985. Bericht des Bundesministeriums für Auswärtige Angelegenheiten*, Wien 1986, p. 20.

9 The then Austrian Foreign Minister Alois Mock referred to this, for example, in 1987 in connection with the international criticism of the controversial wartime past of the Austrian Federal President Kurt Waldheim: "Introductory speech by Vice-Chancellor Dr Alois Mock Federal Minister for Foreign Affairs before the Foreign Cultural Conference on 31 August 1987", in: Federal Ministry for Foreign Affairs (BMAA) (ed.), *Auslandskulturtagung 1987*, Wien 1987, p. 2–9, on p. 4.

10 Andreas Stadler, "Auslandskulturpolitik", in: Martin Senn/Franz Eder et al. (eds.), *Handbuch Außenpolitik Österreichs*, Wiesbaden 2023, p. 269–283, on p. 270.

11 Peter Bachmaier, "Austrian-Bulgarian Cultural Relations", in: Arnold Suppan/Wolfgang Mueller (eds.), *"Peaceful Coexistence" or "Iron Curtain". Austria, Neutrality, and Eastern Europe in the Cold War and Détente, 1955–1989* (Europa Orientalis Vol. 7), Wien-Berlin-Piscataway, NJ 2009, p. 487–508; Alexander Burka, *Was blieb vom Fenster in den Westen? Zur Auslandskulturpolitik Österreichs in Ostmitteleuropa seit 1945 am Beispiel Polens und*

surprise that, with regard to Austria's actions in the Conference on Security and Cooperation in Europe (CSCE) – which Benjamin Gilde has already analysed in detail for the years 1969–1983[12] – the negotiations in the area of cultural cooperation, which were located in Basket III, have so far played only a marginal role in research.[13] The following study aims to contribute to closing this research gap. Specifically, it examines the question of what the Austrian delegation advocated in the context of the Vienna Follow-up Meeting of the CSCE (1986–1989) with regard to so-called "cultural cooperation" (kulturelle Zusammenarbeit), how this approach was (internally) argued by the Austrian foreign ministry and which of the goals pursued could be achieved.

2 Cultural Cooperation in the Context of the CSCE

The cultural sector was part of the CSCE process from the very beginning and was seen as an opportunity to contribute to an understanding between East and West. For instance, in the context of the negotiations on the humanitarian dimension in Geneva (1973–1975), the French president, Georges Pompidou, spoke in favour of infecting the Warsaw Pact states with the "virus of liberty", to which cultural exchange was to make an important contribution.[14] In his comparison of various international agreements in the field of cultural policy, Olaf Schwencke concludes that "no post-war agreement [...] had a similar significance in terms of peace policy and ultimately also cultural policy as the

der Tschechoslowakei/Tschechiens (Politik und Demokratie Vo. 23), Frankfurt am Main-Berlin-Bern et al. 2012.

12 Benjamin Gilde, *Österreich im KSZE-Prozess 1969–1983. Neutraler Vermittler in humanitärer Mission* (Quellen und Darstellungen zur Zeitgeschichte Vol. 98), München 2013.

13 This is consistent with the studies on other states and with CSCE research as a whole: apart from minor publications, the negotiations on cultural cooperation are not at the centre of academic studies. Helmut Altrichter/Hermann Wentker (eds.), *Der KSZE-Prozess. Vom Kalten Krieg zu einem neuen Europa 1975 bis 1990*, München 2011; Anja Hanisch, *Die DDR im KSZE-Prozess 1972–1985. Zwischen Ostabhängigkeit, Westabgrenzung und Ausreisebewegung* (Quellen und Darstellungen zur Zeitgeschichte Vol. 91), München 2012; Philip Rosin, *Die Schweiz im KSZE-Prozess 1972–1983* (Quellen und Darstellungen zur Zeitgeschichte Vol. 99), München 2014; Matthias Peter, *Die Bundesrepublik im KSZE-Prozess 1975–1983. Die Umkehrung der Diplomatie* (Quellen und Darstellungen zur Zeitgeschichte Vol. 105), Berlin 2015; Veronika Heyde, *Frankreich im KSZE-Prozess. Diplomatie im Namen der europäischen Sicherheit*, Berlin-Boston 2017.

14 Daniel Möckli, "The EC Nine, the CSCE, and the changing pattern of European security", in: Andreas Wenger/Vojtech Mastny et al. (eds.), *Origins of the European Security System. The Helsinki process revisited, 1965–75*, London-New York 2008, p. 145–163, on p. 148.

so-called CSCE process."[15] However, cultural cooperation in the implementation of the objectives laid down in the Helsinki Final Act[16] was subject to government control where Warsaw Pact states were involved.[17] For instance, the Austrian diplomat Franz Ceska criticised the fact that the Soviet Union was only interested in sending state-approved events or artists to the West as part of cultural exchange.[18]

Cultural exchange became the focus of the CSCE ten years after the adoption of the Helsinki Final Act. The occasion was the CSCE Cultural Forum, which took place in Budapest from 15 October to 25 November 1985, after the Polish delegation had first proposed a meeting dedicated to cultural heritage at the CSCE Follow-up Meeting in Madrid (1980–1983).[19] Around 600 cultural figures from all 35 CSCE states actively participated in this meeting, the first CSCE meeting in a Warsaw Pact state.[20] The aim of the Cultural Forum was to specify and deepen the agreements on cultural cooperation. However, negotiations were severely hampered by the completely different interpretations regarding the significance of culture in society between East and West. In the discussions, while the representatives of the Warsaw Pact states emphasised that culture and art should not be commercial and should promote peace in society, the representatives of the Western-oriented states stressed the importance of independent artistic and cultural activity.[21] There was also a heated debate about the most appropriate methods of cultural cooperation: foundations, personal contacts, events or treaties between states.[22]

---

15 Olaf Schwencke, *Das Europa der Kulturen – Kulturpolitik in Europa. Dokumente, Analysen und Perspektiven – von den Anfängen bis zum Vertrag von Lissabon* (Edition Umbruch Vol. 26), Essen 2010³, p. 191.

16 Konferenz über Sicherheit und Zusammenarbeit in Europa, Schlussakte, 01.08.1975.

17 Hans-Adolf Jacobsen, "Auswärtige Kulturpolitik", in: Hans-Adolf Jacobsen/Gert Leptin et al. (eds.), *Drei Jahrzehnte Außenpolitik der DDR. Bestimmungsfaktoren, Instrumente, Aktionsfelder* (Internationale Politik und Wirtschaft Vol. 44), München-Wien 1979, p. 235–260, on p. 257.

18 Franz Ceska, "'Insofern war das die aufregendste Sache meines Lebens.'", in: Habel/Hechenblaikner et al. (eds.), *Diplomatie am Ende des Kalten Krieges*, p. 64.

19 Adam D. Rotfeld, "The New Dimensions of the CSCE Process", in: Halina Ognik/Adam D. Rotfeld (eds.), *Cultural Heritage and the CSCE Process. Selected Documents*, Warsaw 1991, p. VII–XIII, on p. XII.

20 For an overview from the perspective of the Austrian foreign ministry see: *Außenpolitischer Bericht 1985*, p. 20–22.

21 Hubertus Knabe, "Der schwierige Kulturdialog in Europa. Anmerkungen zum KSZE-Kulturforum in Budapest", in: *Osteuropa* (1986), issue 5, p. 380–388.

22 Schwencke, *Das Europa der Kulturen*, p. 197.

A total of 198 proposals were formally submitted, twelve of which by Austria and a further six with Austrian support.[23] According to its own records, Austria actively participated in the negotiations and provided the first draft of a paper of the neutral and non-aligned states (N+N), which was the basis for negotiations on a final document. It proved impossible, however, to reach a consensus regarding such a document.[24] The Cultural Forum thereby exposed the lines of conflict not only between the two blocs but also within them: the Hungarian delegation's attempt to adopt at least a three-sentence final declaration at the end of the conference was blocked by Romania, presumably due to the two states' disputes over ethnic minorities.[25]

Although no final document was adopted, the Cultural Forum was considered a success by the Austrian foreign ministry, as it had succeeded in bringing together many cultural representatives across blocs.[26] This assessment was in line with that of various other states, as is evident from the opening statements of the foreign ministers at the Vienna Follow-up Meeting.[27] As the German foreign minister, Hans-Dietrich Genscher, underscored in a speech at the Danube-European Institute in Vienna in August 1986, the Cultural Forum made it possible to hold joint discussions without the participants having to betray their political convictions.[28] In retrospect, the Austrian journalist Burkhard Bischof even associates the Cultural Forum with the first signs of change in Eastern Europe.[29] Moreover, the inclusion of non-diplomats was considered exemplary for the Vienna Follow-up Meeting.[30]

---

23 Der Korb III in der KSZE, in: KSZE; 3. Folgetreffen; Eröffnung auf Aussenministerebene, Österreichisches Staatsarchiv (ÖStA), Archiv der Republik (AdR), BMAA, politische Sektion II/Abteilung 7 Entwicklung (II-Pol.) 1986, GZ 803.00/50-II.7/86.

24 Interparlamentarische Union, Besuch einer Parlamentarierdelegation in Ungarn, ÖStA, AdR, BMAA, II-Pol. 1986, GZ 801.04/10-II.7/86.

25 Knabe, *Der schwierige Kulturdialog*, p. 387 f.

26 *Außenpolitischer Bericht 1985*, p. 21.

27 KSZE; WFT; Eröffnungserklärungen der Außenminister (4.–7.11.1986); Zusammenfassende Information, ÖStA, AdR, BMAA, II-Pol. 1986, GZ 803.00/220-II.7/86.

28 Rede AM Genschers im Donaueuropäischen Institut am 27. August 1986, BMAA, II-Pol. 1986, GZ 803.00/96-II.9/86.

29 Burkhard Bischof, "'Aber für Europa war das Geschehen in Wien ein Wahnsinn.'", in: Habel/Hechenblaikner et al. (eds.), *Diplomatie am Ende des Kalten Krieges*, p. 342.

30 Besuch des HGS in Ungarn; 19./20.6.1986, Information über WFT, Kulturforum, KVAE; Abrüstungsvorschläge zu den bilateralen Beziehungen, ÖStA, AdR, BMAA, II-Pol. 1986, GZ 801.04/29-II.7/86.

3 The Course of Negotiations on Cultural Cooperation at the Vienna Follow-up Meeting

For the Vienna Follow-up Meeting, the Austrian foreign ministry set itself the goal of "analysing the extensive material of the Budapest Cultural Forum and compiling a package of measures from it that could be agreed upon".[31] Preparations were already made within the foreign ministry in the summer of 1986, although assessments of possible proposals changed over the months: while twelve were still being considered in June 1986,[32] the number was down to eight in July[33] and six in September.[34]

In a manner similar to Basket II,[35] the Austrian foreign ministry also liaised with other relevant ministries on the subject of culture in order to take their expertise into account. According to a list from the foreign ministry, at the beginning of October 1986, the Federal Ministry for Education, the Arts and Sport and the Federal Ministry of Science and Research were in favour of supporting or contributing 34 proposals from other states, while ten proposals from other states received a negative assessment. The latter category included, for example, the idea of an "immediate scheme to strengthen the influence of women in culture", which was favoured by eleven states at the Budapest Cultural Forum, including the United States.[36]

By early December 1986, more concrete drafts had been produced on five subject groups, all of which had been submitted to the Budapest Cultural Forum by persons not belonging to the foreign ministry: an exhibition of contemporary graphic art, a CSCE youth orchestra, an exchange of catalogues between art institutions, an exchange of cultural television programmes and a CSCE children's book series.[37] In addition, the submission of the proposal for a symposium on the cultural heritage of the CSCE states, as discussed at the

31 WFT, KSZE-Folgetreffen, Entwurf der österr. Grundlinie, ÖStA, AdR, BMAA, II-Pol. 1986, GZ 803.00/74-II.7/86.

32 WFT; Korb III, Kultur, Vorbesprechung über österreichische Vorschläge vom 13. Juni, ÖStA, AdR, BMAA, II-Pol. 1986, GZ 803.04.06/II-7/86.

33 WFT, KSZE-Folgetreffen, Entwurf der österr. Grundlinie, ÖStA, AdR, BMAA, II-Pol. 1986, GZ 803.00/74-II.7/86.

34 WFT; österreichische Linie Befassung der Vertretungsbehörden, ÖStA, AdR, BMAA, II-Pol. 1986, GZ 803.00/101-II.7/86.

35 See the article by Roland Laimer in this volume.

36 WFT; allfällige Weiterverfolgung von Vorschlägen des Budapester Kulturforums, ÖStA, AdR, BMAA, II-Pol. 1986, GZ 803.04.06/27-II.7/86.

37 KSZE, WFT, Korb III; Präsentierung österreichischer Vorschläge, ÖStA, AdR, BMAA, II-Pol. 1986, GZ 803.04.01/5-II.7/86.

Budapest Cultural Forum (CFB.106),[38] had already agreed with Poland in the summer of that year.[39]

With this approach, the Austrian foreign ministry pitted itself in opposition to Romania, which in the summer of 1986 had announced, in a communication between a civil servant in the Romanian foreign ministry and Andreas Berlakovic, the Austrian ambassador, that it wanted to prevent the direct forwarding of proposals from Budapest.[40] However, this did not change the Austrian position. During a bilateral meeting at the beginning of the Follow-up Meeting, Jankowitsch assured his Hungarian counterpart, Péter Várkonyi, that Austria would endeavour to ensure that the proposals drawn up in Budapest would not be lost.[41]

The Austrian foreign ministry's thinking about the development of proposals on cultural cooperation was based on the assumption that there would be a greater willingness to engage with "Eastern European" culture in Austria if there were better travel and contact opportunities. The aim was therefore to focus on removing these obstacles.[42]

However, from the internal deliberations of the Austrian foreign ministry it is also clear that, although staff wanted to introduce a variety of proposals, they were also aware that cultural activities required a financial outlay, leading to concerns about funding. The foreign ministry therefore wanted to concentrate in particular on proposals that were expected to have a particular foreign policy impact. For example, a youth orchestra was expected to have an "immediate and lively effect", while other ideas, such as the exchange of exhibition catalogues, were classified as "peripheral and administrative measures".[43]

Finally, at the Vienna Follow-up Meeting, proposals were reintroduced by the Cultural Forum in an adapted form and in some cases in new constellations. 14 of the 154 proposals made at the Vienna Follow-up Meeting related

38 WFT; Korb III, Symposium über das kulturelle Erbe der KSZE-Staaten, Stellungnahme der Abteilung II.7, ÖStA, AdR, BMAA, II-Pol. 1986, GZ 803.04.06/15-II.7/86.

39 KSZE, 3. Folgetreffen, Wien, ab 4.11.1986 brain-storming am 4.7.1986, ÖStA, AdR, BMAA, II-Pol. 1986, GZ 803.00/73-II.7/86.

40 Bericht ÖB Bukarest an das BMAA betr. KSZE; Wiener Treffen; Vorbereitung, 14.07.1986, ÖStA, AdR, BMAA, II-Pol, GZ 803.00/77-II.7/86.

41 Gespräch des HBM mit dem ungarischen Außenminister Peter Varkonyi, Protokoll vom 7.11.1986, ÖStA, AdR, BMAA, II-Pol. 1986, GZ 222.18.09/2-II.3/86.

42 Korb III Zusammenarbeit und Austausch im Bereich der Kultur und Bildung, in: KSZE, 3. Folgetreffen, Wien, ab 4.11.1986 brain-storming am 4.7.1986, ÖStA, AdR, BMAA, II-Pol. 1986, GZ 803.00/73-II.7/86.

43 KSZE – Wiener Folgetreffen, Korb III; Bereich Kultur; Überlegungen zu den österreichischen Initiativen, in: Bela Bartok Folklorezentrum, gemeinsamer österr.-ungarischer Vorschlag, ÖStA, AdR, BMAA, II-Pol. 1986, GZ 803.04.06/39-II.7/86.

to cultural cooperation. Three of these – and thus more than in any other area – were joint proposals from N+N and Warsaw Pact states; two were submitted by NATO, N+N and Warsaw Pact states.[44] Austria ultimately supported five proposals in the field of culture.[45]

Most of the proposals concerned specific projects. As Stefan Lehne, a member the Austrian delegation, emphasised, it became clear early on during the Vienna meeting that there was insufficient political will to make decisions on such projects.[46] This applied, for example, to the proposal jointly submitted by Austria and Hungary in December 1986 (WT.7) for the establishment of an international folk art centre to be named in honour of Béla Bartok,[47] a proposal ultimately abandoned due to lack of Western support.[48]

As the Austrian foreign ministry noted in mid-1987, overall interest in the cultural sector at the Vienna Follow-up Meeting was "noticeably lower than in the past". This was probably due, on the one hand, to recent detailed exchanges at the Cultural Forum, which had failed to achieve any concrete results, and, on the other, to interests which continued to diverge.[49] The Austrian foreign ministry also noted a discrepancy between "formal Soviet negotiating positions at the Vienna Follow-up Meeting" and "Western ideas about 'GLASNOST'".[50]

In order to achieve progress in the negotiations on Basket III, in the summer of 1987 Austria and Switzerland decided to draw up a joint "non-paper", which was officially submitted on 30 July 1987. The Austrian foreign ministry's aim was to underline Austria's interest in Basket III, to recapitulate Austrian and Western interests, to remove non-essential and unrealistic proposals, and to facilitate further work in autumn 1987.[51]

---

44 Stefan Lehne/Hanspeter Neuhold, "The Role of the Neutral and Non-Aligned Countries at the Vienna Meeting", in: Arie Bloed/Pieter van Dijk (eds.), *The Human Dimension of the Helsinki Process. The Vienna Follow-up meeting and its Aftermath* (International Studies in Human Rights Vol. 20), Dordrecht-Boston-Norwell 1991, p. 30–53, on p. 53.

45 Stefan Lehne, *The Vienna Meeting of the Conference on Security and Cooperation in Europe, 1986–1989. A Turning Point in East-West Relations*, Boulder-San Francisco-Oxford 1991, p. 213.

46 Ibid., p. 105.

47 Zusammenfassung der 7. Konferenzwoche des Wiener KSZE-Folgetreffens (Stand: 18.12.1986), ÖStA, AdR, BMAA, II-Pol. 1986, GZ 803.00/246-II.7/86.

48 WFT; Zusammenfassung der Sitzungsperiode 22.1.–25.3.1988, ÖStA, AdR, BMAA, II-Pol. 1988, GZ 803.12/16-II.7/88.

49 WFT, Korb III, Zusammenfassung der 3. Sitzungsperiode, 5. Mai bis 31. Juli 1987, ÖStA, AdR, BMAA, II-Pol. 1987, GZ 803.12/41-II.7/87.

50 WFT; Zusammenfassung der Sitzungsperiode Jänner bis April 1987, Korb III, ÖStA, AdR, BMAA, II-Pol. 1987, GZ 803.12/20-II.7/87.

51 WFT; Österreichisch-schweizerische Initiative im Korb III, ÖStA, AdR, BMAA, II-Pol. 1987, GZ 803.04/1-II.7/87.

Building on this, the first points were successfully put beyond dispute in March 1988. These aspects concerned the involvement of NGOs in drafting cultural agreements and the general encouragement of wide-ranging cultural cooperation.[52] By contrast, the proposed paragraph on national minorities, which was initially opposed by Romania and the Soviet Union[53] and to which Bulgaria had long demanded the addition of the phrase "where they exist", proved much more controversial.[54] As with other issues, the Warsaw Pact states did not act as a united bloc when it came to cultural cooperation.

The resistance of individual states to certain points was abandoned in the first half of 1988, with many a change of heart occurring within a few days.[55] Following the submission of an N+N draft for the final document, the area of culture was considered largely uncontroversial in May 1988,[56] which is why the focus turned mainly to other areas.[57] Overall, culture received significant attention only during a few weeks of negotiations, which was undoubtedly due to the other highly controversial and politically explosive issues in Basket III.

In the Concluding Document, the participating states finally formulated sixteen goals for cooperation and exchange in the field of culture.[58] The assessments of diplomats involved in the Vienna Follow-up Meeting differ considerably. For example, Hans-Heinrich Wrede, a delegate for the Federal Republic of Germany, is convinced that the Vienna Follow-up Meeting succeeded in striking a good compromise between the opposing positions with regard to the status of culture in society.[59] Lehne, on the other hand, concludes

52 Zusammenfassung der 51. Konferenzwoche, Stand 3.3.1988, ÖStA, AdR, BMAA, II-Pol. 1988, GZ 803.12/9-II.7/88.

53 Zusammenfassung der 48. Konferenzwoche, ÖStA, AdR, BMAA, II-Pol. 1988, GZ 803.12/7-II.7/88.

54 KSZE, WFT; Zusammenfassung der sechsten Sitzungsperiode vom 15.4. – 5.8.1988, ÖStA, AdR, BMAA, II-Pol. 1988, GZ 803.12/38-II.7/88.

55 In the 54th week of the conference, the USSR agreed to numerous articles in Basket III that had been rejected in the 53rd week of the conference. These included two articles concerning cultural cooperation. Zusammenfassung der 54. Konferenzwoche Stand 24. März 1988, ÖStA, AdR, BMAA, II-Pol. 1988, GZ 803.12/13-II.7/88.

56 Zusammenfassung der 60. Konferenzwoche, ÖStA, AdR, BMAA, II-Pol. 1988, GZ 803.12/22-II.7/88.

57 Zusammenfassung der 61. Konferenzwoche, ÖStA, AdR, BMAA, II-Pol. 1988, GZ 803.12/23-II.7/88.

58 Abschließendes Dokument des Wiener Treffens 1986 der Vertreter der Teilnehmerstaaten der Konferenz für Sicherheit und Zusammenarbeit in Europa, welches auf der Grundlage der Bestimmungen der Schlussakte betreffend die Folgen der Konferenz abgehalten wurde, https://www.osce.org/files/f/documents/c/a/40883.pdf, accessed 22.11.2023.

59 Hans-Heinrich Wrede, *KSZE in Wien. Kursbestimmung für Europas Zukunft*, Köln 1990, p. 116.

that it was mainly Western concerns that were realised, some of which had initially met with considerable Eastern resistance, such as unhindered public access to cultural events.[60] From the perspective of the Austrian foreign ministry, the following points were seen as being of key importance:

- "Encouraging the establishment of cultural institutions",
- the "regulation of unhindered access to cultural events",
- "encouraging direct personal contacts in the cultural sector as well as joint artistic activities, exhibitions and tours" and
- the "substantial expansion of previous regulations concerning national minorities."[61]

4 The Proposed Symposium on Shared Cultural Heritage

Among the measures included in the Concluding Document was a symposium on common cultural heritage, to be held in Krakow. Since – as mentioned above – it proved impossible to reach a consensus on many of the proposals for concrete measures in the field of cultural cooperation, this represents a major exception.[62] As had been discussed in advance in the summer of 1986, the corresponding proposal (WT.6) was submitted by Austria together with Poland in the seventh week of the conference in December 1986.[63] As Wrede emphasises in his memoirs, this was the first time in the entire CSCE process that there had been cooperation across blocs on an important issue,[64] and the proposal was accordingly seen as a "manifestation of their will to overcome the bloc divide".[65] The head of the Austrian delegation, Ambassador Rudolf Torovsky, explained the significance of such a meeting in the plenary session on 17 December 1986 as follows:

> First and foremost, we are concerned with working out what we have in common, with revealing and raising awareness of connecting lines that together make up what we understand to be our common cultural

60 Lehne, *The Vienna Meeting*, p. 168.

61 Bericht über Verlauf und Ergebnis des Wiener KSZE-Folgetreffens, Österreichisches Staatsarchiv (ÖStA), Archiv der Republik (AdR), BMAA, politische Sektion II/Abteilung 7 Entwicklung (II-Pol.) 1989, GZ 804.00/2-II.7/89.

62 Lehne, *The Vienna Meeting*, p. 105.

63 Zusammenfassung der 7. Konferenzwoche des Wiener KSZE-Folgetreffens (Stand: 18.12.1986), ÖStA, AdR, BMAA, II-Pol. 1986, GZ 803.00/246-II.7/86.

64 Wrede, *KSZE in Wien*, p. 118 f.

65 Rotfeld, *The New Dimensions*, p. XII.

> heritage. […] We do not accept any geographical dividing lines in this endeavour: For us, signs of the common cultural heritage of the CSCE States extend from Vladivostok to Hawaii.[66]

In proposing such a symposium, the Austrian foreign ministry was not only pursuing the goal of initiating a process of cooperation on the basis of cultural commonalities. The proposal was also linked to an overall strategic goal, as an internal ministry document shows:

> Austria has traditionally taken the view that broad forms of cooperation should be actively sought within the CSCE framework wherever objectively possible and justified. In this way, the ever-increasing solidification of blocs can be counteracted and the basic democratic, cross-bloc claim of the CSCE can be realised in practice, at least in some areas.[67]

As can be seen from its internal deliberations, the foreign ministry was well aware that there were only a few areas in which cross-bloc proposals stood a realistic chance. In addition to culture, the areas of education and sport were mentioned. After a corresponding attempt at a joint proposal with Hungary at the Bern Meeting of Experts on Human Contacts (1986) had failed, it became the declared aim of the Austrian foreign ministry to realise such a cross-bloc initiative at the Vienna Follow-up Meeting,[68] which explains why Austria had already agreed on submitting, jointly with Poland, a proposal to that effect in the summer of 1986.[69]

The Austro-Polish proposal was – to the surprise of the Austrian foreign ministry – supported by the Federal Republic of Germany, France and Sweden in the fifteenth week of the conference in March 1987;[70] Denmark and Yugoslavia followed in the sixteenth week.[71] Ultimately, fourteen states supported the

66 Erklärung des Leiters der österreichischen Delegation zum Wiener Folgetreffen der KSZE, Botschafter Dr. Rudolf Torovsky, 17.12.1986, in: Zusammenfassung der 7. Konferenzwoche des Wiener KSZE-Folgetreffens (Stand: 18.12.1986), ÖStA, AdR, BMAA, II-Pol. 1986, GZ 803.00/246-II.7/86.

67 Symposium über das kulturelle Erbe der KSZE-Staaten, aktueller Stand (1. Dez. 1986), ÖStA, AdR, BMAA, II-Pol. 1986, GZ 803.04.06/43-II.7/86.

68 Symposium über das kulturelle Erbe der KSZE-Staaten, aktueller Stand (1. Dez. 1986), ÖStA, AdR, BMAA, II-Pol. 1986, GZ 803.04.06/43-II.7/86.

69 KSZE, 3. Folgetreffen, Wien, ab 4.11.1986 brain-storming am 4.7.1986, ÖStA, AdR, BMAA, II-Pol. 1986, GZ 803.00/73-II.7/86.

70 WFT; 15. Konferenzwoche, Zusammenfassung, ÖStA, AdR, BMAA, II-Pol. 1987, GZ 803.12/14-II.7/87.

71 WFT, 16. Konferenzwoche, Zusammenfassung, ÖStA, AdR, BMAA, II-Pol. 1987, GZ 803.12/15-II.7/87.

proposal.[72] Although the US delegation (and it alone) remained quite sceptical for a long time,[73] the proposal was ultimately accepted. In the Vienna Concluding Document, the signatories agreed to hold a "symposium on the cultural heritage of the participating states of the CSCE",[74] which ultimately took place – as planned, but in completely changed political circumstances – in Krakow in 1991.[75] For the first time, a document dedicated exclusively to cultural issues was successfully adopted at this symposium. It emphasised that respect for human rights and fundamental freedoms is an essential prerequisite for the full development of cultural creativity; specifically, various cultural freedoms were enshrined, such as the freedom of artistic creation, the freedom to publish artistic works and the freedom of access to culture. The preservation of monuments and memorials commemorating tragic events in the common past of the participating states was also laid down.[76] The agreements reached became fundamental to the CSCE/OSCE's commitment to the protection of cultural heritage, for example in the context of the OSCE Mission in Kosovo established in 1999, which for many years launched numerous initiatives to protect religious and cultural heritage.[77]

5 Conclusion

The diplomats at the Vienna Follow-up Meeting unanimously recalled the cultural sector as a less prominent subject of negotiation. Lehne, for example, remarks:

> I can remember that a tremendous amount of proposals were made for all kinds of follow-up events on culture, especially by Romania. I think there were around 20 or 25 different events. But most of them never

72 Lehne, *The Vienna Meeting*, p. 105.

73 Zusammenfassung der 73. Konferenzwoche, ÖStA, AdR, BMAA, II-Pol. 1988, GZ 803.12/41-II.7/88. According to Wrede, the US delegation was fundamentally opposed to a large number of CSCE expert meetings and also saw the danger of a too large international stage for a Warsaw Pact state. Wrede, KSZE in Wien, p. 119.

74 Abschließendes Dokument des Wiener Treffens.

75 Konferenz über Sicherheit und Zusammenarbeit in Europa, Dokument des Krakauer Symposiums über das kulturelle Erbe der KSZE-Teilnehmerstaaten, https://www.osce.org/files/f/documents/0/a/24398.pdf, accessed 18.11.2023.

76 Bundesministerium für auswärtige Angelegenheiten, *Außenpolitischer Bericht 1991*, Vienna 1992, p. 69.

77 Protection of Cultural Heritage in Kosovo, https://www.osce.org/files/f/documents/e/b/522892.pdf, accessed 11.4.2024.

> materialised. Overall, culture only played a subordinate role in the Vienna Follow-up Meeting.[78]

The Swedish diplomat Nils Eliasson also remembers a number of topics in the field of culture, while emphasising that, in retrospect, "the focus in my view were [sic] on the human contacts and on the information part of the third basket. That was where the most controversies were taking place and where most of the difficulties on formulation occurred."[79] Due to the disputes in these areas and the developments within the Warsaw Pact, it is not surprising that questions of cultural cooperation were not the focus of the negotiations and have therefore not been central to the accounts published to date.

However, it should be noted that the Austrian foreign ministry recognised the opportunities presented by the subject matter of the negotiations and therefore sought – ultimately successfully – to make cross-bloc proposals. This is in line with the fundamental principle of Austrian foreign policy of seeking to act as a bridge-builder in the cultural sphere. After a similar attempt had failed at the Bern Expert Meeting, a certain opening of the Warsaw Pact can also be observed at the Vienna Follow-up Meeting – at least with the benefit of hindsight, in light of subsequent developments. It should also be noted that, in contrast to the Budapest Cultural Forum, it was possible to overcome differences of opinion even in sensitive areas of cultural exchange, including in relation to national minorities.

Finally, it should be noted that the CSCE also created a framework for communication across bloc borders and had an impact beyond its formal final documents. For example, a proposal to establish a youth orchestra was submitted to the Cultural Forum in Budapest (CFB.9).[80] Although no final document was adopted in Budapest, this orchrestra was finally founded in Vienna in

78 Stefan Lehne, "Es 'zeigte sich sehr rasch, dass 'der Osten' nicht mehr existiert'", in: Habel/Hechenblaikner et al. (eds.), *Diplomatie am Ende des Kalten Krieges*, p. 196.

79 Nils Eliasson, "'Towards the middle of the Vienna meeting, nothing was said at the formal meetings'", in: Habel/Hechenblaikner et al. (eds.), *Diplomatie am Ende des Kalten Krieges*, p. 282.

80 Vorschlag der Delegation Österreichs "KSZE-Jugend-Symphonie-Workshop und -Orchester", in: KSZE; WFT; Anfrage Abg. Höchtl/Ettmayer/Neisser betreffend Menschenrechte, ÖStA, AdR, BMAA, II-Pol. 1986, GZ 803.00/138-II.7/86.

May 1986[81] and still exists today. The proposal (WT.68)[82] submitted by Austria together with Czechoslovakia, the GDR and Hungary at the Vienna Follow-up Meeting had therefore already been overtaken by actual developments at the time of its submission.

---

81 Vermerk über ein Gespräch des Leiters der Abt. KIL, Genossen Rolf Dill, mit dem künstlerischen Leiter des Gustav-Mahler-Jugendorchester, Sitz Wien, Prof. Dr. Hans Landesmann, am 20.5.1987 im Ministerium für Kultur der DDR, Politisches Archiv des Auswärtigen Amts, Berlin (PA-AA), Ministerium für Auswärtige Angelegenheiten der DDR (MfAA), ZR 2684/14.

82 Lehne, *The Vienna Meeting*, p. 213.

The "Neglected Step-Child" of the Vienna CSCE Follow-up Meeting?

Basket II from the Perspective of the Austrian Foreign Ministry

Roland Ernst Laimer

1 Introduction[1]

"No other item on the agenda of the CSCE [Conference for Safety and Security in Europe] process had gained as much international attention and urgency since the closure of the Madrid meeting than the protection of the environment."[2] In these words the Austrian diplomat Stefan Lehne summarised the increased importance given to protecting the environment at the Vienna CSCE Follow-up Meeting. Lehne was involved in the meeting as a member of the Austrian delegation, with responsibility for the issues in Basket III.[3] Basket II, which dealt with matters of economics, science and technology, and environment, was considered to be of relatively minor importance within the CSCE process. Yet environmental questions were growing in importance internationally, in society as well as in politics. Lehne referred to Basket II as the "neglected step-child"[4] of the entire CSCE process, as an "empty basket" in terms of substance.[5]

1 The following discussion is based on the author's master's thesis: Roland Ernst Laimer, *Die KSZE und der Umweltschutz. Korb II beim Wiener KSZE-Folgetreffen (1986–1989) aus der Perspektive der Ballhausplatzdiplomatie*, MA thesis, Innsbruck 2023. It was written as part of the project "Durchbruch bei den Menschenrechten? Das KSZE-Folgetreffen in Wien (1986–1989)" and was funded fully or in part by the Austrian Science Fund (FWF) [project number: I 4139]. The term Ballhausplatzdiplomatie is used synonymously for Austrian foreign policy, the Austrian foreign ministry having been located at Vienna's Ballhausplatz until 2005. See Andrea Brait, *Das Bundeskanzleramt in Wien, Ein österreichischer Gedächtnisort* (Schriften zur Kulturgeschichte Vol. 16), Hamburg 2010. Previously untranslated German language sources were translated for this chapter.

2 Stefan Lehne, *The Vienna Meeting of the Conference on Security and Cooperation in Europe, 1986–1989. A Turning Point in East-West Relations*, Boulder-San Francisco 1991, p. 82.

3 Ibid; Stefan Lehne, "'Es zeigte sich sehr rasch, dass 'der Osten' nicht mehr existiert'", in: Kai Habel/Nina Hechenblaikner et al. (eds.), *Diplomatie am Ende des Kalten Krieges. Erinnerungen an die dritte KSZE-Folgekonferenz in Wien 1986–1989*, Baden-Baden 2025, p. 183–216. On Basket III see the articles by Nina Hechenblaikner and Wanda Jarząbez in this volume.

4 Michael R. Lucas, *The CSCE in the 1990s*, p. 99.

5 Ibid., p. 98.

 | DOI:10.1163/9789004736979_008

But was this really the case? Were the participating states truly as uninterested in Basket II as Lehne claimed?

Since the following essay is unable to cover all fields of negotiation contained in Basket II, it will restrict itself to highlighting cooperation in the field of environmental protection – which, as Lehne stated, was accorded greater weight at the Vienna CSCE Follow-up Meeting.[6] The question to be discussed here concerns the targets set by the Austrian delegation in the negotiations on Basket II at the Vienna CSCE Follow-up Meeting with regard to environmental issues and to what degree these targets were ultimately met.

In order to answer this question, this essay will begin by examining the role of Basket II within the CSCE process and the state of research. The second part of the essay will then analyse three selected sources that throw light on Austria's position in approach to negotiations at the Vienna CSCE Follow-up Meeting. These sources are then compared with the meeting's Concluding Document.[7]

2 State of Research

Unlike Baskets I and III, Basket II has so far received scant attention in research on the CSCE, with few historians have examining the negotiations in the fields of economics, science and technology, and environment. Contemporary perspectives on Basket II at the Vienna CSCE Follow-up Meeting have been provided by the German delegates Ekkehard Eickhoff,[8] Hans-Christian Reichel[9] and Hans-Heinrich Wrede,[10] who are unanimous in recognising greater

6 Austria presented six proposals in the field of environmental protection at the Vienna CSCE Follow-up Meeting: Vienna Meeting (Wiener Treffen, WT.) 8 "Air protection and forest dieback", WT.11 "Cross-border transport and the environment", WT.30 "Transboundary environmental protection and acute environmental accidents", WT.109 "Cross-border transport of hazardous waste", WT.114 "Protection of international watercourses" and WT.127 "European Measurement and Evaluation Programme (EMEP)"; see also Laimer, *Die KSZE und der Umweltschutz*.

7 On the Vienna Concluding Document, see the article by Michael Gehler in this volume.

8 Ekkehard Eickhoff, "Das Dritte KSZE-Folgetreffen in Wien, Implementierung der Wirtschaftsbestimmungen", in: *Europa Archiv* 42 (1987), p. 59–66.

9 Hans-Christian Reichel, "Die Bonner Wirtschaftskonferenz und die Zukunft der KSZE", in: *Europa-Archiv* 45 (1990), p. 461–470; Idem, "'Die Stimmung generell, die war natürlich vorzüglich und, wie ich hinzufügen will, aufregend und spannend'", in: Habel/Hechenblaikner et al. (eds.), *Diplomatie am Ende des Kalten Krieges*, p. 141–163.

10 Hans-Heinrich Wrede, *KSZE in Wien. Kursbestimmung für Europas Zukunft*, Köln 1990.

opportunities for cooperation between the states of the Warsaw Pact, of NATO, and the neutral and non-aligned (N+N) states than in Baskets I and III.[11]

The Finnish historians Simo Laakkonen and Tuomas Räsänen discuss environmental cooperation in northern Europe in the 1970s, arguing that Helsinki Convention on the Protection of the Baltic Sea, adopted in 1972, paved the way for Basket II in the CSCE by implementing cross-bloc cooperation on water protection, or protection of the marine environment.[12] Meanwhile, the Swedish historian Arne Kaijser has shown how Norway attempted to limit air pollution in the Nordic region in cooperation with the Soviet Union.[13] Nor have historians studying the CSCE had much to say about Basket II. An essay by the Finnish historian Juhana Aunesluoma looks at the negotiations on Basket II at the CSCE in Helsinki, where issues of environmental cooperation were discussed at a multilateral diplomatic level between "East" and "West" for the first time.[14]

3 Source Analysis

In order to analyse the Austrian negotiating position at the Vienna CSCE Follow-up Meeting, the files of the foreign ministry, which are kept in the Austrian State Archives, were consulted. These papers consist of official notes containing individual proposals, drafts, statements or weekly reports.[15] The Concluding Document of the Vienna CSCE Follow-up Meeting provided a further source.[16] Methodologically, the essay is based on a critical study of the

11 Laimer, *Die KSZE und der Umweltschutz*, p. 46–47.

12 Simo Laakkonen/Tuomas Räsänen, "Negotiating the Maritime Commons, Protecting the Baltic Sea in a European Context", in: Anna-Katharina Wöbse/Patrick Kupper (eds.), *Greening Europe, Environmental protection in the long twentieth century – a handbook* (Contemporary European History Vol. 1), Berlin-Boston 2022, p. 243–268.

13 Arne Kaijser, "Combatting 'Acid Rain'. Protecting the Common European Sky", in: Wöbse/Kupper (eds.), *Greening Europe*, p. 363–387, on p. 382–383.

14 Juhana Aunesluoma, "Finlandisation in Reverse. The CSCE and the Rise and Fall of Economic Detente", 1968–1975, in: Oliver Bange/Gottfried Niedhart (eds.), *Helsinki 1975 and the Transformation of Europe*, New York-Oxford 2008, p. 98–112, on p. 104.

15 On the study of documents see Druck und Verlag der Österreichischen Staatsdruckerei, *Kanzleiordnung für die Bundesministerien. Erlassen am 10. Dezember 1974*, Wien 1975; Michael Hochedlinger, *Aktenkunde, Urkunden- und Aktenlehre der Neuzeit* (Historische Hilfswissenschaften Vol. 3), Wien-Köln et al. 2009.

16 Concluding Document of the Vienna Meeting 1986 of representatives of the participating states of the Conference on Security and Co-operation in Europe, held on the basis of the provisions of the final act relating to the follow-up to the conference.

files and their subsequent analysis.[17] The selected official documents include an internal exchange of ideas in preparation for the negotiations,[18] the official negotiating line in Basket II (both from 1986)[19] and a statement by the head of the Austrian delegation, Rudolf Torovsky,[20] from April 1988.[21]

4 From Draft to Concluding Document: the Negotiations in Basket II from the Austrian Perspective

4.1 *Initial Thoughts on Basket II*

In early June 1986 the Austrian foreign ministry organised a brainstorming session on all the negotiating baskets. Among the participants were the ambassadors Rudolf Torovsky and Franz Ceska, the envoy Christian Zeileissen, and Stefan Lehne. The foreign ministry hoped "that positive results could be achieved here at the Vienna Follow-up meeting" with regard to environmental questions.[22] This statement should be seen against the background of the environmental discourse and environmental policy in 1980s Austria. The Chernobyl nuclear disaster on 26 April 1986 gave rise to a worldwide rethink

https://www.osce.org/files/f/documents/a/7/40881.pdf, accessed 18.10.2024; on the Vienna Concluding Document see the article by Michael Gehler in this volume.

17 Stefan Jordan, *Theorien und Methoden der Geschichtswissenschaft* (Orientierung Geschichte Vol. 1), Paderborn 2013², p. 49; Georg Eckert/Thorsten Beigel, *Historisch Arbeiten. Handreichung zum Geschichtsstudium*, Göttingen 2019, p. 78–79.

18 Dienstzettel des Bundesministeriums für Auswärtige Angelegenheiten (BMAA) vom 10.7.1986 betreffend "3. KSZE-Folgetreffen in Wien; BMAA-interner Gedankenaustausch zur Vorbereitung", Österreichisches Staatsarchiv (ÖStA), Archiv der Republik (AdR), BMAA, politische Sektion II/Abteilung 7 Entwicklung (II.-Pol.) 1986, Geschäftszahl (GZ) 803.00/47-II. 7/86; Dienstzettel des BMAA vom 7.7.1986 betreffend "KSZE, 3. Folgetreffen, Wien, ab 4.11.1986; brain-storming am 4.7.1986", ÖStA, AdR, BMAA, II-Pol. 1986, GZ 803.00/73-II. 7/86.

19 Dienstzettel des BMAA vom 2.9.1986 betreffend "WFT; österreichische Linie. Befassung der Vertretungsbehörden", ÖStA, AdR, BMAA, II-Pol. 1986, GZ 803.00/101-II. 7/86.

20 The envoy Gerhard Velcovsky was charged with running Basket II at the Vienna CSCE Follow-up Meeting; see also René Pollitzer, "'in meinem Bereich, den Bereichen Umweltschutz, Landwirtschaft und Wirtschaft, war wahrscheinlich die Autonomie der einzelnen Länder, egal welchem Block sie zugehörten, am größten'", in: Habel/Hechenblaikner et al. (eds.), *Diplomatie am Ende des Kalten Krieges*, p. 313–334.

21 Dienstzettel des BMAA vom 3.3.1988 betreffend "WFT; Plenarsitzung am 4. März 1988; Erklärung von Bot. Dr. Torovsky zu Korb II", ÖStA, AdR, BMAA, II.-Pol. 1988, GZ 803.10/2-II. 7/88.

22 "KSZE, 3. Folgetreffen, Wien, ab 4.11.1986; brain-storming am 4.7.1986", GZ 803.00/73-II. 7/86.

on the issue of environmental protection.[23] In addition to Chernobyl, "acid rain" and the associated "forest dieback",[24] air protection with the reduction of chlorofluorocarbons[25] and water protection were also high on the international environmental protection agenda.[26] Austria-specific issues were the anti-nuclear power policy following the Zwentendorf referendum in 1978[27] and the occupation of the Hainburger Au in the winter of 1983/84.[28] This was also a time when parties dedicated to environmental issues, such as the Green Party in Austria, were gaining political influence.[29]

Based on environmental protection agreements such as the Geneva Convention on Long-Range Transboundary Air Pollution,[30] the foreign ministry envisaged further strengthening intergovernmental cooperation on environmental protection at the level of the CSCE. Even in the run-up to the negotiations, the Austrian delegates considered it problematic that the "Western" states held divergent opinions on the matter, with the United States and Great

23 Joachim Radkau, *Die Ära der Ökologie. Eine Weltgeschichte*, München 2011, p. 500; Peter Bilhöfer, *26. April 1986: Tschernobyl. Folgen einer Katastrophe* (Zeitpunkte der Geschichte), Stuttgart 2021.

24 Gerhard Strohmeier, "'Umwelt': Österreichische Mythen, Topoi und Erinnerungen, Die Gedächtnisorte 'Zwentendorf', 'Hainburg' und 'das Waldsterben'", in: Emil Brix/Ernst Bruckmüller et al. (eds.), *Memoria Austriae I. Menschen, Mythen, Zeiten*, Wien 2004, p. 357–391; Richard Hölzl/K. J. Oosthoek, "Transforming Woodlands. European Forest Protection in a Global Context", in: Wöbse/Kupper (eds.), *Greening Europe*, p. 157–184.

25 Radkau, *Die Ära der Ökologie*, p. 547–549.

26 Udo Ernst Simonis/Ernst Ulrich Freiherr von Weizsäcker, "Globale Umweltprobleme. Neun Thesen", in: *Europa-Archiv* 45 (1990), p. 1–12.

27 Robert Kriechbaumer, *Nur ein Zwischenspiel (?). Die Geschichte der Grünen in Österreich* (Schriftenreihe des Forschungsinstitutes für politisch-historische Studien der Dr.-Wilfried-Haslauer-Bibliothek Vol. 66), Wien 2018, p. 16–40, p. 63–92; Andreas Kuchler, "Die Umweltbewegung (1965–1985), Österreich im postmateriellen Zeitalter", in: Oliver Rathkolb/Richard Hufschmied et al. (eds.), *Wasserkraft. Elektrizität. Gesellschaft. Kraftwerksprojekte ab 1880 im Spannungsfeld* (Schriftenreihe Forschung in der Verbund AG, Vol. 104), Wien 2012, p. 226–232.

28 Andreas Kuchler, "Hainburg (1980–1985), Menschen und Medien kippten ein Megaprojekt", in: Rathkolb/Hufschmied et al. (eds.), *Wasserkraft. Elektrizität. Gesellschaft*, p. 245–256; Kriechbaumer, *Nur ein Zwischenspiel (?)*.

29 Franz Schandl/Gerhard Schattauer, *Die Grünen in Österreich. Entwicklung und Konsolidierung einer politischen Kraft*, Wien 1996; Othmar Pruckner, *Eine kurze Geschichte der Grünen. Ereignisse, Persönlichkeiten, Jahreszahlen*, Wien 2005; Kriechbaumer, *Nur ein Zwischenspiel (?)*.

30 United Nations Economic Commission for Europe, 1979 Convention on Long-Range Transboundary Air Pollution (CLRTAP), https://unece.org/sites/default/files/2021-05/1979%20CLRTAP.e.pdf, accessed 3.3.2022; on the treaty see Philippe Sands/Jacqueline Peel et al., *Principles of International Environmental Law*, Cambridge-New York et al. [3]2012.

Britain, for instance, prioritising their economic interests over environmental considerations.[31]

Ideas for potential negotiating points were developed in a brainstorming session. According to the official note, possible proposals for the Vienna CSCE follow-up meeting were already being drafted. In Austria, as the foreign ministry lacked in-depth expertise in areas such as environmental protection, it was up to the relevant ministries to concretise the content of the proposals for Basket II.[32] Austria concurred with Western Germany and Sweden in wanting to list all environmental protection treaties adopted by the CSCE states to date in the Concluding Document in order to achieve more durable results in the future.[33] An important concern for Austria was the inclusion of environmental education, a field that had been developing since the 1970s, in the Concluding Document.[34] According to the Foreign Ministry, such a proposal would be "constructive" and "uncontroversial".[35] Yet ultimately, no proposal on environmental education was tabled, though it is unclear why.[36]

From a territorial perspective, Austria also found the CSCE to be ideally suited for adopting a convention on the protection of international waters from pollution, in which Austria saw great potential for deepening East-West cooperation. The model for this idea was the Baltic or Helsinki Convention.[37] However, debates on hydro-electric plants – a live issue in Austria since the occupation of the Hainburger Au in 1983/84 – were not considered,[38] nor did protests against a projected power plant in the Hungarian Danube in 1988 inform the subsequent course of negotiations.[39]

---

31 "KSZE, 3. Folgetreffen, Wien, ab 4.11.1986; brain-storming am 4.7.1986", GZ 803.00/73-II. 7/86.

32 Pollitzer, "'in meinem Bereich [...]'"; Laimer, *Die KSZE und der Umweltschutz*, p. 49–50.

33 "KSZE, 3. Folgetreffen, Wien, ab 4.11.1986; brain-storming am 4.7.1986", GZ 803.00/73-II. 7/86.

34 "Environmental education" refers mainly to in-school teaching of a responsible engagement with nature; see e.g. Georg Pfligersdorfer/Ulrike Unterbruner (eds.), *Umwelterziehung auf dem Prüfstand, Ergebnisse der Tagung "Umwelterziehung in Österreich": Prüfbericht der OECD, Forschung und Ausblick*, Innsbruck 1994.

35 "KSZE, 3. Folgetreffen, Wien, ab 4.11.1986; brain-storming am 4.7.1986", GZ 803.00/73-II. 7/86.

36 Laimer, *Die KSZE und der Umweltschutz*, p. 52.

37 "KSZE, 3. Folgetreffen, Wien, ab 4.11.1986; brain-storming am 4.7.1986", GZ 803.00/73-II. 7/86; on the Baltic or Helsinki Convention see Laakkonen/Räsänen, "Negotiating the Maritime Commons", p. 257, p. 258–259.

38 Kriechbaumer, *Nur ein Zwischenspiel (?)*, p. 69, p. 84, p. 86.

39 Daniela Neubacher, *Stop Nagymaros! Die Geschichte einer Grenzüberschreitung*, PhD thesis, Budapest 2021, p. 8–9, p. 88, p. 91.

4.2 *The Austrian Negotiating Line in Basket II*

About a month before the start of the Vienna CSCE Follow-up Meeting, the Austrian foreign ministry laid down the official negotiating line for Basket II, essentially reiterating the stances developed in the brainstorming session. Once again, foreign ministry officials emphasised that environmental protection should be one of Austria's priorities at the Vienna CSCE Follow-up Meeting. In the area of economic cooperation expectations were low given the divergence between the economic systems of capitalism in the "West" and real socialism in the "East".[40]

In accordance with the Austrian negotiating line aspects of intergovernmental exchange in the event of transboundary environmental disasters were negotiated at the Vienna CSCE Follow-up Meeting. This proposal arose in view of the Chernobyl disaster in 1986 and was submitted to the foreign ministry at the request of the Austrian parliament, the Nationalrat.[41]

4.3 *Torovsky's Statement on Basket II, March 1988*

Austria's ideas and demands were highly ambitious. Accordingly, they met with considerable resistance as negotiations progressed. Some proposals, such as those on air and water protection, were too progressive (i.e. restrictive) for the other participating states.[42] In a statement dated 4 March 1988, Torovsky expressed his disappointment with the course of the negotiations and the slow progress in the drafting of Basket II, arguing that Austria had scaled back its ambitious goals to a level that was "fundamentally acceptable to all sides. But even these modest ideas were often rejected as unrealistic".[43]

For example, negotiations on the Austrian proposal WT.11 "Cross-border Traffic and Environment" proved difficult[44] as two NATO states, the Netherlands and Turkey, regarded this proposal as a threat to their national transit

40 "WFT; österreichische Linie. Befassung der Vertretungsbehörden", GZ 803.00/101-II. 7/86.

41 Dienstzettel des BMAA vom 10.7.1986 betreffend "Nuklearunfälle, Frage der Information und des Schadenersatzes, Entschließung des Nationalrates vom 11.6.1986", ÖStA, AdR, BMAA, II-Pol. 1986, GZ 803.03.07/4-II. 7/86; Antrag in der 144. Nationalratssitzung von 11. Juni 1986: Stenographisches Protokoll, 144. Sitzung des Nationalrates der Republik Österreich, XVI. Gesetzgebungsperiode, 11.6.1986, https://www.parlament.gv.at/recherchieren/protokolle, accessed 18.4.2023, p. 12636.

42 On the Basket II negotiations at the Vienna CSCE Follow-up Meeting see Laimer, *Die KSZE und der Umweltschutz.*

43 "WFT; Plenarsitzung am 4. März 1988; Erklärung von Bot. Dr. Torovsky zu Korb II", GZ 803.10/2-II. 7/88.

44 On the Austrian proposal WT.11 "Cross-border Traffic and Environment" see Laimer, *Die KSZE und der Umweltschutz*, p. 78–98.

interests.[45] The Austrian government's aim was to use WT. 11 to regulate transit traffic passing through its territory.[46] Yet the Turkish delegation interpreted the expansion of rail transport called for in the proposal as "discrimination" against road transport.[47] It went so far as to question the ecological credentials of rail transport,[48] a charge which the Austrian CSCE delegation was able to refute with an expert opinion.[49]

Moreover, in his statement Torovsky also emphasised the consequences of transboundary environmental disasters. Without an intact environment, he argued, quality of life would decline worldwide. In addition, the costs and consequences of environmental disasters would ultimately lower economic output in all countries – whether NATO, Warsaw Pact or N+N.[50] As examples, Torovsky cited the Chernobyl nuclear disaster and the major fire in the Schweizerhalle near Basel[51] (both 1986).[52]

4.4 *Comparison with the Vienna Concluding Document*

To what extent did the Austrian delegation succeed with its environmental demands? In the Vienna Concluding Document, 16 of the 46 paragraphs from the chapter on Basket II covered environmental questions.[53] The document contained numerous measures against air pollution, with half the points

45 Dienstzettel des BMAA vom 27.8.1987 betreffend "WFT; Zusammenfassung über die Verhandlungsphase vom 5. Mai bis 31. Juli 1987", ÖStA, AdR, BMAA, II-Pol. 1987, GZ 803.12/42-II. 7/87.

46 Laimer, *Die KSZE und der Umweltschutz*, p. 78–98.

47 Dienstzettel des BMAA vom 2.7.1987 betreffend "WFT – Zusammenfassung der 27. Konferenzwoche Stand 2. Juli 1987", GZ 803.12/42–II. 7/87.

48 "WFT; Zusammenfassung über die Verhandlungsphase vom 5. Mai bis 31. Juli 1987", GZ 803.12/42-II. 7/87.

49 Dienstzettel des BMAA vom 29.9.1987 betreffend "WFT; Korb II; Übersendung von Unterlagen über Emissionen", ÖStA, AdR, BMAA, II-Pol. 1987, GZ 803.03.05/9-II. 7/87.

50 "WFT; Plenarsitzung am 4. März 1988; Erklärung von Bot. Dr. Torovsky zu Korb II", GZ 803.10/2-II. 7/88.

51 The conflagration at the Schweizerhalle in Basel on 1 November 1986, in the course of which water used to extinguish the fire became contaminated with chemicals and entered the Rhine, led to the death of fish on a catastrophic scale. See Walter Giger, "Der Rhein rot, die Fische tot. Brandkatastrophe in Schweizerhalle 1986 – Rückblick und Bilanz", in: *UWSF – Z Umweltchem Ökotox* (*Umweltwissenschaften und Schadstoff-Forschung*) 19 (2007), special issue 1, p. 11–23; Andreas Schuler, "Schweizerhalle 1986. Roter Rhein und grüne Wirtschaft", in: *Akzent: Magazin für Kultur und Gesellschaft* (2016), issue 6, Arbeit und Verdienst: Basel und seine Wirtschaft, p. 18–22.

52 "WFT; Plenarsitzung am 4. März 1988; Erklärung von Bot. Dr. Torovsky zu Korb II", GZ 803.10/2-II. 7/88.

53 Concluding Document of the Vienna Meeting 1986.

including demands for the reduction of chlorofluorocarbons and other pollutants potentially damaging to the Earth's climate.[54] The Concluding Document also committed the signatory states to cooperation on water protection[55] and to "improving and coordinating their arrangements for prevention, early warning, exchange of information and mutual assistance in cases of industrial accidents".[56]

Austria's demand for a solution to the transit problem was rebuffed. According to paragraph 38, under the heading of "Cooperation in other areas", the participating states were to "encourage the elaboration of measures for achieving an economically more efficient transport system", which was to be achieved through joint conferences of experts or research efforts.[57] However, Austria's call for a reduction or regulation of transit flows has remained de facto unresolved until nowadays.[58]

5 Conclusion

On questions of environmental cooperation in Basket II, the Austrian delegation at the Vienna CSCE Follow-up Meeting set itself ambitious goals and made forward-looking demands – without being able to secure their full implementation. The other participating states found Austria's proposals for environmental protection to be too restrictive and thereby damaging to their own economic interests. Austria drew up a number of proposals in the run-up to the Vienna CSCE Follow-up Meeting, and the source documents allow the process to be traced, in the manner of a case study, from brainstorming to the official tabling of a proposal and ultimately the completion of a paragraph in the Vienna Concluding Document. Some Austrian proposals – for instance, the proposal for resolving the transit problem – were ahead of their time and addressed issues that are still unresolved.[59] Nor were negotiations in the area of environmental protection frictionless and uncontroversial, as can be seen from the Austrian proposal for WT. 11 "Cross-border Traffic and Environment". With regard to environmental protection, Basket II was therefore rather more

54 Ibid., paragraphs 24–30.
55 Ibid., paragraph 31.
56 Ibid., paragraph 36.
57 Ibid., paragraph 38.
58 Romed Aschwanden/Maria Buck et al. (eds.), *Conflicts d'usage depuis 1950 – Conflitti d'uso dal 1950 – Nutzungskonflikte seit 1950* (Histoire des Alpes – Storia delle Alpi – Geschichte der Alpen 2022/27), Zürich 2022.
59 Laimer, *Die KSZE und der Umweltschutz*, p. 99, p. 107–108.

than the "step-child"[60] which some CSCE delegates found it, in retrospect, to have been.

Basket II still holds much potential for research. Historians have yet to explore and contextualise the various environmental treaties of the 1970s and 1980s. Nor is the Austrian delegates' conduct of the negotiations at the Vienna CSCE Follow-up Meeting fully understood. For instance, the two pioneering figures of the Austrian Green movement, Freda Meißner-Blau and Peter Pilz, appear on the lists of CSCE delegates,[61] yet it remains unknown whether they were involved in the negotiations in Basket II and, if so, what influence they exerted there.

60 Lehne, *The CSCE in the 1990s*, p. 98.

61 Wiener Treffen 1986 der Vertreter der Teilnehmerstaaten der Konferenz über Sicherheit und Zusammenarbeit in Europa, Haupttreffen, Liste der Teilnehmer, Politisches Archiv des Auswärtigen Amts, Berlin (PA-AA), B 28, Zwischenarchiv (ZA), Referat 212, Bd. 153421.

Front Page News or Side Note?

The Human Dimension of the Vienna CSCE Follow-up Meeting in Austrian and West German Newspapers

Nina Hechenblaikner

1 Introduction[1]

The main task of mass media, including newspapers, is to keep the public informed of (current) events. Yet they should be considered not only as sources of information but also in their effects on political structures and processes.[2] Besides situating topical issues in the context of global politics, mass media offer views, commentary and opinions. Analysing the emphases placed by newspapers shows what areas are considered to be of particular relevance by a given media outlet. While it is of course impossible to make direct inferences regarding public opinion from published opinion, a media analysis is able to show what image was intended for public consumption. Although research in the field of contemporary history has paid increasing attention to political communication,[3] an analysis of reporting on the Conference on Security and Cooperation in Europe (CSCE) and its follow-up meetings remains a research desideratum.

1 The research for this article was conducted as part of the project "Durchbruch bei den Menschenrechten? Das KSZE-Folgetreffen in Wien (1986–1989)" and funded wholly or in part by the Austrian Science Fund (FWF) [project number: I 4139]. Previously untranslated German language sources were translated by the author.

2 Peter Maurer, "Einflussfaktoren auf die Handlungsautonomie der Medien im politischen Prozess westlicher Demokratien. Eine theoretische Analyse", in: Barbara Pfetsch/Silke Adam (eds.), *Massenmedien als politische Akteure. Konzepte und Analysen*, Wiesbaden 2008, p. 73–91, on p. 73.

3 For theoretical foundations see e.g. Martin Klimke/Joachim Scharloth (eds.), *1968. Handbuch zur Kultur- und Mediengeschichte der Studentenbewegung*, Stuttgart-Weimar 2007; Barbara Pfetsch/Silke Adam (eds.), *Massenmedien als politische Akteure. Konzepte und Analysen*, Wiesbaden 2008; Thomas Mergel, "Politisierte Medien und medialisierte Politik. Strukturelle Koppelungen zwischen zwei sozialen Systemen", in: Klaus Arnold/Christoph Classen et al. (eds.), *Von der Politisierung der Medien zur Medialisierung des Politischen? Zum Verhältnis von Medien, Öffentlichkeit und Politik im 20. Jahrhundert*, Leipzig 2010, p. 29–50; Otfried Jarren/Patrick Donges, *Politische Kommunikation in der Mediengesellschaft. Eine Einführung* (Springer Link Bücher), Wiesbaden 2011³; Winfried Schulz, *Politische Kommunikation. Theoretische Ansätze und Ergebnisse empirischer Forschung*, Wiesbaden 2011³.

The opening of the third Follow-up Meeting of the CSCE, which spanned from 4–7 November 1986, was met with considerable interest from the international media. Newspapers, radio and television reported on the opening ceremony as well as on the various events (both official and unofficial) that flanked the meeting's opening. For example, the opening speech by Austrian Chancellor Franz Vranitzky, written by the then young diplomat and later Foreign Minister Ursula Plassnik, was particularly praised by the media.[4] At the end of the first week, the Austrian daily Die Presse reported that 1059 journalists representing media from 47 countries had come to Vienna to report about the opening events.[5] It can therefore be stated without a doubt that the start of the third Follow-up Meeting attracted international media attention. This chapter examines how two daily newspapers – the Austrian Die Presse and the West German Frankfurter Allgemeine Zeitung (FAZ) – reported throughout the course of the Follow-up Meeting on one of its focal points, the Human Dimension. These two newspapers are exemplary as national dailies newspapers which aimed primarily at middle-class audiences and were among the newspapers with the highest circulation in their respective countries at the time. On the one hand, the analysis focuses on the question of the continuity of reporting and on the other on that of how the selected media reported on human rights organisations, that were active in the context of the Follow-up Meeting and whether these organisations actively used daily newspapers to draw attention to their concerns. Finally, a case study takes a closer look at everyday journalistic life around the third Follow-up Meeting.

2 The Vienna Follow-up Meeting as a News Subject

The first question to address is whether the Vienna Follow-up Meeting even was the subject of continuous reporting in the two newspapers. The answer is a resounding yes. In the month of the opening of the Follow-up Meeting, Die Presse published 60 articles about the conference; in the same month, the FAZ reported on the Follow-up Meeting in 29 instances. In total, during the period analysed, Die Presse published 536 articles on the CSCE, the FAZ 250.[6] Both

4 E-Mail from Ursula Plassnik to Nina Hechenblaikner, 02.05.2022. The author would like to express her sincere thanks to Dr Plassnik for giving her access to these notes.

5 "Zwischenbilanz im KSZE-Pressenzentrum. Ein 'Barbar' unter 1059 Journalisten", in: *Die Presse*, 11.11.1986, p. 2.

6 This survey includes articles published between September 1986 and March 1898. This period was chosen in order to be able to include the preparations for the meeting and its first repercussions.

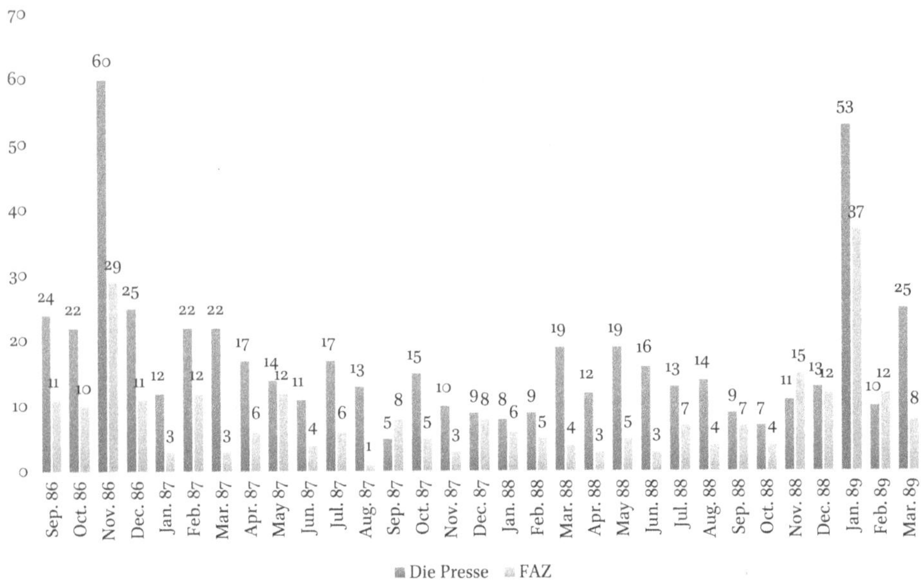

FIGURE 1 Reporting on the CSCE Follow-up Meeting in Vienna
SOURCE: CREATED BY THE AUTHOR

newspapers kept up their reporting on the conference even during breaks in the negotiations.

Both newspapers picked up on the conference even before it opened. The preliminary negotiations, which took place from 23 September to 10 October, were therefore also of interest to them. An article in Die Presse from early October 1986 criticised the fact that only Rudolf Torovsky, the leader of the Austrian delegation, was holding press conferences at this time.[7] Soon after the opening of the conference, the number of reports on the Follow-up Meeting decreased, remaining at a constant level until the numbers rose again for the signing of the Concluding Document in January 1989. According to the journalist Burkhard Bischof, who reported on the Vienna Follow-up Meeting for Die Presse, the dwindling number of articles was due to the fact that during many phases of the negotiations not much was happening that was worth reporting on.[8] Due to the protracted course of the conference and given the scant

7 "Europa in kaiserlichem Glanz. Eifersüchteleien und Strategien rund um die Wiener KSZE-Tagung", in: *Die Presse*, 03.10.1986, p. 3.

8 Burkhard Bischof, "'Aber für Europa war das Geschehen in Wien ein Wahnsinn.'", in: Kai Habel/Nina Hechenblaikner et al. (eds.), *Diplomatie am Ende des Kalten Krieges. Erinnerungen an die dritte KSZE-Folgekonferenz in Wien 1986–1989*, Baden-Baden 2025, p. 343.

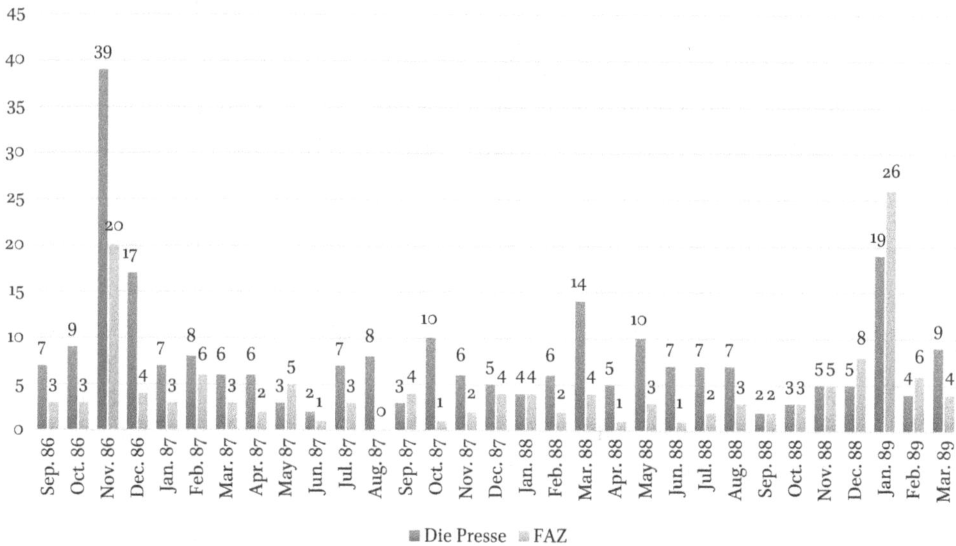

FIGURE 2 Reporting on the Human Dimension of the CSCE Follow-up Meeting in Vienna
SOURCE: CREATED BY THE AUTHOR

information that leaked out in the press conferences, there was not much public interest in the reporting on the Follow-up Meeting. This impression was confirmed by several diplomats who were involved in the negotiations.[9] Bischof also reported that he often had difficulty fleshing out the articles on the CSCE demanded by his editors.[10]

The remainder of this article takes a closer look at reporting on the Human Dimension[11] of the third CSCE Follow-up Meeting. 250 articles on this topic were published in Die Presse, 138 in the FAZ.

The articles most frequently found in both dailies deal with the Human Dimension in general or in connection with other negotiation topics (Die Presse: 120, FAZ: 86). Articles addressing a specific aspect in greater detail are rarer. Most contain additional information on military security (Die Presse: 56, FAZ: 44). A combination of the two subject fields seems obvious given that the

9 Nils Eliasson, "'Towards the middle of the Vienna meeting, nothing was said at the formal meetings.'", in: Ibid, p. 284–285; Stefan Lehne, "Es 'zeigte sich sehr rasch, dass 'der Osten' nicht mehr existiert'", in: Ibid, p. 195.

10 Bischof, "'Aber für Europa war das Geschehen in Wien ein Wahnsinn.'", p. 343.

11 The term Human Dimension refers to all those areas of the CSCE process that deal with aspects of human rights. It covers issues that have had the most direct impact on the lives of people living in a Europe that was divided by the Iron Curtain. E-Mail from Ursula Plassnik to Nina Hechenblaikner, 02.05.2022.

close connection between military and human negotiations was one of the reasons for the success of the CSCE process.[12]

Articles dealing with specific negotiation topics follow the focus of the conference itself. Both Die Presse and FAZ contain numerous items on family reunification (Die Presse: 10, FAZ: 14), religious freedom (Die Presse: 17, FAZ: 11) and the protection of minorities (Die Presse: 25, FAZ: 20). The Soviet proposal to hold a human rights conference in Moscow following the Vienna meeting (WT.2) received a great deal of attention in both media analysed (Die Presse: 41, FAZ: 26). As in the negotiations themselves, the proposal was mentioned in the reporting throughout the course of the Follow-up Meeting. There was hardly any evidence of national priorities in the reporting of Die Presse. It followed the topics that were particularly prominent in the negotiations at the time. In the FAZ, on the other hand, a focus on the question of freedom of movement can be recognised. The problems of "Germans"[13] applying to leave Warsaw Pact states took centre stage. This coincides with the West German government's focus during the human negotiations in Vienna.[14] It can also be seen that both Die Presse and the FAZ spoke most frequently with and about members of their country's delegation.

12 Stefan Lehne, *The Vienna Meeting of the Conference on Security and Cooperation in Europe, 1986–1989. A Turning Point in East-West relations*, Boulder-San Francisco-Oxford 1991, p. 138–139; Douglas Selvage, "The Superpowers and the Conference on Security and Cooperation in Europe, 1977–1983", in: Matthias Peter/Hermann Wentker (eds.), *Die KSZE im Ost-West-Konflikt. Internationale Politik und gesellschaftliche Transformation 1975–1990* (Schriftenreihe der Vierteljahrshefte für Zeitgeschichte Sondernummer), Berlin-Boston 2013, p. 15–58, on p. 34; Michael C. Morgan, "North America, Atlanticism, and the making of the Helsinki Final Act", in: Andreas Wenger/Vojtech Mastny et al. (eds.), *Origins of the European Security System. The Helsinki process revisited, 1965–75*, London-New York 2008, p. 25–45, on p. 31.

13 Most articles do not specify the nationality of the persons concerned.

14 This includes both freedom of movement and freedom of travel for media professionals. Rede Hans-Dietrich Genschers zur Eröffnung des dritten KSZE-Folgetreffens, 7.11.1986. CSCE/WT/PVR.7, Politisches Archiv des Auswärtigen Amtes (PA-AA), B 28, Zwischenarchiv (ZA) (Referat 212), Bd. 153432, p. 85; Korb III Arbeitsunterlagen. Vorbereitungstreffen 23.09.1986, PA-AA, B 28, ZA (Referat 212), Bd. 158438; Intervention des Leiters der Delegation der Bundesrepublik Deutschland, 10.11.1986, PA-AA, B 28, ZA (Referat 212), ZA Bd. 158442. The Federal Republic of Germany (FRG) (co-)submitted seven proposals on these topics. Vorschläge, PA-AA, B 28 (Referat 212), Bd.153448. The focus of the FRG on this issue was not surprising. After all, the people of the two German states were more affected by the division of Europe than anyone else. The West German delegation therefore clearly had the support of N+N during the negotiations. E-Mail from Ursula Plassnik to Nina Hechenblaikner, 02.05.2022.

3 Human Rights Activism and Its Coverage

Human rights organisations had been closely associated with the CSCE process since the signing of the Helsinki Final Act.[15] The follow-up meetings were an important means for activists to draw attention to their concerns. In the course of the CSCE process, the organisations received increasing recognition from delegations and governments[16] and accordingly organised numerous events at the opening of the Vienna Follow-up Meeting. They also distributed reports on the human rights situation in numerous countries to various delegations.[17]

Human rights organisations too criticised the lack of public information about the CSCE.[18] Although informing the public about violations of the Helsinki Final Act was not the primary goal of the groups, they nevertheless sought the attention of the media, as members of human rights organisations also had no direct access to the negotiations. Daily newspapers thus offered an opportunity to attract the attention of delegations. The various groups organised press conferences and sent information to editorial offices.

At the beginning of the Vienna Follow-up Meeting, events held by various organisations received particular media attention. These events included demonstrations, lectures by dissidents, exhibitions and (often publicly staged)

15 Shortly after the signing, so-called "Helsinki groups" were formed in the Warsaw Pact countries. In Western participating states, too, organisations were founded that campaigned for compliance with the human provisions of the Final Act, or the cause was taken up by existing organisations. Examples include Helsinki Watch in the USA, the League for Human Rights and the International Helsinki Federation for Human Rights (IHF).

16 Andrei Zagorski, "The Human Dimension of the CSCE. 1975–1990", in: Nicolas Badalassi/ Sarah B. Snyder (eds.), *The CSCE and the End of the Cold War. Diplomacy, Societies and Human Rights, 1972–1990*, New York 2019, p. 17–42, on p. 30–31.

17 Hester Minnema, "'The [CSCE] process at that time was what was needed.'", in: Habel/ Hechenblaikner et al. (eds.), *Diplomatie am Ende des Kalten Krieges*, p. 371, 376, 383. For instance, the IHF wrote country reports on many Warsaw Pact states especially for the Vienna Follow-up Meeting, which were printed individually as books and distributed to delegation members and other interested parties, e.g. The International Helsinki Federation for Human Rights, *Violations of the Helsinki Accords: Bulgaria. A Report for the Helsinki Review Conference Vienna*, Wien 1986; The International Helsinki Federation for Human Rights, *Violations of the Helsinki Accords: Czechoslovakia. A Report for the Helsinki Review Conference Vienna*, Wien 1986; The International Helsinki Federation for Human Rights, *Violations of the Helsinki Accords: USSR. A Report for the Vienna Review Conference*, Wien 1986.

18 "'Gestern das Baltikum, heute Afghanistan, morgen die ganze Welt'. Schwere Vorwürfe gegen Moskau", in: *FAZ*, 5.11.1986, p. 6.

submissions of reports.[19] So many events took place around the opening of the Follow-up Meeting that Die Presse devoted a separate article to the "chaos of dates in the human rights struggle".[20] However, the various organisations were not only present in Vienna as a group of actors. They also drew attention to the human rights violations suffered by the members of various Helsinki groups.[21]

Besides the "scheduling chaos" at the opening, there were further aspects that were viewed less favourably by the media. A report in Die Presse, for example, criticised that in some cases, the public's interest had apparently been underestimated. This was reflected, among other things, by too few seats and overheated rooms.[22] In another article, the Austrian daily wrote that the unmanageable number of events and demonstrations cast a negative light on the Follow-up Meeting.[23] According to a report in Die Presse, the Soviet ambassador in Vienna felt so disturbed by the numerous activities of various human rights organisations that he complained about them to the Austrian government.[24] In addition, the Soviets insinuated that the people protesting against human rights violations during the opening in Vienna were in the pay of the Americans.[25]

Human rights organisations therefore were definitely covered at the opening of the Vienna Follow-up Meeting. Keeping the attention of the media in the long term, however, involved a great deal of effort for the members of the groups. According to the co-founder of the International Helsinki Federation

19 E.g. "Die Balten wollen in Wien die 'Mauer des Schweigens' durchbrechen. Hilferufe vor dem KSZE-Treffen", in: *FAZ*, 04.11.1986, p. 2; "'Der Gulag existiert weiter'. Vorwürfe gegen Moskau bei Veranstaltungen des 'Helsinki Spiegels' in Wien", in: *FAZ*, 06.11.1986, p. 7; "'Gestern das Baltikum, heute Afghanistan, morgen die ganze Welt'. Schwere Vorwürfe gegen Moskau", in: *FAZ*, 5.11.1986, p. 6; "Erschütternde Berichte. Menschenrechtsgruppen bei der KSZE in Wien", in: *FAZ*, 08.11.1986, p. 6; "Entspannung von unten. Memorandum über Grenzen hinweg", in: *Die Presse*, 04.11.1986, p. 2; "Exilgruppen fordern: Schlußakte als Einheit behandeln", in: *Die Presse*, 04.11.1986, p. 2; "Orlow: Druck des Westens hilft den Bürgerrechtlern", in: *Die Presse*, 04.11.1986, p. 2.

20 "Terminchaos im Menschenrechtskampf. Veranstaltungen am Rand des Wiener KSZE-Folgetreffens: wichtig, aber unkoordiniert", in: *Die Presse*, 30.10.1986, p. 3.

21 "Fast alle Mitglieder der Helsinki-Gruppen in Haft oder im Exil. Dokumentation über Familienzusammenführung und Ausreiseverweigerung", in: *FAZ*, 12.11.1986, p. 6; "'Wir werden Fälle von Menschenrechtsverletzungen beobachten'. Polnisches und tschechoslowakisches Helsinki-Komitee in die 'Internationale Helsinki Föderation für Menschenrechte' aufgenommen", in: *FAZ*, 05.12.1988, p. 6.

22 "Europäisches Chaos über Wien zur KSZE-Eröffnung. Alle Wege führen zum Heldenplatz", in: *Die Presse*, 05.11.1986, p. 3.

23 "'Ohne Menschenrechte kein Friede'. Vranitzky setzt Auftakt für KSZE", in: *Die Presse*, 05.11.1986, p. 1.

24 "Gestern das Baltikum, heute Afghanistan, morgen die ganze Welt".

25 Moskau: USA zahlen Wiener Demonstranten, in: *Die Presse*, 05.11.1986, p. 2.

for Human Rights (IHF), Jana Starek, the media's attention and trust had to be earned.[26] The newspapers tended to always quote the same, already well-known organisations, explained Hester Minnema, an IHF employee. The IHF tried for a long time to be mentioned in the FAZ. To this end, they sent the newspaper reports, articles and other materials. However, the breakthrough only came when the editors needed information that Minnema could provide at short notice. From this point onwards, the IHF was featured regularly in the FAZ's coverage.[27] Die Presse also drew on information provided by the IHF. In an article on human rights violations in various Warsaw Pact states, for example, it quoted directly from reports written by the non-governmental organisation (NGO).[28]

However, various NGOs not only dealt with human rights violations in Warsaw Pact states but also denounced abuses in Western or neutral states. These cases were also taken up in the daily newspapers analysed. The International Society for Human Rights (Internationale Gesellschaft für Menschenrechte, IGFM), for example, reported on refugees from Warsaw Pact countries who had been denied asylum in Finland and Yugoslavia, which the NGO considered to be a violation of human rights. In an article in the FAZ, the IGFM also criticised the way the Finnish head of delegation, Markku Reimaa, dealt with the accusations.[29] After overcoming the first hurdle, some human rights organisations were able to place their concerns in the reporting of the two daily newspapers examined and also express criticism of the actions of neutral and/or Western states.

---

26 Jana Starek, "'Es ist uns vieles von dem, was wir wollten, gelungen'", in: Habel/Hechenblaikner et al. (eds.), *Diplomatie am Ende des Kalten Krieges*, p. 423.

27 Minnema, "'The [CSCE] process at that time was what was needed'", p. 382–383. In the period under examination, the FAZ published six articles discussing the IHF – one each in 1986, 1987 and 1988, and three in 1989; "'Gestern das Baltikum, heute Afghanistan, morgen die ganze Welt'. Schwere Vorwürfe gegen Moskau", in: *FAZ*, 5.11.1986, p. 6; "Rhetorisches Entgegenkommen der Sowjetunion in Wien. Menschenrechte und Abrüstung", in: *FAZ*, 24.09.1987, p. 2; "'Wir werden Fälle von Menschenrechtsverletzungen beobachten'; Petition zur Freilassung Havels", in: *FAZ*, 09.02.1989, p. 2; "Über das schlagende Herz der Partei wird in Prag nicht verhandelt. Schauprozesse offenbaren die Verlegenheit des Regimes", in: *FAZ*, 22.02.1989, p. 7; "Über die Verletzung der Menschenrechte in Rumänien berichtet. Eine Anhörung vor dem Europäischen Parlament/Minderheiten, politische Gefangene, Psychiatrie, Dorfzerstörung", in: *FAZ*, 22.02.1989.

28 "Information als KSZE-Hürde. Rumänien behindert Medien", in: *Die Presse*, 23.07.1987, p. 2.

29 "Die Auslieferung von Flüchtlingen beanstandet. Finnlands KSZE-Delegation will mit der IGFM keine Fälle erörtern", in: *FAZ*, 14.12.1987, p. 5. In an interview conducted in 2022, Reimaa claims that neutral states like Finland had been of virtually no interest to the NGOs and their enquiries. Markku Reimaa, "'The CSCE could defuse the antagonism between the two military alliances.'", in: Habel/Hechenblaikner et al. (eds.), *Diplomatie am Ende des Kalten Krieges*, p. 239.

4 Keeping the Public Informed about the Vienna Follow-up Meeting

Another distinguishing feature of the Vienna Follow-up Meeting lay in the fact that increased attention was paid from various sides to keeping the public informed about the negotiations.[30] The Austrian government had already stated in the preparations for the conference that the CSCE was not only a task for statesmen and diplomats, but that it must also be supported by the public.[31] One step in this direction was the opening of some plenary sessions to the public. Unlike at previous CSCE meetings, interested parties were now able to attend selected sessions.[32] The head of the US delegation, Warren Zimmermann, hoped that this would also lead to an improved and expanded exchange with the media.[33]

The head of the Austrian delegation, Rudolf Torovsky, too emphasised the importance of maintaining a close relationship with the media and of keeping them informed about the status of the negotiations. He was well aware of how difficult it was for the media to present the topics and negotiations of the CSCE to their audience in an understandable and interesting way.[34] In doing so, Torovsky was also fulfilling a wish of the Austrian chancellor, Franz Vranitzky, who at the opening of the third Follow-up Meeting had called for more contact between the negotiations and the public.[35] In the course of the Vienna Follow-up Meeting, Torovsky repeatedly complained about the public's lacking awareness of the CSCE process, which in his opinion contributed to scepticism and negative judgements about the negotiations. According to Torovsky,

30 The Austrian public's general lack of interest in foreign policy issues had already been recognised earlier. Renate Kicker and Wolfgang Benedek speak of a vicious circle of lack of interest and lack of information. Renate Kicker/Ruth Deutschmann, *Die außenpolitische Berichterstattung der Neuen Kronenzeitung. Eine empirische Untersuchung des Jahres 1978* (Grazer rechts- und staatswissenschaftliche Studien), Graz 1981, p. 9.

31 Wiederveröffentlichung der KSZE-Texte durch das BMAA, Entwurf eines Vorwortes des HBM und einer Einführung, 11.02.1986, Österreichisches Staatsarchiv (ÖStA), Archiv der Republik (AdR), Bundesministerium für Auswärtige Angelegenheiten (BMAA), politische Sektion II/Abteilung 7 Entwicklung (II-Pol.) 1986, Geschäftszahl (GZ) 801.01/2-II.7/86.

32 In previous meetings, Western delegations had endeavoured to inform the media about the progress of the negotiations by sending them the texts of their speeches. See Lehne, *The Vienna Meeting of the Conference on Security and Cooperation in Europe, 1986–1989*, p. 86.

33 "Viel Lob für Neutrale und Blockfreie", in: *Die Presse*, 08.10.86, p. 2; "Weitgehende Einigung über KSZE-Konferenz", in: *FAZ*, 7.10.1986, p. 1.

34 "Von Tag zu Tag – Wiener Folgetreffen 'Konferenz für Sicherheit und Zusammenarbeit in Europa'", *Ö1*, 01.06.1987.

35 KSZE; WFT, Eröffnungserklärung von HBM Dr. Peter Jankowitsch, ÖStA, AdR, BMAA, II-Pol. 1986, GZ 803.10/2-II.7/86.

public support was an essential aspect for the CSCE's success.[36] To counteract this deficit, he not only turned to the media but also addressed the citizenry directly – for instance, through lectures at adult education centres.[37] In a programme on the Austrian radio station Ö1, Torovsky addressed the concerns of callers and was confronted with the question of "whether this conference will achieve anything at all", reflecting public scepticism towards the CSCE. Torovsky responded by referring to family reunions, the simplification of visits and the release of political prisoners in the Soviet Union since the signing of the Helsinki Final Act, which he argued were due to the CSCE.[38]

Despite the efforts of various heads of delegation, the third Follow-up Meeting nevertheless remained a marginal topic that attracted little interest outside informed circles. In an article published at its close, the FAZ came to the sobering conclusion that the acronym CSCE was unlikely to mean anything to most people in Western Europe.[39] Bischof too surmised that the coverage of the Vienna Follow-up Meeting was of no importance to the majority of readers.[40] The FAZ judged that the Concluding Document of the Vienna Follow-up Meeting would therefore not find many readers in the West. However, it also recognised that the new resolutions on human rights would be of particular interest to people in the Warsaw Pact states.[41]

5 Behind the Coverage

As shown at the beginning, international press interest was particularly large at the start of the Follow-up Meeting. Numerous journalists from all over the world were present in Vienna to report on the opening and the events held to accompany it. It was important to the organisers to present a good international image. Since, to accomplish this, they depended not least on favourable coverage, great importance was attached to a well-functioning press office.[42] While the media representatives were highly satisfied with the organisation of the press centre, the head of press relations, Martin Sajdik, reported an incident in the press office. An unknown person had ripped the power cord

36 "Bei Konferenz in Venedig: Dialogchance blieb ungenutzt", in: *Die Presse*, 08.02.1988, p. 2.
37 "Der Diplomat und Volksanwalt. Wie Österreichs Delegationsleiter Torovsky den KSZE-Alltag miterlebte", in: *Die Presse*, 18.01.1989, p. 4.
38 In the original: „ob diese Konferenz überhaupt einmal etwas bringen wird", "Von Tag zu Tag – Wiener Folgetreffen 'Konferenz für Sicherheit und Zusammenarbeit in Europa'".
39 "Abschluß in Wien", in: *FAZ*, 17.01.1989, p. 1.
40 Bischof, "'Aber für Europa war das Geschehen in Wien ein Wahnsinn.'", p. 344.
41 "Abschluß in Wien".
42 "Zwischenbilanz im KSZE-Pressenzentrum".

feeding an electric typewriter from the wall and rigged up a new connection for himself, causing several short circuits. Among other things, the system relaying the translation failed during a speech by the US Secretary of State.[43]

In addition, supporting events were organised to "put [the journalists] in a good mood".[44] A welcome party, a trip to a typical Viennese wine tavern[45] and museum tours were laid on for this purpose. However, things did not always run smoothly. On 4 November 1986 the Federal Press Service had invited the more than 1200 journalists accredited at the time to an informal evening get-together. As it was not possible to predict attendance, approximately 150 sandwiches were provided. However, as almost all of those invited turned up, the food was eaten before the official start of the event, according to the report in Die Presse. In order to cater for the attendees, sausage and cheese were swiftly purchased from a nearby delicatessen, though trading laws had to be temporarily suspended due to the late hour. Frozen bread was supplied from the emergency reserve of the Federal Press Service. In addition, officials bought up everything that a nearby "Würstelstand" (hot dog stand) had to offer.[46]

Day-to-day reporting during the conference was beset by fewer incidents. Bischof confirmed the impression recorded by some of his colleagues in reports that Torovsky, the leader of the Austrian delegation, was particularly approachable. He held a press conference every Friday and was also available to answer questions from the media at other times.[47] Bischof also had positive memories of the dissemination of information by West Germany and the USA, with the latter, according to the journalist, being particularly keen to inform "their own" press.[48] This impression was also confirmed in an article by an American journalist in Die Presse. Unlike all delegations, that of the United States initially held its press conferences away from the official press office, using the Hilton Hotel instead.[49]

However, the journalists received at least as much information as at the press conferences at evening events where they were able to exchange views

---

43 Ibid.

44 In the original: „mit einem Rahmenprogramm ‚gütig'stimmen". "Zwischen Ghetto und Weißen Pferden", in: *Die Presse*, 07.11.1986, p. 2.

45 Heurige, taverns specialising in local wine, are a Viennese institution.

46 "Zwischen Ghetto und Weißen Pferden".

47 Bischof, "'Aber für Europa war das Geschehen in Wien ein Wahnsinn.'", p. 337. Several other diplomats also met the media at their request. Hans-Heinrich Wrede, "'Wir mussten aufpassen und geschickt spielen, wir als Bundesrepublik, wenn wir deutsche Themen durchbrachten'", in: Habel/Hechenblaikner et al. (eds.), *Diplomatie am Ende des Kalten Krieges*, p. 123–124.

48 Bischof, "'Aber für Europa war das Geschehen in Wien ein Wahnsinn.'", p. 342.

49 "Zwischenbilanz im KSZE-Pressenzentrum".

with delegation members. According to Bischof, the media representatives responsible for CSCE reporting in Vienna were pretty collegial towards each other. Most of them were keen to help one another and there was a lively exchange of information.[50]

6 Conclusion

In conclusion about the coverage of the Human Dimension of the Vienna Follow-up Meeting it can be noted that the two groups of actors analysed in this chapter had already recognised the importance of keeping the public informed before the opening of the Follow-up Meeting. Vranitzky's opening speech and Torovsky's public appearances and regular press conferences clearly indicate that the Austrian government was keen to maintain the flow of information. The activities of the press office, which offered a supporting programme of networking and entertainment for the benefit of media representatives in addition to handling the daily journalistic routine, show that the host country also wanted to project a favourable image of itself internationally. Human rights organisations also increasingly relied on public attention, which they hoped to gain not least by featuring in the coverage of the daily newspapers.

Nevertheless, in the estimation of delegations and the media alike, the Vienna Follow-up Meeting remained a marginal topic in public perception of foreign policy reporting. Yet this did not deter both Die Presse and the FAZ from reporting on it continuously. The Human Dimension of the conference was a constant feature of the coverage. Despite efforts on many parts, the FAZ drew a sobering conclusion at the meeting's end:

> To most people in Western Europe, not to mention the North Americans, the acronym CSCE means very little: At best, they know that the representatives of 35 states from the West and the East have been discussing European security and respect for human rights in Vienna for more than two years.[51]

According to the daily newspapers analysed and contrary to the wishes of many of those involved, the goal of involving the public in the CSCE process through media coverage was thus not accomplished.

50 Bischof, "'Aber für Europa war das Geschehen in Wien ein Wahnsinn.'", p. 343.

51 "Abschluß in Wien".

Questions of Security

The Role of the Vienna Follow-up Meeting on the Road from the CDE to the CFE Treaty

Jonas Kaiser

1 Introduction[1]

The third Follow-up Meeting to the Conference on Security and Cooperation in Europe (CSCE) took place in Vienna from 4 November 1986 to 19 January 1989. Already well received by contemporary observers,[2] the Vienna Follow-up Meeting was subsequently regarded as an important step in overcoming the East-West conflict.[3] In addition to successes in the field of human rights, groundbreaking successes were also achieved on military and security policy issues,[4] including further negotiations on confidence- and security-building measures (CSBMs) and the mandate for negotiations on conventional armed forces in Europe (CFE Mandate).

This essay provides an insight into one of the core questions of a doctoral project[5] examining the discourse on disarmament, security and peace policy issues within the CSCE in the period from 1984 to 1990, from the Conference

1 Previously untranslated German language sources were translated by the author.

2 From the perspective of the West German delegate Hans-Heinrich Wrede, the contemporary response to the final document of the Vienna Follow-up Meeting was consistently positive; Hans-Heinrich Wrede, *KSZE in Wien. Kursbestimmung für Europas Zukunft*, Köln 1990, p. 147.

3 Hermann Wentker, "Die KSZE als Ordnungsfaktor. Höhenflug und Bedeutungsverlust einer Idealvorstellung europäischer Politik (1989–1991)", in: Tim Geiger/Jürgen Lillteicher/Hermann Wentker (eds.), *Zwei plus Vier. Die internationale Gründungsgeschichte der Berliner Republik*, Berlin-Boston 2021, p. 125–141, on p. 125–126.

4 The Austrian delegate Stefan Lehne points out that the successfully negotiated provisions on human rights and those on military security were equally important and that neither was "less significant"; Stefan Lehne, *The Vienna Meeting of the Conference on Security and Cooperation in Europe, 1986–1989. A Turning Point in East-West Relations* (Austrian Institute for International Affairs Series), Boulder-San Francisco-Oxford 1991, p. IX–X.

5 The project "Von Stockholm nach Wien: Vertrauens- und Sicherheitsbildende Maßnahmen und das KSE-Mandat" ("From Stockholm to Vienna: Confidence- and Security-Building Measures and the CFE Mandate") is part of a joint project of the University of Hildesheim Foundation, the University of Innsbruck, the Graduate Institute of International and Development Studies Geneva and the Institute of Contemporary History Munich–Berlin. It is funded by the German Research Foundation, the Austrian Science Fund (Austria) and the Swiss National Science Foundation.

on Security and Confidence-Building Measures and Disarmament in Europe (CDE) in Stockholm (1984–1986) to the Vienna Follow-up Meeting (1986–1989) and the CSCE Summit in Paris in 1990, at which the Treaty on Conventional Armed Forces in Europe (CFE Treaty) was signed. More specifically, it investigates the role played by the Vienna Follow-up Meeting in this security policy process up to the CFE Treaty.

2 The Titular "S": Security and the CSCE

As the "S" in its name suggests, security was an integral part of the CSCE from the very beginning. The CSCE as such was initially conceived as a European security conference against the backdrop of the Cold War. As early as 1954, at the beginning of the post-Stalinist era, Vyacheslav Molotov, the Soviet foreign minister, proposed such a conference[6] with the aim of dissolving existing alliances, maintaining Europe's post-war political order and forcing the United States out of Europe. Molotov's proposal was not accepted, not least because the two non-European NATO states, the USA and Canada, were to be excluded.[7] During the 1960s, the Warsaw Pact states in particular repeatedly called for a European security conference. But it was not until 1969, against the background of the Harmel Report[8] of 1967 and the much more relaxed international situation,[9] that individual NATO states declared their willingness to hold multilateral talks with the Warsaw Pact states. With the mediation of the neutral and non-aligned (N+N) states, preliminary negotiations began in 1972, and the CSCE was established in Helsinki and Geneva in 1973.

In the context of the CSCE, "security" generally meant conventional security and arms control, referring to troops and heavy weapons systems such as tanks, combat helicopters and artillery. However, in the CSCE process, security

6 Jussi M. Hanhimäki, "'They can write it in Swahili'. Kissinger, the Soviets and the Helsinki Accords, 1973–75", in: *Journal of Transatlantic Studies* 1 (2003), issue 1, p. 37–58, on p. 38–39.

7 Wrede, *KSZE*, p. 20.

8 The report on NATO's political orientation, initiated in 1967 by the then Belgian foreign minister, Pierre Harmel, led to a strategic reorientation of the Alliance: a dual strategy of deterrence on the one hand and détente via diplomatic relations on the other; Johannes Varwick, *NATO in (dis)order. How transatlantic security is being renegotiated*, Bonn 2017, p. 45–46.

9 Matthias Peter/Hermann Wentker, "'Helsinki-Mythos' oder 'Helsinki-Effekt'? Der KSZE-Prozess zwischen internationaler Politik und gesellschaftlicher Transformation. Zur Einleitung", in: Matthias Peter/Hermann Wentker (eds.), *Die KSZE im Ost-West-Konflikt. Internationale Politik und gesellschaftliche Transformation 1975–1990* (Schriftenreihe der Vierteljahrshefte für Zeitgeschichte Sondernummer), München 2012, p. 1–14, on p. 1.

was regarded not as a purely military phenomenon but from a holistic perspective.[10] Even a brief look at the Helsinki Final Act, especially Basket I, reveals the security policy dimension of the CSCE, in which the principles of the inviolability of borders and the territorial integrity of the participating states were just as important in terms of security policy as the agreement on future disarmament talks and an initial catalogue of CSBMs, such as the announcement of military manoeuvres and the invitation of military observers to such manoeuvres.[11] In theory, this particular CSBM was a good building block for making Europe more secure in that it aimed to reduce the military threat posed by armies by enabling realistic assessments of the danger and threat posed by another army. The principle of "everyone watching everyone else" was intended to make war less likely.[12]

3 CSBMs: Implementation, Deficiencies and Attempted Reforms

However, the post-1975 implementation of CSBMs, especially in the area of military manoeuvres, was inadequate. Either manoeuvres were not registered on time, no observers were invited or invitations to observe were repeatedly declined without explanation. The implementation of the Helsinki Final Act by the Warsaw Pact states, especially the Soviet Union, thus came to be perceived as "unsatisfactory" by the Federal Republic of Germany, especially compared with its own conduct. Particular criticism was levelled at the practice both of the selection of manoeuvres to be observed and the states invited to do so.[13] The Austrian journalist Andreas Unterberger came to a similar conclusion, albeit far more strongly worded, accusing the Soviet Union of having "completely hollowed out" the Helsinki CSBM agreements "by tricks, by stretching their wording to breaking point". He too supported this claim with reference to

10 Peter Jankowitsch: "'Das Konferenzgeschehen in Wien war sehr wichtig für das, was sich dann 1989 und später abgespielt hat.'", in. Kai Habel/Nina Hechenblaikner et al. (eds.), *Diplomatie am Ende des Kalten Krieges. Erinnerungen an die dritte KSZE-Folgekonferenz in Wien 1986–1989*, Baden-Baden 2025, p. 97.

11 "Schlussakte von Helsinki vom 01.08.1975", in: Auswärtiges Amt, Referat Öffentlichkeitsarbeit (ed.), *20 Jahre KSZE. 1973–1993. Eine Dokumentation*, Bonn 1993, p. 18–81, on p. 27–31.

12 Erwin Müller explains the CSBM issue succinctly: "Vertrauensbildende Maßnahmen (VBM)", in: Dieter S. Lutz (ed.), *Lexikon Rüstung, Frieden, Sicherheit*, München 1987, p. 316–320.

13 Antwort Staatssekretär Peter Kurt Würzbach vom 27. September 1985 an MdB Helmut Sauer bezüglich dessen Fragen vom 18. September 1985. Betreff: Einladungspraxis KSZE Manöverbeobachter durch die Sowjetunion, Bundesarchiv (BArch), BW 1/284826, p. 2–3.

the lack of announcements of military manoeuvres and the anecdotal accusation of that observers had been deliberately issued with faulty binoculars.[14] It can therefore be concluded that such violations of the Helsinki Final Act could quickly strain relations between the CSCE states by generating mistrust. Confidence- and security-building measures thus inadvertently turned into mistrust- and insecurity-building measures.

Conversely, however, the implementation of CSBMs by Western states also provoked criticism from the Warsaw Pact. West Germany, for instance, for a long time would accept only persons officially accredited at the respective countries' embassies as military observers.[15] These were usually military attachés, "members of your permanent mission in the Federal Republic of Germany."[16] Although this was in line with the provisions of the Helsinki Final Act, Poland was one county to take exception to this German practice, complaining in 1986 that it had "for many years made it impossible to send Polish observers to manoeuvres" since there was "no military department in the embassy of the People's Republic of Poland in Cologne".[17] Such behaviour, though in conformity with the letter of Helsinki Final Act, hardly served the cause of confidence-building.

The entire CSBM system was therefore in need of reform, something of which the participating states were well aware. Thus, in the final phase of the Madrid Follow-up Meeting, the Soviets and above all the French showed an increasingly strong interest in a disarmament and CSBM conference, the later CDE. The fact that this conference was able to take place at all, in Stockholm, was in itself a milestone of political negotiation, the United States, for one, having initially rejected the idea. American concerns regarding the final document of the Madrid Follow-up Meeting – and, explicitly, the mandate for the Stockholm CDE – could only be overcome when improvements were promised in the humanitarian field, especially in the Warsaw Pact. The head of the

14 Andreas Unterberger, "Punktesieg über das Mißtrauen. KVAE-Beschlüsse. Was sie wiegen und wie sie zu umgehen sind", in: *Die Presse*, 25.09.1986, p. 3.

15 Karl-Heinz Lutz, "Vom Schwinden des Misstrauens. Deutsch-deutsche Manöverbeobachtungen 19871989", in: *Militärgeschichte. Zeitschrift für historische Bildung* 35 (2020), issue 3, p. 4–9, on p. 5.

16 KSZE-Vertrauensbildende Maßnahmen. Ankündigung und Einladung von Manöverbeobachtern zu dem NATO-Manöver "Certain Sentinel", 23.12.1985. Anlage: Note des Bundeskanzleramts an die Ständige Vertretung der DDR in Bonn vom 30.12.1985, Politisches Archiv des Auswärtigen Amts, Berlin (PA-AA), B 43, Zwischenarchiv (ZA)/130140, p. 2.

17 Antwort der Botschaft der Volksrepublik Polen auf die Verbalnote des Auswärtigen Amtes der Bundesrepublik Deutschland vom 1. September 1986, 09.09.1986, PA-AA, B 43, ZA/130140, p. 1.

US delegation, Max Kampelman, explicitly linked American acceptance of the CDE to the release of prominent Soviet dissidents, to which effect he had received reassurances from Yuri Andropov, the general secretary of the CPSU.[18] This example illustrates a phenomenon typical of the CSCE, the trade-offs between security and human rights concerns.

4 CDE: the Foundation for Building Confidence and Security?

The aforementioned CDE was brought to a successful conclusion in September 1986, helped by the contemporary awareness of the danger of "the 'accidental' outbreak of war due to mistrust or misjudgement of enemy troop movements".[19] The Stockholm conference heralded vast improvements in the area of CSBMs. The measures already adopted in the Helsinki Final Act were extended and specified in the CDE Final Document,[20] which came into force on 1 January 1987. The registration of manoeuvres and the invitation of observers to them were regulated in detail; furthermore, a control mechanism with on-site inspections was introduced. The USSR's agreement to these inspections came as a great surprise, particularly to the West, since the Soviets had previously considered them tantamount to "legalised espionage".[21] Due to the successful negotiation of several Western positions and, above all, because of the on-site inspections, the Stockholm Final Document was regarded by some observers as a "Western victory on points".[22]

The CDE was of great importance for the Vienna Follow-up Meeting, with the Stockholm provisions already coming into force while it was in progress. Even as further CSBMs were being negotiated in Vienna, the implementation of the most recently adopted measures could be observed in parallel. By and large, the implementation of the Stockholm resolutions went smoothly in

18 Veronika Heyde, *Frankreich im KSZE-Prozess. Diplomatie im Namen der europäischen Sicherheit 1969–1983*, Berlin-Boston 2017, p. 426–430.

19 Unterberger, *Punktesieg*, p. 3.

20 Document of the Stockholm Conference on Confidence- and Security-Building Measures and Disarmament in Europe, convened in accordance with the relevant provisions of the Concluding Document of the Madrid Meeting of the Conference on Security and Co-operation in Europe, Stockholm 1986, https://www.osce.org/files/f/documents/5/d/41238.pdf, accessed 25.6.2023.

21 Wrede, *KSZE*, p. 32.

22 Unterberger, *Punktesieg*, p. 3.

terms both of manoeuvre observations and of inspections. Although the process was not entirely frictionless,[23] no major violations of the Stockholm CDE provisions were identified during the Vienna Follow-up Meeting or beyond. This contributed to a mood of optimism among the CSCE states concerning future CSBMs and disarmament agreements, giving a boost and further substance to their negotiations in Vienna.[24]

5 Security at the Vienna Follow-up Meeting: CSBM and the CSE Mandate

The original plan was to organise the CDE process in two stages. While concrete CSBMs were to be negotiated in the first stage, the Stockholm KVAE, the second was to focus on further disarmament negotiations during the Vienna Follow-up Meeting. In Vienna itself, however, it was decided, mostly in accordance with American demands, to divide this process into further CSBM negotiations involving all 35 CSCE participants on the one hand, and separate negotiations on conventional disarmament (CFE Mandate) with only the 23 member states of NATO and the Warsaw Pact on the other. This division, which would have meant excluding the N+N states from the CFE negotiations, was highly controversial at first. France in particular put up massive resistance, with the so-called mandate dispute overshadowing the Vienna negotiations for almost a year until the summer of 1987 and impeding decision-making processes, particularly in the West.[25]

The concerns of France and the N+N in the context of the mandate dispute were allayed by ensuring a strong integration or "encapsulation" of the CFE

23 There were certainly minor difficulties in the practical implementation of the Stockholm Document, for example during the Swiss manoeuvre "Feuerdorn" in November 1988, where from the German point of view there was a disproportion between the times allocated to observation (13 hours) and transport and the rest of the programme (36 hours). However, this shortcoming was not classified as serious, especially since the manoeuvre observation was carried out largely in accordance with the KVAE document; KVAE-Manöverbeobachtung vom 20.–24.11.1988 in der Schweiz, Bericht aus rüstungskontrollpolitischer Sicht, 14.12.1988, PA-AA, B 43, ZA/144811, p. 1–4.

24 Kurzprotokoll der 6. Sitzung des Unterausschusses für Abrüstung und Rüstungskontrolle, 6. November 1987, BArch, B 136/30771, p. 4–8.

25 A summary of the mandate dispute from the perspective of the Federal Republic of Germany can be found in: Sachstand Konventionelle Rüstungskontrolle, 05.06.1987, BArch, BW 1/30789, p. 2–3.

negotiations within the CFE framework. As part of this close link between the CFE negotiations and the CSCE, regular, mandatory reports were issued by the 23 CFE negotiators to the other twelve CSCE states, providing information on decisions and the status of negotiations. The continuing CSBM and CFE negotiations also took place in close spatial and temporal proximity. Both forums were opened and held at the same time in March 1989 in the Vienna Hofburg, albeit in separate rooms, in order to signal the formal synchronisation and integration of the CFE with the CSCE process.[26]

This CFE mandate can also be counted a success of the Vienna Follow-up Meeting in terms of security policy, as this new forum meant that there was once again a real chance of conventional disarmament. The negotiations over Mutual and Balanced Force Reductions (MBFR), which began in Vienna in 1973, had the function of concluding a treaty on conventional disarmament between East and West. However, by the beginning of 1989, they had become so muddled and hopeless[27] that they were cancelled after 16 years and de facto (if not officially) replaced by the CFE negotiations. From the perspective of the Austrian foreign ministry, the integration of conventional arms control into the CSCE process in itself improved the process of détente between East and West.[28]

In addition to the mandate dispute, dual-capable systems – weapon systems that can be deployed both nuclear and conventionally – were another major bone of contention. As these were essential to France's nuclear force, their integration into the CFE negotiations would also have led to a weakening of French nuclear power, which would also have meant a violation of French security policy. According to Wrede, this problem was solved in a "Solomonic" fashion: the reduction of nuclear weapons within the CFE framework was excluded but the conventional form of dual-capable systems was not.[29] Other contentious questions included the Soviet proposal for the inclusion of naval forces or the question of the area to which any agreement would apply ("From the Atlantic to the Urals"),[30] but none of these issues was as dominant as the mandate dispute.

---

26 Wrede, *KSZE*, p. 90–95.

27 The data dispute, the question of the exchange and disclosure of official figures on troop levels and heavy weapons in the military blocs constituted a serious impediment to MBFR negotiations; "Neuer Nato-Vergleich der Streitkräfte in Europa", in: *FAZ*, 26.11.1988, p. 5.

28 Michael Gehler, *From Saint-Germain to Lisbon. Austria's Long Road from Disintegrated to United Europe 1919–2009*, Wien 2020, p. 546–547.

29 Wrede, *KSZE*, p. 95.

30 Sachstand Konventionelle Rüstungskontrolle, p. 2–3.

6 Achievements in Vienna: Dissolving the Interdependence of Security and Human Rights

A major stumbling block for the mandate for negotiations on conventional disarmament was the interdependence between security and human rights issues. The aforementioned trade-offs between security and human rights also came to the fore in Vienna. The American position was already clear at the beginning of the Follow-up Meeting in December 1986: a mandate for conventional arms control negotiations (the later CFE mandate) could be realised only if the Warsaw Pact made far-reaching concessions in the area of human rights.[31] The West had to take advantage of increased Soviet interest in arms control to achieve further successes in human rights negotiations. In April 1987, during the mandate dispute, France was also of the opinion that further steps in the negotiations on conventional security could be taken only once the East had made concessions in the area of human rights.[32] While for the Warsaw Pact the success of the Vienna Follow-up Meeting was linked to a mandate for conventional disarmament negotiations, for the United States concessions in the area of human rights on the part of the East were essential for a successful conclusion to the conference.[33] However, the Soviet Union had already taken the first symbolic steps in the area of human rights at the beginning of the Vienna Meeting. One such step was the revocation of Andrey Sakharov's exile in December 1986, which was noted favourably by the American public.[34] In the view of the Austrian delegate Stefan Lehne, the participants in Vienna perceived the trade-off between military security and human rights to be, in contrast to the previous follow-up meetings, more than just an impediment to negotiations. In fact, successful negotiations in one area could advance those in another. According to Lehne, the strong interest shown in the CFE mandate by both East and West during the Vienna Follow-up Meeting not only helped to bring it to a successful conclusion but also had a positive influence on the negotiations in the area of human rights.[35]

31 Ministerialdirektor Freiherr von Richthofen, z. Z. Brüssel, an das Auswärtige Amt. 12.12.1986, in: *Akten zur Auswärtigen Politik der Bundesrepublik Deutschland* (AAPD) *1986*, Berlin-Boston 2017, Dok. 362, p. 1879–1893, on p. 1880–1881, p. 1886–1887.

32 Aufzeichnung des Ministerialdirigenten Kastrup. 24.04.1987, in: *AAPD 1987*, Berlin-Boston 2018, Dok. 117, p. 584–588, on p. 585–586.

33 Michael Gehler/Andrea Brait, "The Breakthrough. Freedom and Security at the Vienna CSCE Follow-up Conference 1986–1989", in: Michael Gehler/Wilfried Loth (eds.), *Reshaping Europe*, p. 477–495, on p. 487.

34 Aufzeichnung Kastrup. 24.04.1987, *AAPD 1987*, p. 585.

35 Lehne, *Vienna Meeting*, p. 137–139.

Ultimately, there were significant successes in Vienna both in the area of security and in that of human rights, which would not have been possible without the political change that was taking place in the Soviet Union.[36] The so-called Gorbachev factor[37] formed the essential foundation for the massive reduction of weapons systems, for the Warsaw Pact and above all the Soviet Union had previously long resisted disarmament, which contributed to the failure of the MBFR negotiations. From the mid-1980s at the latest, there was a strong desire in both blocs, East and West, to establish conventional security. On the Soviet side, conventional disarmament was enormously important for the implementation of Gorbachev's glasnost and perestroika reforms. These required large economic and financial resources which were, however, tied up in the military and the defence industry. Disarmament seemed a promising strategy for freeing up these economic resources.[38] According to von Bredow, considerations of security policy also played a role in Gorbachev's disarmament initiative.[39]

The motivation of Western states to limit conventional armaments was also multifaceted. According to the West German delegate Klaus-Jürgen Citron, the primary goal of Western states was stability, i.e. "a stable, secure balance of conventional armed forces at a low level",[40] in contrast to the Soviet Union, which favoured the reduction of conventional weapons stocks over stability. However, Citron was also certain that with the right wording in the CSCE

36 Yuliya von Saal, *KSZE-Prozess und Perestroika in der Sowjetunion. Demokratisierung, Werteumbruch und Auflösung 1985–1991* (Quellen und Darstellungen zur Zeitgeschichte Vol. 100), München 2014, p. 4–8.

37 The term "Gorbachev factor" refers to the dominant influence of Mikhail Gorbachev as general secretary of the CPSU on the politics, economy, military and society of the Soviet Union. Helmut Altrichter, *Russland 1989. Der Untergang des sowjetischen Imperiums*, München 2009, p. 16–19. This also had an impact on the further course of the Cold War. The term was coined by Archie Brown; Archie Brown, *The Gorbachev Factor*, Oxford 1997.

38 Detailed explanations of the domestic political and economic implications of Gorbachev's disarmament policy can be found in e.g. Florian Pressler, "A Triumph of Disarmament? The 1980s and the International Political System", in: Christoph Becker-Schaum/Philipp Gasser et al. (eds.), *The Nuclear Crisis. The Arms Race, Cold war Anxiety, and the German Peace Movement of the 1980s*, New York-Oxford 2016, p. 338–351, on p. 348; Ulrich Herbert, *Geschichte Deutschlands im 20. Jahrhundert*, München 2017, p. 1030; Helmut Altrichter, *Kleine Geschichte der Sowjetunion 1917–1991*, München 2013, p. 160–161, p. 178–179.

39 Wilfried von Bredow, *Der KSZE-Prozess. Von der Zähmung zur Auflösung des Ost-West-Konflikts*, Darmstadt 1992, p. 114.

40 Stenographisches Protokoll der 9. Sitzung des Auswärtigen Ausschusses und der 10. Sitzung des Verteidigungsausschusses, 14.10.1987. Parlamentsarchiv des Deutschen Bundestages (PA-DBT), 3104 Auswärtige Angelegenheiten, 3104/4, 11, WP Prot. 9, p. 46.

negotiations, both goals could be harmonised and the wishes of both sides taken into account. As a border state and potential front in the event of war, West Germany in particular had a genuine interest in conventional disarmament. Trade-offs between human rights and security that might prevent conventional disarmament negotiations were therefore not in the interests of the Federal Republic.[41]

Furthermore, the Intermediate Range Nuclear Forces Treaty (INF) Treaty of 1987 reshuffled the cards with regard to disarmament. In this treaty, the Soviet Union and the United States committed themselves to scrapping their land-based intermediate-range nuclear missiles. This led to a shift in the global arms balance: while NATO was superior in the naval and nuclear fields, the Warsaw Pact was superior in the conventional arms.[42] The nuclear disarmament of the USA increased the threat potential of the Warsaw Pact's conventional superiority. This imbalance was very worrying for some Western states such as Germany, which is why the need for conventional armaments appeared all the more urgent in order to restore the global balance of deterrence.[43]

Despite some difficulties, the negotiations on the CFE mandate were ultimately successful and led to the signing of the CFE Treaty in November 1990,[44] which was regarded as a foundational treaty on conventional disarmament and arms control. It set upper limits for the stationing of heavy weapons systems (battle tanks, armoured combat vehicles, artillery, combat aircraft and attack helicopters) in Europe, thereby shaping the conventional balance in Europe for years after the Cold War. It has endured to this day and remains in force except in the Russian Federation, which de facto withdrew from the CFE Treaty in 2015[45] but formally remained part of the agreement until 2023.[46]

---

41 Richthofen. 12.12.1986, *AAPD 1986*, p. 1880–1881, p. 1886–1887.

42 According to US estimates, the ratio of conventional Warsaw Pact forces to their NATO equivalents was approximately 2:1 in 1987; William W. Kaufmann, *Glasnost, Perestroika and U.S. Defence Spending*, Washington D.C. 1990, p. 32.

43 Gespräch des Bundesministers Genscher mit den Außenministern Howe (Großbritannien), Raimond (Frankreich) und Shultz (USA) in Chevening. 09.12.1986, in: *AAPD 1986*, Berlin-Boston 2017, Dok. 353, p. 1825–1834, on p. 1826–1827.

44 Vertrag über konventionelle Streitkräfte in Europa. Über die vorläufige Anwendung einiger Bestimmungen des Vertrags über konventionelle Streitkräfte in Europa, https://www.auswaertiges-amt.de/blob/207276/b1196519ae7598a29c873570448a59e9/kse-vertrag-data.pdf, accessed 25.6.2023.

45 Kingston Reif, "Russia Completes CFE Treaty Suspension", in: *Arms Control Today*, April 2015, https://www.armscontrol.org/act/2015-04/news-briefs/russia-completes-cfe-treaty-suspension, accessed 25.6.2023.

46 In the context of the Russian-Ukrainian War, Russian President Vladimir Putin announced Russia's final withdrawal from the CFE Treaty in May 2023; "Putin besiegelt

7 Conclusion

Both the West and the Warsaw Pact states were strongly interested in conventional arms control, albeit for different reasons, as were the N+N states. The desire for conventional disarmament became a kind of lowest common denominator in matters of security for all participants in Vienna. It was so great on all sides that, on the one hand, it was possible to resolve security policy conflicts such as the mandate dispute or the question of the inclusion of dual capability systems – which Shevardnadze, the Soviet foreign minister, held to be nothing less than the "question of questions"[47] – and, on the other hand, a further argument was created in favour of achieving success in other areas of the Vienna Follow-up Meeting, particularly in the humanitarian dimension. This in turn required large concessions from the Warsaw Pact in order not to jeopardise the meeting's security policy dimension and thus also the CFE Treaty.

This led to a double tie-break in East-West relations. The first was the Stockholm CDE, which utilised the positive changes in the international climate from 1985 onwards to produce the first concrete arms control document; the second was the Vienna Follow-up Meeting, which met the challenge of transforming this positive starting position into concrete negotiation results and resolving the interdependence between security and human rights, which was particularly obstructive at the beginning, during the implementation phase, into a constructive interrelationship between the two areas of negotiation. The Vienna Follow-up Meeting thus fulfilled something of a pioneering function in the field of security. On the basis of the decisions made and negotiating experience gained in Vienna, it became possible to continue security policy negotiations and sign the CFE Treaty in 1990.

Russlands Austritt aus KSE-Vertrag", in: *Spiegel Online*, 29.05.2023, https://www.spiegel.de/ausland/abruestung-wladimir-putin-besiegelt-russlands-austritt-aus-kse-vertrag-a-60241242-22ab-4122-8f14-d5ed50d5811c, accessed 25.6.2023.

47 Wrede, *KSZE*, p. 95.

Shifting Agendas?

The United States, the Soviet Union, and the Vienna CSCE, 1986–1989

Jussi M. Hanhimäki

1 Introduction

"They can write it in Swahili", was how Henry Kissinger once dismissed the significance of the Helsinki Accords. And while the former national security advisor and secretary of state would later express his appreciation for the role that the Conference on Security and Cooperation in Europe (CSCE) played in bringing about an end to the Cold War, the anecdote does capture a significant point about the United States' thinking about the process.[1] Compared to the challenges elsewhere, Europe in the 1970s and 1980s remained a place of relative stability and continuity, a geopolitical arena divided between two military alliances and a few neutral countries with a very small likelihood of significant change. The transformational events that would occur between 1989 and 1991 and change the face of Europe appeared beyond improbable.[2]

While the CSCE was never central to US foreign policy, it was accorded a certain significance. Few policymakers in the Gerald Ford, Jimmy Carter and Ronald Reagan administrations thought that the CSCE could set in motion a wholesale and dramatic transformation of the Warsaw Pact. Yet there was an intrinsic value in keeping the Soviet bloc on the defensive on the issue of human rights. From the long and arduous multilateral negotiations in the early 1970s through the follow-up meetings in Belgrade (1977–1978) and Madrid (1980–1983), American policymakers saw it as a means of engaging the USSR and perhaps even moderating its behaviour. The CSCE also served as a multilateral forum in which the United States could act as the proverbial leader of the

---

1 Quoted in Jussi M. Hanhimäki, "'They Can Write it in Swahili': Kissinger, the Soviets, and the Helsinki Accords, 1973–1975", in: *Journal of Transatlantic Studies* 1 (2003), issue 1, p. 37–58. See also Henry Kissinger, *Diplomacy*, New York 1994, p. 760.

2 For overviews see: Michael Morgan, *The Final Act: The Helsinki Accords and the Transformation of the Cold War*, Princeton 2018; Sarah Snyder, *Human Rights Activism and the End of the Cold War: A Transnational History of the Helsinki Network*, New York 2011; and Daniel C. Thomas, *The Helsinki Effect: International Norms, Human Rights, and the Demise of Communism*, Princeton 2001. One of the best of many edited collections is Nicolas Badalassi/Sarah B. Snyder (eds.), *The CSCE and the End of the Cold War: Diplomacy, Societies and Human Rights, 1972–1990*, New York 2019.

DOI:10.1163/9789004736979_011

free world, demanding the Soviets' and other Warsaw Pact countries' adherence to the principles of human rights laid out in Basket III of the 1975 Helsinki Final Act. In short, if the Soviet Union remained America's primary foreign and security policy concern, the CSCE was useful as a means both of engaging the Soviets and of holding the "West" together. By the time the Vienna CSCE opened in November 1986, however, Soviet policy on human rights appeared to be in the process of rapid change because of the drive for reform initiated by the country's new leader, Mikhail Gorbachev.

So how, if at all, did American policy Vienna differ from thc previous CSCE follow-up conferences? Did Gorbachev's evident push for openness (glasnost) and economic liberalisation (perestroika) convince the Reagan administration that a serious transformation in Soviet policy – particularly regarding freedom of movement and political rights – was afoot? Or did the Reagan administration remain deeply suspicious about the USSR's motives all the way to the signing of the Concluding Document of the Vienna meetings in early 1989?

2 The Primacy of the USSR: Détente and Confrontation

While US foreign policy was global in nature, the role of the Soviet Union remained fundamental to America's strategic calculations in the 1980s. This is hardly surprising. Ever since the 1940s the Soviet Union had been "Subject A" – as Richard Nixon once put it[3] – for US foreign policy. To be sure, the potentially catastrophic consequences of a thermonuclear war between two superpowers necessitated at least a minimum of diplomatic contact and negotiation to minimise the likelihood of a direct military confrontation that could lead to a global nuclear catastrophe. In the decade after the 1962 Cuban missile crisis, Moscow and Washington had improved bilateral communications to avoid nuclear disaster, signed the Limited Test Ban Treaty (1963), and agreed to combat nuclear proliferation in the form of the Nuclear Non-Proliferation Treaty (1968). Yet even in the heyday of détente summitry in the early 1970s – which produced the first Strategic Arms Limitation Treaty (SALT I), the Anti-Ballistic Missile Treaty (ABM) and a series of other bilateral agreements – competition and proxy military confrontation continued. Detente and Confrontation was how

3 This is what Nixon called the Soviet Union in his much-cited address to the Bohemian Club on 29 July 1967. For the full speech: 2. Address by Richard M. Nixon to the Bohemian Club, Office of the Historian, Foreign Relations of the United States, 1969–1976, Volume I, Foundations of Foreign Policy, 1969–1972, https://history.state.gov/historicaldocuments/frus1969-76v01/d2, accessed 1.7.2023.

the former US diplomat Raymond Garthoff aptly summed up Soviet-American relations.[4] Moscow and Washington may have moved towards détente in the 1970s and 1980s, but the underlying ideological hostility and ongoing geopolitical competition were hardly things of the past.[5]

In fact, concerns about the Soviet Union continued to influence virtually every aspect of American foreign policy in the last decades of the Cold War. The normalisation of Sino-American relations in the 1970s was justified in large part in terms of its perceived benefits for the United States' dealings with the USSR. Already in the mid-1970s Kissinger referred to the People's Republic of China (PRC) as "one of our best NATO allies",[6] and the Sino-American relationship became a tool of America's policy of containment. In practice, this meant that throughout the remainder of the Cold War the United States treated China very differently from the Soviet Union. The Carter administration cast aside concerns about China's questionable human rights record as it moved fully to normalise diplomatic relations in early 1979. Throughout the 1980s a Sino-American strategic partnership (or "strategic association") aimed at containing the Soviet Union continued under the Reagan administration. Even the arrival of Mikhail Gorbachev in the Kremlin at first did nothing to alter the perception that a stronger China translated into an asset for the United States in its ongoing confrontation and competition with the Soviet Union.[7]

Underlying American concerns about the Soviet Union was the perception that in the 1960s and 1970s Moscow had truly gone global. As the United States moved gradually to extricate itself from Vietnam, the Soviet leadership appeared relatively confident in the late 1960s and early 1970s. Moscow rivalled and ultimately overtook China as the principal supporter of North Vietnam and could hence claim some credit for the country's unification 1975. The USSR became increasingly active in Africa (particularly in Angola and the

4 Raymond Garthoff, *Détente and Confrontation: Soviet-American Relations from Nixon to Reagan*, Washington D.C. 1994; For an overview see Jussi M. Hanhimäki, "Détente and the Reconfiguration of Superpower Relations", in: David C. Engerman/May Paul Friedman/Melani McAlister (eds.), *The Cambridge History of America and the World. Volume 4: 1945 to the Present*, New York 2022, p. 512–534.

5 General accounts on the long 1970s include: Jussi M. Hanhimäki, *The Rise and Fall of Détente: American Foreign Policy and the Transformation of the Cold War*, Washington D.C. 2012; Daniel Sargent, *Superpower Transformed: The Remaking of American Foreign Relations in the 1970s*, New York 2015; Barbara Zanchetta, *Transformation of American International Power in the 1970s*, New York 2013.

6 Quoted in Jussi M. Hanhimäki, *Flawed Architect: Henry Kissinger and American Foreign Policy*, New York 2004, p. 419.

7 For a detailed discussion of Sino-American cooperation in the last decades of the Cold War, see: S. Mahmud Ali, *US-China Cold War Collaboration, 1971–1989*, London-New York 2005.

Horn of Africa) in the 1970s while maintaining its close relationship with Castro's Cuba.[8] Towards the end of the decade, various regional conflicts further eroded the basis of détente. Rather remarkably, seen from today's perspective, the 1977–1978 war between Ethiopia and Somalia over the Ogaden Desert was considered, both in Washington and Moscow, as a key conflict in Cold War terms. Carter's national security adviser, Zbigniew Brzezinski, won support within the administration for viewing Soviet bloc aid to Ethiopia as a direct challenge to the United States. On the Soviet side, some leaders believed that by receiving Soviet advisers and Cuban troops, the leftist military regime in Ethiopia would become a shining example of the inevitable triumph of socialism across Africa.[9]

The Soviet invasion of Afghanistan in December 1979 is widely seen as the end of superpower détente. The Carter administration withdrew SALT II from ratification by Congress and issued the so-called Carter Doctrine in January 1980. A year later the new president, Ronald Reagan, made no effort to hide his sentiments about the Soviet Union and its leadership.

> I know of no leader of the Soviet Union since the revolution, and including the present leadership, that has not more than once repeated in the various Communist congresses they hold their determination that their goal must be the promotion of world revolution and a one-world Socialist or Communist state, whichever word you want to use,

Reagan said during his first press conference as president.[10] Under the Reagan Doctrine, the United States claimed to contain Soviet influence all across the globe[11] – most obviously by supporting all manner of "freedom fighters" as long as they were plausibly anti-communist. Whether it was the mujahidin in Afghanistan, the UNITA in Angola or the Contras in Nicaragua, the Reagan administration challenged the Soviet Union and its perceived allies and proxies on a global scale. But such aid was for the most part indirect (and not always

8 The most comprehensive work on these issues remains Odd Arne Westad, *The Global Cold War. Third World Interventions and the Making of Our Times*, Cambridge 2007.

9 Louise Woodroofe, *Buried in the Sands of the Ogaden: The United States, the Horn of Africa, and the Demise of Detente*, Kent, OH 2013.

10 The President's News Conference, January 29, 1981, Ronald Reagan Presidential Library & Museum, https://www.reaganlibrary.gov/archives/speech/presidents-news-conference-1, accessed 7.7.2023.

11 For a compact discussion of the Reagan Doctrine and its impact see: Hal Brands, *Making the Unipolar Moment: U.S. Foreign Policy and the Rise of the Post-Cold War Order*, Ithaca, NY 2016, p. 68–118.

sanctioned by Congress) and its actual impact difficult to measure. American assistance certainly contributed to Soviet troubles in Afghanistan and made it difficult, if not impossible, for the Sandinistas to cement control in Nicaragua. But whether the Reagan offensive – such as it was – helped bring the Soviet Union to the brink of collapse remains a matter of heavily partisan (and heavily "American") debate.[12]

The tensions of the early 1980s did not change everything. Even during Reagan's first term as president, Soviet-American relations continued to bear the imprint of détente. This was most evident when it came to nuclear weapons. Negotiations for an Intermediate-Range Nuclear Forces Treaty (INF) began already in September 1981. There were problems and diversions. The Soviets suspended these talks in November 1983 and despite widespread public protests the Americans began deploying medium-range missiles to Europe in 1984. Yet by 1985 – following the re-election of Reagan and the arrival Mikhail Gorbachev in the Kremlin – bilateral Soviet-American summitry returned. Détente was making a comeback. But it appeared that the focus would remain, as it had done since the Nixon presidency, on reducing the likelihood of nuclear war through bilateral treaties. Throughout the 1980s, the primary agenda in Soviet-American relations remained largely unchanged.

3 CSCE: Pragmatism and Human Rights

There is a simple reason for the virtual absence of the CSCE from the above narrative, which is that none of the American administrations in power in the 1970s and 1980s considered the Helsinki process to be central to their foreign policy. It is easy to see why. The "real" issues – the nuclear arms race and military interventionism – were addressed elsewhere. Compared to the many armed conflicts and changing superpower tactics of the 1970s and 1980s, the Nixon, Ford, Carter, and Reagan administrations viewed the CSCE process as a long-term tool to be used to moderate Soviet behaviour – or at least remind the world of its brutal excesses.

Moreover, the CSCE already carried domestic baggage in the 1970s. "Jerry don't go" ran the Wall Street Journal's memorable headline on 23 July 1975, pleading with President Ford not to go to Helsinki and "capitulate" to the Soviet

12 See Jussi M. Hanhimäki, "Introduction", in: Bernhard Blumenau/Jussi Hanhimäki/Barbara Zanchetta (eds.), *New Perspectives on the End of the Cold War: Unexpected Transformations?*, London 2017, p. 1–12. For a brief account of the "Reagan offensive" in the third world see Westad, *Global Cold War*, p. 331–363.

Union. To many, the Helsinki agreements – and détente in general – amounted to a betrayal of American values and a legitimation of the Soviet sphere. In 1976 the presidential candidates Reagan (who narrowly lost to Gerald Ford in the Republican primaries) and Jimmy Carter (who eventually claimed victory in the general election) were both critical of the Helsinki Final Act. Yet after 1977 the Carter administration came to see the CSCE as a venue for promoting the new president's human rights agenda. Taking over in 1981, the Reagan administration essentially continued in the same vein.[13]

While human rights remained a centrepiece of the United States' agenda during the Belgrade (1977–1978) and Madrid (1980–1983) follow-up meetings, American policymakers never expected fast results. Entrenched totalitarian regimes like the Soviet Union, with well-developed mechanisms and institutions devoted to containing internal dissent, were unlikely suddenly to shift their policies. When it came down to such questions as freedom of movement or the persecution of dissidents, "our expectations must be realistic", a presidential review memorandum of July 1977 noted in advance of the Belgrade follow-up meeting.[14] The Carter administration emphasised the need to monitor Soviet (and other Warsaw Pact countries') compliance with the CSCE human rights provisions. The Reagan administration followed this practice and continued working with Congress and private groups to highlight abuses of human rights in the Soviet bloc. Both administrations also exhibited pragmatism as individual cases were occasionally dealt with via high-level diplomatic channels.[15] There was significant continuity from Carter to Reagan in their approach to the question of human rights and the CSCE. Both administrations viewed the issue of rights as a tool of undermining the legitimacy of totalitarian rule and something that enabled the United States to emphasise a common "Western" agenda. Focusing on human rights was also domestically useful as it provided a basis for engaging with the Congress and private groups. After all, it would be difficult to go wrong by advocating for individual freedom.

From the perspective of advancing human rights, however, the end results of American pressure as well as all the transnational activism that had

---

13 E.g. Sarah B. Snyder, "'Jerry, Don't Go': Domestic Opposition to the 1975 Helsinki Final Act", in: *Journal of American Studies* 44 (2009), issue 1, p. 67–81; Carl J. Bon Tempo, "Helsinki at Home. NGOs, the Helsinki Final Act and Politics in the United States, 1975–1985", in: Badalassi/Snyder (eds.), *The CSCE and the End of the Cold War*, p. 230–246.

14 David F. Schmitz/Vanessa Walker, "Jimmy Carter and the Foreign Policy of Human Rights: The Development of a Post-Cold War Foreign Policy", in: *Diplomatic History* 28 (2004), issue 1, p. 113–143, on p. 126.

15 Christian Philip Peterson, "'Confronting' Moscow. The Reagan Administration, Human Rights and the Final Act", in: *The Historian* 74 (2012), issue 1, p. 57–86.

proliferated since the Helsinki Final Act were not encouraging. Soviet and East European governments had not substantially changed their approaches to political rights or freedom of movement. When engaging with their American and West European counterparts, Warsaw Pact representatives emphasised that human rights were not just political and legal rights but included economic, social and cultural rights. In essence, this implied that there was to be no change in repressive measures brought against the activities of dissidents and human rights groups across the Soviet bloc. ("We are masters in this house", the Soviet foreign minister, Andrei Gromyko, had confidently told his Politburo comrades in the mid-1970s.[16] In the years that followed, the future general secretary (1982–1984) made sure that dissidents were unable to challenge this dictum.) Reagan, in a speech commemorating the tenth anniversary of Helsinki, set out the American view in straightforward terms:

> Sadly, despite some gains, the Soviet Union and several other signatories of the Helsinki Act have failed to keep their promises. Despite the solemn pledge that citizens have the right "to know and act upon" their rights, brave men and women have suffered for taking this commitment by their governments seriously. Those who have tried to exercise freedoms of religion, thought, conscience, and belief have often paid a tragic price. The Helsinki accords called for freer movement of people and ideas across the European divide, but that flow remains impeded, and in the case of the Soviet Union it is but a trickle.[17]

Despite the installation of Gorbachev as general secretary of the Communist Party of the Soviet Union six months earlier, little had changed when it came to human rights. Instead, the focus of a "reset" in Soviet-American relations was on nuclear arms negotiations. In November 1985 Reagan met with Gorbachev in Geneva; the following year they would hold another summit in Reykjavik. Ultimately, the United States and the Soviet Union signed the INF Treaty in 1987, indicating that Soviet-American détente was truly back on track. While

16 As cited in Anatoly Dobrynin, *In Confidence. Moscow's Ambassador to America's Six Cold War Presidents*, New York 1995, p. 346. For Soviet dissidents see Peter Reddaway, *The Dissidents*, Washington DC 2020.

17 Ronald Reagan's statement on the 10th anniversary of the signing of the Final Act of the Conference on Security and Cooperation in Europe, July 30, 1985, Ronald Reagan Presidential Library & Museum, https://www.reaganlibrary.gov/archives/speech/statement-10th-anniversary-signing-final-act-conference-security-and-cooperation, accessed 10.7.2023.

no one anticipated that a major transformation was just around the corner, it would not be business as usual at the Vienna CSCE.

4 Vienna and the Moscow Proposal

Soviet Foreign Minister Eduard Shevardnadze's opening speech in Vienna in November 1986 placed human rights firmly on the Vienna agenda. He issued an invitation for a CSCE meeting, to be held in Moscow, "to consider the whole range of problems, including human contacts, information, culture and education."[18] In other words, the Soviets were taking the initiative on Basket III, on the very issue which the United States and Western European diplomats had been trying to force for over a decade. The Soviet delegation formally submitted the proposal on 10 December 1986. Although both Shevardnadze's speech and the formal proposal were short on detail, they were important demonstrations of a shifting Soviet agenda on human rights. In fact, the Soviets sponsored over thirty proposals in the first four months of the Vienna meeting.[19]

The United States and its Western allies did not take the sudden new Soviet openness at face value. Distrust of Soviet motivations and sincerity was sufficiently deep-seated to effectively place the Moscow proposal on ice for several months pending evidence that Gorbachev was seriously moving towards the Western position on human rights. In other words, the question was whether, after years of keeping human rights on the agenda as a means of putting pressure on the USSR, real progress might now be on the cards. The evidence seemed limited or indeed contrary to Soviet rhetoric, as when the news broke that Anatoly Marchenko, one of the founders of the Moscow Helsinki Watch Group, had died in prison on 10 December 1986, International Human Rights Day.[20]

Despite the promising rhetoric of Gorbachev and Shevardnadze, there was no immediate change in the US approach. A week after the opening of the Vienna Conference, Secretary of State George Shultz had summed up the American approach in a message to President Reagan:

18 Quoted in Chris van Esterik/Hester Minnema, "The Conference that Came in from the Cold", in: Arie Bloed/Pieter van Dijk (eds.), *The Human Dimension of the Helsinki Process. The Vienna Follow-up Meeting and its Aftermath* (International Studies in Human Rights Vol. 20), Dordrecht-Boston-London 1991, p. 1–29, on p. 5.

19 Snyder, *Human Rights Activism*, p. 176–177; Morgan, *Final Act*, p. 244.

20 Snyder, *Human Rights Activism*, p. 177–180.

> On human rights, we will continue in our bilateral contacts to press on emigration and specific cases. The Vienna CSCE Follow-on Meeting will give us another means to keep the spotlight on human rights and to press for improved compliance. Deeds – emigration, specific cases – are our bottom line [...]. Together with our Allies, we should probe the Soviet invitation, expressing our readiness to consider it *if* the Soviets meet our other CSCE objectives, agree to consider Western proposals, and agree to conditions that would make the Moscow meeting meaningful.[21]

In fact, relatively little changed on either side throughout the first year of the Vienna conference. Rhetoric aside, Soviet and other Warsaw Pact diplomats continued to employ a well-tested tactic to deflect Western criticism of their human rights policies by emphasising the importance of economic, social and cultural rights in contrast with political and civil rights. On the Western side, too, old habits died hard. In the fall of 1987 Colin Powell, the US national security adviser, recommended to Reagan that the US should defer a decision on a possible Moscow Conference as long as possible in order "to prolong pressure on the Soviets to improve human rights performance if they wished to keep open the door for a Moscow conference." Should the Soviets insist on a decision on a Moscow conference, then Powell advised that "our decision would be 'no'." Even in early 1988, more than a year after the initial Soviet proposal, National Security Council staff recommended that the US

> should avoid either rejecting or embracing a Moscow human rights meeting prematurely, thus maintaining our best leverage on Soviet human rights performance and the indicators of performance which are the best expression of that leverage.[22]

Change was, however, in the air. In 1987 the Soviet Union improved its human rights record by releasing political prisoners, resolving a number of contested family reunification cases, liberalising emigration policy and curbing radio jamming. In 1988, both at the annual Soviet Communist Party conference and in meetings with Warsaw Pact leaders, Gorbachev kept insisting on the need

---

21 8. Memorandum from Secretary of State Shultz to President Reagan, November 14, 1986, Office of the Historian, Foreign Relations of the United States, 1981–1988, volume VI, Soviet Union, October 1986 – January 1989, Document 8, https://history.state.gov/historicaldocuments/frus1981-88v06/d8, accessed 11.7.2023 (emphasis added).

22 "CSCE Endgame" Fritz W. Ermath to Colin Powell, January 27, 1988, Ronald Reagan Presidential Library, CSCE Vienna 1987 (3) Perina, Rudolf U. Files RAC, Box 1 Colin Powell memo (1987).

for serious human rights reform. Avoiding "serious conversation about human rights", the Soviet leader maintained in a speech to his Warsaw Pact counterparts in July 1988, was "a weak spot in us". Instead of "rewarding" the USSR for such efforts, however, the American delegation kept up the pressure. "Why can't all prisoners of conscience be released?", Warren Zimmermann, the head of the US delegation to Vienna, asked at congressional hearings in August 1988.[23]

But perhaps the most significant and unpredictable factor for Western – and particularly American – restraint in face of the Soviet charm offensive was Gorbachev's push for a "Common European Home". Broad in principle but vague in detail, the Soviet leader started making his case in earnest in the spring of 1987. However, one implication of the concept was particularly alarming for the United States and its allies. As Neil Malcolm put it, Gorbachev essentially maintained – in a manner not entirely dissimilar to Charles de Gaulle's notion of a "Europe from the Atlantic to the Urals" – that while the USSR "was inside the European home by right, the United States was there by invitation, and perhaps only on special occasions."[24]

For Washington, the transatlantic dimension was always embedded in the CSCE process as a complicating factor. While the West European states may, at times, have objected to America's dominant role in NATO, they were far from ready to contemplate a European security system without the United States. At the same time, there was no denying that the United States (and Canada) were geopolitical outsiders and that European political cooperation and economic integration had raised concerns about an emerging transatlantic rivalry since the 1970s. In the 1960s and 1970s several European governments – most spectacularly West Germany with its Ostpolitik – had embarked on independent initiatives vis-à-vis the Soviet bloc that rang alarm bells in Washington.[25] In 1988, as some of these same countries appeared ready to accept the Soviet proposal for a human rights meeting in Moscow, with the West German and French foreign ministers, Hans Dietrich Genscher and Roland Dumas, paying a surprise visit to Vienna on 1 July 1988, to press the negotiators to conclude the meeting as soon as possible. Other NATO allies, including Great Britain and

23 Snyder, *Human Rights Activism*, p. 192–193.

24 Neil Malcolm, "'Common European Home' and Soviet European Policy", in: *International Affairs* 65 (1989), issue 4, p. 659–676, on p. 665.

25 For an overview of transatlantic relations in the Cold War era see Jussi M. Hanhimäki, *Pax Transatlantica, America and Europe in the Post-Cold War Era*, New York 2021, p. 13–41.

Canada, appeared less in a hurry, continuing to demand full compliance on human rights issues from the Soviet bloc.[26]

The pressure seemed to work. Throughout 1988, American negotiators in Vienna and Secretary of State Shultz in his meetings with Shevardnadze insisted that the US would only accept the Soviet Moscow conference proposal if there was clear evidence that the USSR was changing its human rights policies. The Soviets continued to release more political prisoners and allowed more people to emigrate. While there was no wholesale capitulation – human rights violations would continue until the dissolution of the Soviet Union in 1991 – it was becoming increasingly difficult to argue that Gorbachev was making merely token gestures.

In the end, Gorbachev's public diplomacy helped clinch an agreement in Vienna. On 7 December 1988, at the UN General Assembly in New York, the Soviet leader made one of his most cited speeches. After declaring the continuation of the recently relaxed policies on emigration and an end to all jamming of foreign radio broadcasts, Gorbachev announced the unilateral withdrawal of 50,000 Soviet troops from Eastern Europe. Outlining the ongoing political reforms in the USSR, Gorbachev affirmed his commitment to engaging "in the human rights monitoring arrangements in the United Nations and the Conference on Security and Cooperation." There appeared to be no doubt, Gorbachev asserted, that all this meant "we have the preconditions for making 1989 the decisive year."[27]

It was a seminal moment and helped remove the remaining obstacles to an agreement about the human dimension of the Concluding Document of the Vienna CSCE Follow-up Meeting. There would be a Conference on the Human Dimension in Moscow in 1991, but it would be preceded by two other conferences: Paris in 1989 and Copenhagen in 1990. Moreover, the Vienna Concluding Document also included an agreement on a comprehensive human rights monitoring process. In effect, the Soviet Union had accepted most of the human rights demands of the United States and its NATO allies. In 1989, East Europeans expressed their preference by overthrowing communist governments one by one.

26 Esterik/Minnema, "The Conference that Came in from the Cold", in: Bloed/van Dijk (eds.), *The Human Dimension*, p. 24.

27 Snyder, *Human Rights Activism*, p. 209. For the full speech see: Provisional verbatim record of the 72nd meeting, 7 December 1988: General Assembly, 43rd session. United Nations Digital Library, A/43/PV.72, https://digitallibrary.un.org/record/54974?ln=en, accessed 12.7.2023.

5 Conclusion

At a meeting of President Ford's cabinet in August 1975, Henry Kissinger summed up the American approach to the CSCE quite succinctly. The CSCE, he opined, "was never an element of US foreign policy. We never pushed it and stayed a half step behind our allies all through the process. But we didn't want to break with our allies or confront the Soviets on it." Yet Kissinger had seen potential in the Helsinki Accords. "All the new things in the document", he maintained, "are in our favour – peaceful change, human contacts, maneuver notification."[28] That Kissinger considered the likelihood that real change would occur limited does not change the fact that Helsinki provided a framework for highlighting the most obvious deficit of totalitarian systems: their disregard for human rights.

The CSCE never dominated the US foreign policy agenda, but the Soviet Union did. The ability to challenge the USSR on human rights in a multilateral forum was a useful asset employed by successive American administrations throughout the follow-up conferences in the late 1970s and early 1980s. But relatively little had changed in Soviet human rights practices by the time the Vienna conference opened. Scepticism about the nature and purposes of Gorbachev's glasnost and perestroika was dominant as many dissidents continued to languish in jails in the USSR and free speech remained heavily curtailed across Warsaw Pact nations. The Soviet proposal for a human rights conference to be held in Moscow was thus met with doubt and suspicion: was Gorbachev simply disguising his ultimate aim of maximising Soviet power and influence? In the Soviet leader's notion of a "Common European Home", American policymakers instinctively suspected a ploy to drive a wedge between Washington and its NATO partners. In this context, highlighting the gap between the Soviets' human rights rhetoric and practice was not only a strong issue of principle but also made the Vienna meetings a multilateral platform from which the United States could coordinate a common Western position and retain its role as the proverbial leader of the "free world".

The outcome – an effective Soviet acceptance of Western human rights standards – was far beyond what Kissinger or any American policymaker could have expected in 1975 or even at the beginning of 1989. In less than three years after the conclusion of Vienna, the Soviet Union itself was no more. It

28 Memorandum of Conversation, Washington, August 8, 1975, 2 p.m., Office of the Historian, Foreign Relations of the United States, 1969–1976, VOL. XXXIX, European Security, Document 339, https://history.state.gov/historicaldocuments/frus1969-76v39/d339, accessed 13.7.2023.

is impossible to "prove" that this shift in Soviet policy and the outcomes it contributed to was in a result of US policy. But Gorbachev's reforms did not proceed in isolation and each of his statements related to human rights not only raised expectations but also strengthened the arguments in favour of full compliance with the standards embedded in the CSCE. While its causes were multiple, the outcome of the Vienna Follow-up Meeting had shifted the international human rights discourse decisively in favour of the West and undoubtedly contributed to the eventual unravelling of the Cold War order in Europe.

European Political Cooperation at the Vienna CSCE Follow-up Meeting (1986–1989)

Matthias Peter

1 European Political Cooperation and the Conference on Security and Cooperation in Europe (CSCE)

At their council session on 27 October 1970, the foreign ministers of the six member states of the European Community (EC) – Belgium, France, Italy, Luxembourg, the Netherlands and West Germany – adopted the so-called Luxembourg (or "Davignon") Report, committing themselves to greater cooperation in the field of foreign policy. By introducing European Political Cooperation (EPC), they provided themselves with an instrument for the coordination of foreign policy positions that was to flank economic cooperation.[1] By taking this step, the EC sought to strengthen its cohesion and establish itself as a player on the international stage. The long-term goal, as formulated by the heads of state and government in a 1973 document entitled "The European Identity", was a "European Union", in which EC and EPC would be merged, and the fostering of a European identity.[2] From the outset, the CSCE was at the centre of this joint undertaking. This was in accordance with the stated intentions of the EC foreign ministers, who in 1970 had defined the CSCE, alongside the Middle East, as a further focus of EPC's work.[3] Last but not least, the member states of the EC – nine in number since Denmark, the Republic of Ireland and the United Kingdom joined in 1973 – regarded the CSCE process as a suitable

1 Bericht der Außenminister der EG-Mitgliedstaaten über die Politische Einigung vom 27.10.1970 (Davignon-Bericht), in: *Europa-Archiv* 1970, D 520–524.

2 "Declaration on European Identity", 14.12.1973, in: Christopher Hill/Karen E. Smith (eds.), *European Foreign Policy. Key Documents*, London-New York 2000, p. 93–97; *Akten zur Auswärtigen Politik der Bundesrepublik Deutschland* (AAPD) *1973*, München 2004, III, Dok. 422, p. 2059–2062; Berndt von Staden, "Politische Zusammenarbeit der EG-Staaten", in: *Außenpolitik* 23 (1972), p. 200–209, on p. 202; Matthias Peter, *Die Bundesrepublik im KSZE-Prozess 1975–1983. Die Umkehrung der Diplomatie*, (Quellen und Darstellungen zur Zeitgeschichte Vol. 105), Berlin-München-Boston 2015, p. 56–59; Angela Romano, "The European Community and the Belgrade CSCE", in: Vladimir Bilandžić/Dittmar Dahlmann/Milan Kosanović (eds.), *From Helsinki to Belgrade. The First CSCE Follow-up Meeting and the Crisis of Détente* (Internationale Beziehungen: Theorie und Geschichte Vol. 10), Göttingen-Bonn 2012, p. 205–224, on p. 205–207.

3 Runderlass von Staden, 23.11.1970, in: *AAPD 1970*, München 2001, III, Dok. 564, p. 2100–2103.

instrument for countering the bilateralism of the superpowers and formulating distinctly European interests.[4] Just as the CSCE was an important driving force in the development of EPC, the EC member states also influenced the course of the Conference. In particular, they succeeded in adding dynamic elements to the Kremlin's static concept for a European security conference, considerably expanding the topics to be addressed (especially in the humanitarian field), formulating rules for the follow-up to the conference and – as was demonstrated at the first Follow-up Meeting in Belgrade (1977–1978) but above all at the second Follow-up Meeting in Madrid (1980–1983) – making the CSCE an instrument of East-West détente.[5]

However, its claim to act as a unit within the CSCE also made EPC an important forum for EC countries to present their own positions in order to gain the support of their partners for their national goals. This was particularly true for West Germany, part of a divided country in the middle of Europe. In the phase of the realisation and further development of the Final Act after 1975, it sought the backing of its EPC partners in order to push for improved rights for Germans beyond the Iron Curtain. France, on the other hand, which was not part of NATO's military command structure, pursued its special interest in establishing a forum for disarmament and arms control within the CSCE process.[6] Something similar could be said for the United Kingdom in its capacity as transatlantic "bridge builder"[7] or for the Netherlands with its pronounced interest in seeing human rights implemented. In December 1985, just under a year before the start of the Vienna follow-up meeting, the European Council adopted the Single European Act (SEA), which placed EPC on a new footing. With the SEA, the member states – twelve since the accession of Greece (1981) and Portugal and Spain (1986) – also made provisions for the organisational consolidation of their political cooperation. Specifically, this referred to the

4 On the significance of the first phase of the CSCE (1972–1975) for the development of the EPC see the detailed account in Daniel Möckli, *European Foreign Policy during the Cold War. Heath, Brandt, Pompidou and the Dream of Political Unity*, London-New York 2009, p. 99–139.

5 Möckli, *European Foreign Policy*, p. 109–123; Frans A. M. Alting von Geusau, "The Nine and Détente", in: Nils Andrén/Karl E. Birnbaum (eds.), *Belgrade and Beyond: The CSCE Process in Perspective*, Alphen aan den Rijn/Rockville, MD 1980, p. 17–25, on p. 20; Peter, *Die Bundesrepublik im KSZE-Prozess*, p. 314–317, p. 530–532; Romano, *The European Community*, p. 216–224.

6 Veronika Heyde, "Nicht nur Entspannung und Menschenrechte. Die Entdeckung von Abrüstung und Rüstungskontrolle durch die französische KSZE-Politik", in: Matthias Peter/Hermann Wentker (eds.), *Die KSZE im Ost-West-Konflikt. Internationale Politik und gesellschaftliche Transformation 1975–1990* (Schriftenreihe der Vierteljahrshefte für Zeitgeschichte Sondernummer), München 2012, p. 83–98.

7 Kai Hebel, "Die 'Brückenbauer'? Großbritannien als transatlantischer Vermittler in der KSZE 1972–1978", in: Peter/Wentker (eds.), *Die KSZE im Ost-West-Konflikt*, p. 99–120.

establishment of a permanent secretariat and the manner of cooperation with third countries and international organisations.[8] It was precisely against the background of this new step in its development that the subsequent Vienna Follow-up Meeting took on particular significance for EPC. While it had previously been an ad hoc "negotiating sub-system",[9] its institutionalisation also increased its claim to political participation and an enhanced status, especially vis-à-vis the East.

How did the EC countries attempt to live up to this claim and implement their CSCE policies in a field where alliance solidarity, European identity and national interests existed in a state of tension? This question will be explored below with a focus on the Vienna Follow-up Meeting.

2 The Vienna CSCE Follow-up Meeting, 1986–1989

2.1 *Preparations*

The preparations for the Vienna Follow-up Meeting on the part of its Western participants served primarily for the formulation of goals and the agreement on a tactical approach rather than on reaching conclusions on points of substance. "A fundamental unity of purpose and leeway in individual proposals", is how Ekkehard Eickhoff, the head of the West German delegation, summed up the general approach.[10] Already at this stage, familiar national interests came to the fore. The United States once again saw the meeting as an opportunity to criticise the USSR's human rights record and to press Moscow to make progress on humanitarian matters. Accordingly, Washington advocated an extensive phase of implementation criticism and a set end to the conference on 1 August 1987, the anniversary of the signing of the Helsinki Final Act. West Germany, on the other hand, pursued a broader approach aimed at progress in all three baskets and the further expansion of the conference system. To this end, as the political director of the West German foreign ministry, Gerold von Braunmühl, put it, it was important to "integrate our ideas into the starting positions of EPC and NATO for Vienna and at the same time to mould the political declarations of the Western bodies in our favour".[11]

8 Schrifterlass Schilling vom 10.7.1986, in: *AAPD 1986*, Berlin-Boston 2017, II, Dok. 189, p. 997–998.
9 Alting von Geusau, *The Nine and Détente*, p. 18.
10 Eickhoff an Auswärtiges Amt (AA), 16.9.1986, in: *AAPD 1986*, II, Dok. 244, p. 1298–1299. Previously untranslated German language sources were translated by the author.
11 Aufzeichnung Braunmühl vom 18.3.1986, in: *AAPD 1986*, I, Dok. 75, p. 430.

It was therefore hardly surprising that Germany introduced a comprehensive strategy paper, first in EPC and then in NATO, which formed the basis for the West's further coordination. In addition to taking stock of the situation, the paper identified four main areas in which further agreements were to be reached:

- "improvement of the code of conduct contained in the CSCE framework;
- intensification of the dialogue on security and stability including arms control with regard to the balance of conventional forces;
- development of East-West cooperation in Basket 2: economics, science and technology, environment;
- development of the contents of Basket 3: the human dimension, cultural identity, information, education."[12]

In the course of discussions over the summer of 1986, the EC member states succeeded in asserting themselves in the NATO circle on important procedural issues, such as not aiming for a fixed end date for the conference.[13] A compromise was also reached with the United States on the duration of the implementation debate, which was to be concluded at the beginning of February 1987 before entering the proposal phase.

In addition to procedural issues, substantive issues and possible proposals were also discussed during the preparatory phase. The United States, for instance, floated the idea of admitting "Helsinki monitors" in the participating states. Denmark endeavoured to set up a "semi-permanent body" to discuss issues relating to human contacts and family reunification. Greece, for its part, announced that it would propose a further meeting in Vienna on the peaceful settlement of disputes. The Netherlands wished to arrange a meeting of experts on tourism, while Turkey sought stronger protections for migrant workers.[14] All proposals were initially only declarations of intent, but they showed in what material terms the Western participants intended to fill out the general guidelines.

2.2 *The Conference*

Indeed, there was at first no need for concrete proposals, the initial stage being traditionally given over to a critical survey of the implementation of CSCE agreements in the member states. In parallel, until December 1986, the EPC

12 "CSCE Process and Vienna Follow-up Meeting (General Remarks)" (Fernschreiben Nr. 255 Coreu aus Bonn), Politisches Archiv des Auswärtigen Amts, Berlin (PA-AA), B 28, Zwischenarchiv (ZA), Bd. 158449.

13 Eickhoff an AA, 16.9.1986, in: *AAPD 1986*, II, Dok. 244, p. 1298.

14 Eickhoff an AA, 16.9.1986, in: *AAPD 1986*, II, Dok. 244, p. 1296–1300 (cit. p. 1299).

delegations in Vienna were engaged in consultations on the first packages of proposals for Baskets II and III, though no final discussion at the NATO level took place at this stage. What and how many proposals the West would table, and when and by whom they would be tabled, therefore remained an open question at first.[15]

Unlike the West, the Warsaw Pact states began to make proposals even during the implementation debate, the most striking of which was the Kremlin's surprising proposal to discuss humanitarian issues in Moscow as part of a conference on human contacts, information, culture and education.[16] The actual proposal phase, including for EPC, only began in February 1987. 154 proposals were on the table by the summer, although only a small number of them actually became relevant. The Western camp was responsible for a total of 30 proposals. The EPC group focussed on Basket II. The proposals, particularly in the area of trade but also on science and the environment, were tabled jointly.[17]

However, the EPC's main interest was in its so-called "flagship" proposal (WT.19) in the humanitarian field. It was formally registered on 4 February 1987. This proposal provided for a mechanism aimed primarily at improved monitoring of compliance with humanitarian obligations, thereby increasing the pressure to fulfil them. This was achieved, first, by an obligation to provide information on questions of human rights and fundamental freedoms (including those of "private individuals" and "private groups"), second, by the obligation to settle individual humanitarian cases bilaterally upon request, third, by establishing of a notification procedure to keep the other participating states informed and, fourth, by the right of each participating state to request special meetings of the 35 "within the shortest possible time" "to discuss and resolve specific situations or cases". In addition to this strengthened monitoring mechanism, the group was in favour of launching "continuous action" through a series of meetings that would culminate in a major "conference on

15 Eickhoff an AA, 20.12.1986, in: *AAPD 1986*, II, Dok. 374, p. 1947–1957.

16 CSCE/WT.2, Vorschlag der UdSSR bezüglich der Einberufung einer Konferenz von Vertretern der KSZE-Teilnehmerstaaten über die Entwicklung der humanitären Zusammenarbeit, 10.12.1986, PA-AA, B 28, ZA, Bd. 153445.

17 Vorschläge zur Einberufung einer Ost-West-Wirtschaftskonferenz (CSCE/WT.58, 18.02.1987, von den USA unterstützt), zum Umweltschutz (CSCE/WT.89, 27.02.1987, co-sponsord by the USA), zur Biotechnologie (CSCE/WT.116, 13.03.1987, co-sponsored by Iceland, Canada, Norway, Hungary and the USA) sowie zur Reaktorsicherheit (CSCE/WT.E.8, 09.04.1987, EPCZ without Italy and Luxembourg), PA-AA, B 28, ZA, Bd. 153446 and 153448. See also Stefan Lehne, *The Vienna Meeting of the Conference on Security and Cooperation, 1986–1989. A Turning Point in East-West Relations* (Austrian Institute for International Affairs Series), Boulder-San Francisco-Oxford 1991, p. 102, p. 200 (panel II).

the human dimension of the CSCE".[18] Although the time and place of this conference remained open, the French foreign minister, Jean-Bernard Raimond, had already announced that his government would convene a meeting in Paris to mark the 200th anniversary of the Declaration of the Rights of Man.[19]

A look at the individual elements of this key Western proposal shows that its elaboration was exclusively the work of the EPC group. Consequently, it was planned to introduce it as a proposal by the Twelve and not as a "Western" proposal in Vienna. Naturally, this approach caused annoyance among the NATO partners, who felt excluded from having a say. The EPC approach was criticised for contradicting the usual consensus-building practices and weakening Western cohesion in the key area of human rights. Despite these concerns, however, the other NATO partners soon agreed to support the proposal without making any changes. The EPC group finally agreed to explicitly mention them as co-sponsors in the CSCE plenary sessions while "clearly emphasising the identity of the Twelve in the authorship of the proposal".[20] This was finally achieved by naming the "member states of the European Community" followed by the United States, Canada, Iceland, Norway and Turkey as co-sponsors in the proposal's opening sentence.

The other Western proposals were presented in varying constellations. In Basket I, for example, only Belgium, the UK, Canada, the Netherlands, Spain and the USA were responsible for a text on terrorism.[21] Among the plethora of proposals for Basket III, it is worth mentioning the text on facilitating travel submitted by Belgium, Ireland, Italy, Canada, the Netherlands, Norway, Turkey, the United States and West Germany.[22] The different levels of support that characterised these proposals naturally reflected the national priorities that existed within the EPC group. Germany, for example, submitted a total of eight proposals to facilitate humanitarian contacts. It was particularly striking that a total of seven proposals were submitted jointly by Western and Eastern group members, an absolute novelty in the history of the CSCE.[23]

Concrete work on texts subsequently proved difficult, as the EPC states initially felt unable to enter into negotiations on their own "flagship" proposal (WT.19). Differences of opinion persisted, particularly with regard to the precise implementation of the individual measures, but also on the issue of the

18 CSCE/WT.19, Vorschlag über die menschliche Dimension der Schlussakte von Helsinki, 4.2.1987, PA-AA, B 28, ZA, Bd. 153445.

19 Eickhoff an AA, 12.3.1988, in: *AAPD 1988*, Berlin-Boston 2019, I, Dok. 92, p. 521, annot. 11.

20 Eickhoff an AA, 28.1.1987 (Drahtbericht Nr. 84), PA-AA, B 28, ZA, Bd. 153428.

21 CSCE/WT.116, 13.3.1987, PA-AA, B 28, ZA, Bd. 153446.

22 CSCE/WT/E.5, 3.3.1987, PA-AA, B 28, ZA, Bd. 153448.

23 Lehne, *The Vienna Meeting*, p. 102.

human rights conference. It was not until a year later, after a long internal coordination process, that the group presented a non-paper on 19 February 1988 to concretise the four procedural proposals of WT.19.[24] However, this did not settle all disagreements, which principally concerned the question of whether each participating state should be given the right to convene ad hoc meetings of the 35 on individual humanitarian cases, a point on which the Netherlands was particularly insistent. A Belgian compromise formula discussed in the twelve-member group, on the other hand, envisaged agreeing on three or four fixed dates per year instead of an unlimited number of meetings. The disagreement within the EPC group remained unresolved for the time being, so that the coordinator for Basket I – the head of the Austrian delegation, Rudolf Torovsky – was asked to defer the non-paper until further notice. In the meantime, the EPC political committee in Brussels was working flat out to revise the document.[25] Cooperation between the EC partners proved difficult due to Franco-American differences in the talks on a mandate for negotiations on conventional arms control (CAC). The French, who were not part of NATO's military command structure and feared for their defence independence, were vehemently opposed to bloc-to-bloc negotiations, preferring negotiations within the CSCE. However, a CSCE setting was categorically rejected by Washington, as this would give the non-aligned CSCE states a say in military matters.[26] NATO was only able to find a solution at the Ministerial Council in Reykjavik in June 1987. The compromise was that negotiations on conventional disarmament, though formally embedded in the CSCE framework, should be conducted independently between the two military alliances and without any other participating state having the right to object.[27] The Western proposal on military security (CAC and confidence-building measures) was then presented on 10 July 1987.[28]

Another factor that strongly influenced the EPC countries' coordination and approach in Vienna was the question of how to deal with Mikhail Gorbachev's reform policy. The momentum with which the Kremlin leader pushed ahead with his project to transform the USSR unfolded in parallel with the Vienna Follow-up Meeting and also presented the EPC group with the task of rethinking its negotiating concept. The speech given by Hans-Dietrich Genscher at the

---

24 Non-paper, 19.2.1988, in: *AAPD 1988*, I, Dok. 92, p. 519, annot. 8.

25 Vermerk "Sonder-PK zur Menschlichen Dimension der KSZE am 15.3.1988", PA-AA, B 28, ZA, Bd. 133568; Aufzeichnung Richthofen vom 21.3.1988, in: *AAPD 1988*, I, Dok. 92, p. 516–522.

26 Aufzeichnung Hartmann, 10.10.1986, in: *AAPD 1986*, II, Dok. 279, p. 1452–1455.

27 Holik an AA, 11.6.1987, in: *AAPD 1987*, Berlin-Boston 2018, I, Dok. 174, p. 868, annot. 40.

28 CSCE/WT.129, 10.7.1987, PA-AA, B 28, ZA, Bd. 153446.

World Economic Forum in Davos on 1 February 1987, just three months after the opening of the Follow-up Meeting, is a good example of this. Genscher emphasised the opportunities that would arise for the West from the change in Soviet policy and warned against simply sitting "with folded arms" and waiting "to see what Gorbachev will do for us". Instead, Genscher appealed: "Our motto can only be: Let's take Gorbachev seriously, let's take him at his word!"[29]

Genscher's speech also caused quite a stir in Vienna. As the reactions showed, the EPC and NATO were divided into a majority that wanted to wait in Vienna until Gorbachev's reform announcements were followed by concrete steps, and a smaller group of countries, led by West Germany, which considered it possible to conduct negotiations in a manner honouring Moscow's willingness to reform.[30] At a meeting of EPC foreign ministers in Konstanz on 5/6 March 1988, Genscher suggested holding an "in-depth discussion on human rights issues" in the EPC in light of the changed situation in Eastern Europe, which in turn might make it easier for the East to agree to the CAC negotiations.[31] However, this approach met with resistance and exposed Bonn to the suspicion that it was forcing a conclusion of the conference at the expense of Western room for manoeuvre in negotiations on the humanitarian dimension.[32]

Finally, there was a great need for coordination within the Western group on the question of how to react to the Soviet proposal for a human rights conference in Moscow. Reactions in the Western camp ranged from tentative to openly hostile. The US government, recognising that the Kremlin had put itself in a demandeur position with its proposal, began an intensive human rights dialogue with Moscow, focusing on cases of emigration, the release of further prisoners, a reform of Soviet criminal law and religious freedom.[33] On the other hand, Margaret Thatcher, the British prime minister, categorically rejected Moscow as a conference venue, while France, for its part, was not prepared to abandon its own proposed conference in favour of the Soviet capital.[34]

At a further meeting in Brussels on 22 March 1988, the EPC foreign ministers approved a compromise, which they also communicated to Torovsky, on their February non-paper. They reaffirmed the goal of the Twelve to create a mechanism that would enable each participating state to raise individual human

29 Bulletin des Presse- und Informationsamts der Bundesregierung 1987, Bonn 1987, p. 97.

30 Eickhoff an AA, 4.3.1987, in: *AAPD 1987*, I, Dok. 65, p. 305–308.

31 Vermerk über das informelle Treffen der EPZ-Außenminister am 5./6.3.1988 in Konstanz, in: *AAPD 1988*, I, Dok. 92, p. 517, annot. 5.

32 Aufzeichnung Richthofen vom 21.3.1988, in: *AAPD 1988*, I, Dok. 92, p. 516–522.

33 Anatoly Adamishin/Richard Schifter, *Human Rights, Perestroika, and the End of the Cold War*, Washington DC 2009, p. 161–181.

34 Aufzeichnung Richthofen vom 21.3.1988, in: *AAPD 1988*, I, Dok. 92, p. 520.

rights cases in the group of 35. However, the format in which this was to take place – whether as ad hoc conferences or as part of a set number of meetings – was a point deliberately omitted. The EPC group also left all options open with regard to the Moscow human rights conference, arguing instead that the aim in Vienna should be to agree on a mandate for the conference in the first place. The number of conferences and their locations were to be finalised only later. But even this formulation went too far for the UK, which entered a reservation in the EPC group.[35]

2.3 *The "Endgame"*

In the summer of 1988, with the final stages of negotiations looming, further difficulties of coordination between EPC and NATO arose. On 13 May 1988 the coordinators of the neutral and non-aligned (N+N) states drew up a first full draft of a concluding document.[36] Yet it soon became apparent that the time before the sixth period of sessions was scheduled to end on 27 June would not suffice. In spite of progress in many matters, some key points remained unresolved. Within the Western group of states the United States, Canada, Iceland, Norway and Turkey wanted to include further humanitarian improvements in the texts of Baskets II and III even at this late moment. These new requests for amendments in turn divided the EPC states. While some, in particular West Germany and France, did not want to jeopardise the N+N draft, others supported the demands – for instance, for an emphasis on the role of "persons and institutions" in environmental matters – so that the EPC group was repeatedly forced to give in.[37]

In this situation, Genscher and his French counterpart Raimond travelled to Vienna in person to lobby for an early conclusion at the plenary session on 1 July. In so doing, they referred to the guideline that the European Council had set at its meeting three days earlier in Hanover, namely that a successful conclusion in Vienna would open the door to negotiations on conventional disarmament, and argued in favour of continuing the work on the text over the summer.[38] This push did indeed at first enable further progress to be made on the text. However, this momentum fizzled out again in the course of the autumn. As far as the EPC and NATO were concerned, this was due to two

35 Fernschreiben Nr. 221 (Coreu) vom 17.3.1988 und Vermerk Haak vom 25.3.1988, in: *AAPD 1988*, I, Dok. 92, p. 516, annot. 3.

36 On the N+N's full draft see Aufzeichnung Richthofen, 16.5.1988, in: *AAPD 1988*, I, Dok. 153, p. 835–840.

37 Eickhoff an AA, 30.6.1988, in: *AAPD 1988*, I, Dok. 195, p. 1055–1077.

38 Eickhoff an AA, 2.7.1988, in: *AAPD 1988*, II, Dok. 196, p. 1059–1064.

problems. First, there was the Franco-American controversy over the link between the planned disarmament conference and the CSCE. At the Franco-German summit in Bonn on 4 November 1988, François Mitterrand, the French president, suddenly announced that Paris still insisted on a "Conference of 35".[39] This abrupt change of policy also put the brakes on the Vienna negotiations shortly before their conclusion and once again called the EPC consensus into question. Only by further changes of a fairly cosmetic nature, intended underscore the link between the CRC and the CSCE, was Paris persuaded to yield.[40]

Far more threatening was, second, transatlantic opposition to the Moscow Human Rights Conference. For weeks, the American delegation in Vienna withheld its agreement while Washington continued to negotiate directly with Moscow over Soviet concessions. Until the 1988 Christmas break, Warren Zimmermann, the leader of the US delegation, was unable to offer the prospect of a decision by Washington, further and further postponing final discussion of the N+N's full draft. Although the West made a show of outward unity, internally the US government's approach divided NATO and the EPC group into a transatlantic and a continental European camp. Washington's position was supported by Canada and the UK but rejected by the other EPC states.[41] The view in Bonn in particular was that by going it alone, the United States was jeopardising what had already been achieved, not least in the humanitarian field. "The last drop squeezed out of a lemon changes neither the quantity nor the quality of the juice already extracted", Detlev Graf zu Rantzau, the new head of the Bonn delegation, reproached his American and British colleagues.[42] The conflict came to head at a meeting of the EPC heads of delegation in Vienna on 28 December 1988. In view of Moscow's preliminary efforts, the time had now come, Rantzau argued

> for the states of the European Community to call the attention of their American allies to their own positions and to remind them that, as far as they were concerned, the conditions for a swift conclusion to the VFM with a substantial and balanced outcome were in place. It was unacceptable for the countries of the European Community, disregarding their

39 Gespräch Kohl mit Mitterrand und Rocard, 4.11.1988, in: *AAPD 1988*, II, Dok. 313, p. 1661; Aufzeichnung Buerstedde, 11.11.1988, in: Ibid., Dok. 320, p. 1686–1688; Pfeffer an AA, 28.11.1988, in: Ibid., Dok. 343, p. 1797–1800.

40 Hartmann an AA, 5.11.1988 and 6.11.1988, in: *AAPD 1988*, II, Dok. 358, p. 1860, annot. 20.

41 Rantzau an AA, 23.12.1988, in: *AAPD 1988*, II, Dok. 372, p. 1911–1917.

42 Ibid., p. 1915.

> own interests, to be kept silently waiting for the as yet uncertain conclusion of American-Soviet contacts, [a conclusion] which could scarcely bring any qualitative change to the highly satisfactory conclusion to the VFM that already lies within reach; yet by waiting any longer we ran the risk of losing what we have already gained.[43]

And indeed, the disagreement was resolved in early January 1989. Following further talks between American and Soviet negotiators, George Shultz, the US Secretary of State, confirmed in a letter to his Soviet counterpart, Edvard Shevardnadze, that his government acknowledged the progress made in the Kremlin's human rights policy and agreed to holding a conference in Moscow.[44] Once a precise mandate for entering into arms control talks had been completed, the delegates passed the Vienna Concluding Document on 15 January 1989, only a few days before a new administration took office in the United States.[45]

3 Conclusion

Since 1970, EPC provided a forum in which EC member states could coordinate their foreign policy in both its substantive and operative dimensions. Yet EPC did not constitute a homogeneous political bloc. On the contrary, its role at the third CSCE Follow-up Meeting in Vienna was marked by a laborious process of negotiation in Brussels and Vienna. Further, no less difficult coordination took place within the NATO bodies, in which EPC diplomacy was confronted not only by the United States and Canada but also by the non-EPC countries Iceland, Norway and Turkey, which repeatedly felt sidelined by the unity of the EPC group. The EPC group showed itself to be a unified organisation, particularly in the area of Basket II, where it put forward joint proposals. In the humanitarian field, EPC was responsible for a proposal that served as its "flagship". In addition, the EPC countries, in varying constellations, acted as co-sponsors to numerous other proposals.

All those involved took care to ensure that due consideration was given to their respective national interests. As the examples of the CRC mandate and the Moscow human rights conference illustrate, differences in content

43 Rantzau an AA, 28.12.1988 (Drahtbericht Nr. 2020), PA-AA, B 28, ZA, Bd. 153431.

44 The letter is reprinted in Adamishin/Schifter, *Human Rights*, p. 178–179. See also Rantzau an AA, 4.1.1988 (Drahtbericht Nr. 22), PA-AA, B 28, ZA, Bd. 158552.

45 Rantzau an AA, 15.1.1989 (Drahtberichte Nr. 91 und Nr. 92), PA-AA, B 28, ZA, Bd. 158552.

and negotiating tactics repeatedly paralysed the West, both within the NATO framework and in the EPC. The question of how to react to Gorbachev's reform policy also deprived the West of momentum in its negotiations. Finally, the bilateralism between Washington and Moscow on human rights and arms control issues emphasised the overriding role of superpower relations, a factor which the EPC group's political cooperation had to take into account.

Nevertheless, the Vienna Follow-up Meeting was a milestone in the development of EPC as well as in the CSCE process. In particular, the twelve succeeded in opening a new chapter in the CSCE with the "human dimension" mechanism developed in their proposal WT.19. With the Maastricht Treaty approved by the European Council on 11 December 1991, EPC was finally transferred to the Common Foreign and Security Policy (CFSP) and thus placed on a new footing. A platform for harmonising the foreign policy of the EC member states became the foreign policy instrument of the European Union. In a separate declaration on this chapter of the CFSP, the states named the areas in which they found cooperation to be particularly desirable. At the top of the list was the CSCE process.[46]

46 Runderlass Bettzuege, 16.12.1991, in: *AAPD 1991*, Berlin-Boston 2022, II, Dok. 431, p. 1729–1735. See also "Conclusions of the Presidency of the European Council, 26./27.6.1992 in Lisbon", in: *Bulletin of the European Communities*, vol. 25 (1992), no. 6, Brussels 1992, p. 21–22.

Divergent Neutral Strategies

The N+N and the Issue of Disarmament

Kai Habel

1 Introduction

The neutral and non-aligned states (the N+N, or NNAs) represented a third group of countries that had chosen, within the framework of the Conference on Security and Cooperation in Europe (CSCE), not to be incorporated into one of the two antagonistic blocs, NATO and the Warsaw Pact. This group, which could be described as a loose coalition, emerged during the CSCE negotiations in Geneva (1973–1975) and did not extend beyond the Helsinki process. The most important and active N+N states were the four neutrals – Austria, Finland, Sweden and Switzerland – and the non-aligned Yugoslavia. Besides these five countries, the group was composed of four smaller states or microstates, namely Cyprus, Malta, Liechtenstein and San Marino. It should be noted that not all neutral European countries were part of the group; for instance, Ireland and the Holy See, which participated in the CSCE, were not members of the N+N. The N+N took on an ambiguous role during the CSCE negotiations because they were both negotiators who made propositions to defend their national interests and mediators who helped the two blocs to find compromises. Accordingly, the N+N are often described as "intermediaries" or "bridge-builders".[1]

There is not much doubt that, by mediating between Eastern and Western positions that were often diametrically opposed and hence mutually unacceptable, the N+N contributed significantly to the success of the CSCE. The N+N were remarkably active on procedural issues such as setting the agenda or determining the structure of the negotiations – for example, by creating the concept of "baskets".[2] They also proposed the creation of informal working groups that would prove especially productive; they acted as coordinators of the talks; and, apart from these tasks of mediation or administration, they drafted joint proposals, depending on the topic.[3]

1 Thomas Fischer, *Keeping the Process Alive: The N+N and the CSCE Follow-Up from Helsinki to Vienna (1975–1986)*, Zurich 2012, p. 13.

2 Thomas Fischer, *Neutral Power in the CSCE*. Baden-Baden 2009, p. 18.

3 Ibid., p. 365–369.

Efraim Karsh argues that the N+N fulfilled "indispensable functions [that were] instrumental on more than one occasion in keeping the delicate edifice of the CSCE resilient to the pressures of East-West differences."[4] Adrian Hyde-Price considers the group to have "served as a partial buffer in the military confrontation between the blocs, and some of these countries actively contributed diplomatically and politically to easing East-West tensions and establishing a modus vivendi between the two sides."[5] According to Jussi Hanhimäki,

> the neutrals acted as midwives to détente. From the late 1960s onwards, Austria, Finland, Sweden and Switzerland were influential players within the late Cold War context, pulling above their weight in a process that gave rise to a growing set of so-called Helsinki networks that, in the long term, undermined the totalitarian systems of Eastern Europe.[6]

Stefan Lehne and Hanspeter Neuhold, who were both part of the Austrian delegation in Vienna, explain that "the contributions of the NNAs to the success of the CSCE process have [...] exceeded their material power potential."[7] The importance of the N+N throughout the Helsinki process is thus rarely challenged.

In the first two Follow-up Meetings in Belgrade (1977–1978) and Madrid (1980–1983), which were held in extremely tense international contexts, the N+N are seen as the intermediaries that prevented the whole process from falling apart. Yet there is no such consensus regarding the third Follow-up Meeting, held in Vienna (1986–1989). From the outset, it was uncertain whether the N+N would play the same crucial role as before. It was felt, as Thomas Fischer has put it, that "the role of neutral mediators was no longer needed in the CSCE at the Vienna meeting to the same degree as before."[8] One reason why their influence was challenged is that, since Mikhail Gorbachev came to power

4 Efraim Karsh, *Neutrality and Small States*, London-New York 1988, p. 130.

5 Adrian Hyde-Price, "Geopolitics and the Concept of Neutrality in Contemporary Europe", in: Heinz Gärtner (ed.), *Engaged Neutrality. An Evolved Approach to the Cold War*, Lanham 2017, p. 121–142, on p. 121.

6 Jussi M. Hanhimäki, "Non-aligned to What? European Neutrality and the Cold War", in: Sandra Bott/Jussi M. Hanhimäki/Janick Schaufelbuehl/Marco Wyss (eds.), *Neutrality and Neutralism in the Global Cold War. Between or Within the Blocs?* London 2016, p. 17–32, on p. 28.

7 Stefan Lehne/Hanspeter Neuhold, "The Role of the Neutral and Non-Aligned Countries at the Vienna Meeting", in: Arie Bloed/Pieter Van Dijk (eds.), *The Human Dimension of the Helsinki Process. The Vienna Follow-Up Meeting and its Aftermath*, Dordrecht-Boston-London 1991, p. 30–53, on p. 35.

8 Fischer, *Keeping the Process Alive*, p. 148.

in the Soviet Union in 1985, relations between the superpowers had become increasingly relaxed, thereby reducing the necessity and relevance of a mediator. In Vienna, the two blocs could negotiate directly with each other more easily than before.[9]

Another reason why the N+N lost influence was that dissension within the group grew, especially with regard to military issues, thereby reducing the scope for common positions or joint proposals. The topic that created the most significant divisions among the N+N in Vienna was that of conventional disarmament and the states' eventual participation in the negotiations that were to take place after the conclusion of the third Follow-up Meeting. The N+N had divergent views on this question and hence could not agree on whether or not to take part in future negotiations on disarmament.

The paper will endeavour to explain why this subject was so contentious for the N+N and how they eventually managed to find a common ground. This specific issue is worth examining because it touches upon the very understanding of neutrality: the possible involvement of the N+N in disarmament talks raises the questions of what it means to be neutral and what the most appropriate diplomatic strategies are for a neutral state.

2 The N+N and Conventional Disarmament

The CSCE had addressed the issue of disarmament from its inception, even if no concrete measures were discussed. On this subject, the Helsinki Final Act stipulates that "the participating States recognize the interest of all of them in efforts aimed at lessening military confrontation and promoting disarmament."[10] It was then decided, in the course of the second follow-up meeting in Madrid, that conferences on Confidence- and Security-Building Measures (CSBM) and on Disarmament in Europe (CDE) would be held in Stockholm to undertake "new, effective and concrete actions designed to make progress in strengthening confidence and security and in achieving disarmament."[11] The first stage, which took place from 1984 to 1986, consisted in the negotiation of a set of confidence- and

9 Ibid., p. 17.

10 Conference on Security and Co-operation in Europe Final Act, 1 August 1975, p. 13, https://www.osce.org/files/f/documents/5/c/39501.pdf, accessed 16.8.2023.

11 Concluding Document of the Madrid Meeting 1980 of Representatives of the Participating States of the Conference on Security and Cooperation in Europe, held on the Basis of the Provisions of the Final Act Relating to the Follow-Up to the Conference, 6 September 1983, p. 8, https://www.osce.org/files/f/documents/9/d/40871.pdf, p. 9, accessed 23.10.2024.

security-building measures; nonetheless, the Stockholm document reaffirms that the participating states were "determined to achieve progress in disarmament".[12] Despite these expressions of goodwill, concrete disarmament measures had not yet been negotiated in the framework of the CSCE. A big step forward would be taken in Vienna, where the mandate for negotiations on Conventional Armed Forces in Europe would be decided.

Yet here was the point of contention: the N+N states disagreed on whether they should participate in these negotiations or not. All N+N were proponents of confidence- and security-building measures, which appeared to them as effective means of guaranteeing European security and thus their own safety. Disarmament, however, was a completely different issue, chiefly because neutral states considered their military capabilities to be purely defensive and

therefore representing a threat to any country. Consequently, disarming neutral states would not improve European security. It would be meaningless at best, but it might even jeopardise the balance of power within the continent by weakening states that had no territorial ambitions. As possessors of armies, the N+N believed their neutrality to rely on their capacity to defend it against potential aggressors. Following this logic, disarmament would involve nothing less than undermining both their neutral status and their national security.

Yet the choice whether or not to participate in disarmament talks had to take into account another crucial element: the risk of potentially disastrous diplomatic isolation. The CSCE and the rule of unanimity had offered the N+N a remarkable opportunity to exert real influence on the international stage. Participation in the Helsinki process in itself represented an outstanding diplomatic success for the neutral and non-aligned states. Therefore, the N+N were understandably wary of being excluded from negotiations on disarmament, which would have left them unable to influence the discussions. Given the importance of the topic, this alarming possibility left the N+N states witht a choice between two unsatisfactory solutions: they could either participate in future negotiations on disarmament and risk being compelled to reduce their military capabilities, or they could preserve their freedom of action with regard to conventional forces at the cost of some diplomatic alienation.

Caught between undesirable alternatives, most of the N+N were uncertain how to address this dilemma. In this atmosphere of indecision, two countries

12 Document of the Stockholm Conference on Confidence- and Security-Building Measures and Disarmament in Europe Convened in Accordance with the Relevant Provisions of the Concluding Document of the Madrid Meeting of the Conference on Security and Co-Operation in Europe, 19 September 1986, p. 17, https://www.osce.org/files/f/documents/5/d/41238.pdf, accessed 25.6.2023.

stood out from the rest, having chosen different and conflicting solutions: whereas Sweden wanted the N+N to be part of the negotiations on disarmament, Switzerland was absolutely opposed to such a possibility.[13] Even before the start of the Vienna meeting, the Swiss were concerned by the growing importance of the military dimension within the CSCE, evidenced by the successful holding of the Stockholm Conference on Confidence- and Security-Building Measures and Disarmament in Europe (1984–1986).[14] The Swiss thought that this development was problematic mainly for two reasons. First, since the N+N were not major military powers and had geopolitical situations and national interests that were too divergent from each other in terms of security, they did not have much bargaining power on military issues. The Swiss were therefore afraid that the N+N would become less and less influential in a CSCE centred around military questions. Second, they feared that the expansion of military discussions would take place at the expense of other issues, resulting in the formation of a critical imbalance between the three baskets. Since one of the unique features that explained the success of the CSCE was the grouping of military, economic and humanitarian issues under a single negotiation forum that allowed for the conception of "linkage strategies" – for example, making a concession on financial cooperation in exchange for a concession from the other side on, say, confidence-building measures – an unbalanced development might undermine the CSCE's distinctiveness and effectiveness.

As for the other N+N, Finland and Yugoslavia more or less agreed with Sweden. The Finns stated clearly to their partners that the CDE mandate, which provided a unique opportunity to negotiate military security issues on an equal footing with the two alliances and their members, had to be expanded to include disarmament.[15] The Yugoslavs were particularly concerned that the group should formulate a common position as soon as possible in order not to be sidelined by the two military alliances. In an informal working paper shared with their N+N partners, they argued:

13 Commentaires au texte du contre-projet suédois, 23.4.1987, Swiss Federal Archives, Bern, Aktenmaterial zur KSZE-Konferenz in Wien (1985–1987), E5812#2009/67#138*, 76.

14 Rapport final de la délégation suisse à la CDE de Stockholm, 24.11.1986, Swiss Federal Archives, Bern, KSZE: Folgekonferenz in Wien (1986–1988), E2200.49#1996/380#93*, 370.3.

15 Möte med NN-staternas utrikesministrar i Brioni, Jugoslavien, den 23–24 oktober 1986, 27.10.1986, Swedish National Archives, Täby, DU Utlandsmyndighet Repr. arkiv, ESK/OSSE Wien, 1920 års, dossiersystem F1:19, HP 79 NN.

> Neutral and non-aligned countries could well find themselves on the margin of events, i.e. they could be faced with a fait accompli should they fail to make adequate preparations in good time. This practically means that elaboration of their own, joint concept should commence at once.[16]

The Austrians were less convinced than the Swedes, Finns and Yugoslavs, but they did not think that a categorical N+N withdrawal would make sense. In an internal working document, the Austrian foreign ministry wrote:

> The fundamental interest in cutting conventional armaments in Europe and in the participation of the N+N in a negotiation process to that end is contrasted by a realistic assessment of their own military and political weight and by an awareness of the enormous complexity of the matter. A possible solution is seen by some in a negotiating structure divided into 'concentric circles'. According to this, the actual reduction negotiations would take place first in a subsidiary body of the CDE limited to the member states of the military alliances, in which the N+N could participate as observers. In parallel, negotiations on CSBM would continue among all 35 states.[17]

Austria followed a nuanced, pragmatic approach to the issue. Instead of defining a strict objective, it adopted a flexible attitude, well aware of the fact that the structure of the future negotiations on disarmament would ultimately be determined by the superpowers and their respective allies. The Austrian position was therefore to support the extension of the CDE mandate to cover the reduction of conventional armaments and its participation in the negotiations; if this solution should prove too ambitious, the delegation would promote the creation of a dual negotiation structure within the CSCE framework or, at worst, the establishment of an "intermediate phase" consisting in the continuation of CSBM talks in the CDE along with the postponement of the discussions on the disarmament mandate to the next follow-up meeting.[18] Yet

16 Informal working paper (Yugoslavia), 20.11.1986, Österreichisches Staatsarchiv (ÖStA), Archiv der Republik (AdR), BMAA, II-Pol, GZ 803.00/233–II.7/86.

17 Wiener Folgetreffen (WFT), 4.9.1986, ÖStA, AdR, BMAA, II-Pol, GZ 801.04/41–II.7/86 (translated).

18 Zur Zukunft der KVAE, 4.9.1986, ÖStA, AdR, BMAA, II-Pol, GZ 801.04/41–II.7/86 (translated).

the Austrians decided for tactical reasons to remain vague about their intentions until the two blocs' stances became clearer, as explained in another foreign ministry internal document:

> In order not to prejudice a later mediating role, Austria will not present its own proposal for a new CDE mandate in the initial phase of the Vienna follow-up meeting, but will await the development of the positions of the military allies and seek to bring about a coordinated position in the N+N framework.[19]

As for the smaller N+N, Cyprus and Malta supported the Swedish-Finnish-Yugoslavian line, while San Marino was relatively passive.[20] Liechtenstein avoided taking a firm stance, but leant toward the Swiss point of view. Despite Liechtenstein's tacit support and the veiled flexibility of the Austrian position, the Swiss were clearly isolated among the N+N on the major issue of disarmament. It should be noted that, during the opening debate, the N+N states, with the exception of Switzerland, supported the start of disarmament talks in the framework of the CDE.[21]

In a delegation report written in April 1987, half a year after the start of the Vienna negotiations, the Swiss expressed serious pessimism over the situation, stating unambiguously that their position could not be reconciled with that of other N+N countries.[22] Moreover, the report disclosed the existence of tensions among the group, caused by the failure to find a compromise: "These three months of interminable discussions between the N+N have resulted in a deterioration of the atmosphere within the group."[23] These tensions were especially apparent when, on 23 March 1987, Sweden presented its N+N partners with a draft position paper that provided for the involvement of non-military alliance states in disarmament negotiations. Dissatisfied with the draft, the

19 Drittes KSZE-Folgetreffen Wien, österreichische Linie, 8.7.1986, ÖStA, AdR, BMAA, II-Pol, GZ 803.00/74–II.7/86.

20 NN-diskussion om militära frågor, 1.1987, Swedish National Archives, Täby, DU Utlandsmyndighet Repr. arkiv, ESK/OSSE Wien, 1920 års, dossiersystem F1:19, HP 79 NN.

21 Wiener Folgetreffen, Stand vom 14. November 1986, ÖStA, AdR, BMAA, II-Pol, GZ 803.00/223–II.7/86.

22 Rapport de la délégation suisse sur la deuxième session de la réunion de Vienne sur les suites de la CSCE, 27 janvier–10 avril 1987, 4.5.1987, Swiss Federal Archives, Bern, KSZE: Folgekonferenz in Wien (1986–1988), E2200.49#1996/380#93*, 370.26.

23 Ibid. (translated).

Swiss wrote: "The essential elements that we value have been excluded. [...] Elements that are unacceptable to us have been introduced."[24]

Yet if the Swiss were not in a fundamentally weak negotiating position, they had the other participating states to thank for it. Most NATO countries were reluctant to involve the N+N in disarmament talks, while the Warsaw Pact was satisfied with a negotiation format limited to the members of the two military alliances.[25] In fact, the Western bloc was also divided on the issue of disarmament: whereas the United States wanted to negotiate as directly as possible with the Soviet bloc, the French were in favour of involving all 35 CSCE participating states in the talks.[26] One of the twelve founding members of NATO, under President Charles de Gaulle France had decided to withdraw from the organisation's integrated military structure in 1966; therefore, with regard to conventional armaments, French diplomacy supported a negotiation format in which it would be able to counterbalance its isolation within the North Atlantic Alliance by bringing in neutral and non-aligned states. As for the Warsaw Pact countries, although they had initially suggested that they endorsed the participation of all 35 CSCE members, it was becoming gradually clear that a negotiation structure limited to the 23 alliance members was perfectly acceptable to them.[27] In sum, even if the Swiss were isolated within the N+N, their position was strengthened by the superpowers' willingness to negotiate from alliance to alliance.

3 The Limassol and Bern Meetings

Two important meetings took place at the level of foreign ministers in May 1987 that would contribute to and coincide with a shift in the position of the N+N: the first was held in Limassol on 16 and 17 May, the second in Bern on May 26.

The Limassol meeting gathered the foreign ministers and state secretaries of the N+N in order to review the progress of the CSCE negotiations. It should first be noted that the participating countries appeared disunited with regard

---

24 Commentaires au texte du contre-projet suédois, 23.4.1987, Swiss Federal Archives, Bern, Aktenmaterial zur KSZE-Konferenz in Wien (1985–1987), E5812#2009/67#138*, 76 (translated).

25 Sammanträde 1987–04-27 om ESK: s uppföljningsmöte i Wien, 27.4.1987, Swedish National Archives, Täby, Delegationsarkiv, ESK Wien, 1920 års, dossiersystem F1:1, HP 79 A.

26 Frankreich und die KSZE, 16.9.1987, ÖStA, AdR, BMAA, II-Pol, GZ 801.04/33–II.7/87.

27 Wiener KSZE-Folgetreffen: Militärische Sicherheit, 23.6.1987, ÖStA, AdR, BMAA, II-Pol, GZ 801.04/24–II.7/87.

to the level of cohesion that was required among them. Sweden, Yugoslavia and Cyprus insisted on the importance of a "smooth cooperation", arguing that the N+N would not be able to play their role as mediators successfully without a common position. Switzerland expressed its reservations, asserting that differences of opinion within the group should not be dramatised because the N+N was "neither a bloc nor an alliance", implying that no "alliance discipline" was demanded.[28] In addition, the Swiss claimed that in view of the sudden improvement of East-West relations, the CSCE negotiations represented a "sideshow" (*Nebenschauplatz*) in which the N+N needed to understand that they had little influence.[29]

After these preliminary remarks, the participants delved into the heated issue of negotiations on disarmament.[30] Sweden, Yugoslavia and Cyprus declared that a disarmament forum had to be established within the framework of the CSCE, mainly because of two reasons: first, the Madrid mandate and the Stockholm document both stipulated this extension; second, there existed a "functional link" between confidence-building measures and conventional disarmament that justified a joint negotiation. Switzerland expressed its reservations but recognised all the same that the creation of a completely distinct negotiation forum was undesirable. As a consequence of Switzerland's isolation among the N+N, its position had evolved to resemble the aforementioned Austrian "concentric circles" solution.

Switzerland proposed the institution of a "link" between the CSCE and the future negotiations that would take place between the Warsaw Pact and NATO states. The arguments in favor of an intermediate solution were the following: informal meetings between the 23 alliance members had been set up in Vienna on the initiative of France, which wanted the negotiations on disarmament to be incorporated into the CSCE; by contrast, the United States was in favor of establishing a separate 23-state forum that would be unrelated to the Helsinki process; the N+N had to take advantage of this disagreement to advocate for a third way, which would consist in the institution of a relatively autonomous disarmament forum connected to the CSCE framework. The "link" between the two settings would have to be conceived in a way that would enable the N+N not only to be informed of the progress of the discussions but also to be directly consulted about the negotiations. The N+N could also think of a

28 KSZE: N+N-Treffen auf Aussenministerebene in Limassol (Zypern), 16./17. Mai 1987, 21.5.1987, Swiss Federal Archives, Bern, KSZE: Treffen, Vorschläge etc. der Schweiz + N+N (1985–1988), E2200.49#1996/380#92*, 370.25.

29 Ibid.

30 Ibid.

means of contributing to the implementation of the 23-state forum, for example by providing their services throughout the verification phase.

The N+N partners expressed interest in the idea of an intermediate solution. Even if much remained to be done, the seeds of a compromise were starting to grow. A second meeting took place in Bern between the State Secretaries of the four main neutral partners – Austria, Finland, Sweden, and Switzerland – on 26 May. It addressed the most important and contentious topic: how to integrate the issue of conventional disarmament into the CSCE framework. The Swiss again argued in favor of the intermediate solution and the creation of an "institutional link." Both Austria and Finland suggested waiting before proposing an institutional link, arguing that it was preferable to be patient in the present situation. They wanted first to observe how the alliance members would structure their talks in Vienna. Furthermore, Austria wanted to wait for the results of the Intermediate-Range Nuclear Forces (INF) negotiations between the United States and the Soviet Union, which had resumed in March 1986 (and would ultimately lead to the signing of the INF Treaty on 8 December 1987). Although it had been continuously playing for time, Switzerland responded that a wait-and-see attitude would be a tactical mistake that would eventually result in the interests of the N+N being ignored.[31]

The debates within the N+N concerning conventional disarmament were approaching a turning point. In June 1987, all the N+N countries seemed to have accepted the idea of an intermediary solution, even if there was still no concrete design of the so-called "link".[32] This agreement can be explained by the fact that, in the Western camp, the United States and France had reached a compromise at the NATO meeting of foreign ministers held in Reykjavik on 11 and 12 June. The allies had agreed to support a dual negotiation structure in which disarmament would be discussed among the 23 alliance members within the CSCE framework.[33]

After months of discussions, the N+N finally came to an agreement and in March 1988 drafted a "non-paper on military issues" that reflected their common position.[34] The non-paper devised a dual negotiation structure

31 Treffen der Staatssekretäre der vier neutralen Staaten am 26. Mai 1987 in Bern, 3.6.1987, Swiss Federal Archives, KSZE: Treffen, Vorschläge etc. der Schweiz + N+N (1985–1988), E2200.49#1996/380#92*, 370.25.

32 Réunion CSCE de Vienne, rapport de mi-session, 23.6.1987, Swiss Federal Archives, Bern, KSZE: Folgekonferenz in Wien (1986–1988), E2200.49#1996/380#93*, 370.26.

33 Wiener KSZE-Folgetreffen: Militärische Sicherheit, 23.6.1987, ÖStA, AdR, BMAA, II-Pol, GZ 801.04/24–II.7/87.

34 Rapport intermédiaire de la délégation suisse sur la 6ème session de la Réunion de Vienne sur les suites de la CSCE, 10.6.1988, Swiss Federal Archives, Bern, KSZE: Folgekonferenz in Wien (1986–1988), E2200.49#1996/380#93*, 370.26.

consisting of negotiations on confidence- and security-building measures gathering all 35 CSCE participants on the one hand and another set of negotiations on disarmament involving exclusively the 23 alliance members on the other, the two settings being connected by the institutional link. Specifically, this link would consist of meetings "to Exchange Views and Information Concerning the Course of the Negotiation"; at least two of which had to take place in the course of each round of the negotiation. The contentious issue of conventional disarmament had found a solution among the N+N, and the compromise that they had devised in accordance with the military alliances' wishes would ultimately prove acceptable all the participating states and integrated in the Vienna concluding document.

4 Conclusion

The Vienna Follow-up Meeting witnessed the division of the N+N on the issue of disarmament and its place in the CSCE process. The N+N were facing a dilemma to which different countries gave different answers. They were forced to make a choice between two unsatisfactory solutions: either getting involved in disarmament talks but being bound by the obligations that would result from these negotiations, or remaining unrestricted in respect to military policy but being excluded from crucial negotiations in Europe. In other words, the N+N were worried about *diplomatic isolation* on the one hand and *the loss of military independence* on the other. Faced with this choice of evils, the N+N countries had divergent views on which was the greater. The dilemma faced by the N+N was all the more important given that neutral states need to continuously prove that their neutrality is credible by maintaining adequate defence capabilities while ensuring international support through an active diplomacy.

As the meeting progressed and the positions held by the two alliances became clear, the group managed to find a compromise that would be acceptable to all participating states. Regardless of their initial disunity, all the N+N countries were ultimately satisfied with the compromise solution that they had devised. Switzerland, which had been isolated within the group on the matter, avoided possible involvement in disarmament measures that would have jeopardised its military sovereignty. Although they had initially pushed for direct participation in the negotiations, Sweden, Yugoslavia and Finland were finally satisfied that disarmament was incorporated in the CSCE framework and that the N+N obtained the right to ask questions and make comments during the meetings to exchange views and information. As for Austria, it welcomed an intermediate solution that it had envisaged even before the start of the negotiations in Vienna.

Even if Switzerland was isolated within the N+N on the topic of disarmament, its negotiating position was not weak since it was in agreement with most of the military alliances' members, including the US and the Soviet Union, which preferred to negotiate face-to-face without the involvement of potential troublemakers. Because of its disunity, the N+N group was never in a position to challenge the two blocs' will with regard to this complex issue. It was only when it became clear that disarmament would be discussed among the 23 alliance members within the CSCE framework that the N+N managed to formulate a common position.

East German Intelligence Perspectives on the CSCE Follow-up Meeting in Vienna

Simon Graham

1 Introduction[1]

On 7 May 1986 the Main Intelligence Directorate (Hauptverwaltung Aufklärung, HVA), the foreign intelligence service of the East German Ministry for State Security (Ministerium für Staatssicherheit, MfS or "Stasi") said of the impending Third Follow-up Meeting of the Conference on Security and Cooperation in Europe (CSCE) that "the interests of important CSCE participating states are not only so different but also their tactics have become so offensive that tangible results would be difficult to achieve". Consequently, participating states must prepare "for a time when CSCE conferences will end controversially, without agreement".[2] This assessment tallies with the broader objective of the MfS for CSCE meetings, namely to place East Germany on an equal diplomatic footing with West Germany while spoiling attempts to increase scrutiny of East Germany's human rights record.[3] It was primarily produced from the intelligence gathered by more than a dozen HVA officers embedded in the East German delegation over the course of the CSCE.[4] Douglas Selvage and Walter Süß have explained the function of these officers and shown us how they influenced the delegation on behalf of the MfS.[5]

Yet we know that the Vienna Meeting did produce tangible results. It not only produced the Vienna Mechanism for implementing the human dimension of the CSCE but also saw extensive agreement between European states over issues as diverse as conventional armed forces, human rights protections, education, migration, technology and the environment.[6] Thus, we may well

1 Note: previously untranslated German language sources were translated by the author.
2 Aufklärung über das KSZE-Folgetreffen in Wien, BArch, MfS, HVA 41, 206/86, Bl. 167.
3 Oliver Bange, "The Stasi Confronts Western Strategies for Transformation, 1966–1975", in: Jonathan Haslam/Karina Urbach (eds.), *Secret Intelligence in the European States System, 1918–1989*, Stanford 2014, p. 189–196.
4 Douglas Selvage/Walter Süß, *Staatssicherheit und KSZE-Prozess. MfS zwischen SED und KGB (1972–1989)*, Göttingen 2019, p. 83–89.
5 Ibid.
6 Organisation for Security and Cooperation in Europe, Concluding Document of the Third Follow-up Meeting, Vienna, 4 November 1986 to 19 January 1989, Conference on Security and Cooperation in Europe, 19 January 1989, p. 1–81.

DOI:10.1163/9789004736979_014

ask: why did the HVA get its forecast for the Vienna Meeting so wrong and how were its assessments shaped by diplomatic and strategic change in Eastern Europe? I answer these questions in what follows by drawing on sources from the Stasi Records Archive and the Organisation for Security and Cooperation in Europe Documentation Centre in Prague, among others. I also relate these sources to those used in the ground-breaking work of Douglas Selvage and Walter Süß, the difference being that, where Selvage and Süß predominately focus on the role, activities and influence of the MfS at the CSCE, I try to relate the activities and influence of the MfS to the CSCE's diplomatic context.[7] However, it is critical to recognise that this chapter only begins the process of qualifying the nature and quantifying the scale of what was a much larger effort by the Stasi to influence the international order through espionage against the CSCE.

East Berlin approached the CSCE Third Follow-up Meeting in Vienna well aware of the growing distance between East Germany's negotiating positions and those of the Soviet Union.[8] This was a product of the growing divide between the "New Thinking" of the Soviet general secretary, Mikhail Gorbachev, on foreign policy and mutual security, and the general secretary of the Socialist Unity Party of Germany (Sozialistische Einheitspartei Deutschlands, SED), Erich Honecker's, adversarial "two camps" approach to Western Europe. Odd Arne Westad shows that Gorbachev found significant support for his New Thinking in the foreign ministries of Romania, Poland and Hungary, which all presented plans at the Vienna Follow-up Meeting for bridging Europe's East-West divide.[9] In contrast, the East German delegation, along with the Soviet delegation, initially took a more combative approach to the meeting. But whereas the Soviet position moderated over time as New Thinking filtered through to the delegation in Vienna, the East German delegation largely avoided constructive dialogue.[10] It was in this context that the HVA issued the dire prediction that the Vienna Follow-up Meeting may well "end in dispute, without agreement".[11] However, as the meeting progressed, the prediction became increasingly difficult to sustain and by the time it ended on 19 January 1989 the HVA had

7 Selvage/Süß, *Staatssicherheit und KSZE-Prozess*, p. 515–658.

8 Hermann Wentker, *Außenpolitik in engen Grenzen. Die DDR im internationalen System 1949–1989*, München 2007, p. 477–500.

9 Romania ultimately proved to be among the most intractable attendees at the meeting, along with East Germany. Odd Arne Westad, *The Cold War. A World History*, New York 2017, p. 389–391.

10 Ibid.

11 Aufklärung über das KSZE-Folgetreffen in Wien, BArch, MfS, HVA 41, 206/86, Bl. 167.

significantly adjusted its guidance.[12] Thus, on 24 February 1989 the HVA declared that "the final document adopted at this meeting continued the CSCE process substantially in all areas and [...] has unequivocally demonstrated its central role in shaping West-East relations".[13] This stands in stark contrast to the HVA's initial predictions for the meeting, despite the report's internal audience and its purpose of legitimising compromise over the extent of human rights reforms in the Eastern Bloc.[14]

2 The HVA, "New Thinking" and the Vienna Meeting

Throughout this chapter, I suggest that the dramatic change in the HVA's analysis of the prospects of the Vienna Meeting was less a result of deft diplomatic wrangling at the meeting than a product of the seismic shifts in the foreign policies of Eastern Bloc states, precipitated by Gorbachev's New Thinking and his willingness to foster pan-European relations.[15] Consequently, I see halting East German recognition of the successes of the Vienna Follow-up Meeting and the associated changes in security, border and German-German policy as one part of a much larger constellation of changes in the strategic landscape of Central Europe. This is not to detract from the important normalising function of the CSCE but rather to highlight the relationship between "pull" factors like the CSCE and substantial "push" factors in the form of liberalisation and democratisation in the Eastern Bloc.

For example, Alexis Heraclides argues that Soviet delegates at the Vienna Follow-up Meeting were committed to the position that changes in the Soviet Union were driven by Gorbachev's reforms rather than Western pressure.[16]

12 Oliver Bange, "Transformation by Linkage? Arms Control, Human Rights and the Rift Between Moscow and East Berlin in the Late 1980s", in: Nicolas Badalassi/Sarah B. Snyder (eds.), *The CSCE and the End of the Cold War*, New York 2019, p. 305–329, on p. 309.

13 Der Verlauf und die Ergebnisse des Wiener-Folgetreffens aus BRD-Sicht, BArch, MfS, HVA 761, 83/89, Bl. 175

14 Aufklärung über das KSZE-Folgetreffen in Wien, BArch, MfS, HVA 41, 206/86, Bl. 167; Der Verlauf und die Ergebnisse des Wiener-Folgetreffens aus BRD-Sicht, BArch, MfS, HVA 761, 83/89, Bl. 175.

15 Angela Romano, "The EC and the Socialist World. The Ascent of a Key Player in Cold War Europe", in: Ulrich Krotz/Kiran Klaus Patel/Federico Romero (eds.), *Europe's Cold War Relations. The EC Towards a Global Role*, London 2020, p. 51–70, on p. 61; Westad, *The Cold War*, p. 389–391; Sylvia Woodby, *Gorbachev and the Decline of Ideology in Soviet Foreign Policy*, Boulder 1989, p. 118.

16 Alexis Heraclides, *Security and Cooperation in Europe. The Human Dimension 1972–1992*, London 1993, p. 83.

This position that the West was not (and could not) be the instigator of change in the Soviet Union is not surprising in and of itself. Rather, what is interesting is the fact that Soviet delegates eventually came publicly to recognise the centrality of New Thinking in Moscow's renewed willingness to engage with CSCE processes on a "trust but verify" basis, and to make and support proposals across the so-called Iron Curtain.[17] Indeed, on 5 September 1986 the Soviet foreign minister, Eduard Shevardnadze, is recorded as having told Pierre Aubert, his Swiss counterpart, that in conversation with Gorbachev, he had praised the CSCE process to date as "very constructive" and occurring "in an atmosphere of 'benevolent openness'".[18]

However, Hans-Heinrich Wrede, a member of the delegation of the Federal Republic of Germany at the Vienna meeting, rightly cautions against overstating the impact of Gorbachev's agenda, especially in the early stages of the Vienna Follow-up Meeting.[19] Unlike the Hungarian and Polish delegations, the East German delegation was staunchly opposed to the kind of openness and East-West engagement that Shevardnadze and Gorbachev had begun to support. Indeed, the growing diversity in positions among the Warsaw Pact states arguably contributed to the East German government's interest in intelligence from the Vienna Follow-up Meeting. Such intelligence, it was hoped, would help both in understanding relations between reformers and hardliners in Moscow and in addressing East Germany's perennial problem of how to relate to West Germany.[20]

Nevertheless, the East German delegation still showed deference to the Soviet delegation's position when considering whether to support East-West

17 J. Simon Rofe, "Trust between Adversaries and Allies: President George H. W. Bush, Trust and the End of the Cold War", in: Christian Ostermann/Martin Klimke/Reinhild Kreis (eds.), *Trust, But Verify. The Politics of Uncertainty and the Transformation of the Cold War Order, 1969–1991*, Stanford 2016, p. 53–55.

18 Conversation between the Head of the Swiss Federal Department for Foreign Affairs, Pierre Aubert, and Soviet Minister of Foreign Affairs Eduard Shevardnadze, Memorandum of Conversation, 5–6 September 1986, Moscow, Swiss Federal Archives, Bern, Beziehungen der Schweiz zum Empfangsstaat (1985–1988), CH-BAR#E2200.157-04#1997/151#45*, https://dodis.ch/54262, accessed 21.11.2021, p. 10.

19 Hans-Heinrich Wrede, "Die Weiterentwicklung des KSZE-Prozesses. Das Folgetreffen in Wien", in: Wolfgang Wagner et al. (eds.), *Die Internationale Politik 1987–1988*, Berlin 2015, p. 111–122, on p. 115.

20 Ziele für das KSZE-Folgetreffen, BArch, MfS, HVA, ZAIG 5342, Bl. 6; Walter Süß, "Die Wiener KSZE-Folgekonferenz und der Handlungsspielraum des DDR-Sicherheitsapparates 1989", in: Matthias Peter/Hermann Wentker (eds.), *Die KSZE im Ost-West-Konflikt. Internationale Politik und gesellschaftliche Transformation 1975–1990* (Schriftenreihe der Vierteljahrshefte für Zeitgeschichte Sondernummer), München 2012, p. 219–232, on p. 220–221, p. 227.

proposals – at least until the latter moderated its position in mid-1988. For example, on 24 April 1987 the HVA distributed a classified report entitled "Western Assessments of the Second Round of the Vienna CSCE Follow-up Meeting" to high-ranking members of the Stasi and the Ministry of Foreign Affairs, addressing discussions which took place at the CSCE from January 27, 1987 until April 10, 1987.[21] This report synthesised intelligence from three sources, two of whom had access to the internal discussions of the West German delegation, having infiltrated the West German foreign intelligence service (Bundesnachrichtendienst, BND), and one who was briefly in attendance at the Vienna Follow-Up Meeting.[22] In the report, it is argued that the states of the Warsaw Pact "found themselves in a better tactical position overall" than they had been in when the meeting began in late 1986 and attributed this to taking a more active role in making "proposals covering the entire range of the CSCE process". Yet the report also reveals that Moscow had less control over the pace of reforms in the East than Shevardnadze and Gorbachev appreciated.[23]

The HVA was wary not only of runaway reforms in Moscow but also of cracks emerging between the Warsaw Pact delegations because this disunity could then be exploited by the Western delegations to force further concessions. This prioritisation of ideas of unity and solidarity by the Stasi and the ruling SED in the mid-1980s is well-established in the broader literature on East German political development.[24] However, it is significant that we see this kind of thought also guiding the analysis of intelligence provided by sources close to the Vienna Follow-up Meeting because it helps us to understand why East German policymakers were so critical of their allies' efforts to engage with the CSCE process despite Moscow's growing acceptance of a diversity of positions among Pact members. For example, in HVA's report of 24 April 1987 Hungary

21 Westliche Wertungen zur 2. Runde des Wiener KSZE-Folgetreffens, BArch, MfS, HVA 46, 150/87, Bl. 31–37.

22 Sources include: XV378/68 Gerald, XV381/69 Harry, XV/3690/74 Florian, in: Douglas Selvage/Walter Süß, *Staatssicherheit und KSZE-Prozess. MfS zwischen SED und KGB (1972–1989) – Tabellenanhang*, Göttingen 2019, p. 83.

23 Westliche Wertungen zur 2. Runde des Wiener KSZE-Folgetreffens, BArch, MfS, HVA 46, 150/87, Bl. 31–32

24 Ilko-Sascha Kowalczuk, *End Game. The 1989 Revolution in East Germany*, Oxford 2022, p. 29–31; Esther von Richthofen, *Bringing Culture to the Masses. Control, Compromise and Participation in the GDR*, Oxford 2009, p. 189–191; A. James McAdams, *Germany Divided. From the Wall to Reunification*, Princeton 2020, p. 122–123; Selvage/Süß, *Staatssicherheit und KSZE-Prozess*, p. 515–531.

and Romania are singled out for criticism, the former for its engagement with the West and the latter for resisting close coordination with Moscow.[25]

This is consistent with the pattern of HVA reporting on the CSCE process, where the service's strongest criticisms tended to be reserved for their allies. The accusation of schism against the Hungarian delegation was especially strongly prosecuted because of the Hungarian Basket III proposals on cross-border tourism and travel echoed those of West Germany.[26] The HVA report argues that "what is striking and unparalleled in [the Hungarian delegation's proposals] is the clarity in its explicit linkage to important Western concerns".[27] Furthermore, the report notes that "Hungarian support for the Western proposal for the protection of national minorities" made it "the first Warsaw Pact state in the history of the CSCE to have joined a Western human rights proposal as a co-contributor".[28] Arguably, domestic concern in Hungary over discrimination against the Hungarian minority in Romania (Székely Land) was the primary motivation for the East-West consensus.[29] Yet this "remarkable step" by Hungary was interpreted and firmly criticised by the HVA as a West German attempt "to use CSCE tools to solve an internal bloc problem". The HVA's critique that the CSCE was being appropriated by some Warsaw Pact states to circumvent Pact processes and take unilateral action to the detriment of other members also formed a trope in the HVA's analysis of the Vienna Follow-up Meeting.[30]

3 Seeing Opposition on All Sides

In mid-1987 the HVA drew on unnamed sources within the Italian government to access the Italian delegation's assessment of how the CSCE process was progressing and found that internal division was not unique to the delegations

25 Westliche Wertungen zur 2. Runde des Wiener KSZE-Folgetreffens, BArch, MfS, HVA 46, 150/87, Bl. 33.

26 Stefan Lehne, *The Vienna Meeting of the Conference on Security and Cooperation in Europe, 1986–1989. A Turning Point in East-West Relations*, London 2019, p. 135–167.

27 Westliche Wertungen zur 2. Runde des Wiener KSZE-Folgetreffens, BArch, MfS, HVA 46, 150/87, Bl. 36.

28 See the article by Willi Schrenk in this volume.

29 Andrea Brait/Michael Gehler, "The CSCE Vienna Follow-up Meeting and Alois Mock, 1986–1989", in: Helmut Wohnout et al. (eds.), *Christian Democracy and the Fall of Communism*, Leuven 2019, p. 75–92, on p. 84.

30 Selvage/Süß, *Staatssicherheit und KSZE-Prozess*, p. 540–569 and p. 611–618.

from Warsaw Pact states. There was in fact greater division among Western states than East Berlin had initially appreciated.[31] Similarly, during the fourth round of talks at the Vienna Follow-up Meeting (September to December 1987), the HVA sought to highlight how the West German delegation was displeased with the "tactic of unlimited procrastination" that some NATO members – namely the United States, Canada, Britain and the Netherlands – were pursuing in the negotiations.[32] Instead, the West German delegation argued that "the West has nothing to gain from" attempting to maximise the symbolic concessions extracted from East Germany and should instead focus on gradual but tangible improvements in human rights.[33]

This kind of division was also identified in relation to Western military force reduction targets and there was supposedly "complete agreement in rejecting isolated American reductions".[34] Overall, the analysis is helpful not only because it highlights the changing priorities of *both* the Eastern and Western "camps" but also enables us to find points of interconnection and agreement across strategic alliances. Indeed, the CSCE Vienna Follow-up Meeting was arguably one of the key forums for this kind of trust and confidence building.[35] It had the effect of eroding established loyalties to Washington D.C. and incentivising autonomy from Moscow while highlighting the viability of alternative structures and relationships (such as the N+N group) based on common geographies and histories, if not ideologies.[36] This was precisely the point being made by a representative of the Italian foreign ministry in writing that

> the CSCE remains, in the current bipolar system, the best example of polyphonic dynamism in the international arena. As a result of this, medium powers, like Italy, have the possibility to play a proactive role, and therefore also a political one, of considerable importance.[37]

---

31 Westliche Wertungen zur 2. Runde des Wiener KSZE-Folgetreffens, BArch, MfS, HVA 46, 150/87, Bl. 34.

32 Westliche Wertungen zum Stand und zu den Perspektiven des Wiener KSZE-Folgetreffens, BArch, MfS, HVA 50, 388/87, Bl. 259. Also see: BRD-Wertungen zum Stand und zu den Perspektiven des Wiener KSZE-Folgetreffens, BArch, MfS, HVA/MD, SIRA-TDB 12, SA8750333; Die Haltung der BRD-Regierung zum Wiener KSZE-Folgetreffen, BArch, MfS, HVA/MD, SIRA-TDB 12, SA8750328 (System der Informationsrecherche der HVA (SIRA)).

33 Ibid.

34 Ibid.

35 Marie-France Desjardins, *Rethinking Confidence-Building Measures. Obstacles to Agreement and the Risks of Overselling the Process*, London 2014, p. 15–18.

36 Kii-Jong Hong, *The CSCE Security Regime Formation. An Asian Perspective*, London 1997, p. 84–85.

37 Bilancio dei progressi della CSCE, Italian Ministry of Foreign Affairs, East-West Relations, 24 November 1987, History and Public Policy Program Digital Archive, Istituto Luigi Sturzo, Archivio Giulio Andreotti, NATO Series, Box 172, Subseries 1, Folder 085, p. 5.

However, a polyphonic Europe was not what the HVA or the East German government wanted to see. This kind of alternative, and the freedoms and associations that it implied, constituted the so-called "internationalisation of opposition" that the Stasi had so fiercely opposed from 1975 on. Consequently, it was not without reason that calls of this kind, which internationalised questions of human rights, were met with alarm by the HVA analysts. This fear was compounded by the HVA's belief that "the outcome of the Vienna meeting could not be predicted with certainty".[38]

The fears came to a head in the first half of 1988. On 18 January 1988 the Central Information Group issued a report entitled "Assessment of the actual political-ideological attacks by the NATO states against the European socialist states against the background of the Vienna Follow-up Meeting".[39] This report was widely circulated throughout the upper echelons of the Stasi and SED bureaucracies and also dispatched to Moscow for consideration by the Committee for State Security (Komitet gosudarstvennoy bezopasnosti, KGB).[40] It is significant because it provides a summary of the thinking that underpinned the largely hostile approach of the MfS to the first half of the Vienna Follow-up Meeting. The administration saw the CSCE process as having been used by Western European states as a "framework" to "polemicise against" and interfere with the internal policies of Warsaw Pact, particularly in relation to the control of political dissent.[41]

Moreover, the Stasi report suggested that Western demands around human rights amounted to blackmail because they had become "a prerequisite for further comprehensive steps towards [military] disarmament and an essential yardstick for the results of the regional détente process". This assessment was coupled with the prediction that the West could use the tactic "in further negotiations as a lever to enforce its own demands and to deepen differences of opinion between the states of the Warsaw Treaty". Discrediting Gorbachev's New Thinking, along with his ideas of Glasnost and Perestroika, was

38 Westliche Wertungen zum Stand und zu den Perspektiven des Wiener KSZE-Folgetreffens, BArch, MfS, HVA 50, 388/87, Bl. 260–261; Ergebnisse der KSZE in Wien, BArch, MfS, BdL/Doc., 8932, Bl. 1–18. Also see: Bewertung des KSZE-Folgetreffens, BArch, MfS, ZAIG, 4883, Bl. 1–45; Ergebnisse der KSZE in Wien, BArch, MfS, BdL/Doc. 8937, Bl. 1–2, BRD-Wertungen zum Stand und zu den Perspektiven des Wiener KSZE-Folgetreffens, BArch, MfS, HVA/MD, SIRA-TDB 12, SA8750333; Die Haltung der BRD-Regierung zum Wiener KSZE-Folgetreffen, BArch, MfS, HVA/MD, SIRA-TDB 12, SA8750328 (SIRA).

39 Gegnerische Angriffe während des Wiener Folgetreffens, BArch, MfS, ZAIG 6053, 20/88, Bl. 3–12.

40 Selvage/Süß, *Staatssicherheit und KSZE-Prozess*, p. 84.

41 Gegnerische Angriffe während des Wiener Folgetreffens, BArch, MfS, ZAIG 6053, 20/88, Bl. 3–4.

supposedly central to the Western effort to drive a wedge between Pact members.[42] However, we must not uncritically accept the Stasi's assessment that there was significant Western opposition to Gorbachev's reforms. Threaded throughout the Group's extensive treatment of the issue is the hypothesis that Western attempts at "measuring" Gorbachev's reforms "against bourgeois ideas of democracy and values" were intended to exacerbate activism by Helsinki groups and erode unity among Pact members.[43] The report suggests that evidence for this hypothesis could be found in attempts by unnamed politicians from NATO countries to meet with dissidents during official visits to socialist countries and efforts to promote the "intensification of such encounters on a 'private' level".[44] Yet the tone of the Stasi analysis is particularly conspiratorial and pays little attention to alternative explanations for Western criticism, which in fact was more concerned with the lack of implementation of Gorbachev's reforms.

Arguably, the strongest explanation of Western hesitancy to endorse Gorbachev's reforms in early 1988, despite his personal popularity among Western audiences, was not a Machiavellian effort to sow division amongst Warsaw Pact states but rather suspicion that Gorbachev's reforms were temporary and, in part, designed to neutralise a key area of Western advantage in international forums including the CSCE.[45] Jussi Hanhimäki makes the compelling argument that human rights were a central part of reinvention of the Western liberalism that emerged from the Helsinki Process in the late 1970s and became a defining feature of Western criticism of the Soviet alliance in the 1980s.[46] The decline in Soviet interest was matched across the Eastern Bloc, but where Gorbachev sought to reinvigorate human rights discourse through the Vienna Follow-up Meeting, Honecker and the SED steadfastly refused to entertain such questions.[47]

42 Rofe, "Trust between Adversaries and Allies", in: Ostermann/Klimke/Kreis (eds.), *Trust, But Verify*, p. 53–55; Westad, *The Cold War*, p. 389–391.

43 Akira Iriye/Petra Goedde, "Introduction: Human Rights as History", in: Akira Iriye/Petra Goedde/William Hitchcock (eds.), *The Human Rights Revolution. An International History*, New York 2012, p. 3–26, on p. 9; Gegnerische Angriffe während des Wiener Folgetreffens, BArch, MfS, ZAIG 6053, 20/88, Bl. 4.

44 Gegnerische Angriffe während des Wiener Folgetreffens, BArch, MfS, ZAIG 6053, 20/88, Bl. 6.

45 Vladislav M. Zubok, *A Failed Empire. The Soviet Union in the Cold War from Stalin to Gorbachev*, Chapel Hill 2009, p. 317.

46 See the article by Jussi Hanhimäki in this volume.

47 Gegnerische Angriffe während des Wiener Folgetreffens, BArch, MfS, ZAIG 6053, 20/88, Bl. 6.

Human rights increasingly became a focal point for "cross-bloc initiatives" as the Vienna Follow-up Meeting progressed, reflecting the convergence of Western interests since the mid-1970s and Gorbachev's program of reforms in the mid-1980s.[48] However, Stasi observers largely interpreted human rights discourse through the lens of a wider Western plot to use agreement with Soviet-aligned states to sow division among Warsaw Pact members. For example, the Central Information Group's report of 18 January 1988 report argues that Hungary had shown considerable interest in working with Western states on proposals related to the human dimension of the CSCE in solidarity with the Hungarian minority in Romania.[49] Yet this was understood to reflect Western efforts to exacerbate and internationalise differences between Pact members. Such an interpretation helps to explain why members of the Western delegations accused the East German delegation of having an "inflexible attitude" towards negotiations – the East German delegation saw themselves as playing the role of "brakeman" in relation first and foremost to the more reform-minded Pact members like Hungary and Poland but to also the West. This interpretation also accounts for the growing isolation of East Germany at the CSCE, even among its allies – an isolation of which East Berlin was all too aware.[50]

4 East German Pressure Points in Vienna

Pressure on East Germany from its allies, particularly the Soviet Union, rather than from its adversaries in the West, and the associated need to limit reputational damage within the Soviet alliance, were arguably the decisive factors in efforts by the MfS to construct a façade of receptiveness to the CSCE meeting.[51] However, to understand this development in the East German approach to the CSCE we need to understand the changes occurring in Moscow during 1988. Throughout that year, tensions increased between the Soviet delegation in Vienna and the reform-minded foreign minister, Shevardnadze, in Moscow, with the former taking far more conservative positions than the latter.[52] For

48 Ibid., Bl. 6–9.

49 Selvage/Süß, *Staatssicherheit und KSZE-Prozess,* p. 642–643; Gegnerische Angriffe während des Wiener Folgetreffens, BArch, MfS, ZAIG 6053, 20/88, Bl. 9.

50 Ibid.

51 Ziele für das KSZE-Folgetreffen, BArch, MfS, HVA, ZAIG 5342, Bl. 6–10; Selvage/Süß, *Staatssicherheit und KSZE-Prozess,* p. 647–658.

52 Harm Hazewinkel, "Paris, Copenhagen, and Moscow", in: Arie Bloed/Pieter van Dijk, *The Human Dimension of the Helsinki Process. The Vienna Follow-up Meeting and Its Aftermath,* Leiden 2021, p. 128–132.

example, in a conversation between George Shultz, the US Secretary of State, and Shevardnadze on 21. April 1988, Shevardnadze betrayed his frustration with the delegation, complaining that "We tell them one thing [...] They do something different".[53]

Heraclides helps to explain these tensions – between Moscow and the Soviet delegation in Vienna on the one hand and among Warsaw Pact members on the other – by arguing that from early 1987 on, the alliance was divided into two factions. The East German, Czechoslovak, Bulgarian and Romanian delegations were resistant to domestic political reforms, including the freedom of movement proposals in Basket III, whereas the Hungarian and Polish delegates begrudgingly recognised the need for modest reforms and expressed willingness to negotiate.[54] The position of the Soviet delegation shifted from that of the former "hardliner" faction towards that of the latter "moderate" faction as the Vienna Meeting progressed – but without ever quite matching, despite Shevardnadze's and Gorbachev's private endorsement.[55] This was a consequence of the pace of reform at the highest echelons of the Soviet Politburo eclipsing that occurring both among the rank and file in the Soviet Ministry of Foreign Affairs and in East Berlin, Prague, Sofia and Bucharest. Wrede describes this change in the Soviet Politburo as "a much-noticed about-face", which led to Shevardnadze consistently holding, in his communications with the foreign ministers of the Warsaw Pact states, that "respect for human rights was a pillar of the international security system" to which the Soviet Union was committed.[56] Meanwhile, Sarah Snyder sees the changing Soviet position at the Vienna Follow-up Meeting as a key barometer of the larger reforms that Gorbachev was pursuing in Moscow.[57]

Simultaneously with the "about-face" over human rights that had occurred in Moscow, a less dramatic change seems to have been underway in East Berlin. Where Moscow proactively sought the measured extension of human

53 "Conversation between US Secretary of State George Shultz and Soviet Minister of Foreign Affairs Eduard Shevardnadze", Memorandum of Conversation: The Secretary's Initial Meeting with Shevardnadze, 21 April 1988, Moscow, The National Security Archive, https://nsarchive2.gwu.edu/NSAEBB/NSAEBB251/7.pdf, accessed 21.11.2023, p. 9–10.

54 Heraclides, *Security and Cooperation in Europe*, p. 92.

55 "Conversation between US Secretary of State George Shultz and Soviet Minister of Foreign Affairs Eduard Shevardnadze", Memorandum of Conversation: The Secretary's Initial Meeting with Shevardnadze, 21 April 1988, Moscow, The National Security Archive, https://nsarchive2.gwu.edu/NSAEBB/NSAEBB251/7.pdf, accessed 21.11.2023, p. 9–10.

56 Wrede, *Die Weiterentwicklung des KSZE-Prozesses*, p. 113.

57 Snyder, Sarah B., "Principles Overwhelming Tanks: Human Rights and the End of the Cold War", in: Akira Iriye/Petra Goedde/William Hitchcock (eds.), *The Human Rights Revolution. An International History*, Oxford 2012, p. 265–284, on p. 265.

rights – evident in the Soviet proposal for the Moscow Meeting of the Conference on the Human Dimension of the CSCE – the change in East Germany was predominately reactive.[58] It was a reluctant response to changes being driven by Gorbachev and Shevardnadze from SED figures like Egon Krenz and Wolfgang Herger designed to prop up one-party rule against internal criticism rather than a rethinking of the place of human rights in East German politics and diplomacy.[59] Thus, from late 1988 on, Stasi commentary on the Vienna Follow-up Meeting increasingly treated Basket III concessions as a fait accompli and prescriptive comments were focused on how to increase East German influence over the kind and extent of the concessions being made.[60]

For example, on 26 September 1988 the HVA produced a summary of the outcome of the sixth round of talks at the Vienna Follow-up Meeting, concluding that they had reduced "contentious negotiations [freedom of movement] to core political problems" and thereby restricted the opportunity for Western delegations to criticise East Germany, albeit without succeeding in halting the negotiations altogether.[61] Nevertheless, the report predicts that "decisions about the Human Dimension Conference, including the Soviet proposal to host it in Moscow, were likely to be particularly difficult".[62] The difficulty was attributed to the Soviet "about-face" and Moscow's inability to secure "a unified line within the framework of the Warsaw Treaty", which meant that "East Germany felt compelled to modify its behaviour". This HVA analysis supports the argument that a lesser, unwilling "about-face" over human rights in general, if not freedom of movement in particular, was occurring in East Berlin in the wake of Gorbachev's reforms.

The HVA believed that East Germany had been forced into a "defensive position" at the Vienna Follow-Up Meeting by the (expected) criticism of the Western delegations on the one hand and, on the other, the (unexpected)

---

58 Sandra Gubin, "Between Regimes and Realism – Transnational Agenda Setting. Soviet Compliance with CSCE Human Rights Norms", in: *Human Rights Quarterly* 17 (1995), issue 2, p. 278–302, on p. 297–300; Yuliya von Saal, "Die Folgen des KSZE-Prozesses in der Sowjetunion der Perestroika. Der KSZE-Faktor in der Eigendynamik des Wertewandels", in: Matthias Peter/Hermann Wentker (eds.), *Die KSZE im Ost-West-Konflikt. Internationale Politik und gesellschaftliche Transformation 1975–1990* (Schriftenreihe der Vierteljahrshefte für Zeitgeschichte Sondernummer), München 2012, p. 296–303.

59 Charles Maier, *Dissolution. The Crisis of Communism and the End of East Germany*, London 1999, p. 3–51; Daniel Chirot, "What Happened in Eastern Europe in 1989?", in: Vladimir Tismaneanu (ed.), *The Revolutions of 1989*, London 2005, p. 19–50.

60 Selvage/Süß, *Staatssicherheit und KSZE-Prozess*, p. 621–646.

61 Der Stand und die Perspektiven des KSZE-Folgetreffens in Wien aus BRD-Sicht, BArch, MfS, HVA 53, 418/88, Bl. 5–6.

62 Ibid., Bl. 7.

willingness of the Soviet Union to make concessions.[63] East Berlin was particularly concerned that these concessions might extend to the humanitarian cases of East Germans who had been prevented from emigrating to West Germany.[64] This helps to explain why the HVA officers embedded within the East German delegation were tasked with "making every effort to limit the active role of Helsinki groups" in criticising East Germany on the sidelines of the Vienna Follow-Up Meeting.[65] The objective of these measures was to thwart what Wrede describes as the campaign of "discussion and discrete diplomacy to raise human rights violations with the delegation from East Germany".[66] However, the measures of August–September 1988 were assessed by the HVA as having been relatively ineffective, providing East Germany only with "a little breathing room" in the face of "sustained and massive criticism from the West".[67]

Four months later, on 15 December 1988, the efficacy of the East German government's measures was reviewed in a report produced by the Central Information Group and distributed to the office of Erich Honecker, the Ministry of National Defence (Ministerium für Nationale Verteidigung, MfNV) and the KGB in Moscow.[68] The report argues that NATO sought "long-term, controllable and evolutionary processes that neither exceeded the tolerance of the Soviet Union nor provided conservative forces in Warsaw Pact states with pretexts for limiting the internal reforms". The report also explains that the Vienna Follow-up Meeting had become an important forum for critiquing East Germany's human rights record and that the exploitation of this function of the meeting was "one of the most important successes of their [the West's] CSCE policy".[69] This analysis highlights the fear within the MfS that the CSCE Meeting might cause the proliferation of Helsinki groups in East Germany

63 Ibid.

64 Selvage/Süß, *Staatssicherheit und KSZE-Prozess*, p. 611–618, p. 632–635; Der Stand und die Perspektiven des KSZE-Folgetreffens in Wien aus BRD-Sicht, BArch, MfS, HVA 53, 418/88, Bl. 8; Die Position der DDR beim Wiener Folgetreffen, BArch, MfS, ZAIG, 4246, Bl. 2–4; Arie Bloed, "Institutional Aspects of the Helsinki Process After the Follow-up Meeting of Vienna", in: *Netherlands International Law Review* 36 (1989), issue 3, p. 360.

65 Der Stand und die Perspektiven des KSZE-Folgetreffens in Wien aus BRD-Sicht, BArch, MfS, HVA 53, 418/88, Bl. 8.

66 David H. Shumaker, *Gorbachev and the German question. Soviet–West German relations, 1985–1990*, London 1995, p. 53–62; Wrede, *Die Weiterentwicklung des KSZE-Prozesses*, p. 113.

67 Der Stand und die Perspektiven des KSZE-Folgetreffens in Wien aus BRD-Sicht, BArch, MfS, HVA 53, 418/88, Bl. 8.

68 Einschätzung über aktuelle politisch-ideologische Angriffsrichtungen der NATO gegen die Warschauer Vertragsstaaten, insbesondere die DDR, vor dem Hintergrund des KSZE-Folgetreffens in Wien, BArch, MfS, ZAIG 6067, 540/88, Bl. 3–13.

69 Ibid., Bl. 4–5.

and is particularly noteworthy because the report directly connects this illusory threat to internal security threat to the Soviet Union's commitment to "maximalist positions" on human rights.[70] It was in this context that the report delivered an ominous warning to both Honecker and the leadership of the East German security apparatus that "the progress of the CSCE process will also force the East German leadership to revise its positions".[71]

5 Conclusion

The Vienna Follow-up Meeting ended on 19 January 1989, only a month after the report by the Central Information Group warned that East Germany's leaders could not resist the CSCE process in perpetuity, especially given the concerted pressure from Moscow to sign the Concluding Document.[72] The effect of the meeting's Concluding Document was quickly felt in the Soviet Union, with the HVA concluding that the Vienna Follow-up Meeting had accelerated "the opening of the media to debates on sometimes sensitive domestic political and historical topics in the course of Perestroika and Glasnost [and] also led to a liberalisation of the information system as a whole".[73] More broadly, the HVA argued that the Vienna Follow-up Meeting had ensured that the CSCE had established a "central role in shaping West-East relations" and, pointedly, that this "would not have been possible without the reform policy of the Communist Party of the Soviet Union's general secretary, M. Gorbachev".[74] Thus,

70 Christiane Olivo, *Creating a Democratic Civil Society in Eastern Germany. The Case of the Citizen Movements and Alliance* 90, New York 2001, p. 61–90; Peter Voss/Christiane Gern/Karl-Dieter Opp, *Origins of a Spontaneous Revolution. East Germany, 1989*, Ann Arbor 1995, p. 19–20, p. 60–71; Douglas Selvage, "The Limits of Repression. Soviet Bloc Security Services vs. Transnational Helsinki Networks, 1976–1986", in: Nicolas Badalassi/Sarah B. Snyder (eds.), *The CSCE and the End of the Cold War, Diplomacy, Societies and Human Rights 1972–1990*, New York-Oxford 2019, p. 207–229, on p. 210–211; Einschätzung über aktuelle politisch-ideologische Angriffsrichtungen der NATO gegen die Warschauer Vertragsstaaten, insbesondere die DDR, vor dem Hintergrund des KSZE-Folgetreffens in Wien, BArch, MfS, ZAIG 6067, 540/88, Bl. 5.

71 Einschätzung über aktuelle politisch-ideologische Angriffsrichtungen der NATO gegen die Warschauer Vertragsstaaten, insbesondere die DDR, vor dem Hintergrund des KSZE-Folgetreffens in Wien, BArch, MfS, ZAIG 6067, 540/88, Bl. 5.

72 Süß, *Die Wiener KSZE-Folgekonferenz*, p. 220–227.

73 Ergebnisse des KSZE-Folgetreffens für die Sowjetunion, BArch, MfS, HVA 761, 163/89, Bl. 5.

74 Der Verlauf und die Ergebnisse des Wiener-Folgetreffens aus BRD-Sicht, BArch, MfS, HVA 761, 83/89, Bl. 175–177.

Wrede's observation of a Soviet "about-face" is far more than a retroactive label – it can be found in contemporary East German analysis.

However, even more significant is the fact that the HVA analysis departs from much of the negative commentary of Vienna Follow-up Meeting in 1986–88 in concluding that "the numerous new, substantial texts for the specification of human rights and human contacts will benefit the people in both German states".[75] This rhetorical shift is corroborated by the wide-ranging speech of Erich Mielke, East German minister for state security, to the college of the Ministry of State Security in late 1989, in which he acknowledged that Gorbachev's reforms and the Vienna Follow-Up Meeting would necessitate controlled, measured change in East Germany.[76] Arguably, the HVA got its forecast of 7 May 1986 for the Vienna Meeting so wrong because it at first underestimated the magnitude of the diplomatic opportunities that Gorbachev's New Thinking created in Europe and reacted too slowly to the strategic realignment precipitated by that diplomacy. It was not until the end of the Vienna Follow-up Meeting on 19 January 1989 that the HVA fully recognised the implications of the changes that occurred throughout the meeting in Vienna and adjusted its guidance to the SED accordingly. This was not quite the "about-face" that took place in Moscow during 1986–87. However, the Vienna Follow-up Meeting did lead the Honecker government and the HVA to the cynical realisation that both institutions needed to distract from East Germany's poor human rights record more effectively in international forums like the CSCE or risk significant reputational damage within the Soviet alliance, not to mention among Western and N+N states.[77]

---

75 Ibid.

76 Ziele für das KSZE-Folgetreffen, BArch, MfS, ZAIG, 5342, Bl. 1–64.

77 Auftritt der DDR in der KSZE, BArch, MfS, ZAIG, 5351, Bl. 40–52; Die DDR und internationale Organisationen, BArch, MfS, BdL/Dok. 5299 and Bl. 1–3; Bewertung des KSZE-Folgetreffens, BArch, MfS, ZAIG, 4883, Bl. 1–45.

A German-German Conflict in a Multilateral Framework

The Debate on Compulsory Currency Exchange at the Vienna Follow-up Meeting

Willi Schrenk

The Federal Republic of Germany considered the Vienna Concluding Document a resounding foreign policy success. Detlev Graf zu Rantzau, the second leader of the West German delegation, went so far as to describe the outcomes of the Vienna Follow-up Meeting as "a development unprecedented in Europe's post-war history" and as "in every regard satisfactory to the Federal Republic of Germany".[1] The German Democratic Republic, by contrast, was most dissatisfied with the Concluding Document. In the meeting's final months, the East Germans found themselves under increasing pressure from both East and West. The more liberal policies pursued by the Soviet Union under Gorbachev meant that old certainties no longer applied within the Warsaw Pact. Instead, East Germany, together with Romania, gradually found itself in an isolated position within the Eastern alliance.[2] In the last days of the Vienna Follow-up Meeting, it found itself compelled, under Soviet pressure, to accede to two demands which it had previously been alone among the participating states in blocking: the abolition of the compulsory currency exchange at the inner-German border and the legalisation of the activities of so-called "Helsinki groups" in the CSCE states.[3]

The present chapter examines one of the most hotly-fought disputes between the two German states at the meeting, that concerning the abolition of the compulsory exchange of a specified minimum amount of currency on entry to the GDR. This debate was of great importance to both German states

1 "Botschafter Graf zu Rantzau, Wien (KSZE-Delegation), an das Auswärtige Amt, Delegationsbericht Nr. 505", in: *Akten zur Auswärtigen Politik der Bundesrepublik Deutschland* (AAPD) *1989*, München 2020, I, Dok. 7, p. 29–36, on p. 29. Previously untranslated German language sources were translated by the author.

2 On the isolation of the GDR during the Vienna Follow-up Conference see Benno-Eide Siebs, *Die Außenpolitik der DDR 1976–1989. Strategien und Grenzen,* Paderborn-München-Wien-Zürich 1999, p. 351–353.

3 On the Helsinki and human rights groups in the CSCE process see e.g. Sarah B. Snyder, *Human Rights Activism and the End of the Cold War. A Transnational History of the Helsinki Network*, New York 2011.

DOI:10.1163/9789004736979_015

and reflects their general approach to the Vienna Follow-up Meeting. The present analysis is concerned particularly with the strategies and other factors that determined the course of negotiations and their ultimate outcome.

1 The History of Compulsory Currency Exchange Prior to the Vienna Follow-up Meeting

Compulsory currency exchange (CCE) for visitors to East Germany from the "non-socialist economic area" was introduced in December 1964. From that time on, travellers from West Germany, West Berlin and other Western states were obliged by law to exchange a fixed sum of Deutschmarks (DM) into East German marks (Ostmark) at a rate of one to one, which corresponded neither to the rates offered by West German bureaux de change nor to the respective currencies' real value. The minimum sum to be exchanged was adjusted over the years, as were the shifting exemptions for old-age pensioners and minors, who were permitted to exchange smaller sums or none at all. Since 1989 the standard sum had been fixed at DM 25.[4] From 1 August 1984 the daily rate was lowered to DM 15 for pensioners, with under-14s fully exempt from CCE.[5]

From the very beginning, CCE on crossing the East German border was a contentious issue between the German states, with the Federal Republic regarding it as a major obstacle to contact between people in East and West. This was particularly true for West Germans who had relatives in the GDR and especially in divided Berlin, but also in other regions along the inner-German border, as every visit to East Germany meant a financial burden. From the perspective of the GDR, the compulsory purchase of Ostmark at high rates was an important source of hard currency, since the money could not be exchanged back into Deutschmarks when returning to the West. In the 1980s, income from the minimum exchange rate averaged around DM 300 million per annum. Another purpose of this rule was to protect the GDR economy from unofficial foreign currency trading in the Federal Republic, particularly in West Berlin. Although the introduction of Ostmarks cheaply bought in West Berlin into the GDR was prohibited, it was frequently practised and allowed visitors

4 Gesetzblatt der DDR 1964, II, Nr. 114 vom 28.11.1964; Gesetzblatt der DDR 1973, I, Nr. 51 vom 06.11.1973; Gesetzblatt der DDR 1974, I, Nr. 54 vom 05.11.1974; Gesetzblatt der DDR 1974, I, Nr. 61 vom 10.12.1974; Gesetzblatt der DDR 1980, I, Nr. 29 vom 09.10.1980.

5 This was part of a series of humanitarian concessions to which the GDR had committed itself in return for the granting of a loan of just under a billion marks by the Federal Republic. See "Gespräch des Bundeskanzlers Kohl mit Premierministerin Thatcher in Berlin (West) vom 25.09.1987", in: *AAPD 1987*, München 2018, II, Dok. 269, p. 1359–1360.

from the West to buy subsidised products in the GDR for a fraction of their value in West Germany. One Deutschmark usually bought four to eight Ostmarks, sometimes even more. In 1987 alone, the damage to the GDR economy from this practice was estimated at DM 500 to 600 million. The Socialist Unity Party of Germany (SED) assumed that abolishing or lowering CCE rates would exacerbate this problem.[6] In addition to its economic benefits, the GDR also regarded CCE an effective means of distancing itself from West Germany. It was not in the interests of the party leadership to bring people in East and West too close together.[7]

Even if comparable regulations also applied in other Warsaw Pact states, the debate about abolishing CCE at the Vienna Follow-up Conference must be seen as a specifically German-German problem fundamentally linked to the division of Germany. Due to family ties between the two Germanies, significantly more visitors from the West travelled to the GDR than to other Eastern states. In this respect, the negotiations in Vienna addressed a fairly commonplace problem for many people in the two German states that did not exist elsewhere in the Eastern bloc.

2 The Negotiations on Compulsory Currency Exchange

The debate on the abolition of CCE was based on two proposals tabled at the Follow-up Meeting in late February and early March 1987. The first, headed "Foreign travel and family visits" (WT.93), was tabled by Austria and Switzerland in Basket III[8] and suggested the abolition of minimum exchange rates not overall but only for family visits. The second proposal (WT.101) was supported by a broad alliance of the states of the European Community, Canada, the United States, Norway and Switzerland. It was located in Basket II and contained demands for the promotion of tourism, including that "All requirements for tourists to exchange certain amounts of money into the national currency shall be abolished."[9] The negotiations on the abolition of CCE were thus conducted in two baskets (something which applied only to few debates at the Follow-up Meeting) and their outcome was ultimately enshrined in

6 Douglas Selvage/Walter Süß, *Staatssicherheit und KSZE-Prozess. MfS zwischen SED und KGB (1972–1989)*, Göttingen 2019, p. 644–647.

7 See e.g. Siebs, *Die Außenpolitik der DDR 1976–1989*, p. 128.

8 CSCE/WT.93 vom 27.2.1987, Politisches Archiv des Auswärtigen Amts, Berlin (PA-AA), B 28, Zwischenarchiv (ZA) (Referat 212), Bd. 153446.

9 CSCE/WT.101 vom 03.03.1987, PA-AA, B 28, ZA (Referat 212), Bd. 153446.

two passages of the Vienna Concluding Document. Neither proposal directly addressed the German-German dimension of abolishing CCE.[10]

As would become apparent in the further course of the meeting, the inclusion of the proposal in Basket III by neutral states had considerable tactical advantages for West Germany. Foreign ministry documents also indicate that there had been previous agreements between the Federal Republic and the neutral states. Looking back in the summer of 1988, the West German delegation reported that it had succeeded in persuading the neutral states to "submit additional proposals in this area (see WT.93), which also took account of concerns relating to Germany-Germany policy".[11] In an assessment of the Concluding Document, Detlev Graf zu Rantzau, the second head of the West German delegation, stated that the "quality of the VCD [Vienna Concluding Document] in the area of human rights and Basket III was undoubtedly due to the fact that Western neutrals fully shared our understanding of human rights."[12] In this connection, Rantzau explicitly mentioned the neutral proposal on CCE.[13]

Both proposals were initially rejected by the Warsaw Pact states and by the GDR in particular. The East German diplomats repeatedly stated that no agreement on the abolition or reduction of CCE could be reached in Vienna. In support of this line, they argued that CCE was a specifically German-German problem that should not be dealt with at the multilateral level of the CSCE.[14] Within the Warsaw Pact, however, there were few objections to an agreement on CCE being included in the Vienna Concluding Document. Instead, the Soviet Union pressed for compromises with the West in the area of human rights early on in order to achieve progress in disarmament in return, a line initially supported by Hungary and Poland. As early as 1987, the GDR had reason to worry about being isolated within its own alliance.[15]

10 The West German diplomat Hans-Heinrich Wrede, in the short chapter on the debate on CCE in his memoirs of the Follow-up Meeting, only dealt with proposal WT.93, thereby bolstering the interpretation of the conflict something other than an explicitly German-German problem. Hans-Heinrich Wrede, *KSZE in Wien. Kursbestimmung für Europas Zukunft*, Köln 1990, p. 109–112.

11 Delegationsbericht 400 (A) vom 29.06.1988, PA-AA, B 28, ZA (Referat 212), Bd. 153444.

12 Botschafter Graf zu Rantzau an das Auswärtige Amt, in: *AAPD 1989*, p. 92.

13 Ibid. p. 90.

14 Zum Vorschlag WT 93. Österreich/Schweden vom 27.2.1987 über Auslandsreisen zu Familienbesuchen, PA-AA, M 21/286995; Standpunkt der sozialistischen Staaten zu den NATO/EG-Vorschlägen WT 101, 105, 115, 117, 118 vom 17.03.1987, PA-AA, M 21/286995.

15 For example, the GDR delegation wrote in a report to East Berlin on 28 September 1987 that its allies had "apparently [...] no problems" with an agreement to abolish CCE. This willingness of the USSR and other WVO states to agree to Western proposals in the humanitarian field jeopardised the "substantial interests" of the GDR; Ergebnisse Abstimmung

Overall, West Germany was unable to make any significant progress on the issue of CCE until May 1988, when the follow-up conference gained considerable momentum with the first draft of a Concluding Document, drawn up by the N+N.[16] Although it found its stance confirmed by the adoption of a phrasing based on proposal WT.93 in the full draft, the Federal Republic doubted that the agreement would be included in the Vienna final document "in view of the fierce resistance announced by the GDR".[17] Instead, Bonn expected to be able to use the discussion of the issue in Vienna as leverage in bilateral negotiations with East Berlin.[18] The GDR, by contrast, found itself increasingly isolated in the following months. From the summer of 1988, only Romania continued to support its position.[19] Until the end of the Follow-up Meeting, these two states, as conservative hardliners, consistently opposed the policies of the more liberal Warsaw Pact states.[20]

At a meeting between the German delegations in July 1988, the East German diplomats declared that, though they were isolated on this issue, no concessions could be made. Instead, they indicated that they wanted to negotiate this matter directly with Bonn in order to prevent a debate in Vienna. As a result of this threat, the Federal Republic adopted a new strategy, henceforth arguing that the original proposal on CCE had been tabled not by itself but rather by neutral states. Moreover, many Western states were in favour of abolishing CCE, which was why the issue, contrary to East German assertions, could not be treated as a specifically German-German problem. Bonn had recognised that the Federal Republic's chances of success in this bilateral debate were significantly higher in Vienna than in direct talks with East Berlin.[21]

This negotiating strategy proved to be extremely effective over the following months. However, its success was possible only due to the lack of support the GDR received from its allies. In this debate, as in others, the Soviet Union simply ignored the interests of the GDR. Hannsgerd Protsch, for example, who had supported the East German delegation in the area of Basket III since April 1988 and who worked for the Ministry for State Security (MfS) under the code

Staaten Warschauer Vertrages zu Österr.-Schweizer non-paper Korb III, Teil menschliche Kontakte vom 28.09.1987, PA-AA M 21/289595.

16 On the N+N's full proposal: CSCE/WT.137 vom 13.05.1988, PA-AA, B 28, ZA (Referat 212), Bd. 158445; Lehne, The Vienna Meeting, p. 118–119.

17 Delegationsbericht Nr. 373 vom 13.05.1988, PA-AA, B 28, ZA (Referat 212), Bd. 153444.

18 Ibid.

19 Anlage Nr. 1 zur Vorlage für das Politbüro des ZK der SED vom 16. Juni 1988. Informationen zum gegenwärtigen Stand des Wiener KSZE-Folgetreffens, BArch, DP 1/6124.

20 See e.g. Siebs, *Die Außenpolitik der DDR 1976–1989*, p. 352.

21 Delegationsbericht Nr. 412 (I) vom 22.7.1988, PA-AA, B 28, ZA (Referat 212), Bd. 153444.

name "Paul", reported to his case officer on 11 August 1988 that the GDR would ultimately have to agree to all demands in order not to jeopardise progress on conventional disarmament. The Soviet delegation had already informed him confidentially that it too would agree to the abolition of the minimum exchange rate if doing so was necessary to achieve its objectives in military matters,[22] leaving Protsch to conclude that "it [was] all over" in the negotiations on Basket III.[23]

The final months of the conference were marked by tough negotiations in the few areas that remained unresolved. However, while more and more agreements were reached, the GDR blocked agreements on CCE and on legalising the activities of Helsinki groups until shortly before the end of the conference. It was not until December 1988 that the East German foreign minister, Oskar Fischer, suggested that his government cease to block progress on the two contentious issues, as the GDR was in danger of being the only participant to prevent the successful conclusion of the Follow-up Meeting. He also stressed, however, that national legislation should take precedence and that the provisions should not be implemented.[24] This was intended at least to limit the damage to the international reputation of the East German state, since its responsibility for the failure of the Follow-up Conference would have meant a severe loss of face.

Unlike their East German colleagues, the West German delegation expressed a high degree of satisfaction with the final weeks of the Follow-up Meeting. In an assessment of Basket III in the N+N's revised full draft of 3 January 1989, the delegation wrote that the section was "unreservedly acceptable" and stressed "that the GDR's efforts to eliminate the text on minimum exchange [...] have failed".[25] This also applied to the corresponding phrasing in Basket II.[26]

The GDR's resistance to the inclusion of a commitment to abolishing CCE in the Vienna Concluding Document finally ended with the visit of the leader of the Soviet delegation, Yuri Kashlev, to East Berlin on 5 January 1989. Kashlev had the task of obtaining the agreement of the general secretary of the Central Committee of the SED, Erich Honecker, to the final document. Under pressure from the Soviet Union, Honecker finally consented, but asked Kashlev to

22 Selvage/Süß, *Staatssicherheit und KSZE-Prozess*, p. 622–623.
23 Ibid., p. 623.
24 Ibid., p. 641–642.
25 Delegationsbericht Nr. 484 vom 03.01.1989, PA-AA, B 28, ZA (Referat 212), Bd. 153431.
26 Delegationsbericht Nr. 492 vom 04.01.1989, PA-AA, B 28, ZA (Referat 212), Bd. 153432.

inform Gorbachev that neither the abolition of the minimum exchange rate nor the legalisation of Helsinki groups in the GDR would be implemented de facto.[27]

In a final attempt to bend the new resolutions in its favour, the East German delegation sparked a dispute within the German translation group in Vienna on 11 January 1989 by trying to obtain a weaker translation from the English. The GDR wished to see the English verb "consider" translated as prüfen ("examine") instead of the stronger in Erwägung ziehen ("take into consideration"). However, this attempt was prevented by referring a German-English dictionary produced in East Germany, which did not support that country's desired translation.[28]

Ultimately, the negotiations ended with a commitment to the abolition of CCE being included in two places in the Concluding Document. Under the heading "Co-operation in other areas" in the section "Co-operation in the field of economics, of science and technology and of the environment", the document pledged its signatories to "consider in a positive spirit the progressive phasing out, for foreign tourists, of minimum exchange requirements" and to "allow the reconversion of legally acquired local currency". In addition, in the provisions for "Human Contacts" in the "Co-operation in Humanitarian and Other Fields" section, that the participating states agreed to

> consider the scope for gradually reducing and eventually eliminating any requirement which might exist for travellers to obtain local currency in excess of actual expenditure, giving priority to persons travelling for the purpose of family meetings. They will accord such persons the opportunity in practice to bring in or to take out with them personal possessions or gifts.[29]

27 Selvage/Süß, *Staatssicherheit und KSZE-Prozess*, p. 644–647; Peter Steglich/Günter Leuschner, *KSZE – Fossil oder Hoffnung?*, Berlin 1996, p. 194–196.

28 Delegationsbericht Nr. 504 (B) vom 16.01.1989, PA-AA, B 28, ZA (Referat 212), Bd. 153432. It was at this point that, according to Peter Steglich, the conversation "at last turned embarrassing" for "the long-suffering East German diplomats in the Hofburg"; Steglich/Leuschner, *KSZE*, p. 197; Wrede, *KSZE in Wien*, p. 111.

29 Concluding Document of the Vienna Meeting 1986 of representatives of the participating states of the Conference on Security and Co-operation in Europe, held on the basis of the provisions of the final act relating to the follow-up to the conference. https://www.osce.org/files/f/documents/a/7/40881.pdf, accessed 22.10.2024, p. 21, p. 26.

3 The Debate after the Vienna Follow-up Meeting

As Kashlev had already been told, the SED leadership was not prepared to comply with the new agreements by abolishing CCE after the end of the Follow-up Meeting. Its argument was based on the premise that the laws of the sovereign participating states always took precedence over the documents of the CSCE. As a report on the results of the Follow-up Conference declared,

> Of decisive importance is the statement in the Vienna Concluding Document that each state determines its own internal order and that the implementation of the provisions of the Vienna Meeting takes place within the framework of its laws, regulations, practices and policies. This confirms the principle that the implementation of the provisions of the Vienna Concluding Document in national legislation will be carried out by the free sovereign decision of the participating states.[30]

In fact, however, the Concluding Document stipulated that the participating states should "ensure that their laws, regulations, practices and policies conform with their obligations under international law and are brought into harmony with the provisions of the Declaration on Principles and other CSCE commitments."[31] The GDR's interpretation thus deliberately ignored parts of the agreements reached in Vienna. It used this argument to counter any future criticism from the West that the Concluding Document had not been implemented.

Moreover, the SED's decision to amend the passage on CCE when publishing the Vienna Concluding Document in Neues Deutschland, the party's mouthpiece and the GDR's largest-circulation daily newspaper, also attracted a strong international response. Large parts of the final document were published in the issue of 21 January 1989. However, the original wording on CCE, "consider", was rendered as prüfen ("examine"), the translation unsuccessfully demanded by the GDR in Vienna.[32] In response to West German criticism the GDR had published a manipulated version of the Concluding Document, the head of

30 Anlage Nr. 3 zum Protokoll Nr. 4 der Sitzung des Politbüros des ZK der SED vom 24.1.1989, Bericht über Verlauf und Ergebnisse des Treffens der Außenminister der KSZE-Staaten zum Abschluss des Wiener Folgetreffens, BArch, DY 30/44286.

31 Concluding Document of the Vienna Meeting, p. 4; Selvage/Süß, *Staatssicherheit und KSZE-Prozess*, p. 645–646.

32 *Neues Deutschland*, 21./22.01.1989. The participating states had pledged themselves to publication in the Vienna Concluding Document.

the East German delegation, Peter Steglich, replied – in a conversation with an employee of the permanent mission of the Federal Republic in the GDR, undersecretary (Ministerialrat) Ernst-Jörg von Studnitz – that his delegation had agreed to the version used in Vienna only so as not to block the conclusion of the meeting. However, the GDR was still convinced that "consider" could also be translated as prüfen. Ultimately, "the text published in Neues Deutschland was the GDR's version of the Concluding Document."[33] The GDR's awkward manoeuvring over this matter was a result of its difficult situation. Since implementation of the Vienna agreements was out of the question, it felt it had no choice but to resort to this transparent stratagem. In his memoirs of the Follow-up Meeting, the deputy head of the GDR delegation, Hans Voß, described this behaviour as "not only unique in the history of the CSCE" but also as a "great folly".[34]

4 Conclusion

The analysis of the negotiations on a possible abolition of CCE at the inner-German border at the Vienna Follow-up Conference, which ultimately ended with the adoption of this demand in the Concluding Document, has revealed several aspects that characterised this debate throughout. For example, the tactically advantageous cooperation between West Germany and the neutrals was a constant influence felt throughout the conference, from the tabling of proposal WT.93 to the protection of West German interests in the various neutral non-papers and finally the Concluding Document. Analysis of the relevant archival sources leads to the conclusion that this proposal, or at least its more precise elaboration, originated not with the neutrals but rather in a West German initiative. Cooperation with the neutral states allowed the Bonn delegation to conduct negotiations on the abolition of CCE without being accused of pursuing its immediate national interest or adopting a strident tone vis-à-vis its Eastern counterpart.

---

33 Vermerk über ein Gespräch des Genossen Steglich, Abteilungsleiter im Bereich G/P, mit Herrn von Studnitz, Ministerialrat in der Ständigen Vertretung der BRD in der DDR, am 27. Januar 1989, PA-AA, M 21/286895.

34 Hans Voß, "Konstruktivität und Dilemma der DDR-Außenpolitik. Ein Bericht des stellvertretenden Delegationsleiters der DDR über das Wiener Folgetreffen des KSZE (1986–1989)", in: *1999. Zeitschrift für Sozialgeschichte des 20. und 21. Jahrhunderts* 8 (1993), issue 1, p. 91–99, on p. 98.

This attitude on the part of the West German diplomats, which they sustained throughout the Follow-up Meeting, also played a significant part in their success. The delegation avoided confrontation and polemics as far as possible. As a result, it left little room for attack from the East German diplomats, who were unable to exclude the debate on CCE from the Follow-up Meeting by accusing it of being a bilateral issue unfit for discussion in a multilateral forum. While both delegations were aware of the German-German dimension of the issue, the question of its treatment as a specifically German-German problem was another feature of this debate. The East German diplomats always addressed this fact openly, while the West German delegation would deny it at certain times, thereby guarding itself against criticism that it was turning the CSCE into a venue for *querelles allemandes*.

The success of this strategy was due not least to the GDR's increasing isolation. In the course of the Vienna Follow-up Meeting, its support within the Eastern alliance dwindled ever further, reaching the point of conflict between the GDR and its most important ally, the Soviet Union. Moreover, the SED found itself compelled to agree to more and more Western demands as the conference went on. With gritted teeth, it had to follow the new, more liberal course on which Gorbachev led Soviet foreign policy.

Four theses emerge from the present study. First, West Germany achieved a bilateral success within a multilateral framework. In Vienna, the Federal Republic succeeded in solving a bilateral problem in its favour by making it part of the multilateral CSCE process. By contrast, it would hardly have been possible to persuade the GDR to agree to a corresponding agreement in a bilateral setting. Moreover, Bonn benefited from the GDR's isolation within the Eastern alliance. Second, West Germany successfully deployed a strategy of conflict avoidance. Its delegation in Vienna practised restraint and avoided confrontation. This tactful approach towards the GDR on the part of the Federal Republic's diplomats and the efficient use of informal agreements with the Western and neutral states offered the East German delegation very little room for attack. This was important in maintaining the appearance that German-German disputes would not be discussed in Vienna, as the GDR repeatedly tried to exclude the debate from the multilateral conference as a bilateral conflict. Third, East Germany was isolated from its allies. Due to its increasing isolation within the Warsaw Pact, the GDR came under pressure from both East and West, which ultimately led to its agreeing to previously unacceptable concessions in the humanitarian field. Of fundamental importance for this change was Gorbachev's reform policy and the resulting rapprochement between the USSR and the West. At the end of the Vienna Follow-up Conference, the GDR had formally to agree to the abolition of CCE in order not to be the only participant to block the end of the conference.[35] Fourth, West Germany's cooperation with the neutral states was strategically adept. This gave its delegation tactical advantages over the GDR, which were highly relevant to the outcome of the Follow-up Meeting. The role of the N+N in supporting negotiation proposals bearing the Western imprint, not least by tabling proposals itself, was an important factor in the West's success.

It should also be stressed that this development was a novelty in relations between the two Germanies. In an assessment of the "Effects of the Vienna CSCE Follow-up Meeting on German-German Relations", an employee of the West German Federal Chancellery wrote on 15 February 1989 that whereas "the standard of human facilitation achieved in bilateral relations with the GDR generally" had previously "exceeded the CSCE's stipulations", "now, for the first time, the CSCE standard in various areas exceeds what has been achieved at the bilateral level".[36]

---

35 On the disintegration of the Eastern alliance in Vienna see Stefan Lehne, *The Vienna Meeting of the Conference on Security and Cooperation in Europe, 1986–1989. A Turning Point in East-West relations*, Boulder-San Francisco-Oxford 1991, p. 76–78.

36 Auswirkungen des Wiener KSZE-Folgetreffens auf die innerdeutschen Beziehungen vom 15.02.21989, BArch, B 136/20201.

Human Rights, the Vienna Follow-up Meeting, and Political Transformation in the Eastern Bloc

The Case of Poland

Wanda Jarząbek

1 Introduction

After the Second World War, the countries of Central and Eastern Europe were placed into the USSR's sphere of influence, which had drastic consequences for the conditions under which these societies had to function. Undemocratic political systems led to the restriction of human rights and the freedom of political and economic activity. Accordingly, more freedom and the restoration of democracy were among the principal demands of the anti-Communist opposition. In some countries, as in Poland, these aims also included the restoration of independence. In the late 1960s, a growing interest in economic as well as social contacts could be observed on both sides of the Iron Curtain. There was also a greater willingness to talk about slowing down the arms race and taking confidence-building measures to reduce the threat of armed conflict.

The Conference on Security and Cooperation in Europe (CSCE) was a product of this détente. After the Helsinki Final Act (1975), all states participating in the conference recognised the results as meeting their expectations to some extent. The formula for the talks worked well, no one felt the loser (which would have been psychologically disastrous), and everyone found reasons to continue the dialogue. There were also critics of Helsinki – including, for example, some of the political émigrés from Eastern bloc countries living the West, among them many Poles – who held that the CSCE was a confirmation of the existing division into blocs in Europe and thus a de facto recognition of the USSR's right to its sphere of influence.[1] This, they believed, perpetuated both the bloc system and the Communist regimes, making their liquidation more difficult. This view was shared by those observers of public life who considered Communism a criminal ideology by its very nature, directed against human rights and freedom, and feared that the CSCE would contribute to the gradual legitimisation of Communism as a political system of equal standing to democracy and to a renewed recognition of the USSR's sphere of influence.

1 Wanda Jarząbek, *Polska Rzeczpospolita Ludowa wobec polityki wschodniej Republiki Federalnej Niemiec w latach 1966–1976*, Warszawa 2011, p. 440–443.

DOI:10.1163/9789004736979_016

Although the CSCE seemingly confirmed the political status quo in Europe, the Final Act did in fact contain the potential to undermine Communist system. Much, however, depended on whether there would be the will to apply its provisions and whether the circumstances in which to do so would arise. Some effects of the Final Act were difficult to forecast, such as its impact on social activism in East and West.[2] The human rights issues of the time were multidimensional. In this chapter, I will concentrate on the question of the political rights negotiated at the Vienna Follow-up Meeting, especially their impact on the events of 1989 and the transition to democracy.[3]

2 The Problem of Human Rights In Poland before the Vienna Follow-up Meeting

The authorities of the People's Republic of Poland soon discovered that the provisions of the Final Act regarding the observance of basic human rights could be applied in practice. They were aware of a continuing lack of public support, even if some people were satisfied with the situation. Opposition to the Communist system had been a continuous phenomenon in Poland since 1944. The wave of protests in 1976 had mostly economic grounds but took place at nearly the same time as the protests against changes to the constitution, which would have enshrined the alliance with the USSR, the leading role of the Communist Party and special rights of the state in education and the activities of social organisations. Many participants in the protests were arrested, many lost their jobs. Various groups supporting the arrested emerged, as did groups demanding respect for civil and human rights. Independent trade unions were also formed. After the signing of the Final Act, some of the organisations ceased to operate clandestinely, others remained underground.[4] Some organisations began at that time, though not on a wide scale and not universally, to refer to the stipulations of the Helsinki Final Act: to freedom of

2 Daniel C. Thomas, *The Helsinki Effect: International Norms, Human Rights, and the Demise of Communism*, Princeton 2001; Sara B. Snyder, *Human Rights Activism and the End of the Cold War. A Transnational History of the Helsinki Network*, Cambridge-New York 2011.

3 Essential research for this article was done within the framework of the National Science Centre (Poland) project DEC-2022/45/B/HS3/00603.

4 Andrzej Anusz/Łukasz Perzyna, *Konfederacja. Rzecz o KPN*, Warszawa 2009; Andrzej Friszke, *Opozycja polityczna w PRL 1945–1980*, London 1994; Paweł Sasanka, *Czerwiec 1976. Geneza, przebieg, konsekwencje*, Warszawa 2006; Grzegorz Waligóra, *Ruch Obrony Praw Człowieka i Obywatela 1977–1981*, Warszawa 2006; Paweł Zaremba, *Młodopolacy*, Gdańsk 2000.

thought, the free exchange of ideas, the right to build social organisations. The question of political rights now came to be of great interest.

Standing up for human rights, however, was selective. A good example is the reaction of Western European countries to the anti-government protests in Poland in 1976, whose participants were treated brutally by the authorities. Yet the problem of freedom of expression and protest, including the persecution of those involved in the protests, were not the subject of discussions between Western European politicians and the authorities of the People's Republic of Poland. Western interventions were limited to issues affecting their citizens, such as mixed marriages and visas for journalists. The issues of the freedom to express political views or support for the Polish anti-communist opposition activists were not raised at all initially and only tentatively later. The exception among Western countries was the United States, and its policy indeed made a difference.[5] Reports of human rights violations began to be appear in the press and in 1977, after the wave of repression against the political opposition and striking workers in Poland, a hearing was held in the US Congress.[6] Soon the Polish opposition realised that the Final Act could be used to inform people in the West about the true nature of "real socialism". The creation of groups with names that included "Helsinki" – e.g. the Helsinki Commission in Poland as late as 1978 – was due to the fact that this name was recognisable in the West. The Belgrade Follow-up Meeting (1977–1978) had become a forum for discussing human rights violations, and the Polish opposition wanted to use the upcoming Madrid Follow-up Meeting (1980–1983) to provide more examples of human rights violations in Poland. The so-called Madrid Report could not be presented by one of its authors, Zbigniew Romaszewski of the Helsinki Commission, as the Communist authorities would not issue him a passport, but it was translated into English and sent to the delegations attending the conference.[7]

5 Breck Walker, "'Neither Shy or Demagogic' – The Carter Administration Goes to Belgrade", in: Vladislav Bilandžić/Dietmar Dahlmann/Milan Kosanović (eds.), *From Helsinki to Belgrade. The First CSCE Follow-up Meeting in Belgrade 1977/78*, Belgrade 2008, p. 207–230; Wanda Jarząbek, "Basket III provisions in the policies of France and the Federal Republic of Germany toward the Polish People's Republic (1975–1980): A Comparative Approach", in: Jakub Tyszkiewicz (ed.), *Human Rights and Political Dissent in Central Europe. Between the Helsinki Accords and the Fall of the Berlin Wall*, London-New York 2022, p. 39–52.

6 Wanda Jarząbek, *Hope and Reality: Poland and the Conference on Security and Cooperation in Europe, 1964–1989* (Cold War International History Project Working Paper Series Vol. 56), Washington 2008, p. 45–46.

7 *Raport o przestrzeganiu praw człowieka w Polsce*, Warszawa, Wydawnictwo 3 maja 1980. Przyg. Komisja Helsińska, translation: The Helsinki Committee, *Prologue to Gdansk. Report on the Observation of the Human and Civil Rights in the Polish People's Republic*, New York 1980.

After the rise of the Solidarity (Solidarność) trade union it turned out that the readiness to rise up was much greater than assumed, and observers began to believe that change in Poland might challenge the existing equilibrium in East-West relations. For this reason, at the government level, the first question concerned Solidarity's willingness to compromise, whether it was ready, in exchange for a certain degree of liberalisation – increasing the scope of freedom of speech, expanding the right of association – to accept the so-called political realities. This meant accepting the membership of Poland and other countries in the sphere of influence of the USSR, which was a Communist, totalitarian state. and this, in turn, meant asking whether Solidarity understood that the protection of human rights had therefore also to be limited, especially when it came to demands that implied domestic political change.[8] Solidarity's activities aroused great sympathy in Western societies, which was also of significance for the authorities of these countries. The imposition of martial law in Poland by the Communist authorities in December 1981 was aimed primarily at ending the growing movement, which publicised the problem of human rights violations in the Eastern bloc – including political, civil and labour rights – and demanded the democratisation of the political system. The situation was also dangerous for the USSR because it threatened the functioning of the Eastern bloc. After the end of martial law in July 1983, the domestic situation, including the economy, remained difficult.[9]

The authorities tried to stop uncontrolled social activism. They agreed to register various organisations but did not give permission for the re-registration of Solidarity (it had been a legal organisation since September 1980, signalling a break with the monopoly for groups allied with the Communist Party). In 1984, only one trade union centre, Ogólnopolskie Porozumienie Związków Zawodowych (OPZZ), was legalised and took over Solidarity's assets, e.g. its offices and equipment. An amendment to the Trade Union Act essentially eliminated the pluralism of trade unions. Some activists returned to clandestine activity, but Solidarity cadres were quite weakened, as one of the ways to get rid of

8 Helen Sjursen, *The United States, Western Europe and the Polish Crisis. International Relations in the Second Cold War*, Houndmills-Basingstoke 2003; the question of ability to self-limitation becomes a topic in L. Wałesa's talks with French politicians: Jarząbek, *Basket III*, p. 45–46.

9 Gunter Dehnert, "Entspannung gegen das Volk – Sanktionen für das Volk? Die Solidarność nach Ausrufung des Kriegsrechts und die Nachfolgekonferenz von Madrid", in: Matthias Peter/Hermann Wentker (eds.), *Die KSZE im Ost-West-Konflikt. Internationale Politik und gesellschaftliche Transformation 1975–1990* (Schriftenreihe der Vierteljahrshefte für Zeitgeschichte Sondernummer), München 2012, p. 249–266, on p. 249.

people who might challenge the system was to persuade them to leave Poland. Activists often received proposals to do while they were still interned.

The repressiveness of the state increased compared to the 1970s. Under a 1985 amendment to Poland's penal code, summary courts could bring defendants to trial 48 hours after arrest and could hand down prison sentences of up to three years. Defendants were not permitted to choose their own defence counsel but were assigned one by the court. In 1986 alone, some 400 people were sentenced in this way for their political activities.[10] The number of secret service officers grew, peaking in 1988. The authorities began to violate the secrecy of correspondence on a large scale. Previously, compared to other Eastern bloc countries, Poland had been quite liberal. Now a significant proportion of letters arrived with clear signs of having been opened and bearing the stamp "Item arrived damaged". It was made mandatory to pack parcels to be sent abroad at the post office, supervised by a customs officer. The wiretapping of telephone conversations became widespread, and militia were entitled to search private residences without a court order. Censorship increased, and academic freedom was severely curtailed by a law passed in 1982.

In contrast, especially after 1986, so-called "second circulation" or underground publications could in principle be sold at places of worship and universities without much harassment from the authorities. By contrast, foreign radio broadcasts, primarily Radio Free Europe and Voice of America, were jammed in order to minimise access to alternative sources of knowledge about the world and, above all, about events in Poland, Polish history and literature. Although the issuing of passports was formally liberalised, in practice there was even greater control than before. Some academics and people working in certain industries were not given permission to travel for fear that they would remain abroad. Workers' rights and human rights were violated on a wide scale, generally much more than in the period between 1956 and 1980. Also, it could be observed that the authorities were unwilling to cooperate with various organisations. For example, the authorities did not agree to a visit to Poland by a representative of the UN in 1983 to investigate the state of human rights and did not cooperate with the International Labour Organization. Foreign correspondents were frequently warned by Polish officials not to contact opposition figures. Surveillance of foreign correspondents by the secret service also increased, not least by means of an obligation to hire Polish staff as technical assistants.

10 According to the data passed by the Polish opposition to the US Congress and included to its Annual Report for 1986.

Information on violations of the Helsinki Final Act regularly featured in reports sent back to Western countries, especially the United States. Warsaw's diplomacy followed the reports and publications on these issues, but there was little readiness to change course.[11] Talks with American officers made it clear that the US was not going to stop speaking about violations or the individuals concerned (the "naming names" strategy), as this approach had proved its usefulness.[12]

3 The Authorities of the Polish People's Republic and the Vienna Follow-up Meeting

According to the routine existing in the Warsaw Pact, preparations for the upcoming meeting in Vienna took place within the bloc's structures, including a meeting of the Warsaw Pact countries' experts on the CSCE on 30 July 1986 and followed by a meeting of deputy foreign ministers on 2 September, both in Warsaw. These meetings made it clear that the individual countries wanted to present their own initiatives, not those coming from Moscow – even if they conflicted with the interests of other countries in the bloc (especially, but not exclusively, in the area of the human rights).[13] Some were aimed at the bloc's organisation, i.e. the Hungarian proposal to lay the groundwork for better contacts within the Eastern bloc and to remove border barriers. Hungary wanted minorities issues to be dealt more extensively; Bulgaria was opposed. So was Poland, due primarily to the question of the German minority.[14] In bilateral consultation before the Vienna Follow-up Meeting, Polish diplomats tried to prevent the West German side from discussing this question during the conference. Yet as Ekkehard Eickhoff, the leader of the German delegation, made clear, domestic considerations made it impossible not to raise this question, though he promised to do so in such a way as "not to attack Poland".[15] For its

11 Notatka w sprawie XX raportu prezydenta USA wraz z fragmentami raportu, 24.06.1986, Archiwum Ministerstwa Spraw Zagranicznych (AMSZ), DSiP, z. 26/93, w. 1.

12 Notatka informacyjna, 16.07.1986, AMSZ, DSiP, z. 26/93, w. 1.

13 Notatka informacyjna o naradzie ministrów spraw zagranicznych UW, 5.09.1986, AMSZ, DSiP, z. 26/93, w. 1.

14 In the case of Poland, this related to the growing number of citizens who declared themselves as belonging to the German minority. According to the government, many were simply looking for legal grounds to emigrate because of the poor economic situation and standard of living.

15 Quoted according to the Polish note from this conversation, Notatka informacyjna o konsultacjach z MSZ RFN, 27.08.1986, AMSZ, DSiP, z. 26/93, w. 1.

part, the Polish side regarded the way in which the questions of the German minority in Poland (which it described as an "alleged" minority) and family reunification were reported by the West German delegation as not objective, and the Polish foreign minister summoned the West German ambassador in Warsaw to voice his government's displeasure.[16]

As restrictions on human rights were severe at the time, both in Poland and the USSR, neither country wanted the implementation of the Final Act in the area of human rights and the structures to become the subject of intense talks. They preferred other topics – including confidence-building measures and disarmament – to dominate the meeting. These tactics had already been used at the Belgrade and Madrid Follow up-Conferences.[17] It was believed that the Western countries wanted to focus on human rights and were not in a hurry to push for progress in other areas because they believed that time was working in their favour and that the situation in the countries of the bloc would evolve towards concessions in this area.[18]

The Vienna talks were still ongoing when strikes began in Poland in the spring of 1988. Despite the dire economic situation, the government, misreading the collective mood, did not expect large-scale protests. This time the strikes were often organised by a younger generation of activists not always affiliated with Solidarity.[19] The protesters now also included students from several Polish universities. Although Solidarity remained the strongest opposition force, it was not the only one. Environmental and pacifist movements also sprang up, and some Solidarity activists, dissatisfied with what they felt to be the excessively cautious stance of the union's leadership, founded *Solidarność Walcząca* (Fighting Solidarity). The USSR entered into talks with some opposition activists in Poland, which was regarded as a form of pressure on the Polish government as well as on Solidarity as a whole. The Polish government itself then made attempts to talk not only with the striking workers but also with other anti-Communist opposition groups. The first meetings took place in August 1988, and a Round Table was planned for autumn before being postponed to February 1989. The question of more profound reforms became very pressing.

16 Notatka informacyjna T. Olechowskiego, 8.12.1986, AMSZ, DSiP, z. 26/93, w. 1.

17 Notatka informacyjna o naradzie ministrów spraw zagranicznych UW, 5.09.1986, AMSZ, DSiP, z. 26/93, w. 1.

18 Notatka informacyjna o przebiegu i rezultatach III sesji spotkania wiedeńskiego KBWE oraz rozmów 23 państw UW i NATO w sprawie broni konwencjonalnej, 3.08.1987, AMSZ, DSiP, z. 26/93, w. 1.

19 On the changes in Poland: Antoni Dudek, *Reglamentowana rewolucja. Rozkład dyktatury komunistycznej w Polsce 1988–1990*, Kraków 2004.

Nearly at the same time, the Eastern bloc countries agreed to accept the Final Document of the Vienna Follow-up Conference and with it an expanded catalogue of commitments on the flow of information and civil liberties. According to the Polish report, the Soviet Union – under widespread pressure, including from within the bloc – finally agreed to change its stance on the flow of information. In Poland, the flow of information was no longer a very important question for the authorities, as access to alternative sources of information had recently increased and, being difficult to suppress, was accepted as an existing fact. Yet the law remained a barrier for independent publishers and was sometimes enforced, and state media remained closed to dissident voices. A big problem for the Polish authorities was the pluralism of organisations in general and, after the legalisation of Solidarity, of trade unions in particular.

Various Polish ministries were consulted on the act's final draft, which met with little enthusiasm from the director of the investigation Department in the ministry of the interior, who was opined that the activities of the Polish delegation as well as those of other Eastern bloc countries had been "not optimal", for instance in accepting a definition of human rights that matched the "Western" model of democracy. What is interesting is that the director of Department I (intelligence) had no remarks to make on the draft document.[20] He probably was able to understand the spirit of the times. The foreign ministry found the changes to be necessary, perceiving them as a symbol of the ongoing rapprochement between East and West in the field of human rights as well as signalling agreement in the fields of disarmament and trade.[21]

The Polish delegation stressed the importance of creating a new mechanism for cooperation in the field of human rights protection and the expansion of the range of problems to be observed and evaluated. Another point concerned the scheduling of meetings, for example a meeting on the mandatory exchange of information and more meetings on human rights, which later took place in Paris, Copenhagen and Moscow. Much attention was paid to details concerning easing the flow of information. That included, among other things, the removal of legal restrictions on tuning into Western radio stations, an end to jamming broadcasts (which the Polish authorities had already stopped doing earlier) at the beginning of 1989, and the permission for more live broadcasts on television from other countries, which was to promote freedom of expression and to make the role of censorship more difficult. The

20 Exchange of views between ministries, Archiwum Instytutu Pamięci Narodowej (Archiwum IPN), MSW II 1820.

21 Notatka informacyjna: Spotkanie wiedeńskie, T. Olechowski, 25.01.1989, AMSZ, z. 29, w. 174, t. 2109.

Polish foreign minister, in an evaluation note on the results of Vienna, wrote that the arrangements were favourable from the point of view of Poland, creating a good climate for internal reform. It was hoped that they made it possible to reactivate relations with the West. The next step was to prepare a list of tasks for the government to be carried out in connection with the adoption of the Final Document.[22]

With regard to the problems related to principle VII and Basket III discussed in this chapter, the issue of Poland's accession to multilateral agreements on human rights needs to be examined first of all. Among the models considered by the government were the Optional Protocol to the International Covenant on Civil and Political Rights and the UN Conventions on the Prohibition of Hostage-taking and on Refugees. The ministries involved recommended revising existing legislation to align with the Final Act, including the right to a lawyer from the moment of arrest in case of provisions on criminal proceedings, to transfer all rights related to detentions to the common judiciary (any special proceedings), to limit the application of the death penalty and to review provisions on the rights of national minorities. Work on a new law of association was ongoing at that time in Poland, albeit slowly, and it was recommended that it should include, among other points, the possibility to create organisations devoted to human rights. The security services stressed that the Final Act's stipulations should include changes in passport regulations, guarantees for the secrecy of correspondence and other communications, and a prohibition on confiscating foreign printed material.[23]

At a meeting on 20 February 1989, the Polish government adopted guidelines on how to implement the Final Act's provisions. These guidelines provided for several important changes in domestic legislation, including a reformed press law, the liberalisation of the rules for allotting paper to non-state publishers (a de facto legalisation of the so called "second circulation" press) and the lifting of restrictions on books and journals imported from abroad. In the case of Poland, this was of great importance even for books in Polish, since Polish émigrés of various factions had established several publishing houses in Western countries and these publications could not previously be legally sold in Poland. There were no plans to abolish censorship, but its role was to be limited to matters relating to state and military secrets. Also liberalised was the ownership of what were then the latest means of communication. It was no

22 Wnioski i zobowiązania wynikające dla Polski z Dokumentu Końcowego Spotkania Wiedeńskiego KBWE, 08.02.1989, AMSZ, z. 29, w.174, t. 2109.

23 Ibid.

longer necessary to obtain permission to own satellite dishes or fax machines, although their owners were subject to registration.[24]

The determination of the West (including neutral countries) to put pressure on the USSR with regard to human rights had visibly increased during the Vienna Follow-up Meeting. But this was already a different USSR and a different Eastern bloc – it was losing the arms race, sinking into economic crisis, unable to modernise its economies by own efforts and in debt to Western countries. If the bloc was not yet on the edge of disintegration, its Communist elites certainly recognised the need for internal reforms if they were to retain power. Social processes that had long been unfolding in certain Warsaw Pact countries – especially in Poland, Hungary and Czechoslovakia – soon came to fruition, leading to a rejection of the Communist system in favour of democracy.

4 Conclusion

Transformation in the Eastern bloc countries was not the result solely of the CSCE. Many factors contributed to the ultimate collapse of the bloc, including, first and foremost, the economic inefficiency of USSR, the fact that Moscow lost the arms race and was forced to change its policy. But domestic conditions in the various countries of the bloc, their political and cultural traditions, were also very important. The Soviet bloc was not a monolith. The countries whose political and cultural traditions differed from those of the USSR – above all Czechoslovakia, Hungary and Poland – and in which people still remembered a time before Communism were less inclined to believe official propaganda, not least because they also had increasing access to other information. Communism failed to gain sufficient social legitimacy in these states, where a strong tendency to reject Communism manifested itself in, among other things, the emergence of a fairly well-organised opposition. It should not be forgotten that the initial goal of the CSCE had not been regime change in Eastern Europe and the dissolution of existing spheres of influence but rather rapprochement between the blocs. Might rapprochement itself have led to regime change, to democratisation, to the abolition of spheres of influence, which (incidentally) many politicians did not consider to be bad in themselves? This seems unlikely, which is why anti-Communist social activity and protests should not be downplayed. They played a very important role in forcing the authorities to liberalise or to some degree deviate from certain regulations in the post-1945 period.

24 Notatka informacyjna o kierunkach realizacji przez Polskę postanowień spotkania wiedeńskiego KBWE w dziedzinie informacji, 15.03.1989, AMSZ, z. 29, w.174, t. 2109.

Public protests showed an unwillingness to continue with real socialism and a desire to change it or to reject it altogether. Social protests also changed Western attitudes toward the bloc and influenced politicians' decisions. The CSCE might have become a tool for top-down change in the East-West system, but it seems that it became primarily a tool for bottom-up changes by creating better conditions for opposition movements. Economic decline, growing social discontent and the weakening of the Communist authorities were ultimately seized upon by Western political elites and contributed, among other factors, to the collapse of the Eastern bloc and the USSR.

The significance of the CSCE process for the political transition was that it created a catalogue of human rights commitments which implicitly supported the activities of anti-system groups in the Eastern bloc. Their emergence and activities provided Western politicians with arguments to raise when discussing problems of access to information, the right to express political views and dissatisfaction, and the expansion of political rights with Eastern bloc governments. The Vienna Follow-up Meeting preceded the so-called Autumn of Nations and the disintegration of the Eastern bloc. The proximity of these events may influence assessments of the Follow-up Meeting's significance to their unfolding. This influence cannot be completely negated, but nor should it be overstated, especially in case of Poland. The struggle against the Communist system had been ongoing since its inception and was supported by the Catholic Church, which enjoyed great authority. Communism was widely regarded as a tool of Russian expansionism in its new guise, rejected by much of the population as promoting alien values and an unattractive economic system.

Due to a combination of several factors, the CSCE became a facilitator and, in a sense, an accelerator of anti-Communist processes in the Eastern bloc, but I do not think that it can be regarded as having initiated them. But the commitments contained in the Helsinki Final Act and the Vienna Final Concluding Document, including the projected next steps (implemented in Paris and Copenhagen), were important for the democratisation of domestic life in countries that had liberated themselves from Soviet domination and for the spread of new human rights standards throughout the European continent.

The Vienna CSCE Follow-up Meeting and Czechoslovakia

Miroslav Kunštát

1 Introduction

A synthesis of the foreign policy of Communist Czechoslovakia in the period from 1985 to 1990 – the years of so-called perestroika and its cautious Czechoslovak adaptation – has yet to be written.[1] However, studies of individual aspects, together with the published memoirs of some of the key actors involved, confirm that the years directly preceding the collapse of the Communist regimes witnessed a widening scope for individual Warsaw Pact countries to set their own policies and priorities.[2] In the Czechoslovak case, this is evident both in bilateral relations with certain neighbouring states, especially in the West (West Germany, Austria),[3] and in important multilateral forums – including, from 1986 to 1989, the Vienna CSCE Follow-up Meeting. This amended, rather low-key approach, in tandem with a palpable generational shift and the increasing professionalisation of the Czechoslovak foreign service (the previous foreign minister, Bohuslav Chňoupek, was replaced by the pragmatic career diplomat Jaromír Johanes in October 1988), is also reflected in Communist Czechoslovakia's last official outline of its foreign policy, dating from the end of May 1989.[4]

---

1 Unfortunately, the relevant archive holdings from this period (especially in the Archiv Ministerstva zahraničních věcí České republiky [Archive of the Ministry of Foreign Affairs of the Czech Republic in Prague, AMZV Prague]) have been only partially inventoried and therefore are available only to a limited extent. Previously untranslated sources in this text were translated.

2 The penultimate Communist prime minister, Lubomír Štrougal, mentions, for example, the repeated demands (ignored by the Soviet side until 1990) made by Gustáv Husák, the Czechoslovak president and general secretary of the KSČ, to Mikhail Gorbachev, finally to withdraw Soviet troops from Czechoslovakia in accordance with the Moscow Memorandum of August 1968 because the situation in the country had long been "consolidated"; see Lubomír Štrougal, *Paměti a úvahy* [Memories and Reflections], Praha 2009, p. 281–283.

3 Miroslav Kunštát/Tomáš Vilímek, "Die deutsch-tschechoslowakischen Beziehungen im Zeichen der Perestroika", in: Edita Ivaničková/Miloš Řezník/Volker Zimmermann (eds.), *Das Jahr 1989 im deutsch-tschechisch-slowakischen Kontext*, Essen 2013, p. 117–150; Miroslav Kunštát, "Die Tschechoslowakei und Österreich vor dem Umbruch 1989/90", in: Andrea Brait/Michael Gehler (eds.), *Grenzöffnung 1989. Innen- und Außenperspektiven und die Folgen für Österreich*, Wien et al. 2014, p. 367–384.

4 Fond Porady kolegia ministra [Consultations of the College of Ministers], AMZV Prague, Sign. V/7-KM 1953–89, Inv. No. 914, 917. See Jindřich Dejmek, *Diplomacie Československa. Nástin*

 | DOI:10.1163/9789004736979_017

The Czechoslovak leadership wanted to shift the existing modus vivendi between East and West towards a new quality of relations based on closer cooperation, particularly – and despite continuing systemic competition – in the areas of trade, science and technology. At the Vienna Meeting, however, the Czechoslovak delegation took a particularly cautious and defensive approach to the issues of the so-called Third Basket (i.e. humanitarian issues), which is not surprising given the systematic human rights violations in Czechoslovakia in the 1970s and 1980s. Yet under pressure from the West, including some neutral states – and, as negotiations proceeded, also from the Soviet Union and some other socialist states (Poland, Hungary) – it was prepared to make compromises in this area at the end of the Vienna Meeting. However, the multi-stage consultation and control mechanism on the human dimension agreed in Vienna led to its activation in the case of Czechoslovakia immediately after the conclusion of the Vienna Meeting, in response to the behaviour of the Czechoslovak police and authorities towards the demonstrators on Wenceslas Square in Prague during the so-called "Palach Week" (15–21 January 1989). The police cracked down very harshly at the time, arresting up to 1,000 people, including the dissident and later president, Václav Havel. The Netherlands, France, the United States, Sweden and Austria deployed the first stage of the mechanism in the run-up to the subsequent Paris Conference on the Human Dimension (May/June 1989).[5] These immediate consequences of the Vienna Meeting also indicate that the relationship between perestroika-era Czechoslovakia and this phase of the Helsinki Process was necessarily ambivalent. The following brief analysis outlines which priorities the Czechoslovak delegation tried to push through during the Vienna Meeting within the framework of its negotiating mandate, how it reacted to the development of the negotiations in individual areas ("baskets") and which compromise solutions it was ultimately prepared to accept.

dějin ministerstva zahraničních věcí a diplomacie 1918–1992 [Czechoslovak Diplomacy. An outline of the history of the foreign ministry and the foreign service], VOL. I, Praha 2012, p. 224–229.

5 The demonstrations took place on the twentieth anniversary of the self-immolation of the student Jan Palach as a desperate protest against the Soviet occupation. See: Jana Starek, "Das Ringen um die Einhaltung der Menschenrechte in der Tschechoslowakei und die solidarische Haltung Österreichs zur Zeit der Folgetreffen der Konferenz für Sicherheit und Zusammenarbeit (KSZE)", in: Hildegard Schmoller/Miroslav Kunštát/Monika Březinová (eds.), *Vom 20. Jahrhundert ins neue Jahrtausend. Österreich und die Tschechoslowakei/Tschechien 1986–2016*, Wien 2022, p. 21–58, on p. 46–47.

2 Official Czechoslovak Diplomacy at the Vienna Meeting – a Difficult Mission

The most important priorities of the Czechoslovak government in the CSCE process in the second half of the 1980s were formulated in the directive "Orientation of Czechoslovak foreign policy and important contact formats". Revised each year, it was drawn up by the foreign ministry, subsequently approved by the presidium of the Central Committee (CC) of the Communist Party of Czechoslovakia (Komunistická strana Československa, KSČ) and finally by the government.[6] In January 1984, this guideline still contained rigid and strongly defensive phrasings expressive of a deep wariness. For example, it proposed "significantly to reduce" political relations with countries – particularly the West Germany, the United Kingdom and Italy – that had agreed to the deployment of medium-range missiles on their territory. The CSCE mechanism itself received a positive assessment because it "is currently – alongside the UN bodies – the only functioning international forum for the continuation of dialogue between East and West". In the run-up to the planned CSCE meeting of experts on human rights and fundamental freedoms in Ottawa (June 1984), the elaboration of a detailed "socialist conception of human rights protection" and the active struggle against the "bourgeois view of and Western approach to" this issue were called for.[7] The supposed danger of "ideological diversion" was also raised in connection with the planned CSCE Cultural Forum in Budapest (October/November 1985). Against the background of the concept of a "common European culture", Western states were accused of creating the conditions for the disruption of Europe's political realities and of fomenting "political-ideological diversion" in the socialist states.[8] However, this rather wary stance was not consistently maintained. Around the same time, in January 1985, government officials in Prague were gratified to note that their Western counterparts at bilateral meetings or in multilateral forums supposedly no longer raised "confrontational issues, including the traditional "disregard" for human rights in the Czechoslovak Socialist Republic and in the socialist countries", instead speaking out in favour of dialogue. However, the same directive (1985) repeatedly warned that the West would not abandon a

6 Zaměření československé zahraniční politiky a hlavní stykové akce [Orientation of Czechoslovak foreign policy and important contact formats], AMZV Prague, ZPO-T, 1984, 1985–86, 1987–1989, Inv. No. 4–7.

7 Zaměření československé zahraniční politiky a hlavní stykové akce v roce 1984 [Orientation of Czechoslovak foreign policy and important contact formats in 1984], AMZV Prague, ZPO-T, 1984, 1985–86, 1987–1989, Inv. No. 4.

8 Ibid., Inv. No. 5–6.

"policy of differentiation towards the countries of the socialist community" in order to drive a wedge between the individual socialist countries and the USSR.[9] In the following two years, however, the concept of a "policy of differentiation" was also adopted by Prague and applied to Western countries, with the directive calling for the expansion of cooperation with social democratic and socialist parties in particular and explicitly referring to "useful contacts with representatives of progressive forces, including the SPD [Social Democratic Party of Germany]". Gradually, Prague also adopted the vocabulary of Soviet perestroika and repeatedly emphasised that "the innovative approach of the Soviet Communists [...] is also inspiring for our activities." In connection with the meeting of the foreign ministers of the Warsaw Pact countries in Bucharest in October 1986, however, it was noted that the mutual coordination of the positions of the member states in the run-up to the Vienna Meeting was not easy, with Prague criticising the positions of Hungary and Romania in particular.[10]

The most important topics presented by the Czechoslovak delegation in the individual rounds of the Vienna Meeting negotiations or relating specifically to Czechoslovakia (especially as the subject of criticism from Western countries in the context of the implementation debates in the Third Basket) can be summarised in the following points:

1. In the area of the First Basket (military and security issues), the main issue was the "Czechoslovak initiative to create a zone of trust, cooperation and good neighbourly relations along the line of contact between the Warsaw Pact and NATO". This project was based on the earlier or parallel initiatives of the East German ruling party, the Socialist Unity Party of Germany (SED), and the SPD, i.e. the proposal for a chemical weapons-free zone in Europe (to which the GDR subsequently added a nuclear weapons-free corridor in Central Europe), later also supported by the KSČ and hence by Czechoslovakia. On the fringes of the disarmament conference in Geneva, there were repeated – albeit ultimately unsuccessful – consultations between the official delegations of the two Germanies and of Czechoslovakia on this topic from 1988 onwards. As late as 1989, this initiative – as an "unequivocal peace offensive" – was mentioned at almost every meeting of Czechoslovak and East German

9 Ibid., Inv. No. 6.

10 Vyhodnocení "Zaměření československé zahraniční politiky a hlavních stykových akcí v roce 1986" [Evaluation of the "Orientation of Czechoslovak foreign policy and important contact formats in 1986"], n.d., probably January 1987, AMZV Prague, ZPO-T, 1984, 1985–86, 1987–1989, Inv. No. 7.

politicians. It was intended to symbolise the harmony between the two states not only in Geneva and Vienna but also after the conclusion of the Vienna Meeting, for instance during Erich Honecker's visit to Prague in May 1989. However, the "Czechoslovak Initiative" was fully elaborated and approved by the presidium of the CC of the KSČ and by the government only after the conclusion of the Vienna Meeting in February 1989. From today's perspective, the terminology used seems more striking than the concrete measures proposed. The Prague government regarded the initiative not only as "Czechoslovakia's concrete contribution to the realisation of the idea of a common European home" but as nothing less than "the building block of a common European identity" in need of further cultivation.[11]

2. In the area of the Second Basket, Czechoslovakia sought support for its prestige project, the "CSCE Economic Forum", which it intended to hold in Prague. The evaluation report for 1987 states that the Czechoslovak delegation in Vienna was confronted with attempts "to impede progress in the military, security and economic fields by making concessions in the humanitarian dimension."[12] Prague then tried to "shift" a substantial part of the issues that were uncomfortable for Czechoslovakia (persecution of dissidents, restriction of religious freedom, etc.) to a conference on humanitarian cooperation in Moscow proposed by the Soviet Union. However, West Germany also sought to organise the Economic Forum, with Chancellor Helmut Kohl having already proposed the convening of a CSCE economic conference in May 1986 at the Interparliamentary Conference on Security and Cooperation in Europe.[13]

Given the strength of West Germany's negotiating position at the Vienna Meeting, it is not surprising that Bonn ended up being chosen as the venue for the Economic Forum. Prague's attempts to find a compromise solution with the

11 Ibid., Inv. No. 7. See also the minutes of the conversation between Miloš Jakeš and Erich Honecker on 3 May 1989 in Prague, Stiftung Archiv der Parteien und Massenorganisationen der DDR im Bundesarchiv (SAPMO-BArch), Büro Erich Honecker, DY/30/2439; Dokumenty k československé zahraniční politice [Documents on Czechoslovak Foreign Policy], vol. 36 (1989), p. 360–369.

12 Vyhodnocení "Zaměření československé zahraniční politiky a hlavních stykových akcí v roce 1987" [Evaluation of the "Orientation of Czechoslovak foreign policy and important contact formats in 1987"], n.d., probably January 1988, AMZV Prague, ZPO-T, Inv. No. 7.

13 Helmut Kohl, "Rede zur Eröffnung der VI. Interparlamentarischen KSZE-Konferenz am 26.5.1986 in Bonn", in: *Bulletin des Presse- und Informationsamts der Bundesregierung 1986*, Bonn 1986, p. 496–501, on p. 501. See also Ralf Roloff, *Auf dem Weg zur Neuordnung Europas. Die Regierungen Kohl/Genscher und die KSZE-Politik der Bundesrepublik Deutschland von 1986 bis 1992*, Vierow b. Greifswald 1995, p. 179–186.

West German government (i.e. to hold at least part of the forum in Prague) were unsuccessful. In Prague's view, despite the Soviet Union's support for the Czechoslovak proposals, the decisive factor was American ingratitude. According to the Czechoslovak ambassador in Vienna, Marek Venuta, the United States suspected the Prague initiative of being a clandestine attempt to "facilitate the transfer of cutting-edge Western technology to the socialist states."[14]

3. Negotiations on the Third Basket were particularly difficult for the Czechoslovak delegation. Western criticism of human and civil rights violations in Czechoslovakia – and thus of repeated breaches of the CSCE Final Act – was justified and, above all, well-founded. The Prague regime hoped that the West would be content with cosmetic changes and for a long time blocked even those passages of the Concluding Document (or even some Soviet compromise proposals) that other socialist states had ultimately agreed to, particularly in the area of controlling the right to religious freedom. It was only after an urgent telephone conversation between the Soviet foreign minister, Eduard Shevardnadze, and his Czechoslovak counterpart Bohuslav Chňoupek on 19 May 1988 that Prague changed its position.[15] On the question of religious freedom, Prague stubbornly rejected formulations "that would give the Vatican the exclusive right to appoint bishops or other religious personnel" and demanded a direct link between the rights of religious communities and the need to comply with the constitutional framework. In the course of negotiations on this issue, Czechoslovakia became completely isolated, but in the end agreed to a compromise text that also took into account national legislation.[16]

A new element in the Czechoslovak proposals in negotiations at the Vienna Meeting was the postulate of "people's diplomacy", which was striking from a domestic policy perspective in particular. The mass organisations of the Czechoslovak National Front, including its four nominally non-communist

14 Vyhodnocení "Zaměření československé zahraniční politiky a hlavních stykových akcí v roce 1987", AMZV Prague, ZPO-T, Inv. No. 7. See also Information from the Czechoslovak ambassador in Vienna, Marek Venuta, for the foreign minister's consultation on the fourth round of negotiations at the VFM, Vienna, 31 March 1988, AMZV Prague, ZPO-T, Inv. No. 18.

15 Information on the telephone conversation between Bohuslav Chňoupek and Eduard Shevardnadze, AMZV Prague, ZPO-T, Inv. No. 7, Inv. No. 18; On the personal relationship between Chňoupek and Shevardnadze, see also Bohuš Chňoupek, *Memoáre in claris* [Memoirs in claris], Bratislava 1998, p. 87–90.

16 Informace o 5. kole jednání Vídeňské následné schůzky pro kolegium ministra zahraničí, 05.04.1988 [Information on the fifth round of negotiations of the Vienna Follow-up Meeting for the College of the Minister of Foreign Affairs, 05.04.1988], AMZV Prague, Porady kolegia 1953–1989 [Consultations of the College 1953–1989], Sign. KM-020/88.

member parties, were to be invited to participate in shaping Czechoslovak foreign policy, especially in European affairs, using contacts with their "natural partners" in the West. In the case of the Christian-orientated Czechoslovak People's Party, for example, this would have meant reviving contacts with the Austrian People's Party (ÖVP) and the German Christian Democratic Union (CDU) as well as its Bavarian sister party, the Christian Social Union (CSU), contacts which had been tentatively established at the time of the Prague Spring of 1968.[17]

During the negotiations in the Third Basket, Prague criticised pro foro interno the poor and sometimes completely lacking coordination between the individual Warsaw Pact states. These states indeed did not act as a monolithic bloc in Vienna, as had been the case in earlier phases of the CSCE process. Informal mechanisms, such as the meetings of the heads of delegation and ambassadors of the Warsaw Pact states in Austria, rather served the purpose of exchanging information. A degree of closer coordination did exist, above all between Czechoslovakia, the Soviet Union and the GDR. There was mutual support, particularly in the area of East-West travel (family visits, family reunification, abolition of exit visas, compulsory currency exchange for Western visitors to socialist states, etc.). However, there were also differences in the countries' approaches to this issue. While Czechoslovakia wanted to facilitate travel opportunities for its citizens to the "capitalist West" as quickly as possible, the GDR took a different line. The GDR observed the measures introduced by Prague at the beginning of 1988 – the private foreign currency accounts of Czechoslovak citizens could also be used, de facto without restriction, for individual travel to other Western countries from 1 April 1988 – with some concern. There were also complaints about the lack of information.[18]

3 The Vienna Meeting and the Czechoslovak Dissidents

The Vienna Follow-up Meeting provided several impulses and suggestions for the unofficial human rights organisations and initiatives in the Communist

17 Zaměření československé zahraniční politiky a hlavní stykové akce v roce 1988 [Orientation of Czechoslovak foreign policy and important contact formats in 1988], AMZV Prague, Porady kolegia 1953–1989, Inv. No. 18.

18 See here the information "Valuta-Konten für die CSSR-Bürger" (for internal circulation only), 21 January 1988, BArch, DC 900, Allgemeiner Deutscher Nachrichtendienst (ADN), No. 2204001; internal party statement by Alexander Schalck-Golodkowski to Politburo member and Secretary of the Central Committee of the SED Günter Mittag, 27 January 1988, SAPMO-BArch, Büro Günter Mittag, DY/30/3196.

states of Eastern Europe. In Czechoslovakia, the most prominent such group was Charter 77, founded in 1977. Since the humanitarian dimension was to become an important part of the Follow-up Meeting's agenda, Czechoslovak human rights campaigners (including Václav Havel, Václav Benda, Jaroslav Šabata and Jiří Dienstbier) had already been involved, in the run-up to the Vienna Meeting, in drafting the "Milan Appeal". This appeal, formulated as a "suggestion package" for the Vienna Meeting, was adopted at the International Peace Forum in Milan in May 1986. The Prague Supplement to the Milan Appeal identified a certain crisis in the Helsinki process (including its "hegemonisation" by the two major powers) and called for the formation of a cross-bloc "European democratic community" in the spirit of the earlier "Prague Appeal of Charter 77". This included an explicit appreciation of the new party programme of the Communist Party of the Soviet Union (CPSU), particularly its foreign policy articles.[19]

Charter 77 also sent a moderately optimistic message of greeting to the opening of the Vienna Meeting,[20] in line with documents drawn up in parallel by other Czechoslovak exile organisations. A joint Czechoslovak-Polish memorandum was drafted on the occasion by The Council of Free Czechoslovakia, together with the Polish "government-in-exile". Eighteen Czech and Slovak groups sent another petition to Vienna, demanding that Charter 77 be "upgraded" to an independent control and monitoring body of the CSCE in the field of human rights, etc.[21] The letter of 25 September 1987 from Charter 77 spokespersons Jan Litomiský, Libuše Šilhánová and Jan Vohryzek to the delegates of the Vienna Meeting acknowledged the interest in and commitment to human rights issues on the part of several delegations and the consideration already given to the numerous proposals made by non-governmental organisations (NGOs), including the Charter 77 signatories. Charter 77 supported the Soviet proposal to organise an international forum on humanitarian issues

19 Blanka Císařovská/Vilém Prečan, *Charta 77 – Dokumenty 1977–1989* [Charter 77 – Documents 1977–1989], Vol. 2, Praha 2007, doc. D333, p. 768–774. On the "Prague Appeal of Charter 77" see also Tomáš Vilímek, *Solidarita napříč hranicemi. Opozice v ČSSR a NDR po roce 1968* [Solidarity across the border. The post-1968 opposition in Czechoslovakia and the GDR], Praha 2010, p. 226–240.

20 Ibid., doc. D352, p. 805–806.

21 *Americké listy* 46 (1986); *Nový domov* 37 (1986), issue 24. See "Rada svobodného Československa a československé organizace na vídeňském zasedání KBSE v Evropě" [Council of Free Czechoslovakia and the Czechoslovak Organisations at the Vienna CSCE Meeting in Europe], in: *Rada svobodného Československa* [Council of Free Czechoslovakia], Toronto 1990, p. 142–145; Francis D. Raška, *Fighting Communism from Afar. The Council of Free Czechoslovakia, Boulder*, CO 2008, p. 173–175.

and aspects in Moscow – subject, of course, to the forum being open to NGOs (including Soviet ones) "that are seriously concerned with these issues".[22]

Charter 77 also sent the Czechoslovak government and the Vienna Meeting delegations very specific and detailed proposals on various parts of the Concluding Document of the Vienna Meeting, including a proposal for the improved protection of minorities drawn up by *Výbor pro ochranu práv maďarské menšiny* (Committee for the Protection of the Rights of the Hungarian Minority) with the participation of Charter 77.[23] In their "Call for Solidarity with the Romanian People" (2 January 1988), Stanislav Devátý, Miloš Hájek and Bohumír Janát (the Charter 77 spokespersons at the time) appealed to the Vienna Meeting delegates and the European public to draw attention to the catastrophic social and political situation of the Romanian people under Nicolae Ceaușescu's regime.[24] However, repeated direct and indirect references to the Vienna Meeting appear in other documents of Charter 77 and other citizens' initiatives as a topical reference and legitimising motif, e.g. in the extensive declaration of 1 December 1988 on the fortieth anniversary of the United Nations (UN) Charter of Human Rights.[25] A letter of 17 January 1989 to the states and delegations participating in the Vienna Meeting drew attention to the extreme contrast between the provisions of the Concluding Document adopted close to that date and the demonstrations in Prague that were being forcibly suppressed by the police – demonstrations which, as already mentioned, marked the twentieth anniversary of the self-immolation of the Prague student Jan Palach. Human rights activists such as Dana Němcová, Saša Vondra and Václav Havel were arrested in the course of these events.[26] On 10 February 1989, Charter 77 and the Czechoslovak Helsinki Committee formulated a joint statement on the Concluding Document of the Vienna Meeting, highlighting the contradiction between the official statements of the Czechoslovak delegation (the "constructive" speech by the foreign minister, Jaromír Johanes) and the previous practice of the Czechoslovak authorities. Yet the statement also proclaimed a fundamental willingness to cooperate and participate in the implementation of the CSCE decisions, including with organs of the Czechoslovak state.[27]

---

22 Císařovská/Prečan, *Charta 77*, doc. D414, p. 922–923.

23 Ibid., doc. D.435, p. 962–964; *Listy* 18 (1988), issue 1, p. 82–83.

24 Císařovská/Prečan, *Charta 77*, doc. D422, p. 971–972; Vilém Prečan, *Charta 77. 1977–1989. Od morální k demokratické revoluci* [Charter 77. From moral to democratic revolution], Scheinfeld-Schwarzenberg-Bratislava 1990, p. 331–332.

25 Císařovská/Prečan, *Charta 77*, doc. D504, p. 1054–1056.

26 Ibid., doc. D515, p. 1068–1070.

27 Ibid., doc. D521, p. 1080–1081; Československý helsinský výbor [Czechoslovak Helsinki Committee], *Stanoviska a dokumenty* [Statements and Documents], Vol.1, Praha 1992, p. 5–8.

In connection with subsequent attempts (after the "bad" experiences with the aforementioned mass demonstrations in Prague) to place further legal restrictions on freedom of assembly, other documents and related initiatives were produced that referred to the resolutions of the Vienna Meeting and the specific articles of the Vienna Final Document (especially Article 13). These included the joint letter of Charter 77, České děti (Czech Children), Demokratická iniciativa (Democratic Initiative, which had already been founded as a "political party" in 1988), Polsko-československá Solidarita (Polish-Czechoslovak Solidarity) and others to the governments participating in the Vienna Meeting.[28] The contradiction between the existing practice of Czechoslovak human rights policy and the commitments made in Vienna was analysed in more detail in the joint letter of 5 May 1989 from three Czechoslovak human rights organisations to the participants of the Paris CSCE conference on the humanitarian dimension.[29] However, the authorities prevented the participation of Czechoslovak NGO representatives Zdeněk Jičínský, Radim Palouš and Michael Dymáček in the first session of the conference.[30] Until the start of the "Velvet Revolution" in the second half of November 1989, the Concluding Document of the Vienna Meeting and other CSCE decisions in the humanitarian field were constantly invoked both by active critics of the regime and by increasingly vocal citizens from the so-called "grey zone" as well as in society at large.

4 Conclusion

At least outwardly, the Prague regime repeatedly expressed satisfaction with the results of the Vienna Meeting and with the "further deepening of the Helsinki process, in which Czechoslovakia sees a reliable guarantee for security and cooperation in Europe", as Johanes, for instance, put it in October 1989. He even conceded that in the area of human rights and humanitarian issues it would be necessary to make "the necessary adjustments to our legal system", to facilitate travel abroad and to draft a new law on religious freedom and religious communities.[31] The shortcomings in this area were to be monitored by the newly established Committee of the Czechoslovak Public for

28 Císařovská/Prečan, *Charta 77*, doc. D524, p. 1085–1086.

29 Ibid., doc. D 551, p. 1119–1121.

30 Jiří Dienstbier, *Lidská dimenze měřená v Paříži* [Human dimension measured in Paris], in: *Lidové noviny* 2 (1989), issue 6, p. 1.

31 Vystoupení ministra zahraničních věcí ČSSR Jaromíra Johanese na výboru ministrů zahraničních věcí členských států Varšavské smlouvy, Varšava 26. října 1989 [Statement by ČSSR Foreign Minister Jaromír Johanes to the Committee of Foreign Ministers

Human Rights and Humanitarian Cooperation, headed by Zdeněk Dienstbier, a respected professor of medicine at the University of Prague. The Committee was to become something of an informal "ombudsman's office" in matters of human rights. A broader public was also to be represented in the new Czechoslovak Committee for European Security and Cooperation.[32]

A demonstration in Prague by opposition citizens' groups was announced for 10 December 1989, UN Human Rights Day, this time approved by the relevant authorities. How far the Communist regime was prepared to retreat is difficult to assess in retrospect. The "Velvet Revolution" in Czechoslovakia, which began on 17 November 1989, led to a radical change in the political and economic system, leaving the reforms and cosmetic improvements promised by the KSČ pushed to the sidelines.

Yet the Helsinki process did not at first come to a standstill. On the contrary, it accelerated in many respects, and the new democratic Czechoslovakia played an active role in this process. This phase of the CSCE's history was successfully concluded in Paris (18–21 November 1990) with the signing of the Treaty on the Reduction of Conventional Armed Forces in Europe and the Joint Declaration on the End of the Cold War by twenty-two states. At the end of the meeting, the Paris Charter for a New Europe was signed. While Czechoslovakia had been one of the much-criticised outsiders during the Vienna Meeting in 1986–89, Prague even became the seat of its secretariat after the signing of the Charter for a New Europe and the establishment of a permanent Committee of Senior Officials. Later, after the dissolution of Czechoslovakia (1 January 1993), the indifferent attitude of the new Czech government under Prime Minister Václav Klaus led to the CSCE Secretariat being relocated to Vienna. The small Prague office of the CSCE's successor organisation, the Organisation for Security and Cooperation in Europe (OSCE), still houses the organisation's documentation centre and archive (OSCE Documentation Centre Prague, DCiP), which is freely accessible to researchers.

---

of the Warsaw Pact Member States, Warsaw 26 October 1989], AMZV Prague, ZPO-T, Inv. No. 34.

32 Výsledky vídeňské následné schůzky KBSE. Informační materiál pro předsednictvo ÚV KSČ, 1. únor 1989 [Results of the Vienna CSCE Follow-up Meeting. Information material for the Presidium of the Central Committee of the KSČ, 1 February 1989], AMZV Prague, ZPO-T, Inv. No. 18.

Bibliography

Ali, S. Mahmud, *US-China Cold War Collaboration, 1971–1989*, London-New York 2005.

Alting von Geusau, Frans A. M., "The Nine and Détente", in: Nils Andrén/Karl E. Birnbaum (eds.), *Belgrade and Beyond. The CSCE Process in Perspective*, Alphen aan den Rijn-Rockville MD 1980, p. 17–25.

Altrichter, Altrichter, *Russland 1989. Der Untergang des sowjetischen Imperiums*, München 2009.

Altrichter, Helmut, *Kleine Geschichte der Sowjetunion 1917–1991*, München 2013.

Altrichter, Helmut/Wentker, Hermann (eds.), *Der KSZE-Prozess. Vom Kalten Krieg zu einem neuen Europa 1975 bis 1990* (Zeitgeschichte im Gespräch Vol. 11), München 2011.

Anusz, Andrzej/Perzyna, Łukasz, *Konfederacja. Rzecz o KPN*, Warszawa 2009.

Aschwanden, Romed/Buck, Maria et al. (eds.), *Conflicts d'usage depuis 1950 – Conflitti d'uso dal 1950 – Nutzungskonflikte seit 1950* (Histoire des Alpes – Storia delle Alpi – Geschichte der Alpen Vol. 2022/27), Zürich 2022.

Aunesluoma, Juhana, "Finlandisation in Reverse. The CSCE and the Rise and Fall of Economic Detente, 1968–1975", in: Oliver Bange/Gottfried Niedhart (eds.), *Helsinki 1975 and the Transformation of Europe*, New York-Oxford 2008, p. 98–112.

Bundesministerium für Auswärtige Angelegenheiten, *Außenpolitischer Bericht 1985. Bericht des Bundesministeriums für Auswärtige Angelegenheiten*, Wien 1986.

Bachmaier, Peter, "Austrian-Bulgarian Cultural Relations", in: Arnold Suppan/Wolfgang Mueller (eds.), *"Peaceful Coexistence" or "Iron Curtain". Austria, Neutrality, and Eastern Europe in the Cold War and Détente, 1955–1989* (Europa Orientalis Vol. 7), Wien-Berlin-Piscataway, NJ 2009, p. 487–508.

Bacia, Horst, "Die Stockholmer Konferenz über Vertrauensbildung und Abrüstung in Europa vor der entscheidenden Phase. Eine Zwischenbilanz", in: *Europa-Archiv 41* (1986), p. 69–78.

Bacia, Horst, "Die Stockholmer Konferenz – Schlußverhandlungen, Ergebnis und Ausblick", in: *Europa-Archiv 42* (1987), p. 369–378.

Badalassi, Nicolas/Snyder, Sara B. (eds.), *The CSCE and the End of the Cold War. Diplomacy, Societies and Human Rights, 1972–1990*, New York 2019.

Baev, Jordan, "Bulgaria and the Warsaw Pact consultations on the CSCE Process. From Helsinki to Belgrade", in: Vladimir Bilandžić/Dittmar Dahlmann et al. (eds.), *From Helsinki to Belgrade. The First CSCE Follow-up Meeting and the Crisis of Détente* (Internationale Beziehungen: Theorie und Geschichte Vol. 10), Göttingen-Bonn 2012, p. 107–118.

Bange, Oliver/Niedhart, Gottfried (eds.), *Helsinki 1975 and the Transformation of Europe*, New York-Oxford 2008.

Bange, Oliver, "Der KSZE-Prozess und die sicherheitspolitische Dynamik des Ost-West-Konflikts 1970–1990", in: Oliver Bange/Bernd Lemke (eds.), *Wege zur Wiedervereinigung. Die beiden deutschen Staaten in ihren Bündnissen 1970 bis 1990* (Beiträge zur Militärgeschichte Vol. 75), München 2013, p. 87–104.

Bange, Oliver, "The Stasi Confronts Western Strategies for Transformation, 1966–1975", in: Jonathan Haslam/Karina Urbach (eds.), *Secret Intelligence in the European States System, 1918–1989*, Stanford 2014, p. 170–208.

Bange, Oliver, "Transformation by Linkage? Arms Control, Human Rights and the Rift Between Moscow and East Berlin in the Late 1980s", in: Nicolas Badalassi/Sarah B. Snyder (eds.), *The CSCE and the End of the Cold War*, New York 2019, p. 305–329.

Baudet, Floribert, "'It was Cold War and we wanted to win'. Human rights, 'Détente', and the CSCE", in: Andreas Wenger/Vojtech Mastny et al. (eds.), *Origins of the European Security System. The Helsinki Process Revisited, 1965–75* (CSS Studies in Security and International Relations), London-New York 2008, p. 183–198.

Békés, Csaba, "The Warsaw Pact, the German Question and the Birth of the CSCE Process, 1961–1970", in: Oliver Bange/Gottfried Niedhart (eds.), *Helsinki 1975 and the Transformation of Europe*, New York-Oxford 2008, p. 113–128.

Békés, Csaba, "Der Warschauer Pakt und der KSZE-Prozess", in: Torsten Diedrich/Winfried Heinemann/Christian F. Ostermann (eds.), *Der Warschauer Pakt. Von der Gründung bis zum Zusammenbruch 1955 bis 1991*, Berlin 2009, p. 225–244.

Bilandžić, Vladimir/Dittmar Dahlmann et al. (eds.), *From Helsinki to Belgrade. The First CSCE Follow-up Meeting and the Crisis of Détente* (Internationale Beziehungen: Theorie und Geschichte Vol. 10), Göttingen-Bonn 2012.

Bilhöfer, Peter, *26. April 1986: Tschernobyl. Folgen einer Katastrophe* (Zeitpunkte der Geschichte), Stuttgart 2021.

Birnbaum, Karl E., "Die KSZE nach der Stockholmer Konferenz als Rahmen für die Zusammenarbeit zwischen Ost und West in Europa", in: *Europa-Archiv 42* (1987), p. 171–178.

Birnbaum, Karl E./Ingo Peters, "Die beiden deutschen Staaten auf dem Wiener KSZE-Folgetreffen", in: Karl E. Birnbaum/Ingo Peters (eds.), *Zwischen Abgrenzung und Verantwortungsgemeinschaft. Zur KSZE-Politik der beiden deutschen Staaten 1984–1989*, Baden-Baden 1991, p. 71–105.

Bischof, Burkhard, "'Aber für Europa war das Geschehen in Wien ein Wahnsinn.'", in: Kai Habel/Nina Hechenblaikner et al. (eds.), *Diplomatie am Ende des Kalten Krieges. Erinnerungen an die dritte KSZE-Folgekonferenz in Wien 1986–1989*, Baden-Baden 2025, p. 335–348.

Bischof, Günter, "Rezension zu: Benjamin Gilde, Österreich im KSZE-Prozess 1969–1983. Neutraler Vermittler in humanitärer Mission, München 2013", in: *sehepunkte 14* (2014), issue 2, http://www.sehepunkte.de/2014/02/24330.html, accessed 9.9.2023.

Bischof, Günter/Ruggenthaler, Peter, *Österreich und der Kalte Krieg*, Graz 2022.

Bloed, Arie, "Institutional Aspects of the Helsinki Process After the Follow-up Meeting of Vienna", in: *Netherlands International Law Review* 36 (1989), issue 3, p. 342–363.

Bloed, Arie/van Dijk, Pieter (eds.), *The Human Dimension of the Helsinki Process. The Vienna Follow-up Meeting and its Aftermath* (International Studies in Human Rights Vol. 20), Dordrecht-Boston-Norwell 1991.

Bon Tempo, Carl J., "Helsinki at Home: NGOs, the Helsinki Final Act and Politics in the United States, 1975–1985", in: Nicolas Badalassi/Sarah B. Snyder (eds.), *The CSCE and the End of the Cold War. Diplomacy, Societies and Human Rights, 1972–1990*, New York 2019, p. 230–246.

Borchard, Michael/Karner, Stefan et al. (eds.), *Entspannung im Kalten Krieg. Der Weg zum Moskauer Vertrag und zur KSZE*, Graz-Wien 2020.

Borcke, Astrid von, *Die Abrüstungsvorschläge Gorbatschows und das „neue Denken". Indizien aus der sowjetischen Innenpolitik* (Berichte des Bundesinstituts für Ostwissenschaftliche und Internationale Studien Vol. 32), Köln 1987.

Brait, Andrea, *Das Bundeskanzleramt in Wien, Ein österreichischer Gedächtnisort* (Schriften zur Kulturgeschichte Vol. 16), Hamburg 2010.

Brait, Andrea, "'die große Trennungslinie, die an unserer Haustür vorbeiführt, überbauen'. Zur Vermittlerfunktion der österreichischen Kulturaußenpolitik zwischen Ost und West", in: Maximilian Graf/Agnes Meisinger (eds.), *Österreich im Kalten Krieg. Neue Forschungen im internationalen Kontext* (Zeitgeschichte im Kontext Vol. 11), Göttingen 2016, p. 259–295.

Brait, Andrea, "Österreichisch-tschechische Kulturdiplomatie zwischen 1918 und 2018 aus der Perspektive des österreichischen Außenministeriums", in: *Paginae Historiae* 27 (2019), issue 2, p. 184–234.

Brait, Andrea/Michael Gehler, "The CSCE Vienna Follow-up Meeting and Alois Mock, 1986–1989", in: Helmut Wohnout/Michael Gehler et al. (eds.), *Christian Democracy and the Fall of Communism* (Civitas. Studies in Christian Democracy Vol. 1), Leuven 2019, p. 75–92.

Brands, Hal, *Making the Unipolar Moment: U.S. Foreign Policy and the Rise of the Post-Cold War Order*, Ithaca, NY 2016.

Bredow, Wilfried von, *Der KSZE-Prozeß. Von der Zähmung zur Auflösung des Ost-West-Konflikts*, Darmstadt 1992.

Breitenmoser, Christoph, *Sicherheit für Europa*, Zürich 1996.

Brett, Rachel, "The Human Dimension Mechanism of the CSCE and the CSCE Response to Minorities", in: Michael R. Lucas (ed.), *The CSCE in the 1990s. Constructing European Security and Cooperation* (Demokratie, Sicherheit, Frieden Vol. 83), Baden-Baden 1993, p. 143–160.

Brix, Emil, "Austrian Cultural and Public Diplomacy After the End of the Cold War", in: Günter Bischof/Ferdinand Karlhofer (eds.), *Austria's International Position after the End of the Cold War* (Contemporary Austrian Studies Vol. 22), Innsbruck 2013, p. 95–107.

Brown, Archie, *The Gorbachev Factor*, Oxford 1997.

Brown, Archie, "Mikhail Gorbachev and the Politics of Perestroika", in: *Russian History 49* (2022), issue 2–4, p. 123–145.

Brown, Martin D./Angela Romano, "Executors or Creative Deal-Makers? The Role of the Diplomats in the Making of the Helsinki CSCE", in: Nicolas Badalassi/Sarah B. Snyder (eds.), *The CSCE and the End of the Cold War. Diplomacy, Societies and Human Rights, 1972–1990*, New York 2019, p. 43–73.

Bruns, Wilhelm, "Mehr Substanz in den Ost-West-Beziehungen. Zur dritten KSZE-Folgekonferenz in Wien", in: *Aus Politik und Zeitgeschichte* (1989), issue 12, p. 3–9.

Burka, Alexander, *Was blieb vom Fenster in den Westen? Zur Auslandskulturpolitik Österreichs in Ostmitteleuropa seit 1945 am Beispiel Polens und der Tschechoslowakei/Tschechiens* (Politik und Demokratie Vol. 23), Frankfurt am Main-Berlin-Bern et al. 2012.

Casey, Steven (ed.), *The Cold War. Volume IV: From Détente to the End of the Cold War* (Critical Concepts in Military, Strategic, and Security Studies), Abingdon-Oxon 2013.

Ceska, Franz, "Détente und KSZE-Prozess. Österreich zwischen Helsinki (1975) und Madrid (1983)", in: Oliver Rathkolb/Otto M. Maschke et al. (eds.), *Mit anderen Augen gesehen. Internationale Perzeptionen Österreichs 1955–1990. Österreichische Nationalgeschichte nach 1945, Band 2* (Schriftenreihe des Forschungsinstitutes für politisch-historische Studien der Dr.-Wilfried-Haslauer-Bibliothek, Salzburg Vol. 6/2), Wien-Köln-Weimar 2002, p. 507–521.

Ceska, Franz, "'Insofern war das die aufregendste Sache meines Lebens.'", in: Kai Habel/Nina Hechenblaikner et al. (eds.), *Diplomatie am Ende des Kalten Krieges. Erinnerungen an die dritte KSZE-Folgekonferenz in Wien 1986–1989*, Baden-Baden 2025, p. 49–78.

Chirot, Daniel, "What Happened in Eastern Europe in 1989?", in: Vladimir Tismaneanu (ed.), *The Revolutions of 1989*, London 2005, p. 19–50.

Chňoupek, Bohuš, *Memoáre in claris* [*Memoiren in claris*], Bratislava 1998.

Crome, Erhard/Franzke, Jochen, "Die SED-Führung und die Wiener KSZE-Konferenz 1986 bis 1989. Dokumente aus dem Parteiarchiv", in: *Deutschland Archiv 26* (1993), p. 905–914.

Cuccia, Deborah, "The European Common House: The Soviet Prescription for Reshaping Europe", in: Michael Gehler/Wilfried Loth (eds.), *Reshaping Europe. Towards a Political, Economic and Monetary Union, 1984–1989* (Publications of the European Liaison Committee of Historians Vol. 20), Baden-Baden 2020, p. 443–459.

David, Dewitt/Rattinger, Hans (eds.), *East-West Arms Control. Challenges for the Western Alliance*, London-New York 1992.

Dehnert, Gunter, "'Eine neue Beschaffenheit der Lage'. Der KSZE-Prozess und die polnische Opposition 1975–1989", in: Helmut Altrichter/Hermann Wentker (eds.), *Der*

KSZE-*Prozess. Vom Kalten Krieg zu einem neuen Europa 1975 bis 1990* (Zeitgeschichte im Gespräch Vol. 11), München 2011, p. 87–98.

Dehnert, Gunter, "Entspannung Gegen das Volk – Sanktionen für das Volk? Die Solidarność nach Ausrufung des Kriegsrechts und die Nachfolgekonferenz von Madrid", in: Matthias Peter/Hermann Wentker (eds.), *Die KSZE im Ost-West-Konflikt. Internationale Politik und gesellschaftliche Transformation 1975–1990* (Schriftenreihe der Vierteljahrshefte für Zeitgeschichte Sondernummer), München 2012, p. 249–266.

Dejmek, Jindřich, *Diplomacie Československa. Nástin dějin ministerstva zahraničních věcí a diplomacie 1918–1992* [*Tschechoslowakische Diplomatie. Skizze einer Geschichte des Außenministeriums und des Auswärtigen Dienstes*], VOL. I, Praha 2012.

Delbrück, Jost/Ropers, Norbert et al. (eds.), *Grünbuch zu den Folgewirkungen der KSZE*, Köln 1977.

Desjardins, Marie-France, *Rethinking Confidence-Building Measures. Obstacles to Agreement and the Risks of Overselling the Process*, London 2014.

Deutsche Gesellschaft für Friedens- und Konfliktforschung (ed.), *DGFK-Jahrbuch 1979/80. Zur Entspannungspolitik in Europa*, Baden-Baden 1980.

Deutsche Gesellschaft für Friedens- und Konfliktforschung (ed.), *DGFK-Jahrbuch 1982/83. Zur Lage Europas im globalen Spannungsfeld*, Baden-Baden 1983.

Dewitt, David/Rattinger, Hans (eds.), *East-West Arms Control. Challenges for the Western Alliance*, London-New York 1992.

Dietrich, Frenzke/Uschakow, Alexander (eds.), *Die Oststaaten, das sowjetische Bündnissystem und die KSZE vor und nach Helsinki*, Köln 1980.

Długołęcki, Piotr, "Diplomatic file. An Unknown Context of the Rapacki Plan", in: *The Polish Quarterly of International Affairs* 20 (2011), p. 59–71.

Dobrynin, Anatoly, *In Confidence. Moscow's Ambassador to America's Six Cold War Presidents*, New York 1995.

Dobrynin, Anatolij F., *Sugubo doveritel'no*, Moscow 2016.

Domber, Gregory F., "Transatlantic Relations, Human Rights, and Power Politics", in: Poul Villaume/Odd Arne Westad (eds.), *Perforating the Iron Curtain. European Détente, Transatlantic Relations, and the Cold War, 1965–1985*, Copenhagen 2010, p. 195–214.

Dudek, Antoni, *Reglamentowana rewolucja. Rozkład dyktatury komunistycznej w Polsce 1988–1990*, Kraków 2004.

Eckel, Jan/Moyn, Samuel (eds.), *Moral für die Welt? Menschenrechtspolitik in den 1970er Jahren*, Göttingen 2012.

Eckel, Jan, *Die Ambivalenz des Guten. Menschenrechte in der internationalen Politik seit den 1940ern*, Göttingen 2014.

Eickhoff, Ekkehard, "Das KSZE-Expertentreffen über Menschenrechte in Ottawa – eine Bewertung", in: *Europa-Archiv* 40 (1985), p. 573–580.

Eickhoff, Ekkehard, "Das Dritte KSZE-Folgetreffen in Wien, Implementierung der Wirtschaftsbestimmungen", in: *Europa Archiv* 42 (1987), p. 59–66.

Fischer, Per, "Das Ergebnis von Belgrad. Das KSZE-Folgetreffen in seiner Bedeutung für den Entspannungsprozeß", in: *Europa-Archiv 33* (1978), p. 221–230.
Fischer, Thomas, "Die Sowjetunion, Österreich und die finnische KSZE-Initiative vom 5. Mai 1969", in: Wolfgang Mueller/Michael Portmann (eds.), *Osteuropa vom Weltkrieg zur Wende* (Zentraleuropa-Studien Vol. 10), Wien 2007, p. 313–339.
Fischer, Thomas, "A Mustard Seed Grew Into a Bushy Tree", in: *Cold War History 9* (2009), p. 177–201.
Fischer, Thomas, "Austria and the Helsinki Process", in: Arnold Suppan/Wolfgang Mueller (eds.), *"Peaceful Coexistence" or "Iron Curtain". Austria, Neutrality, and Eastern Europe in the Cold War and Détente, 1955–1989* (Europa Orientalis Vol. 7), Wien-Berlin-Piscataway, NJ 2009, p. 168–202.
Fischer, Thomas, *Neutral Power in the CSCE: The N+N States and the Making of the Helsinki Accords 1975*, Baden-Baden 2009.
Fischer, Thomas, *Keeping the Process Alive. The N+N and the CSCE Follow-Up from Helsinki to Vienna (1975–1986)* (Zürcher Beiträge zur Sicherheitspolitik Vol. 84), Zurich 2012.
Friszke, Andrzej, *Opozycja polityczna w PRL 1945–1980*, London 1994.
Gaddis, John Lewis, *Der Kalte Krieg. Eine neue Geschichte*, München 2008.
Garthoff, Raymond, *Détente and Confrontation: Soviet-American Relations from Nixon to Reagan*, Washington D.C. 1994.
Gehler, Michael, "Neutralität und Neutralisierungspläne für Mitteleuropa?", in: Dominik Geppert/Udo Wengst (eds.), *Neutralität – Chance oder Chimäre?. Konzepte des Dritten Weges für Deutschland und die Welt 1945–1990*, München 2005, p. 105–131.
Gehler, Michael, "Die Affäre Waldheim. Eine Fallstudie zur Instrumentalisierung der NS-Vergangenheit zur politischen Vorteilsverschaffung 1986–1988", in: *Geschichte in Wissenschaft und Unterricht 69* (2018), issue 1/2, p. 67–85.
Gehler, Michael, *From Saint-Germain to Lisbon. Austria's Long Road from Disintegrated to United Europe 1919–2009*, Wien 2020.
Gehler, Michael/Brait, Andrea, "The Breakthrough. Freedom and Security at the Vienna CSCE Follow-up Conference 1986–1989", in: Michael Gehler/Wilfried Loth (eds.), *Reshaping Europe. Towards a Political, Economic and Monetary Union, 1984–1989*, Baden-Baden 2020, p. 477–495.
Ghebali, Victor-Yves, *La diplomatie de la Détente: La CSCE, d'Helsinki à Vienne (1973–1989)*, Brüssel 1989.
Gienow-Hecht, Jessica C./Donfried, Mark C. (eds.), *Searching for a Cultural Diplomacy*, New York-Oxford 2010.
Giger, Walter, "Der Rhein rot, die Fische tot. Brandkatastrophe in Schweizerhalle 1986 – Rückblick und Bilanz", in: *UWSF – Z Umweltchem Ökotox (Umweltwissenschaften und Schadstoff-Forschung) 19* (2007), special issue 1, p. 11–23.

Gilde, Benjamin, *Österreich im KSZE-Prozess 1969–1983. Neutraler Vermittler in humanitärer Mission* (Quellen und Darstellungen zur Zeitgeschichte Vol. 98), München 2013.

Grachev, Andrei, "Gorbachev and the 'New Political Thinking'", in: Wolfgang Mueller/Michael Gehler et al. (eds.), *The Revolutions of 1989. A Handbook* (Internationale Geschichte/International History Vol. 2), Wien 2015, p. 33–46.

Graf, Maximilian, "Kreisky und Polen. Schlaglichter auf einen vernachlässigten Aspekt der österreichischen 'Ostpolitik'", in: Lucile Dreidemy et al. (eds.), *Bananen, Cola, Zeitgeschichte. Oliver Rathkolb und das lange 20. Jahrhundert*, Vol. 2, Wien 2015, p. 692–706.

Graf, Maximilian, *Österreich und die DDR 1949–1990. Politik und Wirtschaft im Schatten der deutschen Teilung*, Wien 2016.

Graf, Maximilian, "European Détente and the CSCE. Austria and the East-Central European Theatre in the 1970s and 1980s", in: Nicolas Badalassi/Sarah B. Snyder (eds.), *The CSCE and the End of the Cold War. Diplomacy, Societies and Human Rights, 1972–1990*, New York, NY 2019, p. 249–274.

Graf, Maximilian, "Österreich und die 'polnische Krise' im Kontext 1980–1983", in: Peter Ruggenthaler/Wanda Jarząbek (eds.), *Österreich – Polen. Stationen gemeinsamer Geschichte im 20. Jahrhundert*, Graz 2021, p. 201–221.

Graf-Steiner, Anna, *Brückenbauer im Kalten Krieg. Österreich und der lange Weg zur KSZE-Schlussakte*, Graz-Wien-Berlin 2023.

Graf-Steiner, Anna/Reginbogin, Herbert R., "Austria: The NPT, Diplomacy, and National Identity", in: Pascal Lottaz/Yoko Iwama (eds.), *Neutral Europe and the Creation of the Nonproliferation Regime 1958–1968*. London-New York 2023, p. 169–184.

Graf-Steiner, Anna, "Kreisky, the Soviet Union, and the Helsinki Process", in: Günter Bischof/Michael Burri (eds.), *Bruno Kreisky: A Reassessment* (Austrian and Habsburg Studies Vol. 39), New York-Oxford 2025, p. 167–202.

Grinevsky, Oleg/Hansen, Lynn M., *Making Peace. Confidence and Security in a New Europe*, New York 2009.

Groth, Michael, "Fortschritte im KSZE-Prozeß. Das dritte Folgetreffen in Wien", in: *Europa-Archiv* (1989), p. 95–102.

Grozev, Kostadin/Baev, Jordan, "Bulgaria, Balkan Diplomcy and the Road to Helsinki", in: Oliver Bange/Gottfried Niedhart (eds.), *Helsinki 1975 and the Transformation of Europe*, New York-Oxford 2008, p. 160–174.

Gubin, Sarah, "Between Regimes and Realism – Transnational Agenda Setting. Soviet Compliance with CSCE Human Rights Norms", in: *Human Rights Quarterly* 17 (1995), issue 2, p. 278–302.

Habel, Kai/Hechenblaikner, Nina et al. (eds.), *Diplomatie am Ende des Kalten Krieges. Erinnerungen an die dritte KSZE-Folgekonferenz in Wien 1986–1989*, Baden-Baden 2025.

Haftendorn, Helga, "The Link between CSCE and MBFR: Two sprouts from one bulb", in: Andreas Wenger/Vojtech Mastny/Christian Nuenlist (eds.), *Origins of the European Security System. The Helsinki process revisited 1965–1975*, New York 2008, p. 237–258.

Hakkarainen, Petri, *A State of Peace in Europe. West Germany and the CSCE, 1966–1975*, New York-Oxford 2011.

Hanhimäki, Jussi M., "Ironies and Turning Points. Détente in Perspective", in: Odd Arne Westad (ed.), *Reviewing the Cold War. Approaches, Interpretations, Theory* (Cold War History Vol. 1), London 2001, p. 326–342.

Hanhimäki, Jussi M., "'They can write it in Swahili'. Kissinger, the Soviets, and the Helsinki Accords, 1973–75", in: *Journal of Transatlantic Studies 1* (2003), p. 37–58.

Hanhimäki, Jussi M., *Flawed Architect: Henry Kissinger and American Foreign Policy*, New York 2004.

Hanhimäki, Jussi M., *The Rise and Fall of Détente. American Foreign Policy and the Transformation of the Cold War*, Washington D.C. 2012.

Hanhimäki, Jussi M., "Non-aligned to what? European neutrality and the Cold War", in: Sandra Bott/Jussi M. Hanhimäki et al. (eds.), *Neutrality and Neutralism in the Global Cold War. Between or within the blocs?* (Cold War History Vol. 34), Abingdon-Oxon-New York, NY 2016, p. 17–32.

Hanhimäki, Jussi M., "Introduction", in: Bernhard Blumenau/Jussi Hanhimäki/Barbara Zanchetta (eds.), *New Perspectives on the End of the Cold War. Unexpected Transformations?*, London 2017, p. 1–12.

Hanhimäki, Jussi M., "Détente and the Reconfiguration of Superpower Relations", in: David C. Engerman/May Paul Friedman/Melani McAlister (eds.), *The Cambridge History of America and the World. Volume 4: 1945 to the Present*, New York 2022, p. 512–534.

Hanisch, Anja, *Die DDR im KSZE-Prozess 1972–1985. Zwischen Ostabhängigkeit, Westabgrenzung und Ausreisebewegung* (Quellen und Darstellungen zur Zeitgeschichte Vol. 91), München 2012.

Hazewinkel, Harm, "Paris, Copenhagen, and Moscow", in: Arie Bloed/Pieter van Dijk, *The Human Dimension of the Helsinki Process. The Vienna Follow-up Meeting and Its Aftermath*, Leiden 2021, p. 128–132.

Hebel, Kai, "Die 'Brückenbauer'? Großbritannien als transatlantischer Vermittler in der KSZE 1972–1978", in: Matthias Peter/Hermann Wentker (eds.), *Die KSZE im Ost-West-Konflikt. Internationale Politik und gesellschaftliche Transformation 1975–1990* (Schriftenreihe der Vierteljahrshefte für Zeitgeschichte Sondernummer), München 2012, p. 99–120.

Hechenblaikner, Nina, "Die humanitäre Dimension des KSZE-Prozesses und das Ende des Kalten Krieges", in: Beate Fieseler/Oksana Nagornaia (eds.), *Der Zerfall der Sowjetunion und das Ende der DDR als historische Zäsuren*, Wiesbaden 2024, p. 15–26.

Hechenblaikner, Nina, "Diplomatie und ihre Einflüsse. Prägende Akteursgruppen für die Verhandlungen zur humanitären Dimension beim KSZE-Folgetreffen in Wien (1986–1989)", in: *Österreichische Zeitschrift für Geschichtswissenschaften 35* (2024), issue 2, p. 154–173.

Heraclides, Alexis, *Security and Cooperation in Europe. The Human Dimension 1972–1992,* London 1993.

Herbert, Ulrich, *Geschichte Deutschlands im 20. Jahrhundert,* München 2017.

Heyde, Veronika, "Nicht nur Entspannung und Menschenrechte. Die Entdeckung von Abrüstung und Rüstungskontrolle durch die französische KSZE-Politik", in: Matthias Peter/Hermann Wentker (eds.), *Die KSZE im Ost-West-Konflikt. Internationale Politik und gesellschaftliche Transformation 1975–1990* (Schriftenreihe der Vierteljahrshefte für Zeitgeschichte Sondernummer), München 2012, p. 83–98.

Heyde, Veronika, *Frankreich im KSZE-Prozess. Diplomatie im Namen der europäischen Sicherheit* (Quellen und Darstellungen zur Zeitgeschichte Vol. 113), Berlin-Boston 2017.

Hochedlinger, Michael, *Aktenkunde, Urkunden- und Aktenlehre der Neuzeit* (Historische Hilfswissenschaften 3), Wien-Köln et al. 2009.

Hoffmann, Stefan-Ludwig (ed.), *Moralpolitik. Geschichte der Menschenrechte im 20. Jahrhundert,* Göttingen 2010.

Hollings, Christopher, *Scientific Communication Across the Iron Curtain,* Cham 2016.

Hölzl, Richard/Oosthoek, K.J., "Transforming Woodlands. European Forest Protection in a Global Context", in: Anna-Katharina Wöbse/Patrick Kupper (eds.), *Greening Europe, Environmental protection in the long twentieth century – a handbook* (Contemporary European History Vol. 1), Berlin-Boston 2022, p. 157–184.

Hong, Kii-Jong, *The CSCE Security Regime Formation. An Asian Perspective,* London 1997.

Hunt, Lynn, *Inventing Human Rights. A History,* London 2007.

Hyde-Price, Adrian, "Geopolitics and the Concept of Neutrality in Contemporary Europe", in: Heinz Gärtner (ed.), *Engaged Neutrality. An Evolved Approach to the Cold War,* Lanham 2017, p. 121–142.

Ionescu, Mihail E., "Romania, Ostpolitik and the CSCE 1967–1975", in: Oliver Bange/Gottfried Niedhart (eds.), *Helsinki 1975 and the Transformation of Europe,* New York-Oxford 2008, p. 129–143.

Iriye, Akira/Goedde, Petra, "Introduction: Human Rights as History", in: Akira Iriye/Petra Goedde/William Hitchcock (eds.), *The Human Rights Revolution. An International History,* New York 2012, p. 3–26.

Jacobsen, Hans-Adolf, "Auswärtige Kulturpolitik", in: Hans-Adolf Jacobsen/Gert Leptin et al. (eds.), *Drei Jahrzehnte Außenpolitik der DDR. Bestimmungsfaktoren, Instrumente, Aktionsfelder* (Internationale Politik und Wirtschaft Vol. 44), München-Wien 1979, p. 235–260.

Jankowitsch, Peter, "'Das Konferenzgeschehen in Wien war sehr wichtig für das, was sich dann 1989 und später abgespielt hat.'", in: Kai Habel/Nina Hechenblaikner et al. (eds.), *Diplomatie am Ende des Kalten Krieges. Erinnerungen an die dritte KSZE-Folgekonferenz in Wien 1986–1989*, Baden-Baden 2025, p. 79–104.

Jarząbek, Wanda, *Hope and Reality: Poland and the Conference on Security and Cooperation in Europe, 1964–1989* (Cold War International History Project (CWIHP) Working Paper Series Vol. 56), Washington D.C. 2008.

Jarząbek, Wanda, "Preserving the Status Quo or Promoting Change. The Role of the CSCE in the Perception of Polish Authorities", in: Oliver Bange/Gottfried Niedhart (eds.), *Helsinki 1975 and the Transformation of Europe*, New York-Oxford 2008, p. 144–159.

Jarząbek, Wanda, *Polska Rzeczpospolita Ludowa wobec polityki wschodniej Republiki Federalnej Niemiec w latach 1966–1976*, Warszawa 2011.

Jarząbek, Wanda, "Lost illusions? The Polish government and human rights issues from Helsinki to Belgrade, 1975–1978", in: Vladimir Bilandžić/Dittmar Dahlmann et al. (eds.), *From Helsinki to Belgrade. The First CSCE Follow-up Meeting and the Crisis of Détente* (Internationale Beziehungen: Theorie und Geschichte Vol. 10), Göttingen-Bonn 2012, p. 305–320.

Jarząbek, Wanda, "Troublesome Human Rights. The Polish Strategy between the Belgrade and Madrid CSCE Follow-up Conferences", in: Matthias Peter/Hermann Wentker (eds.), *Die KSZE im Ost-West-Konflikt. Internationale Politik und gesellschaftliche Transformation 1975–1990* (Schriftenreihe der Vierteljahrshefte für Zeitgeschichte Sondernummer), München 2012, p. 121–135.

Jarząbek, Wanda, "Basket III provisions in the policies of France and the Federal Republic of Germany toward the Polish People's Republic (1975–1980): A Comparative Approach", in: Jakub Tyszkiewicz (ed.), *Human Rights and Political Dissent in Central Europe. Between the Helsinki Accords and the Fall of the Berlin Wall*, London-New York 2022, p. 39–52.

Jordan, Stefan, *Theorien und Methoden der Geschichtswissenschaft* (Orientierung Geschichte Vol. 1), Paderborn 2013².

Kaiser, Jens, "Zwischen angestrebter Eigenständigkeit und traditioneller Unterordnung. Zur Ambivalenz des Verhältnisses von sowjetischer und DDR-Außenpolitik in den achtziger Jahren", in: *Deutschland Archiv 24* (1991), p. 478–495.

Kaiser, Jonas, "Von Stockholm über Wien nach Paris. Vertrauens- und Sicherheitsbildende Maßnahmen und das KSE-Mandat im Rahmen des KSZE Prozesses 1984–1990", in: Beate Fieseler/Oksana Nagornaia (eds.), *Der Zerfall der Sowjetunion und das Ende der DDR als historische Zäsuren*, Wiesbaden 2024, p. 1–13.

Karsh, Efraim, *Neutrality and Small States*, London-New York 1988.

Kastl, Jörg, "Das KSZE-Folgetreffen von Madrid. Verlauf und Schlußdokument aus der Sicht der Bundesrepublik Deutschland", in: *Europa-Archiv 20* (1983), p. 617–626.

Kaufmann, William W., *Glasnost, Perestroika and U.S. Defense Spending*, Washington D.C. 1990.

Kicker, Renate/Deutschmann, Ruth, *Die außenpolitische Berichterstattung der Neuen Kronenzeitung. Eine empirische Untersuchung des Jahres 1978* (Grazer rechts- und staatswissenschaftliche Studien), Graz 1981.

Kieninger, Stephan, *The Diplomacy of Détente. Cooperative Security Policies from Helmut Schmidt to George Shultz* (Cold War History), London 2018.

Kissinger, Henry, *Diplomacy*, New York 1994.

Klimke, Martin/Scharloth, Joachim (eds.), *1968. Handbuch zur Kultur- und Mediengeschichte der Studentenbewegung*, Stuttgart-Weimar 2007.

Knabe, Hubertus, "Der schwierige Kulturdialog in Europa. Anmerkungen zum KSZE-Kulturforum in Budapest", in: *Osteuropa* (1986), issue 5, p. 380–388.

Kowalczuk, Ilko-Sascha, *End Game. The 1989 Revolution in East Germany*, Oxford 2022.

Kramer, Mark/Makko, Aryo/Ruggenthaler, Peter (eds.), *The Soviet Union and Cold War Neutrality and Nonalignment in Europe*, Lanham-Boulder et al. 2021.

Kriechbaumer, Robert, *Nur ein Zwischenspiel (?). Die Geschichte der Grünen in Österreich* (Schriftenreihe des Forschungsinstitutes für politisch-historische Studien der Dr.-Wilfried-Haslauer-Bibliothek Vol. 66), Wien 2018.

Kuchler, Andreas, "Die Umweltbewegung (1965–1985), Österreich im postmateriellen Zeitalter", in: Oliver Rathkolb/Richard Hufschmied et al. (eds.), *Wasserkraft. Elektrizität. Gesellschaft. Kraftwerksprojekte ab 1880 im Spannungsfeld* (Schriftenreihe Forschung in der Verbund AG Vol. 104), Wien 2012, p. 226–232.

Kunštát, Miroslav/Vilímek, Tomáš, "Die deutsch-tschechoslowakischen Beziehungen im Zeichen der Perestroika", in: Edita Ivaničková/Miloš Řezník/Volker Zimmermann (eds.), *Das Jahr 1989 im deutsch-tschechisch-slowakischen Kontext*, Essen 2013, p. 117–150.

Kunštát, Miroslav, "Die Tschechoslowakei und Österreich vor dem Umbruch 1989/90", in: Andrea Brait/Michael Gehler (eds.), *Grenzöffnung 1989. Innen- und Außenperspektiven und die Folgen für Österreich*, Wien et al. 2014, p. 367–384.

Laakkonen, Simo/Räsänen, Tuomas, "Negotiating the Maritime Commons, Protecting the Baltic Sea in a European Context", in: Anna-Katharina Wöbse/Patrick Kupper (eds.), *Greening Europe, Environmental protection in the long twentieth century – a handbook* (Contemporary European History Vol. 1), Berlin-Boston 2022, p. 243–268.

Laimer, Roland Ernst, *Die KSZE und der Umweltschutz. Korb II beim Wiener KSZE-Folgetreffen (1986–1989) aus der Perspektive der Ballhausdiplomatie*, phil. Masterarbeit Innsbruck 2023.

Lehne, Stefan, *The Vienna Meeting of the Conference on Security and Cooperation in Europe, 1986–1989. A Turning Point in East-West Relations* (Austrian Institute for International Affairs Series), Boulder-San Francisco-Oxford 1991.

Lehne, Stefan/Neuhold, Hanspeter, "The Role of the Neutral and Non-Aligned Countries at the Vienna Meeting", in: Arie Bloed/Pieter van Dijk (eds.), *The Human*

Dimension of the Helsinki Process. The Vienna Follow-Up Meeting and its Aftermath, Dordrecht-Boston-London 1991, p. 30–53.

Lehne, Stefan, "Es 'zeigte sich sehr rasch, dass ‚der Osten'nicht mehr existiert'", in: Kai Habel/Nina Hechenblaikner et al. (eds.), *Diplomatie am Ende des Kalten Krieges. Erinnerungen an die dritte KSZE-Folgekonferenz in Wien 1986–1989*, Baden-Baden 2025, p. 183–216.

Liedermann, Helmut, "Von Helsinki über Belgrad nach Madrid. Die Konferenz über Sicherheit und Zusammenarbeit in Europa aus der Sicht eines österreichischen Konferenzteilnehmers", in: Peter Fischer/Heribert Köck/Alfred Verdross (eds.), *Völkerrecht und Rechtsphilosophie. Internationale Festschrift für Stephan Verosta zum 70. Geburtstag*, Berlin 1980, p. 427–443.

Liedermann, Helmut, "Some Reflections on the Humanitarian Dimension of the CSCE Process", in: Hanspeter Neuhold (ed.), *CSCE: N+N Perspectives. The Process of the Conference on Security and Co-operation in Europe from the Viewpoint of the Neutral and Non-Aligned Participating States*, Wien 1987, p. 135–143.

Liedermann, Helmut, "Österreichs Image im ehemaligen Jugoslawien", in: Oliver Rathkolb/Otto M. Maschke/Stefan August Lütgenau (eds.), *Mit anderen Augen gesehen. Internationale Perzeptionen Österreichs 1955–1990* (Österreichische Nationalgeschichte nach 1945 Vol. 2), Wien 2002, p. 523–562.

Liedermann, Helmut, "Österreichs Rolle beim Zustandekommen der KSZE", in: Oliver Rathkolb/Otto M. Maschke/Stefan August Lütgenau (eds.), *Mit anderen Augen gesehen. Internationale Perzeptionen Österreichs 1955–1990* (Österreichische Nationalgeschichte nach 1945 Vol. 2), Wien 2002, p. 487–505.

Loth, Wilfried/Soutou, Georges-Henri (eds.), *The Making of Détente. Eastern and Western Europe in the Cold War, 1965–75* (Cold War History Vol. 20), London 2008.

Loth, Wilfried, "Der KSZE-Prozess 1975–1990: eine Bilanz", in: Matthias Peter/Hermann Wentker (eds.), *Die KSZE im Ost-West-Konflikt. Internationale Politik und gesellschaftliche Transformation 1975–1990* (Schriftenreihe der Vierteljahrshefte für Zeitgeschichte Sondernummer), München 2012, p. 323–331.

Lucas, Michael R. (ed.), *The CSCE in the 1990s. Constructing European Security and Cooperation* (Demokratie, Sicherheit, Frieden Vol. 83), Baden-Baden 1993.

Lutz, Karl-Heinz, "Vom Schwinden des Misstrauens. Deutsch-deutsche Manöverbeobachtungen 1987–1989", in: *Militärgeschichte. Zeitschrift für historische Bildung 35* (2020), issue 3, p. 4–9.

Maier, Charles, *Dissolution. The Crisis of Communism and the End of East Germany*, London 1999.

Malcolm, Neil, "The 'Common European Home' and Soviet European Policy", in: *International Affairs* 65 (1989), issue 4, p. 659–676.

Mariager, Rasmus/Molin, Karl et al. (eds.), *Human Rights in Europe during the Cold War* (Cold War History), New York 2014.

Martini, Stephan, *Die sicherheitspolitische Funktion der KSZE im entspannungspolitischen Konzept der Bundesrepublik Deutschland 1975–1990*, Berlin 2006.

Mastny, Vojtech, "Did Gorbachev liberate Eastern Europe?", in: Olav Njølstad (ed.), *The Last Decade of the Cold War. From Conflict Escalation to Conflict Transformation* (Cold War History Vol. 5), London-New York 2004, p. 402–423.

Mastny, Vojtech/Byrne, Malcolm (eds.), *A Cardboard Castle? An Inside History of the Warsaw Pact, 1955–1991*, Budapest 2005.

Maurer, Peter, "Einflussfaktoren auf die Handlungsautonomie der Medien im politischen Prozess westlicher Demokratien. Eine theoretische Analyse", in: Barbara Pfetsch/Silke Adam (eds.), *Massenmedien als politische Akteure. Konzepte und Analysen*, Wiesbaden 2008, p. 73–91.

McAdams, A. James, *Germany Divided. From the Wall to Reunification*, Princeton 2020.

Meissner, Boris (ed.), *Oststaaten und europäische Sicherheit 1972–1975. Analysen und Dokumentation*, Köln 1977.

Meneguzzi Rostagni, Carla (ed.), *The Helsinki Process. A Historical Reappraisal*, Padova 2005.

Mergel, Thomas, "Politisierte Medien und medialisierte Politik. Strukturelle Koppelungen zwischen zwei sozialen Systemen", in: Klaus Arnold/Christoph Classen et al. (eds.), *Von der Politisierung der Medien zur Medialisierung des Politischen? Zum Verhältnis von Medien, Öffentlichkeit und Politik im 20. Jahrhundert*, Leipzig 2010, p. 29–50.

Miedema, Christie, *Not a Movement of Dissidents. Amnesty International Beyond the Iron Curtain* (Schriftenreihe Menschenrechte im 20. Jahrhundert Vol. 4), Göttingen 2019.

Mihr, Anja, *Amnesty International in der DDR. Der Einsatz für Menschenrechte im Visier der Stasi*, Berlin 2002.

Mikkonen, Simo/Pia Koivunen (eds.), *Beyond the Divide. Entangled Histories of Cold War Europe*, New York-Oxford 2015.

Mikkonen, Simo/Suutari, Pekka (eds.), *Music, Art and Diplomacy. East-West Cultural Interactions and the Cold War*, London-New York 2016.

Minnema, Hester, "'The [CSCE-]process at that time was what was needed.'", in: Kai Habel/Nina Hechenblaikner et al. (eds.), *Diplomatie am Ende des Kalten Krieges. Erinnerungen an die dritte KSZE-Folgekonferenz in Wien 1986–1989*, Baden-Baden 2025, p. 365–384.

Möckli, Daniel, *European Foreign Policy during the Cold War. Heath, Brandt, Pompidou and the Dream of Political Unity*, London-New York 2009.

Morgan, Michael C., "North America, Atlanticism, and the making of the Helsinki Final Act", in: Andreas Wenger/Vojtech Mastny et al. (eds.), *Origins of the European Security System. The Helsinki process revisited, 1965–75*, London-New York 2008, p. 25–45.

Morgan, Michael C., *The Final Act. The Helsinki Accords and the Transformation of the Cold War*, Princeton-Oxford 2018.

Moyn, Samuel, *The Last Utopia. Human Rights in History*, Cambridge 2010.

Müller, Erwin, "Vertrauensbildende Maßnahmen (VBM)", in: Dieter S. Lutz (ed.), *Lexikon Rüstung, Frieden, Sicherheit*, München 1987, p. 316–320.

Mueller, Wolfgang, *A Good Example of Peaceful Coexistence? The Soviet Union, Austria and Neutrality, 1955–1991*, Vienna 2011.

Mueller, Wolfgang, "The Revolutions of 1989: An Introduction", in: Wolfgang Mueller/ Michael Gehler et al. (eds.), *The Revolutions of 1989. A Handbook* (Internationale Geschichte/International History Vol. 2), Wien 2015, p. 3–30.

Müller, Benjamin, "Von der Konfrontation zum Dialog. Charta 77, Menschenrechte und 'Samtene Revolution' in der Tschechoslowakei 1975–1989", in: Helmut Altrichter/Hermann Wentker (eds.), *Der KSZE-Prozess. Vom Kalten Krieg zu einem neuen Europa 1975 bis 1990* (Zeitgeschichte im Gespräch Vol. 11), München 2011, p. 99–110.

Neubacher, Daniela, *Stop Nagymaros! Die Geschichte einer Grenzüberschreitung*, phil. Diss. Budapest 2021.

Neuhold, Hanspeter (ed.), *CSCE: N+N Perspectives. The Process of the Conference on Security and Cooperation in Europe from the Viewpoint of the Neutral and Non-aligned Participating States*, Wien 1987.

Nuti, Leopoldo (ed.), *The Crisis of Détente in Europe. From Helsinki to Gorbachev, 1975–1985* (Cold War History Vol. 23), London 2009.

Olivo, Christiane, *Creating a Democratic Civil Society in Eastern Germany. The Case of the Citizen Movements and Alliance 90*, New York 2001.

OSZE-Büro für demokratische Institutionen und Menschenrechte, *OSZE-Verpflichtungen im Bereich der menschlichen Dimension. Band 1, Thematische Zusammenstellung*, Warschau 2023.

Peter, Matthias/Wentker, Hermann (eds.), *Die KSZE im Ost-West-Konflikt. Internationale Politik und gesellschaftliche Transformation 1975–1990* (Schriftenreihe der Vierteljahrshefte für Zeitgeschichte Sondernummer), München 2012.

Peter, Matthias/Wentker, Hermann, "'Helsinki-Mythos' oder 'Helsinki-Effekt'? Der KSZE-Prozess zwischen internationaler Politik und gesellschaftlicher Transformation. Zur Einleitung", in: Matthias Peter/Hermann Wentker (eds.), *Die KSZE im Ost-West-Konflikt. Internationale Politik und gesellschaftliche Transformation 1975–1990* (Schriftenreihe der Vierteljahrshefte für Zeitgeschichte Sondernummer), München 2012, p. 1–14.

Peter, Matthias, *Die Bundesrepublik im KSZE-Prozess 1975–1983. Die Umkehrung der Diplomatie* (Quellen und Darstellungen zur Zeitgeschichte Vol. 105), Berlin-München-Boston 2015.

Peter, Matthias, "Saving Détente. The Federal Republic of Germany and the CSCE in the 1980s", in: Nicolas Badalassi/Sarah B. Snyder (eds.), *The CSCE and the End of the*

Cold War. Diplomacy, Societies and Human Rights, 1972–1990, New York, NY 2019, p. 275–304.

Peterson, Christian P., "'Confronting' Moscow: The Reagan Administration, Human Rights and the Final Act", in: *The Historian* 74 (2012), issue 1, p. 57–86.

Peterson, Christian P., *Globalizing Human Rights. Private Citizens, the Soviet Union, and the West*, New York-London 2012.

Pfetsch, Barbara/Adam, Silke (eds.), *Massenmedien als politische Akteure. Konzepte und Analysen*, Wiesbaden 2008.

Pfligersdorfer, Georg/Unterbruner, Ulrike (eds.), *Umwelterziehung auf dem Prüfstand, Ergebnisse der Tagung „Umwelterziehung in Österreich": Prüfbericht der OECD, Forschung und Ausblick*, Innsbruck 1994.

Pollitzer, René, "'in meinem Bereich, den Bereichen Umweltschutz, Landwirtschaft und Wirtschaft, war wahrscheinlich die Autonomie der einzelnen Länder, egal welchem Block sie zugehörten, am größten'", in: Kai Habel/Nina Hechenblaikner et al. (eds.), *Diplomatie am Ende des Kalten Krieges. Erinnerungen an die dritte KSZE-Folgekonferenz in Wien 1986–1989*, Baden-Baden 2025, p. 313–334.

Pressler, Florian, "A Triumph of Disarmament? The 1980s and the International Political System", in: Christoph Becker-Schaum/Philipp Gasser et al. (eds.), *The Nuclear Crisis. The Arms Race, Cold war Anxiety, and the German Peace Movement of the 1980s*, New York-Oxford 2016, p. 338–351.

Pruckner, Othmar, *Eine kurze Geschichte der Grünen. Ereignisse, Persönlichkeiten, Jahreszahlen*, Wien 2005.

Radchenko, Sergey, *Two Suns in the Heavens*, Stanford 2009.

Radkau, Joachim, *Die Ära der Ökologie. Eine Weltgeschichte*, München 2011.

Raška, Francis D., *Fighting Communism from Afar. The Council of Free Czechoslovakia*, Boulder 2008.

Reagan, Ronald, *An American Life*, New York 1990.

Reddaway, Peter, *The Dissidents*, Washington D.C. 2020.

Reichel, Hans-Christian, "'Die Stimmung generell, die war natürlich vorzüglich und, wie ich hinzufügen will, aufregend und spannend'", in: Kai Habel/Nina Hechenblaikner et al. (eds.), *Diplomatie am Ende des Kalten Krieges. Erinnerungen an die dritte KSZE-Folgekonferenz in Wien 1986–1989*, Baden-Baden 2025, p. 141–163.

Reichel, Hans-Christian, "Die Bonner Wirtschaftskonferenz und die Zukunft der KSZE", in: *Europa-Archiv* 45 (1990), p. 461–470.

Reif, Kingston, "Russia Completes CFE Treaty Suspension", in: *Arms Control Today*, April 2015, https://www.armscontrol.org/act/2015-04/news-briefs/russia-completes-cfe-treaty-suspension, accessed 25.6.2023.

Reimaa, Markku, "'The CSCE could defuse the antagonism between the two military alliances'", in: Kai Habel/Nina Hechenblaikner et al. (eds.), *Diplomatie am Ende des*

Kalten Krieges. Erinnerungen an die dritte KSZE-Folgekonferenz in Wien 1986–1989, Baden-Baden 2025, p. 233–251.

Rentola, Kimmo, "Der Vorschlag einer europäischen Sicherheitskonferenz und die stille Krise zwischen Finnland und der Sowjetunion 1968–1971", in: Dominik Geppert/Udo Wengst (eds.), *Neutralität-Chance oder Chimäre? Konzepte des Dritten Weges für Deutschland und die Welt 1945–1990*, Oldenburg 2005, p. 177–202.

Rey, Marie-Pierre, "Gorbachev's New Thinking and Europe, 1985–1989", in: Frédéric Bozo/Marie-Pierre Rey et al. (eds.), *Europe and the End of the Cold War. A Reappraisal* (Cold War History Vol. 19), London-New York 2008, p. 23–35.

Richardson-Little, Ned, *The Human Rights Dictatorship. Socialism, Global Solidarity and Revolution in East Germany* (Human Rights in History 20), Cambridge 2020.

Richthofen, Esther von, *Bringing Culture to the Masses. Control, Compromise and Participation in the GDR*, Oxford 2009.

Rofe, Simon J., "Trust between Adversaries and Allies: President George H.W. Bush, Trust and the End of the Cold War", in: Christian Ostermann/Martin Klimke/Reinhild Kreis (eds.), *Trust, But Verify. The Politics of Uncertainty and the Transformation of the Cold War Order, 1969–1991*, Stanford 2016, p. 63–84.

Roloff, Ralf, *Auf dem Weg zur Neuordnung Europas. Die Regierungen Kohl/Genscher und die KSZE-Politik der Bundesrepublik Deutschland von 1986 bis 1992*, Vierow 1995.

Romano, Angela, *From Détente in Europe to European Détente. How the West Shaped the Helsinki CSCE* (Euroclio Vol. 44), Bruxelles-New York 2009.

Romano, Angela, "The European Community and the Belgrade CSCE", in: Vladimir Bilandžić/Dittmar Dahlmann/Milan Kosanović (eds.), *From Helsinki to Belgrade. The First CSCE Follow-up Meeting and the Crisis of Détente* (Internationale Beziehungen: Theorie und Geschichte Vol. 10), Göttingen-Bonn 2012, p. 205–224.

Romano, Angela, "The EC and the Socialist World. The Ascent of a Key Player in Cold War Europe", in: Ulrich Krotz/Kiran Klaus Patel/Federico Romero (eds.), *Europe's Cold War Relations. The EC Towards a Global Role*, London 2020, p. 51–70.

Rosin, Philip, "Neutralität in der Menschenrechtsfrage? Die Schweiz in Belgrad und Madrid", in: Matthias Peter/Hermann Wentker (eds.), *Die KSZE im Ost-West-Konflikt. Internationale Politik und gesellschaftliche Transformation 1975–1990* (Schriftenreihe der Vierteljahrshefte für Zeitgeschichte Sondernummer), München 2012, p. 173–189.

Rosin, Philip, *Die Schweiz im KSZE-Prozess 1972–1983. Einfluss durch Neutralität* (Quellen und Darstellungen zur Zeitgeschichte Vol. 99), München 2014.

Rotfeld, Adam D., "The New Dimensions of the CSCE Process", in: Halina Ognik/Adam D. Rotfeld (eds.), *Cultural Heritage and the CSCE Process. Selected Documents*, Warsaw 1991, p. VII–XIII.

Ruggenthaler, Peter/Steiner, Anna, "Der Weg nach Helsinki. Entspannung mit Bonn als letzte Etappe auf dem Weg zur Einberufung der Konferenz über Sicherheit und Zusammenarbeit in Europa", in: Michael Borchard/Stefan Karner et al. (eds.),

Entspannung im Kalten Krieg. Der Weg zum Moskauer Vertrag und zur KSZE, Graz-Wien 2020, p. 677–701.

Saal, Yuliya von, "Die Folgen des KSZE-Prozesses in der Sowjetunion der Perestroika. Der KSZE-Faktor in der Eigendynamik des Wertewandels", in: Matthias Peter/Hermann Wentker (eds.), *Die KSZE im Ost-West-Konflikt. Internationale Politik und gesellschaftliche Transformation 1975–1990* (Schriftenreihe der Vierteljahrshefte für Zeitgeschichte Sondernummer), München 2012, p. 296–303.

Saal, Yuliya von, *KSZE-Prozess und Perestroika in der Sowjetunion. Demokratisierung, Werteumbruch und Auflösung 1985–1991* (Quellen und Darstellungen zur Zeitgeschichte Vol. 100), München 2014.

Sands, Philippe/Peel, Jaqueline et al., *Principles of International Environmental Law*, Cambridge-New York et al. [3]2012.

Sargent, Daniel, *Superpower Transformed: The Remaking of American Foreign Relations in the 1970s*, New York 2015.

Sasanka, *Paweł, Czerwiec 1976. Geneza, przebieg, konsekwencje*, Warszawa 2006.

Schandl, Franz/Schattauer, Gerhard, *Die Grünen in Österreich. Entwicklung und Konsolidierung einer politischen Kraft*, Wien 1996.

Schlotter, Peter, "Heiße Luft oder Magna Charta? Der KSZE-Prozeß nach dem dritten Folgetreffen", in: Hanne-Margret Birckenbach/Uli Jäger/Christian Wellmann (eds.), *Jahrbuch Frieden 1990. Ereignisse, Entwicklungen, Analysen*, München 1989, p. 74–81.

Schlotter, Peter, *Die KSZE im Ost-West-Konflikt. Wirkung einer internationalen Institution* (Studien der Hessischen Stiftung Friedens- und Konfliktforschung Vol. 32), Frankfurt am Main-New York 1999.

Schmidt, Hans-Joachim, "Die Anfangsphase der Wiener Verhandlungen über konventionelle Streitkräfte in Europa (VKSE)", in: Erwin Müller/Götz Neuneck (eds.), *Abrüstung und Konventionelle Stabilität in Europa* (Demokratie, Sicherheit, Frieden Vol. 63), Baden-Baden 1990, p. 11–36.

Schmitt, Burkard, *Frankreich und die Nukleardebatte der Atlantischen Allianz 1956–1966*, München 1998.

Schmitz, David F./Walker, Vanessa, "Jimmy Carter and the Foreign Policy of Human Rights: The Development of a Post-Cold War Foreign Policy", in: *Diplomatic History 28* (2004), issue 1, p. 113–143.

Schneider, Gerd/Toyka-Seid, Christiane, *Entspannungspolitik*, https://www.bpb.de/kurz-knapp/lexika/das-junge-politik-lexikon/320215/entspannungspolitik/, accessed 12.11.2023.

Schuler, Andreas, "Schweizerhalle 1986. Roter Rhein und grüne Wirtschaft", in: *Akzent: Magazin für Kultur und Gesellschaft* (2016), issue 6, Arbeit und Verdienst: Basel und seine Wirtschaft, p. 18–22.

Schulz, Winfried, *Politische Kommunikation. Theoretische Ansätze und Ergebnisse empirischer Forschung*, Wiesbaden 2011[3].

Schwencke, Olaf, *Das Europa der Kulturen – Kulturpolitik in Europa. Dokumente, Analysen und Perspektiven – von den Anfängen bis zum Vertrag von Lissabon* (Edition Umbruch Vol. 26), Essen 2010[3].

Selvage, Douglas, *The Warsaw Pact and Nuclear Nonproliferation, 1963–1965* (The Cold War International History Project Working Paper Series Vol. 32), Washington D.C. 2001.

Selvage, Douglas, "Poland and the Sino-Soviet Rift, 1963–1965", in: *CWIHP e-Dossier 10*, 2004, https://www.wilsoncenter.org/publication/poland-and-the-sino-soviet-rift-1963-1965, accessed 9.9.2023.

Selvage, Douglas, "The Superpowers and the Conference on Security and Cooperation in Europe, 1977–1983", in: Matthias Peter/Hermann Wentker (eds.), *Die KSZE im Ost-West-Konflikt. Internationale Politik und gesellschaftliche Transformation 1975–1990* (Schriftenreihe der Vierteljahrshefte für Zeitgeschichte Sondernummer), München 2012, p. 15–58.

Selvage, Douglas/Süß, Walter, *Staatssicherheit und KSZE-Prozess. MfS zwischen SED und KGB (1972–1989)* (Analysen und Dokumente Vol. 54), Göttingen 2019.

Selvage, Douglas, "The Limits of Repression. Soviet Bloc Security Services vs. Transnational Helsinki Networks, 1976–1986", in: Nicolas Badalassi/Sarah B. Snyder (eds.), *The CSCE and the End of the Cold War, Diplomacy, Societies and Human Rights 1972–1990*, New York-Oxford 2019, p. 207–229.

Shumaker, David H., *Gorbachev and the German question. Soviet–West German relations, 1985–1990*, London 1995.

Siebs, Benno-Eide, *Die Außenpolitik der DDR 1976–1989. Strategien und Grenzen*, Paderborn-München-Wien-Zürich 1999.

Signitzer, Benno, "Public Relations and Public Diplomacy: Some Conceptual Explorations", in: Ansgar Zerfass/Betteke van Ruler et al. (eds.), *Public relations research. European and International Perspectives and Innovations*, Wiesbaden 2008, p. 205–218.

Simonis, Ernst Udo/Weizsäcker, Ernst Ulrich von, "Globale Umweltprobleme. Neun Thesen", in: *Europa-Archiv 45* (1990), p. 1–12.

Sjursen, Helen, *The United States, Western Europe and the Polish Crisis. International Relations in the Second Cold War*, Houndmills-Basingstoke 2003.

Snyder, Sarah B., "'Jerry, Don't Go': Domestic Opposition to the 1975 Helsinki Final Act" , in: *Journal of American Studies 44* (2009), issue 1, p. 67–81.

Snyder, Sarah B., "The foundation for Vienna. A reassessment of the CSCE in the mid-1980s", in: *Cold War History 10* (2010), issue 4, p. 493–512.

Snyder, Sarah B., *Human rights activism and the end of the Cold War. A Transnational History of the Helsinki Network* (Human Rights in History), New York 2011.

Snyder, Sarah B., "Principles Overwhelming Tanks: Human Rights and the End of the Cold War", in: Akira Iriye/Petra Goedde/William Hitchcock (eds.), *The Human Rights Revolution. An International History*, Oxford 2012, p. 265–284.

Soutou, Georges-Henri, "Paris und der 'Prager Frühling'", in: Stefan Karner et al. (eds.), *Prager Frühling. Das internationale Krisenjahr 1968. Band 1: Beiträge*, Köln-Weimar-Wien 2008, p. 356–357.

Spanger, Hans-Joachim/Handl, Vladimir, *Wie weiter bei der Vertrauensbildung? Zu den Wiener VSBM-Verhandlungen und darüber hinaus* (HSFK-Report Vol. 6), Frankfurt am Main 1989.

Speech of the Polish FM Adam Rapacki before the General Assembly of the United Nations on Dec. 14, 1964, in: Friedrich-Karl Schramm/Wolfram-Georg Riggert/Alois Friedel (eds.), *Sicherheitskonferenz in Europa. Dokumentation 1954–1972*, Frankfurt a. M. 1972, p. 415–416.

Staden, Berndt von, "Politische Zusammenarbeit der EG-Staaten", in: *Außenpolitik 23* (1972), p. 200–209.

Stadler, Andreas, "Auslandskulturpolitik", in: Martin Senn/Franz Eder et al. (eds.), *Handbuch Außenpolitik Österreichs*, Wiesbaden 2023, p. 269–283.

Starek, Jana, "'Es ist uns vieles von dem, was wir wollten, gelungen'", in: Kai Habel/Nina Hechenblaikner et al. (eds.), *Diplomatie am Ende des Kalten Krieges. Erinnerungen an die dritte KSZE-Folgekonferenz in Wien 1986–1989*, Baden-Baden 2025, p. 385–432.

Starek, Jana, "Das Ringen um die Einhaltung der Menschenrechte in der Tschechoslowakei und die solidarische Haltung Österreichs zur Zeit der Folgetreffen der Konferenz für Sicherheit und Zusammenarbeit (KSZE)", in: Hildegard Schmoller/Miroslav Kunštát/Monika Březinová (eds.), *Vom 20. Jahrhundert ins neue Jahrtausend. Österreich und die Tschechoslowakei/Tschechien 1986–2016*, Wien 2022, p. 21–58.

Steglich, Peter/Leuschner, Günter, *KSZE – Fossil oder Hoffnung?*, Berlin 1996.

Steininger, Rolf, "Entspannung und Abrüstung im Kalten Krieg. Der KSZE-Prozess und seine Auswirkungen auf die innenpolitischen Situationen in Ost und West", in: Andreas H. Apelt/Robert Grünbaum/Jens Schöne (eds.), *2 x Deutschland. Innerdeutsche Beziehungen 1972–1990*, Halle 2013, p. 111–126.

Stöver, Bernd, *Der Kalte Krieg. Geschichte eines radikalen Zeitalters 1947–1991*, München 2007.

Strohmeier, Gerhard, "'Umwelt': Österreichische Mythen, Topoi und Erinnerungen, Die Gedächtnisorte 'Zwentendorf', 'Hainburg' und 'das Waldsterben'", in: Emil Brix/Ernst Bruckmüller et al. (eds.), *Memoria Austriae I. Menschen, Mythen, Zeiten*, Wien 2004, p. 357–391.

Štrougal, Lubomír, *Paměti a úvahy* [Erinnerungen und Überlegungen], Praha 2009.

Suri, Jeremi, "Détente and human rights. American and West European perspectives on international change", in: *Cold War History 8* (2008), issue 4, p. 527–545.

Süß, Walter, "Die Wiener KSZE-Folgekonferenz und der Handlungsspielraum des DDR-Sicherheitsapparates 1989", in: Matthias Peter/Hermann Wentker (eds.), *Die KSZE im Ost-West-Konflikt. Internationale Politik und gesellschaftliche Transformation*

1975–1990 (Schriftenreihe der Vierteljahrshefte für Zeitgeschichte Sondernummer), München 2012, p. 219–232.

The International Helsinki Federation for Human Rights, *Violations of the Helsinki Accords: Bulgaria. A Report for the Helsinki Review Conference Vienna*, Wien 1986.

The International Helsinki Federation for Human Rights, *Violations of the Helsinki Accords: Czechoslovakia. A Report for the Helsinki Review Conference Vienna*, Wien 1986.

The International Helsinki Federation for Human Rights, *Violations of the Helsinki Accords:* USSR. *A Report for the Vienna Review Conference*, Wien 1986.

Thomas, Daniel C., *The Helsinki Effect: International Norms, Human Rights, and the Demise of Communism*, Princeton 2001.

Thomas, Daniel C., "Human Rights Ideas, the Demise of Communism and the End of the Cold War", in: *Journal of Cold War Studies* 7 (2005), issue 2, p. 110–141.

Tudyka, Kurt P., "Nichtstaatliche Organisationen und die OSZE", in: *OSZE-Jahrbuch 7* (2001), p. 503–513.

Van Esterik, Chris/Minnema, Hester, "The Conference that Came in from the Cold", in: Arie Bloed/Pieter van Dijk (eds.), *The Human Dimension of the Helsinki Process. The Vienna Follow-up Meeting and its Aftermath* (International Studies in Human Rights Vol. 20), Dordrecht-Boston-London 1991, p. 1–29.

Varwick, Johannes, *NATO in (Un-)Ordnung. Wie transatlantische Sicherheit neu verhandelt wird*, Bonn 2017.

Villaume, Poul/Westad, Odd Arne (eds.), *Perforating the Iron Curtain. European Détente, Transatlantic Relations, and the Cold War, 1965–1985*, Copenhagen 2010.

Volle, Hermann/Wagner, Wolfgang (eds.), *KSZE. Konferenz über Sicherheit und Zusammenarbeit in Europa in Beiträgen und Dokumenten aus dem Europa-Archiv*, Bonn 1976.

Volle, Hermann/Wagner, Wolfgang (eds.), *Das Belgrader KSZE-Folgetreffen. Der Fortgang des Entspannungsprozesses in Europa. In Beiträgen und Dokumenten aus dem Europa-Archiv*, Bonn 1978.

Volle, Hermann/Wagner, Wolfgang (eds.), *Das Madrider KSZE-Folgetreffen. Der Fortgang des KSZE-Prozesses in Europa. In Beiträgen und Dokumenten aus dem Europa-Archiv*, Bonn 1984.

Voß, Hans, "Konstruktivität und Dilemma der DDR-Außenpolitik. Ein Bericht des stellvertretenden Delegationsleiters der DDR über das Wiener Folgetreffen des KSZE (1986–1989)", in: *1999. Zeitschrift für Sozialgeschichte des 20. und 21.* Jahrhunderts 8 (1993), issue 1, p. 91–99.

Voss, Peter/Gern, Christiane/Opp, Karl-Dieter, *Origins of a Spontaneous Revolution. East Germany, 1989*, Ann Arbor 1995.

Waligóra, Grzegorz, *Ruch Obrony Praw Człowieka i Obywatela 1977–1981*, Warszawa 2006.

Walker, Breck, "'Neither Shy or Demagogic'– The Carter Administration Goes to Belgrade", in: Vladislav Bilandžić/Dietmar Dahlmann/Milan Kosanović (eds.): *From Helsinki to Belgrade. The First CSCE Follow-up Meeting in Belgrade 1977/78*, Belgrade 2008, p. 207–230.

Wawra, Ernst, "Ein Schandfleck der westlichen Diplomatie? Der KSZE-Prozess und die Bürger- und Menschenrechtsbewegung in der Sowjetunion 1976–1982", in: Helmut Altrichter/Hermann Wentker (eds.), *Vom Kalten Krieg zu einem neuen Europa 1975 bis 1990* (Zeitgeschichte im Gespräch 11), München 2011, p. 63–73.

Wegener Friis, Thomas, "Dänemark – NATO-Horchposten zur Ostsee", in: Stefan Karner et al. (eds.), *Prager Frühling. Das internationale Krisenjahr 1968. Band 1: Beiträge*, Köln-Weimar-Wien 2008, p. 617–631.

Wenger, Andreas/Mastny, Vojtech et al. (eds.), *Origins of the European Security System. The Helsinki Process Revisited, 1965–75*, London-New York 2008.

Wentker, Hermann, *Außenpolitik in engen Grenzen. Die DDR im internationalen System 1949–1989*, München 2007.

Wentker, Hermann, "Die KSZE als Ordnungsfaktor. Höhenflug und Bedeutungsverlust einer Idealvorstellung europäischer Politik (1989–1991)", in: Tim Geiger/Jürgen Lillteicher et al. (eds.), *Zwei plus Vier. Die internationale Gründungsgeschichte der Berliner Republik* (Schriftenreihe der Vierteljahrshefte für Zeitgeschichte Vol. 123), Berlin-Boston 2021, p. 125–141.

Westad, Odd Arne, *The Global Cold War. Third World Interventions and the Making of Our Times*, Cambridge 2007.

Westad, Odd Arne, *The Cold War. A World History*, New York 2017.

Woodby, Sylvia, *Gorbachev and the Decline of Ideology in Soviet Foreign Policy*, Boulder 1989.

Woodroofe, Louise, *Buried in the Sands of the Ogaden: The United States, the Horn of Africa, and the Demise of Detente*, Kent, OH 2013.

Wrede, Hans-Heinrich, *KSZE in Wien. Kursbestimmung für Europas Zukunft*, Köln 1990.

Wrede, Hans-Heinrich, "Die Weiterentwicklung des KSZE-Prozesses. Das Folgetreffen in Wien", in: Wolfgang Wagner et al. (eds.), *Die Internationale Politik 1987–1988*, Berlin 2015, p. 111–122.

Wuthe, Paul, *Für Menschenrechte und Religionsfreiheit in Europa. Die Politik des Heiligen Stuhls in der KSZE/OSZE* (Theologie und Frieden Vol. 22), Stuttgart 2002.

Zagorskij, Andrej, *Chel'sinkskij Process*, Moscow 2005.

Zagorski, Andrei, "The Human Dimension of the CSCE, 1975–1990", in: Nicolas Badalassi/Sarah B. Snyder (eds.), *The CSCE and the End of the Cold War. Diplomacy, Societies and Human Rights, 1972–1990*, New York 2019, p. 17–42.

Zanchetta, Barbara, *Transformation of American International Power in the 1970s*, New York 2013.

Zaremba, Paweł, *Młodopolacy*, Gdańsk 2000.

Zielinski, Michael, *Die neutralen und blockfreien Staaten und ihre Rolle im KSZE-Prozeß* (Nomos Universitätsschriften – Politik Vol. 13), Baden-Baden 1990.

Zubok, Vladislav M., *A Failed Empire. The Soviet Union in the Cold War from Stalin to Gorbachev*, Chapel Hill 2009.

Index

www.ingramcontent.com/pod-product-compliance
Lightning Source LLC
Chambersburg PA
CBHW071247230926
51849CB00001B/255
9789004736962